From Reading, Writing

SECOND EDITION

From Reading, Writing

SECOND EDITION

Anthony C. Winkler ■ Jo Ray McCuen
Glendale Community College

Harcourt Brace College Publishers

Fort Worth Philadelphia San Diego New York Orlando Austin San Antonio
Toronto Montreal London Sydney Tokyo

Publisher: Ted Buchholz
Acquisitions Editor: Stephen T. Jordan
Project Editor: Margaret Allyson
Production Manager: Erin Gregg
Book Designer: Beverly Baker

ISBN: 0-15-500146-9
Library of Congress Number: 92-72259

Cover photograph: © 1992 Elle Schuster

Address for Editorial Correspondence: Harcourt Brace Jovanovich, Inc., 301
Commerce Street, Suite 3700, Fort Worth, TX 76102.

Address for Orders: Harcourt Brace Jovanovich, Inc., 6277 Sea Harbor Drive,
Orlando, FL 32887. 1-800-782-4479, or 1-800-433-0001 (in Florida).

Printed in the United States of America

3 4 5 6 7 8 9 0 1 016 9 8 7 6 5 4 3 2

Preface

This second edition of *From Reading, Writing* continues to embody the pedagogic relationship between reading and writing that was central to the first. We still believe that a causal relationship exists between habitual reading and writing well, and we still attempt to promote reading not only as an end in itself but as an indispensable means of acquiring one's own writing voice and range of compositional skills.

Nevertheless, although the basic pedagogy of this new edition still remains faithful to its title, we have, at the wise urging of users, made some significant changes.

The first and most obvious change is an entirely new Chapter 1, "The Reading and Writing Process." Here we have collected essays that give pragmatic advice to the student on reading and writing. Simultaneously, we have dropped the addendum section of the previous edition, in which many of the essays in this new Chapter 1 previously appeared. The new Chapter 1 is prefaced by our essay, "The Reading and Writing Process," which defines what we know about the writing process and specifically suggests how students can use their reading skills to improve their own writing.

The second major change to this edition is the addition of a new headnote, "Preparing to Read This Selection Critically," before each reading. In it we give students practical advice about what to look for as they read, alerting them to assumptions or biases that may underlie an author's ideas, and suggesting questions they should ask as they think about an author's assertions.

Our third significant change is to focus the apparatus after each selection on critical thinking by grouping the questions under three headings, "Thinking Critically about this Reading," "Understanding the Writer's Process," and "Examining the Writer's Language." As always, the emphasis is on understanding the skills exemplified in the article rather than on mere rote recognition of rhetorical techniques.

Users of the previous edition pointed out that some of its stories were commonly taught in second-semester composition classes. To avoid repetition, we have replaced several of the more familiar stories with fresher ones not likely to be encountered later. Four stories are new to this edition. One is by the South African and recent Nobel laureate Nadine Gordimer. "The Open Window" by Saki, a perennial favorite of short-fiction editors, and stories by the American writers Andre Dubus and Ann Petry, are unlikely to be found in second semester composition anthologies. As in the first edition, the stories are used to generate a chapter writing assignment, thus further cementing the link between reading and writing.

This new edition contains 60 selections: 10 stories; 10 student essays with annotations that show the painstaking process of revision between first and final drafts; and 40 essays, articles, and excerpts. The selections range in cultural diversity from discussions of the ways of Eskimo women to the burial practices of South Africans. They span space and time from the diary excerpt of a pre-Civil War slaveholder in the American South to the descriptions by a Nazi architect of afternoon dinners at Hitler's table. They vary in voice and tone from the resigned observations of a homeless, unemployed editor to the rich descriptiveness of a renowned English travel writer.

Twenty-one of the selections are new to this edition. For each selection the teachers' manual continues to provide a basic comprehension test, printed on standard typewriter paper format, designed to be simple to copy and administer, and intended to enforce the quite practical requirement that students actually do the reading.

As in the previous edition, all the selections are organized under the traditional rhetorical types most commonly taught. And as before, all are intended not only to stimulate students to read and think, but also to inspire them to grow and blossom as writers.

Many users of the previous edition have contributed ideas to this revision, and we are grateful for all their suggestions. We are especially indebted to Betty Bamberg (University of Southern California), Carroll Wilson (Raritan Valley Community College), and Branson Woodard (Liberty University).

Contents

Introduction

1

The Reading and Writing Process

2

Narration

3

Description

4

D e f i n i t i o n

5

Using Examples

How to Write with Examples   **240**

6

Explaining Process

7

Classification

8

Comparing / Contrasting

9

A n a l y z i n g   C a u s e

MILTON MAYER   *What You Will Be*   **487**

The author warns an audience of college graduates that without a studied effort to avoid their parents' and grandparents' attitudes, they will end up being just as corrupted by materialistic desires as were their forebears.

OLIVER SACKS   *The Man Who Mistook His Wife for a Hat*   **496**

A New York neurologist struggles to find the cause of a bizarre perceptual disability in a patient who literally mistakes his wife for a hat.

JOSEPH SOBRAN   *The Cruel Logic of Liberation*   **508**

A journalist exposes a perceived inconsistency in the argument that women should be free to do as they please with a pregnancy without consulting the father.

SCOTT PECK   *Why We Fall in Love*   **512**

"The honeymoon always ends. The bloom of romance always fades." So warns a Connecticut psychiatrist who analyzes why we fall in love and with what consequence.

ANN PETRY   *Like A Winding Sheet*   **520**

A husband's brutal treatment of the wife he genuinely loves demonstrates starkly how inner rage occasioned by racism can explode into irrational and destructive behavior.

10

Argumentation

Thematic Table of Contents

Cultural Diversity

Formal Education

Human Personality

Interaction of Male and Female

Language and Literature

Life's Spiritual Side

Science as Friend or Enemy

Social Problems

Various Faces of Nature

War and Peace

Introduction

THE CASE FOR READING

Writers begin as readers. No doubt there are exceptions to this statement, but offhand we can think of none. If you hate to read and cannot bear even to be in the same room with a book, most likely you will write a graceless style with no sense of idiom and no feel for the texture of your language. The hard fact is that writers generally learn their craft by imitating the examples of syntax, appropriateness, and style encountered while reading. In recognition of this truth, colleges and universities routinely use reading tests to place incoming students into writing programs.

Reading Teaches Usage Standards

Reading teaches about word usage in a way a dictionary does not and also teaches about the modern conventions and standards nowadays observed by writers. For it is plain that writing styles gradually change over the years and that every age sooner or later evolves its own pet standards and conventions about writing. For example, consider this 1892 newspaper account that describes the final hours of English poet Alfred, Lord Tennyson:

> As the day advanced a change came over the scene, a change almost awful to those who watched the deathbed. Slowly the sun went down, the blue died out of the sky, and upon the valley below there fell a perfectly white mist. The hills, as our representative was told, put on their purple garments to watch this strange, white stillness; there was not a sound in the air, and, high above, the clear cloudless sky shone

1

like a pale glittering dome. All nature seemed to be watching, waiting.

Then the stars came out and looked in at the big mullioned window, and those within saw them grow brighter and brighter, until at last a moon—a harvest moon for splendour, though it was an October moon—sailed slowly up and flooded the room with golden light. The bed on which Lord Tennyson lay, now very near to the gate of death, and with his left hand still resting on his Shakespeare, was in deep darkness; the rest of the room lit up with the glory of the night, which poured in through the uncurtained windows. And thus, without pain, without a struggle, the greatest of England's poets passed away.

Although the Victorians doted on this kind of syrupy journalism, our own age has no stomach for it; any reporter today who wrote in the style of this account soon would be pounding the pavements looking for work. We prefer our journalism to deliver the straight stuff in a workmanlike prose with no sentimental gushing by the writer (even the tabloids write about two-headed baboon babies with relative restraint). The minimum that reading can teach is elementary but useful lessons about the tastes and standards that govern contemporary writing; and these lessons can provide you with a valuable gauge for judging the quality of your own work.

Aside from acquainting you with the standards observed by this generation of editors, reading is also invaluable schooling for your own internal editor. That each of us has within us an internal editor who judges our own written work is a suggestion lately made by researchers. The fact is that writing is solitary labor usually done in the privacy of the office or home and never, like a comedian's act, before a live audience. Yet, we all write for different audiences for whom we must occasionally tailor our styles. How are we able to do it? Because, suggest researchers in writing, of our internal editor who acts as judge and jury over final copy. No matter for whom you are writing, it is always your internal editor who must finally decide whether your text is appropriate. It is this same internal editor who profits most from the lessons about syntax, diction, and prevailing standards of good and bad taught by a lifetime of reading. If you do not habitually read, your internal editor will lack the experience necessary to make the judgments about style and conventions needed to guide your hand. Read for the sake of your internal editor, if for no one else.

Reading Teaches Thinking

The more you think, the better at thinking you are likely to become. A great deal of writing is nothing less than thinking transcribed on paper, and an enormous amount of reading requires us to think as we read. Doubtless other mediums can stimulate us to think, but writing has the advantage of separating ideas from the emotional slush that often accompanies thought in a conversation. You have before you the ideas of the writer undistracted by facial tics, speech peculiarities, or oddities of manner. You can grapple with thought expressed in nearly its purest form. And you can, if you choose to annotate your books in the manner recommended by Mortimer Adler in "How to Mark a Book," even engage your author in debate with marginal comment and rebuttal.

Our questions at the end of each essay are designed partly to encourage thinking by inference and summary. The first of these, thinking by inference, means to draw conclusions from an author's words. To think inferentially about a work is to unravel its assumptions by making deductions and forming conclusions as you read. For example, in "I Want a Wife," Judy Syfers sketches a satirical stereotype of the perfect wife and shows this poor creature at the beck and call of a demanding husband. But she also, in portraying the husband as a selfish and egotistic taskmaster, implies a portrait of the ideal husband. So we ask you to infer from her sketch a composite of how a helping and loving husband would be if Syfers, and feminists, got their way. To do so requires you to think inferentially about Syfers's opinions.

Thinking by summary is the ability to grasp and express the gist of an author's idea accurately and compactly. You are encouraged to see the whole picture and to avoid overconcentrating on a single part.

Many years ago this kind of thinking was commonly taught through exercises in précis writing. (A précis is a brief abstract of a longer work that accurately summarizes its main points.) Students would be given a work of, say, 2,000 words and asked to condense it into a précis of 300 words. Some of our questions intend to promote this kind of thinking by encouraging you to read essays for their overall significance and not to become bogged down by minor details.

Finally, we also ask questions that prompt you to see the relationship between an author's ideas and your own life. It is doubtful that we truly understand an idea if we cannot grasp its potential effect on our personal lives. To understand an essay's meaning is to fathom the possible real-world consequences of its ideas. Our questions probe for such consequences and encourage you to think about them as you read.

The Rhetorical Modes and Writing

The essays in this book are grouped within chapters organized by the rhetorical mode they exemplify. What, you might ask, are the rhetorical modes, and why do books of this kind so insistently teach them? The rhetorical modes are patterns of thinking that a writer may use to organize and write about a subject. They are taught because experience shows that they help students learn how to write. What follows is an example of how rhetorical modes are commonly used. Our case is not hypothetical; it actually happened.

A senior editor had gotten into a tiff with her landlord over longstanding maintenance problems the landlord had vowed repeatedly to remedy but had never actually fixed. In a rage, she sat down to write the landlord a final letter threatening legal action.

The situation is familiar enough, and if the editor had had no training in writing, she might have been tempted to splatter her anger all over the page in an unrestrained outburst. But in factual or expository writing, it is better to make your case with precision and effect than merely to air your grievances. After some thought, the editor decided to shame the landlord into action by contrasting the apartment she now rented with the one she had occupied in another city from which she had recently moved. She wrote a letter pointing out that her present quarters badly needed painting, whereas her former apartment had been spick and span; that where she now lived there was frequently pooled water in the walkways leading to the building and garbage deposited in an unsightly bin placed right before the front entrance, whereas in her former residence the walkways had been immaculately maintained and the garbage bin discreetly hidden behind a wooden screen.

Whether or not the editor's letter worked its desired effect is not the point. What we wish to underscore is that writing is usually more effective if its means and ends are premeditated. The editor could have merely let the landlord have her anger with both barrels. But by expressing her complaints and rage into an invidious comparison/contrast designed to embarrass and shame, she obtained the reaction she hoped for. Knowing how to write by rhetorical modes gives any writer this advantage of premeditation; it allows you to conceptualize an assignment by specific rhetorical means.

Let us say, for example, that an instructor assigns an essay on any subject related to modern careers. This almost bottomless subject is enough to drive any inexperienced writer to wail, "I don't know what to say!" But if you know how to *write* by the rhetorical modes, you automatically know how to *think* by the rhetorical modes and therefore how to use them to compress any vague assignment into a compact topic. You could, for instance, decide to view the subject as a possible classification and so immediately narrow your focus from modern careers to *kinds* of modern careers. Once you've made that decision, "Kinds of Careers in the Computer Industry," which is a suitable topic for an essay, is only a hairbreadth away.

The rhetorical modes are useful means to an end. When you are given a blanket assignment, such as to write about any topic related to modern careers, it's very much like being told to go to a grocery store and buy a carton of eggs. If you know how to think by the rhetorical modes, you have a map and can choose from several alternative ways of getting there. You can take one route and write a causal analysis, or take another and do a classification. You may write a description and so take the highway, or do a narrative and take the back road. But if you have no concept of the rhetorical modes, you are working without a map and must determine for yourself how to get to the store, buy eggs, and get back. It can be done, of course. But it is harder to do.

Some assignments will plainly tell you which road to take and thus spare you having to find your own way. For example, if you were asked to write an essay contrasting the satire in Pope's "The Rape of the Lock" with that in Swift's "A Modest Proposal," you know exactly what you must do. But if you were asked simply to write on satire, knowing the rhetorical modes can help you select the final topic and plan the essay. You could adopt several approaches to such an assignment based on the rhetorical modes. You could write a *definition* of satire, a *classification* of the kinds of satire, a *causal analysis* of what makes a work satirical, a historical discussion of satire with the inclusion of many *examples,* or a *comparison/ contrast* of the works of two famous satirists.

Finally, the rhetorical modes can also help you learn and master techniques of writing in the abstract. Writing is a complex undertaking that tends to vary with every different assignment. The basic rules of diction and syntax aside, it is difficult to isolate common techniques of organization and form that are universally applicable to different topics. Within limits, the rhetorical modes allow us to do exactly that—to demonstrate and impart some elementary writing techniques in the abstract. So once you have mastered the basic form of the process essay, you can explain any process, from how to skin a deer to how to perform a belly dance. And once you know how to write a comparison/contrast, you can apply the basic techniques to an essay that compares tropical fish or to one that contrasts monetary systems.

In any case, the trick is to practice the lessons of the rhetorical modes—but not slavishly. Indeed, as you read these essays you will quickly see that considerable variation exists among even those written in the same rhetorical mode. Good writing is always distinctive and original and can never be produced in cookie-cutter fashion. Use the organizing techniques of the rhetorical modes until you have a better idea. Then always opt for your own distinctive way of writing over the method you learned from a book, any book, even this one.

1

The Reading and Writing Process

Reading is a process; so is writing. By "process" we mean that both require the taking of sequential steps over a lapse of time. We have already pointed out that virtually all writers are habitual readers. And while not all readers are habitual writers, it is still a pragmatic truth that habitual readers usually make better writers. Nor should this revelation be a surprise, since most learned processes improve with practice. The archer who shoots regularly is more likely to hit the bull's-eye reliably than is the one who hasn't touched a bow in years, and there is no magic or happenstance whatever in any of this. Practice, if it does not always make perfect, certainly does make better.

We bring all this up, at the risk of sounding inanely elementary, to point out another truth: Often, many students who think they cannot write well just do not understand the writing process. It is not that they cannot write, but simply that they do not know how to write and have a mistaken idea about what the writing process entails. Over and over again English teachers have found this to be true.

For example, many beginning writers will take one swipe at composing an essay, be dissatisfied, and interpret the outcome as damning evidence that they have no gift for writing. Professional writers, on the other hand, understand that writing is typically done in numerous sittings and passes over the interval of days, weeks, even months or years, depending on the length of the assignment. This essay you are now reading, for example, was composed over days, revised and reread numerous times, tinkered with, changed, and edited in several passes. And all this was done not because the writer is inept or neurotic, but because this stop–and–go method is part of the typical and expected writing process.

Reading and Writing

One study looked at how amateur and professional writers work and found a single surprising difference centered around how they react when stuck in the middle of writing. The amateurs, when stuck, nibble on the tip of their pen, beat a tattoo with the ballpoint on the desktop, and stare aimlessly around the room with glassy eyes. The stuck professionals, on the other hand, go back to the first word and reread what they had written, making revisions and changes in the text as they read. By the time they've reached the logjam they usually have a good idea where they went wrong and what to do. If they're still stuck, they reread the material again, doing so over and over until they become unstuck.

For all writers, amateurs as well as professionals, periodically bogging down on the page is an inevitable part of the whole writing process. But how you view and react to this certain event is likely to affect your composition efforts drastically. If you see it as a necessary and usual part of the writing process and remain untroubled by it, you most likely will profit from the experience of rereading and taking a closer look at your work. On the other hand, if you mistake being temporarily stuck as yet another sign of your writing ineptness, this falsely negative attitude will make writing only harder labor.

Writing as an Individualistic Act

The writing process is, above all, an individualistic act, even an idiosyncratic one. What works for one writer often will not work for the other. Some writers like to generate an outline, a plan, and follow it to the letter as they write. Other writers prefer just to sit and write, spending their time on revising and doctoring the shape of the essay during the act of composing it. Neither method is particularly right or wrong. If one method works especially well for you, use it.

However, experienced writers know that the best writing is preceded always by exhaustive reading about the subject, that it is impossible even for seasoned professionals to write well about a subject they do not truly know. Yet every year many students will attempt to put pen to paper about topics and subjects they only vaguely understand, subsequently blaming the unhappy results on imagined bad writing skills.

Reading about a subject should always precede writing about it. Consider different opinions and perspectives. Make notes about your reactions to your reading. Once you start the actual writing, you should also incessantly reread your own text as a prelude to rewriting it. Professional writers habitually reread and rewrite their work. They reread to assess how their words might strike an audience, to gauge clarity, persuasiveness, and conviction; they rewrite to find a slightly better word, to create an improved sentence, to structure a stronger paragraph. The process is akin to systematic whittling of a stubborn piece of wood. Gradually, the repeated rereading and rewriting will yield a sharper, better, and more readable page.

The essays in this chapter underscore these points, some with specific advice for reading, others with similarly specific prescriptions for writing. All emphasize the relationship between the skills of reading and writing. Mitchell Stephens speculates on the decline of reading and its consequences not only to the individual, but to the nation. Mortimer Adler tells us that we must make books our own by scribbling our reactions to them in the margins. Paul Roberts and Donald Hall teach the nuts and bolts of essay writing, while F. L. Lucas, a veteran teacher of writing, muses on style and the struggles to find one; and a student, David Beckham, tells us how he writes with a word processor.

Read before you write; read while you write; read after you write: That is what anyone who wishes to write well must do, repetitively and continuously. Writing is not an isolated skill that pops up like a convenient, nomadic muse just as you sit at your desk, pen and paper in hand, ready to begin. It is rather more like the seed planted many moons before and cultivated through countless hours spent in solitude with writers and books. It blossoms through care, labor, habit, and practice. It is a skill learned by trial and error, and by mimicry. Those who write best of all are always numbered among the best, the most industrious, the most persistent readers.

THE DEATH OF READING?

Mitchell Stephens

Mitchell Stephens is an Associate Professor of Journalism at New York University. A former free-lance writer and journalist, he is the author of numerous articles and essays and has been a news writer for the Chicago Tribune, Newsday, *and* NBC Radio. *His books include* Writing and Reporting the News *(1986), and* A History of News *(1988).*

Preparing to Read This Selection Critically

Begin with the title, which often will crisply sum up an author's central argument or thesis. Ask yourself, what does the author mean by "reading"? And how can "reading" suffer "death"? Pay attention to the evidence the author cites in support of his thesis, and ask yourself if there are other, equally reasonable, explanations that account for the author's interpretation of the evidence. The author relies heavily on testimonial evidence—the opinions of experts. Ask yourself if the credentials of the expert are enough to qualify him or her as an authoritative spokesperson on the subject.

What's missing from these pictures? Three people sit in a doctor's waiting room. One stares at the television that rests on an end table, the second fiddles with a hand-held video game; the head of the third is wrapped in earphones. A couple of kids, waiting for bedtime, lie on the floor of a brightly painted room, busily manipulating the controls of a video game. Two hundred people sit in an airplane. Some have brought their own tapes, some doze, most stare up at a small movie screen. **1**

What is missing from these pictures, and increasingly from our lives, is the activity through which most of us learned much of what we know of the wider world. What's missing is the force that, according to a growing consensus of historians, established our patterns of thought and, in an important sense, made our civilization. What's missing is the venerable, increasingly dated activity that you—what's the matter? bored with all your CDs and videotapes?—are engaged in right now. **2**

Ironically, but not coincidentally, reading has begun fading from our culture at the very moment that its importance to that culture is finally being established. Its decline, many theorists believe, is as profound as, say, the fall of communism, and some have taken to prophesying that the downturn in reading could result in the modern world's cultural and political decline. "A mode of thinking is being lost," laments Neil Postman, whose book, *Amusing Ourselves to Death*, is a warning about the consequences of a falloff in reading. "We are losing a sort of psychic habit, a logic, a sense of complexity, an ability to spot contradictions and even falsity." Postman, a professor of communication arts at New York University, believes this loss is now being felt in our cultural activities and in our politics, as well as in our children's SAT scores, and that it could get worse. But of course such prophecies are delivered in print, so no one pays much heed. **3**

4   The anecdotal evidence that reading is in decline is copious and compelling. "When I go out socially in Washington," confides Daniel Boorstin, a historian and former librarian of Congress, "I'm careful not to embarrass my dinner companions by asking what they have read lately. Instead I say, 'I suppose you don't have much time to read books nowadays.' " That is a courtesy, alas, for which most of us would be grateful. The fact is that few of us, and few of our friends and few of our children, have the time to read as much as we would like. We're too busy working or working out or playing or—OK, let's admit it—watching TV. Our homes barely make room for reading. Those old islands of quiet—libraries, studies and dens—long ago were invaded by flat screens and Nintendos. Now they are called "family rooms" or, more accurately, "television rooms." And our architects seem to have given up providing us with book-shelves; instead they busy themselves designing "entertainment centers." So we haven't quite gotten around to Stephen M. Hawking's *A Brief History of Time* yet. We're saving Amy Tan's latest novel for vacation, maybe. And that pile of unread *New Yorkers* or *Rolling Stones* or *Los Angeles Times Magazines* keeps growing, each unread issue an additional piece of anecdotal evidence.

5   Those whose livelihoods depend on our reading suggest, optimistically, that the widespread notion that it is in decline is an oversimplification. "I believe that people who used to read a lot of books read less now," concedes Alberto Vitale, chairman of Random House, the nation's largest publisher of trade (nontext) books. "But in my opinion, there are many *more* people reading books." The optimists do have some statistics on their side. Books, the oldest form of print, seem to be doing reasonably well. Publishers, in fact, are churning out more and more of them: 133,196 new titles listed in *Books in Print* in the past year. That is about 16 times the number of titles printed 40 years ago (one of the reasons "keeping up" may seem so much harder for us than it did for our parents and grand-parents). And publishers are selling more, too: about 2 billion books in 1990, an 11% increase over 1985. Reports of the death of the book seem greatly exaggerated.

6   Ah, but are those books actually being read? Not, in many cases, from cover to cover. A recent Gallup Poll found many more people in 1990 than in 1957 who say they are currently reading a book or novel, but many fewer now than in 1975 who say they have completed a book in the past week. In a society where professional success now requires acquaintance with masses of esoteric

information, books are often purchased to be consulted, not read. About 15% of the new titles in *Books in Print* are scientific or technical books. Fiction and general-interest nonfiction works would seem to be designed to be read, but lately these books also serve other functions. Their authors often employ them as routes to movie contracts or to tenure or to the intellectual renown that apparently comes with having catalogued definitively, in two or three dense volumes, how George Bernard Shaw, say, spent each of his evenings. Their publishers increasingly see these books not as collections of sentences and paragraphs that might be clarified and sharpened but as product that must be publicized and marketed so the balance sheets of the large conglomerates they now work for might tilt in the right direction. Given the pace of modern life, the readers of these books, too, may have other purposes in mind—a quick, conversation-enhancing skim perhaps. "People tend to read too rapidly," moans Russell Jacoby, author of *The Last Intellectual.* "They tend to read while commuting, watching a game on TV or playing Nintendo." Jacoby, who recently taught history at UC Riverside, keeps threatening to open "slow-reading centers."

And books increasingly have another function for those who 7
purchase them. They have begun replacing the bottle of Scotch or the tie as gifts—giving them about the same chance of being opened as those ties had of being worn. The number of bookstores in the United States has been growing in recent decades, at a rate second only to that of fast-food restaurants, but according to statistics supplied by the American Booksellers Assn., more than one quarter of all their sales are in November and December—for the holidays.

In 1985, Michael Kinsley of the *New Republic* conducted an 8
experiment. Notes offering a $5 reward to anyone who saw them and called the magazine were hidden about three-quarters of the way through 70 copies of the hottest nonfiction books in Washington, D.C., bookstores. These were the books that all of Washington seemed to be talking about. "Washington" was apparently basing its comments on the reviews and maybe a quick skim. No one called.

"Fortunately for booksellers," Kinsley wrote, "their prosperity 9
depends on people buying books, not on people actually reading the bulky things." (Kinsley's advice to authors who would like their words actually to be read: "Cut out the middleman, and just write the review.")

Those of us with less disposable income, or less inclination to 10
dispose of it in bookstores, can still get our books from libraries."You

can't say people take books out of the library just to put them on the coffee table," says Simon Michael Bessie, chairman of the Center for the Book at the Library of Congress.

11   And library use is up. Public-library circulation in the United States has grown from 4.7 "units" per capita per year in 1980 to 6.1 in 1989, according to a study by the Library Research Center at the University of Illinois. However, the "units" we are checking out of the library now include not only lots of school and business readings but also cassettes, CDs and videotapes.

12   Here is perhaps the most frightening of the statistics on books: According to the Gallup Poll, the number of Americans who admitted to having read *no* books during the past year—and this is not an easy thing to admit to a pollster—doubled from 1978 to 1990, from 8% to 16%. "I cannot live without books," Thomas Jefferson, whose collection helped start the Library of Congress, told John Adams. More and more of us apparently can.

13   Magazines would appear to be better suited to our hectic lives, if for no other reason than that they require much less of a time commitment than do books. Gathering evidence to confirm or deny this surmise, however, is not easy. There are too many different kinds of magazines and too many individual variations in their popularity. We do know that the magazine business has been in dire straits lately, but this has been caused by a falloff in advertising, not necessarily in circulation.

14   The best indicator of whether we are spending more or less time with magazines may be "time-use" studies such as those compiled at the University of Maryland. These show that the proportion of the population that reads a magazine on a typical day dropped from 38% in 1946 to 28% in 1985. Magazine publishers, however, can take some encouragement from the fact that most of that drop had occurred by the 1950s.

15   The statistics on newspaper readership are much less ambiguous and much grimmer. According to the University of Maryland time-use studies, the share of the adult population that "read a newspaper yesterday" has declined from 85% in 1946 to 73% in 1965 to 55% in 1985. The numbers on per capita newspaper circulation and the percentage of American homes that receive a daily newspaper form similar graphs—graphs you could ski down.

16   "What has changed is the strength of the habit of reading a newspaper," notes Al Gollin of the Newspaper Advertising Bureau. "It used to be one of those things that almost everybody did." No

more. Americans on average now read newspapers much less frequently than they did 30 years ago, 20 years ago, even 10 years ago.

And young people have been losing the newspaper habit even 17 faster than their parents. "We are developing a generation that has no interest in reading except insofar as it is assigned in school," concludes Daniel Kevles, professor of humanities at Caltech. "They don't read newspapers or magazines. I sense a general lack of interest in public affairs among my students." A recent *Times Mirror* survey found that only 30% of Americans under the age of 35 said they had read a newspaper the previous day, compared to 67% in 1965.

The Gulf War provided further evidence of how far the news- 18 paper has fallen. According to a survey by Birch/Scarborough, a grand total of 8.9% of us said we kept up with war news primarily through newspapers. The days when we found most of our news set in type on a page are long gone.

Those time-use studies actually discovered a slight increase 19 from 1965 to 1985 in the amount of time people said they spend reading books and magazines: from 1.7 to 1.9 hours a week. But if you throw in newspapers, the total time people spent with reading as their primary activity has dropped more than 30% in those years, from 4.2 hours a week to 2.8.

And this drop has occurred at the same time that the amount 20 of education Americans obtain has been rising dramatically. The percentage of Americans who have completed four years of high school has more than tripled since 1940, according to the Bureau of the Census Current Population Survey, and the percentage of Americans completing four years of college has more than quadrupled.

If education still stimulated the desire to read, all the statistics 21 on reading would be shooting up. That they are not may say something about the quality of our educational system and about the interests of the students it now attracts. It certainly says something about reading and its future. If dramatically increased exposure to an educational system based on the printed word cannot get us to read, what will?

Reading's troubles are not difficult to explain. A hundred years 22 ago, on days when no circus was in town, people looking for entertainment had three alternatives: fulfilling biological needs, talking or reading. Those looking for information were restricted to the latter two. Many of our ancestors, to be sure, were unable to read, but those who could relied upon it, as Thomas Jefferson did, with a desperation that is difficult for us to imagine.

23   Books, in those days, had a unique power to transport. "There is no Frigate like a Book," wrote 19th-Century poet Emily Dickinson, "To take us Lands away." Now, of course, there are many easier ways of getting there.

24   "Our society is particularly ingenious at thinking up alternatives to the book," notes Boorstin. Indeed, we have thought up an entire communications revolution, and there have not been many of those in human history. The first such revolution was the development of language hundreds of thousands of years ago; the second, the development of reading and writing in the Middle East about 5,000 years ago; the third, the invention of the printing press 500 years ago.

25   The fourth communications revolution—ours—began, perhaps, with the experiments of Samuel Morse, Guglielmo Marconi and Thomas Edison in the 19th Century, and it has been picking up steam ever since. Movies, recordings, radio, telephones, computers, photocopiers and fax machines are all part of it. But, of course, the most powerful product of this revolution, so far, and the one that has posed the largest threat to reading, has been television.

26   Some print lovers have taken heart from the recent troubles of the TV networks or from the fact that the amount of time the average American family keeps the TV on each day, as measured by Nielsen, finally leveled off in the mid-1980s—at about seven hours a day. But, of course, we have since supplemented broadcast and even cable TV with other equally diverting forms of programming.

27   The first television wave washed over us in the 1950s and '60s. But then, while we were still getting used to having this perky new friend in our bedrooms, a second wave hit. In 1982, only 5.5% of American homes had videocassette recorders. Now 72.5% of them do, and, according to Nielsen, videotapes keep the set on an average of an extra half-hour each day in those homes. Add still more minutes for video games. So much for that leveling-off.

28   Russell Jacoby and his wife have found a sure way to protect themselves and their two children from the siren songs of the tube: When their set was stolen a number of years ago, they simply didn't replace it. But most of the rest of us now share our homes with one or more TV sets, which we turn on more than we would like to admit. "Everyone lies about how much time they and their families spend watching TV," Jacoby asserts. It is a wonder that we manage to find the time to read even as much as we do.

"There are only so many hours in the day," says Alberto Vitale   29
of Random House, wistfully.

As a youth, Abraham Lincoln is reported to have spent so many   30
hours buried in his books that the neighbors labeled him lazy. When
Lincoln arrived in Congress, his fellow congressmen, by one account, dismissed him as a "bookworm." That insult is not heard
much nowadays, nor are readers disparaged as lazy.

Instead, the more dedicated parents among us feel guilty if we   31
don't manage to read to our children each evening, hoping the kids
will pick up the habit we parents are rapidly losing. The First Lady
campaigns for literacy. We end TV shows with pleas to read books.
And, according to the Gallup Poll, 61% of us proclaim reading "more
rewarding" than watching television; 73% lament that we read too
few books; 92% attest that reading is a "good use" of our time. And
45% of the poll's respondents believe, against all the evidence, that
they will be "reading more in the months and years ahead."

Reading certainly is well-loved now that it is in decline. Yet it   32
is no longer something that we ache to do. How many kids today
surreptitiously finish books by flashlight under the covers? Instead,
reading, like eating broccoli, has now become something that we
feel we *should* do (always a bad sign).

Some teen-agers and—says Michael Silverblatt, host of   33
KCRW's "Bookworm" show—some Southern Californians actually
find it hip to pretend to read *less* than they really do, but the vast
majority of us sincerely, vigorously and guiltily genuflect in front
of the printed page. Never in human history has reading been more
respected.

This is not surprising. One of the characteristics of any tech-   34
nological revolution is nostalgia for the old order. Socrates, who
lived a few hundred years after the invention of the Greek alphabet,
when writing was transforming Greek culture, strenuously argued
the superiority of the oral culture it was replacing. According to
Plato's (written) account, Socrates predicted that the use of writing
would weaken memories and deprive "learners" of the chance to
question what they were being taught.

Such nostalgia for the methods of oral tradition—memoriza-   35
tion, rhetoric, recital—kept them alive in the schools well into this
century. Now similar calls are going out to defend the schools
against the incursions of the new information technologies so that
our educational institutions can serve as repositories of another fading tradition—reading.

36   We did not realize that we were living in the age of print until it began to end. Only then did we gain the perspective to see the effects of reading on our thoughts. Those effects are profound, as anthropological studies of societies without reading have begun to show.

37   For example, the following statements were presented to members of a mostly preliterate tribe in a remote area of the Soviet Union: "In the far north, where there is snow, all bears are white. Novaya Zembla is in the far north, and there is always snow there." Then these people were asked what color the bears are in Novaya Zembla. A typical response, as reported by Father Walter Ong in his book *Orality and Literacy:* "I don't know. I've seen a black bear. I've never seen any others. Each locality has its own animals." These people could not solve this simplest of logical problems.

38   It is not that such preliterate people are less intelligent than we are. They simply think differently—"situationally." When words are written down, not just enunciated, they are freed from the subjective situations and experiences ("I've seen a black bear") in which they were imbedded. Written words can be played with, analyzed, rearranged and organized into categories (black bears, white bears, places where there is always snow). The correspondences, connections or contradictions among various statements can be carefully examined. As investigators such as Ong and anthropologist Jack Goody have explained, our system of logic—our ability to find principles that apply independently of situations—is a product of literacy. This logic, which goes back to the Egyptians, Hebrews and Greeks, led to mathematics and philosophy and history. Among its accomplishments is our culture.

39   And when written words are set in print, they gain additional powers. Our sentences grow even less connected to our persons as they are spelled out in the interchangeable letters of movable type. Our thoughts grow more abstract, more removed from the situations in which we happen to find ourselves. Superstitions, biases and legendary characters like dragons and kings have difficulty fitting into these straight, precise lines of type. Charts, maps and columns of figures can be duplicated exactly for the first time. According to seminal media theorist Marshall McLuhan and historian Elizabeth Eisenstein, the scientific revolution and the Enlightenment were both products of the printing press.

40   "Reading is central to our culture," states Ong, a professor of humanities at Saint Louis University. "It is connected to virtually

all the forces that shaped our culture." Among those who ponder such matters, there is no longer much controversy about that. The question, as we leave the age of print for the uncharted waters of this new electronic age, is whether we risk losing much of what reading enabled us to gain.

Neil Postman, for one, fears that the answer is yes. "New communications technologies giveth," he proclaims, "and they taketh away." On the debit side Postman would place recent developments in art, education, religion, journalism and politics—all of which, in his view, are losing the seriousness and intellectual content print gave them as they are transformed into "show business" to meet the needs of electronic media. 41

Reading demands that we sit still, be quiet and concentrate hard enough to decode a system of symbols and follow extended arguments. This is an injunction that increasingly is falling on earphone-plugged ears. Television and its electronic brethren are much less strict. We can be cleaning, daydreaming or half-dozing; they don't seem to care. All television demands is our gaze. Dazzling collages of imagery and rhythm are assembled just to get us to open our eyelids a bit wider. 42

Kings used to turn thumbs down on spectacles that bored them; we simply press thumb to remote control, zapping any scene, exposition or argument that takes much more than a fraction of a minute to unfold. "Thinking," Postman writes, "does not play well on TV." 43

Our entertainers, pundits, professors, ministers and leaders, therefore, are judged not so much on their ability to reason but on their ability to project a diverting image. Amuse us or we'll change the channel. Whether or not the points being made are valid is of less importance. Somehow this does not seem what Jefferson and the other founders had in mind when they entrusted us with governing a country. 44

Pessimists like Postman do not have much difficulty convincing us that life on a late-20th-Century couch can be frivolous and vegetable-like. We already feel guilty that we are watching "the boob tube" rather than reading. However, making the case that life in that supposed golden age of reading was really much more noble than life today is more difficult. 45

As his example of political discourse before TV, Postman chooses those astoundingly literate, three-hour-long debates between Lincoln and Stephen A. Douglas in 1858. But 18th- and 19th- 46

Century American politics was not all conducted on this level. The slogans with which William Henry Harrison made his case for the presidency in 1840, for example—"Log Cabin and Hard Cider," "Tippecanoe and Tyler, too"—are as vacuous as anything concocted by Ronald Reagan's media wizards.

47   The arguments against TV are based on a certain amount of such false nostalgia. People then did not read quite so much, and their reading material was not quite so exemplary as those pining for a lost golden age suggest. "We have no figures on how much or how well books were read in the past," Ong notes. "All we have are the comments of bibliophiles. There is no evidence, for example, that all the copies of the books printed in the 16th and 17th centuries were read. There is plenty of evidence that a lot of them were not read." Nevertheless, the doomsayers do have some harder evidence on their side.

48   There is, to begin with, the decline in writing skills, much fretted over by educators in recent years. Written language demands stricter rules of syntax and grammar than spoken language, and these are the rules, first codified in printed dictionaries and grammar books, that we learn (or now fail to learn) in school. The sentences of the electronic age, because they are supplemented by images, can get away with playing by looser rules. Try, sometime, to diagram the sentences of a TV–football "analyst."

49   It is not surprising, therefore, that students who watch and listen more and read less are losing command of their writing. As anyone who has seen that rare thing, a letter written by a student, knows, young people today often have considerable difficulty filling a page with clear, exact sentences. Their performance on recent SATs raises the question of whether they also have difficulty producing clear, exact thought.

50   The average score on the SAT verbal test, taken by a large number of college-bound high school students, was 466 (on a scale of 200 to 800) in 1968. Then, as the first TV generation began taking the test, scores began tumbling. The average score leveled off from 1978 to 1987, but now, with the arrival of the MTV kids, it has begun skidding again—down to 422 this year.

51   The College Boards do not test a representative sample of American teen-agers. More—and perhaps less qualified—students are now going to college and therefore taking the test, which may be driving scores down. Still, the correspondence between verbal

scores and the two waves of TV's assault upon reading is hard to overlook.

The decline in SAT scores has a lot to do with not reading," 52 asserts College Board President Donald M. Stewart. Why? "The ability to read is linked to the ability to process, analyze and comprehend information," Stewart explains. "I guess that's called thinking."

Michael Silverblatt of "Bookworm" uses an analogy that young 53 people might find more persuasive: "Just as people who don't work out can't do certain things with their bodies, people who don't read can't do certain things with their minds."

Boorstin puts the problem even more bluntly. He calls people 54 who do not read "self-handicapped" and says, "A person who doesn't read books is only half-alive." And if the members of a society stop reading? "Then you have a half-alive society."

From the perspective of enthusiasts of the new culture of vid- 55 eos, videotapes, video games and CDs, all this must sound like the whining of a ragged, nearly defeated old order. Not everyone is convinced that all that is deep and serious in our society is in fact under siege. "I know a number of extremely intelligent adults who don't read more than a book or two a year but still remain healthy, active contributors to society," says Wendy Lesser, editor of *Three Penny Review*, a respected Berkeley literary publication. "I think if you can get people to learn to discriminate between good and bad TV programs, you've done more for them than you would by simply forcing them to read a book, however trashy."

And even those who believe that the decline in reading does 56 herald some profound cultural changes are not convinced those changes will necessarily be for the worse. Perhaps, they might argue, the logic inculcated by writing and print is not the only way of processing information about the world. Perhaps an immersion in electronic forms of communication might lead to different but equally valid ways of being smart—forms of intelligence that go unrecognized by SAT tests. "I'm listening to that argument with more and more sympathy," concedes Stewart of the College Boards.

It is possible, moreover, that electronic forms of communication 57 have more potential than is currently being expressed in either the vapid fantasies of Madonna videos or the static talk shows and costume dramas of public television. These media might be capable, given time, of creating a culture as profound and deep as that of reading. These technologies might, in other words, have more to "giveth" than we can yet imagine.

58   It took 2,000 years of writing before an alphabet was developed. It took a century and a half of printing before someone thought to print a novel or a newspaper. New communications technologies do not arrive upon the scene fully grown; they need time to develop the methods and forms that best exploit their potential.

59   Our communications revolution, from this perspective, is still quite young. TV has been around for only half a century. Most of its programming is still recycled theater—mini-dramas and comedies; its more stylistically adventurous forms—commercials and music videos—are little more than demonstrations of the visual capabilities of the medium.

60   Television's technicians have mastered the art of mating laugh track to quip; they can make everything from cats to toothbrushes dance. But TV still may not have stumbled upon the grammar and syntax of video—the patterns and relations of images and sounds that will enable us to communicate complex ideas with clarity and exactness. Television may not yet have discovered the forms that will do for that medium what the novel and the newspaper did for print.

61   TV today grapples with difficult subjects only by getting slow and boring. It is possible to imagine a television program that would be difficult for the opposite reason: because it is too fast, too busy, too full of information. Perhaps such super-dense television would be able to plumb depths quickly enough to fit the video generation's short attention spans, or perhaps this TV would be stimulating enough to stretch those attention spans.

62   Does television really have such potential? Does a whole culture's worth of new perspectives, new ideas, new creations in fact lie slumbering in our television sets, just waiting for programming capable of awakening them? "Possibly," Daniel Kevles comments with some skepticism, "but I think any more intelligent programming will still have to coexist with MTV and action dramas."

63   Still, if the electronic media can, even intermittently, transform themselves into vehicles for ideas with the reach and capacity of print, it would be good news for our society. The Postmans of the world could rest easy: We would not go giggling off into decadence and dictatorship. But such a development would represent still more bad news for reading.

64   Is reading likely to survive the electronic age? Of course, Daniel Boorstin says. He scoffs at the notion that books, magazines or newspapers are going to disappear any time soon. Boorstin calls this the

"displacement fallacy" and points out that radio survived and prospered after the introduction of TV, despite many gloomy predictions to the contrary. "New technologies tend to discover unique opportunities for the old," Boorstin maintains.

Not every outdated communication technology succeeds in 65 finding such an opportunity. Consider smoke signals, for example, or town criers or the telegram. Nevertheless, Boorstin has a point.

Books already have found some new functions for them- 66 selves—as reference manuals, for example. Magazines have survived in part by discovering audiences too small and specialized for TV to reach. And newspapers? Well, maybe *USA* Today, with its brief, snappy stories, is responding to a new opportunity presented by the TV generation's shortened attention spans. Or maybe newspapers are still searching for their niche in the electronic age.

Print and electronics also collaborate more than is generally 67 recognized. According to the preliminary results of a study by Robert Kubey, a communications professor at Rutgers University, words appear in about 20% of the images in a sample of 30 channels available on cable. And the alphabet has recently found a new life for itself on the keyboards of computers.

"I'm using about 20 times as much paper since I started using 68 a computer," Ong adds. "A new technology does not wipe out what went before; it transforms and enhances it. When people started writing, they didn't quit talking." Indeed, they probably spoke more logically.

However, the introduction of writing undoubtedly did cause 69 people to spend less time talking—because of the old not-enough-hours-in-the-day problem. And it probably did cause them to rely less on speech for communicating important information. So, whatever new forms print may assume in response to electronics, it is unlikely that print will regain its position as our major source of information or entertainment.

Reading still plays and, for the foreseeable future, will continue 70 to play, a crucial role in our society. Nevertheless, there is no getting around the fact that reading's role has diminished and likely will continue to shrink.

This does not mean we should begin turning first-grade classes 71 over to video lessons. Until the new technologies grow up a bit, it would not hurt any of us to read more to our children or take a book with us the next time we must sit and wait. And perhaps it was not a bad idea that you chose, instead of watching the Rams game or renting *Dances With Wolves*, to make it through this article.

Thinking Critically About This Reading

1. What kind of evidence does the author cite to support his contention that reading is in decline? What objection to this evidence might a conscientious reader legitimately raise?

2. The author quotes an expert who criticizes people for reading "too rapidly." What do you find wrong with reading "too rapidly"?

3. The author quotes Socrates as decrying the introduction of a written culture and arguing for the superiority of the oral one it was replacing. What similar argument could an alert reader make against the author's views? What counter argument could a defender of reading make?

4. If a Gallup poll on reading were conducted during the days of the founding fathers, what would you expect the results to show— more or less reading than today? Why?

5. What distinction between literacy and reading is implied in this article? What are the advantages of being literate, and how is literacy related to our sense of logic?

Understanding the Writer's Process

1. Aside from introducing his topic, what other purpose does the writer's opening rhetorical question serve?

2. What implicit definition of reading does the author propose and how does it fit in with his thesis?

3. The author repeatedly cites statistics that seem to contradict his thesis about the decline of reading, for example, the statistics in paragraph 26. How does he then use these same figures to support his thesis?

4. In paragraph 8, the author describes an experiment conducted by a *New Republic* writer which seems to prove that books are being bought but not read. What other explanation can you suggest to account for the results of this experiment?

5. In arguing that reading is in decline, the author frequently cites opinions from commentators who disagree with his thesis. What

purpose do you think the author achieves by this citing of the opposition?

Examining the Writer's Language

1. Define the meanings of the following words used in this essay: copious (paragraph 4), esoteric (6), surreptitiously (32), repositories (35), vacuous (46), bibliophiles (47), inculcated (56), vapid (57).
2. What is the meaning of "per capita newspaper circulation" in paragraph 15?
3. What is a "siren song" as used by the author in paragraph 28 in "the siren songs of the tube"? Explain the origin of this phrase.
4. In paragraph 41, the author quotes Neil Postman as saying, "New communications technologies giveth, and they taketh away." To what does this odd phrasing "giveth" and "taketh" allude?
5. In paragraph 27, what does the author's description of the advent of television imply about his attitude toward that technology?

Suggestions for Writing

1. Write an essay of any type about your own reading habits.
2. Defend or attack the proliferation of video in our daily lives, including television.

HOW TO MARK A BOOK

Mortimer Adler

Mortimer Adler—American educator, writer, and son of a jewelry salesman—was born in New York City in 1902. He received his Ph.D. from Columbia in 1928 and taught for many years at the University of Chicago. Adler planned and oversaw publication of the fifteenth edition of the Encyclopaedia Britannica, *which appeared in 1974. Since then he has been an honorary trustee of the Aspen Institute for Humanistic Studies.*

Adler's many published works include the best-seller
How to Read a Book (1940), Six Great Ideas *(1981),*
and How to Talk and Listen *(1982).*

Preparing to Read This Selection Critically

In "How to Mark a Book," Adler advocates a method of reading that flies in the face of the modern way, which tends to stress speed even if the cost is some initial loss of comprehension. "Never reread a passage" is advice that many teachers of speed reading urge on their students. But Adler says the opposite: He advocates that we reread, we rethink, we pause to ponder and argue, and always we note not only what the author is saying, but how we feel about his message. This is an essay rich in such suggestions and one we would urge you to read and savor slowly, perhaps even taking the time to make notes in the margins as the author suggests.

1   You know you have to read "between the lines" to get the most out of anything. I want to persuade you to do something equally important in the course of your reading. I want to persuade you to "write between the lines." Unless you do, you are not likely to do the most efficient kind of reading.

2   I contend, quite bluntly, that marking up a book is not an act of mutilation but of love.

3   You shouldn't mark up a book which isn't yours. Librarians (or your friends) who lend you books expect you to keep them clean, and you should. If you decide that I am right about the usefulness of marking books, you will have to buy them. Most of the world's great books are available today, in reprint editions, at less than a dollar.

4   There are two ways in which one can own a book. The first is the property right you establish by paying for it, just as you pay for clothes and furniture. But this act of purchase is only the prelude to possession. Full ownership comes only when you have made it a part of yourself, and the best way to make yourself a part of it is by writing in it. An illustration may make the point clear. You buy a beefsteak and transfer it from the butcher's icebox to your own. But you do not own the beefsteak in the most important sense until you consume it

and get it into your bloodstream. I am arguing that books, too, must be absorbed in your bloodstream to do you any good.

Confusion about what it means to *own* a book leads people to   5
a false reverence for paper, binding, and type—a respect for the physical thing—the craft of the printer rather than the genius of the author. They forget that it is possible for a man to acquire the idea, to possess the beauty, which a great book contains, without staking his claim by pasting his bookplate inside the cover. Having a fine library doesn't prove that its owner has a mind enriched by books; it proves nothing more than that he, his father, or his wife, was rich enough to buy them.

There are three kinds of book owners. The first has all the   6
standard sets and best-sellers—unread, untouched. (This deluded individual owns woodpulp and ink, not books.) The second has a great many books—a few of them read through, most of them dipped into, but all of them as clean and shiny as the day they were bought. (This person would probably like to make books his own, but is restrained by a false respect for their physical appearance.) The third has a few books or many—everyone of them dog-eared and dilapidated, shaken and loosened by continual use, marked and scribbled in from front to back. (This man owns books.)

It is false respect, you may ask, to preserve intact and unblem-   7
ished a beautifully printed book, an elegantly bound edition? Of course not. I'd no more scribble all over a first edition of *Paradise Lost* than I'd give my baby a set of crayons and an original Rembrandt! I wouldn't mark up a painting or a statue. Its soul, so to speak, is inseparable from its body. And the beauty of a rare edition or of a richly manufactured volume is like that of a painting or a statue.

But the soul of a book *can* be separated from its body. A book   8
is more like the score of a piece of music than it is like a painting. No great musician confuses a symphony with the printed sheets of music. Arturo Toscanini reveres Brahms, but Toscanini's score of the C-minor Symphony is so thoroughly marked up that no one but the maestro himself can read it. The reason why a great conductor makes notations on his musical scores—marks them up again and again each time he returns to study them—is the reason why you should mark your books. If your respect for magnificent binding or typography gets in the way, buy yourself a cheap edition and pay your respects to the author.

9   Why is marking up a book indispensable to reading? First, it keeps you awake. (And I don't mean merely conscious; I mean wide awake.) In the second place, reading, if it is active, is thinking, and thinking tends to express itself in words, spoken or written. The marked book is usually the thought-through book. Finally, writing helps you remember the thoughts you had, or the thoughts the author expressed. Let me develop these three points.

10   If reading is to accomplish anything more than passing time, it must be active. You can't let your eyes glide across the lines of a book and come up with an understanding of what you have read. Now an ordinary piece of light fiction, like say, *Gone with the Wind*, doesn't require the most active kind of reading. The books you read for pleasure can be read in a state of relaxation, and nothing is lost. But a great book, rich in ideas and beauty, a book that raises and tries to answer great fundamental questions, demands the most active reading of which you are capable. You don't absorb the ideas of John Dewey[1] the way you absorb the crooning of Mr. Vallee.[2] You have to reach for them. That you cannot do while you're asleep.

11   If, when you've finished reading a book, the pages are filled with your notes, you know that you read actively. The most famous *active* reader of great books I know is President Hutchins, of the University of Chicago. He also has the hardest schedule of business activities of any man I know. He invariably reads with a pencil, and sometimes, when he picks up a book and pencil in the evening, he finds himself, instead of making intelligent notes, drawing what he calls "caviar factories" on the margins. When that happens, he puts the book down. He knows he's too tired to read, and he's just wasting time.

12   But, you may ask, why is writing necessary? Well, the physical act of writing, with your own hand, brings words and sentences more sharply before your mind and preserves them better in your memory. To set down your reaction to important words and sentences you have read, and the questions they have raised in your mind, is to preserve those reactions and sharpen those questions.

13   Even if you wrote on a scratch pad, and threw the paper away when you had finished writing, your grasp of the book would be surer. But you don't have to throw the paper away. The margins

[1] John Dewey (1859–1952), educational philosopher who had a profound influence on learning through experimentation.
[2] Rudy Vallee was a popular singer of the 1920s, famous for his crooning high notes.

(top and bottom, as well as side), the end-papers, the very space between the lines, are all available. They aren't sacred. And, best of all, your marks and notes become an integral part of the book and stay there forever. You can pick up the book the following week or year, and there are all your points of agreement, disagreement, doubt, and inquiry. It's like resuming an interrupted conversation with the advantage of being able to pick up where you left off.

And that is exactly what reading a book should be: a conversation between you and the author. Presumably he knows more about the subject than you do; naturally, you'll have the proper humility as you approach him. But don't let anybody tell you that a reader is supposed to be solely on the receiving end. Understanding is a two-way operation; learning doesn't consist in being an empty receptacle. The learner has to question himself and question the teacher. He even has to argue with the teacher, once he understands what the teacher is saying. And marking a book is literally an expression of your differences, or agreements of opinion, with the author.

There are all kinds of devices for marking a book intelligently and fruitfully. Here's the way I do it:

1. *Underlining*: of major points, of important or forceful statements.

2. *Vertical lines at the margin*: to emphasize a statement already underlined.

3. *Star, asterisk, or other doo-dad at the margin*: to be used sparingly, to emphasize the ten or twenty most important statements in the book. (You may want to fold the bottom corner of each page on which you use such marks. It won't hurt the sturdy paper on which most modern books are printed, and you will be able to take the book off the shelf at any time and, by opening it at the folded-corner page, refresh your recollection of the book.)

4. *Numbers in the margin*: to indicate the sequence of points the author makes in developing a single argument.

5. *Numbers of other pages in the margin*: to indicate where else in the book the author made points relevant to the point marked; to tie up the ideas in a book, which, though they may be separated by many pages, belong together.

6. *Circling of key words or phrases.*

7. *Writing in the margin, or at the top or bottom of the page, for the sake of*: recording questions (and perhaps answers) which a passage raised in your mind; reducing a complicated discussion to a simple statement; recording the sequence of major points right

through the books. I use the end-papers at the back of the book to make a personal index of the author's points in the order of their appearance.

23   The front end-papers are, to me, the most important. Some people reserve them for a fancy bookplate. I reserve them for fancy thinking. After I have finished reading the book and making my personal index on the back end-papers, I turn to the front and try to outline the book, not page by page, or point by point (I've already done that at the back), but as an integrated structure, with a basic unity and an order of parts. This outline is, to me, the measure of my understanding of the work.

24   If you're a die-hard anti-book-marker, you may object that the margins, the space between the lines, and the end-papers don't give you room enough. All right. How about using a scratch pad slightly smaller than the page-size of the book—so that the edges of the sheets won't protrude? Make your index, outlines, and even your notes on the pad, and then insert these sheets permanently inside the front and back covers of the book.

25   Or, you may say that this business of marking books is going to slow up your reading. It probably will. That's one of the reasons for doing it. Most of us have been taken in by the notion that speed of reading is a measure of our intelligence. There is no such thing as the right speed for intelligent reading. Some things should be read quickly and effortlessly, and some should be read slowly and even laboriously. The sign of intelligence in reading is the ability to read different things differently according to their worth. In the case of good books, the point is not to see how many of them you can get through, but rather how many can get through you—how many you can make your own. A few friends are better than a thousand acquaintances. If this be your aim, as it should be, you will not be impatient if it takes more time and effort to read a great book than it does a newspaper.

26   You may have one final objection to marking books. You can't lend them to your friends because nobody else can read them without being distracted by your notes. Furthermore, you won't want to lend them because a marked copy is a kind of intellectual diary, and lending it is almost like giving your mind away.

27   If your friend wishes to read your *Plutarch's Lives, Shakespeare,* or *The Federalist Papers,* tell him gently but firmly to buy a copy. You will lend him your car or your coat—but your books are as much a part of you as your head or your heart.

Thinking Critically About This Reading

1. What objections might one who reads strictly for pleasure raise to the author's scheme of marking books?

2. What is your definition of a *great book*? What examples of great books can you give?

3. How do your own reading habits differ from the author's system?

4. Most speed-reading courses work to suppress the tendency of the typical reader to internally repeat an author's words. Do you hear an author's words as you read? In what way does hearing an author's words help or hinder your comprehension?

5. Do you think the author's system would work for reading fiction as well as nonfiction? Why? Why not?

Understanding the Writer's Process

1. Why does the author make a separate paragraph of the single sentence comprising paragraph 2?

2. In paragraph 6, the author classifies the three types of book owners. What primary technique for achieving coherence does the author employ?

3. Comment on the author's use of rhetorical questions throughout this essay. What assumption does he make about the reader by using rhetorical questions?

4. In explaining and justifying his scheme for marking books, where and how does the author use testimonial evidence to support it?

5. How does the author ensure that a reader can follow the steps of his process explanation on how to mark a book?

Examining the Writer's Language

1. Define the meanings of the following words as used in this essay: mutilation (paragraph 2), dilapidated (6), integral (13), integrated (23), protrude (24).

2. How would you characterize the diction of this essay? For what kind of audience do you think this essay was originally written?

3. What language characteristics identify this as an informal essay? Cite some specific instances.

4. How does the author address the reader? What is the effect of this address?

5. What analogy does the author use in paragraph 4 to clarify his assertion that purchasing a book is not the same as owning it? Aside from its aptness or inaptness, what is unusual about his analogy?

Suggestions for Writing

1. Write a process essay outlining the sequence you observe in reading a book.

2. Write an essay about the one book above all others you found most memorable and moving. Say why it affected you as it did.

HOW TO SAY NOTHING IN 500 WORDS

Paul Roberts

> *Paul McHenry Roberts (1917–1967) was a popular English teacher and textbook writer for over twenty years, first at San Jose State College and later at Cornell University. His several books on English and linguistics include* Understanding Grammar *(1954),* Patterns of English *(1956), and* Understanding English *(1958).*

Preparing to Read This Selection Critically

This essay is regarded as a minor classic of English instruction not only for its sharply irreverent description of the writing classroom, but also for the wealth of practical if unconventional suggestions it offers the beginner scribbler. Roberts not only preaches, he practices. Every suggestion he gives for sharpening writing he practices here with grace and wit. He advises student writers to "call a fool a fool," and does. Ask yourself, as you read, whether the unorthodox techniques suggested by Roberts would work in your particular writing class. How, for example, would your instructor react if you wrote an essay in praise of communism?

It's Friday afternoon, and you have almost survived another 1 week of classes. You are just looking forward dreamily to the weekend when the English instructor says: "For Monday you will turn in a five-hundred-word composition on college football."

Well, that puts a good hole in the weekend. You don't have 2 any strong views on college football one way or the other. You get rather excited during the season and go to all the home games and find it rather more fun than not. On the other hand, the class has been reading Robert Hutchins in the anthology and perhaps Shaw's "Eighty-Yard Run," and from the class discussion you have got the idea that the instructor thinks college football is for the birds. You are no fool. You can figure out what side to take.

After dinner you get out the portable typewriter that you got 3 for high school graduation. You might as well get it over with and enjoy Saturday and Sunday. Five hundred words is about two double-spaced pages with normal margins. You put in a sheet of paper, think up a title, and you're off:

WHY COLLEGE FOOTBALL SHOULD BE ABOLISHED

College football should be abolished because it's bad for the school and also for the players. The players are so busy practicing that they don't have any time for their studies.

This, you feel, is a mighty good start. The only trouble is that it's only thirty-two words. You still have four hundred and sixty-eight to go, and you've pretty well exhausted the subject. It comes to you that you do your best thinking in the morning, so you put away the typewriter and go to the movies. But the next morning you have to do your washing and some math problems, and in the afternoon you go to the game. The English instructor turns up too, and you wonder if you've taken the right side after all. Saturday night you have a date, and Sunday morning you have to go to church. (You can't let English assignments interfere with your religion.) What with one thing and another, it's ten o'clock Sunday night before you get out the typewriter again. You make a pot of coffee and start to fill out your views on college football. Put a little meat on the bones.

Satire — witty, reproof. (lesson)
Clever & humorous, sold.

WHY COLLEGE FOOTBALL
SHOULD BE ABOLISHED

In my opinion, it seems to me that college football should be abolished. The reason why I think this to be true is because I feel that football is bad for the college in nearly every respect. As Robert Hutchins says in his article in our anthology in which he discusses college football, it would be better if the colleges had race horses and had races with one another, because then the horses would not have to attend classes. I firmly agree with Mr. Hutchins on this point, and I am sure that many other students would agree too.

One reason why it seems to me that college football is bad is that it has become too commercial. In the olden times when people played football just for the fun of it, maybe college football was all right, but they do not play football just for the fun of it now as they used to in the old days. Nowadays college football is what you might call a big business. Maybe this is not true at all schools, and I don't think it is especially true here at State, but certainly this is the case at most colleges and universities in America nowadays, as Mr. Hutchins points out in his very interesting article. Actually the coaches and alumni go around to the high schools and offer the high school stars large salaries to come to their colleges and play football for them. There was one case where a high school star was offered a convertible if he would play football for a certain college.

Another reason for abolishing college football is that it is bad for the players. They do not have time to get a college education, because they are so busy playing football. A football player has to practice every afternoon from three to six and then he is so tired that he can't concentrate on his studies. He just feels like dropping off to sleep after dinner, and then the next day he goes to his classes without having studied and maybe he fails the test.

(Good ripe stuff, so far, but you're still a hundred and fifty-one words from home. One more push.)

Also I think college football is bad for the colleges and the universities because not very many students get to participate in it. Out of a college of ten thousand students only seventy-five or a hundred play football, if that many. Football is what you might call a spectator sport. That means that most people go to watch it but do not play it themselves.

(Four hundred and fifteen. Well, you still have the conclusion, and when you retype it, you can make the margins a little wider.)

> These are the reasons why I agree with Mr. Hutchins that college football should be abolished in American colleges and universities.

On Monday you turn it in, moderately hopeful, and on Friday   4
it comes back marked "weak in content" and sporting a big "D."

This essay is exaggerated a little, not much. The English in-   5
structor will recognize it as reasonably typical of what an assignment on college football will bring in. He knows that nearly half of the class will contrive in five hundred words to say that college football is too commercial and bad for the players. Most of the other half will inform him that college football builds character and prepares one for life and brings prestige to the school. As he reads paper after paper all saying the same thing in almost the same words, all blood-less, five hundred words dripping out of nothing, he wonders how he allowed himself to get trapped into teaching English when he might have had a happy and interesting life as an electrician or a confidence man.

Well, you may ask, what can you do about it? The subject is   6
one on which you have few convictions and little information. Can you be expected to make a dull subject interesting? As a matter of fact, this is precisely what you are expected to do. This is the writer's essential task. All subjects, except sex, are dull until somebody makes them interesting. The writer's job is to find the argument, the approach, the angle, the wording that will take the reader with him. This is seldom easy, and it is particularly hard in subjects that have been much discussed: College Football, Fraternities, Popular Music, Is Chivalry Dead?, and the like. You will feel that there is nothing you can do with such subjects except repeat the old bro-mides. But there are some things you can do which will make your papers, if not throbbingly alive, at least less insufferably tedious than they might otherwise be.

AVOID THE OBVIOUS CONTENT

Say the assignment is college football. Say that you've decided   7
to be against it. Begin by putting down the arguments that come to your mind: it is too commercial, it takes the students' minds off their studies, it is hard on the players, it makes the university a kind of circus instead of an intellectual center, for most schools it

is financially ruinous. Can you think of any more arguments, just off hand? All right. Now when you write your paper, *make sure that you don't use any of the material on this list.* If these are the points that leap to your mind, they will leap to everyone else's too, and whether you get a "C" or a "D" may depend on whether the instructor reads your paper early when he is fresh and tolerant or late, when the sentence "In my opinion, college football has become too commercial," inexorably repeated, has brought him to the brink of lunacy.

8   Be against college football for some reason or reasons of your own. If they are keen and perceptive ones, that's splendid. But even if they are trivial or foolish or indefensible, you are still ahead so long as they are not everybody else's reasons too. Be against it because the colleges don't spend enough money on it to make it worthwhile, because it is bad for the characters of the spectators, because the players are forced to attend classes, because the football stars hog all the beautiful women, because it competes with baseball and is therefore un-American and possibly Communist-inspired. There are lots of more or less unused reasons for being against college football.

9   Sometimes it is a good idea to sum up and dispose of the trite and conventional points before going on to your own. This has the advantage of indicating to the reader that you are going to be neither trite nor conventional. Something like this:

> We are often told that college football should be abolished because it has become too commercial or because it is bad for the players. These arguments are no doubt very cogent, but they don't really go to the heart of the matter.

Then you go to the heart of the matter.

TAKE THE LESS USUAL SIDE

10   One rather simple way of getting into your paper is to take the side of the argument that most of the citizens will want to avoid. If the assignment is an essay on dogs, you can, if you choose, explain that dogs are faithful and lovable companions, intelligent, useful as guardians of the house and protectors of children, indispensable in police work—in short, when all is said and done, man's best friends. Or you can suggest that those big brown eyes conceal, more often than not, a vacuity of mind and an inconstancy of purpose; that the dogs you have known most intimately have been mangy, ill-

tempered brutes, incapable of instruction; and that only your nobility of mind and fear of arrest prevent you from kicking the flea-ridden animals when you pass them on the street.

Naturally personal convictions will sometimes dictate your approach. If the assigned subject is "Is Methodism Rewarding to the Individual?" and you are a pious Methodist, you have really no choice. But few assigned subjects, if any, will fall in this category. Most of them will lie in broad areas of discussion with much to be said on both sides. They are intellectual exercises, and it is legitimate to argue now one way and now another, as debaters do in similar circumstances. Always take the side that looks to you hardest, least defensible. It will almost always turn out to be easier to write interestingly on that side. 11

This general advice applies where you have a choice of subjects. If you are to choose among "The Value of Fraternities" and "My Favorite High School Teacher" and "What I Think About Beetles," by all means plump for the beetles. By the time the instructor gets to your paper, he will be up to his ears in tedious tales about a French teacher at Bloombury High and assertions about how fraternities build character and prepare one for life. Your views on beetles, whatever they are, are bound to be a refreshing change. 12

Don't worry too much about figuring out what the instructor thinks about the subject so that you can cuddle up with him. Chances are his views are no stronger than yours. If he does have convictions and you oppose him, his problem is to keep from grading you higher than you deserve in order to show he is not biased. This doesn't mean that you should always cantankerously dissent from what the instructor says; that gets tiresome too. And if the subject assigned is "My Pet Peeve," do not begin, "My pet peeve is the English instructor who assigns papers on 'my pet peeve.' " This was still funny during the War of 1812, but it has sort of lost its edge since then. It is in general good manners to avoid personalities. 13

SLIP OUT OF ABSTRACTION

If you will study the essay on college football [near the beginning of this essay], you will perceive that one reason for its appalling dullness is that it never gets down to particulars. It is just a series of not very glittering generalities: "football is bad for the colleges," "it has become too commercial," "football is big business," "it is bad for the players," and so on. Such round phrases thudding 14 against the reader's brain are unlikely to convince him, though they may well render him unconscious.

15   If you want the reader to believe that college football is bad for the players, you have to do more than say so. You have to display the evil. Take your roommate, Alfred Simkins, the second-string center. Picture poor old Alfy coming home from football practice every evening, bruised and aching, agonizingly tired, scarcely able to shovel the mashed potatoes into his mouth. Let us see him staggering up to the room, getting out his econ textbook, peering desperately at it with his good eye, falling asleep and failing the test in the morning. Let us share his unbearable tension as Saturday draws near. Will he fail, be demoted, lose his monthly allowance, be forced to return to the coal mines? And if he succeeds, what will be his reward? Perhaps a slight ripple of applause when the third-string center replaces him, a moment of elation in the locker room if the team wins, of despair if it loses. What will he look back on when he graduates from college? Toil and torn ligaments. And what will be his future? He is not good enough for pro football, and he is too obscure and weak in econ to succeed in stocks and bonds. College football is tearing the heart from Alfy Simkins and, when it finishes with him, will callously toss aside the shattered hulk.

16   This is no doubt a weak enough argument for the abolition of college football, but it is a sight better than saying, in three or four variations, that college football (in your opinion) is bad for the players.

17   Look at the work of any professional writer and notice how constantly he is moving from the generality, the abstract statement, to the concrete example, the facts and figures, the illustrations. If he is writing on juvenile delinquency, he does not just tell you that juveniles are (it seems to him) delinquent and that (in his opinion) something should be done about it. He shows you juveniles being delinquent, tearing up movie theatres in Buffalo, stabbing high school principals in Dallas, smoking marijuana in Palo Alto. And more than likely he is moving toward some specific remedy, not just a general wringing of the hands.

18   It is no doubt possible to be *too* concrete, too illustrative or anecdotal, but few inexperienced writers err this way. For most the soundest advice is to be seeking always for the picture, to be always turning general remarks into seeable examples. Don't say, "Sororities teach girls the social graces." Say, "Sorority life teaches a girl how to carry on a conversation while pouring tea, without sloshing the tea into the saucer." Don't say, "I like certain kinds of popular

music very much." Say, "Whenever I hear Gerber Sprinklittle play 'Mississippi Man' on the trombone, my socks creep up my ankles."

GET RID OF OBVIOUS PADDING

The student toiling away at his weekly English theme is too 19 often tormented by a figure: five hundred words. How, he asks himself, is he to achieve this staggering total? Obviously by never using one word when he can somehow work in ten.

He is therefore seldom content with a plain statement like "Fast 20 driving is dangerous." This has only four words in it. He takes thought, and the sentence becomes:

> In my opinion, fast driving is dangerous.

Better, but he can do better still:

> In my opinion, fast driving would seem to be rather dangerous.

If he is really adept, it may come out:

> In my humble opinion, though I do not claim to be an expert on this complicated subject, fast driving, in most circumstances, would seem to be rather dangerous in many respects, or at least so it would seem to me.

Thus four words have been turned into forty, and not an iota of content has been added.

Now this is a way to go about reaching five hundred words, 21 and if you are content with a "D" grade, it is as good a way as any. But if you aim higher, you must work differently. Instead of stuffing your sentences with straw, you must try steadily to get rid of the padding, to make your sentences lean and tough. If you are really working at it, your first draft will greatly exceed the required total, and then you will work it down, thus:

> It is thought in some quarters that fraternities do not contribute as much as might be expected to campus life.
>
> Some people think that fraternities contribute little to campus life.
>
> The average doctor who practices in small towns or in the country must toil night and day to heal the sick.
>
> Most country doctors work long hours.
>
> When I was a little girl, I suffered from shyness and embarrassment in the presence of others.

I was a shy little girl.

It is absolutely necessary for the person employed as a marine fireman to give the matter of steam pressure his undivided attention at all times.

The fireman has to keep his eye on the steam gauge.

22   You may ask how you can arrive at five hundred words at this rate. Simple. You dig up more real content. Instead of taking a couple of obvious points off the surface of the topic and then circling warily around them for six paragraphs, you work in and explore, figure out the details. You illustrate. You say that fast driving is dangerous, and then you prove it. How long does it take to stop a car at forty and at eighty? How far can you see at night? What happens when a tire blows? What happens in a head-on collision at fifty miles an hour? Pretty soon your paper will be full of broken glass and blood and headless torsos, and reaching five hundred words will not really be a problem.

CALL A FOOL A FOOL

23   Some of the padding in freshman themes is to be blamed not on anxiety about the word minimum but on excessive timidity. The student writes "In my opinion, the principal of my high school acted in ways that I believe every unbiased person would have to call foolish." This isn't exactly what he means. What he means is, "My high school principal was a fool." If he was a fool, call him a fool. Hedging the thing about with "in-my-opinion's" and "it-seems-to-me's" and "as-I-see-it's" and "at-least-from-my-point-of-view's" gains you nothing. Delete these phrases whenever they creep into your paper.

24   The student's tendency to hedge stems from a modesty that in other circumstances would be commendable. He is, he realizes, young and inexperienced, and he half suspects that he is dopey and fuzzy-minded beyond the average. Probably only too true. But it doesn't help to announce your incompetence six times in every paragraph. Decide what you want to say and say it as vigorously as possible, without apology and in plain words.

25   Linguistic diffidence can take various forms. One is what we call *euphemism*. This is the tendency to call a spade "a certain garden implement" or women's underwear "unmentionables." It is stronger in some eras than others and in some people than others but it always operates more or less in subjects that are touchy or taboo:

death, sex, madness, and so on. Thus we shrink from saying "He died last night" but say instead "passed away," "left us," "joined his Maker," "went to his reward." Or we try to take off the tension with a lighter cliché: "kicked the bucket," "cashed in his chips," "handed in his dinner pail." We have found all sorts of ways to avoid saying *mad:* "mentally ill," "touched," "not quite right upstairs," "feebleminded," "innocent," "simple," "off his trolley," "not in his right mind." Even such a now plain word as *insane* began as a euphemism with the meaning "not healthy."

Modern science, particularly psychology, contributes many polysyllables in which we can wrap our thoughts and blunt their force. To many writers there is no such thing as a bad schoolboy. Schoolboys are maladjusted or unoriented or misunderstood or in the need of guidance or lacking in continued success toward satisfactory integration of the personality as a social unit, but they are never bad. Psychology no doubt makes us better men and women, more sympathetic and tolerant, but it doesn't make writing any easier. Had Shakespeare been confronted with psychology, "To be or not to be" might have come out, "To continue as a social unit or not to do so. That is the personality problem. Whether 'tis a better sign of integration at the conscious level to display a psychic tolerance toward the maladjustments and repressions induced by one's lack of orientation in one's environment or—" But Hamlet would never have finished the soliloquy.

Writing in the modern world, you cannot altogether avoid modern jargon. Nor, in an effort to get away from euphemism, should you salt your paper with four-letter words. But you can do much if you will mount guard against those roundabout phrases, those echoing polysyllables that tend to slip into your writing to rob it of its crispness and force.

BEWARE OF PAT EXPRESSIONS

Other things being equal, avoid phrases like "other things being equal." Those sentences that come to you whole, or in two or three doughy lumps, are sure to be bad sentences. They are no creation of yours but pieces of common thought floating in the community soup.

Pat expressions are hard, often impossible, to avoid, because they come too easily to be noticed and seem too necessary to be dispensed with. No writer avoids them altogether, but good writers avoid them more often than poor writers.

30   By "pat expressions" we mean such tags as "to all practical intents and purposes," "the pure and simple truth," "from where I sit," "the time of his life," "to the ends of the earth," "in the twinkling of an eye," "as sure as you're born," "over my dead body," "under cover of darkness," "took the easy way out," "when all is said and done," "told him time and time again," "parted the best of friends," "stand up and be counted," "gave him the best years of her life," "worked her fingers to the bone." Like other clichés, these expressions were once forceful. Now we should use them only when we can't possibly think of anything else.

31   Some pat expressions stand like a wall between the writer and thought. Such a one is "the American way of life." Many student writers feel that when they have said that something accords with the American way of life or does not they have exhausted the subject. Actually, they have stopped at the highest level of abstraction. The American way of life is the complicated set of bonds between a hundred and eighty million ways. All of us know this when we think about it, but the tag phrase too often keeps us from thinking about it.

32   So with many another phrase dear to the politician: "this great land of ours," "the man in the street," "our national heritage." These may prove our patriotism or give a clue to our political beliefs, but otherwise they add nothing to the paper except words.

COLORFUL WORDS

33   The writer builds with words, and no builder uses a raw material more slippery and elusive and treacherous. A writer's work is a constant struggle to get the right word in the right place, to find that particular word that will convey his meaning exactly, that will persuade the reader or soothe him or startle or amuse him. He never succeeds altogether—sometimes he feels that he scarcely succeeds at all—but such successes as he has are what make the thing worth doing.

34   There is no book of rules for this game. One progresses through everlasting experiment on the basis of ever-widening experience. There are few useful generalizations that one can make about words as words, but there are perhaps a few.

35   Some words are what we call "colorful." By this we mean that they are calculated to produce a picture or induce an emotion. They are dressy instead of plain, specific instead of general, loud instead of soft. Thus, in place of "Her heart beat," we may write, "Her heart

pounded, throbbed, fluttered, danced." Instead of "He sat in his chair," we may say, "He *lounged, sprawled, coiled."* Instead of "It was hot," we may say, "It was *blistering, sultry, muggy, suffocating, steamy, wilting."*

However, it should not be supposed that the fancy word is 36 always better. Often it is as well to write "Her heart beat" or "It was hot" if that is all it did or all it was. Ages differ in how they like their prose. The nineteenth century liked it rich and smoky. The twentieth has usually preferred it lean and cool. The twentieth century writer, like all writers, is forever seeking the exact word, but he is wary of sounding feverish. He tends to pitch it low, to understate it, to throw it away. He knows that if he gets too colorful, the audience is likely to giggle.

See how this strikes you: "As the rich, golden glow of the 37 sunset died away along the eternal western hills, Angela's limpid blue eyes looked softly and trustingly into Montague's flashing brown ones, and her heart pounded like a drum in time with the joyous song surging in her soul." Some people like that sort of thing, but most modern readers would say, "Good grief," and turn on the television.

COLORED WORDS

Some words we would call not so much colorful as colored— 38 that is, loaded with associations, good or bad. All words—except perhaps structure words—have associations of some sort. We have said that the meaning of a word is the sum of the contexts in which it occurs. When we hear a word, we hear with it an echo of all the situations in which we have heard it before.

In some words, these echoes are obvious and discussable. The 39 word *mother*, for example, has, for most people, agreeable associations. When you hear *mother* you probably think of home, safety, love, food, and various other pleasant things. If one writes, "She was like a mother to me," he gets an effect which he would not get in "She was like an aunt to me." The advertiser makes use of the associations of *mother* by working it in when he talks about his product. The politician works it in when he talks about himself.

So also with such words as *home, liberty, fireside, contentment,* 40 *patriot, tenderness, sacrifice, childlike, manly, bluff, limpid.* All of these words are loaded with associations that would be rather hard to indicate in a straightforward definition. There is more than a literal difference between "They sat around the fireside" and "They sat around the stove." They might have been equally warm and happy around the stove, but *fireside* suggests leisure, grace, quiet tradition, congenial company, and *stove* does not.

41   Conversely, some words have bad associations. *Mother* suggests pleasant things, but *mother-in-law* does not. Many mothers-in-law are heroically lovable and some mothers drink gin all day and beat their children insensible, but these facts of life are beside the point. The point is that *mother* sounds good and *mother-in-law* does not.

42   Or consider the word *intellectual*. This would seem to be a complimentary term, but in point of fact it is not, for it has picked up associations of impracticality and ineffectuality and general dopiness. So also such words as *liberal, reactionary, Communist, socialist, capitalist, radical, schoolteacher, truck driver, undertaker, operator, salesman, huckster, speculator.* These convey meaning on the literal level, but beyond that—sometimes, in some places—they convey contempt on the part of the speaker.

43   The question of whether to use loaded words or not depends on what is being written. The scientist, the scholar, try to avoid them; for the poet, the advertising writer, the public speaker, they are standard equipment. But every writer should take care that they do not substitute for thought. If you write, "Anyone who thinks that is nothing but a Socialist (or Communist or capitalist)" you have said nothing except that you don't like people who think that, and such remarks are effective only with the most naive readers. It is always a bad mistake to think your readers more naive than they really are.

COLORLESS WORDS

44   But probably most student writers come to grief not with words that are colorful or those that are colored but with those that have no color at all. A pet example is *nice*, a word we would find it hard to dispense with in casual conversation but which is no longer capable of adding much to a description. Colorless words are those of such general meaning that in a particular sentence they mean nothing. Slang adjectives like *cool* ("That's real cool") tend to explode all over the language. They are applied to everything, lose their original force, and quickly die.

45   Beware also of nouns of very general meaning, like *circumstances, cases, instances, aspects, factors, relationships, attitudes, eventualities,* etc. In most circumstances you will find that those cases of

writing which contain too many instances of words like these will in this and other aspects have factors leading to unsatisfactory relationships with the reader resulting in unfavorable attitudes on his part and perhaps other eventualities, like a grade of "D." Notice also what *etc.* means. It means "I'd like to make this list longer, but I can't think of any more examples."

Thinking Critically About This Reading

1. In your view, is it ethical for a student to write an essay on a topic chosen simply because he or she thinks it likely to provide relief to the overworked instructor?

2. By implication, how is the author suggesting the student view the instructor? Is this a legitimate view for a student to take of a writing instructor?

3. Why is it not enough for student writers simply to "write from the heart," as they were encouraged to do during the 1960s?

4. What risk does the student writer run who takes the author's advice and calls a fool a fool in his or her essays?

5. Do you agree with Roberts that padding in freshman writing is caused by excessive timidity? If not, what other reason can you suggest for it?

Understanding the Writer's Process

1. From whose point of view is this essay mainly written? What does the writer gain by using this point of view?

2. In paragraph 6, what lead-in to the instructional discussion that follows does the author use? Comment on its effectiveness.

3. In paragraph 15, the author suggests that you show rather than tell your opposition to college football. Does the author practice what he preaches? Cite specific examples from the essay that support your answer.

4. What primary rhetorical technique does the author use to make his suggestions on writing specific and clear?

5. The author offers a series of specific suggestions about writing a 500-word essay. In what logical sequence does the author present his suggestions?

Examining the Writer's Language

1. Define the meanings of the following words as used in this essay: bromides (paragraph 6), inexorably (7), vacuity (10), inconstancy (10), cantankerously (13), adept (20), diffidence (25), euphemism (25), congenial (40).

2. Cite examples of the effective use of colloquial diction in this essay. Substitute a standard word for the colloquial one and say what effect the change has on the writer's style.

3. "Whenever I hear Gerber Sprinklittle play 'Mississippi Man' on the trombone, my socks creep up my ankles." The author suggests this as an alternative to "I like certain kinds of popular music very much." Which of the two sentences do you think would be more acceptable in an English class? Why? How could you rewrite the first sentence to make it conventionally acceptable yet preserve its superior specificity?

4. Identify at least two uses of verbal irony in this essay.

5. How would you characterize the tone of this essay? What does it contribute to the author's pedagogy?

Suggestions for Writing

1. Write an essay on college football, heeding the advice of Paul Roberts.

2. Write an essay explaining the process you follow in writing college essays.

REVISING

Donald Hall

> *Donald Hall (b. 1928) is a poet, essayist, short-story writer, and author of numerous books on poetry and poets. He was born in Connecticut and educated at Harvard and Oxford, where his poem "Exile" won the Newdegate Prize. Hall earned a reputation for writing poetry that reached out to the social themes of post-World War II. He explains his approach by stating that*

"Man learns by love, and not by metaphor." Hall
wrote, among other works, To the Loud Wind and
Other Poems *(1955),* Exiles and Marriages *(1955),* The
Dark Houses *(1958), and* A Roof of Tiger Lilies *(1964).*
A skilled editor, he has published the widely acclaimed
Oxford Book of American Literary Anecdotes *as well*
as the new Oxford Book of Children's Verse in Amer-
ica. *He is also the author of a widely used textbook,*
On Writing Well *(1984), from which the following ex-*
cerpt is reprinted.

Preparing to Read This Selection Critically

Many freshmen enter college with profound misconceptions about writers and writing. Many, for example, believe that naturalness and ease in written
expression are sure signs of a gift for writing and that,
conversely, the struggle to pen words on paper is clear
evidence of no writing talent. Veteran writers, on the
other hand, know that to sound natural and easy on paper
takes constant revision. For the fact is that virtually all
writers are persistent revisers who struggle daily to write.
In this essay, Hall reinforces this ancient truth about writing by showing us the example of Jim Beck, who takes
two stabs at an essay titled, "How I Came to College."
Beck's struggle to express himself in his own voice is
typical of how most writers, beginners as well as veterans,
work.

Almost all writers, almost all the time, need to revise. We need   1
to revise because spontaneity is never adequate. Writing that is
merely emotional release for the writer becomes emotional chaos
for the reader. Even when we write as quickly as our hand can move,
we slide into emotional falsity, into cliché or other static. And we
make leaps by private association that leave our prose unclear. And
we often omit steps in thinking or use a step that we later recognize
as bad logic. Sometimes we overexplain the obvious. Or we include
irrelevant detail. First drafts remain first drafts. They are the material
that we must shape, a marble block that the critical brain chisels
into form. We must shape this material in order to pass it from mind
to mind; we shape our material into a form that allows other people

to receive it. This shaping often requires us, in revising, to reorganize whole paragraphs, both the order of sentences and the sentences themselves. We must drop sentences and clauses that do not belong; we must expand or supply others necessary to a paragraph's development. Often we must revise the order of paragraphs; often we must write new paragraphs to provide coherent and orderly progress.

2   Good writing is an intricate interweaving of inspiration and discipline. A student may need one strand more than the other. Most of us continually need to remember both sides of writing: *we must invent, and we must revise.* In these double acts, invention and revision, we are inventing and revising not just our prose style but our knowledge of ourselves and of the people around us. When Confucius recommended "Make it new," he told us to live what Socrates called "the examined life." It was a moral position. By our language, we shall know ourselves—not once and for all, by a break-through, but continually, all our lives. Therefore, the necessity to write well arises from the need to understand and to discriminate, to be genuine and to avoid what is not genuine, in ourselves and in others. By understanding what our words reveal, we can under-stand ourselves; by changing these words until we arrive at our own voices, we change ourselves; by arriving at our own voices, we are able to speak to others and be heard.

THEMES AND REVISIONS

3   On the first day of class, the assignment was to write for twenty minutes on the topic "How I Came to College." Here is an im-promptu theme by Jim Beck.

> Education is of paramount importance to today's youth.
> No one can underestimate the importance of higher education.
> It makes us well-rounded individuals and we must realize that
> all work and no play is not the way to go about it, but studies
> is the most important part, without a doubt. Therefore I decided
> when I was young that I would go to college and applied myself
> to studies in high school so that I would be admitted. I was
> admitted last winter and my family was very happy as was I.
> Coming here has been a disappointment so far because people
> are not very friendly to freshmen and everyone has their own
> clique and the whole place is too big. But I expect that it will
> get better soon and I will achieve my goal of a higher education
> and being a well-rounded person.

Repetition at the end of the impromptu gives it some unity. 4
When Jim says that "people are not very friendly to freshmen," the
reader glimpses Jim Beck and his feelings. But through most of the
paragraph, the writer is not being himself. You can tell that he is
not being himself because he is sounding like so many other people.
Doubtless he thinks that he writes for a teacher who wants to hear
this sort of language. Really, he makes contact with no audience at
all. Jim is assembling an impromptu from the cliché collection in
the why-I-want-to-go-to-college box. When he says *paramount importance*, does he really know what *paramount* means? Does he mean
that *today's youth* is genuinely different from yesterday's or tomorrow's? And how far into history does *today* extend? What does *well-
rounded* mean? Why say *individual* instead of *person* or *people? Importance* is vague, and saying it twice makes it vaguer. In the sentence
of complaint, where the reader briefly senses an actual writer, Jim
would have done better to *show* his loneliness in an anecdote, instead
of just *telling* us about it. Showing makes contact; telling avoids it.

Later in the term, when he had a free theme, Jim wrote an 5
essay which was not so much a revision of his impromptu as a new
start and which *really* told how he came to college.

The Race to College
Jim Beck

It's horrible now, and I don't know if it will get any better.
The only people who pay attention to me are the people who
are trying to beat me out for the track team. My roommate is
stoned all day and gets A's on his papers anyway. I hate him
because he hates me because I'm a jock. My classes are boring
lectures and the sections are taught by graduate students who
pick on the students because the professors pick on them.

But I remember wanting to come here so bad! Nobody
from Hammerton named Beck had ever been to college. Everybody knew the Becks were stupid. This went for my father,
who never got through high school, and for my grandfather,
who died before I was born, and who was the town drunk. It
went for my two older brothers who went bad, as they say in
Hammerton. Steve got a dishonorable discharge from the Marines and he works on a farm outside town and gets drunk on
Fridays and Saturdays. Curt stole a car and did time at Jackson
and nobody has heard from him since. My sister had a three-
month baby and the town liked to talk about that.

I was different. Everybody told me I was. My mother told
me I wasn't a Beck. My father told me I was going to bring back

the family's good name. (I never knew it had one.) In grammar school the teachers all told me how much better I was than my brothers. By the time I was in sixth grade my father and the school Principal were talking about the University.

My father isn't really dumb. Sometimes people look dumb because it's expected of them. He's worked at the same grocery for twenty years, I guess. Now that I made it to the University, he wants to be called Manager, because he's the only man there besides Mr. Roberts who owns it. (The rest of the help are— is?—kids who bag and an old lady cashier.) When I went back for a weekend everybody treated me as if I won the Olympics.

I said the Principal and my father were talking about my going to the University. All through junior high I said I didn't want to go. I was scared. No Beck could do that. Bad things kept happening to my family. My father had an accident and totalled the car and lost his license and for a year we didn't have a car at all. He had to walk home two miles every night pushing a basket of groceries. When I said I would quit school and get a job, everybody jumped on me.

It wasn't that I was an A student. It was just that I tried hard at everything I did. I got B's mostly. Now with B's, the counsellors kept telling me, I could be admitted to the University, but I wouldn't get a scholarship. I needed mostly A's for that, and then when I got to the University would lose the scholarship if I couldn't keep the grades up. Then my brother Steve, who was a pretty good athlete once, suggested athletics.

I was too skinny for football, too short for basketball, I could barely swim and my school didn't have a swimming team anyway. There is one sport you can practice with no money and no equipment. I started to run when I was in my last year of junior high. It felt good right away. I ran to and from school. I went over to the high school and did laps. The high school coach noticed me and asked me to go out the next year. Running long distances hurts a lot. Sometimes you get a stitch in your left side and suddenly it shifts to your right side. I didn't exactly mind the pain. I studied it. I studied it in order to go to the University, the way I studied everything else.

In my Senior year I was all-state and held two high-school records (600 and half-mile) and I had an athletic scholarship to the University. Now I am here, the first Beck to make it. I don't know why I'm here or why I ran so hard or where I go from here. Now that I am here, the race to get here seems pointless. Nothing in my classes interests me. I study, just as I did before, in order to pass the course or even get a good grade. I run to win, but what am I running for? I will never be a great runner.

Sometimes when I cannot sleep I imagine packing my bags and going back to Hammerton. But I can't do that. They would say, "He's a Beck, all right."

Jim's essay has the two most important features of good writing: it has unity, which means the focus, the point, the coming together of many details; and it has the voice of a real person speaking out of experience with a minimum of tired phrases, of borrowed clothing. It has discipline, and it has feeling. Although Jim is discouraged and feels aimless and melancholy, his mind has made an enormous stride toward knowing and being able to present itself. He revised, using his own experience in his own language. *And* he was disciplined; he used tighter sentence structure, and he found a narrative structure that contained and shaped his thought. Therefore he made contact with his readers.

This revision was the product of much hard work, of which only a portion went to the actual revision. Jim's daily writing—with which he struggled at first and which he later enjoyed—was a source of improvement. He began to find his own, unpompous voice. He also revised other essays after reading his teacher's comments, and after discussing these comments in conferences. Jim Beck also talked with his English teacher during office hours, and thought about his writing and his ideas while he ran cross-country in the autumn of his freshman year.

Thinking Critically About This Reading

1. Reviewing what the author says in paragraph 1, what do you conclude about revising? What is it? Why must it be done? Generally, how much revising of papers submitted as class requirements do you do?

2. What is the main criticism leveled at Jim Beck's essay? Is this a criticism that might apply to many other college students? Why? Why not?

3. What sentence hints at the possibility that Jim is a feeling human being? Take that sentence and, using it as a topic sentence, develop a paragraph reflecting a genuine personality.

4. What does the author consider the two most important features of good writing? In which paragraph are they mentioned? What other features of good writing do you consider important?

5. The author mentions several aspects of improving writing that do not involve putting words on paper. Which of these aspects do you consider most important? Why?

Understanding the Writer's Process

1. What is the author's major strategy in presenting this segment on revising? How appropriate is the strategy?
2. Why does the author mention the "repetition at the end of the impromptu"?
3. What is your opinion of Jim Beck's revision? If you were evaluating the essay, what would you say about it?

Examining the Writer's Language

1. In paragraph 1, what metaphor is used to describe the act of revising an essay? How effective is the image?
2. In the first sentence of paragraph 2, the author uses the phrase "intricate interweaving." If one were to substitute "strong mixture," would the meaning of the sentence remain intact? Why? Why not? Explain your answer fully.
3. Through what means does the final sentence of paragraph 2 achieve a sense of harmony?
4. In paragraph 6, what comparison does the writer draw in order to stress the effect of "tired phrases"? Explain the comparison.

Suggestions for Writing

1. Write for 20 consecutive minutes on the topic "How I Came to College." Then spend another 20 consecutive minutes revising and editing what you have written. Evaluate the final draft. What improvements did you make?
2. Write an essay on some bothersome aspect of your family life. Try to project a completely genuine voice.

WHAT IS STYLE?

F. L. Lucas

F. L. Lucas (1894–1967) was a professor of literature at Cambridge University during the course of four decades. As such, he was best known for his interest in the classics and for his insistence that students write English correctly and with style. While Lucas experimented with a variety of literary forms, his most memorable and most prolific work was in the field of literary criticism. His publications include such major works as The Decline and Fall of the Romantic Ideal *(1934),* Greek Poetry for Everyman *(1951),* Greek Drama for Everyman *(1954), and* The Art of Living *(1959).*

Preparing to Read This Selection Critically

This selection is replete with numerous literary sayings and allusions and is best read with a good dictionary near at hand. Widely reprinted and considered one of the more definitive essays on style, "What Is Style?" practices what it preaches, exemplifies what it defines. Lucas was a Cambridge don steeped in the culture of the Classics, and he ranges abroad into scholarship to support his definition. We are regaled with witticisms and saws from both famous and obscure literary figures, and it helps to know who these people are if we are to appreciate their wit. As you read, ask yourself whether Lucas's genteel discussion of style is as applicable to the office memo or newsletter note as it was to the informal essay.

When it was suggested to Walt Whitman that one of his works 1 should be bound in vellum, he was outraged—"Pshaw!" he snorted, "—hangings, curtains, finger bowls, chinaware, Matthew Arnold!" And he might have been equally irritated by talk of style; for he boasted of "my barbaric yawp"—he would *not* be literary; his readers should touch not a book but a man. Yet Whitman took the pains to rewrite *Leaves of Grass* four times, and his style is unmistakable. Samuel Butler maintained that writers who bothered about their style became unreadable but he bothered about his own. "Style" has got a bad name by growing associated with precious and superior persons who, like Oscar Wilde, spend a morning putting in a comma, and the afternoon (so he said) taking it out again. But such abuse of "style" is misuse of English. For the word means merely "a way of expressing oneself, in language, manner, or appearance"; or, secondly, "a *good* way of so expressing oneself "—as when one says, "Her behavior never lacked style." '

2   Now there is no crime in expressing oneself (though to try to impress oneself on others easily grows revolting or ridiculous). Indeed one cannot help expressing oneself, unless one passes one's life in a cupboard. Even the most rigid Communist, or Organizationman, is compelled by Nature to have a unique voice, unique fingerprints, unique handwriting. Even the signatures of the letters on your breakfast table may reveal more than their writers guess. There are blustering signatures that swish across the page like cornstalks bowed before a tempest. There are cryptic signatures, like a scrabble of lightning across a cloud, suggesting that behind is a lofty divinity whom all must know, or an aloof divinity whom none is worthy to know (though, as this might be highly inconvenient, a docile typist sometimes interprets the mystery in a bracket underneath). There are impetuous squiggles implying that the author is a sort of strenuous Sputnik streaking around the globe every eighty minutes. There are florid signatures, all curlicues and danglements and flamboyance, like the youthful Disraeli (though these seem rather out of fashion). There are humble, humdrum signatures. And there are also, sometimes, signatures that are courteously clear, yet mindful of a certain simple grace and artistic economy—in short, of style.

3   Since, then, not one of us can put pen to paper, or even open his mouth, without giving something of himself away to shrewd observers, it seems mere common sense to give the matter a little thought. Yet it does not seem very common. Ladies may take infinite pains about having style in their clothes, but many of us remain curiously indifferent about having it in our words. How many women would dream of polishing not only their nails but also their tongues? They may play freely on that perilous little organ, but they cannot often be bothered to tune it. And how many men think of improving their talk as well as their golf handicap?

4   No doubt strong silent men, speaking only in gruff monosyllables, may despise "mere words." No doubt the world does suffer from an endemic plague of verbal dysentery. But that, precisely, is bad style. And consider the amazing power of mere words. Adolf Hitler was a bad artist, bad statesman, bad general, and bad man. But largely because he could tune his rant, with psychological nicety, to the exact wave length of his audiences and make millions quarrelsome-drunk all at the same time by his command of windy

nonsense, skilled statesmen, soldiers, scientists were blown away like chaff, and he came near to rule the world. If Sir Winston Churchill had been a mere speechifier, we might well have lost the war; yet his speeches did quite a lot to win it.

No man was less of a literary aesthete than Benjamin Franklin; yet this tallow-chandler's son, who changed world history, regarded as "a principal means of my advancement" that pungent style which he acquired partly by working in youth over old *Spectators*; but mainly by being Benjamin Franklin. The squinting demagogue, John Wilkes, as ugly as his many sins, had yet a tongue so winning that he asked only half an hour's start (to counteract his face) against any rival for a woman's favor. "Vote for you!" growled a surly elector in his constituency. "I'd sooner vote for the devil!" "But in case your friend should not stand . . . ?" Cleopatra, the ensnarer of world conquerors, owed less to the shape of her nose than to the charm of her tongue. Shakespeare himself has often poor plots and thin ideas; even his mastery of character has been questioned; what does remain unchallenged is his verbal magic. Men are often taken, like rabbits, by the ears. And though the tongue has no bones, it can sometimes break millions of them.

"But," the reader may grumble, "I am neither Hitler, Cleopatra, nor Shakespeare. What is all this to me?" Yet we all talk—often too much; we all have to write letters—often too many. We live not by bread alone but also by words. And not always with remarkable efficiency. Strikes, lawsuits, divorces, all sorts of public nuisance and private misery, often come just from the gaggling incompetence with which we express ourselves. Americans and British get at cross-purposes because they use the same words with different meanings. Men have been hanged on a comma in a statute. And in the valley of Balaclava a mere verbal ambiguity, about *which* guns were to be captured, sent the whole Light Brigade to futile annihilation.

Words can be more powerful, and more treacherous, than we sometimes suspect; communication more difficult than we may think. We are all serving life sentences of solitary confinement within our own bodies; like prisoners, we have, as it were, to tap in awkward code to our fellow men in their neighboring cells. Further, when A and B converse, there take part in their dialogue not two characters, as they suppose, but six. For there is A's real self—call it A_1; there is also A's picture of himself—A_2; there is also B's picture of A—A_3. And there are three corresponding personalities of B. With

six characters involved even in a simple tête-à-tête, no wonder we
fall into muddles and misunderstandings.

8   Perhaps, then, there are five main reasons for trying to gain
some mastery of language:

> We have no other way of understanding, informing, mis-
> informing, or persuading one another.
>
> Even alone, we think mainly in words; if our language is
> muddy, so will our thinking be.
>
> By our handling of words we are often revealed and
> judged. "Has he written anything?" said Napoleon of a can-
> didate for an appointment. "Let me see his *style*."
>
> Without a feeling for language one remains half-blind and
> deaf to literature.
>
> Our mother tongue is bettered or worsened by the way
> each generation uses it. Languages evolve like species. They can
> degenerate; just as oysters and barnacles have lost their heads.
> Compare ancient Greek with modern. A heavy responsibility,
> though often forgotten.

9   Why and how did I become interested in style? The main answer, I suppose, is that I was born that way. Then I was, till ten,
an only child running loose in a house packed with books, and in
a world (thank goodness) still undistracted by radio and television.
So at three I groaned to my mother, "Oh, I *wish* I could read," and
at four I read. Now travel among books is the best travel of all, and
the easiest, and the cheapest. (Not that I belittle ordinary travel—
which I regard as one of the three main pleasures in life.) One learns
to write by reading good books, as one learns to talk by hearing
good talkers. And if I have learned anything in writing, it is largely
from writers like Montaigne, Dorothy Osborne, Horace Walpole,
Johnson, Goldsmith, Montesquieu, Voltaire, Flaubert and Anatole
France. Again, I was reared on Greek and Latin, and one can learn
much from translating Homer or the Greek Anthology, Horace or
Tacitus, if one is thrilled by the originals and tries, however vainly,
to recapture some of that thrill in English.

10   But at Rugby I could *not* write English essays. I believe it stupid
to torment boys to write on topics that they know and care nothing
about. I used to rush to the school library and cram the subject, like
a python swallowing rabbits; then, still replete as a postprandial
python, I would tie myself in clumsy knots to embrace those ac-
cursed themes. Bacon was wise in saying that reading makes a full

man; talking, a ready one; writing, an exact one. But writing from
an empty head is futile anguish.

At Cambridge, my head having grown a little fuller, I suddenly 11
found I *could* write—not with enjoyment (it is always tearing oneself
in pieces)—but fairly fluently. Then came the War of 1914–18; and
though soldiers have other things than pens to handle, they learn
painfully to be clear and brief. Then the late Sir Desmond MacCarthy
invited me to review for the *New Statesman:* it was a useful apprenticeship, and he was delightful to work for. But I think it was
well after a few years to stop; reviewers remain essential, but there
are too many books one *cannot* praise, and only the pugnacious
enjoy amassing enemies. By then I was an ink-addict—not because
writing is much pleasure, but because not to write is pain; just as
some smokers do not so much enjoy tobacco as suffer without it.
The positive happiness of writing comes, I think, from work when
done—decently, one hopes, and not without use—and from the letters of readers which help to reassure, or delude, one that so it is.

But one of my most vivid lessons came, I think, from service 12
in a war department during the Second World War. Then, if the
matter one sent out was too wordy, the communication channels
might choke; yet if it was not absolutely clear, the results might be
serious. So I emerged, after six years of it, with more passion than
ever for clarity and brevity, more loathing than ever for the obscure
and the verbose.

For forty years at Cambridge I have tried to teach young men 13
to write well, and have come to think it impossible. To write really
well is a gift inborn; those who have it teach themselves; one can
only try to help and hasten the process. After all, the uneducated
sometimes express themselves far better than their "betters." In language, as in life, it is possible to be perfectly correct—and yet perfectly tedious, or odious. The illiterate last letter of the doomed
Vanzetti was more moving than most professional orators; 18th Century ladies, who should have been spanked for their spelling, could
yet write far better letters than most professors of English; and the
talk of Synge's Irish peasants seems to me vastly more vivid than
the latter styles of Henry James. Yet Synge averred that his characters
owed far less of their eloquence to what he invented for them than
to what he had overheard in the cottages of Wicklow and Kerry:

> CHRISTY. It's little you'll think if my love's a poacher's, or
> an earl's itself, when you'll feel my two hands stretched around
> you, and I squeezing kisses on your puckered lips, till I'd feel

> a kind of pity for the Lord God in all ages sitting lonesome in
> His golden chair.
>   PEGEEN. That'll be right fun, Christy Mahon, and any girl
> would walk her heart out before she'd meet a young man was
> your like for eloquence, or talk at all.

14   Well she might! It's not like that they talk in universities—
more's the pity.

15   But though one cannot teach people to write well, one can
sometimes teach them to write rather better. One can give a certain
number of hints, which often seem boringly obvious—only experience shows they are not.

16   One can say: Beware of pronouns—they are devils. Look at
even Addison, describing the type of pedant who chatters of style
without having any:

> Upon enquiry I found my learned friend had dined that
> day with Mr. Swan, the famous punster; and desiring *him* to
> give me some account of Mr. Swan's conversation, *he* told me
> that *he* generally talked in the Paronomasia, that *he* sometimes
> gave it to the Ploce, but that in *his* humble opinion *he* shone
> most in the Antanaclasis.

What a sluttish muddle of *he* and *him* and *his*! It all needs rewording.
Far better repeat a noun, or a name, than puzzle the reader, even
for a moment, with ambiguous pronouns. Thou shalt not puzzle thy
reader.

17   Or one can say: Avoid jingles. The B.B.C. news bulletins seem
compiled by earless persons, capable of crying around the globe:
"The enemy is re*port*ed to have seized this im*port*ant *port*, and re-
inforcements are hurrying up in sup*port*." Any fool, once told, can
hear such things to be insupportable.

18   Or one can say: Be sparing with relative clauses. Don't string
them together like sausages, or jam them inside one another like
Chinese boxes or the receptacles of Buddha's tooth. Or one can say:
Don't flaunt jargon, like Addison's Mr. Swan, or the type of modern
critic who gurgles more technical terms in a page than Johnson used
in all his *Lives* or Sainte-Beuve in thirty volumes. But dozens of such
snippety precepts, though they may sometimes save people from
writing badly, will help them little toward writing well. Are there
no general rules of a more positive kind, and of more positive use?

19   Perhaps. There *are* certain basic principles which seem to me
observed by many authors I admire, which I think have served me

and which may serve others. I am not talking of geniuses, who are a law to themselves (and do not always write a very good style, either); nor of poetry, which has different laws from prose; nor of poetic prose, like Sir Thomas Browne's or De Quincey's which is often more akin to poetry; but of the plain prose of ordinary books and documents, letters and talk.

The writer should respect truth and himself; therefore honesty. 20 He should respect his readers; therefore courtesy. These are two of the cornerstones of style. Confucius saw it, twenty-five centuries ago: "The Master said, The gentleman is courteous, but not pliable: common men are pliable, but not courteous."

First, honesty. In literature, as in life, one of the fundamentals 21 is to find, and be, one's true self. One's true self may indeed be unpleasant (though one can try to better it); but a false self, sooner or later, becomes disgusting—just as a nice plain woman, painted to the eyebrows, can become horrid. In writing, in the long run, pretense does not work. As the police put it, anything you say may be used as evidence against you. If handwriting reveals character, writing reveals it still more. You cannot fool *all* your judges *all* the time.

Most style is not honest enough. Easy to say, but hard to prac- 22 tice. A writer may take to long words, as young men to beards—to impress. But long words, like beards, are often the badge of charlatans. Or a writer may cultivate the obscure, to seem profound. But even carefully muddied puddles are soon fathomed. Or he may cultivate eccentricity, to seem original. But really original people do not have to think about being original—they can no more help it than they can help breathing. They do not need to dye their hair green. The fame of Meredith, Wilde or Bernard Shaw might now shine brighter, had they struggled less to be brilliant; whereas Johnson remains great, not merely because his gifts were formidable but also because, with all his prejudice and passion, he fought no less passionately to "clear his mind of cant."

Secondly, courtesy—respect for the reader. From this follow 23 several other basic principles of style. Clarity is one. For it is boorish to make your reader rack his brains to understand. One should aim at being impossible to misunderstand—though men's capacity for misunderstanding approaches infinity. Hence Molière and Po Chu-i tried their work on their cooks; and Swift his on his men-servants—"which, if they did not comprehend, he would alter and amend, until they understood it perfectly." Our bureaucrats and pundits, unfortunately, are less considerate.

24   Brevity is another basic principle. For it is boorish, to waste your reader's time. People who would not dream of stealing a penny of one's money turn not a hair at stealing hours of one's life. But that does not make them less exasperating. Therefore there is no excuse for the sort of writer who takes as long as a marching army corps to pass a given point. Besides, brevity is often more effective; the half can say more than the whole, and to imply things may strike far deeper than to state them at length. And because one is particularly apt to waste words on preambles before coming to the substance, there was sense in the Scots professor who always asked his pupils—"Did ye remember to tear up that fir-r-st page?"

25   Here are some instances that would only lose by lengthening.

> *It is useless to go to bed to save the light, if the result is twins.* (Chinese proverb.)
> *My barn is burnt down—*
> * Nothing hides the moon.* (Complete Japanese poem.)
> *Je me regrette.*[1] (Dying words of the gay Vicomtesse d'Houdetot.)
> *I have seen their backs before.* (Wellington, when French marshals turned their backs on him at a reception.)
> *Continue until the tanks stop, then get out and walk.* (Patton to the Twelfth Corps, halted for fuel supplies at St. Dizier, 8/30/44.)

26   Or there is the most laconic diplomatic note on record: when Philip of Macedon wrote to the Spartans that, if he came within their borders, he would leave not one stone of their city, they wrote back the one word—"If."

27   Clarity comes before even brevity. But it is a fallacy that wordiness is necessarily clearer. Metternich when he thought something he had written was obscure would simply go through it crossing out everything irrelevant. What remained, he found, often became clear. Wellington, asked to recommend three names for the post of Commander-in-Chief, India, took a piece of paper and wrote three times—"Napier." Pages could not have been clearer—or as forcible. On the other hand the lectures, and the sentences, of Coleridge became at times bewildering because his mind was often "wiggle-waggle"; just as he could not even walk straight on a path.

28   But clarity and brevity, though a good beginning, are only a beginning. By themselves, they may remain bare and bleak. When

---

[1] "I shall miss myself."

Calvin Coolidge, asked by his wife what the preacher had preached on, replied "Sin," and, asked what the preacher had said, replied, "He was against it," he was brief enough. But one hardly envies Mrs. Coolidge.

An attractive style requires, of course, all kinds of further gifts— 29 such as variety, good humor, good sense, vitality, imagination. Variety means avoiding monotony of rhythm, of language, of mood. One needs to vary one's sentence length (this present article has too many short sentences; but so vast a subject grows here as cramped as a djin in a bottle); to amplify one's vocabulary; to diversify one's tone. There are books that petrify one throughout, with the rigidly pompous solemnity of an owl perched on a leafless tree. But ceaseless facetiousness can be as bad; or perpetual irony. Even the smile of Voltaire can seem at times a fixed grin, a disagreeable wrinkle. Constant peevishness is far worse, as often in Swift; even on the stage too much irritable dialogue may irritate an audience, without its knowing why.

Still more are vitality, energy, imagination gifts that must be 30 inborn before they can be cultivated. But under the head of imagination two common devices may be mentioned that have been the making of many a style—metaphor and simile. Why such magic power should reside in simply saying, or implying, that A is like B remains a little mysterious. But even our unconscious seems to love symbols; again, language often tends to lose itself in clouds of vaporous abstraction, and simile or metaphor can bring it back to concrete solidity; and, again, such imagery can gild the gray flats of prose with sudden sun-glints of poetry.

If a foreigner may for a moment be impertinent, I admire the 31 native gift of Americans for imagery as much as I wince at their fondness for slang. (Slang seems to me a kind of linguistic fungus; as poisonous, and as short-lived, as toadstools.) When Matthew Arnold lectured in the United States, he was likened by one newspaper to "an elderly macaw pecking at a trellis of grapes"; he observed, very justly, "How lively journalistic fancy is among the Americans!" General Grant, again, unable to hear him, remarked: "Well, wife, we've paid to see the British lion, but as we can't hear him roar, we'd better go home." By simile and metaphor, these two quotations bring before us the slightly pompous, fastidious, inaudible Arnold as no direct description could have done.

Or consider how language comes alive in the Chinese say- 32 ing that lending to the feckless is "like pelting a stray dog with dumplings," or in the Arab proverb: "They came to shoe the pasha's horse, and the beetle stretched forth his leg"; in the Greek phrase for a perilous cape—"stepmother of ships"; or the Hebrew adage that "as the climbing up a sandy way is to the feet of the aged, so is a wife full of words to a quiet man"; in Shakespeare's phrase for a little England lost in the world's vastness—"in a great Poole, a Swan's nest"; or Fuller's libel on tall men—"Ofttimes such who are built four stories high are observed to have little in their cockloft"; in Chateaubriand's "I go yawning my life"; or in Jules Renard's portrait of a cat, "well buttoned in her fur." Or, to take a modern instance, there is Churchill on dealing with Russia:

> Trying to maintain good relations with a Communist is like wooing a crocodile. You do not know whether to tickle it under the chin or beat it over the head. When it opens its mouth, you cannot tell whether it is trying to smile or preparing to eat you up.

What a miracle human speech can be, and how dull is most that one hears! Would one hold one's hearers, it is far less help, I suspect, to read manuals on style than to cultivate one's own imagination and imagery.

33   I will end with two remarks by two wise old women of the civilized 18th Century.

34   The first is from the blind Mme du Deffand (the friend of Horace Walpole) to that Mlle de Lespinasse with whom, alas, she was to quarrel so unwisely: "You must make up your mind, my queen, to live with me in the greatest truth and sincerity. You will be charming so long as you let yourself be natural, and remain without pretension and without artifice." The second is from Mme de Charrière, the Zélide whom Boswell had once loved at Utrecht in vain, to a Swiss girl friend: "Lucinde, my clever Lucinde, while you wait for the Romeos to arrive, you have nothing better to do than become perfect. Have ideas that are clear, and expressions that are simple." ("*Ayez des idées nettes et des expressions simples.*") More than half the bad writing in the world, I believe, comes from neglecting those two very simple pieces of advice.

35   In many ways, no doubt, our world grows more and more complex; sputniks cannot be simple; yet how many of our complexities remain futile, how many of our artificialities false. Simplicity too can be subtle—as the straight lines of a Greek temple, like the Parthenon at Athens, are delicately curved, in order to look straighter still.

Thinking Critically About This Reading

1. The author insists that everyone has style, even people who claim not to have it or want it. Do you agree with this view? Why? Why not?

2. How successful does the author consider courses in teaching students how to write well? Do you agree with his view? Explain your answer.

3. In paragraph 8, the author gives five reasons why one should learn to write with good style. As his first reason, he cites the fact that we have no other way to communicate than through language. Do you think that communication absolutely must involve writing? Or is it enough to know how to speak persuasively? (Some futurists speculate that soon all communication will occur via personal television monitors and the like—so why bother with the painful task of learning how to write well?)

4. According to the author, how much pleasure is derived from writing well? Does your personal experience match his?

5. What does the author mean when he says the cornerstones of good style are honesty and courtesy? What are some further requirements that complement courtesy? How would you explain each of these general requirements to a friend?

Understanding the Writer's Process

1. Why do you suppose the author used a question as his title?

2. In paragraph 1, what is the purpose of the allusions to Matthew Arnold, Samuel Butler, and Oscar Wilde?

3. In paragraph 13, what strategy does the author use to prove his point? What is his point?

4. What condemnation does Lucas assign to long-winded writers?

5. In paragraph 25, the author gives several examples of brief but highly effective writing. What additional examples can you provide? Set a dramatic stage, and then create an effective but brief statement. For example, you might compose a tombstone epitaph for someone you especially admire or dislike. Or, you might compose a retort to someone who has maligned you. Or, you might imagine a wondrous natural scene and fashion a brief but fitting description.

6. How does the author tie the second paragraph to the first? Choose two other paragraphs from the essay and comment on the author's method of creating coherence.

Examining the Writer's Language

1. Using a college dictionary, define the following words: endemic (paragraph 4), aesthete (5), demagogue (5), gaggling (6), tête-à-tête (7), degenerate (8), replete (10), postprandial (10), pugnacious (11), verbose (12), odious (13), pedant (16).
2. How do you characterize the author's style in paragraph 2? How pleasing is it?
3. What stylistic characteristic exists in the second sentence of paragraph 6? What is its purpose?
4. What is your reaction to the python image in paragraph 10? How does your own reaction to essay assignments compare with that of Lucas?
5. Who is the "Vanzetti" alluded to in paragraph 13? Find the name in an encyclopedia of American history. Read Vanzetti's speech to the court and comment on its style.

Suggestions for Writing

1. Write an essay in which you state the influences in your past that have the strongest effect on your style of writing.
2. Write an essay either defending or attacking Lucas's two basic rules of good style—courtesy and brevity. Or, write an essay in which you establish your own such rules.

THE PROPER TOOL (STUDENT ESSAY)

David Beckham

David Beckham is attending Glendale Community College in California to prepare for a second career as a scriptwriter for the cinema. He grew up in Texas, working for his father in the cement business and on

*a family–owned ranch. In 1982 he moved to California,
where he worked as a film projectionist and became
fascinated with the movie business. He is a recipient
of the Glendale College Poetry Scholarship, and his
work was published in the 1991 edition of the* Spring
Harvest Poetry Anthology *of California State Poly-
technic University.*

Since well before the beginning of recorded history, mankind   1
has made enormous progress in the ability to communicate ideas
and information. From the codification of impulsive grunts into a
recognizable spoken language through the development of devices
such as cave paintings, cuneiform, hieroglyphs, and abstract symbols
there has been an irregular, but continuous, development in the tools
of expression. As writing surfaces developed from mud tablets
through parchment and papyrus to the present standards of acid–
free bond, so writing implements have moved from burnt sticks and
rocks through styli and feathers, steel nibs and typewriters, to the
word processor and laser jet printer. Mankind, the great toolmaker
and great communicator, has made steady progress in the state of
both arts, and both arts come together today in the word processor.

Many levels of usage are possible with the word processor.   2
They range from treating it as a glorified typewriter to using it as a
state–of–the–art tool for written communication. It is this latter use
that deserves consideration here, as the former use might be compared to driving a Ferrari only on trips to the corner grocery store.
As a communication tool, the word processor shines brightly in a
number of areas. These might be divided up into pre–writing, writing, and polishing.

When one first approaches a writing project, whether it be a
letter, an essay, a poem, or a novel, one begins with a collection of
ideas and a desire to communicate something. Few people are mentally organized enough to put anything more ambitious than a
thank–you note down on paper in optimum order at the first draft.
The word processor lends itself to the pre–writing step of the writing
process. One can brainstorm ideas in any order, putting down single
words, fragments, or complete sentences as they come. The order
and development can follow after. The *block* and *move text* functions

of the word processor make this a simple task. As ideas are ordered and subordinated by repositioning with the word processor, they can be fleshed out into sentence outline form if that level of organization is necessary. Those sentences can then be directly developed into paragraphs, since the word processor allows the writer to add and subtract text before, behind, and/or within what is already there. Simple keystrokes shape the format into a more and more elegant presentation of the author's ideas, like a sculptor adding, removing, and reshaping bits of clay in the production of a masterpiece. For simpler projects, single–word reminders of important concepts, correctly ordered, can float a line or two ahead of the cursor reminding the author of the direction to take. When a particular topic word or sentence has been adequately treated, the cursor keys move the process forward into the next paragraph.

3   The writing part of the whole process is made much easier as well by the modern, full–featured word processor. One can type at one's best speed, without worrying unduly about typographical errors, because the word processor will be able to check one's spelling at the end of the whole effort. No need to worry about coming to the end of the line or the end of the page at this stage, as the word processor will take care of such picayune details with *word wrap* and *automatic pagination* features that are built into the program. Get stuck for a word or wonder if the one just typed is the correct choice— call up the *thesaurus* while the cursor is on the questionable syllables and see if the definition offered is what is wanted. If no word will come to mind, type in a synonym or two and look among the choices; a couple of keystrokes will insert the favored one in the appropriate place in the text. When major inspirations occur during the writing process, such as improved order of paragraphs in one's five–paragraph essay, the new order can be accommodated with a few *block moves*. And the order of the related items in the introduction and conclusion can be adjusted as easily.

4   It is, perhaps, in polishing that the word processor shines most as the modern tool of expression. Once the text is completed, it can be read directly on the screen, scrolling through it a line, or a screen, or a page at a time. Changes can be made as they suggest themselves. But it is after the *document* has been printed on paper that the greatest satisfaction comes. The beautiful, clean, carefully formatted copy that comes out of the printer can be folded, stapled, mutilated and otherwise assaulted by the critical eye of the author turned editor. Slashing red or blue marks can temper the purpleness

of the ambitious scrivener's prose. The communication can be made to suit its original purpose. The changes can be made in the document filed on the *disk* and a new copy printed. The great labor of getting a truly polished clean final draft is gone. There is no more excuse for sloppy written communication.

What other conclusion could one reach than that the word 5 processor is the latest in the long evolution of communication tools humanity has developed? By slickening the processes of pre–writing, writing, and polishing text, the word processor places the possibility of artistic and elegant written communication within the grasp of its master. The word processor may not provide one with anything to say, but, if used well, the tool will greatly enhance one's ability to say it.

Plot → chain of events
chronologically
flashback

"Wow! Well, what happened next, Gramps? — AFTER you found the cheese sitting on the little block of wood!"

2

Narration

Plot → chain of events
1 chronologically
2 flashback
3 past to present

70 2 *Narration*

HOW TO WRITE A NARRATION

In its most common form, the narration is a story: It has a beginning, a middle, and an end. Something happens and someone is affected. Things are not exactly the same at the end of the story as they were at the start. If they are, the story is either silly and boring or its teller is playing with our expectations. For most of us do indeed have strong expectations about narration. We expect events to occur in a plot based on a climactic sequence; we expect characters to behave with reasonable consistency; and, most of all, we expect to be entertained—whether amused, aroused, or scared out of our wits.

Virtually every reader is familiar with the common forms of narration: novel, short story, fable, anecdote, and fairy tale. But there are also less familiar and factual instances of narration, such as the minutes of a meeting or a police report. What such forms share with, say, a novel is the relating of events in some significant and patterned sequence. For the focus of all good narratives is on the connection between successive events and actions. Events flow, action follows action, cause triggers effect, and everything is related by the storyteller in some rational sequence. This telling of events by sequence is a feature unique to the narrative form and distinguishes it, for example, from a causal analysis.

Characters (people) {realistic}
3D → us (people)
flat → has one trait (stereotyping)

1. Decide on Your Point of View

All narrations are either subjective or objective. A subjective narration relates your own experience from the *I* point of view. Here is an example from a student paper: "I recently visited a retirement home and had an experience that taught *me* that growing old gracefully is an art." On the other hand, an objective narration tells someone else's story using the third person pronouns *he* or *she*: "Kim Pham, an immigrant from Vietnam, worked in a basement sewing uniforms in order to pay for her tuition. One evening she. . . ."

The point of view you should use will depend on the intent of your narration. Telling your own story will necessarily entail use of the subjective point of view; telling someone else's, the objective. Many instructors, however, discourage subjective writing on the ground that its excessively personal nature does not adequately prepare a student for the kind of writing the workplace demands. Before

1st person —→ I
2nd person —→ You

3rd person → Us Them We (objective) (knows what's going

beginning your narration, then, be sure you are permitted to use either point of view.

2. Make a Point

Theme - what's your message.
Actions revolved around the theme.

All good narratives make a point. But this point does not have to be profound, preachy, or moralistic. Nor does it have to be an ideological and farfetched declaration, such as "Communists deserve to go to hell" or "Eat vegetables lest you die." However, your narration must have a point—be it simple or deep, hinted or trumpeted. Your first date was a repulsive experience; skydiving is not for timid souls; catching a rainbow in a photograph of Stonehenge was a thrilling accomplishment—each of these modest assertions could easily be the point of a separate narration. Proving this point, called the theme, is what endows the narration with movement.

For example, let us take a narration on the perennial theme of how you spent your summer vacation. Your last summer vacation was intolerable and wretched. You hated it. Of all the summer vacations in your life, it was the most beastly. That is your beginning point; you put it down in a thesis:

> Last summer was the most dreadful, horrible, and boring summer of my life.

You are off to a good start because you have made an unmistakable point. All you need to do now is dress up the paragraph a little and add impact to your thesis. Your feeling of gloom about last summer is the beginning of your narration. Now comes its body. Here is what one student wrote:

> What hurts most in retrospect is that I had such high expectations. I would fly to Chicago, work as an intern on a local newspaper, meet fascinating strangers who would soon turn into intimate friends with whom I would have scintillating discussions. Instead, I had to work as a short-order cook in a dingy coffee-shop.

3. Include Only Significant Details

In the body of the narration you must share with the reader every significant moment of torment, woe, and grief inflicted by that dreadful summer. Notice that we said every *significant* moment. The hangnail you suffered in July does not qualify. Writing a paragraph on how you butted your head against the kitchen cabinet one day in August will only make your reader fidgety (unless, of course, you knocked yourself unconscious and ended up in the hospital with a concussion). The trick in the middle of this narration is to focus only on major traumas that prove your point—namely, that last summer was a horror. If you have no traumas worth relating, if somehow your memories of last summer seem trivial and petty, then you are making the wrong point. "My last summer was the most trivial and petty I've ever lived through" is really what your narration ought to be about.

4. Pace Your Narrative   *spend more time focusing the main point.*

Pacing means focusing the narration only on major episodes and events that prove its point. Uneventful stretches of time are summarily dismissed. "Time passed," writes an author in a story, "and puff! a year goes up in smoke." Of course, as everyone who has ever watched the clock ticking away knows, life is not lived that way. But life is narrated that way. For a good narration expends ink only on those periods of time in which episodes, events, and incidents relevant to its point occurred. So about your boring summer, you might write:

> July passed in a daze of hourly drudgery and toil. I worked overtime everyday in the restaurant, fried my quota of 500 eggs, and returned home after twelve hours in the kitchen splattered with grease and grime, looking as scruffy and wilted as a basted rasher of bacon. The first two weeks I spent a lot of time with Marylou, but then she left and I sank to my chin in the hole of boredom. I tried to read, but couldn't stand the tedious details of a Henry James novel. I rented videos and fell asleep because they were so insipid. I went for lonely walks. . . .

Abandoning Marylou so abruptly may strike you as unjust; if you feel strongly about the slight, you should change the point of your narration. But given your current point—that the summer was dreadfully boring—Marylou is an intrusion you must dispose of quickly through pacing.

Pacing also entails relating the incidents of your narrative in a climactic sequence. For example, if being evicted by your crotchety landlady was the worst moment of that dreadful summer, save that episode for last: telling it first will blunt the climax. After making the reader feel every pebble of boredom and bad luck pelting down on your head, you let fall the tree limb of eviction. Then you end your narration. To do otherwise—to drop the limb first and do the pelting after—would ruin the climactic effect your narration might otherwise have had.

5. Plan Your Narrative

Although many writers plot their narratives down to the villain's last leer, we do not recommend such rigid planning for everyone. Some of us simply do not write well when confined by a hidebound plan. But it can be helpful to make a thumbnail sketch of the narration, if only to remind you of what comes next. Begin by jotting down your main point: working in a gas station is a course in human relations; some relatives can be demonic; contrary to popular belief, dogs are bungling brutes. Write this at the top of a piece of scratch paper; keep it under your nose as you write. Occasionally, glance at what is written there; remind yourself of the thesis. Under your main point, arrange the events of your story in climactic order. Narrate them that way, saving the worst or the best for last. And when you are finished, be sure to reread what you have written to see if it indeed proves your announced point. Nothing is so irksome as a narration in which the writer promises to tell one story but ends up telling another.

A HELL ON WHEELS

Diane

Nothing is known about Diane, except what she briefly tells us in this article: She was, at the time of writing, a 57–year–old divorced former editor whose parents had died recently and who did not have enough money to make the down payment on an apartment. The editors respected her desire for privacy and made no further inquiries about her true identity.

Preparing to Read This Selection Critically

This article purports to be the recounting of an episode of homelessness by a woman from a professional, middle–class background. Since the author reveals little biographically about herself, a reader is left to judge her credibility by inferring information about her from the text. Notice, for example, the phrasing and style of the writing. She tells us that she was formerly employed as an editor—what evidence of this do you see in the text? Examine also the verisimilitude of her story. What details of her account do you find most believable, or most unbelievable? Ask yourself, if this is not a true story, does it at least have the probability of truthfulness on its side?

1   I need anonymity so call me Diane. I try not to be seen as I watch you prosperous–looking people walking from your cars to your offices. If you saw me, your faces would mirror your suspicion and disapproval.

2   Yet I was one of you. And at least some of you are dancing on the same tightrope over the same abyss into which I have fallen.

3   None of you know I am here in the car just a few feet away from you—or what it is like once you get here.

4   I can tell you, courtesy of a typewriter for which no one would pay me five desperately needed dollars.

5   Last night my money added up to $38.67, so I found a cheaper motel. But tonight I will start sleeping in my car.

6   I must eat on $6.23 for the next 10 days. Then there will be a paycheck—enough to keep me in a motel again for about a week. After that, it will be back to the car until the next payday.

7   Yes, I work for a living, but this job may end soon. And since the pay isn't enough for a deposit on an apartment or even a room, it would be hard to mourn its loss. Except that I have no money, no home, no evident prospects.

8   My downward spiral from a middle–class Orange County lifestyle began a few years ago. I was divorced and in my 50s, earning $40,000 a year as an editor, when my mother died of cancer. As the only child, I was left to care for an aged father advancing steadily into the dementia of Alzheimer's.

9   I quit my job, moved to his apartment in Florida and cared for him for two years. We survived on my savings and his annuity. And

in 1989 he died, leaving me broke and drained of self-confidence and the ability to concentrate.

News reports told of high unemployment among "older work-   10
ers," meaning anyone over 40. I was 57. Where did I fit in?

I didn't.   11

Now I drive through the streets of Newport Beach looking for   12
a place to spend the night.

There seems something wrong with each street-side parking   13
space. Here is a house whose windows look directly into my car.
Here a space is too near the intersection–with heavy traffic. To remain anywhere, I must remain invisible. Yet the one quiet area is
also isolated. There is danger in isolation.

Finally, I drive slowly past the Sheraton hotel, with its many   14
parked cars and empty parking spaces. It seems so civilized. I used
to come here for business lunches when I worked across the street.
Aware of the irony, I check into a space facing the street.

The back seat of my 5–year–old Oldsmobile is too short for   15
sleeping, but the front seats recline. My legs dangle toward the brake
and accelerator, yet it seems comfortable enough to think of getting
some sleep.

I drop my seat back, but tense whenever footsteps approach.   16
I dread waking to find someone staring at me, so a large, black,
cotton knit jacket I place over my head makes me feel nicely invisible. If I were dressed entirely in black, I'd be even less visible. From
now on I shall prepare for the night like a cat burglar.

The night is filled with the noise of airplanes, police helicop-   17
ters, traffic, auto alarms, slamming doors and voices. But for about
five hours, it is almost silent. I sleep soundly for two hours, then
fitfully for the next hour and a half. To avoid discovery, I must leave
before daylight.

This is the first night of what will become four months of living   18
out of my car—long hours of solitude, physical discomfort, boredom
and sometimes hunger. And a few middle–of–the–night frights.

But it will teach me much about myself—and that line beyond   19
which lies permanent hopelessness.

When I awaken, the night sky is beginning to pale. I hear a   20
soft, staccato padding of feet and cautiously raise an eye to window
level. A jogger sets out from the hotel. It's time to leave. I drive
toward the fast-food restaurants on Bristol Street.

I sit impatiently in McDonald's parking lot for its 6 o'clock   21
opening. I can wait for coffee, but I need the restroom. I take my
dish-washing detergent along and manage a passable sponge bath.

22   I need exercise to pull me out of my stupor. I drive to Park Newport and walk briskly along the bluff as if I were a resident, nodding back to those who say good morning. When I get back to the car it is 7:35 and I am still sleepy. But I can think of nowhere to sleep in the daytime without attracting unwelcome attention. Finally, at 9, the library is open and I can check job ads in out-of-town papers.

23   The day crawls on, uneventfully. I won't return to the Sheraton before 9 p.m., for there is too much activity and too much chance of being noticed. So at 6, I'm sitting in my car in a Coco's parking lot, alone in the dark with only my stereo for company and empty hours ahead.

24   My mind summons old memories:

25   ■ Mother meticulously reviewing financial records with me so that I would know "how to handle things in case anything happens to us." I was surprised at how little they had left after 14 years of retirement. A small, dwindling cash reserve, Social Security and a small, fixed annuity financed their lives in a rented apartment.

26   ■ Father after Mother's death, grief-stricken and demented. Sometimes he knew me, but in an instant his eyes would change, and I knew before he spoke that he believed I was Mother.

27   ■ Father raving and threatening suicide if he had to enter "a home." He asked me to stay and take care of him. "You'll never have to work again," he said and waved proudly at the apartment. "You're going to get all this when I go, you know." It was pointless to explain that he had so little and I had only enough savings to last a year.

28   ■ Me selling our possessions to pay the bills, until he died and I returned broke to California.

29   Now, in Coco's parking lot, living out of a car does not seem the worst thing that can happen to anyone. I know better.

30   Morning. I drive to Ralphs and spend 69 cents of my remaining $2.56 for a can of tuna.

31   This is the time, from 6 until 9 a.m., when you are most exposed. People out and about now seem to have an evident purpose. Police cars make rounds up side streets and through parking lots. Gardeners descend on shopping centers to mow and groom and pick up litter.

32   Carrying my tuna back to the car, I find a wallet full of cash and credit cards in the parking lot. I take it to the market manager. As I walk back to my car, I wonder: How hungry or desperate would

I have to be to have kept that wallet? I don't know, but I'm not there now and I'm thankful.

I am startled by a glimpse of myself in a mirror. I must wash 33 my hair. It's not a matter of vanity. After three days without a shampoo, I'm beginning to look a little too much like a bag lady.

A shampoo isn't easy. You have to plan. I weigh the options 34 and decide to use the restroom at the main Newport Beach Public Library. It is clean and often quiet.

I fill my purse with a plastic water bottle, a bottle of dish- 35 washing detergent and a washcloth. I wait for the restroom to empty, then enter the spacious handicapped stall.

I remove my jacket and T–shirt and pour water over my head. 36 Then the restroom door swings open. I freeze. Semi–soaped and dripping, I stand motionless until the occupant of the next stall leaves.

The prospect of being seen now—with soaked hair and deter- 37 gent in hand—is mortifying. I finish, pull on my shirt and leave the restroom looking as if I have been swimming. I cross to the library exit quickly, not looking back. It is a new, low moment in my life.

I awaken the next morning at 4:30 after sleeping almost five 38 hours.

This is a go–to–work day for me. I work a 40–hour week in 39 four days. But while most people yearn for quitting time, I now look forward to the hours in the office, that place of blissful luxury.

It has hot water, coffee, tea, drinking water, a newspaper, a 40 restroom, my own chair and a place to leave the car. I hope I will be alert enough to do a good day's work.

I manage to perform well. Only in the warm, airless afternoon 41 do I suddenly drop off over my papers and yank instantly awake. I pull through the fog, pour more coffee and focus on my work.

The irony is I work for a firm that publishes books advertising 42 apartment rentals and their vast array of comforts and amenities.

Occasionally, someone looks at me oddly. There are expres- 43 sions on faces I haven't seen before, but no one is aggressively rude. And always I am on guard, ready for any attempt to make me leave or any rude remark. I am so constantly on guard for hostility that I don't realize I have become unprepared to deal with anything else.

One weekday morning, I linger long in my car at Coco's at 44 Fashion Island, alternately reading and thinking. A voice wafts into my open window.

"Are you all right?" 45

46   Startled, I look out and see, a few car–widths away, a well–groomed, attractive man in his 30s approaching his Mercedes. He pauses tentatively and looks at me with an expression of kindly concern in his acutely intelligent eyes.

47   "What?"

48   "Are you all right? I wondered if you had car trouble. I saw you here earlier."

49   "I'm fine," I say abruptly and turn away. "I'm waiting for an appointment."

50   "Oh." He moves into his car and leaves.

51   I was rude to someone genuinely concerned about a stranger. I was caught off–guard, and now, oddly, tears flow. I must be more tired than I thought. I have been thrown off balance by a moment of kindness and concern.

52   Now the tears cut loose. I keep seeing a stranger's kind, puzzled face and hearing a gentle "Are you all right?"

53   Of course I'm not all right! But I can't say that to him—or anyone.

54   I'm down to 43 cents, so I shop carefully. I buy two bananas for 29 cents; I can't think of anything I can buy with my remaining 14 cents.

55   As I leave the grocery store, a healthy–looking man in his 30s asks, "Excuse me, have you got a spare dollar?"

56   "No, I haven't," I say, but he has already turned away. He doesn't want words; he wants a dollar.

57   As days go by, I become increasingly aware of homeless people, from those living in automobiles to the fully homeless afoot. They are unseen when you live a "normal" life. They try to go unnoticed.

58   One man comes every night to check the coin–return slots of the newspaper racks and telephones near Coco's. He is about 50. Nothing distinguishes him from anyone else except the telltale hesitancy of his movements.

59   At dawn, a woman in her 40s, dressed for the office and driving a Buick just a few years old, pulls up to the racks and begins methodically fingering the coin slots. She sees me, freezes like a deer in headlights, then squares her shoulders and leaves.

60   I am struck by a posture of studied dignity that denies what the fingers are doing.

61   At midday, in Mariners Park, I eat my lunch of bread, tuna and an orange, then toss my refuse into the trash bin. An old, white–

haired man darts from nowhere and puts his hand deep into the trash can, searching through my impoverished rubbish.

One night late, I awaken abruptly. I hear the sound of a key 62 being slowly worked into my door lock and turned, just inches from my ear. My scalp tingles. The key does not work and is slowly withdrawn.

I listen warily. I can lunge for the horn if need be. That could 63 bring someone out of the hotel—and probably end my tenancy at the Sheraton. I wait, unmoving and unseeing under my nighttime shroud.

In a few minutes, I hear a key working slowly in the lock of 64 a car door or a trunk to the left of me. It opens and soon closes softly. Then it is quiet. I lie awake, adrenaline rushing, and finally sleep fitfully.

This unexplained event is a cold wash of reality: I am no more 65 immune from danger than anyone else.

This payday has loomed larger in my mind with each passing 66 day. I feel increasing urgency to buy some fresh food, to have a bed to sleep in for a few nights, to soak in a tub. Such expectation allowed me very little sleep last night.

But the paychecks from out of state are delayed; they won't 67 be here until tomorrow.

Tonight I eat my last saved slice of bread and margarine. And, 68 with a wary eye on the gas tank, which reads empty, I drive to the Sheraton yet again.

The paychecks arrive. I check into a motel and almost instantly 69 fall asleep, unable to enjoy the luxury of tub and television until tomorrow.

I wish I had discovered earlier how much money can be saved 70 by sleeping in the car. It's the only way I know now to save enough to rent a room near my office. Allowing for a night at a motel once a week to catch up on sleep, for laundry and for general self–repair, it will probably take two months or so to save up.

But will I be able to keep up the rent? 71

When I returned to California from Florida, I finally landed a 72 low–paying but full–time job and was promised rapid advancement. Now I find that the promises are not going to be kept by the corporation that bought this company.

There is a 49–year–old man in the office, desperate to hold his 73 job after a year of unemployment. He is the butt of contemptuous jokes. I did not want to become like him. I do *not* become like him, an "old person" in a low–paying job, acting always out of fear.

74   I have taken a stand: Live up to the promises the company made me or I quit. They praise me but won't budge.

75   I quit, and they look surprised. It was hardly noble or heroic. When you are already living out of your car, it is easier to give up a job. If you have a home, you can imagine losing it.

76   The downward spiral continues in earnest. Until now, the auto life has had a rhythm based on paydays. But there are no more paychecks to come.

77   My son, who lives in Tennessee, is suspicious. He's been aware that I'm having money problems, but my lack of a permanent phone number and address prompts him to ask me outright if I'm sleeping in my car.

78   I've tried carefully to keep this from him. Maybe it's a mother's protectiveness, but I don't want to burden him and his young family with my financial problems. So when he asks, I laugh it off.

79   I start walking almost everywhere. Occasionally, I sell minor possessions to buy gas and food, but there is not much left to sell. The gas tank is precariously low; I worry about running out of gas in the street and not having a penny to do anything about it.

80   It's harder to look for a new job. Without motel room telephones and the workplace, there is no way to leave call–back numbers when responding to ads. I can walk major distances, but it means arriving hot, sweaty and too tired to impress anybody. Most time now is spent simply solving the problems of getting from one day to the next.

81   I walk as much as 25 miles a day. Now, after seven days of exceptional walking, my left knee is stunningly painful, and the right knee echoes the pain. There are other unfamiliar pains running down the front of my legs. But if I don't start walking, I won't get a gallon of gas into the car and I won't get any food.

82   So I grit my teeth and walk, overriding the pain with necessity. For the next three days, I continue to walk many miles. The pain fills every part of my brain.

83   Now I am hobbling, so crippled that I can hardly get in and out of the car. One day of rest makes no improvement, nor do two, nor three. Movement is excruciating.

84   I have come to a critical time. My days have become a self–defeating spiral of non–accomplishment. Everything I do now is

devoted to simple survival. If I don't do something to halt it, I could be on my way into a rougher homelessness. But what can I do?

Editor's note: The author lived in her car for about four months until her son finally learned of the situation and took her into his home in Tennessee. However, he soon will be relocating to another state, and "Diane" says she intends to return to Orange County, California, where she hopes to restart her writing career.

Thinking Critically About This Reading

1. Based on what the writer tells us in this article, what can you infer about her character?

2. What psychological effects of homelessness are implicitly revealed in this article?

3. What can you infer from this article about the causes of homelessness?

4. What do you think—based on this article—the government could do to relieve the plight of people in Diane's circumstances?

5. What moral obligation, if any, do you think the government has toward the homeless?

Understanding the Writer's Process

1. In her opening paragraphs, what tack does the author take to engage the readers' interest in her tale?

2. In what kind of paragraphs does the author write her story? Why is this kind of paragraph suitable for her narrative?

3. How does the writer structure her story to enhance its readability and appeal?

4. Missing from the author's narrative is any complaining about her plight. What effect does this lack have on your reaction to her as a narrator?

5. What literary form does this narrative most closely resemble? What advantages does this particular form afford a writer?

Examining the Writer's Language

1. Define the meanings of the following words used in this essay: dementia (paragraph 8), staccato (20), meticulously (25), excruciating (83).

2. How does the author manipulate the tense of her narrative for maximum dramatic effect?

3. What technique does the author use in paragraph 11 for added emphasis?

4. The author expends considerable ink describing the first night she slept in her car, and after that merely refers to occasional episodes that occurred during subsequent nights. What is the rhetorical logic behind this treatment?

5. Beginning writers frequently are warned against the overuse of the "I" pronoun in their essays. The author of this article uses "I" repeatedly throughout her work, yet it does not seem excessive. How does the writer manage to avoid the pitfalls associated with the overuse of the "I" pronoun?

Suggestions for Writing

1. Write an essay drawing a character portrait of Diane, the writer of this article. Use references from the article itself as supporting details for your opinions of her.

2. Narrate any temporary brush with homelessness or dispossession you might have suffered.

GRADUATION

Maya Angelou

Maya Angelou (b. 1928) is a pseudonym for Marguerite Johnson. In spite of an early life filled with tragedy and sorrow—she was raped at eight and was an unwed mother at sixteen—she enjoys a versatile and accomplished career as an American actress, singer, dancer, director, teacher, writer, linguist, and political activist. She is especially well-known for her four-volume autobiography chronicling her experiences as a black woman in America. This selection is taken from the first and most popular volume, I Know Why the Caged Bird Sings *(1970).*

Preparing to Read This Selection Critically

"Graduation" tells the story of a 12–year–old black child's graduation from grammar school. Written in the first-person point of view, it dramatically recreates for us the thrill and excitement of the moment as seen through the eyes of its youthful teller. The author occasionally interrupts her narrative for an adult aside, but for the most part she stays within character. We are treated to a wealth of innocent detail as seen by the sensitive and perceptive mind of the narrator. Notice, for example, her occasional ironic remarks about the educational opportunities available to blacks of her generation. All is well until the climactic moment of the ceremony itself. And then the dream world collapses abruptly under the weight of a grim racial reality.

The children in Stamps[1] trembled visibly with anticipation. 1
Some adults were excited too, but to be certain the whole young population had come down with graduation epidemic. Large classes were graduating from both the grammar school and the high school. Even those who were years removed from their own day of glorious release were anxious to help with preparations as a kind of dry run. The junior students who were moving into the vacating classes' chairs were tradition-bound to show their talents for leadership and management. They strutted through the school and around the campus exerting pressure on the lower grades. Their authority was so new that occasionally if they pressed a little too hard it had to be overlooked. After all, next term was coming, and it never hurt a sixth grader to have a play sister in the eighth grade, or a tenth-year student to be able to call a twelfth grader Bubba. So all was endured in a spirit of shared understanding. But the graduating classes themselves were the nobility. Like travelers with exotic destinations on their minds, the graduates were remarkably forgetful. They came to school without their books, or tablets or even pencils. Volunteers fell over themselves to secure replacements for the missing equipment. When accepted, the willing workers might or might not be thanked, and it was of no importance to the pregraduation rites. Even teachers were respectful of the now quiet and aging seniors, and tended to speak

[1] An Arkansas town.

to them, if not as equals, as beings only slightly lower than themselves. After tests were returned and grades given, the student body, which acted like an extended family, knew who did well, who excelled, and what piteous ones had failed.

2   Unlike the white high school, Lafayette County Training School distinguished itself by having neither lawn, nor hedges, nor tennis court, nor climbing ivy. Its two buildings (main classrooms, the grade school and home economics) were set on a dirt hill with no fence to limit either its boundaries or those of bordering farms. There was a large expanse to the left of the school which was used alternately as a baseball diamond or basketball court. Rusty hoops on swaying poles represented the permanent recreational equipment, although bats and balls could be borrowed from the P.E. teacher if the borrower was qualified and if the diamond wasn't occupied.

3   Over this rocky area relieved by a few shady tall persimmon trees the graduating class walked. The girls often held hands and no longer bothered to speak to the lower students. There was a sadness about them, as if this old world was not their home and they were bound for higher ground. The boys, on the other hand, had become more friendly, more outgoing. A decided change from the closed attitude they projected while studying for finals. Now they seemed not ready to give up the old school, the familiar paths and classrooms. Only a small percentage would be continuing on to college—one of the South's A&M (agricultural and mechanical) schools, which trained Negro youths to be carpenters, farmers, handymen, masons, maids, cooks and baby nurses. Their future rode heavily on their shoulders, and blinded them to the collective joy that had pervaded the lives of the boys and girls in the grammar school graduating class.

4   Parents who could afford it had ordered new shoes and ready-made clothes for themselves from Sears and Roebuck or Montgomery Ward. They also engaged the best seamstresses to make the floating graduating dresses and to cut down secondhand pants which would be pressed to a military slickness for the important event.

5   Oh, it was important, all right. Whitefolks would attend the ceremony, and two or three would speak of God and home, and the Southern way of life, and Mrs. Parsons, the principal's wife, would play the graduation march while the lower-grade graduates paraded down the aisles and took their seats below the platform.

The high school seniors would wait in empty classrooms to make their dramatic entrance.

In the Store I was the person of the moment. The birthday 6 girl. The center. Bailey[2] had graduated the year before, although to do so he had had to forfeit all pleasures to make up for his time lost in Baton Rouge.

My class was wearing butter-yellow piqué dresses, and 7 Momma launched out on mine. She smocked the yoke into tiny crisscrossing puckers, then shirred the rest of the bodice. Her dark fingers ducked in and out of the lemony cloth as she embroidered raised daisies around the hem. Before she considered herself finished she had added a crocheted cuff on the puff sleeves, and a pointy crocheted collar.

I was going to be lovely. A walking model of all the various 8 styles of fine hand sewing and it didn't worry me that I was only twelve years old and merely graduating from the eighth grade. Besides, many teachers in Arkansas Negro schools had only that diploma and were licensed to impart wisdom.

The days had become longer and more noticeable. The faded 9 beige of former times had been replaced with strong and sure colors. I began to see my classmates' clothes, their skin tones, and the dust that waved off pussy willows. Clouds that lazed across the sky were objects of great concern to me. Their shiftier shapes might have held a message that in my new happiness and with a little bit of time I'd soon decipher. During that period I looked at the arch of heaven so religiously my neck kept a steady ache. I had taken to smiling more often, and my jaws hurt from the unaccustomed activity. Between the two physical sore spots, I suppose I could have been uncomfortable, but that was not the case. As a member of the winning team (the graduating class of 1940) I had outdistanced unpleasant sensations by miles. I was headed for the freedom of open fields.

Youth and social approval allied themselves with me and we 10 trammeled memories of slights and insults. The wind of our swift passage remodeled my features. Lost tears were pounded to mud and then to dust. Years of withdrawal were brushed aside and left behind, as hanging ropes of parasitic moss.

My work alone had awarded me a top place and I was going 11 to be one of the first called in the graduating ceremonies. On the

[2] The author's brother.

classroom blackboard, as well as on the bulletin board in the auditorium, there were blue stars and white stars and red stars. No absences, no tardinesses, and my academic work was among the best of the year. I could say the preamble to the Constitution even faster than Bailey. We timed ourselves often: "We the people of the United States in order to form a more perfect union. . . ." I had memorized the Presidents of the United States from Washington to Roosevelt in chronological as well as alphabetical order.

12   My hair pleased me too. Gradually the black mass had lengthened and thickened, so that it kept at last to its braided pattern, and I didn't have to yank my scalp off when I tried to comb it.

13   Louise and I had rehearsed the exercises until we tired out ourselves. Henry Reed was class valedictorian. He was a small, very black boy with hooded eyes, a long, broad nose and an oddly shaped head. I had admired him for years because each term he and I vied for the best grades in our class. Most often he bested me, but instead of being disappointed I was pleased that we shared top places between us. Like many Southern Black children, he lived with his grandmother, who was as strict as Momma and as kind as she knew how to be. He was courteous, respectful and softspoken to elders, but on the playground he chose to play the roughest games. I admired him. Anyone, I reckoned, sufficiently afraid or sufficiently dull could be polite. But to be able to operate at a top level with both adults and children was admirable.

14   His valedictory speech was entitled "To Be or Not to Be." The rigid tenth-grade teacher had helped him write it. He'd been working on the dramatic stresses for months.

15   The weeks until graduation were filled with heady activities. A group of small children were to be presented in a play about buttercups and daisies and bunny rabbits. They could be heard throughout the building practicing their hops and their little songs that sounded like silver bells. The older girls (nongraduates, of course) were assigned the task of making refreshments for the night's festivities. A tangy scent of ginger, cinnamon, nutmeg and chocolate wafted around the home economics building as the budding cooks made samples for themselves and their teachers.

16   In every corner of the workshop, axes and saws split fresh timber as the woodshop boys made sets and stage scenery. Only the graduates were left out of the general bustle. We were free to sit in the library at the back of the building or look in quite detachedly, naturally, on the measures being taken for our event.

Even the minister preached on graduation the Sunday before.   17
His subject was, "Let your light so shine that men will see your
good works and praise your Father, Who is in Heaven." Although
the sermon was purported to be addressed to us, he used the occasion to speak to backsliders, gamblers and general ne'er do-wells.
But since he had called our names at the beginning of the service
we were mollified.

Among Negroes the tradition was to give presents to children   18
going only from one grade to another. How much more important
this was when the person was graduating at the top of the class.
Uncle Willie and Momma had sent away for a Mickey Mouse watch
like Bailey's. Louise gave me four embroidered handkerchiefs. (I
gave her crocheted doilies.) Mrs. Sneed, the minister's wife, made
me an undershirt to wear for graduation, and nearly every customer
gave me a nickel or maybe even a dime with the instruction "Keep
on moving to higher ground," or some such encouragement.

Amazingly the great day finally dawned and I was out of bed   19
before I knew it. I threw open the back door to see it more clearly,
but Momma said, "Sister, come away from that door and put your
robe on."

I hoped the memory of that morning would never leave me.   20
Sunlight was itself young, and the day had none of the insistence
maturity would bring it in a few hours. In my robe and barefoot in
the backyard, under cover of going to see about my new beans, I
gave myself up to the gentle warmth and thanked God that no
matter what evil I had done in my life He had allowed me to live
to see this day. Somewhere in my fatalism I had expected to die,
accidentally, and never have the chance to walk up the stairs in the
auditorium and gracefully receive my hard-earned diploma. Out of
God's merciful bosom I had won reprieve.

Bailey came out in his robe and gave me a box wrapped in   21
Christmas paper. He said he had saved his money for months to
pay for it. It felt like a box of chocolates, but I knew Bailey wouldn't
save money to buy candy when we had all we could want under
our noses.

He was as proud of the gift as I. It was a soft-leather-bound   22
copy of a collection of poems by Edgar Allan Poe, or, as Bailey and
I called him, "Eap." I turned to "Annabel Lee" and we walked up
and down the garden rows, the cool dirt between our toes, reciting
the beautifully sad lines.

23   Momma made a Sunday breakfast although it was only Friday. After we finished the blessing, I opened my eyes to find the watch on my plate. It was a dream of a day. Everything went smoothly and to my credit. I didn't have to be reminded or scolded for anything. Near evening I was too jittery to attend to chores, so Bailey volunteered to do all before his bath.

24   Days before, we had made a sign for the Store, and as we turned out the lights Momma hung the cardboard over the doorknob. It read clearly: CLOSED. GRADUATION.

25   My dress fitted perfectly and everyone said that I looked like a sunbeam in it. On the hill, going toward the school, Bailey walked behind with Uncle Willie, who muttered, "Go on, Ju." He wanted him to walk ahead with us because it embarrassed him to have to walk so slowly. Bailey said he'd let the ladies walk together, and the men would bring up the rear. We all laughed, nicely.

26   Little children dashed by out of the dark like fireflies. Their crepe-paper dresses and butterfly wings were not made for running and we heard more than one rip, dryly, and the regretful "uh uh" that followed.

27   The school blazed without gaiety. The windows seemed cold and unfriendly from the lower hill. A sense of ill-fated timing crept over me, and if Momma hadn't reached for my hand I would have drifted back to Bailey and Uncle Willie, and possibly beyond. She made a few slow jokes about my feet getting cold, and tugged me along to the now-strange building.

28   Around the front steps, assurance came back. There were my fellow "greats," the graduating class. Hair brushed back, legs oiled, new dresses and pressed pleats, fresh pocket handkerchiefs and little handbags, all homesewn. Oh, we were up to snuff, all right. I joined my comrades and didn't even see my family go in to find seats in the crowded auditorium.

29   The school band struck up a march and all classes filed in as had been rehearsed. We stood in front of our seats, as assigned, and on a signal from the choir director, we sat. No sooner had this been accomplished than the band started to play the national anthem. We rose again and sang the song, after which we recited the pledge of allegiance. We remained standing for a brief minute before the choir director and the principal signaled to us, rather desperately I thought, to take our seats. The command was so unusual that our carefully rehearsed and smooth-running machine was thrown off. For a full minute we fumbled for our chairs and bumped into each

other awkwardly. Habits change or solidify under pressure, so in our state of nervous tension we had been ready to follow our usual assembly pattern: the American national anthem, then the pledge of allegiance, then the song every Black person I knew called the Negro National Anthem. All done in the same key, with the same passion and most often standing on the same foot.

Finding my seat at last, I was overcome with a presentiment 30 of worse things to come. Something unrehearsed, unplanned, was going to happen, and we were going to be made to look bad. I distinctly remember being explicit in the choice of pronoun. It was "we," the graduating class, the unit, that concerned me then.

The principal welcomed "parents and friends" and asked the 31 Baptist minister to lead us in prayer. His invocation was brief and punchy, and for a second I thought we were getting on the high road to right action. When the principal came back to the dais, however, his voice had changed. Sounds always affected me profoundly and the principal's voice was one of my favorites. During assembly it melted and lowed weakly into the audience. It had not been in my plan to listen to him, but my curiosity was piqued and I straightened up to give him my attention.

He was talking about Booker T. Washington, our "late great 32 leader," who said we can be as close as the fingers on the hand, etc. . . . Then he said a few vague things about friendship and the friendship of kindly people to those less fortunate than themselves. With that his voice nearly faded, thin, away. Like a river diminishing to a stream and then to a trickle. But he cleared his throat and said, "Our speaker tonight, who is also our friend, came from Texarkana to deliver the commencement address, but due to the irregularity of the train schedule, he's going to, as they say, 'speak and run.' " He said that we understood and wanted the man to know that we were most grateful for the time he was able to give us and then something about how we were willing always to adjust to another's program, and without more ado—"I give you Mr. Edward Donleavy."

Not one but two white men came through the door off-stage. 33 The shorter one walked to the speaker's platform, and the tall one moved to the center seat and sat down. But that was our principal's seat, and already occupied. The dislodged gentleman bounced around for a long breath or two before the Baptist minister gave him his chair, then with more dignity than the situation deserved, the minister walked off the stage.

34   Donleavy looked at the audience once (on reflection, I'm sure that he wanted only to reassure himself that we were really there), adjusted his glasses and began to read from a sheaf of papers.

35   He was glad "to be here and to see the work going on just as it was in the other schools."

36   At the first "Amen" from the audience I willed the offender to immediate death by choking on the word. But Amens and Yes, sir's began to fall around the room like rain through a ragged umbrella.

37   He told us of the wonderful changes we children in Stamps had in store. The Central School (naturally, the white school was Central) had already been granted improvements that would be in use in the fall. A well-known artist was coming from Little Rock to teach art to them. They were going to have the newest microscopes and chemistry equipment for their laboratory. Mr. Donleavy didn't leave us long in the dark over who made these improvements available to Central High. Nor were we to be ignored in the general betterment scheme he had in mind.

38   He said that he had pointed out to people at a very high level that one of the first-line football tacklers at Arkansas Agricultural and Mechanical College had graduated from good old Lafayette County Training School. Here fewer Amen's were heard. Those few that did break through lay dully in the air with the heaviness of habit.

39   He went on to praise us. He went on to say how he had bragged that "one of the best basketball players at Fisk sank his first ball right here at Lafayette County Training School."

40   The white kids were going to have a chance to become Galileos and Madame Curies and Edisons and Gauguins, and our boys (the girls weren't even in on it) would try to be Jesse Owenses and Joe Louises.

41   Owens and the Brown Bomber were great heroes in our world, but what school official in the white-goddom of Little Rock had the right to decide that those two men must be our only heroes? Who decided that for Henry Reed to become a scientist he had to work like George Washington Carver, as a bootblack, to buy a lousy microscope? Bailey was obviously always going to be too small to be an athlete, so which concrete angel glued to what country seat had decided that if my brother wanted to become a lawyer he had to first pay penance for his skin by picking cotton and hoeing corn and studying correspondence books at night for twenty years?

The man's dead words fell like bricks around the auditorium   42
and too many settled in my belly. Constrained by hard-learning manners I couldn't look behind me, but to my left and right the proud
graduating class of 1940 had dropped their heads. Every girl in my
row had found something new to do with her handkerchief. Some
folded the tiny squares into love knots, some into triangles, but most
were wadding them, then pressing them flat on their yellow laps.

On the dais, the ancient tragedy was being replayed. Professor   43
Parsons sat, a sculptor's reject, rigid. His large, heavy body seemed
devoid of will or willingness, and his eyes said he was no longer
with us. The other teachers examined the flag (which was draped
stage right) or their notes, or the windows which opened on our
now-famous playing diamond.

Graduation, the hush-hush magic time of frills and gifts and   44
congratulations and diplomas, was finished for me before my name
was called. The accomplishment was nothing. The meticulous maps,
drawn in three colors of ink, learning and spelling decasyllabic
words, memorizing the whole of *The Rape of Lucrece*³—it was for
nothing. Donleavy had exposed us.

We were maids and farmers, handymen and washerwomen,   45
and anything higher that we aspired to was farcical and presump-
tuous.

Then I wished that Gabriel Prosser and Nat Turner⁴ had killed   46
all whitefolks in their beds and that Abraham Lincoln had been
assassinated before the signing of the Emancipation Proclamation,
and that Harriet Tubman⁵ had been killed by that blow on her head
and Christopher Columbus had drowned in the *Santa Maria*.

It was awful to be a Negro and have no control over my life.   47
It was brutal to be young and already trained to sit quietly and listen
to charges brought against my color with no chance of defense. We
should all be dead. I thought I should like to see us all dead, one on
top of the other. A pyramid of flesh with the whitefolks on the bottom,
as the broad base, then the Indians with their silly tomahawks and
teepees and wigwams and treaties, the Negroes with their mops and
recipes and cotton sacks and spirituals sticking out of their mouths.
The Dutch children should all stumble in their wooden shoes and

---

³ Long narrative poem by William Shakespeare.
⁴ Prosser and Turner were leaders of slave rebellions during the early 1800s in Virginia.
⁵ American Black Abolitionist leader.

break their necks. The French should choke to death on the Louisiana Purchase (1803) while silkworms ate all the Chinese with their stupid pigtails. As a species, we were an abomination. All of us.

48   Donleavy was running for election, and assured our parents that if he won we could count on having the only colored paved playing field in that part of Arkansas. Also—he never looked up to acknowledge the grunts of acceptance—also, we were bound to get some new equipment for the home economics building and the workshop.

49   He finished, and since there was no need to give any more than the most perfunctory thank-you's, he nodded to the men on the stage, and the tall white man who was never introduced joined him at the door. They left with the attitude that now they were off to something really important. (The graduation ceremonies at Lafayette County Training School had been a mere preliminary.)

50   The ugliness they left was palpable. An uninvited guest who wouldn't leave. The choir was summoned and sang a modern arrangement of "Onward, Christian Soldiers," with new words pertaining to graduates seeking their place in the world. But it didn't work. Elouise, the daughter of the Baptist minister, recited "Invictus"[6] and I could have cried at the impertinence of "I am the master of my fate, I am the captain of my soul."

51   My name had lost its ring of familiarity and I had to be nudged to go and receive my diploma. All my preparations had fled. I neither marched up to the stage like a conquering Amazon, nor did I look in the audience for Bailey's nod of approval. Marguerite Johnson, I heard the name again, my honors were read, there were noises in the audience of appreciation, and I took my place on the stage as rehearsed.

52   I thought about colors I hated: ecru, puce, lavender, beige and black.

53   There was shuffling and rustling around me, then Henry Reed was giving his valedictory address, "To Be or Not to Be." Hadn't he heard the whitefolks? We couldn't *be*, so the question was a waste of time. Henry's voice came out clear and strong. I feared to look at him. Hadn't he got the message? There was no "nobler in the mind" for Negroes because the world didn't think we had minds, and they let us know it. "Outrageous fortune"? Now, that was a joke. When the ceremony was over I had to tell Henry Reed some

---

[6] Poem by William Ernest Henley.

things. That is, if I still cared. Not "rub," Henry, "erase." "Ah, there's the erase." Us.

Henry had been a good student in elocution. His voice rose   54
on tides of promise and fell on waves of warnings. The English teacher had helped him to create a sermon winging through Hamlet's soliloquy. To be a man, a doer, a builder, a leader, or to be a tool, an unfunny joke, a crusher of funky toadstools. I marveled that Henry could go through with the speech as if we had a choice.

I had been listening and silently rebutting each sentence with   55
my eyes closed; then there was a hush, which in an audience warns that something unplanned is happening. I looked up and saw Henry Reed, the conservative, the proper, the A student, turn his back to the audience and turn to us (the proud graduating class of 1940) and sing, nearly speaking,

> "Lift ev'ry voice and sing
> Till earth and heaven ring
> Ring with the harmonies of Liberty . . ."

It was the poem written by James Weldon Johnson. It was the music composed by J. Rosamond Johnson. It was the Negro National Anthem. Out of habit we were singing it.

Our mothers and fathers stood in the dark hall and joined the   56
hymn of encouragement. A kindergarten teacher led the small children onto the stage and the buttercups and daisies and bunny rabbits marked time and tried to follow:

> "Stony the road we trod
> Bitter the chastening rod
> Felt in the days when hope, unborn, had died.
> Yet with a steady beat
> Have not our weary feet
> Come to the place for which our fathers sighed?"

Each child I knew had learned that song with his ABC's and   57
along with "Jesus Loves Me This I Know." But I personally had never heard it before. Never heard the words, despite the thousands of times I had sung them. Never thought they had anything to do with me.

On the other hand, the words of Patrick Henry had made such   58
an impression on me that I had been able to stretch myself tall and trembling and say, "I know not what course others may take, but as for me, give me liberty or give me death."

59 And now I heard, really for the first time:

> "We have come over a way that with tears
> has been watered,
> We have come, treading our path through
> the blood of the slaughtered."

60 While echoes of the song shivered in the air, Henry Reed bowed his head, said "Thank you," and returned to his place in the line. The tears that slipped down many faces were not wiped away in shame.

61 We were on top again. As always, again. We survived. The depths had been icy and dark, but now a bright sun spoke to our souls. I was no longer simply a member of the proud graduating class of 1940; I was a proud member of the wonderful, beautiful Negro race.

62 Oh, Black known and unknown poets, how often have your auctioned pains sustained us? Who will compute the lonely nights made less lonely by your songs, or the empty pots made less tragic by your tales?

63 If we were a people much given to revealing secrets, we might raise monuments and sacrifice to the memories of our poets, but slavery cured us of that weakness. It may be enough, however, to have it said that we survive in exact relationship to the dedication of our poets (include preachers, musicians and blues singers).

Thinking Critically About This Reading

1. What obvious differences existed between the facilities of white and black schools? How do you think these differences might have affected the quality of education in each school?

2. Schools are usually funded by property-tax assessments against the homes in their district. What effect do you think this method of funding is likely to have on the facilities of schools in rich and poor neighborhoods? What advantages would a national and uniform system of school funding likely have? What disadvantages?

3. Some feminists have argued that sex roles, not race, exert the greater influence on human development. From the descriptions of how the boys and girls separately prepared for the graduation ceremony, what conclusions can you infer about the influence of sex roles on their lives?

4. From her reactions to the graduation incident, what can you deduce about the author's self-concept as a black child? How is the self-concept of any child likely to affect his or her adult behavior?

5. Why was the writer so mortified at the outbreak of "amen's" and "yes sir's" from the audience at the beginning of the white man's speech? What does this reaction reveal about her?

Understanding the Writer's Process

1. How do you characterize the tone of paragraph 5?

2. In paragraph 6, how does the author emphasize her own importance in the approaching ceremony? What might an unforgiving grammarian object to in this paragraph?

3. Although the narrative opens on a note of expectation and eagerness, we are not surprised at the sudden and dismal turn in the ceremony. How did the author prepare us for the unpleasantness ahead? What is the technique called that writers use to hint at coming events?

4. The author continually refers to herself and her people as "Negroes," a term which, having fallen into disuse and disfavor, has been replaced by the more forthright "black." What justification can she have for using this obsolete, and somewhat disfavored, term to refer to her race?

Examining the Writer's Language

1. Define the meanings of the following words: piqué (paragraph 7), shirred (7), trammeled (10), mollified (17), presentiment (30), constrained (42), farcical (45).

2. Identify the figures of speech used in paragraph 10 and explain their meanings.

3. Identify and explain the technical dressmaking terms used in paragraph 7. What do these words contribute to the author's narrative?

4. The author describes her indignant and angry reaction to the bigoted speech of the white guest. In paragraph 42, how does she characterize the reactions of her fellow students? Why is this an effective method of characterization?

Suggestions for Writing

1. Narrate any experience or incident that left you feeling demeaned and angry.

2. Narrate an encounter with prejudice—directed against you as a student, a female, a male, a member of a racial or religious minority, or otherwise—and tell how you coped with it.

SHOOTING AN ELEPHANT

George Orwell

> *George Orwell, the pen name of Eric Blair (1903–1950), was born in Bengal, India and educated at Eton. While serving with the imperial police in Burma, Orwell lived through the events related in "Shooting an Elephant." He fought on the Republican side in the Spanish Civil War, was severely wounded, and recorded the experience in a memoir,* Homage to Catalonia *(1938). Writing a prose style that has been described as one of "singular directness and honesty," Orwell is best known for two influential political novels that warn against totalitarian regimes,* Animal Farm *(1945) and* Nineteen Eighty–Four *(1949), the latter published just before his death at age 47.*

Preparing to Read This Selection Critically

The charm of this essay, indeed, the power and persuasiveness of it, lies in its author's honesty. Orwell is candid about the conflicts he suffered while serving as a policeman in colonial Burma. In narrating his experience with the elephant, he does not attempt to put a heroic face on his emotions or to excuse himself with show or bravado. As you read, ask yourself how the native Burmese must have felt under the rule of the colonial English. Ask yourself how this white policeman must have looked to them when he appeared with the elephant gun. Do you think the Burmese spectators would have jeered at the narrator had he not shot the elephant, or do you think this belief symptomatic of the persecution Orwell suffered?

In Moulmein, in Lower Burma, I was hated by large numbers 1 of people—the only time in my life that I have been important enough for this to happen to me. I was sub-divisional police officer of the town, and in an aimless, petty kind of way anti-European feeling was very bitter. No one had the guts to raise a riot, but if a European woman went through the bazaars alone somebody would probably spit betel juice over her dress. As a police officer I was an obvious target and was baited whenever it seemed safe to do so. When a nimble Burman tripped me up on the football field and the referee (another Burman) looked the other way, the crowd yelled with hideous laughter. This happened more than once. In the end the sneering yellow faces of young men that met me everywhere, the insults hooted after me when I was at a safe distance, got badly on my nerves. The young Buddhist priests were the worst of all. There were several thousand of them in the town and none of them seemed to have anything to do except stand on street corners and jeer at Europeans.

All this was perplexing and upsetting. For at that time I had 2 already made up my mind that imperialism was an evil thing and the sooner I chucked up my job and got out of it the better. Theoretically—and secretly, of course—I was all for the Burmese and all against their oppressors, the British. As for the job I was doing, I hated it more bitterly than I can perhaps make clear. In a job like that you see the dirty work of Empire at close quarters. The wretched prisoners huddling in the stinking cages of the lock-ups, the grey, cowed faces of the long-term convicts, the scarred buttocks of the men who had been flogged with bamboos—all these oppressed me with an intolerable sense of guilt. But I could get nothing into perspective. I was young and ill-educated and I had had to think out my problems in the utter silence that is imposed on every Englishman in the East. I did not even know that the British Empire is dying, still less did I know that it is a great deal better than the younger empires that are going to supplant it. All I knew was that I was stuck between my hatred of the empire I served and my rage against the evil-spirited little beasts who tried to make my job impossible. With one part of my mind I thought of the British Raj as an unbreakable tyranny, as something clamped down, in *saecula saeculorum,*[1] upon the will of prostrate peoples; with another part I thought that the greatest joy in the world would be to drive a bayonet into a Buddhist priest's guts. Feelings like these are the normal by-products of imperialism; ask any Anglo-Indian official, if you can catch him off duty.

3   One day something happened which in a roundabout way was enlightening. It was a tiny incident in itself, but it gave me a better glimpse than I had had before of the real nature of imperialism— the real motives for which despotic governments act. Early one morning the sub-inspector at a police station the other end of the town rang me up on the 'phone and said that an elephant was ravaging the bazaar. Would I please come and do something about it? I did not know what I could do, but I wanted to see what was happening and I got on to a pony and started out. I took my rifle, an old .44 Winchester and much too small to kill an elephant, but I thought the noise might be useful *in terrorem.*[2] Various Burmans stopped me on the way and told me about the elephant's doings. It was not, of course, a wild elephant, but a tame one which had gone "must." It had been chained up, as tame elephants always are when their attack of "must" is due, but on the previous night it had broken its chain and escaped. Its mahout, the only person who could manage it when it was in that state, had set out in pursuit, but had taken the wrong direction and was now twelve hours' journey away, and in the morning the elephant had suddenly reappeared in the town. The Burmese population had no weapons and were quite helpless against it. It had already destroyed somebody's bamboo hut, killed a cow and raided some fruit-stalls and devoured the stock; also it had met the municipal rubbish van and, when the driver jumped out and took to his heels, had turned the van over and inflicted violences upon it.

4   The Burmese sub-inspector and some Indian constables were waiting for me in the quarter where the elephant had been seen. It was a very poor quarter, a labyrinth of squalid bamboo huts, thatched with palm-leaf, winding all over a steep hillside. I remember that it was a cloudy, stuffy morning at the beginning of the rains. We began questioning the people as to where the elephant had gone and, as usual, failed to get any definite information. That is invariably the case in the East; a story always sounds clear enough at a distance,

---

[1] Latin, "for ever and ever."—Ed.
[2] Latin, "as a warning."—Ed.

but the nearer you get to the scene of events the vaguer it becomes. Some of the people said that the elephant had gone in one direction, some said that he had gone in another, some professed not even to have heard of any elephant. I had almost made up my mind that the whole story was a pack of lies, when we heard yells a little distance away. There was a loud, scandalized cry of "Go away, child! Go away this instant!" and an old woman with a switch in her hand came round the corner of a hut, violently shooing away a crowd of naked children. Some more women followed, clicking their tongues and exclaiming; evidently there was something that the children ought not to have seen. I rounded the hut and saw a man's dead body sprawling in the mud. He was an Indian, a black Dravidian coolie, almost naked, and he could not have been dead many minutes. The people said that the elephant had come suddenly upon him round the corner of the hut, caught him with its trunk, put its foot on his back and ground him into the earth. This was the rainy season and the ground was soft, and his face had scored a trench a foot deep and a couple of yards long. He was lying on his belly with arms crucified and head sharply twisted to one side. His face was coated with mud, the eyes wide open, the teeth bared and grinning with an expression of unendurable agony. (Never tell me, by the way, that the dead look peaceful. Most of the corpses I have seen looked devilish.) The friction of the great beast's foot had stripped the skin from his back as neatly as one skins a rabbit. As soon as I saw the dead man I sent an orderly to a friend's house nearby to borrow an elephant rifle. I had already sent back the pony, not wanting it to go mad with fright and throw me if it smelt the elephant.

The orderly came back in a few minutes with a rifle and five 5 cartridges, and meanwhile some Burmans had arrived and told us that the elephant was in the paddy fields below, only a few hundred yards away. As I started forward practically the whole population of the quarter flocked out of the houses and followed me. They had seen the rifle and were all shouting excitedly that I was going to shoot the elephant. They had not shown much interest in the elephant when he was merely ravaging their homes, but it was different now that he was going to be shot. It was a bit of fun to them, as it would be to an English crowd; besides they wanted the meat. It made me vaguely uneasy. I had no intention of shooting the elephant—I had merely sent for the rifle to defend myself if necessary— and it is always unnerving to have a crowd following you. I marched down the hill, looking and feeling a fool, with the rifle over my shoulder and an ever-growing army of people jostling at my heels. At the bottom, when you got away from the huts, there was a metalled road and beyond that a miry waste of paddy fields a thousand yards across, not yet ploughed but soggy from the first rains and dotted with coarse grass. The elephant was standing eight yards from the road, his left side towards us. He took not the slightest notice of the crowd's approach. He was tearing up bunches of grass, beating them against his knees to clean them and stuffing them into his mouth.

6   I had halted on the road. As soon as I saw the elephant I knew with perfect certainty that I ought not to shoot him. It is a serious matter to shoot a working elephant—it is comparable to destroying a huge and costly piece of machinery—and obviously one ought not to do it if it can possibly be avoided. And at that distance, peacefully eating, the elephant looked no more dangerous than a cow. I thought then and I think now that his attack of "must" was already passing off; in which case he would merely wander harmlessly about until the mahout came back and caught him. Moreover, I did not in the least want to shoot him. I decided that I would watch him for a little while to make sure that he did not turn savage again, and then go home.

7   But at that moment I glanced round at the crowd that had followed me. It was an immense crowd, two thousand at the least and growing every minute. It blocked the road for a long distance on either side. I looked at the sea of yellow faces above the garish clothes—faces all happy and excited over this bit of fun, all certain that the elephant was going to be shot. They were watching me as they would watch a conjurer about to perform a trick. They did not like me, but with the magical rifle in my hands I was momentarily worth watching. And suddenly I realized that I should have to shoot the elephant after all. The people expected it of me and I had got to do it; I could feel their two thousand wills pressing me forward, irresistibly. And it was at this moment, as I stood there with the rifle in my hands, that I first grasped the hollowness, the futility of the white man's dominion in the East. Here was I, the white man with his gun, standing in front of the unarmed native crowd—seemingly the leading actor of the piece; but in reality I was only an absurd puppet pushed to and fro by the will of those yellow faces behind. I perceived in this moment that when the white man turns tyrant it is his own freedom that he destroys. He becomes a sort of hollow,

posing dummy, the conventionalized figure of a sahib. For it is the condition of his rule that he shall spend his life in trying to impress the "natives," and so in every crisis he has got to do what the "natives" expect of him. He wears a mask, and his face grows to fit it. I had got to shoot the elephant. I had committed myself to doing it when I sent for the rifle. A sahib has got to act like a sahib; he has got to appear resolute, to know his own mind and do definite things. To come all that way, rifle in hand, with two thousand people marching at my heels, and then to trail feebly away, having done nothing—no, that was impossible. The crowd would laugh at me. And my whole life, every white man's life in the East, was one long struggle not to be laughed at.

But I did not want to shoot the elephant. I watched him beating   8 his bunch of grass against his knees, with that preoccupied grand-motherly air that elephants have. It seemed to me that it would be murder to shoot him. At that age I was not squeamish about killing animals, but I had never shot an elephant and never wanted to. (Somehow it always seems worse to kill a *large* animal.) Besides, there was the beast's owner to be considered. Alive, the elephant was worth at least a hundred pounds; dead, he would only be worth the value of his tusks, five pounds, possibly. But I had got to act quickly. I turned to some experienced-looking Burmans who had been there when we arrived, and asked them how the elephant had been behaving. They all said the same thing: he took no notice of you if you left him alone, but he might charge if you went too close to him.

It was perfectly clear to me what I ought to do. I ought to walk   9 up to within, say, twenty-five yards of the elephant and test his behavior. If he charged, I could shoot; if he took no notice of me, it would be safe to leave him until the mahout came back. But also I knew that I was going to do no such thing. I was a poor shot with a rifle and the ground was soft mud into which one would sink at every step. If the elephant charged and I missed him, I should have about as much chance as a toad under a steam-roller. But even then I was not thinking particularly of my own skin, only of the watchful yellow faces behind. For at that moment, with the crowd watching me, I was not afraid in the ordinary sense, as I would have been if I had been alone. A white man mustn't be frightened in front of "natives"; and so, in general, he isn't frightened. The sole thought in my mind was that if anything went wrong those two thousand Burmans would see me pursued, caught, trampled on and reduced to a grinning corpse like that Indian up the hill. And if that happened it was quite probable that some of them would laugh. That would never do. There was only one alternative. I shoved the cartridges into the magazine and lay down on the road to get a better aim.

10   The crowd grew very still, and a deep, low, happy sigh, as of people who see the theatre curtain go up at last, breathed from innumerable throats. They were going to have their bit of fun after all. The rifle was a beautiful German thing with cross-hair sights. I did not then know that in shooting an elephant one would shoot to cut an imaginary bar running from ear-hole to ear-hole. I ought, therefore, as the elephant was sideway on, to have aimed straight at his ear-hole; actually I aimed several inches in front of this, thinking the brain would be further forward.

11   When I pulled the trigger I did not hear the bang or feel the kick—one never does when a shot goes home—but I heard the devilish roar of glee that went up from the crowd. In that instant, in too short a time, one would have thought, even for the bullet to get there, a mysterious, terrible change had come over the elephant. He neither stirred nor fell, but every line of his body had altered. He looked suddenly stricken, shrunken, immensely old, as though the frightful impact of the bullet had paralyzed him without knocking him down. At last, after what seemed a long time—it might have been five seconds, I dare say—he sagged flabbily to his knees. His mouth slobbered. An enormous senility seemed to have settled upon him. One could have imagined him thousands of years old. I fired again into the same spot. At the second shot he did not collapse but climbed with desperate slowness to his feet and stood weakly upright, with legs sagging and head drooping. I fired a third time. That was the shot that did for him. You could see the agony of it jolt his whole body and knock the last remnant of strength from his legs. But in falling he seemed for a moment to rise, for as his hind legs collapsed beneath him he seemed to tower upward like a huge rock toppling, his trunk reaching skywards like a tree. He trumpeted, for the first and only time. And then down he came, his belly towards me, with a crash that seemed to shake the ground even where I lay.

12   I got up. The Burmans were already racing past me across the mud. It was obvious that the elephant would never rise again, but he was not dead. He was breathing very rhythmically with long rattling gasps, his great mound of a side painfully rising and falling. His mouth was wide open—I could see far down into caverns of pale pink throat. I waited a long time for him to die, but his breathing

did not weaken. Finally I fired my two remaining shots into the spot where I thought his heart must be. The thick blood welled out of him like red velvet, but still he did not die. His body did not even jerk when the shots hit him, the tortured breathing continued without a pause. He was dying, very slowly and in great agony, but in some world remote from me where not even a bullet could damage him further. I felt that I had got to put an end to that dreadful noise. It seemed dreadful to see the great beast lying there, powerless to move and yet powerless to die, and not even to be able to finish him. I sent back for my small rifle and poured shot after shot into his heart and down his throat. They seemed to make no impression. The tortured gasps continued as steadily as the ticking of a clock.

In the end I could not stand it any longer and went away. I   13
heard later that it took him half an hour to die. Burmans were bringing dahs and baskets even before I left, and I was told they had stripped his body almost to the bones by the afternoon.

Afterwards, of course, there were endless discussions about   14
the shooting of the elephant. The owner was furious, but he was only an Indian and could do nothing. Besides, legally I had done the right thing, for a mad elephant has to be killed, like a mad dog, if its owner fails to control it. Among the Europeans opinion was divided. The older men said I was right, the younger men said it was a damn shame to shoot an elephant for killing a coolie, because an elephant was worth more than any damn Coringhee coolie. And afterwards I was very glad that the coolie had been killed; it put me legally in the right and it gave me a sufficient pretext for shooting the elephant. I often wondered whether any of the others grasped that I had done it solely to avoid looking a fool.

Thinking Critically About This Reading

1. In your opinion, does the individual have a moral obligation to carry out the commands and duties of an empire he or she regards as evil? Why or why not?

2. What are the real motives for which despotic governments act? Do you agree or disagree with the author's opinions on this subject? What other motive might account for the behavior of a despotic regime?

3. The author claims that invariably in the East a story sounds clearer from afar than it turns out to be as one approaches its center. What explanation can you give for this paradox?

4. What does the author mean by, "when the white man turns tyrant it is his own freedom that he destroys"? What exactly does the author mean by "freedom"? Can this also be said of other races, or only of whites? Why or why not?

5. Under what social circumstances must we all wear a mask and grow a face to fit it? What terms might a social scientist use to describe this kind of social coercion?

Understanding the Writer's Process

1. List some features of this essay that support the headnote's characterization of Orwell's style as possessing "singular directness and honesty."

2. What is the primary aim of this essay? Where does the author tell what he intends to do? How closely does he stick to his stated purpose?

3. Throughout the essay, the author candidly confesses his innermost feelings and fears to the reader. How do these revelations contribute to the believability of the story and to a reader's possible acceptance of Orwell's conclusions?

4. The author occasionally uses "you" as an indefinite pronoun, which is usually considered bad form in writing. Find examples of this use in the narrative and state what it adds to the author's account.

5. As a writer, Orwell is renowned for his keenly descriptive eye and a fine sense of telling detail. Cite some examples characteristic of this ability.

Examining the Writer's Language

1. What is the meaning of "must" as it is used in this essay to describe the bizarre behavior of an elephant?

2. In another famous essay, Orwell lays down this rule about good writing: "Never use a foreign phrase, a scientific word or a jargon word if you can think of an everyday English equivalent." Twice in this essay he uses Latin phrases. What justification can you suggest for this use?

3. In paragraph 1, Orwell writes, "No one had the guts to raise a riot. ..." What difference would it make to the particular

sentence if you substituted a more formal equivalent of "guts," such as "courage" or "fortitude"?

4. Be sure you know the meanings of the following words as they are used in the context of this essay: Raj (paragraph 2), prostrate (2), labyrinth (4), ravaging (5), metalled road (5), conventionalized (7).

5. Orwell occasionally uses unfamiliar terms such as "must," "mahout," "dahs," "sahib," "Dravidian coolie," and "Coringhee coolie" that were foreign to most English readers (for whom this piece was originally written). What do you think is gained by the use of these exotic words?

Suggestions for Writing

1. Write a narrative essay telling about any experience where pressure from others caused you to act against your better judgment.

2. Write an essay on the peer pressures to which college students are typically subjected.

WOMEN IN THE ESKIMO WORLD

Gontran de Poncins

Jean–Pierre Gontran de Montaigne de Poncins (1900–1962), writer, world traveler, and adventurer, was born into an aristocratic French family and briefly studied painting at the Ecole des Beaux–Arts. Becoming restless with civilization, Poncins journeyed first to the South Seas, China, and India, finally arriving in 1938 in the Northwest Territories of Canada where he lived with nomadic Eskimos for a year. Out of this experience came Kabloona *(1941) (Eskimo for "white man"), which is regarded as a classic of ethnography, and from which this excerpt comes.*

Preparing to Read This Selection Critically

Bearing in mind that Poncins was a Frenchman who lived only a year among the Eskimos, ask yourself whether any of his prejudices might be reflected in his narrative. Do you think, for example, that his generalization about Eskimo women is sound? Can a sweeping generalization such as the one with which Poncins opens his narrative be accurately made about any people? What similar generalization could you make about American women and how could you support it?

1 Women were behind everything in this Eskimo world. If one native abandoned a given group in order to go off and live with another you could be sure it was done at the instigation of his wife. If a couple suddenly grew into a triangular household, you were virtually certain that it was the wife and not the husband who had dictated the choice of the permanent friend. And if, one day, that triangle was reduced to a couple again as the result of a murder, there was never any doubt but that it was the wife who had plotted and prompted the murder. But I have a story to tell you . . .

2 My story is of Ekaluk who came out of the porch of the igloo one morning and looked round.

3 Little plumes of snow were running before the wind over the plain and powdering the earth with a fine layer of white. Nothing else stirred. Near by, two puppies lay asleep on the snow. The igloos were hushed and seemingly deserted. The men had gone off to fish through the ice of a lake whose unbroken surface stretched into infinity. All these things the young man saw with an eye quick to seize details in this vast landscape. And he saw, too, receding in the distance, a dark form that he knew to be Ohokto, hurrying on foot to his fishing. Watching him, there dropped into Ekaluk's mind the words spoken a half hour before by Kanaiok, his mistress and Ohokto's wife: "Why don't you do it? Now is the time!"

4 This was not the first time that Kanaiok had urged him to do it. In the beginning, Ekaluk had taken her into his sleeping-bag as a matter of desire and convention, in the common way of neighboring Eskimos. Ohokto had of course not taken it amiss; and besides, he was no longer young. But things had not stopped there: Ekaluk had ended by taking a fancy to the young woman—in Eskimo fashion, naturally; not out of love, but simply because he wanted a woman to himself. And he had come to live in their igloo. Still Ohokto had said nothing. He had merely grown more silent. Now Ekaluk had got it into his head that Kanaiok would make him a

proper wife. He liked her. She could sew skins wonderfully. She was an excellent housewife, for there was always tea and *baneks* in her igloo. And Kanaiok, for her part, found Ekaluk's body more agreeable than her husband's. It was less intelligent, but it was younger, warmer.

Like most Eskimo women, Kanaiok was both clever and per- 5 sistent, and she soon achieved a complete ascendancy over this young, simple–minded, and violent lover. "Why not?" she would urge. "Do away with Ohokto, and we'll go off to another camp and live together. I'll sew you the handsomest clothes in the world, and your igloo will be the one that all men will most willingly visit."

Ekaluk was not bright. He had no words to say what he felt. 6 But these things troubled his mind. More and more violently he desired this woman for himself alone. And Kanaiok gave him no peace, harassed him ceaselessly; and when Ekaluk, angered by her persistence, flew into a rage and beat her, she would be silent for several days. Then she would begin again: Doubtless Ekaluk was a coward; she had thought him a man. Since this was how he was, she would say no more. As a matter of fact, if you wanted a man, a real one, there was Ohokto; and indeed she was lucky to be his wife.

This sort of mockery worked on Ekaluk. It was a spur in the 7 side of the young animal (he might have been twenty–two years old). And this morning he had made up his mind to do the thing as soon as he got the chance—for an Eskimo never kills face to face, but always from behind. He would stab Ohokto from behind. Already he could see himself doing it. Kanaiok knew what was going through his mind. She had been quick to flatter him, to cajole him this morning; and when Ohokto had left, she, snuffing with elaborate casualness the wick of the seal-oil lamp, had whispered a quantity of things into Ekaluk's ear.

All this was stirring confusedly in Ekaluk's mind as he went 8 forward to his sled, turned it right side up, and harnessed his dogs. Ohokto had not been out of sight ten minutes when Ekaluk's sled was gliding down the declivity that led to the lake.

He knew he was going to kill, but he knew not how. A mind 9 like his could make no plans in advance. He knew merely that when the occasion offered itself, he, a hunter and an Eskimo, would seize it. All that he was sure of was that this was the day when the thing would be done. Kanaiok's voice rang in his ears, and all of a sudden his blood began to beat in his chest. He whipped up the dogs, and they, seeming to understand, trotted rapidly through the grey air. Already a silhouette was visible on the ice. It was Ohokto.

10   Ohokto was on his knees over a hole in the ice, in the customary posture. In front of him three heavy blocks of snow formed a rampart against the wind. He was kneeling on a bed of crushed ice over which he had spread his caribouskin. Ohokto was motionless, a statue of immobility. Eskimos are able to kneel like this for hours without the slightest movement, without the least fatigue, watching the fish pass slowly to and fro under the ice as in a dream. Only the left hand is in motion, the hand that does the jigging and rises and falls with the regularity of the tick-tock of a clock while five or six feet under the ice the decoy—fins made of bone—flutters in the same rhythm. Within reach of the right hand lies the great three-pronged harpoon, ready for the kill.

11   Ohokto is motionless. The wind may veer, the blizzard may come, nothing will budge Ohokto. His is the patience of the hunter, and his concern with the kill is so concentrated that nothing can distract him from it. He does not so much as turn his head when Ekaluk draws near.

12   The easiest thing in the world to do is to stop one's dogs: they seem always ready to rest. A whispered "Hoo!" will cut them short and turn their heads towards the driver. Ekaluk has stopped his team at about fifty yards from the hole, instinctively concerned not to frighten the fish. He strokes them with his whip, and they lie down. The whip is then slipped under the straps along the sled.

13   For an Eskimo, there is nothing so automatic as to pick up one's snow–knife at the moment of getting off a sled. Ekaluk's knife is in his hand as he goes towards Ohokto. A blizzard has come up, and Ekaluk moves at the center of a whirling wall of snow through which he can see a bare hundred feet. Probably there are other natives out on the lake, but in this wall of snow Ekaluk is as good as invisible to them—and besides, what he is up to is his own affair.

14   As he walks slowly forward towards his still motionless friend, a gleam of consciousness pierces his brain. He is about to kill Ohokto from behind. Two strokes of a spear in the ice will make a hole down which he can send Ohokto; and if ever the police come—they never come in the winter—clever the man who can find a body under eight feet of ice!

15   Now the thing is very clear in Ekaluk's mind. But at the moment when he stands over his friend, Ohokto straightens up and murmurs mysteriously:

"Angi-y-uk." (Big ones.) 16

Big fish! After days of harpooning fish so small that they were 17
not worth bringing in, so that Ekaluk had preferred to spend his
hours with Kanaiok in the igloo! And now the big fish are back! It
must have been the new moon last night that brought them.

It was at this moment that Ekaluk forgot the purpose of his 18
coming and forgot the murderous knife in his hand. He knelt without
a word beside Ohokto, who had returned to his knees as soon as
he had spoken, and side by side the man who had been about to
kill and the man who had been about to die peered together above
the hole. One after another they speared great fish, violently red of
flesh; and it was as if the fish had been sent to save Ohokto from
murder.

Ekaluk had forgotten; for Ekaluk was first of all a hunter, and 19
fish or seal spoke louder to his instinct than woman or murder.
Frozen instantly, hard as wood, the fish were piled on Ekaluk's sled,
the dogs were on their feet, and the sled was away.

Neither man spoke. The Spirit of Fishing filled them both, each 20
for himself. From time to time Ekaluk would call out to his dogs,
or Ohokto would jump down from the sled to release a tangled trace
and quickly remount again. They had crossed the great lake called
Kakivok–tar–yik and were nearing the camp when by one of the
recurrent miracles of the Arctic the wind suddenly shifted, the grey
veil vanished from the air, and the sinking sun was revealed—a sun
of mercy.

And then Ekaluk remembered. Two hundred yards ahead, 21
Kanaiok was waiting for him, prepared to leave with him. His dogs
were already slowing down; and at the moment when they stopped
dead he stepped behind Ohokto and sank the snow–knife into his
back. Ohokto toppled over like a sack of grain. Lying in his heavy
overcoat on the ground, his short arms motionless, he looked like
a grotesque dead doll. Ekaluk ran past the dogs, struck his harpoon
into the snow, and crawled on all fours into the porch.

Thinking Critically About This Reading

1. Assuming that Poncins is right and that women are the instigators
   of most mischief in the Eskimo world, what explanation do you
   think might reasonably account for their conniving behavior?

2. The author generalizes more about Eskimo women than about
   Eskimo men. What general truths can a reader reasonably infer
   about Eskimo men from this story?

3. In your estimation, how do Eskimo women compare/contrast with American women?

4. What do you speculate might have been the outcome of this story of murder?

5. In what general ways does this Eskimo love triangle differ from a similar situation in our world?

Understanding the Writer's Process

1. What poetic license does the writer take with the material? Point to specific instances.

2. How does the author manipulate the tense of his narrative for dramatic effect? Point to specific examples.

3. In his descriptions of the three Eskimos, the author does not particularize any with unique features or traits. Why do you think he chose not to individualize his characters?

4. In neither the excerpt reprinted here nor in the original book from which this selection came does the author give a sequel to this story. How can you explain this omission?

5. What does the use of exclamation marks in paragraph 17 implicitly tell us about Ekaluk?

Examining the Writer's Language

1. Define the meanings of the following words used in this essay: ascendancy (paragraph 5), cajole (7), declivity (8).

2. In paragraph 6, the author uses indirect discourse to explain the kinds of things Kanaiok might have said to Ekaluk. Why is this more effective than using direct discourse?

3. At the end of paragraph 7, the writer tells us that on the fateful morning Kanaiok had whispered "a quantity of things in Ekaluk's ear." Why do you think he chose not to share with us the specific things she said?

4. How would you characterize the author's description of the sun at the end of paragraph 20?

5. How does the author use language to reflect the thinking processes of Ekaluk?

Suggestions for Writing

1. Make a generalization about a group of people, then write a narration that supports or illustrates it.
2. Write a narration about a love triangle.

THE CODE

Richard T. Gill

> *Richard T. Gill (b. 1927) was born in Long Island, New York, and educated at Harvard University. A former assistant professor of economics at Harvard, Gill has been the principal bass of the New York Metropolitan opera since 1973. He occasionally contributes stories to the* New Yorker *and* Atlantic Monthly, *and is the author of* Economic Development: Past and Present *(3rd ed., 1973) and* Economics and the Public Interest *(2nd ed., 1972).*

Preparing to Read This Selection Critically

One of the questions students usually ask after reading "The Code" is: "Did this really happen to the writer?" Whether or not it did is beside the point. Fiction deals in plausibility more than in realism or truth, and the story as the writer tells it is troublingly plausible. Yet the author does not tell us all we want to know. As you read, ask yourself why the narrator simply didn't summon the minister to his father's deathbed. Was it because he could not witness his father's terror of death? Was it because of his own true–believer stubbornness? We are given strong inklings but no explicit answer. Also ask yourself what, if anything, the son could have said, but failed to say, to ease his father's last moments. What would you have done, in the narrator's place?

I

I remember, almost to the hour, when I first began to question my 1
religion. I don't mean that my ideas changed radically just at that

time. I was only twelve, and I continued to go to church faithfully and to say something that could pass for prayers each night before I went to sleep. But I never again felt quite the same. For the first time in my life, it had occurred to me that when I grew up I might actually leave the Methodist faith.

2   It all happened just a few days after my brother died. He was five years old, and his illness was so brief and his death so unexpected that my whole family was almost crazed with grief. My three aunts, each of whom lived within a few blocks of our house, and my mother were all firm believers in religion, and they turned in unison, and without reservation, to this last support. For about a week, a kind of religious frenzy seized our household. We would all sit in the living room—my mother, my aunts, my two sisters, and I, and sometimes Mr. Dodds, the Methodist minister, too—saying prayers in low voices, comforting one another, staying together for hours at a time, until someone remembered that we had not had dinner or that it was time for my sisters and me to be in bed.

3   I was quite swept up by the mood that had come over the house. When I went to bed, I would say the most elaborate, intricate prayers. In the past, when I had finished my "Now I lay me down to sleep," I would bless individually all the members of my immediate family and then my aunts, and let it go at that. Now, however, I felt that I had to bless everyone in the world whose name I could remember. I would go through all my friends at school, including the teachers, the principal, and the janitor, and then through the names of people I had heard my mother and father mention, some of whom I had never even met. I did not quite know what to do about my brother, whom I wanted to pray for more than for anyone else. I hesitated to take his name out of its regular order, for fear I would be committed to believing that he had really died. But then I *knew* that he had died, so at the end of my prayers, having just barely mentioned his name as I went along, I would start blessing him over and over again, until I finally fell asleep.

4   The only one of us who was unmoved by this religious fervor was my father. Oddly enough, considering what a close family we were and how strongly my mother and aunts felt about religion, my father had never shown the least interest in it. In fact, I do not think that he had ever gone to church. Partly for this reason, partly because he was a rather brusque, impatient man, I always felt that he was something of a stranger in our home. He spent a great deal

of time with us children, but through it all he seemed curiously unapproachable. I think we all felt constrained when he played with us and relieved when, at last, we were left to ourselves.

At the time of my brother's death, he was more of a stranger 5 than ever. Except for one occasion, he took no part in the almost constant gatherings of the family in the living room. He was not going to his office that week—we lived in a small town outside Boston—and he was always around the house, but no one ever seemed to know exactly where. One of my aunts—Sarah, my mother's eldest sister—felt very definitely that my father should not be left to himself, and she was continually saying to me, "Jack, go upstairs and see if you can find him and talk to him." I remember going timidly along the hallway on the second floor and peeking into the bedrooms, not knowing what I should say if I found him and half afraid that he would scold me for going around looking into other people's rooms. One afternoon, not finding him in any of the bedrooms, I went up into the attic, where we had a sort of playroom. I remember discovering him there by the window. He was sitting absolutely motionless in an old wicker chair, an empty pipe in his hands, staring out fixedly over the treetops. I stood in the doorway for several minutes before he was aware of me. He turned as if to say something, but then, looking at me or just above my head—I was not sure which—he seemed to lose himself in his thoughts. Finally, he gave me a strangely awkward salute with his right hand and turned again to the window.

About the only times my father was with the rest of us were 6 when we had meals or when, in the days immediately following the funeral, we all went out to the cemetery, taking fresh flowers or wreaths. But even at the cemetery he always stood slightly apart— a tall, lonely figure. Once, when we were at the grave and I was nearest him, he reached over and squeezed me around the shoulders. It made me feel almost embarrassed as though he were breaking through some inviolable barrier between us. He must have felt as I did, because he at once removed his arm and looked away, as though he had never actually embraced me at all.

It was the one occasion when my father was sitting in the 7 living room with us that started me to wondering about my religion. We had just returned from the cemetery—two carloads of us. It was three or four days after the funeral and just at the time when, the shock having worn off, we were all experiencing our first clear realization of what had happened. Even I, young as I was, sensed that there was a new air of desolation in our home.

8   For a long time, we all sat there in silence. Then my aunts, their eyes moist, began talking about my brother, and soon my mother joined in. They started off softly, telling of little things he had done in the days before his illness. Then they fell silent and dried their eyes, and then quickly remembered some other incident and began speaking again. Slowly the emotion mounted, and before long the words were flooding out. "God will take care of him!" my Aunt Sarah cried, almost ecstatically. "Oh, yes, He will! He will!" Presently, they were all talking in chorus—saying that my brother was happy at last and that they would all be with him again one day.

9   I believed what they were saying and I could barely hold back my tears. But swept up as I was, I had the feeling that they should not be talking that way while my father was there. The feeling was one that I did not understand at all at the moment. It was just that when I looked over to the corner where he was sitting and saw the deep, rigid lines of his face, saw him sitting there silently, all alone, I felt guilty. I wanted everyone to stop for a while—at least until he had gone upstairs. But there was no stopping the torrent once it had started.

10   "Oh, he was too perfect to live!" Aunt Agnes, my mother's youngest sister, cried. "He was never a bad boy. I've never seen a boy like that. I mean he was never even naughty. He was just too perfect."

"Oh, yes. Oh, yes," my mother sighed.

"It's true," Aunt Sarah said. "Even when he was a baby, he never really cried. There was never a baby like him. He was a saint."

"He *was* a saint!" Aunt Agnes cried. "That's why he was taken from us!"

"He was a perfect baby," my mother said.

"He was taken from us," Aunt Agnes went on, "because he was too perfect to live."

11   All through this conversation, my father's expression had been growing more and more tense. At last, while Aunt Agnes was speaking, he rose from his chair. His face was very pale, and his eyes flashed almost feverishly. "Don't talk like that, Agnes!" he exclaimed, with a strange violence that was not anger but something much deeper. "I won't have you talking like that any more. I don't want anybody talking like that!" His whole body seemed to tremble. I had never seen him so worked up before. "Of course he was a bad boy

at times!" he cried. "Every boy's bad once in a while. What do you have to change him for? Why don't you leave him as he was?"

"But he was such a perfect baby," Aunt Sarah said.   12

"He *wasn't* perfect!" my father almost shouted, clenching his fist. "He was no more perfect than Jack here or Betty or Ellen. He was just an ordinary little boy. He wasn't perfect. And he wasn't a saint. He was just a little boy, and I won't have you making him over into something he wasn't!"

He looked as though he were going to go on talking like this,   13
but just then he closed his eyes and ran his hand up over his forehead and through his hair. When he spoke again, his voice was subdued. "I just wish you wouldn't talk that way," he said. "That's all I mean." And then, after standing there silently for a minute, he left the living room and walked upstairs.

I sat watching the doorway through which he had gone. Sud-   14
denly, I had no feeling for what my mother and my aunts had been saying. It was all a mist, a dream. Out of the many words that had been spoken that day, it was those few sentences of my father's that explained to me how I felt about my brother. I wanted to be with my father to tell him so.

I went upstairs and found him once again in the playroom in   15
the attic. As before, he was silent and staring out the window when I entered, and we sat without speaking for what seemed to me like half an hour or more. But I felt that he knew why I was there, and I was not uncomfortable with him.

Finally, he turned to me and shook his head. "I don't know   16
what I can tell you, Jack," he said, raising his hands and letting them drop into his lap. "That's the worst part of it. There's just nothing I can say that will make it any better."

Though I only half understood him then, I see now that he   17
was telling me of a drawback—that he had no refuge, no comfort, no support. He was telling me that you were all alone if you took the path that he had taken. Listening to him, I did not care about the drawback. I had begun to see what a noble thing it was for a man to bear the full loss of someone he had loved.

II

By the time I was thirteen or fourteen I was so thoroughly committed   18
to my father's way of thinking that I considered it a great weakness in a man to believe in religion. I wanted to grow up to face life as he did—truthfully, without comfort, without support.

19   My attitude was never one of rebellion. Despite the early regimen of Sunday school and church that my mother had encouraged,
she was wonderfully gentle with me, particularly when I began to
express my doubts. She would come into my room each night after
the light was out and ask me to say my prayers. Determined to be
honest with her, I would explain that I could not say them sincerely,
and therefore should not say them at all. "Now Jack," she would
reply, very quietly and calmly, "you mustn't talk like that. You'll
really feel much better if you say them." I could tell from the tone
of her voice that she was hurt, but she never tried to force me in
any way. Indeed, it might have been easier for me if she *had* tried
to oppose my decision strenuously. As it was, I felt so bad at having
wounded her that I was continually trying to make things up—
running errands, surprising her by doing the dishes when she went
out shopping—behaving, in short, in the most conscientious, considerate fashion. But all this never brought me any closer to her
religion. On the contrary, it only served to free me for my decision
not to believe. And for that decision, as I say, my father was responsible.

20   Part of his influence, I suppose, was in his physical quality.
Even at that time—when he was in his late forties and in only moderately good health—he was a most impressive figure. He was tall
and heavy-chested, with leathery, rough-cast features and with an
easy, relaxed rhythm in his walk. He had been an athlete in his
youth, and, needless to say, I was enormously proud of his various
feats and told about them, with due exaggeration, all over our neighborhood. Still, the physical thing had relatively little to do with the
matter. My father, by that time, regarded athletes and athletics with
contempt. Now and again, he would take me into the back yard to
fool around with boxing gloves, but when it came to something
serious, such as my going out for football in high school, he invariably put his foot down. "It takes too much time," he would tell
me. "You ought to be thinking of college and your studies. It's nonsense what they make of sports nowadays!" I always wanted to
remind him of *his* school days, but I knew it was no use. He had
often told me what an unforgivable waste of time he considered his
youth to have been.

21   Thus, although the physical thing was there, it was very much
in the background—little more, really, than the simple assumption
that a man ought to know how to take care of himself. The real
bond between us was spiritual, in the sense that courage, as opposed

to strength, is spiritual. It was this intangible quality of courage that I wanted desperately to possess and that, it seemed to me, captured everything that was essential about my father.

We never talked of this quality directly. The nearest we came 22
to it was on certain occasions during the early part of the Second World War, just before I went off to college. We would sit in the living room listening to a speech by Winston Churchill, and my father would suddenly clap his fist against his palm. "My God!" he would exclaim, fairly beaming with admiration. "That man's got the heart of a tiger!" And I would listen to the rest of the speech, thrilling to every word, and then, thinking of my father, really, I would say aloud that, of all men in the world, the one I would most like to be was Churchill.

Nor did we often talk about religion. Yet our religion—our re- 23
jection of religion—was the deepest statement of the bond between us. My father, perhaps out of deference to my mother and my sisters and aunts, always put his own case very mildly. "It's certainly a great philosophy," he would say of Christianity. "No one could question that. But for the rest . . ." Here he would throw up his hands and cock his head to one side, as if to say that he had tried, but simply could not manage the hurdle of divinity. This view, however mildly it may have been expressed, became mine with absolute clarity and certainty. I concluded that religion was a refuge, without the least foundation in fact. More than that, I positively objected to those—I should say those *men*, for to me it was a peculiarly masculine matter— who turned to religion for support. As I saw it, a man ought to face life as it really is, on his own two feet, without a crutch, as my father did. That was the heart of the matter. By the time I left home for college, I was so deeply committed to this view that I would have considered it a disloyalty to him, to myself, to the code we had lived by, to alter my position in the least.

I did not see much of my father during the next four years or 24
so. I was home during the summer vacation after my freshman year, but then, in the middle of the next year, I went into the Army. I was shipped to the Far East for the tail end of the war, and was in Japan at the start of the Occupation. I saw my father only once or twice during my entire training period, and, naturally, during the time I was overseas I did not see him at all.

While I was away, his health failed badly. In 1940, before I 25
went off to college, he had taken a job at a defense plant. The plant was only forty miles from our home, but he was working on the

night shift, and commuting was extremely complicated and tiresome. And, of course, he was always willing to overexert himself out of a sense of pride. The result was that late in 1942 he had a heart attack. He came through it quite well, but he made no effort to cut down on his work and, as a consequence, suffered a second, and more serious, attack, two years later. From that time on, he was almost completely bedridden.

26   I was on my way overseas at the time of the second attack, and I learned of it in a letter from my mother. I think she was trying to spare me, or perhaps it was simply that I could not imagine so robust a man as my father being seriously ill. In any event, I had only the haziest notion of what his real condition was, so when, many months later, I finally did realize what had been going on, I was terribly surprised and shaken. One day, some time after my arrival at an American Army post in Japan, I was called to the orderly room and told that my father was critically ill and that I was to be sent home immediately. Within forty-eight hours, I was standing in the early-morning light outside my father's bedroom, with my mother and sisters at my side. They had told me, as gently as they could, that he was not very well, that he had had another attack. But it was impossible to shield me then. I no sooner stepped into the room and saw him than I realized that he would not live more than a day or two longer.

27   From that moment on, I did not want to leave him for a second. Even that night, during the periods when he was sleeping and I was of no help being there, I could not get myself to go out of the room for more than a few minutes. A practical nurse had come to sit up with him, but since I was at the bedside, she finally spent the night in the hallway. I was really quite tired, and late that night my mother and my aunts begged me to go to my room and rest for a while, but I barely heard them. I was sure he would wake up soon, and when he did, I wanted to be there to talk to him.

28   We did talk a great deal that first day and night. It was difficult for both of us. Every once in a while, my father would shift position in the bed, and I would catch a glimpse of his wasted body. It was a knife in my heart. Even worse were the times when he would reach out for my hand, his eyes misted, and begin to tell me how he felt about me. I tried to look at him, but in the end I always looked down. And, knowing that he was dying, and feeling desperately guilty, I would keep repeating to myself that he knew how I felt, that he would understand why I looked away.

There was another thing, too. While we talked that day, I had 29 a vague feeling that my father was on the verge of making some sort of confession to me. It was, as I say, only the vaguest impression, and I thought very little about it. The next morning, however, I began to sense what was in the air. Apparently, Mr. Dodds, the minister, whom I barely knew, had been coming to the house lately to talk to my father. My father had not said anything about this, and I learned it only indirectly, from something my mother said to my eldest sister at the breakfast table. At the moment, I brushed the matter aside. I told myself it was natural that Mother would want my father to see the minister at the last. Nevertheless, the very mention of the minister's name caused something to tighten inside me.

Later that day, the matter was further complicated. After lunch, 30 I finally did go to my room for a nap, and when I returned to my father's room, I found him and my mother talking about Mr. Dodds. The conversation ended almost as soon as I entered, but I was left with the distinct impression that they were expecting the minister to pay a visit that day, whether very shortly or at suppertime or later in the evening, I could not tell. I did not ask. In fact, I made a great effort not to think of the matter at all.

Then, early that evening, my father spoke to me. I knew before 31 he said a word that the minister *was* coming. My mother had straightened up the bedroom, and fluffed up my father's pillows so that he was half sitting in the bed. No one had told me anything, but I was sure what the preparations meant. "I guess you probably know," my father said to me when we were alone, "we're having a visitor tonight. It's—ah—Mr. Dodds. You know, the minister from your mother's church."

I nodded, half shrugging, as if I saw nothing the least unusual 32 in the news. "He's come here before once or twice," my father said. "Have I mentioned that? I can't remember if I've mentioned that."

"Yes, I know. I think Mother said something, or perhaps you did. I don't remember."

"I just thought I'd let you know. You see, your mother wanted me to talk to him. I—I've talked to him more for her sake than anything else."

"Sure. I can understand that."

"I think it makes her feel a little better. I think—" Here he 33 broke off, seeming dissatisfied with what he was saying. His eyes turned to the ceiling, and he shook his head slightly, as if to erase the memory of his words. He studied the ceiling for a long time before he spoke again. "I don't mean it was all your mother exactly," he said. "Well, what I mean is he's really quite an interesting man. I think you'd probably like him a good deal."

"I know Mother has always liked him," I replied. "From what I gather most people seem to like him very much."

"Well, he's that sort," my father went on, with quickening interest. "I mean, he isn't what you'd imagine at all. To tell the truth, I wish you'd talk to him a little. I wish you'd talk things over with him right from scratch." My father was looking directly at me now, his eyes flashing.

"I'd be happy to talk with him sometime," I said. "As I say, everybody seems to think very well of him."

34   "Well, I wish you would. You see, when you're lying here day after day, you get to thinking about things. I mean, it's good to have someone to talk to." He paused for a moment. "Tell me," he said, "have you ever . . . have you ever wondered if there wasn't some truth in it? Have you ever thought about it that way at all?"

35   I made a faint gesture with my hand. "Of course, it's always possible to wonder," I replied. "I don't suppose you can ever be completely certain one way or the other."

"I know, I know," he said, almost impatiently. "But have you ever felt—well, all in a sort of flash—that it *was* true? I mean, have you ever had that feeling?"

36   He was half raised up from the pillow now, his eyes staring into me with a feverish concentration. Suddenly, I could not look at him any longer. I lowered my head.

"I don't mean permanently or anything like that," he went on. "But just for a few seconds. The feeling that you've been wrong all along. Have you had that feeling—ever?"

37   I could not look up. I could not move. I felt that every muscle in my body had suddenly frozen. Finally, after what seemed an eternity, I heard him sink back into the pillows. When I glanced up a moment later, he was lying there silent, his eyes closed, his lips parted, conveying somehow the image of the death that awaited him.

38   Presently, my mother came to the door. She called me into the hall to tell me that Mr. Dodds had arrived. I said that I thought my father had fallen asleep but that I would go back and see.

It was strangely disheartening to me to discover that he was awake. He was sitting there, his eyes open, staring grimly into the gathering shadows of the evening.

"Mr. Dodds is downstairs," I said matter-of-factly. "Mother wanted to know if you felt up to seeing him tonight."

For a moment, I thought he had not heard me; he gave no sign of recognition whatever. I went to the foot of the bed and repeated myself. He nodded, not answering the question but simply indicating that he had heard me. At length, he shook his head. "Tell your mother I'm a little tired tonight," he said. "Perhaps—well, perhaps some other time."

"I could ask him to come back later, if you'd like."

"No, no, don't bother. I—I could probably use the rest."

I waited a few seconds. "Are you sure?" I asked. "I'm certain he could come back in an hour or so."

Then, suddenly, my father was looking at me. I shall never forget his face at that moment and the expression burning in his eyes. He was pleading with me to speak. And all I could say was that I would be happy to ask Mr. Dodds to come back later, if he wanted it that way. It was not enough. I knew, instinctively, at that moment that it was not enough. But I could not say anything more.

As quickly as it had come, the burning flickered and went out. He sank back into the pillows again. "No, you can tell him I won't be needing him tonight," he said, without interest. "Tell him not to bother waiting around." Then he turned on his side, away from me, and said no more.

So my father did not see Mr. Dodds that night. Nor did he ever see him again. Shortly after midnight, just after my mother and sisters had gone to bed, he died. I was at his side then, but I could not have said exactly when it occurred. He must have gone off in his sleep, painlessly, while I sat there awake beside him.

In the days that followed, our family was together almost constantly. Curiously enough, I did not think much about my father just then. For some reason, I felt the strongest sense of responsibility toward the family. I found myself making the arrangements for the funeral, protecting Mother from the stream of people who came to the house, speaking words of consolation to my sisters and even to my aunts. I was never alone except at night, when a kind of oblivion seized me almost as soon as my head touched the pillow. My sleep was dreamless, numb.

Then, two weeks after the funeral, I left for Fort Devens, where I was to be discharged from the Army. I had been there three days when I was told that my terminal leave would begin immediately and that I was free to return home. I had half expected that when I was at the Fort, separated from the family, something would break inside me. But still no emotion came. I thought of my father often during that time, but, search as I would, I could find no sign of feeling.

45   Then, when I had boarded the train for home, it happened. Suddenly, for no reason whatever, I was thinking of the expression on my father's face that last night in the bedroom. I saw him as he lay there pleading with me to speak. And I knew then what he had wanted me to say to him—that it was really all right with me, that it wouldn't change anything between us if he gave way. And then I was thinking of myself and what I had said and what I had *not* said. Not a word to help! Not a word!

46   I wanted to beg his forgiveness. I wanted to cry out aloud to him. But I was in a crowded train, sitting with three elderly women just returning from a shopping tour. I turned my face to the window. There, silent, unnoticed, I thought of what I might have said.

Thinking Critically About This Reading

1. How do you explain the narrator's compulsion to bless everyone in his prayers—including people he had barely heard of—after the death of his brother?

2. Early in his life, the narrator makes an association between religion and women and becomes convinced that religious belief is unmanly. Does your experience with religion confirm or deny this association? If so, what explanation can you offer to account for the varying appeal religion has on the sexes?

3. Why did running errands for his mother free the author to disbelieve in God?

4. It is commonly said that there are no atheists in a foxhole. What does this adage mean? How can it be said to apply to this story?

5. Why didn't the father simply insist on seeing the minister in spite of his son's tacit disapproval? Explain his motive for this final refusal.

Understanding the Writer's Process

1. From what viewpoint does the narrator tell his story? Why is this a useful viewpoint in this narrative?

2. Do you believe this story really happened? How does the writer persuade us of its credibility?

3. The story is formally divided into two numbered parts. What justification exists for the formal break that occurs at the end of paragraph 17?

4. Comment on the pacing of this story. How does the writer signal the passing of time inconsequential to his plot?

5. What is your opinion of the story's ending? Why did the narrator not come right out and tell us what consolations he might have spoken to his dying father?

Examining the Writer's Language

1. Define the following words: unison (paragraph 1), brusque (2), inviolable (6), intangible (21), deference (23).

2. "He was sitting there, his eyes open, staring grimly into the gathering shadows of the evening." What metaphorical meaning does this image have in the context of paragraph 38, where it occurs?

3. Does the diction of this story characterize the narrator in any way? Why? Why not?

Suggestions for Writing

Using "The Code" as a point of reference, narrate an incident from your past that gave you insight into yourself, someone else, or life in general.

STUDENT ESSAY (IN PROCESS) NARRATION

Jennifer Cooper

Jennifer Cooper returned to college after nearly thirty years in the workplace. Following World War II, her family settled in Kenya, where she went to school, worked as a secretary, and married a big-game hunter. She and her husband lived on a farm with their daughter until 1964, when Jennifer returned to London. Five

years later, she settled in Stockholm, where she lived
and worked for the next ten years until 1980, when
she moved to California. She now lives and attends
school in that state and is working on a degree in art
history. As a writer, Jennifer is a perfectionist who
revises and edits her work many times before submit-
ting it for evaluation.

<u>First Draft</u>   Jennifer Cooper

                                          Eng. 101

There Are Fairies at the Bottom of My Garden

tense, (I can
remember)   All I can remember about that first,
                still peaceful Sunday in September, ~~was~~ *is* the
                blissful, childish feeling of being absolutely
                safe. Uncle Will held me on his knee as he sat
                at the kitchen table, carefully filled his
                pipe, and then leaned back and puffed away con-
more
accurate   tentedly. I remember the feel of his soft
                scratchy Shetland sweater
                ~~cashmere sweater~~—the rise and fall of his belly
                as he talked and chuckled with a rich, deep re-
                sonance. I remember the smell of the tobacco, *delete*
                and the sharp tingle in my nostrils as ~~Luke~~ {my *name and*
                father} uncorked the sherry. I remember the hot *parentheses*
                aromatic smells from the oven as my mother
                checked the ~~joint,~~ the Yorkshire pudding, and *clearer,*
                the *blackberry tart* ~~sponge cake~~ she was baking. There were *please*
                sounds, too: The cocker spaniel sprawled out on
                the floor, still panting after the morning romp
                in Richmond Park; my cousin Chris chuff-chuf-
                fing his trains all over the kitchen floor,

make word picture clearer

Aunt Amy's shrill ~~interjections,~~ the strict genius of Mozart ~~classical music on~~ wafting over the wireless, and ~~the clinking sounds~~ clinked with plates, tones as she fussed and ~~of cutlery~~ and glasses. ~~being put on a tray for lunch.~~

fuzzy, fuzzy

Today, is also a peaceful Sunday in September, ~~but~~ and it is forty-seven years later, ~~and~~ also half a world away ~~oceans and continents away~~ from that day when my innocent, young parents turned on their wireless and heard the Town Crier read a Proclamation from the King. War was declared, and an enemy ~~had to~~ must be vanquished. Our way of life was in ~~terrible~~ jeopardy and had to be preserved at all ~~cost,~~ costs, but ~~No one~~ knew that day at what, infinite cost, ~~though, and~~ no one ~~guessed that half a century later we would still be paying the price of victory.~~ } *wordy*

jeopardy is terrible— no need to qualify

In that we were neither maimed nor killed, our family survived the blitz. At the sound of the sirens blaring out their horrendous warnings, we polite~~ly~~ formed queues and took our places in the air-raid shelters, so unbelievably crowded, gloomy, and airless. At the sound of the "all clear," like thousands all over London, we would shuffle up the steps, clutching each a ~~treasured possession,~~ personal treasure and emerge into the ~~cold~~ gray dawn of a new English day, not sure whether we would find our street still ~~standing.~~ It was amazing how well-organized we became. Every man, woman, and child was involved, one way or another, in the war effort, fighting for King and country. The smallest children, like me, were issued ~~with~~ red, rubbery-smelling Mickey Mouse gas masks. Medium-sized children, like Chris, received blue ones. Grown-

delete "ly"

word order!

streets don't "stand"

new para

delete

insert

-delete

-delete - boring

ups had black ~~ones~~. There was daily gas-mask drills for everyone. ~~Mine was so tight I inevitably ended up with a sick headache~~. All had to wear identity bracelets. I have mine still.

∧ insert — Engraved on the front is the inscription ~~It says~~ "J. COOPER CJQN 47/3," ~~on it. The pretty oval plate has Jennifer engraved on the convex front~~. *overstated*

delete - avoid British nomen- clature

Then there were our play things. Along with our tops, ~~skipping~~ ropes, and crayons were the pieces of shrapnel we found at bomb sites. Shrapnel was like ~~currency~~ *money* at school. A good *∧ insert* bit could buy a square of chocolate or a toffee, and that could be nibbled on for a whole week. People on the outskirts of London often ~~found~~ *salvaged* the most highly-prized barter of all—para-

tidy up this bit →

chutes! Those ~~soft~~, ~~shimmering,~~ voluminous yards of ∧ silk were ∧ *luxurious, worth more than their weight in* ~~as precious as~~ gold. Once an uncle found a solid brass shell case. It must have been a foot tall. Every Sunday, out came

∧ insert describes war

the Brasso as he proudly polished his ✓ *latest* war relic. Then he would set it back in its place on the embroidered shawl draped over the piano, and it gleamed and glistened among the sepia photos of brides *and,* ∧ groups, and naked newborns lying on rugs. It seemed to act as a talisman. It seemed to say: "Just you try it, Hitler; just you *dare to* ~~try~~ ∧ marching your goose-stepping, jack-booted S.S. men down **our** street, and see what you get!"

∧ insert "ever" adverb

Throughout all this disaster, I don't ∧ remember being frightened, but as the bombing continued unabated *ly,* ∧ my body started to let me down in curious ways. The first time I ever fainted was when we saw ~~and~~

heard, ~~and~~ smelt, and felt London burning. So
dismayed were my parents by this latest assault
~~on London~~, that without further ado they ~~set~~
~~about moving~~ us, bag and baggage, out to the
country. They had found a tiny cottage in the
grounds of the Old Malt House in a hamlet called
Stanstead in the Weald of Kent. ~~Kent.~~ With its
rolling green ~~temperate~~ landscape, its vast expanses of sky, its fields of barley and aromatic
hops, and its carefully tended apple orchards, Kent
was justly known as "the garden of England." ~~There is a pattern and orderliness in~~
~~nature, sot that~~ After the chaos and unremitting noise of war, the joy of ~~finding out about~~
life in the country was like balm to the soul—
a magical voyage of discovery. ~~We lived~~ Living close
to nature, and we fell in love with life again.

Our idyll, ~~and truly, that's how I ex-~~
~~perienced it,~~ was to be short-lived. The Kentish countryside became a ghastly battleground. We were surrounded ~~on all sides~~ by ca-
bles held ~~up~~ aloft by balloons, ~~put there~~ and anchored in the ground to stop the
rockets and pilotless planes ~~(or doodle bugs)~~
from reaching their pre-programmed targets in
London. By now, my mother had ~~an infant and~~ a
new baby, and as well as a toddler we had to live in a dug-out ~~(or An-~~
~~derson)~~ shelter in the back garden. My mother
had received word that her lovely family home in Battersea had been reduced to a smouldering pile
of rubble. Plainclothesmen from Whitehall came
~~down~~ ~~to our house in the country~~ to tell us that a young soldier had
been found hanged at his barracks. It turned out to be my cousin, Harry.
~~dead.~~ ~~They~~ Those men took my father away ~~to~~ identify the
body. with them so that he could And my father, by now an outpatient at a
distant, overcrowded hospital, was too ill to

[margin annotations:] wordy; delete; insert for accuracy; dash; insert; wordy; yawn!; unnecessary—delete; repetition; better sense; no need to explain; no need to over explain; insert: most of the time

return to his job in Woolwich. My mother, always so valiant, was scared to death. I couldn't bear to see her like that. Shd would hug the newest baby to her and rock back and forth in her chair, *by the fire* trying to stifle the deep, shuddering sobs that filled her whole body, ~~that shook my whole being~~, *sob!* by burying her face in the baby's soft, tiny shape. When I could stand it no longer, I would run out into the garden, leaving my father holding the other baby, powerless to comfort her.

I often wonder whether I would *ever* have found the fairies at the bottom of my garden if I'd *had* been raised in peacetime. I had searched and searched for them in our London garden but *had* never *even caught a glimpse* ~~found a sign~~ of ~~a~~ one. It wasn't until we moved to the country that I finally found them. Oh joy! Oh jubilation! There they were, shimmering, bobbing, translucent blue *delete ,* light forms, who *pulled* ~~invited~~ me in to *laughing,* their secret fairy rings; who taught me to bob and sway and swirl, drift and surge like waves eddying on a beach; who filled my bruised young *spirit* ~~soul~~ with light and *repetition* hope; and who gave me the eternal key to their secret garden. I can go there even now; it is always there for me. You see, *in my heart* I always knew *italics* there *must be* ~~were~~ fairies at the bottom of my garden, too. *What I had not realized was, that in order for me to see them, my heart first had to break.*

for an ending to pull the whole paragraph up more sharply.

insert **All through the long night that followed their visit, I heard his sister crying.*

Final Draft   Jennifer Cooper

Eng. 101

There Are Fairies at the Bottom of My Garden

All I can remember about that first,
still peaceful Sunday in September, is the
blissful, childish feeling of being absolutely
safe. Uncle Will held me on his knee as he sat
at the kitchen table, carefully filled his
pipe, and then leaned back and puffed away con-
tentedly. I remember the feel of his scratchy
Shetland sweater—the rise and fall of his
belly—as he talked and chuckled with a rich,
deep resonance. I remember the smell of the tobacco, and the sharp tingle in my nostrils as
my father uncorked the sherry. I remember the
delicious smells from the oven as my mother
checked the roast beef, the Yorkshire pudding,
and the blackberry tart she was baking. There
were sounds, too: the cocker spaniel still
panting after the morning romp in Richmond
Park, my cousin Chris chuff-chuffing his
trains all over the kitchen floor, the strict
genius of Mozart wafting over the wireless, and
then Aunt Amy's shrill tones as she fussed and
clinked with plates and glasses.

Today, forty-seven years later, it is
also a peaceful Sunday in September; and today
it is also half a world away from that day when
my innocent, young parents turned on their
wireless and heard the Town Crier read a Proclamation from the King. War was declared and an

enemy must be vanquished. Our way of life was in jeopardy and had to be preserved at all costs, but at what infinite cost, no one knew that day.

In that we were neither maimed nor killed, our family survived the blitz. At the sound of the sirens blaring out their horrendous warnings, we formed polite queues and took our places in the air-raid shelters, so unbelievably crowded, gloomy, and airless. At the sound of the "all clear," like thousands all over London, we would shuffle up the steps, each clutching a personal treasure, and emerge into the grey dawn of a new English day, not sure that our street would still be there.

It was amazing how well-organized we became. Every man, woman, and child was involved, one way or another, in the war effort, fighting for King and country. The smallest children, like me, were issued red, rubbery-smelling Mickey Mouse gas masks. Medium-sized children, like Chris, received blue ones. Grown-ups had black. Gas-mask drill was a daily routine. All had to wear identity bracelets. I have mine still. Engraved on the front is the inscription "J. COOPER CJQN 47/3."

Then there were our play things. Along with our tops, jump ropes, and crayons were the pieces of shrapnel we found at bomb sites. Shrapnel was like money at school. A good bit could buy a square of chocolate or a toffee, and that could be nibbled on for a whole week. People on the outskirts of London often sal-

vaged the most highly-prized barter of all—
parachutes! Those voluminous yards of luxurious silk were worth far more than their weight
in gold. Once an uncle found a solid brass shell
case. It must have been a foot tall. Every Sunday, out came the Brasso as he proudly polished
his latest war relic. Then he would set it back
in its place on the embroidered shawl draped
over the piano, and it gleamed and glistened
among the sepia photos of brides, groups, and
naked newborns lying on rugs. It seemed to act
as a talisman. It seemed to say: "Just you try
it, Hitler! Just you dare march your goose-
stepping, jackbooted S.S. men down our street,
and see what you get!"

Throughout all this disaster, I don't
ever remember being frightened, but as the
bombing continued unabatedly, my body started
to let me down in curious ways. The first time
I ever fainted was when we saw, heard, smelled,
and felt the heat of London burning. So dismayed were my parents by this latest assault,
that without further ado they moved us, bag and
baggage, out to the country. They had found a
tiny cottage in the grounds of the Old Malt
House in a hamlet called Stanstead in the Weald
of Kent. With its rolling green landscape, vast
expanses of sky, its fields of barley and aromatic hops, and its carefully tended apple orchards, Kent was justly known as "the garden of
England." After the chaos and unremitting
noise of war, the joy of life in the country was
like a balm to the soul—a magical voyage of dis-

covery. Living close to nature, we fell in love with life again.

Our idyll was to be short-lived. The Kentish countryside became a ghastly battleground. We were surrounded by cables held aloft by balloons and anchored in the ground to stop the rockets and pilotless planes from reaching their pre-programmed targets in London. By now, my mother had a new baby as well as a toddler, and most of the time we had to live in a dug-out in the back garden. My mother had received word that her lovely family home in Battersea had been reduced to a pile of smouldering rubble. Plainclothesmen came down from Whitehall to tell us that a young soldier had been found hanged at his barracks. It turned out to be my cousin Harry. Those men took my father away with them so that he could identify the body. All through the long night that followed their visit, I heard his sister crying. And my father, by now an outpatient at a distant, overcrowded hospital, was too shellshocked to return to his work in Woolwich. My mother, always so valiant, seemed defeated. I couldn't bear to see her like that. She would hug the newest baby to her and rock back and forth in her chair by the fire, trying to stifle the deep, shuddering sobs that filled her whole body by burying her face in the baby's soft, tiny shape. When I could stand it no longer, I would run out into the garden, leaving my father holding the other baby, powerless to comfort her.

I often wonder whether I would ever have found the fairies at the bottom of my garden if I had been raised in peacetime. I had searched and searched for them in our London garden but had never even caught a glimpse of one. It wasn't until we moved to the country that I finally found them. Oh joy! Oh jubilation! There they were, shimmering, bobbing, translucent blue light forms who pulled me, laughing, into their secret fairy rings; who taught me to bob and sway and swirl, drift and surge like waves eddying on a beach; who filled my bruised young spirit with light and hope; and who gave me the eternal key to their secret garden. I can go there even now; it is always there for me. You see, in my heart I always knew there must be fairies at the bottom of my garden, too. What I had not realized was, that in order for me to see them, my heart first had to break.

3

Description

HOW TO WRITE A DESCRIPTION

Focus, or concentration, contributes more to vivid written description than either the size of the writer's vocabulary or the splattering of adjectives across the page. Here is an example of what we mean. The author is describing a medieval inn partly through the eyes, but mainly through the nose, of a weary traveler:

> In one corner was a travelling family, a large one; thence flowed into the common stock the peculiar sickly smell of neglected brats. Garlic filled up the interstices of the air. And all this with closed window, and intense heat of the central furnace, and the breath of at least forty persons.
>
> They had just supped.
>
> Now Gerard, like most artists, had sensitive organs, and the potent effluvia struck dismay into him. But the rain lashed him outside, and the light and the fire tempted him in.
>
> He could not force his way all at once through the palpable perfumes, but he returned to the light again and again like a singed moth. At last he discovered that the various smells did not entirely mix, no fiend being there to stir them around. Odor of family predominated in two corners; stewed rustic reigned supreme in the center; and garlic in the noisy group by the window. He found, too, by hasty analysis, that of these the garlic described the smallest aerial orbit, and the scent of reeking rustic darted farthest—a flavor as if ancient goats, or the fathers of all foxes, had been drawn through a river, and were here dried by Nebuchadnezzar.
>
> CHARLES READE, *The Cloister and the Hearth*

The essential characteristic of this vivid description is its focus. Instead of trying to give us a sweeping view of the dingy inn, the writer zooms in on how awful it smells. The stink of the inn is the *dominant impression* of this description; the writer's every word, image, and metaphor aims only to direct this stench to our nostrils.

1. Focus on a Dominant Impression

Vivid descriptions invariably focus on a single dominant impression and unremittingly deliver it. Nothing distracts from the dominant impression; every word and image is devoted to rendering it keener and sharper. By *dominant impression*, we mean a feature of the scene that is characteristic of it. Not all scenes have strikingly characteristic features, and writers must often steep themselves in the aura of a place before they can sum up its dominant impression. Yet some scenes possess a dominant impression that leaps out at you. For example, a freeway at rush hour is anything but a placid scene. Usually it is a tangled skein of motorists jockeying for position or nosing from one lane to another. To describe a freeway scene at rush hour, you should word your dominant impression so as to portray the madcap antics of the drivers, the choking fumes of the cars, the background grind and roar of traffic. You might write, as your dominant impression, "The San Diego Freeway at rush hour is a bedlam of traffic noise, choking fumes, and aggressive drivers." Then you would support that dominant impression with specific images and details.

The dominant impression of your description should be the heart of the person, place, or scene you are attempting to describe. If you are describing an elderly aunt who is dull, use her dullness as your dominant impression. If you are writing a description of a Christmas shopping scene, word your dominant impression to portray the frazzled throng of weary shoppers, the harried salesclerks, the dazzling glitter of Christmas lights. What you must avoid in your dominant impression is the mention of every speck in the scene you are describing. For example, among the streaming throngs in the department store at Christmas, there are bound to be a few souls who are calm and composed and seemingly immune to the shopping frenzy. But since these wise few are not at all representative of the overall scene, you should leave them out lest they dilute the description. So if your sister is basically a bundle of nerves, that is how you should paint her on the page—even if you have glimpsed her occasionally in rare moments of serenity.

2. Use Images in Your Descriptions

Most of us know the basics about imagery, especially the simile and the metaphor. We know that the simile is an image based on an explicit comparison. For example, Flannery O'Connor describes the crest of a peabiddy with this simile: "This looks at first like a bug's antennae and later like the head feathers of an Indian." On the other hand, we also know that the metaphor is an image based on an indirect comparison with no obvious linking word—such as *as* or *like*—used to cement it. For example, in "Once More to the Lake," E. B. White uses metaphors to describe a thunderstorm:

"Then the kettle drum, then the snare, then the bass drum and the cymbals, then crackling light against the dark, and the gods grinning and licking their chops in the hills." This is how a thunderstorm seems to the writer: it makes noises *like* many drums and flashes wicked lights against the hills that look *like* gods licking their chops. Even though the writer omits the *like* that might have made the comparison explicit, we still get the picture.

Aside from these basic images, which every writer occasionally uses, there are certain hard-won lessons about descriptive imagery that can be imparted. The first is that vivid images do not miraculously drip off the pen but are usually the result of the writer's reworking the material repeatedly. If nothing original or fresh occurs to you after sitting at your desk for a scant few minutes of trying to write a description, all it means is that you have not sat long enough or tried hard enough. Reread what you have written. Try to picture in your mind the person, place, or thing you are struggling to describe. Cut a word here, replace another there. Persistently scratch away at what you have written, and soon you will be astonished at how much better it begins to get.

The second lesson to impart about writing vivid images is summed up in the adage, "Less is more." Overdoing a descriptive passage is not just possible, it is quite likely. If you are unhappy with a description you have written, instead of stuffing it with more adjectives, try taking some out. Here is an example of a bloated and overdone description. The speaker is trying his utmost to describe his feelings as he says goodbye to his sweetheart:

> . . . I am just in time to hear the toll of a parting bell strike its heavy weight of appalling softness against the weakest fibers of a heart of love, arousing and tickling its dormant action, thrusting the dart of evident separation deeper into its tubes of tenderness, and fanning the flame, already unextinguishable, into volumes of blaze.
>
> AMANDA MCKITTRICK ROS, *Delina Delaney*

This is, of course, wretched stuff. One can see the writer hyperventilating at the pen as she tries desperately to infuse her hero's words with passion. She fails miserably from too much effort.

3. Appeal to All the Reader's Senses

Most of us are so unabashedly visual that we are tempted to deliver only looks in our descriptions. But there is usually much more to a scene than its looks. You might also write about how it sounds, smells, or feels to the touch. The best descriptions draw on all kinds of images and appeal to as many senses as are appropriate. Here is an example. The writer is describing a World War I troop train leaving an African station at night carrying soldiers to the front:

> . . . The men began to sing the jingle that was so popular then—"Marching to Tabora"; and the shouts and cheers, the whistles, the hissing and chugging of the engine, filled the station as a kettle fills with steam. Everything seemed to bubble over; men waved from windows; Dick gave a hunting cry; the red hair of Pioneer Mary flared under a lamp; the guard jumped into his moving van; and we watched the rear light of the last coach vanish, and heard the chugging die away. A plume of sparks, a long coil of dancing fireflies, spread across the black ancient shoulder of the crater Menegai; and gradually the vast digesting dark of Africa swallowed up all traces of that audacious grub, the hurrying train.
>
> ELSPETH HUXLEY, The Flame Trees of Thika

This description is a mixture of appeals to our senses of sight and sound. The men sing and cheer, the engine chugs and hisses. We see Pioneer Mary's red hair and the sparks from the train's engine. We are regaled with a clever simile, "filled the station as a kettle fills with steam" and treated to a riveting metaphor, "the vast digesting dark of Africa swallowed up all traces of that audacious grub, the hurrying train." Did the author really just sit down and calmly mine this rich descriptive vein without effort? We do not know for certain, but most likely not. If her experience is at all typical, she hit this mother lode of imagery only after persistent and labored digging.

ONCE MORE TO THE LAKE

E. B. White

For many years Elwyn Brooks White (1899–1985) was admired and beloved as a contributor to the New Yorker, *where he built an enviable reputation as an incisive essayist with an unerring eye for the telling*

detail. He is the author of many books, including One
Man's Meat *(1942),* Here Is New York *(1949), and two
nearly universally loved books for children,* Stuart Little *(1945) and the venerable* Charlotte's Web *(1952).*

Preparing to Read This Selection Critically

This is a frankly nostalgic essay about an annual
summer vacation haunt and as such will ring with sights
and sounds familiar to many readers. But White has a
deeper, darker purpose than merely regaling us with
childhood memories of his favorite summer lake. He is
taking us on a trek through memory, showing us himself
as boy and man, as son and father, and leading us and
himself irresistibly to an ominous truth. He begins with
innocent and carefree recollections of his childhood days,
amassing a vivid array of sensory details to delight us
with the sights and smells of the summertime lake. It is
only at the very end, when we are fully lulled into his
dreamy nostalgia, that we see to what dark place we have
been led.

1   *August 1941*
One summer, along about 1904, my father rented a camp on
a lake in Maine and took us all there for the month of August. We
all got ringworm from some kittens and had to rub Pond's Extract
on our arms and legs night and morning, and my father rolled over
in a canoe with all his clothes on; but outside of that the vacation
was a success and from then on none of us ever thought there was
any place in the world like that lake in Maine. We returned summer
after summer—always on August 1 for one month. I have since
become a salt-water man, but sometimes in summer there are days
when the restlessness of the tides and the fearful cold of the sea
water and the incessant wind that blows across the afternoon and
into the evening make me wish for the placidity of a lake in the
woods. A few weeks ago this feeling got so strong I bought myself
a couple of bass hooks and a spinner and returned to the lake where
we used to go, for a week's fishing and to revisit old haunts.

2   I took along my son, who had never had any fresh water up
his nose and who had seen lily pads only from train windows. On
the journey over to the lake I began to wonder what it would be

like. I wondered how time would have marred this unique, this holy spot—the coves and streams, the hills that the sun set behind, the camps and the paths behind the camps. I was sure that the tarred road would have found it out, and I wondered in what other ways it would be desolated. It is strange how much you can remember about places like that once you allow your mind to return into the grooves that lead back. You remember one thing, and that suddenly reminds you of another thing. I guess I remembered clearest of all the early mornings, when the lake was cool and motionless, remembered how the bedroom smelled of the lumber it was made of and of the wet woods whose scent entered through the screen. The partitions in the camp were thin and did not extend clear to the top of the rooms, and as I was always the first up I would dress softly so as not to wake the others, and sneak out into the sweet outdoors and start out in the canoe, keeping close along the shore in the long shadows of the pines. I remembered being very careful never to rub my paddle against the gunwale for fear of disturbing the stillness of the cathedral.

The lake had never been what you would call a wild lake. 3 There were cottages sprinkled around the shores, and it was in farming country although the shores of the lake were quite heavily wooded. Some of the cottages were owned by nearby farmers, and you would live at the shore and eat your meals at the farmhouse. That's what our family did. But although it wasn't wild, it was a fairly large and undisturbed lake and there were places in it that, to a child at least, seemed infinitely remote and primeval.

I was right about the tar: it led to within half a mile of the 4 shore. But when I got back there, with my boy, and we settled into a camp near a farmhouse and into the kind of summertime I had known, I could tell that it was going to be pretty much the same as it had been before—I knew it, lying in bed the first morning smelling the bedroom and hearing the boy sneak quietly out and go off along the shore in a boat. I began to sustain the illusion that he was I, and therefore, by simple transposition, that I was my father. This sensation persisted, kept cropping up all the time we were there. It was not an entirely new feeling, but in this setting it grew much stronger. I seemed to be living a dual existence. I would be in the middle of some simple act, I would be picking up a bait box or laying down a table fork, or I would be saying something and suddenly it would be not I but my father who was saying the words or making the gesture. It gave me a creepy sensation.

5   We went fishing the first morning. I felt the same damp moss covering the worms in the bait can, and saw the dragonfly alight on the tip of my rod as it hovered a few inches from the surface of the water. It was the arrival of this fly that convinced me beyond any doubt that everything was as it always had been, that the years were a mirage and that there had been no years. The small waves were the same, chucking the rowboat under the chin as we fished at anchor, and the boat was the same boat, the same color green and the ribs broken in the same places, and under the floorboards the same fresh water leavings and débris—the dead helgramite, the wisps of moss, the rusty discarded fishhook, the dried blood from yesterday's catch. We stared silently at the tips of our rods, at the dragonflies that came and went. I lowered the tip of mine into the water, tentatively, pensively dislodging the fly, which darted two feet away, poised, darted two feet back, and came to rest again a little farther up the rod. There had been no years between the ducking of this dragonfly and the other one—the one that was part of memory. I looked at the boy, who was silently watching his fly, and it was my hands that held his rod, my eyes watching. I felt dizzy and didn't know which rod I was at the end of.

6   We caught two bass, hauling them in briskly as though they were mackerel, pulling them over the side of the boat in a business-like manner without any landing net, and stunning them with a blow on the back of the head. When we got back for a swim before lunch, the lake was exactly where we had left it, the same number of inches from the dock, and there was only the merest suggestion of a breeze. This seemed an utterly enchanted sea, this lake you could leave to its own devices for a few hours and come back to, and find that it had not stirred, this constant and trustworthy body of water. In the shallows, the dark, water-soaked sticks and twigs, smooth and old, were undulating in clusters on the bottom against the clean ribbed sand, and the track of the mussel was plain. A school of minnows swam by, each minnow with its small individual shadow, doubling the attendance, so clear and sharp in the sunlight. Some of the other campers were in swimming, along the shore, one of them with a cake of soap, and the water felt thin and clear and unsubstantial. Over the years there had been this person with the cake of soap, this cultist, and here he was. There had been no years.

7   Up to the farmhouse to dinner through the teeming dusty field, the road under our sneakers was only a two-track road. The middle track was missing, the one with the marks of the hooves and the

splotches of dried, flaky manure. There had always been three tracks to choose from in choosing which track to walk in; now the choice was narrowed down to two. For a moment I missed terribly the middle alternative. But the way led past the tennis court, and something about the way it lay there in the sun reassured me; the tape had loosened along the backline, the alleys were green with plantains and other weeds, and the net (installed in June and removed in September) sagged in the dry noon, and the whole place steamed with midday heat and hunger and emptiness. There was a choice of pie for dessert, and one was blueberry and one was apple, and the waitresses were the same country girls, there having been no passage of time, only the illusion of it as in a dropped curtain—the waitresses were still fifteen; their hair had been washed, that was the only difference—they had been to the movies and seen the pretty girls with the clean hair.

Summertime, oh, summertime, pattern of life indelible with 8 fade-proof lake, the wood unshatterable, the pasture with the sweet-fern and the juniper forever and ever, summer without end; this was the background, and the life along the shore was the design, the cottages with their innocent and tranquil design, their tiny docks with the flagpole and the American flag floating against the white clouds in the blue sky, the little paths over the roots of the trees leading from camp to camp and the paths leading back to the out-houses and the can of lime for sprinkling, and at the souvenir counters at the store the miniature birch-bark canoes and the post-cards that showed things looking a little better than they looked. This was the American family at play, escaping the city heat, wondering whether the newcomers in the camp at the head of the cove were "common" or "nice," wondering whether it was true that the people who drove up for Sunday dinner at the farmhouse were turned away because there wasn't enough chicken.

It seemed to me, as I kept remembering all this, that those 9 times and those summers had been infinitely precious and worth saving. There had been jollity and peace and goodness. The arriving (at the beginning of August) had been so big a business in itself, at the railway station the farm wagon drawn up, the first smell of the pineladen air, the first glimpse of the smiling farmer, and the great importance of the trunks and your father's enormous authority in such matters, and the feel of the wagon under you for the long ten-mile haul, and at the top of the last long hill catching the first view of the lake after eleven months of not seeing this cherished body

of water. The shouts and cries of the other campers when they saw
you, and the trunks to be unpacked, to give up their rich burden.
(Arriving was less exciting nowadays, when you sneaked up in your
car and parked it under a tree near the camp and took out the bags
and in five minutes it was all over, no fuss, no loud wonderful fuss
about trunks.)

10   Peace and goodness and jollity. The only thing that was wrong
now, really, was the sound of the place, an unfamiliar nervous sound
of the outboard motors. This was the note that jarred, the one thing
that would sometimes break the illusion and set the years moving.
In those other summertimes all motors were inboard; and when
they were at a little distance, the noise they made was a sedative,
an ingredient of summer sleep. They were one-cylinder and two-
cylinder engines, and some were make-and-break and some were
jump-spark, but they all made a sleepy sound across the lake. The
one-lungers throbbed and fluttered, and the twin-cylinder ones
purred and purred, and that was a quiet sound, too. But now the
campers all had outboards. In the daytime, in the hot mornings,
these motors made a petulant, irritable sound; at night in the still
evening when the afterglow lit the water, they whined about one's
ears like mosquitoes. My boy loved our rented outboard, and his
great desire was to achieve single-handed mastery over it, and authority, and he soon learned the trick of choking it a little (but not
too much), and the adjustment of the needle valve. Watching him
I would remember the things you could do with the old one-cylinder
engine with the heavy flywheel, how you could have it eating out
of your hand if you got really close to it spiritually. Motorboats in
those days didn't have clutches, and you would make a landing by
shutting off the motor at the proper time and coasting in with a
dead rudder. But there was a way of reversing them, if you learned
the trick, by cutting the switch and putting it on again exactly on
the final dying revolution of the flywheel, so that it would kick back
against compression and begin reversing. Approaching a dock in a
strong following breeze, it was difficult to slow up sufficiently by
the ordinary coasting method, and if a boy felt he had complete
mastery over his motor, he was tempted to keep it running beyond
its time and then reverse it a few feet from the dock. It took a cool
nerve, because if you threw the switch a twentieth of a second too
soon you would catch the flywheel when it still had speed enough
to go up past center, and the boat would leap ahead, charging bull-
fashion at the dock.

We had a good week at the camp. The bass were biting well   11
and the sun shone endlessly, day after day. We would be tired at
night and lie down in the accumulated heat of the little bedrooms
after the long hot day and the breeze would stir almost imperceptibly
outside and the smell of the swamp drift in through the rusty screens.
Sleep would come easily and in the morning the red squirrel would
be on the roof, tapping out his gay routine. I kept remembering
everything, lying in bed in the mornings—the small steamboat that
had a long rounded stern like the lip of a Ubangi, and how quietly
she ran on the moonlight sails, when the older boys played their
mandolins and the girls sang and we ate doughnuts dipped in sugar,
and how sweet the music was on the water in the shining night,
and what it had felt like to think about girls then. After breakfast
we would go up to the store and the things were in the same place—
the minnows in a bottle, the plugs and spinners disarranged and
pawed over by the youngsters from the boy's camp, the Fig Newtons
and the Beeman's gum. Outside, the road was tarred and cars stood
in front of the store. Inside, all was just as it had always been, except
there was more Coca-Cola and not so much Moxie and root beer
and birch beer and sarsaparilla. We would walk out with the bottle
of pop apiece and sometimes the pop would backfire up our noses
and hurt. We explored the streams, quietly, where the turtles slid
off the sunny logs and dug their way into the soft bottom; and we
lay on the town wharf and fed worms to the tame bass. Everywhere
we went I had trouble making out which was I, the one walking at
my side, the one walking in my pants.

One afternoon while we were at that lake a thunderstorm came   12
up. It was like the revival of an old melodrama that I had seen long
ago with childish awe. The second-act climax of the drama of the
electrical disturbance over a lake in America had not changed in
any important respect. This was the big scene, still the big scene.
The whole thing was so familiar, the first feeling of oppression and
heat and a general air around camp of not wanting to go very far
away. In midafternoon (it was all the same) a curious darkening of
the sky, and a lull in everything that had made life tick; and then
the way the boats suddenly swung the other way at their moorings
with the coming of a breeze out of the new quarter, and the pre-
monitory rumble. Then the kettle drum, then the snare, then the
bass drum and cymbals, then crackling light against the dark, and
the gods grinning and licking their chops in the hills. Afterward the
calm, the rain steadily rustling in the calm lake, the return of light

and hope and spirits, and the campers running out in joy and relief to go swimming in the rain, their bright cries perpetuating the deathless joke about how they were getting simply drenched, and the children screaming with delight at the new sensation of bathing in the rain, and the joke about getting drenched linking the generations in a strong indestructible chain. And the comedian who waded in carrying an umbrella.

13   When the others went swimming my son said he was going in, too. He pulled his dripping trunks from the line where they had hung all through the shower and wrung them out. Languidly, and with no thought of going in, I watched him, his hard little body, skinny and bare, saw him wince slightly as he pulled up around his vitals the small, soggy, icy garment. As he buckled the swollen belt, suddenly my groin felt the chill of death.

Thinking Critically About This Reading

1. The author writes at length about the lake where he spent many vacations as a child. How important are childhood haunts in the recollection of your own early years?

2. The author vividly recalls that as a child he was struck by the serenity and beauty of the lake. What impact on a child's development are places of physical beauty likely to have? What is the likely effect on an adult whose childhood has been passed mainly among ugly surroundings?

3. Most people at one time or another look back nostalgically on their childhood. What explanation can you give for this seemingly universal longing?

4. Why do you think the author keeps insisting that nothing has changed, that everything is as it once was?

5. None of us can know exactly when we are going to die, although—like the author—we all get occasional glimpses of our mortality. Would it be better—through some inconceivable breakthrough in genetic engineering—if upon birth everyone could be assigned a distant death-date and made aware of it? Why? Why not?

Understanding the Writer's Process

1. The first paragraph specifically mentions the date when this essay was written and when the author first visited the lake as a child.

Why are these dates mentioned? What do their inclusion add to the overall impact and meaning of this essay?

2. In his very first recollection of the lake, the author mentions two memorable events: catching ringworm from kittens and seeing his father capsize a canoe. Why do you think he chooses to begin with these two rather trivial memories?

3. By what rhetorical mode, other than description, is this essay developed?

4. In paragraph 5, the author mentions the "dead helgramite" in the bottom of the fishing boat. What is "dead helgramite"? Why do you think the author chose to be so specific?

5. How does paragraph 8 differ in tone from the other paragraphs of this essay? What is the writer attempting to do in this paragraph?

Examining the Writer's Language

1. Define the meanings of the following words as used in the context of this essay: incessant (paragraph 1), primeval (3), transposition (4), tentatively (5), pensively (5), undulating (6), unsubstantial (6), petulant (10), perpetuating (12), languidly (13).

2. In paragraph 2, the writer uses the indefinite "you," a structure that style books usually scold against. Why does it seem to work well in this particular essay?

3. What does the author mean by "common" or "nice" (paragraph 8) when used to describe people? What are the equivalents of these words in today's usage?

4. In paragraph 4, the writer says: "It gave me a creepy sensation." What objection might a stickler for conventional English raise against this sentence? What justification could the author give for its wording?

5. Around what dominant sense-impression is the description in paragraph 10 built?

Suggestions for Writing

1. Write an essay describing the scene of the most memorable vacation you took as a child.

2. Write an essay describing White's writing style and speculating about why he was so beloved as a writer. Use this essay as a model of White's style and make specific references to that style.

STORM AT SEA

H. M. Tomlinson

Henry Major Tomlinson (1873–1958), English novelist and travelogue writer, successively worked as a dock worker, journalist, and war correspondent before becoming literary editor of the magazines Nation *and, later,* Athenaeum. *Among his best-known works are* Galleons Reach *(1927, novel);* All Our Yesterdays *(1930, semifictional account of World War I); and* The Sea and the Jungle *(1912, travelogue), from which this description was taken.*

Preparing to Read This Selection Critically

Since this excerpt is taken from a longer source, it might seem to begin or to end somewhat abruptly. But the core technique it practices—the use of a dominant impression and subsequent reinforcing details in its descriptive passages—is exercised with consummate skill. Notice particularly the unwavering focus on the subject being described, a storm at sea, and the accumulation of vivid details that underscore the dominant impression.

1   The sun died at birth. The wind we had lost we found again as a gale from the south-east. The waters quickly increased again, and by noon the saloon was light and giddy with the racing of the propeller. I moved about like an infant learning to walk. We were 201 miles from the Mumbles, course S.W.½W.; it was cold, and I was still looking for the pleasures of travel. The Doctor came to introduce himself, like a good man, and tried me with such things as fevers, Shaw, Brazilian entomology, the evolution of sex, the medical profession under socialism, the sea and the poets. But my

thoughts were in retreat, with the black dog in full cry. It was too cold and damp to talk even of sex. When my oil lamp began to throw its rays of brown smell, the Doctor, tired of the effort to exalt the sour dough which was my mind, left me. It was night. O, the sea and the poets!

2 By next morning the gale, now from the southwest, like the seas, was constantly reinforced with squalls of hurricane violence. The Chief put a man at the throttle. In the early afternoon the waves had assumed serious proportions. They soared by us in broad sombre ranges, with hissing white ridges, an inhospitable and subduing sight. They were a quite different tribe of waves from the volatile and malicious natives of the Bristol Channel. Those channel waves had no serried ranks in the attack; they were but a horde of undisciplined savages, appearing to assault without design or plan, but getting at us as they could, depending on their numbers. The waves in the channel were smaller folk, but more athletic, and very noisy; they appeared to detach themselves from the sea, and to leap at us, shouting.

3 These western ocean waves had a different character. They were the sea. We did not have a multitude of waves in sight, but the sea floor itself might have been undulating. The ocean was profoundly convulsed. Our outlook was confined to a few heights and hollows, and the moving heights were swift, but unhurried and stately. Your alarm, as you saw a greater hill appear ahead, tower, and bear down, had no time to get more than just out of the stage of surprise and wonder when the "Capella's" bows were pointing skyward on a long up-slope of water, the broken summit of which was too quick for the "Capella"—the bows disappeared in a white explosion, a volley of spray, as hard as shot, raked the bridge, the foredeck filled with raging water, and the wave swept along our run, dark, severe, and immense; with so little noise too; with but a faint hissing of foam, as in a deliberate silence. The "Capella" then began to run down a valley.

4 The engines were reduced to half speed; it would have been dangerous to drive her at such seas. Our wet and slippery decks were bleak, wind-swept, and deserted. The mirror of water on the iron surfaces, constantly renewed, reflected and flashed the wild lights in the sky as she rolled and pitched, and somehow those reflections from her polish made the steamer seem more desolate and forlorn. Not a man showed anywhere on the vessel's length, except merely to hurry from one vantage to another—darting out of

[handwritten margin notes:] action and music aroused by the storm' / abstract comparison / Paragraph 2. 3 uses / Doctor. / Act as is narrator.

the ship's interior, and scurrying to another hole and vanishing abruptly, like a rabbit.

5   The gale was dumb till it met and was torn in our harsh opposition, shouting and moaning then in anger and torment as we steadily pressed our iron into its ponderable body. You could imagine the flawless flood of air pouring silently express till it met our pillars and pinnacles, and then flying past rift, the thousand punctures instantly spreading into long shrieking lacerations. The wounds and mouths were so many, loud, and poignant, that you wondered you could not see them. Our structure was full of voices, but the weighty body which drove against our shrouds and funnel guys, and kept them strongly vibrating, was curiously invisible. The hard jets of air spurted hissing through the winches. The sound in the shrouds and stays began like that of something tearing, and rose to a high keening. The deeper notes were amidships, in the alleyways and round the engine-room casing; but there the ship itself contributed a note, a metallic murmur so profound that it was felt as a tremor rather than heard. It was almost below human hearing. It was the hollow ship resonant, the steel walls, decks, and bulkheads quivering under the drumming of the seas, and the regular throws of the crank-shaft far below.

6   It was on this day the "Capella" ceased to be a marine engine to me. She was not the "Capella" of the Swansea docks, the sea waggon squatting low in the water, with bows like a box, and a width of beam which made her seem a wharf fixture. To-day in the Atlantic her bluff bows rose to meet the approaching bulk of each wave with such steady honesty, getting up heavily to meet its quick wiles, it is true, but often with such success that we found ourselves perched at a height above the gloom of the hollow seas, getting more light and seeing more world; though sometimes the hill-top was missed; she was not quick enough, and broke the inflowing ridge with her face. She behaved so like a brave patient thing that now her portrait, which I treasure, is to me that of one who has befriended me, a staunch and homely body who never tired in faithful well-doing. She became our little sanctuary, especially near dayfall, with those sombre mounts close round us bringing twilight before its time.

7   Your glance caught a wave passing amidships as a heaped mass of polished obsidian, having minor hollows and ridges on its slopes, conchoidal fractures in its glass. It rose directly and acutely from your feet to a summit that was awesome because the eye travelled

to it over a long and broken up-slope; this hill had intervened suddenly to obscure thirty degrees of light; and the imagination shrank from contemplating water which overshadowed your foothold with such high dark bulk toppling in collapse. The steamer leaning that side, your face was quite close to the beginning of the bare mobile down, where it swirled past in a vitreous flux, tortured lines of green foam buried far but plain in its translucent deeps. It passed; and the light released from the sky streamed over the "Capella" again as your side of her lifted in the roll, the sea falling down her iron wall as far as the bilge. The steamer spouted violently from her choked valve, as it cleared the sea, like a swimmer who battles, and then gets his mouth free from a smother.

Her task against those head seas and the squalls was so hard and continuous that the murmur of her heart, which I fancied grew louder almost to a moaning when her body sank to the rails, the panic of her cries when the screw raced, when she lost her hold, her noble and rhythmic labourings, the sense of her concentrated and unremitting power given by the smoke driving in violence from her swaying funnel, the cordage quivering in tense curves, the seas that burst in her face as clouds, falling roaring inboard then to founder half her length, she presently to raise her heavy body slowly out of an acre of foam, the cascades streaming from her in veils,— all this was like great music. I learned why a ship has a name. It is for the same reason that you and I have names. She has happenings according to her own weird. She shows perversities and virtues her parents never dreamed into the plans they laid for her. Her heredity cannot be explained by the general chemics of iron and steel and the principles of the steam engine; but something counts in her of the moods of her creators, both of the happy men and the sullen men whose bright or dark energies poured into her rivets and plates as they hammered, and now suffuse her body. Something of the "Capella" was revealed to me, "our" ship. She was one for pride and trust. She was slow, but that slowness was of her dignity and size; she had valour in her. She was not a light yacht. She was strong and hard, taking heavy punishment, and then lifting her broad face over the seas to look for the next enemy. But was she slow? She seemed but slow. The eye judged by those assailing hills, so vast and whelmingly quick. The hills were so dark, swift, and great, moving barely inferior to the clouds which travelled with them, the collapsing roof which fell over the seas, flying with the same impulse as the waters. There was the uplifted ocean, and pressing down to

it, sundered from it only by the gale—the gale forced them apart—
the foundered heavens, a low ceiling which would have been night
itself but that it was thinned in patches by some solvent day. And
our "Capella," heavy as was her body, and great and swift as were
the hills, never failed to carry us up the long slopes, and over the
white summits which moved down on us like the marked approach
of catastrophe. If one of the greater hills but hit us, I thought——

9   One did. Late that afternoon the second mate, who was on
watch, saw such a wave bearing down on us. It was so dominantly
above us that instinctively he put his hand in his pocket for his
whistle. It was his first voyage in an ocean steamer; he was not long
out of his apprenticeship in "sails," and so he did not telegraph to
stop the engines. The Skipper looked up through the chartroom window, saw the high gloom of this wave over us, and jumped out for
the bridge ladder to get at the telegraph himself. He was too late.

10   We went under. The wave stopped us with the shock of a
grounding, came solid over our fore-length, and broke on our structure amidships. The concussion itself scattered things about my
cabin. When the "Capella" showed herself again the ventilators had
gone, the windlass was damaged, and the iron ends of the drum on
the forecastle head, on which a steel hawser was wound, had been
doubled on themselves, like tinfoil.

11   By day these movements of water on a grand scale, the harsh
and deep noises of gale and breaking seas, and the labouring of the
steamer, no more than awed me. At least, my sight could escape.
But courage went with the light. At dusk, the eye, which had the
liberty during the hours of light to range up the inclines of the sea
to distant summits, and note that these dangers always passed, was
imprisoned by a dreadful apparition. When there was more night
than day in the dusk you saw no waves. You saw, and close at hand,
only vertical shadows, and they swayed noiselessly without pro-
gressing on the fading sky high over you. I could but think the ocean
level had risen greatly, and was see-sawing much superior to us all
round. The "Capella" remained then in a precarious nadir of the
waters. Looking aft from the Chief's cabin I could see of our ship
only the top of our mainmast, because that projected out of the
shadow of the hollow into the last of the day overhead; and often
the sheer apparitions oscillating around us swung above the truck
of it, and the whole length vanished. The sense of onward movement
ceased because nothing could be seen passing us. At dusk the
steamer appeared to be rocking helplessly in a narrow sunken place

which never had an outlet for us; the shadows of the seas erect over us did not move away, but their ridges pitched at changing angles. You know the Sussex chalk hills at evening, just at that time 12 when, from the foot of them, they lose all detail but what is on the skyline, become an abrupt plane before you of unequal height. That was the view from the "Capella," except that the skyline moved. And when we passed a barque that evening it looked as looks a solitary bush far on the summit of the downs. The barque did not pass us; we saw it fade, and the height it surmounted fade, as shadows do when all light has gone. But where we saw it last a green star was adrift and was ranging up and down in the night.

Thinking Critically About This Reading

1. In his description, the narrator tells us little about his personal feelings but focuses, instead, almost entirely on the storm. What can you infer about his feelings during the storm? Why do you think he chose not to describe how he felt?

2. What can you infer about the doctor from his brief appearance in the description?

3. How did the storm affect the narrator's attitude toward the Capella?

4. What inferences about the ship's command can you draw from the narrator's description of the way the ship was handled during the storm?

5. How would you characterize the audience for whom this was written? How can you tell?

Understanding the Writer's Process

1. Aside from the focus of the writing on the storm, what other device does the author use to structure and hold together his unfolding description?

2. What rhetorical device does the author use in paragraphs 2 and 3 to flesh out his description of the waves?

3. How would you express the dominant impression that implicitly underlies the author's description of the storm?

4. What literary device does the author employ in paragraphs 6 and 8 to describe the Capella?

5. Although the author plainly uses "I" throughout the description, in paragraph 7 he reverts to the use of "your." What is the rhetorical logic behind this switch?

Examining the Writer's Language

1. Define the meanings of the following words used in this essay: keening (paragraph 5), obsidian (7), conchoidal fractures (7), vitreous (7), nadir (11), oscillating (11).
2. What does the author mean by "the black dog in full cry" in paragraph 1?
3. To appeal to what principal sense does the author structure his description in paragraph 5?
4. What is the meaning of Capella, the name of the ship on which the author voyaged?
5. What figure of speech does the author use in paragraph 12 of this description?

Suggestions for Writing

1. Write a description of any destructive force in nature that you have personally witnessed or experienced.
2. Write an essay describing any experience or event in which you felt your life endangered.

A SLAVEHOLDER'S JOURNAL

Thomas B. Chaplin

Thomas B. Chaplin (1822–1890), hereditary owner of Tombee Plantation on St. Helena Island, South Carolina, left behind the only known diary of a slaveholder and plantation owner. After the Civil War, in which he fought on the side of the Confederates, Chaplin succeeded in winning the right to reclaim his plantation which he had been forced to flee in 1861. Penniless and exhausted, he died before he could return to Tombee.

Preparing to Read This Selection Critically

In 1849, Chaplin served on a makeshift jury of inquest to inquire into the death of a slave owned by James Sandiford, a neighboring plantation owner. The excerpt from his journal describes what he saw and reveals a struggle between his conscience and his sense of obligation to a fellow slaveholder. As Chaplin's biographer writes, "Troublesome thoughts, such as the idea that Negroes are people, kept threatening to break into his [Chaplin's] consciousness, but he kept disavowing them, from pride, lethargy, and the need to keep his world view intact." As you read, pay attention to this expression of internal conflict.

Feb. 17th. Saturday. Clear and cold. Run out, staked & burnt   1
off the root patch, 4 acres. Isaac & Anthony with me. Put Sancho
with Summer carting. 4 hands getting poles for the fence. Women
cleaning cotton ginned yesterday.

Hear that Edw. Chaplin intends to sell all of his Negroes and   2
go regularly into merchandising. One of his fellows came here today
to ask me to buy him, fellow Cuff. That was out of the question for
me to do, to sell one year & buy the next would be *fine* speculation
on my part.

Feb. 19th. Monday. I received a summons while at breakfast,   3
to go over to J. H. Sandiford's[1] at 10 o'clock a.m. this day and sit
on a jury of inquest on the body of Roger, a Negro man belonging
to Sandiford. Accordingly I went. About 12 m. there were 12 of us
together (the number required to form a jury), viz.—Dr. Scott, foreman, J. J. Pope, J.E.L. Fripp, W.O.P. Fripp, Dr. M. M. Sams, Henry
Fripp, Dr. Jenkins, Jn. McTureous, Henry McTureous, P. W. Perry,
W. Perry & myself. We were sworn by J. D. Pope, magistrate, and
proceeded to examine the body. We found it in an outhouse used
as a corn house, and meat house (for there were both in the house).
Such a shocking sight never before met my eyes. There was the
poor Negro, who all his life had been a complete cripple, being
hardly able to walk & used his knees more than his feet, in the most

---

[1] James H. Sandiford (1795–1868), planter. His first and second wives were Perrys, and he was related through marriage to the McTureouses. Sandiford eventually moved to St. Mary's, Georgia.

shocking situation, but *stiff dead*. He was placed in this situation by his *master*, to punish him, as he says, *for impertinence*. And what [was] this punishment—this *poor cripple* was sent by his master (as Sandiford's evidence goes) on Saturday the 17th inst., before daylight (cold & bitter weather, as everyone knows, though Sandiford says, "It was *not very* cold"), in a paddling boat down the river to get oysters, and ordering him to return before high water, & cut a bundle of marsh. The poor fellow did not return before ebb tide, but he brought 7 baskets of oysters & a small bundle of marsh (more than the primest of my fellows would have done. Anthony[2] never brought me more than 3 baskets of oysters & took the whole day). His master asked him why he did not return sooner & cut more marsh. He said that the wind was too high. His master said he would whip him for it, & set to work with a cowhide to do the same. The fellow hollered & when told to stop, said he would not, as long as he was being whipped, for which impertinence he received 30 cuts. He went to the kitchen and was talking to another Negro when Sandiford slipped up & overheard this confab, heard Roger, as he says, say, that if he had sound limbs, he would not take a flogging from any white man, but would shoot them down, and turn his back on them (another witness, the Negro that Roger was talking to, says that Roger did not say this, but "that he would turn his back on them if they shot him down," which I think is much the most probable of the two speeches). Sandiford then had him confined, or I should say, murdered, in the manner I will describe. Even if the fellow had made the speech that Sandiford said he did, and even worse, it by no means warranted the punishment he received. The fellow was a cripple, & could not escape from a slight confinement, besides, I don't think he was ever known to use a gun, or even know how to use one, so there was little apprehension of his putting his threat (if it can be called one) into execution. For these *crimes*, this man, this demon in human shape, this pretended Christian, member of the Baptist Church, had this poor cripple Negro placed in an open outhouse, the wind blowing through a hundred cracks, his clothes wet to the waist, without a single blanket & in freezing weather, with his back against a partition, shackles on his wrists, & chained to a bolt in the floor and a chain around *his neck*, the chain passing through the partition behind him, & fastened on the other side—in this position the poor wretch was left for the night,

[2] One of Chaplin's slaves.

a position that none but the "most *bloodthirsty* tyrant" could have placed a human being. My heart chills at the idea, and my blood boils at the base tyranny—The wretch returned to his victim about daylight the next morning & found him, as anyone might expect, dead, *choked, strangled,* frozen to death, *murdered.* The verdict of the jury was, that Roger came to his death by choking by a chain put around his neck by his master—*having slipped from the position in which he was placed.* The verdict should have been that Roger came to his death by inhumane treatment to him by his master—by placing him, in very cold weather, in a cold house, with a chain about his neck & fastened to the wall, & otherways chained so that he could in no way assist himself should he slip from the position in which he was placed & must consequently choke to death without immediate assistance. Even should he escape being frozen to death, which we believe would have been the case from the fact of his clothes being wet & the severity of the weather, my *individual* verdict would be *deliberately* but *upremeditatedly murdered* by his master James H. Sandiford.

Thinking Critically About This Reading

1. Although Chaplin does not say, how do you suppose he voted in this inquest? Defend your answer.

2. Chaplin tells us the specific finding of the jury. What is the gist of that verdict in equivalent modern terms?

3. What consequences from this verdict do you think befell the murderer?

4. Aside from reacting to an obvious injustice, what else do you think might have made Chaplin so angry and bitter in his denunciation of Sandiford?

5. What can you infer about Sandiford from Chaplin's journalizing about him?

Understanding the Writer's Process

1. What elements identify this excerpt as being from a private journal not intended for publication?

2. On what dominant impression is the description of the body primarily based?

3. How does Chaplin periodically emphasize his sense of outrage throughout the excerpt?

4. In this entry, how does Chaplin use bracketed text?

Examining the Writer's Language

1. This excerpt was written more than a hundred years ago. What characteristics of language, if any, identify its age?

2. Chaplin writes, ". . . another witness, the Negro that Roger was talking to, says that Roger did not say this, but 'that he would turn his back on them if they shot him down,' which I think is much the most probable of the two speeches." What might a grammarian object to in this sentence?

3. In the sentence that begins, "The wretch returned to his victim . . .," describing the condition in which Sandiford found Roger the next morning, what rhetorical technique does Chaplin use for emphasis?

4. Why do you think Chaplin was so exact in his description of the way Sandiford had shackled Roger to the walls of the outhouse?

Suggestions for Writing

1. Write an essay in which you infer and describe Chaplin's emotions and feelings at the time he wrote this entry.

2. Describe any experience in which you have gone along with the opinion of the majority even though you felt it was wrong.

FLYING OVER AFRICA

Isak Dinesen

Isak Dinesen is a pseudonym for the aristocratic Danish writer, Baroness Karen Blixen (1885–1962). In 1914 she married her cousin, the Baron Bron Blixen, and settled with him on a coffee plantation in British East Africa where she lived the experiences memorialized in her best-known book, Out of Africa *(1937).*

*In literary circles, Dinesen is known mainly as a writer
of supernatural fables and tales of the grotesque, including such titles as* Seven Gothic Tales *(1934),* Winter's Tales *(1943), and* Last Tales *(1957).*

Preparing to Read This Selection Critically

What makes this description of aerial views of Africa
even more remarkable than the vivid writing is that it
was penned at a time when flying was still a novelty,
and describing the earth as seen from the heavens still
an unknown art. Dinesen was friendly with Denys Finch–
Hatton, an English big–game hunter and adventurer and,
as she tells us in this excerpt, often went flying with him
over the Kenyan highlands. Notice that in her metaphors
and descriptions Dinesen reaches for religious imagery
to express the startling view of the world the new technology of the airplane suddenly had opened to her. Pay
attention to the mythological and religious allusions she
uses to describe the experience. Finch–Hatton was killed
in a solo flight aboard the same Moth airplane Dinesen
flew in, and was buried in the Ngong hills of Kenya.

To Denys Finch-Hatton I owe what was, I think, the greatest, 1
the most transporting pleasure of my life on the farm: I flew with
him over Africa. There, where there are few or no roads and where
you can land on the plains, flying becomes a thing of real and vital
importance in your life; it opens up a world. Denys had brought
out his Moth machine; it could land on my plain on the farm only
a few minutes from the house, and we were up nearly every day.

You have tremendous views as you get up above the African 2
highlands, surprising combinations and changes of light and col-
ouring, the rainbow on the green sunlit land, the gigantic upright
clouds and big wild black storms, all swing round you in a race and
a dance. The lashing hard showers of rain whiten the air askance.
The language is short of words for the experiences of flying, and
will have to invent new words with time. When you have flown
over the Rift Valley and the volcanoes of Suswa and Longonot, you
have travelled far and have been to the lands on the other side of
the moon. You may at other times fly low enough to see the animals
on the plains and to feel towards them as God did when he had

just created them, and before he commissioned Adam to give them
names.

3   But it is not the visions but the activity which makes you happy,
and the joy and glory of the flyer is the flight itself. It is a sad
hardship and slavery to people who live in towns, that in all their
movements they know of one dimension only; they walk along the
line as if they were led on a string. The transition from the line to
the plane into the two dimensions, when you wander across a field
or through a wood, is a splendid liberation to the slaves, like the
French Revolution. But in the air you are taken into the full freedom
of the three dimensions; after long ages of exile and dreams the
homesick heart throws itself into the arms of space. The laws of
gravitation and time,

>   ". . . in life's green grove, Sport like tame beasts, none
> knew how gentle they could be!"

4   Every time that I have gone up in an aeroplane and looking
down have realised that I was free of the ground, I have had the
consciousness of a great new discovery. "I see:" I have thought,
"This was the idea. And now I understand everything."

5   One day Denys and I flew to Lake Natron, ninety miles South-
East of the farm, and more than four thousand feet lower, two thousand feet above Sea level. Lake Natron is the place from where they
take soda. The bottom of the lake and the shores are like some sort
of whitish concrete, with a strong, sour and salt smell.

6   The sky was blue, but as we flew from the plains in over the
stony and bare lower country, all colour seemed to be scorched out
of it. The whole landscape below us looked like delicately marked
tortoise-shell. Suddenly, in the midst of it was the lake. The white
bottom, shining through the water, gives it, when seen from the air,
a striking, an unbelievable azure-colour, so clear that for a moment
you shut your eyes at it; the expanse of water lies in the bleak tawny
land like a big bright aquamarine. We had been flying high, now
we went down, and as we sank our own shade, dark-blue, floated
under us upon the light-blue lake. Here live thousands of Flamin-
goes, although I do not know how they exist in the brackish water,—
surely there are no fish here. At our approach they spread out in
large circles and fans, like the rays of a setting sun, like an artful
Chinese pattern of silk or porcelain, forming itself and changing, as
we looked at it.

We landed on the white shore, that was white-hot as an oven, 7
and lunched there, taking shelter against the sun under the wing of
the aeroplane. If you stretched out your hand from the shade, the
sun was so hot that it hurt you. Our bottles of beer when they first
arrived with us, straight out of the ether, were pleasantly cold, but
before we had finished them, in a quarter of an hour, they became
as hot as a cup of tea.

While we were lunching, a party of Masai warriors appeared 8
on the horizon, and approached quickly. They must have spied the
aeroplane landing from a distance, and resolved to have a close look
at it, and a walk of any length, even in a country like this, means
nothing to a Masai. They came along, the one in front of the other,
naked, tall and narrow, their weapons glinting; dark like peat on the
yellow grey sand. At the feet of each of them lay and marched a
small pool of shadow, these were, besides our own, the only shadows
in the country as far as the eye reached. When they came up to us
they fell in line, there were five of them. They stuck their heads
together and began to talk to one another about the aeroplane and
us. A generation ago they would have been fatal to us to meet. After
a time one of them advanced and spoke to us. As they could only
speak Masai and we understood but little of the language, the conversation soon slackened, he stepped back to his fellows and a few
minutes later they all turned their back upon us, and walked away,
in single file, with the wide white burning salt-plain before them.

"Would you care," said Denys, "to fly to Naivasha? But the 9
country lying between is very rough, we could not possibly land
anywhere on the way. So we shall have to go up high and keep up
at twelve thousand feet."

The flight from Lake Natron to Naivasha was *Das ding an sich.*[1] 10
We took a bee-line, and kept at twelve thousand feet all the way,
which is so high that there is nothing to look down for. At Lake
Natron I had taken off my lambskin-lined cap, now up here the air
squeezed my forehead, as cold as iced water; all my hair flew backwards as if my head was being pulled off. This path, in fact, was
the same as was, in the opposite direction, every evening taken by
the Roc, when, with an Elephant for her young in each talon, she
swished from Uganda home to Arabia. Where you are sitting in
front of your pilot, with nothing but space before you, you feel that
he is carrying you upon the outstretched palms of his hands, as the

[1] "The thing in itself."

Djinn carried Prince Ali through the air, and that the wings that bear you onward are his. We landed at the farm of our friends at Naivasha; the mad diminutive houses, and the very small trees surrounding them, all threw themselves flat upon their backs as they saw us descending.

11   When Denys and I had not time for long journeys we went out for a short flight over the Ngong Hills, generally about sunset. These hills, which are amongst the most beautiful in the world, are perhaps at their loveliest seen from the air, when the ridges, bare towards the four peaks mount, and run side by side with the aeroplane, or suddenly sink down and flatten out into a small lawn.

12   Here in the hills there were Buffaloes. I had even, in my very young days,—when I could not live till I had killed a specimen of each kind of African game,—shot a bull out here. Later on, when I was not so keen to shoot as to watch the wild animals, I had been out to see them again. I had camped in the hills by a spring half way to the top, bringing my servants, tents, and provisions with me, and Farah[2] and I had been up in the dark, ice cold mornings to creep and crawl through bush and long grass, in the hope of catching a glimpse of the herd; but twice I had had to go back without success. That the herd lived there, neighbours of mine to the West, was still a value in the life on the farm, but they were serious-minded, self-sufficient neighbours, the old nobility of the hills, now somehow reduced; they did not receive much.

13   But one afternoon as I was having tea with some friends of mine from up-country, outside the house, Denys came flying from Nairobi and went over our heads out Westwards; a little while after he turned and came back and landed on the farm. Lady Delamere and I drove down to the plain to fetch him up, but he would not get out of his aeroplane.

14   "The Buffalo are out feeding in the hills," he said, "come out and have a look at them."

"I cannot come," I said, "I have got a tea-party up at the house."

"But we will go and see them and be back in a quarter of an hour," said he.

15   This sounded to me like the propositions which people make to you in a dream. Lady Delamere would not fly, so I went up with him. We flew in the sun, but the hillside lay in a transparent brown

[2] Dinesen's Somali servant, Farah Aden.

shade, which soon we got into. It did not take us long to spy the Buffalo from the air. Upon one of the long rounded green ridges which run, like folds of a cloth gathered together at each peak, down the side of the Ngong mountain, a herd of twenty-seven Buffalo were grazing. First we saw them a long way below us, like mice moving gently on a floor, but we dived down, circling over and along their ridge, a hundred and fifty feet above them and well within shooting distance; we counted them as they peacefully blended and separated. There was one very old big black bull in the herd, one or two younger bulls, and a number of calves. The open stretch of sward upon which they walked was closed in by bush; had a stranger approached on the ground they would have heard or scented him at once, but they were not prepared for advance from the air. We had to keep moving above them all the time. They heard the noise of our machine and stopped grazing, but they did not seem to have it in them to look up. In the end they realised that something very strange was about; the old bull first walked out in front of the herd, raising his hundredweight horns, braving the un-seen enemy, his four feet planted on the ground,—suddenly he be-gan to trot down the ridge and after a moment he broke into a canter. The whole clan now followed him, stampeding headlong down, and as they switched and plunged into the bush, dust and loose stones rose in their wake. In the thicket they stopped and kept close together, it looked as if a small glade in the hill had been paved with dark grey stones. Here they believed themselves to be covered to the view, and so they were to anything moving along the ground, but they could not hide themselves from the eyes of the bird of the air. We flew up and away. It was like having been taken into the heart of the Ngong Hills by a secret unknown road.

When I came back to my tea party, the teapot on the stone table was still so hot that I burned my fingers on it. The Prophet had the same experience when he upset a jug of water, and the Archangel Gabriel took him, and flew with him through the seven heavens, and when he returned, the water had not yet run out of the jug.

In the Ngong Hills there also lived a pair of eagles. Denys in the afternoons used to say: "Let us go and visit the eagles." I have once seen one of them sitting on a stone near the top of the moun-tain, and getting up from it, but otherwise they spent their life up in the air. Many times we have chased one of these eagles, careening and throwing ourselves on to one wing and then to the other, and

I believe that the sharp-sighted bird played with us. Once, when we were running side by side, Denys stopped his engine in mid air, and as he did so I heard the eagle screech.

18   The Natives liked the aeroplane, and for a time it was the fashion on the farm to portray her, so that I would find sheets of paper in the kitchen, or the kitchen wall itself, covered with drawings of her, with the letters ABAK carefully copied out. But they did not really take any interest in her or in our flying.

19   Natives dislike speed, as we dislike noise, it is to them, at the best, hard to bear. They are also on friendly terms with time, and the plan of beguiling or killing it does not come into their heads. In fact the more time you can give them, the happier they are, and if you commission a Kikuyu to hold your horse while you make a visit, you can see by his face that he hopes you will be a long, long time about it. He does not try to pass the time then, but sits down and lives.

20   Neither do the Natives have much sympathy with any kind of machinery or mechanics. A group of the young generation have been carried away by the enthusiasm of the European for the motor-car, but an old Kikuyu said to me of them that they would die young, and it is likely that he was right, for renegades come of a weak line of the nation. Amongst the inventions of civilisation which the Natives admire and appreciate are matches, a bicycle and a rifle, still they will drop these the moment there is any talk of a cow.

21   Frank Greswolde-Williams, of the Kedong Valley, took a Masai with him to England as a Sice, and told me that a week after his arrival he rode his horses in Hyde Park as if he had been born in London. I asked this man when he came back to Africa what he found very good in England. He thought my question over with a grave face and after a long time courteously said that the white men had got very fine bridges.

22   I have never seen an old Native who, for things which moved by themselves without apparent interference by man or by the forces of Nature, expressed anything but distrust and a certain feeling of shame. The human mind turns away its eye from witchcraft as from something unseemly. It may be forced to take an interest in the effects of it, but it will have nothing to do with the inside working, and no one has ever tried to squeeze out of a witch the exact recipe for her brew.

23   Once, when Denys and I had been up, and were landing on the plain of the farm, a very old Kikuyu came up and talked to us:

"You were up very high to-day," he said, "we could not see   24
you, only hear the aeroplane sing like a bee."

I agreed that we had been up high.

"Did you see God?" he asked.

"No, Ndwetti," I said, "we did not see God."

"Aha, then you were not up high enough," he said, "but now   25
tell me: do you think that you will be able to get up high enough
to see him?"

"I do not know, Ndwetti," I said.

"And you, Bedâr," he said, turning to Denys, "what do you   26
think? Will you get up high enough in your aeroplane to see God?"

"Really I do not know," said Denys.

"Then," said Ndwetti, "I do not know at all why you two go   27
on flying."

Thinking Critically About This Reading

1. For ten years the author lived among the Kikuyu of Kenya, who
   were later to wage the bloody guerrilla Mau-Mau war against
   the white settlers. What is her attitude toward the natives? Do
   you perceive in this excerpt any inkling of conflict between the
   natives and expatriate whites that might have foreshadowed the
   coming war?

2. What was the natives' attitude toward time? In what way is this
   attitude better or worse than our own?

3. The author writes about flying in a rapturous, almost religious
   tone. What feelings does flying arouse in you?

4. The author admits that when young she had the ambition to kill
   a specimen of each kind of African game. What impression on
   you did this revelation make?

5. How would you explain the attitude of the old Kikuyu man
   toward Dinesen and Finch-Hatton's constant flying excursions
   (see paragraphs 22–27)?

Understanding the Writer's Process

1. Dinesen was primarily a fabulist, a writer of tales. What is the
   difference between a fable and a novel? Can you discern in this
   excerpt any hint that the writer's special gift was telling tales?

2. Even though she wrote this many years later, in the first three paragraphs the author uses the present tense to describe the transports of flying. What justification can she have for this use? What effect does the use of this tense have on the description?

3. What dominant sense-impression is used in paragraph 6 to describe Lake Natron as it appeared to the flyers?

4. In paragraph 10, the author refers to the flight path of the mythical Roc and to a Djinn who carried Prince Ali in his outstretched palms. What is this figure called and what does its use add to a description?

5. How would you characterize the overall dominant impression on which the writer's description of flying over Africa is based?

Examining the Writer's Language

1. Explain the meanings of the following words as used in the context of this excerpt: askance (paragraph 2), diminutive (10), careening (17).

2. The author says that the language is short of words that express the experiences of flying. She wrote this opinion in the 1930s. Has the language become more capable of expressing the ecstasy of flight, or are we still searching for words?

3. The author's dialogue, what little there is of it, uses none of the contractions commonly found in colloquial speech, but is strictly formal and correct. Why do you think she wrote such formal dialogue?

4. "The mad diminutive houses, and the very small trees surrounding them, all threw themselves flat upon their backs as they saw us descending." What does this mean? What figure of speech is the author using here?

5. Comment on the vocabulary used by the author in the description in paragraph 4. How would you characterize her diction?

Suggestions for Writing

1. Write an essay describing your hometown.

2. Describe any unforgettable place you have ever visited.

THE FAT GIRL

Andre Dubus

Andre Dubus (b. 1936), American writer, has taught at Bradford College, Bradford, Massachusetts, and is frequently a visiting professor of writing at other colleges and universities. His stories have been published in various literary magazines such as Sewanee Review, Carlton Miscellany, *and* North American Review. *His first novel,* The Lieutenant, *was greeted with rave reviews. Among his other work are the short–story collections* Separate Flights *(1975),* Finding a Girl in America *(1980),* We Don't Live Here Anymore *(1984), and* Land Where My Fathers Died *(limited edition, 1984).*

Preparing to Read This Selection Critically

"The Fat Girl" explores the social consequences of obesity in a society that worships thinness. Louise, we are told, began secretly to engorge herself at age nine and became fat. From this beginning we are treated in painful detail to the social consequences and shunning that inevitably follow. Ask yourself, as you read, why Louise became fat, whether her obesity was caused by a faulty metabolism or by overindulging parents. Also ask yourself whether Louise is depicted as a sharply drawn character or serves as a stick figure used to make a point about obesity in American society. Pay particular attention to the meaning that food seems to acquire for Louise as she develops and grows. Is this portrait of a fat person representative of the way the obese among us are treated or do you think it exaggerated?

Her name was Louise. Once when she was sixteen a boy kissed   1
her at a barbecue; he was drunk and he jammed his tongue into her mouth and ran his hands up and down her hips. Her father kissed her often. He was thin and kind and she could see in his eyes when he looked at her the lights of love and pity.

It started when Louise was nine. You must start watching what   2
you eat, her mother would say. I can see you have my metabolism.

Louise also had her mother's pale blonde hair. Her mother was slim
and pretty, carried herself erectly, and ate very little. The two of
them would eat bare lunches, while her older brother ate sandwiches
and potato chips, and then her mother would sit smoking while
Louise eyed the bread box, the pantry, the refrigerator. Wasn't that
good, her mother would say. In five years you'll be in high school
and if you're fat the boys won't like you; they won't ask you out.
Boys were as far away as five years, and she would go to her room
and wait for nearly an hour until she knew her mother was no longer
thinking of her, then she would creep into the kitchen and, listening
to her mother talking on the phone, or her footsteps upstairs, she
would open the bread box, the pantry, the jar of peanut butter. She
would put the sandwich under her shirt and go outside or to the
bathroom to eat it.

3   Her father was a lawyer and made a lot of money and came
home looking pale and happy. Martinis put color back in his face,
and at dinner he talked to his wife and two children. Oh give her
a potato, he would say to Louise's mother. She's a growing girl. Her
mother's voice then became tense: If she has a potato she shouldn't
have dessert. She should have both, her father would say, and he
would reach over and touch Louise's cheek or hand or arm.

4   In high school she had two girl friends and at night and on
week-ends they rode in a car or went to movies. In movies she was
fascinated by fat actresses. She wondered why they were fat. She
knew why she was fat: she was fat because she was Louise. Because
God had made her that way. Because she wasn't like her friends
Joan and Marjorie, who drank milk shakes after school and were
all bones and tight skin. But what about those actresses, with their
talents, with their broad and profound faces? Did they eat as heed-
lessly as Bishop Humphries and his wife who sometimes came to
dinner and, as Louise's mother said, gorged between amenities? Or
did they try to lose weight, did they go about hungry and angry
and thinking of food? She thought of them eating lean meats and
salads with friends, and then going home and building strange large
sandwiches with French bread. But mostly she believed they did
not go through these failures; they were fat because they chose to
be. And she was certain of something else too: she could see it in
their faces: they did not eat secretly. Which she did: her creeping
to the kitchen when she was nine became, in high school, a ritual
of deceit and pleasure. She was a furtive eater of sweets. Even her
two friends did not know her secret.

Joan was thin, gangling, and flat-chested; she was attractive 5
enough and all she needed was someone to take a second look at
her face, but the school was large and there were pretty girls in
every classroom and walking all the corridors, so no one ever needed
to take a second look at Joan. Marjorie was thin too, an intense,
heavy-smoking girl with brittle laughter. She was very intelligent,
and with boys she was shy because she knew she made them uncomfortable, and because she was smarter than they were and so
could not understand or could not believe the levels they lived on.
She was to have a nervous breakdown before earning her Ph.D. in
philosophy at the University of California, where she met and married a physicist and discovered within herself an untrammelled passion: she made love with her husband on the couch, the carpet, in
the bathtub, and on the washing machine. By that time much had
happened to her and she never thought of Louise. Joan would finally
stop growing and begin moving with grace and confidence. In college she would have two lovers and then several more during the
six years she spent in Boston before marrying a middle-aged editor
who had two sons in their early teens, who drank too much, who
was tenderly, boyishly grateful for her love, and whose wife had
been killed while rock-climbing in New Hampshire with her lover.
She would not think of Louise either, except in an earlier time, when
lovers were still new to her and she was ecstatically surprised each
time one of them loved her and, sometimes at night, lying in a man's
arms, she would tell how in high school no one dated her, she had
been thin and plain (she would still believe that: that she had been
plain; it had never been true) and so had been forced into the weekend and night-time company of a neurotic smart girl and a shy fat
girl. She would say this with self-pity exaggerated by Scotch and
her need to be more deeply loved by the man who held her.

She never eats, Joan and Marjorie said of Louise. They ate 6
lunch with her at school, watched her refusing potatoes, ravioli,
fried fish. Sometimes she got through the cafeteria line with only a
salad. That is how they would remember her: a girl whose hapless
body was destined to be fat. No one saw the sandwiches she made
and took to her room when she came home from school. No one
saw the store of Milky Ways, Butterfingers, Almond Joys, and Her-
sheys far back on her closet shelf, behind the stuffed animals of her
childhood. She was not a hypocrite. When she was out of the house
she truly believed she was dieting; she forgot about the candy, as
a man speaking into his office dictaphone may forget the lewd pho-

tographs hidden in an old shoe in his closet. At other times, away from home, she thought of the waiting candy with near lust. One night driving home from a movie, Marjorie said: 'You're lucky you don't smoke; it's in*cred*ible what I go through to hide it from my parents.' Louise turned to her a smile which was elusive and mysterious; she yearned to be home in bed, eating chocolate in the dark. She did not need to smoke; she already had a vice that was insular and destructive.

7   She brought it with her to college. She thought she would leave it behind. A move from one place to another, a new room without the haunted closet shelf, would do for her what she could not do for herself. She packed her large dresses and went. For two weeks she was busy with registration, with shyness, with classes; then she began to feel at home. Her room was no longer like a motel. Its walls had stopped watching her, she felt they were her friends, and she gave them her secret. Away from her mother, she did not have to be as elaborate; she kept the candy in her drawer now.

8   The school was in Massachusetts, a girls' school. When she chose it, when she and her father and mother talked about it in the evenings, everyone so carefully avoided the word boys that sometimes the conversations seemed to be about nothing but boys. There are no boys there, the neuter words said; you will not have to contend with that. In her father's eyes were pity and encouragement; in her mother's was disappointment, and her voice was crisp. They spoke of courses, of small classes where Louise would get more attention. She imagined herself in those small classes; she saw herself as a teacher would see her, as the other girls would; she would get no attention.

9   The girls at the school were from wealthy families, but most of them wore the uniform of another class: blue jeans and work shirts, and many wore overalls. Louise bought some overalls, washed them until the dark blue faded, and wore them to classes. In the cafeteria she ate as she had in high school, not to lose weight nor even to sustain her lie, but because eating lightly in public had become as habitual as good manners. Everyone had to take gym, and in the locker room with the other girls, and wearing shorts on the volleyball and badminton courts, she hated her body. She liked her body most when she was unaware of it: in bed at night, as sleep gently took her out of her day, out of herself. And she liked parts of her body. She liked her brown eyes and sometimes looked at them in the mirror:

they were not shallow eyes, she thought; they were indeed windows of a tender soul, a good heart. She liked her lips and nose, and her chin, finely shaped between her wide and sagging cheeks. Most of all she liked her long pale blonde hair, she liked washing and drying it and lying naked on her bed, smelling of shampoo, and feeling the soft hair at her neck and shoulders and back.

Her friend at college was Carrie, who was thin and wore thick 10 glasses and often at night she cried in Louise's room. She did not know why she was crying. She was crying, she said, because she was unhappy. She could say no more. Louise said she was unhappy too, and Carrie moved in with her. One night Carrie talked for hours, sadly and bitterly, about her parents and what they did to each other. When she finished she hugged Louise and they went to bed. Then in the dark Carrie spoke across the room: 'Louise? I just wanted to tell you. One night last week I woke up and smelled chocolate. You were eating chocolate, in your bed. I wish you'd eat it in front of me, Louise, whenever you feel like it.'

Stiffened in her bed, Louise could think of nothing to say. In 11 the silence she was afraid Carrie would think she was asleep and would tell her again in the morning or tomorrow night. Finally she said Okay. Then after a moment she told Carrie if she ever wanted any she could feel free to help herself; the candy was in the top drawer. Then she said thank you.

They were roommates for four years and in the summers they 12 exchanged letters. Each fall they greeted with embraces, laughter, tears, and moved into their old room, which had been stripped and cleansed of them for the summer. Neither girl enjoyed summer. Carrie did not like being at home because her parents did not love each other. Louise lived in a small city in Louisiana. She did not like summer because she had lost touch with Joan and Marjorie; they saw each other, but it was not the same. She liked being with her father but with no one else. The flicker of disappointment in her mother's eyes at the airport was a vanguard of the army of relatives and acquaintances who awaited her: they would see her on the streets, in stores, at the country club, in her home, and in theirs; in the first moments of greeting, their eyes would tell her she was still fat Louise, who had been fat as long as they could remember, who had gone to college and returned as fat as ever. Then their eyes dismissed her, and she longed for school and Carrie, and she wrote letters to her friend. But that saddened her too. It wasn't simply that Carrie was her only friend, and when they finished college they might never see each other again. It was that her existence in the world was so divided; it had begun when she was a child creeping to the kitchen; now that division was much sharper, and her friendship with Carrie seemed disproportionate and perilous. The world she was destined to live in had nothing to do with the intimate nights in their room at school.

13   In the summer before their senior year, Carrie fell in love. She wrote to Louise about him, but she did not write much, and this hurt Louise more than if Carrie had shown the joy her writing tried to conceal. That fall they returned to their room; they were still close and warm, Carrie still needed Louise's ears and heart at night as she spoke of her parents and her recurring malaise whose source the two friends never discovered. But on most week-ends Carrie left, and caught a bus to Boston where her boy friend studied music. During the week she often spoke hesitantly of sex; she was not sure if she liked it. But Louise, eating candy and listening, did not know whether Carrie was telling the truth or whether, as in her letters of the past summer, Carrie was keeping from her those delights she may never experience.

14   Then one Sunday night when Carrie had just returned from Boston and was unpacking her overnight bag, she looked at Louise and said: 'I was thinking about you. On the bus coming home tonight.' Looking at Carrie's concerned, determined face, Louise prepared herself for humiliation. 'I was thinking about when we graduate. What you're going to do. What's to become of you. I want you to be loved the way I love you. Louise, if I help you, *really* help you, will you go on a diet?'

15   Louise entered a period of her life she would remember always, the way some people remember having endured poverty. Her diet did not begin the next day. Carrie told her to eat on Monday as though it were the last day of her life. So for the first time since grammar school Louise went into a school cafeteria and ate everything she wanted. At breakfast and lunch and dinner she glanced around the table to see if the other girls noticed the food on her tray. They did not. She felt there was a lesson in this, but it lay beyond her grasp. That night in their room she ate the four remaining candy bars. During the day Carrie rented a small refrigerator, bought an electric skillet, an electric broiler, and bathroom scales.

On Tuesday morning Louise stood on the scales, and Carrie   16
wrote in her notebook: *October 14: 184 lbs.* Then she made Louise
a cup of black coffee and scrambled one egg and sat with her while
she ate. When Carrie went to the dining room for breakfast, Louise
walked about the campus for thirty minutes. That was part of the
plan. The campus was pretty, on its lawns grew at least one of every
tree native to New England, and in the warm morning sun Louise
felt a new hope. At noon they met in their room, and Carrie broiled
her a piece of hamburger and served it with lettuce. Then while
Carrie ate in the dining room Louise walked again. She was weak
with hunger and she felt queasy. During her afternoon classes she
was nervous and tense, and she chewed her pencil and tapped her
heels on the floor and tightened her calves. When she returned to
her room late that afternoon, she was so glad to see Carrie that she
embraced her; she had felt she could not bear another minute of
hunger, but now with Carrie she knew she could make it at least
through tonight. Then she would sleep and face tomorrow when it
came. Carrie broiled her a steak and served it with lettuce. Louise
studied while Carrie ate dinner, then they went for a walk.

That was her ritual and her diet for the rest of the year, Carrie   17
alternating fish and chicken breasts with the steaks for dinner, and
every day was nearly as bad as the first. In the evenings she was
irritable. In all her life she had never been afflicted by ill temper
and she looked upon it now as a demon which, along with hunger,
was taking possession of her soul. Often she spoke sharply to Carrie.
One night during their after-dinner walk Carrie talked sadly of night,
of how darkness made her more aware of herself, and at night she
did not know why she was in college, why she studied, why she
was walking the earth with other people. They were standing on a
wooden foot bridge, looking down at a dark pond. Carrie kept talking; perhaps soon she would cry. Suddenly Louise said: 'I'm sick of
lettuce. I never want to see a piece of lettuce for the rest of my life.
I hate it. We shouldn't even buy it, it's immoral.'

Carrie was quiet. Louise glanced at her, and the pain and ir-   18
ritation in Carrie's face soothed her. Then she was ashamed. Before
she could say she was sorry, Carrie turned to her and said gently:
'I know. I know how terrible it is.'

Carrie did all the shopping, telling Louise she knew how hard   19
it was to go into a supermarket when you were hungry. And Louise
was always hungry. She drank diet soft drinks and started smoking
Carrie's cigarettes, learned to enjoy inhaling, thought of cancer and

emphysema but they were as far away as those boys her mother had talked about when she was nine. By Thanksgiving she was smoking over a pack a day and her weight in Carrie's notebook was one hundred and sixty-two pounds. Carrie was afraid if Louise went home at Thanksgiving she would lapse from the diet, so Louise spent the vacation with Carrie, in Philadelphia. Carrie wrote her family about the diet, and told Louise that she had. On the phone to Philadelphia, Louise said: 'I feel like a bedwetter. When I was a little girl I had a friend who used to come spend the night and Mother would put a rubber sheet on the bed and we all pretended there wasn't a rubber sheet and that she hadn't wet the bed. Even me, and I slept with her.' At Thanksgiving dinner she lowered her eyes as Carrie's father put two slices of white meat on her plate and passed it to her over the bowls of steaming food.

20   When she went home at Christmas she weighed a hundred and fifty-five pounds; at the airport her mother marvelled. Her father laughed and hugged her and said: 'But now there's less of you to love.' He was troubled by her smoking but only mentioned it once; he told her she was beautiful and, as always, his eyes bathed her with love. During the long vacation her mother cooked for her as Carrie had, and Louise returned to school weighing a hundred and forty-six pounds.

21   Flying north on the plane she warmly recalled the surprised and congratulatory eyes of her relatives and acquaintances. She had not seen Joan or Marjorie. She thought of returning home in May, weighing the hundred and fifteen pounds which Carrie had in October set as their goal. Looking toward the stoic days ahead, she felt strong. She thought of those hungry days of fall and early winter (and now: she was hungry now: with almost a frown, almost a brusque shake of the head, she refused peanuts from the stewardess): those first weeks of the diet when she was the pawn of an irascibility which still, conditioned to her ritual as she was, could at any moment take command of her. She thought of the nights of trying to sleep while her stomach growled. She thought of her addiction to cigarettes. She thought of the people at school: not one teacher, not one girl, had spoken to her about her loss of weight, not even about her absence from meals. And without warning her spirit collapsed. She did not feel strong, she did not feel she was committed to and within reach of achieving a valuable goal. She felt that somehow she had lost more than pounds of fat; that some time during her dieting she had lost herself too. She tried to re-

member what it had felt like to be Louise before she had started living on meat and fish, as an unhappy adult may look sadly in the memory of childhood for lost virtues and hopes. She looked down at the earth far below, and it seemed to her that her soul, like her body aboard the plane, was in some rootless flight. She neither knew its destination nor where it had departed from; it was on some passage she could not even define.

During the next few weeks she lost weight more slowly and once for eight days Carrie's daily recording stayed at a hundred and thirty-six. Louise woke in the morning thinking of one hundred and thirty-six and then she stood on the scales and they echoed her. She became obsessed with that number, and there wasn't a day when she didn't say it aloud, and through the days and nights the number stayed in her mind, and if a teacher had spoken those digits in a classroom she would have opened her mouth to speak. What if that's me, she said to Carrie. I mean what if a hundred and thirty-six is my real weight and I just can't lose anymore. Walking hand-in-hand with her despair was a longing for this to be true, and that longing angered her and wearied her, and every day she was gloomy. On the ninth day she weighed a hundred and thirty-five and a half pounds. She was not relieved; she thought bitterly of the months ahead, the shedding of the last twenty and a half pounds.

On Easter Sunday, which she spent at Carrie's, she weighed one hundred and twenty pounds, and she ate one slice of glazed pineapple with her ham and lettuce. She did not enjoy it: she felt she was being friendly with a recalcitrant enemy who had once tried to destroy her. Carrie's parents were laudative. She liked them and she wished they would touch sometimes, and look at each other when they spoke. She guessed they would divorce when Carrie left home, and she vowed that her own marriage would be one of affection and tenderness. She could think about that now: marriage. At school she had read in a Boston paper that this summer the cicadas would come out of their seventeen year hibernation on Cape Cod, for a month they would mate and then die, leaving their young to burrow into the ground where they would stay for seventeen years. That's me, she had said to Carrie. Only my hibernation lasted twenty-one years.

Often her mother asked in letters and on the phone about the diet, but Louise answered vaguely. When she flew home in late May she weighed a hundred and thirteen pounds, and at the airport her mother cried and hugged her and said again and again: You're so

22

23

24

beautiful. Her father blushed and bought her a martini. For days her relatives and acquaintances congratulated her, and the applause in their eyes lasted the entire summer, and she loved their eyes, and swam in the country club pool, the first time she had done this since she was a child.

25   She lived at home and ate the way her mother did and every morning she weighed herself on the scales in her bathroom. Her mother liked to take her shopping and buy her dresses and they put her old ones in the Goodwill box at the shopping center; Louise thought of them existing on the body of a poor woman whose cheap meals kept her fat. Louise's mother had a photographer come to the house, and Louise posed on the couch and standing beneath a live oak and sitting in a wicker lawn chair next to an azalea bush. The new clothes and the photographer made her feel she was going to another country or becoming a citizen of a new one. In the fall she took a job of no consequence, to give herself something to do.

26   Also in the fall a young lawyer joined her father's firm, he came one night to dinner, and they started seeing each other. He was the first man outside her family to kiss her since the barbecue when she was sixteen. Louise celebrated Thanksgiving not with rice dressing and candied sweet potatoes and mince meat and pumpkin pies, but by giving Richard her virginity which she realized, at the very last moment of its existence, she had embarked on giving him over thirteen months ago, on that Tuesday in October when Carrie had made her a cup of black coffee and scrambled one egg. She wrote this to Carrie, who replied happily by return mail. She also, through glance and smile and innuendo, tried to tell her mother too. But finally she controlled that impulse, because Richard felt guilty about making love with the daughter of his partner and friend. In the spring they married. The wedding was a large one, in the Episcopal church, and Carrie flew from Boston to be maid of honor. Her parents had recently separated and she was living with the musician and was still victim of her unpredictable malaise. It overcame her on the night before the wedding, so Louise was up with her until past three and woke next morning from a sleep so heavy that she did not want to leave it.

27   Richard was a lean, tall, energetic man with the metabolism of a pencil sharpener. Louise fed him everything he wanted. He liked Italian food and she got recipes from her mother and watched him eating spaghetti with the sauce she had only tasted, and ravioli

and lasagna, while she ate antipasto with her chianti. He made a lot of money and borrowed more and they bought a house whose lawn sloped down to the shore of a lake; they had a wharf and a boathouse, and Richard bought a boat and they took friends waterskiing. Richard bought her a car and they spent his vacations in Mexico, Canada, the Bahamas, and in the fifth year of their marriage they went to Europe and, according to their plan, she conceived a child in Paris. On the plane back, as she looked out the window and beyond the sparkling sea and saw her country, she felt that it was waiting for her, as her home by the lake was, and her parents, and her good friends who rode in the boat and waterskied; she thought of the accumulated warmth and pelf of her marriage, and how by slimming her body she had bought into the pleasures of the nation. She felt cunning, and she smiled to herself, and took Richard's hand.

But these moments of triumph were sparse. On most days she 28 went about her routine of leisure with a sense of certainty about herself that came merely from not thinking. But there were times, with her friends, or with Richard, or alone in the house, when she was suddenly assaulted by the feeling that she had taken the wrong train and arrived at a place where no one knew her, and where she ought not to be. Often, in bed with Richard, she talked of being fat: 'I was the one who started the friendship with Carrie, I chose her, I started the conversations. When I understood that she was my friend I understood something else: I had chosen her for the same reason I'd chosen Joan and Marjorie. They were all thin. I was always thinking about what people saw when they looked at me and I didn't want them to see two fat girls. When I was alone I didn't mind being fat but then I'd have to leave the house again and then I didn't want to look like me. But at home I didn't mind except when I was getting dressed to go out of the house and when Mother looked at me. But I stopped looking at her when she looked at me. And in college I felt good with Carrie; there weren't any boys and I didn't have any other friends and so when I wasn't with Carrie I thought about her and I tried to ignore the other people around me, I tried to make them not exist. A lot of the time I could do that. It was strange, and I felt like a spy.'

If Richard was bored by her repetition he pretended not to be. 29 But she knew the story meant very little to him. She could have been telling him of a childhood illness, or wearing braces, or a broken heart at sixteen. He could not see her as she was when she was fat. She felt as though she were trying to tell a foreign lover about her life in the United States, and if only she could command the language he would know and love all of her and she would feel complete. Some of the acquaintances of her childhood were her friends now, and even they did not seem to remember her when she was fat.

30 Now her body was growing again, and when she put on a maternity dress for the first time she shivered with fear. Richard did not smoke and he asked her, in a voice just short of demand, to stop during her pregnancy. She did. She ate carrots and celery instead of smoking, and at cocktail parties she tried to eat nothing, but after her first drink she ate nuts and cheese and crackers and dips. Always at these parties Richard had talked with his friends and she had rarely spoken to him until they drove home. But now when he noticed her at the hors d'oeuvres table he crossed the room and, smiling, led her back to his group. His smile and his hand on her arm told her he was doing his clumsy, husbandly best to help her through a time of female mystery.

31 She was gaining weight but she told herself it was only the baby, and would leave with its birth. But at other times she knew quite clearly that she was losing the discipline she had fought so hard to gain during her last year with Carrie. She was hungry now as she had been in college, and she ate between meals and after dinner and tried to eat only carrots and celery, but she grew to hate them, and her desire for sweets was as vicious as it had been long ago. At home she ate bread and jam and when she shopped for groceries she bought a candy bar and ate it driving home and put the wrapper in her purse and then in the garbage can under the sink. Her cheeks had filled out, there was loose flesh under her chin, her arms and legs were plump, and her mother was concerned. So was Richard. One night when she brought pie and milk to the living room where they were watching television, he said: 'You already had a piece. At dinner.'

32 She did not look at him.

33 'You're gaining weight. It's not all water, either. It's fat. It'll be summertime. You'll want to get into your bathing suit.'

34 The pie was cherry. She looked at it as her fork cut through it; she speared the piece and rubbed it in the red juice on the plate before lifting it to her mouth.

35 'You never used to eat pie,' he said. 'I just think you ought to watch it a bit. It's going to be tough on you this summer.'

In her seventh month, with a delight reminiscent of climbing 36
the stairs to Richard's apartment before they were married, she returned to her world of secret gratification. She began hiding candy
in her underwear drawer. She ate it during the day and at night
while Richard slept, and at breakfast she was distracted, waiting for
him to leave.

She gave birth to a son, brought him home, and nursed both 37
him and her appetites. During this time of celibacy she enjoyed her
body through her son's mouth; while he suckled she stroked his
small head and back. She was hiding candy but she did not conceal
her other indulgences: she was smoking again but still she ate between meals, and at dinner she ate what Richard did, and coldly
he watched her, he grew petulant, and when the date marking the
end of their celibacy came they let it pass. Often in the afternoons
her mother visited and scolded her and Louise sat looking at the
baby and said nothing until finally, to end it, she promised to diet.
When her mother and father came for dinners, her father kissed her
and held the baby and her mother said nothing about Louise's body,
and her voice was tense. Returning from work in the evenings Richard looked at a soiled plate and glass on the table beside her chair
as if detecting traces of infidelity, and at every dinner they fought.

'Look at you,' he said. 'Lasagna, for God's sake. When are you 38
going to start? It's not simply that you haven't lost any weight. You're
gaining. I can see it. I can feel it when you get in bed. Pretty soon
you'll weigh more than I do and I'll be sleeping on a trampoline.'

'You never touch me anymore.' 39

'I don't want to touch you. Why should I? Have you *looked* at 40
yourself?'

'You're cruel,' she said. 'I never knew how cruel you were.' 41

She ate, watching him. He did not look at her. Glaring at his 42
plate, he worked with fork and knife like a hurried man at a lunch
counter.

'I bet you didn't either,' she said. 43

That night when he was asleep she took a Milky Way to the 44
bathroom. For a while she stood eating in the dark, then she turned
on the light. Chewing, she looked at herself in the mirror; she looked
at her eyes and hair. Then she stood on the scales and looking at
the numbers between her feet, one hundred and sixty-two, she remembered when she had weighed a hundred and thirty-six pounds
for eight days. Her memory of those eight days was fond and amusing, as though she were recalling an Easter egg hunt when she was

six. She stepped off the scales and pushed them under the lavatory and did not stand on them again.

45   It was summer and she bought loose dresses and when Richard took friends out on the boat she did not wear a bathing suit or shorts; her friends gave her mischievous glances, and Richard did not look at her. She stopped riding on the boat. She told them she wanted to stay with the baby, and she sat inside holding him until she heard the boat leave the wharf. Then she took him to the front lawn and walked with him in the shade of the trees and talked to him about the blue jays and mockingbirds and cardinals she saw on their branches. Sometimes she stopped and watched the boat out on the lake and the friend skiing behind it.

46   Every day Richard quarrelled, and because his rage went no further than her weight and shape, she felt excluded from it, and she remained calm within layers of flesh and spirit, and watched his frustration, his impotence. He truly believed they were arguing about her weight. She knew better: she knew that beneath the argument lay the question of who Richard was. She thought of him smiling at the wheel of his boat, and long ago courting his slender girl, the daughter of his partner and friend. She thought of Carrie telling her of smelling chocolate in the dark and, after that, watching her eat it night after night. She smiled at Richard, teasing his anger.

47   He is angry now. He stands in the center of the living room, raging at her, and he wakes the baby. Beneath Richard's voice she hears the soft crying, feels it in her heart, and quietly she rises from her chair and goes upstairs to the child's room and takes him from the crib. She brings him to the living room and sits holding him in her lap, pressing him gently against the folds of fat at her waist. Now Richard is pleading with her. Louise thinks tenderly of Carrie broiling meat and fish in their room, and walking with her in the evenings. She wonders if Carrie still has the malaise. Perhaps she will come for a visit. In Louise's arms now the boy sleeps.

48   'I'll help you,' Richard says. 'I'll eat the same things you eat.'

49   But his face does not approach the compassion and determination and love she had seen in Carrie's during what she now recognizes as the worst year of her life. She can remember nothing about that year except hunger, and the meals in her room. She is hungry now. When she puts the boy to bed she will get a candy bar from her room. She will eat it here, in front of Richard. This room will be hers soon. She considers the possibilities: all these

rooms and the lawn where she can do whatever she wishes. She knows he will leave soon. It has been in his eyes all summer. She stands, using one hand to pull herself out of the chair. She carries the boy to his crib, feels him against her large breasts, feels that his sleeping body touches her soul. With a surge of vindication and relief she holds him. Then she kisses his forehead and places him in the crib. She goes to the bedroom and in the dark takes a bar of candy from her drawer. Slowly she descends the stairs. She knows Richard is waiting but she feels his departure so happily that, when she enters the living room, unwrapping the candy, she is surprised to see him standing there.

Thinking Critically About This Reading

1. What underlying social attitudes toward fat people are implicitly reflected in this story?

2. What is Louise like, aside from being fat?

3. Why does Louise eat to excess? In the depiction of her character, what does the author imply about obesity?

4. If you were grossly overweight, how would you expect society to treat you, and what would you do about it?

5. How do you think the story would have unfolded and what do you think its outcome would have been had Louise been a man?

Understanding the Writer's Process

1. In paragraph 2, the author cites some comments addressed to Louise by her mother, but omits the quotation marks. What point is implicitly made by this omission?

2. How many times do you suppose the exchange reported in paragraph 3 took place between Louise's mother and father, and how do you know?

3. In describing Louise's two girl friends in paragraph 5, what point about Louise is the author indirectly making?

4. What technique of fiction is prominently at work in the brief paragraph 7?

5. In paragraph 9 the author tells us that the girls at the private college in Massachusetts were wealthy but wore "the uniform of

another class." What class does he mean? What does this information tell us about the school?

Examining the Writer's Language

1. Define the meanings of the following words used in this essay: untrammelled (paragraph 5), insular (6), malaise (13), stoic (21), irascibility (21), recalcitrant (23), innuendo (26), pelf (27).

2. In his description in paragraph 6 of the candy Louise eats, how does the author underscore the depth and strength of her secret passion?

3. The author writes in paragraph 6 that Louise "yearned to be home in bed, eating chocolate in the dark." What does this sentence slyly suggest about her passion for food?

4. In paragraph 17, Louise snaps at Carrie about lettuce, "We shouldn't even buy it, it's immoral." Why does she regard lettuce as immoral? To what is she alluding?

5. In paragraph 46 we are told about the quarrels between Louise and Richard: "He truly believed they were arguing about her weight. She knew better: she knew that beneath the argument lay the question of who Richard was." What does this last sentence mean?

Suggestions for Writing

1. Write an essay exploring the stereotypes and myths our society generally holds about fat people.

2. After doing some preliminary research, write an essay on the medical and psychological causes of obesity.

Writing Assignment Based on "The Fat Girl"

With the vivid descriptions of "The Fat Girl" in mind, describe an animal, a person, a place, or a thing that you have closely observed. Be sure your description uses a dominant impression that your details and images support.

STUDENT ESSAY
(IN PROCESS) DESCRIPTION

Mary Beth Stevens

Mary Beth Stevens currently is attending college full time, planning to major in electrical engineering. Her area of interest is the future of artificial intelligence and high technology. She is also a talented illustrator. Throughout the semester, Mary Beth wrote several excellent essays on Arabic culture and politics; however, her favorite essay was the vivid description that follows.

First Draft   Mary Beth Stevens

Eng. 101

Amiera

Leave out first sentence for better opening   ~~Her name is Amiera.~~ Her ancestors were worshiped. Their bodies were embalmed and preserved as shrines. Her family's image has been painted on canvas and sculpted in stone hundreds of thousands of times. ~~Such~~ Works of art *bearing her image* ∧ appeared in China, Japan, and Thailand. They further appeared at the French court, in stately English mansions, and on ancient pottery. They were even stamped on ancient friezes. Volumes of poetry have been written about members of her family, and these honored beings have been figured in literature since the beginning.

You cannot impress her. You cannot court her. You cannot intimidate her. It is not that she sneers at you. It is that she has perspec-

tive, she has things pulled together, and she
is well organized as she sits and watches the
charade of life acted out around her. She seems
to know the punch lines. She knows how the play
will end, so she makes herself comfortable and
waits.

Provide a physical description

~~She~~ *Amiera* has a temper and passion. She gets
hungry and she is very lusty sexually, but all

Amiera is not so much beautiful as seductively mysterious. She is naturally spotted in three magnificent colors.-- honey bronze, seal brown, and smoke black. Her hypnotic eyes are distinctly almond shaped. They are luminescent gooseberry green with an amber cast, creating an effect of mindboggling fascination.

of these things seem to be only diversions. She
knows what is essential and when to expect important events. Meanwhile, she passes the time
playing with a mouse, dawdling with a bit of
fluff, or whacking at a spool dangled by a bit
of thread. Or she can just wait, paws to breast,
like a sphynx. She likes her warm places, but
she is ~~very very~~ *nevertheless* "cool" in the way many teen-
agers like to be cool. The ultimate compliment
during the 50's era was to call someone a "cool

Explain the "cool cat" image

cat." ~~These all are traits most people, I~~ *meaning that the person was unflappable, poised in the face of stress, and in charge of the environment* ~~believe, would want to have said about themselves, even those with~~ allergies.

Rewrite for more precision

If one listens carefully to her sound,
her voice can be very expressive. ~~Although~~ *Whereas* many *avoid repetition of "although"*
of her distant great relatives have the power
than enables them to roar, *with awesome might* she dares not
although she *sometimes* appears to try, *but immediately thinks* ~~(this would be~~ *better, as*
socially unacceptable. My Amiera (Arabic *if such an*

Improve for con-ciseness

~~meaning~~ for ("Princess"), makes one of the most satis- *extravagance* fying sounds in the world: She purrs. I have *would be* never heard a~~n~~ *satisfying* explanation for the purr ~~that I felt comfortable with~~, but I certainly feel comfortable with the phenomenon itself. ~~When I hear~~ Amiera's purr ~~it~~ is a form of high praise, like a gold star on a test paper. I think ~~a lot~~ *many* of us wish we could purr, and in that sponta- neous verbal (yet nonverbal) way tell each other how much we approve. Purring people would have to feel good about themselves and each other. Imagine how you would feel if you bumped into someone in an elevator and ~~they~~ *that person* purred instead of glared at you. And instead of mut- tering a self-conscious "Excuse me," you ~~could~~ *would* purr back.

~~For~~ While my Amiera ~~may be~~ *is* linked to me by her needs, *and our mutual affection for each other* ~~her affection and my love~~, she is also linked to "dark voices" and magic talis- mans, ~~(often she is a talisman herself), as I am~~ *At certain moments her green eyes become* ~~through her; linked that is. I~~ *shall never fully* ~~know not what and perhaps dare not guess~~, that higher wisdom of ~~the~~ voluptuous hedonistic materialis~~s~~*m* which ~~the most ardent cat lover cannot deny~~ is truly the essence of being a cat.

two deep wells of mystery. Amiera is in tune with the occult; she receives messages from places beyond blue mists and grey clouds.

<u>Final Draft</u>   Mary Beth Stevens

Eng. 101

Amiera

Her ancestors were worshiped. Their
bodies were embalmed and preserved as shrines.
Her family's image has been painted on canvas
and sculpted in stone hundreds of thousands of
times. Works of art bearing her image appeared
in China, Japan, and Thailand. They further
appeared at the French court, in stately English mansions, and on ancient pottery. They
were even stamped on ancient friezes. Volumes
of poetry have been written about members of
her family, and these honored beings have been
figured in literature since the beginning.

You cannot impress her. You cannot court
her. You cannot intimidate her. It is not that
she sneers at you. It is that she has perspective, she has things pulled together, and she
is well organized as she sits and watches the
charade of life acted out around her. She seems
to know the punch lines. She knows how the play
will end, so she makes herself comfortable and
waits.

Amiera is not so much beautiful as
seductively mysterious. She is naturally spotted in three magnificent colors—honey bronze,
seal brown, and smoke black. Her hypnotic eyes
are distinctly almond shaped. They are a
luminescent gooseberry green with an amber

cast, creating an effect of mind-boggling fascination.

Amiera has a temper and passion. She gets hungry and she is very lusty sexually, but all of these things seem to be only diversions. She knows what is essential and when to expect important events. Meanwhile, she passes the time playing with a mouse, dawdling with a bit of fluff, or whacking at a spool dangled by a bit of thread. Or she can just wait, paws to breast, like a sphinx. She likes her warm places, but she is nevertheless "cool" in the way many teenagers like to be cool. The ultimate compliment during the 50's era was to call someone a "cool cat," meaning that the person was unflappable, poised in the face of stress, and in charge of the environment.

If one listens carefully to her sound, her voice can be expressive. Although many of her great relatives have the power to roar with awesome might, she dares not although she sometimes appears to try, but immediately thinks better, as if such an extravagance would be socially unacceptable. My Amiera (Arabic for "Princess") makes one of the most satisfying sounds in the world: She purrs. I have never heard a satisfactory explanation for the purr, but I certainly feel comfortable with the phenomenon itself. When I hear Amiera's purr, it is a form of high praise, like a gold star on a test paper. I think many of us wish we could purr, and in that spontaneous verbal (yet non-verbal) way tell each other how much we approve. Purring people would have to feel good about themselves and each other. Imagine how you would feel if you bumped into someone in an elevator and that person purred instead of glared at you. And instead of muttering a self-conscious "Excuse me," you would purr back.

While my Amiera is linked to me by her needs and our mutual affection for each other, she is also linked to "dark voices" and magic talismans. At certain moments her green eyes become two deep wells of mystery. Amiera is in tune with the occult; she receives messages from places beyond blue mists and grey clouds.

I shall never fully understand that higher wisdom of voluptuous hedonistic materialism which is truly the essence of being a cat.

4

Definition

HOW TO WRITE A DEFINITION

Even if you never have formally defined a word in writing, it is certain you at some time or another have informally defined a word in speech. This definition may have been as simple as explaining to someone unfamiliar with basketball what a "slam-dunk" is. Or you may have had to clarify for a heartbroken wooer what you meant when you blurted out that you were not "in love."

The formal definition practiced in essays is not vastly unlike these hasty oral definitions we all must tackle occasionally in daily life. In both cases we say what we mean by a certain abstract word, phrase, or term. For usually it is the abstract word, the one with no tangible object behind it, that requires defining. A concrete word may mystify a reader or listener, but only if the object behind it cannot be produced. To define *apple* to a person who has never seen one only requires plunking down the fruit on the table. With an abstract word such as *love*, however, there is nothing to plunk down. You can only elaborate with more words on what you mean by *love* until satisfied that your reader or listener cannot mistake the definition you intend for that bottomless word.

Formal or informal, most definitions are lexical. Typically, a lexical definition—the kind found in dictionaries—specifies the category to which a word belongs while setting it apart from others in that same category. For example, *Webster's New World Dictionary* defines *love* as "a deep and tender feeling of affection for or attachment or devotion to a person or persons. . . ." This tells us that *love* belongs to the category of *feelings* but differs from other feelings in its depth, tenderness, and devotion to persons. The definition you include in an essay will invariably begin as a lexical definition. You may write that " 'The slam-dunk' is a basketball shot in which . . ." and then show how the "slam-dunk" differs from other basketball shots. Once that is done, however, you must flesh out your definition by one or all of the following methods.

1. Begin with an Etymological Explanation

The etymology of a word is its earliest meaning and all good dictionaries routinely list it in brackets after the word. For example, *Webster's New World Dictionary* provides the following bracketed etymology for *inamorata:* "[It., fem. of innamorato, lover, orig. pp. of innamorare, to fall in love. . . .] This tells us that *inamorata* came into English from the Italian feminine form of *innamorato,* which means "lover," and that *innamorato* was originally the past participle of the Italian verb meaning "to fall in love."

Does this sort of information help in defining a word? Not always, but it can, especially if the word has a rich etymological history. Here is an example of how etymology may be used in a definition:

> There are life-forms which, in the course of evolution, have developed poisons designed to kill, or to prevent themselves from being eaten. Venoms are produced by a variety of animals from jellyfish to reptiles. Plants develop a variety of poisonous substances designed to taste bad to an animal that nibbles and to kill if the animal persists.
>
> Pride of place, however, must be taken by the product of a bacterium which is to be found everywhere and which harms no one—ordinarily. It is *Clostridium botulinum.* "Clostridium" is Latin for "little spindle," which describes its shape, and "botulinum" is from the Latin word *botulus,* which means "sausage," where it has sometimes been detected.
>
> ISAAC ASIMOV, *"World's Deadliest Poison. . . .
The Botulin Spore," Science Digest,* January
1972.

In this case, the etymology tells us where the bacterium has been found and what it looks like—useful preliminary information for a definition.

Whether or not citing etymology in a definition is worth the trouble depends on the word. Newer words tend to have dull etymologies not worth the mention. For example, the etymology of *hype* is listed in *Webster's New World Dictionary* as "a clipped form of hypodermic." But hype, in its present meaning, is so far removed from *hypodermic* that citing this etymology would be pointless. Use common sense. If the etymology of the word adds to your definition, include it. Otherwise, ignore it altogether.

2. Elaborate on Your Definition with Examples

Examples can clarify an abstract term by demonstrating its practical effects. A case in point is "What Is Poverty?" an essay in which the writer overwhelms us with scads of instances and illustrations about her own suffering under poverty. She shows us her dirty, smelly self; her shabby home; her neglected and worm-riddled children. She tells us how she scrimped to buy a jar of Vaseline to soothe her baby's diaper rash but had to pass up the purchase because the price had risen two cents. She shares her drab and cheerless life with us: from the indifference and callousness she suffers from welfare workers to the sexual harassment she must endure from a neighbor in exchange for a ride to the health clinic. These examples contribute a seamy and shocking intimacy to the meaning of *poverty*.

3. Say What the Term Does Not Mean

Sometimes it is helpful to define a word by saying what it does not mean. Many writers practice this technique as an aside. For example, Frank DeFord begins a definition of *cystic fibrosis* by saying, "It [cystic fibrosis] has nothing to do with cysts." But a more elaborate practice of this technique involves saying at length what the defined term is not. Here is an example from an essay defining a sophisticated man:

> Now, here we have come to the crux of the situation, for I maintain that a man who has never traveled in other countries and been exposed to other societies cannot be sophisticated. I am not speaking of package tours or cruise trips, but of a reasonable familiarity with foreign cities and peoples of arts and customs; an education reading alone cannot provide. For sophistication to me suggests, primarily, a refinement of the senses. The eye that has not appreciated Michelangelo's David in Florence or the cathedral of Chartres is not a sophisticated eye; nor is the tongue that has not tasted the best fettucine in Rome or the best wine in Paris. The hand that has not felt the rough heat of an ancient wall in Siena or the sweating cold of a Salzburg stein of beer is an innocent hand. So are the fingers that have not traveled, in conscious and specific savoring, over the contours of many different women.
>
> MARYA MANNES, *"The Sophisticated Man"*

To say what a word does not mean often requires contrasting it with another word of similar meaning. For example, a student wrote a paper for us defining love in which she drew a contrast between *love* and *infatuation*:

> Love, however, is not the same as infatuation. Love is different from infatuation in that it lasts longer and is more profound and caring. Infatuation is only the passion of the moment or the

feeling aroused by someone's popularity or looks. It may be based on nothing more than sexual attraction. Usually, infatuation is the brief whirlwind affair that blows fast and furious for a while. But love is not necessarily fast or furious, and it is never based only on physical attraction or sexuality. Love means caring deeply for another to the point that you would do anything, even give up your own life, for that person. In religion, love is symbolized by the life and the crucifixion of Jesus. On the battlefield, it is told in countless stories about one soldier dying in place of another. In everyday life, it is a willingness to sacrifice personal wants and happiness for the happiness of the other.

Your definition essay is finished when you are satisfied that no one reading it could mistake the meaning you attach to the word, phrase, or term. In complexity and length, therefore, your essay will naturally vary with the word you are attempting to define. Some simple and straightforward words such as *slam-dunk* or *drudgery* or *routine* can be put to bed in a few paragraphs. Such complex terms as *freedom* or *dignity* or *self-determination* will require many detailed examples, greater amplification, and more ink.

WHAT IS POVERTY?

Jo Goodwin Parker

During preparation of America's Other Children: Public Schools Outside Suburbia, *a book published in 1971, a professor at the University of Oklahoma received this unsolicited submission by mail from West Virginia. Nothing factual is known about the essay's author. We do not know whether she really is a member of the desperately poor as she claims, or is a professional who works with the poor and is moved by their plight.*

Preparing to Read This Selection Critically

This essay attempts to define poverty by showing us its worst characteristics and effects. The writer avoids the traditional niceties of a more academic definition, concentrating instead on depicting, in harrowing and graphic detail, what it means to be poor. She catalogues want, deprivation, need, lack, and misery. If this essay had come out several years ago, before the spread of homelessness with the attendant media coverage of people sleeping on city grates, it might have been greeted with incredulity. Today we are more likely to accept it as true. Ask yourself, however, whether you found it puzzling that such an intelligent writer, with so sensitive an eye for detail, could have become so mired in this wretchedness. Do you find her story plausible, or do you think, as some have suggested, that this was written by someone who works with the poor in an attempt to draw sympathy to their plight? Does it matter?

1   You ask me what is poverty? Listen to me. Here I am, dirty, smelly, and with no "proper" underwear on and with the stench of my rotting teeth near you. I will tell you. Listen to me. Listen without pity. I cannot use your pity. Listen with understanding. Put yourself in my dirty, worn out, ill-fitting shoes, and hear me.

2   Poverty is getting up every morning from a dirt- and illness-stained mattress. The sheets have long since been used for diapers. Poverty is living in a smell that never leaves. This is a smell of urine, sour milk, and spoiling food sometimes joined with the strong smell of long-cooked onions. Onions are cheap. If you have smelled this smell, you did not know how it came. It is the smell of the outdoor privy. It is the smell of young children who cannot walk the long dark way in the night. It is the smell of the mattresses where years of "accidents" have happened. It is the smell of the milk which has gone sour because the refrigerator long has not worked, and it costs money to get it fixed. It is the smell of rotting garbage. I could bury it, but where is the shovel? Shovels cost money.

3   Poverty is being tired. I have always been tired. They told me at the hospital when the last baby came that I had chronic anemia caused from poor diet, a bad case of worms, and that I needed a corrective operation. I listened politely—the poor are always polite. The poor always listen. They don't say that there is no money for iron pills, or better food, or worm medicine. The idea of an operation is frightening and costs so much that, if I had dared, I would have laughed. Who takes care of my children? Recovery from an operation

takes a long time. I have three children. When I left them with "Granny" the last time I had a job, I came home to find the baby covered with fly specks, and a diaper that had not been changed since I left. When the dried diaper came off, bits of my baby's flesh came with it. My other child was playing with a sharp bit of broken glass, and my oldest was playing alone at the edge of a lake. I made twenty-two dollars a week, and a good nursery school costs twenty dollars a week for three children, I quit my job.

Poverty is dirt. You say in your clean clothes coming from your 4 clean house, "Anybody can be clean." Let me explain about housekeeping with no money. For breakfast I give my children grits with no oleo or cornbread without eggs and oleo. This does not use up many dishes. What dishes there are, I wash in cold water and with no soap. Even the cheapest soap has to be saved for the baby's diapers. Look at my hands, so cracked and red. Once I saved for two months to buy a jar of Vaseline for my hands and the baby's diaper rash. When I had saved enough, I went to buy it and the price had gone up two cents. The baby and I suffered on. I have to decide every day if I can bear to put my cracked, sore hands into the cold water and strong soap. But you ask, why not hot water? Fuel costs money. If you have a wood fire it costs money. If you burn electricity, it costs money. Hot water is a luxury. I do not have luxuries. I know you will be surprised when I tell you how young I am. I look so much older. My back has been bent over the wash tubs for so long, I cannot remember when I ever did anything else. Every night I wash every stitch my school age child has on and just hope her clothes will be dry by morning.

Poverty is staying up all night on cold nights to watch the fire, 5 knowing one spark on the newspaper covering the walls means your sleeping children die in flames. In summer poverty is watching gnats and flies devour your baby's tears when he cries. The screens are torn and you pay so little rent you know they will never be fixed. Poverty means insects in your food, in your nose, in your eyes, and crawling over you when you sleep. Poverty is hoping it never rains because diapers won't dry when it rains and soon you are using newspapers. Poverty is seeing your children forever with runny noses. Paper handkerchiefs cost money and all your rags you need for other things. Even more costly are antihistamines. Poverty is cooking without food and cleaning without soap.

Poverty is asking for help. Have you ever had to ask for help, 6 knowing your children will suffer unless you get it? Think about asking for a loan from a relative, if this is the only way you can imagine asking for help. I will tell you how it feels. You find out where the office is that you are supposed to visit. You circle that block four or five times. Thinking of your children, you go in. Everyone is very busy. Finally, someone comes out and you tell her that you need help. That never is the person you need to see. You go see another person, and after spilling the whole shame of your poverty all over the desk between you, you find that this isn't the right office after all—you must repeat the whole process, and it never is any easier at the next place.

7   You have asked for help, and after all it has a cost. You are again told to wait. You are told why, but you don't really hear because of the red cloud of shame and the rising black cloud of despair.

8   Poverty is remembering. It is remembering quitting school in junior high because "nice" children had been so cruel about my clothes and my smell. The attendance officer came. My mother told him I was pregnant. I wasn't, but she thought that I could get a job and help out. I had jobs off and on, but never long enough to learn anything. Mostly I remember being married. I was so young then. I am still young. For a time, we had all the things you have. There was a little house in another town, with hot water and everything. Then my husband lost his job. There was unemployment insurance for a while and what few jobs I could get. Soon, all our nice things were repossessed and we moved back here. I was pregnant then. This house didn't look so bad when we first moved in. Every week it gets worse. Nothing is ever fixed. We now had no money. There were a few odd jobs for my husband, but everything went for food then, as it does now. I don't know how we lived through three years and three babies, but we did. I'll tell you something, after the last baby I destroyed my marriage. It had been a good one, but could you keep on bringing children in this dirt? Did you ever think how much it costs for any kind of birth control? I knew my husband was leaving the day he left, but there were no good-byes between us. I hope he has been able to climb out of this mess somewhere. He never could hope with us to drag him down.

9   That's when I asked for help. When I got it, you know how much it was? It was, and is, seventy-eight dollars a month for the four of us; that is all I ever can get. Now you know why there is no soap, no needles and thread, no hot water, no aspirin, no worm medicine, no hand cream, no shampoo. None of these things forever

and ever and ever. So that you can see clearly, I pay twenty dollars a month rent, and most of the rest goes for food. For grits and corn-meal, and rice and milk and beans. I try my best to use only the minimum electricity. If I use more, there is that much less for food.

Poverty is looking into a black future. Your children won't play   10
with my boys. They will turn to other boys who steal to get what they want. I can already see them behind the bars of their prison instead of behind the bars of my poverty. Or they will turn to the freedom of alcohol or drugs, and find themselves enslaved. And my daughter? At best, there is for her a life like mine.

But you say to me, there are schools. Yes, there are schools.   11
My children have no extra books, no magazines, no extra pencils, or crayons, or paper and the most important of all, they do not have health. They have worms, they have infections, they have pink-eye all summer. They do not sleep well on the floor, or with me in my one bed. They do not suffer from hunger, my seventy-eight dollars keeps us alive, but they do suffer from malnutrition. Oh yes, I do remember what I was taught about health in school. It doesn't do much good. In some places there is a surplus commodities program. Not here. The county said it cost too much. There is a school lunch program. But I have two children who will already be damaged by the time they get to school.

But, you say to me, there are health clinics. Yes, there are health   12
clinics and they are in the towns. I live out here eight miles from town. I can walk that far (even if it is sixteen miles both ways), but can my little children? My neighbor will take me when he goes; but he expects to get paid, *one way or another*. I bet you know my neighbor. He is that large man who spends his time at the gas station, the barbershop, and the corner store complaining about the gov-ernment spending money on the immoral mothers of illegitimate children.

Poverty is an acid that drips on pride until all pride is worn   13
away. Poverty is a chisel that chips on honor until honor is worn away. Some of you say that you would do *something* in my situation, and maybe you would, for the first week or the first month, but for year after year after year?

Even the poor can dream. A dream of a time when there is   14
money. Money for the right kinds of food, for worm medicine, for iron pills, for toothbrushes, for hand cream, for a hammer and nails and a bit of screening, for a shovel, for a bit of paint, for some sheeting, for needles and thread. Money to pay *in money* for a trip

to town. And, oh, money for hot water and money for soap. A dream of when asking for help does not eat away the last bit of pride. When the office you visit is as nice as the offices of other governmental agencies, when there are enough workers to help you quickly, when workers do not quit in defeat and despair. When you have to tell your story to only one person, and that person can send you for other help and you don't have to prove your poverty over and over and over again.

I have come out of my despair to tell you this. Remember I did not come from another place or another time. Others like me are all around you. Look at us with an angry heart, anger that will help you help me. Anger that will let you tell of me. The poor are always silent. Can you be silent too?

Thinking Critically About This Reading

1. The writer paints an utterly bleak picture of her situation. Leaving aside such obvious platitudes as *bad luck,* what do you see as the primary cause of her desperate state?

2. Are you convinced that the author is not overstating her helplessness? If in her shoes, what would you do differently?

3. What do you think the future holds for the writer's children?

4. Social welfare programs are nearly always dispensed in an atmosphere the recipients find demeaning. Why is this necessarily so? Should welfare recipients be made to feel shame over having to seek public help?

5. Having read this essay, how do you feel about the writer? Are you sorry for her, contemptuous of her, or otherwise? Why? Why not?

Understanding the Writer's Process

1. What primary technique does the writer use to rivet the focus of this essay on its subject? Comment on its effectiveness.

2. Although this essay is primarily a definition, it also contains a definite argumentative edge. Against whom or what is the writer arguing? How does she make us aware of the opposition's case before rebutting it?

3. The writer omits any but the broadest personal details about herself. Is this an effective strategy? How would more personal information about her likely influence our reaction to this essay?

4. Along the way, the writer inevitably resorts to description as a technique for defining her hopeless condition. In paragraph 2, on what dominant impression is the description based?

5. How is the beginning of this essay related to its ending? Is this an effective way to link the beginning of an essay with its ending?

Examining the Writer's Language

1. How do the writer's syntax and diction underscore the believability of this self-portrait?

2. By whom do you think this piece was written? By someone named Jo Goodwin Parker who is really as destitute as she claims, or by someone who works with the poor and is sympathetic to their plight? What evidence from the language of this piece can you cite to support your belief?

3. Explain the meaning of the italicized passages in paragraphs 12, 13, and 14.

4. The writer does not personalize any mention of contact with hospital or welfare workers. In paragraph 3, she writes that "they" told her she needed an operation. In paragraph 6, she refers to the anonymous welfare worker as a "person." Explain the effect of this.

5. What primary technique does the writer use to vividly depict her unconscionable situation? Does she rely on imagery and metaphor? How does she manage to convey the depth of her want and despair?

Suggestions for Writing

1. Analyze this piece, telling why you think it is the authentic story of its writer, or why you think it is not meant as a real poor person's story but as a composite. Cite evidence from the text to support your view.

2. Using this essay as a model, write an extended definition of any one of the following terms:

Comfort is . . .
Love is . . .
Beauty is . . .
Sex appeal is . . .
Anxiety is . . .
Courage is . . .

I WANT A WIFE

Judy Syfers

Judy Syfers (b. 1937 in San Francisco), who calls herself a "disenfranchised (and fired) housewife" and disclaims being a writer, nevertheless wrote the essay that has become the feminist manifesto and is as widely reprinted as any other that graces the anthology circuit. Educated at the University of Iowa, where in 1962 she earned a B.F.A. in painting, she now lives and works as a secretary in San Francisco.

Preparing to Read This Selection Critically

The essay that follows, first published in 1970 when it was greeted as a feminist manifesto, achieves definition by indirection. The writer satirically depicts the perfect wife as one who is unstinting of herself and her energies, primarily for the benefit of a selfish, demanding husband. In case you might object that you know no such wife, remember that the writer was drawing, in broad strokes, the traditional definition of the wife as helpmate to the husband while at the same time registering her protests to the role as burdensome to women. Ask yourself whether you think her definition of this stereotypic wife still applies today. Or, have women since freed themselves from this oppressive role?

1   I belong to that classification of people known as wives. I am a Wife. And, not altogether incidentally, I am a mother.

Not too long ago a male friend of mine appeared on the scene 2
fresh from a recent divorce. He had one child, who is, of course,
with his ex-wife. He is obviously looking for another wife. As I
thought about him while I was ironing one evening, it suddenly
occurred to me that I, too, would like to have a wife. Why do I want
a wife?

I would like to go back to school so that I can become eco- 3
nomically independent, support myself, and, if need be, support
those dependent on me. I want a wife who will work and send me
to school. And while I am going to school I want a wife to take care
of my children. I want a wife to keep track of the children's doctor
and dentist appointments. And to keep track of mine, too. I want a
wife to make sure that my children eat properly and are kept clean.
I want a wife who will wash the children's clothes and keep them
mended. I want a wife who is a good nurturant attendant to my
children, who arranges for their schooling, makes sure they have
an adequate social life with their peers, takes them to the park, the
zoo, etc. I want a wife who takes care of the children when they
are sick, a wife who arranges to be around when the children need
special care, because, of course, I cannot miss classes at school. My
wife must arrange to lose time at work and not lose the job. It may
mean a small cut in my wife's income from time to time, but I guess
I can tolerate that. Needless to say, my wife will arrange and pay
for the care of the children while my wife is working.

I want a wife who will take care of *my* physical needs. I want 4
a wife who will keep the house clean. A wife who will pick up after
me. I want a wife who will keep my clothes clean, ironed, mended,
replaced when need be, and who will see to it that my personal
things are kept in their proper place so that I can find what I need
the minute I need it. I want a wife who cooks the meals, a wife who
is a *good* cook. I want a wife who will plan the menus, do the
necessary shopping, prepare the meals, serve them pleasantly, and
then do the cleaning up while I do my studying. I want a wife who
will care for me when I am sick and sympathize with my pain and
loss of time from school. I want a wife to go along when our family
takes a vacation so that someone can continue to care for me and
my children when I need a rest and change of scene.

I want a wife who will not bother me with rambling complaints 5
about a wife's duties. But I want a wife who will listen to me when
I feel the need to explain a rather difficult point I have come across

in my course of studies. And I want a wife who will type my papers for me when I have written them.

6   I want a wife who will take care of the details of my social life. When my wife and I are invited out by my friends, I want a wife who will take care of the babysitting arrangements. When I meet people at school that I like and want to entertain, I want a wife who will have the house clean, prepare a special meal, serve it to me and my friends, and not interrupt when I talk about the things that interest me and my friends. I want a wife who will have arranged that the children are fed and ready for bed before my guests arrive so that the children do not bother us. I want a wife who takes care of the needs of my guests so that they feel comfortable, who makes sure that they have an ashtray, that they are passed the hors d'oeuvres, that they are offered a second helping of the food, that their wine glasses are replenished when necessary, that their coffee is served to them as they like it.

7   And I want a wife who knows that sometimes I need a night out by myself.

8   I want a wife who is sensitive to my sexual needs, a wife who makes love passionately and eagerly when I feel like it, a wife who makes sure that I am satisfied. And, of course, I want a wife who will not demand sexual attention when I am not in the mood for it. I want a wife who assumes the complete responsibility for birth control, because I do not want more children. I want a wife who will remain sexually faithful to me so that I do not have to clutter up my intellectual life with jealousies. And I want a wife who understands that *my* sexual needs may entail more than strict adherence to monogamy. I must, after all, be able to relate to people as fully as possible.

9   If, by chance, I find another person more suitable as a wife than the wife I already have, I want the liberty to replace my present wife with another one. Naturally, I will expect a fresh, new life; my wife will take the children and be solely responsible for them so that I am left free.

10   When I am through with school and have a job, I want my wife to quit working and remain at home so that my wife can more fully and completely take care of a wife's duties.

11   My God, who *wouldn't* want a wife?

Thinking Critically About This Reading

1. This essay first appeared in the December 1971 issue of *MS* magazine. Are Syfers's criticisms still applicable to the conditions of

married women today, or have they become dated and inapplicable?

2. Based on your observations and experiences, what do you think is the worst feature about marriage? What do you think is the best?

3. Some have argued that the unrealistic expectations people bring to marriage are a major cause of the high divorce rate. Discuss your view on this issue.

4. By implication, what composite portrait does the author draw of the ideal husband?

5. Assuming you could have one, would you (man or woman) want to be married to a *wife* exactly like the one described in this essay? Why? Why not?

Understanding the Writer's Process

1. What is the overwhelming characteristic of the tone used throughout this essay?

2. What primary technique does the writer use in this essay to maintain focus and coherence?

3. Into what five areas does the author break down and describe the duties of the perfect wife? Why are these areas appropriate or inappropriate?

4. From whose viewpoint is this backhanded definition of a wife constructed? How can you tell?

5. Comment on the author's use of italics throughout this essay.

Examining the Writer's Language

1. Define the meanings of the following words as used in the context of this essay: nurturant (paragraph 3), adherence (8).

2. This essay was originally published in a popular women's magazine. What characteristics of its style and language identify it as written for a popular audience?

3. Nowhere in the essay does the writer use a pronoun to refer to the *wife* she wants. Why?   *Not feeding into stereotype*

4. What are the characteristics of most paragraphs in this essay? How do these paragraphs differ from those you are expected to write in class?

Suggestions for Writing

1. Write an essay defining the perfect mate as you envision him or her.

2. Imitating the author's presentation, write an essay on one of the following topics:

> I want a husband . . .
> I want a teacher . . .
> I want a boss . . .
> I want a job . . .
> I want an English class . . .

WHAT IS AN AMERICAN?

Michel-Guillaume Jean de Crèvecœur

> *Michel-Guillaume Jean de Crèvecœur (1735–1813), migrated as a young man to what was then the French colony of Louisiana in the New World. After fighting against the British in the French and Indian Wars (1756–63), he settled in New York as a farmer. Following the Revolutionary War, in which Crèvecœur fought on the side of the Loyalists, he returned permanently to France in 1790. The excerpt comes from his* Letters from an American Farmer, *written in French, and published in 1782.*

Preparing to Read This Selection Critically

Crèvecœur is more high–flown in expressing his opinions than we are accustomed to nowadays and, on first encounter, his style might strike the reader as bookish. Be prepared to read the excerpt slowly, then, and carefully, as you would the work of any ancient writer. Some parts of it will even require rereading. The aim of Crèvecœur is to praise his adopted America, but he describes a land so distant from us in time and development as to seem foreign. Nevertheless, the underlying principle of American life that Crèvecœur so lavishly praises—freedom for the individual—is one to which most Americans still theoretically subscribe.

I wish I could be acquainted with the feelings and thoughts   1
which must agitate the heart and present themselves to the mind
of an enlightened Englishman, when he first lands on this continent.
He must greatly rejoice, that he lived at a time to see this fair country
discovered and settled; he must necessarily feel a share of national
pride, when he views the chain of settlements which embellishes
these extended shores. When he says to himself, this is the work of
my countrymen, who, when convulsed by factions, afflicted by a
variety of miseries and wants, restless and impatient, took refuge
here. They brought along with them their national genius, to which
they principally owe what liberty they enjoy, and what substance
they possess. Here he sees the industry of his native country, displayed in a new manner, and traces in their works the embryos of
all the arts, sciences, and ingenuity which flourish in Europe. Here
he beholds fair cities, substantial villages, extensive fields, an immense country filled with decent houses, good roads, orchards,
meadows, and bridges, where an hundred years ago all was wild,
woody, and uncultivated!

What a train of pleasing ideas this fair spectacle must suggest!   2
It is a prospect which must inspire a good citizen with the most
heartfelt pleasure. The difficulty consists in the manner of viewing
so extensive a scene. He is arrived on a new continent; a modern
society offers itself to his contemplation, different from what he had
hitherto seen. It is not composed, as in Europe, of great lords who
possess every thing, and of a herd of people who have nothing.
Here are no aristocratical families, no courts, no kings, no bishops,
no ecclesiastical dominion, no invisible power giving to a few a very
visible one; no great manufacturers employing thousands, no great
refinements of luxury. The rich and the poor are not so far removed
from each other as they are in Europe.

Some few towns excepted, we are all tillers of the earth, from   3
Nova Scotia to West Florida. We are a people of cultivators, scattered
over an immense territory, communicating with each other by means
of good roads and navigable rivers, united by the silken bands of
mild government, all respecting the laws without dreading their
power, because they are equitable. We are all animated with the
spirit of industry, which is unfettered, and unrestrained, because
each person works for himself. If he travels through our rural

districts, he views not the hostile castle, and the haughty mansion, contrasted with the claybuilt hut and miserable cabin, where cattle and men help to keep each other warm, and dwell in meanness, smoke, and indigence. A pleasing uniformity of decent competence appears throughout our habitations. The meanest of our log-houses is a dry and comfortable habitation. Lawyer or merchant are the fairest titles our towns afford; that of a farmer is the only appellation of the rural inhabitants of our country. It must take some time ere he can reconcile himself to our dictionary, which is but short in words of dignity, and names of honour. There, on a Sunday, he sees a congregation of respectable farmers and their wives, all clad in neat homespun, well mounted, or riding in their own humble waggons. There is not among them an esquire, saving the unlettered magistrate. There he sees a parson as simple as his flock, a farmer who does not riot on the labour of others. We have no princes, for whom we toil, starve, and bleed: we are the most perfect society now existing in the world. Here man is free as he ought to be; nor is this pleasing equality so transitory as many others are. Many ages will not see the shores of our great lakes replenished with inland nations, nor the unknown bounds of North America entirely peopled. Who can tell how far it extends? Who can tell the millions of men whom it will feed and contain? for no European foot has as yet travelled half the extent of this mighty continent!

4   The next wish of this traveller will be to know whence came all these people? They are a mixture of English, Scotch, Irish, Dutch, Germans, and Swedes. From this promiscuous breed, the race now called Americans have arisen. The eastern provinces must indeed be excepted, as being the unmixed descendants of Englishmen. I have heard many wish they had been more intermixed also: for my part, I am no wisher; and think it much better as it has happened. They exhibit a most conspicuous figure in this great and variegated picture; they too enter for a great share in the pleasing perspective displayed in these thirteen provinces. I know it is fashionable to reflect on them; but I respect them for what they have done; for the accuracy and wisdom with which they have settled their territory; for the decency of their manners; for their early love of letters; their ancient college, the first in this hemisphere; for their industry, which to me, who am but a farmer, is the criterion of every thing. There never was a people, situated as they are, who, with so ungrateful a soil, have done more in so short a time. Do you think that the monarchical ingredients

which are more prevalent in other governments, have purged them from all foul stains? Their histories assert the contrary.

In this great American asylum, the poor of Europe have by some means met together, and in consequence of various causes; to what purpose should they ask one another, what countrymen they are? Alas, two thirds of them had no country. Can a wretch who wanders about, who works and starves, whose life is a continual scene of sore affliction of pinching penury; can that man call England or any other kingdom his country? A country that had no bread for him, whose fields procured him no harvest, who met with nothing but the frowns of the rich, the severity of the laws, with jails and punishments; who owned not a single foot of the extensive surface of this planet? No! Urged by a variety of motives, here they came. Everything has tended to regenerate them; new laws, a new mode of living, a new social system; here they are become men: in Europe they were as so many useless plants, wanting vegetative mould, and refreshing showers; they withered, and were mowed down by want, hunger, and war: but now, by the power of transplantation, like all other plants, they have taken root and flourished! Formerly they were not numbered in any civil list of their country, except in those of the poor; here they rank as citizens. By what invisible power has this surprising metamorphosis been performed? By that of the laws and that of their industry. The laws, the indulgent laws, protect them as they arrive, stamping on them the symbol of adoption; they receive ample rewards for their labours; these accumulated rewards procure them lands; those lands confer on them the title of freemen; and to that title every benefit is affixed which men can possibly require. This is the great operation daily performed by our laws. From whence proceed these laws? From our government. Whence that government? It is derived from the original genius and strong desire of the people, ratified and confirmed by government. This is the great chain which links us all, this is the picture which every province exhibits.

What attachment can a poor European emigrant have for a country where he had nothing? The knowledge of the language, the love of a few kindred as poor as himself, were the only cords that tied him: his country is now that which gives him land, bread, protection, and consequence: *Ubi panis ibi patria,*[1] is the motto of all emigrants. What then is the American, this new man? He is either

---

[1] Where there is bread there is my country.

an European, or the descendant of an European; hence that strange mixture of blood, which you will find in no other country. I could point out to you a man, whose grandfather was an Englishman, whose wife was Dutch, whose son married a French woman, and whose present four sons have now four wives of different nations. *He* is an American, who, leaving behind him all his ancient prejudices and manners, receives new ones from the new mode of life he has embraced, the new government he obeys, and the new rank he holds. He becomes an American by being received in the broad lap of our great *Alma Mater.*

7   Here individuals of all nations are melted into a new race of men, whose labours and posterity will one day cause great change in the world. Americans are the western pilgrims, who are carrying along with them that great mass of arts, sciences, vigour, and industry, which began long since in the east; they will finish the great circle. The Americans were once scattered all over Europe; here they are incorporated into one of the finest systems of population which has ever appeared, and which will hereafter become distinct by the power of the different climates they inhabit. The American ought, therefore, to love this country much better than that wherein either he or his forefathers were born. Here the rewards of his industry follow with equal steps the progress of his labour; his labour is founded on the basis of nature, *self-interest;* can it want a stronger allurement? Wives and children, who before in vain demanded of him a morsel of bread, now, fat and frolicsome, gladly help their father to clear those fields whence exuberant crops are to arise to feed and to clothe them all; without any part being claimed, either by a despotic prince, a rich abbot, or a mighty lord. Here religion demands but little of him; a small voluntary salary to the minister, and gratitude to God; can he refuse these? The American is a new man, who acts upon new principles; he must therefore entertain new ideas, and form new opinions. From involuntary idleness, servile dependence, penury, and useless labour, he has passed to toils of a very different nature, rewarded by ample subsistence.—This is an American.

Thinking Critically About This Reading

1. If Crèvecœur were alive today, what about modern America do you think he would find most astoundingly different from his day?

2. What do you think Crèvecœur would find the least changed about modern America?

3. Crèvecœur writes about eighteenth–century Americans: "We are all animated with the spirit of industry, which is unfettered, and unrestrained, because each person works for himself." Do you regard "industry" as still the animating spirit of America? If not, what do you think is the animating spirit uniting modern Americans?

4. Crèvecœur mentions the uninhabited vastness of the land with unknown bounds "entirely unpeopled." Now that the bounds are known and are everywhere peopled, what effect do you think this change has had on modern America?

5. Crèvecœur alleges that "industry" and "freedom" are the defining traits of an eighteenth–century American. What two traits do you regard as similarly definitive of a modern American?

Understanding the Writer's Process

1. Crèvecœur writes from the perspective of a newcomer from Europe visiting America for the first time. What are the advantages of using this viewpoint?

2. Aside from defining an American, what other rhetorical strategies does Crèvecœur draw on to enlighten his imaginary visitor about America?

3. A definition usually can be clarified not only by saying what a thing is, but also by asserting what it is *not*. What, according to Crèvecœur, is an American not?

4. Crèvecœur frequently uses rhetorical questions throughout his essay. What are some examples of this use and how effective is it?

5. From his arguments and the points he covers, what can you infer about the audience for whom Crèvecœur intended this letter?

Examining the Writer's Language

1. Define the meanings of the following words used in Crèvecœur's essay: ecclesiastical (paragraph 2), indigence (3), appellation (3), penury (5), metamorphosis (5), exuberant (7).

2. What would strike a modern reader as odd about the following sentence? "Here he beholds fair cities, substantial villages, extensive fields, an immense country filled with decent houses,

good roads, orchards, meadows, and bridges, where an hundred years ago all was wild, woody, and uncultivated!"

3. In the following sentence, what likely word would a modern writer use instead of "animated"? "We are all animated with the spirit of industry, which is unfettered, and unrestrained, because each person works for himself."

4. Crèvecœur writes: "From this promiscuous breed, the race now called Americans have risen." What is the meaning of "promiscuous" as Crèvecœur uses it in this sentence? What is the usual meaning of that word?

5. What does *Alma Mater* mean in the context of the following sentence? "He becomes American by being received in the broad lap of our great *Alma Mater*." What does the word usually mean?

Suggestions for Writing

1. Write an essay that defines the modern American.

2. Should all immigrants to America be forced to learn and speak English? Write an essay for or against this idea.

WE CAN CREATE A DECENT SOCIETY

James Michener

James Michener (b. 1907), popular American writer, was orphaned in New York City at birth and reared by adoptive parents in Doylestown, Pennsylvania, taking their surname as his own. As a young man, Michener rode boxcars and hitchhiked across America. He attended Swarthmore College and subsequently worked as an editor, teacher, and writer. Tales of the South Pacific (1948, Pulitzer Prize), his first novel, was based on his experiences in the Navy, in which he served during World War II, eventually attaining the rank of lieutenant commander. His other enormously popular novels include The Bridges at Toko–Ri (1953), The Source (1965), Centennial (1974),

Chesapeake *(1978),* Space *(1982),* Poland *(1983),* Texas *(1985),* Alaska *(1988), and* Caribbean *(1989).*

Preparing to Read This Selection Critically

In this personal political credo, writer James Michener tells us why he is a humanist and a liberal and, in the process, indirectly sketches a sharp definition of both terms. With the conservative temper of the times, neither designation is particularly popular, but Michener is unapologetic about what he believes. As you read, ask yourself whether your own political views differ significantly from Michener's. What do you think is the role of government in the individual's life? Do you think, as Michener alleges of former President Ronald Reagan, that the patriotism of the liberal is suspect? Where would you place yourself on the political spectrum, and why?

As I approached the age of 82, I was confronted by a savage   1
rejection of everything decent I had stood for. In the 1988 election, President Reagan announced that anyone who was a liberal—he used the phrase "the L word" as if it were fatally contaminated—was outside the mainstream of American life and intimated that the liberal's patriotism was suspect. Vice President Bush, seeking our highest office, went a lot farther by shouting that anyone who did not wish to recite the Pledge of Allegiance daily was probably false to the honored traditions of our nation; and his running mate, Senator Quayle, declared: "Michael Dukakis is a member of the American Civil Liberties Union, while George Bush is a member of the National Rifle Association," as if that made the former a loathsome traitor and the latter a great patriot. I found all this denigration of liberals personally offensive.

As I was being rejected from the mainstream of American life,   2
I stumbled into a situation which forced me to evaluate aspects of my political life. I was living in Florida so as to be near the Caribbean Sea, about which I was doing extensive research. Because I wanted to catch the flavor of the area, I not only read newspapers and watched television but also listened for the first time in my life to what is accurately termed "talk radio," keeping my set tuned permanently to a small station that provided a running report on topics

of real concern to the local citizens. What I learned from this listening was invaluable.

3   Tuesday and Wednesday nights were assigned to a soft–spoken, congenial, well–informed commentator who conducted a local call–in show that became a must for me because in it, he abused, vilified and scorned every noble cause to which I had devoted my entire life. It seemed to me he was against any law that sought to improve the lot of the poor, any tax that endeavored to improve the quality of our national life, any act in Congress that hoped to better the condition of the nation as a whole, any movement that tried to lessen police brutality, any bill that struggled to maintain a fair balance between the contending forces in our society, and any move to improve education, protect public health or strengthen the supervision of agencies running wild.

4   His scorn for all Democratic politicians was boundless, with Kennedy, McGovern, Carter, Mondale and Dukakis bearing the brunt of his vilification week after week. It seemed that he saw nothing wrong with Nixon, Ford, Bush or Quayle, while his admiration for Reagan verged on the worshipful. I could never quite determine what kind of government he was for, but at various intervals I guessed that what he really wanted was some version of either Robert Welch's United States, or Lyndon LaRouche's. It also seemed that if he had his way, blacks, women, children and the poor would suffer even worse constraints than they do at present, and that millionaires, tycoons, big businessmen and generals would prosper as never before. Every man in our public life whom I distrusted I heard him enshrine as a hero; and every cause for which I had worked he denigrated with a scorn that was brilliant, clever and heartless.

5   It was extremely fortunate that I had come upon him, because he possessed such a strong native intelligence that he made his positions almost palatable. Sometimes after I heard him sign off on midweek nights, I started my evening walk with considerable fear. "God, I hope no one who listens to his show and agrees with him knows that I'm a liberal, because if he did, he could shoot me . . . He's speaking about you, kiddo, and don't forget it."

6   These diatribes caused me to stop, take a long, hard look at myself and determine where I might possibly have gone wrong. As I engaged in this introspection, I learned one valuable trick: "Listen carefully to this fellow. Identify, specify what he's saying. Then adopt a position 180 degrees in the opposite direction, as far from

him as you can get, and you'll be on the right track." He forced me to define my beliefs and renew my opposition to all things I intuitively detested. Had he been a lamebrain or a mere ranter, I could have dismissed him; but because he was so able in his marshaling of facts, street rumors and inherited positions, such as a reverence for the Pledge of Allegiance and a maniacal hatred of the ACLU, I had to clarify my own thinking—and this confirmed who I was and what I believed.

I decided that I was both a humanist and a liberal, each of the   7 most dangerous and vilified type, and so I shall be increasingly until I die.

I am a humanist because I think humanity can, with constant   8 moral guidance, create reasonably decent societies. I think that young people who want to understand the world can profit from studying the works of Plato and Socrates, the austere analyses of Immanuel Kant, the behavior of the three Thomases—Aquinas, More and Jefferson—and the political leadership of Abraham Lincoln and Franklin Roosevelt. I like the educational theories of John Dewey and the pragmatism of William James. I am terrified of restrictive religious doctrine, having learned from history that when men who adhere to any form of it are in control, common men like me are in peril. I do not believe that pure reason can solve the perpetual problems unless it is modified by poetry and art and social vision.

In the later decades of my life, I have learned to be suspicious   9 of those well–meaning men who were noisy liberals or even Communists in their youth, only to become hard–edged and even savage right–wingers in their maturity, trampling upon the very flags under which they once had marched so proudly. I find such men abhorrent, never to be trusted; I do not associate with those among my acquaintances who have taken that craven course, because they are turncoats who will once again become liberals when the bankruptcy of their present allegiances becomes evident.

So I am a humanist. And if you want to charge me with being   10 the most virulent kind—a secular humanist—I accept the accusation, but I do not want to be accused of atheism. No man who loves the book of Deuteronomy and the first chapter of the General Epistle of St. James, as I do, can be totally anti–religious.

A charge that *can* be lodged against me is that I am a knee–   11 jerk liberal, for I confess to that sin. When I find that a widow has been left penniless and alone with three children, my knee jerks. When I learn that funds for a library have been diminished almost to the vanishing point, my knee jerks. When I find that a playground for children is being closed down while a bowling alley for grown men is being opened, my knee jerks. When men of ill intent out back on teachers' salaries and lunches for children, my knee jerks. When the free flow of ideas is restricted, when health services are denied to whole segments of the population, when universities double their fees, my knee jerks. When I hear that all the universities in Texas, combined, graduated two future teachers qualified to teach calculus but more than 500 trained to coach football, my knee jerks. And I hope never to grow so old or indifferent that I can listen to wrong and immoral choices being made without my knee flashing a warning.

12   Why does it jerk? To alert me that I have been passive and inattentive too long, to remind me that one of the noblest purposes for which human beings are put on earth is to strive to make their societies better, to see to it that gross inequalities are not perpetuated. And to halt them requires both effort and financial contributions, usually in the form of taxes. The best money I have spent in my life was not that used to make me either happier or more comfortable, but the taxes I have paid to the various governments under which I have lived. In general, governments have spent their share of my money more wisely and with better results than I have spent my own funds, and one aspect of my life about which I am most ashamed is that I spent most of a decade living in three states that had no state income tax—Texas, Florida and Alaska—and the deficiencies that the first two suffered because of that lack were evident daily. I like states like New York, Massachusetts and California, which do tax and spend their income wisely.

13   One of the sickest economic preachments has been the trickle–down theory: "If you allow the very rich to make as much money as they can without governmental restraint, they will magnanimously allow some of their largesse to trickle down to the peasants below." Most advocates of the theory do not express it in those blunt terms, but I have found that that is what they mean. I am not for across–the–board redistribution of wealth, and I know that wealthy people invest their money in enterprises that create employment, and I can cite a dozen other constructive uses of great wealth. But I still believe that society prospers most when there are laws to bring that wealth back into circulation, when there are taxes to provide social services that otherwise might not be available, when there is governmental surveillance to ensure proper business

practices and to prevent manipulation of financial markets, and when profits are plowed into research and the education of new generations.

When I have been dead 10 years and a family comes to tend 14 the flowers on the grave next to mine, and they talk about the latest pitiful inequity plaguing their town, they will hear a rattling from my grave and can properly say: "That's Jim again. His knee is still jerking."

Thinking Critically About This Reading

1. Michener labels himself a liberal and a humanist and tells us what he believes. By inference, what do conservatives—whose views Michener claims are in direct opposition to his own—believe?

2. Michener says that both President Ronald Reagan and George Bush questioned the patriotism of liberals during the 1988 presidential campaign. What is there about the beliefs and world view of liberals that would cause politicians to question their patriotism?

3. What is a secular humanist?

4. On which side of the political fence do you think Jesus Christ would be if he were alive today, based on his Biblical preachments? Why?

5. What is your definition of patriotism? Which of the two political factions, liberalism or conservatism, do you regard as more truly patriotic?

Understanding the Writer's Process

1. Michener mentions the talk radio host to whom he listened daily in Florida. What rhetorical function does this host play in this article?

2. Michener characterizes the conservative talk show host as "soft-spoken, congenial, well–informed" who was also "brilliant, clever, and heartless." Why do you think Michener is so temperate about one with whom he utterly disagrees?

3. Michener writes: "These diatribes caused me to stop, take a long, hard look at myself and determine where I might possibly have

gone wrong." How would you characterize the tone of this sentence?

4. In paragraph 7 Michener makes a blunt declaration of what he is and stands for. How does he add emphasis to his declaration?

5. What rhetorical technique does Michener use in paragraph 11 to emphasize what he believes?

Examining the Writer's Language

1. Define the meanings of the following words used in Michener's essay: denigration (paragraph 1), vilified (3), diatribes (6), introspection (6), abhorrent (9), craven (9), virulent (10), magnanimously (13), largesse (13).

2. Who are Robert Welch and Lyndon LaRouche (paragraph 4)? Look up these names and define them.

3. Michener admits that he is a "knee–jerk liberal." What is a knee–jerk liberal?

4. What is the American Civil Liberties Union to which Michael Dukakis was said to belong? What does this organization do and stand for?

5. What is the proper name for the "trickle–down" theory, and where did it come from?

Suggestions for Writing

1. Write an essay defining your own political beliefs.

2. In an essay, attack or defend the principles of liberalism as Michener explains them.

THE CONVERT

Lerone Bennett, Jr.

Lerone Bennett, Jr. (b. 1928, Clarksdale, Mississippi) is an editor of Ebony *magazine and a contributor of short stories, articles, and poems to many popular*

Booker, Booker ! If ya's a man, if ya's a father, if ya's a friend, go wit Aaron [handwritten]

periodicals. He was educated at Morehouse College (A.B. 1949) and did graduate work at Atlanta University. He is the author of many books—among them What Manner of Man: A Biography of Martin Luther King, Jr. (1964), The Challenge of Blackness (1972), and The Shaping of Black America (1975)— and is a member of the Board of Trustees of the Martin Luther King, Jr. Memorial Center.

"They say you are going to chicken out, Papa." [handwritten]

Preparing to Read This Selection Critically

Written from the viewpoint of a hapless black deacon, "The Convert" tells the moving story of a Mississippi minister during the early days of the Civil Rights struggle: Suddenly, and fatally, he resolves to stand up for his personal dignity and constitutional rights against an evil and intransigent system of segregation. In the process of the story, we not only learn about the narrator, we also are treated to the unremittingly harsh view of a society that existed in America little over a generation ago. What effect does the use of religious symbolism and imagery have on the telling of the story? Who has been converted, and to what?

A man don't know what he'll do, a man don't know what he is till he gets his back pressed up against a wall. Now you take Aaron Lott: there ain't no other way to explain the crazy thing he did. He was going along fine, preaching the gospel, saving souls, and getting along with the white folks; and then, all of a sudden, he felt wood pressing against his back. The funny thing was that nobody knew he was hurting till he preached that Red Sea sermon where he got mixed up and seemed to think Mississippi was Egypt. As chairman of the deacons board, I felt it was my duty to reason with him. I appreciated his position and told him so, but I didn't think it was right for him to push us all in a hole. The old fool—he just laughed. 1

"Brother Booker," he said, "the Lord—He'll take care of me." 2

I knew then that the man was heading for trouble. And the very next thing he did confirmed it.

He looked at me like I was Satan. 3

"I sweated over this thing," he said. "I prayed. I got down on my knees and I asked God not to give me this cup. But He said I was the one. I hear Him, Booker, right here"—he tapped his chest—"in my heart."

4   The old fool's been having visions, I thought. I sat down and tried to figure out a way to hold him, but he got up, without saying a word, and started for the door.

5   "Wait!" I shouted. "I'll get my coat."

"I don't need you," he said. "I just came by to tell you so you could tell the board in case something happened."

6   "You wait," I shouted, and ran out of the room to get my coat.

We got in his beat-up old Ford and went by the parsonage to get his suitcase. Rachel—that was his wife—and Jonah were sitting in the living room, wringing their hands. Aaron got his bag, shook Jonah's hand, and said, "Take care of your Mamma, boy." Jonah nodded. Aaron hugged Rachel and pecked at her cheek. Rachel broke down. She throwed her arms around his neck and carried on something awful. Aaron shoved her away.

7   "Don't go making no fuss over it, woman. I ain't gonna be gone forever. Can't a man go to a church meeting 'thout women screaming and crying."

8   He tried to make light of it, but you could see he was touched by the way his lips trembled. He held his hand out to me, but I wouldn't take it. I told him off good, told him it was a sin and a shame for a man of God to be carrying on like he was, worrying his wife and everything.

9   "I'm coming with you," I said. "Somebody's gotta see that you don't make a fool of yourself."

10   He shrugged, picked up his suitcase, and started for the door. Then he stopped and turned around and looked at his wife and his boy and from the way he looked I knew that there was still a chance. He looked at the one and then at the other. For a moment there, I thought he was going to cry, but he turned, quick-like, and walked out of the door.

11   I ran after him and tried to talk some sense in his head. But he shook me off, turned the corner, and went on up Adams Street. I caught up with him and we walked in silence, crossing the street in front of the First Baptist Church for whites, going on around the Confederate monument.

12   "Put it off, Aaron," I begged. "Sleep on it."

He didn't say nothing.

"What you need is a vacation. I'll get the board to approve, full pay and everything."

He smiled and shifted the suitcase over to his left hand. Big 13 drops of sweat were running down his face and spotting up his shirt. His eyes were awful, all lit up and burning.

"Aaron, Aaron, can't you hear me?"

We passed the feed store, Bill Williams' grocery store, and the movie house.

"A man's gotta think about his family, Aaron. A man ain't 14 free. Didn't you say that once, didn't you?"

He shaded his eyes with his hand and looked into the sun. He put the suitcase on the ground and checked his watch.

"Why don't you think about Jonah?" I asked. "Answer that. Why don't you think about your own son?"

"I am," he said. "That's exactly what I'm doing, thinking about 15 Jonah. Matter of fact, he started *me* to thinking. I ain't never mentioned it before, but the boy's been worrying me. One day he was downtown here and he asked me something that hurt. 'Daddy,' he said, 'how come you ain't a man?' I got mad, I did, and told him: 'I am a man.' He said that wasn't what he meant. 'I mean,' he said, 'how come you ain't a man where white folks concerned.' I couldn't answer him, Booker, I'll never forget it till the day I die. I couldn't answer my own son, and I been preaching forty years."

"He don't know nothing 'bout it," I said. "He's hot-headed, 16 like my boy. He'll find out when he grows up."

"I hopes not," Aaron said, shaking his head. "I hopes not."

Some white folks passed and we shut up till they were out of 17 hearing. Aaron, who was acting real strange, looked up in the sky and moved his lips. He came back to himself, after a little bit, and he said: "This thing of being a man, Booker, is a big thing. The Supreme Court can't make you a man. The NAACP can't do it. God Almighty can do a lot, but even He can't do it. Ain't nobody can do it but you."

He said that like he was preaching and when he got through 18 he was all filled up with emotion and he seemed kind of ashamed— he was a man who didn't like emotion outside the church. He looked at his watch, picked up his bag and said, "Well, let's git it over with."

We turned into Elm and the first thing I saw at the end of the 19 street was the train station. It was an old red building, flat like a slab. A group of white men were fooling around in front of the door.

Manhood - State or period of being an adult male, manly qualities of courage and fortitude.

I couldn't make them out from that distance, but I could tell they weren't the kind of white folks to be fooling around with.

20   We walked on, passing the dry goods store, the barber shop, and the new building that was going up. Across the street from that was the sheriff's office. I looked in the window and saw Bull Sampson sitting at his desk, his feet propped up on a chair, a fat brown cigar sticking out of his mouth. A ball about the size of a sweet potato started burning in my stomach.

21   "Please Aaron," I said. "Please. You can't get away with it. I know how you feel. Sometimes I feel the same way myself, but I wouldn't risk my neck for these niggers. They won't appreciate it; they'll laugh at you."

22   We were almost to the station and I could make out the faces of the men sitting on the benches. One of them must have been telling a joke. He finished and the group broke out laughing.

23   I whispered to Aaron: "I'm through with it. I wash my hands of the whole mess."

I don't know whether he heard me or not. He turned to the right without saying a word and went on in the front door. The string-beany man who told the joke was so shocked that his cigarette fell out of his mouth.

24   "Y'all see that," he said. "Why, I'll—"

"Shut up," another man said. "Go git Bull."

25   I kept walking fast, turned at the corner, and ran around to the colored waiting room. When I got there, I looked through the ticket window and saw Aaron standing in front of the clerk. Aaron stood there for a minute or more, but the clerk didn't see him. And that took some not seeing. In that room, Aaron Lott stood out like a pig in a chicken coop.

26   There were, I'd say, about ten or fifteen people in there, but didn't none of them move. They just sat there, with their eyes glued on Aaron's back. Aaron cleared his throat. The clerk didn't look up; he got real busy with some papers. Aaron cleared his throat again and opened his mouth to speak. The screen door of the waiting room opened and clattered shut.

27   It got real quiet in that room, hospital quiet. It got so quiet I could hear my own heart beating. Now Aaron knew who opened that door, but he didn't bat an eyelid. He turned around real slow and faced High Sheriff Sampson, the baddest man in South Mississippi.

Its more honorable to be a man in the eyes of justice, than in the eyes of society.

Mr. Sampson stood there with his legs wide open, like the men 28 you see on television. His beefy face was blood-red and his gray eyes were rattlesnake hard. He was mad; no doubt about it. I have never seen him so mad.

"Preacher," he said, "you done gone crazy?" He was talking lowlike and mean.

"Nosir," Aaron said. "Nosir, Mr. Sampson." 29

"What you think you doing?"

"Going to St. Louis, Mr. Sampson."

"You must done lost yo' mind, boy."

Mr. Sampson started walking towards Aaron with his hands 30 on his gun. Twenty or thirty men pushed through the front door and fanned out over the room. Mr. Sampson stopped about two paces from Aaron and looked him up and down. That look had paralyzed hundreds of niggers, but it didn't faze Aaron none—he stood his ground.

"I'm gonna give you a chance, preacher. Git on over to the 31 nigger side and git quick."

"I ain't bothering nobody, Mr. Sampson."

Somebody in the crowd yelled: "Don't reason wit' the nigger, Bull. Hit em."

Mr. Sampson walked up to Aaron and grabbed him in the 32 collar and throwed him up against the ticket counter. He pulled out his gun.

"Did you hear me, deacon. I said, 'Git.' "

"I'm going to St. Louis, Mr. Sampson. That's cross state lines. The court done said—"

Aaron didn't have a chance. The blow came from nowhere. 33 Laying there on the floor with blood spurting from his mouth, Aaron looked up at Mr. Sampson and he did another crazy thing: he grinned. Bull Sampson jumped up in the air and came down on Aaron with all his two hundred pounds. It made a crunchy sound. He jumped again and the mob, maddened by the blood and heat, moved in to help him. They fell on Aaron like mad dogs. They beat him with chairs; they beat him with sticks; they beat him with guns.

Till this day, I don't know what come over me. The first thing 34 I know I was running and then I was standing in the middle of the white waiting room. Mr. Sampson was the first to see me. He backed off, cocked his pistol, and said: "Booker, boy, you come one mo' step and I'll kill you. What's a matter with you niggers today? All y'all gone crazy?"

cover-up for society - help the problems get worse.

35   "Please don't kill him," I begged. "You ain't got no call to treat him like that."

"So you saw it all, did you? Well, then, Booker you musta saw the nigger preacher reach for my gun?"

"He didn't do that, Mr. Sampson," I said. "He didn't—"

36   Mr. Sampson put a big hairy hand on my tie and pulled me to him.

"Booker," he said sweetly. "You saw the preacher reach for my gun, didn't you?"

37   I didn't open my mouth—I couldn't I was so scared—but I guess my eyes answered for me. Whatever Mr. Sampson saw there musta convinced him 'cause he throwed me on the floor besides Aaron.

38   "Git this nigger out of here," he said, "and be quick about it."

Dropping to my knees, I put my hand on Aaron's chest; I didn't feel nothing. I felt his wrist; I didn't feel nothing. I got up and looked at them white folks with tears in my eyes. I looked at the women, sitting crying on the benches. I looked at the men. I looked at Mr. Sampson. I said, "He was a good man."

39   Mr. Sampson said, "Move the nigger."

A big sigh came out of me and I wrung my hands.

He grabbed my tie and twisted it, but I didn't feel nothing. My eyes were glued to his hands; there was blood under the fingernails, and the fingers—they looked like fat little red sausages. I screamed and Mr. Sampson flung me down on the floor.

He said, *"Move the nigger."*

40   I picked Aaron up and fixed his body over my shoulder and carried him outside. I sent for one of my boys and we dressed him up and put him away real nice-like and Rachel and the boy came and they cried and carried on and yet, somehow, they seemed prouder of Aaron than ever before. And the colored folks—they seemed proud, too. Crazy. Didn't they know? Couldn't they see? It hadn't done no good. In fact, things got worse. The Northern newspapers started kicking up a stink and Mr. Rivers, the solicitor, announced they were going to hold a hearing. All of a sudden, Booker Taliaferro Brown became the biggest man in that town. My phone rang day and night: I got threats, I got promises, and I was offered bribes. Everywhere I turned somebody was waiting to ask me: "Whatcha gonna do? Whatcha gonna say?" To tell the truth, I didn't know myself. One day I would decide one thing and the next day I would decide another.

It was Mr. Rivers and Mr. Sampson who called my attention   41
to that. They came to my office one day and called me a shifty, no-
good nigger. They said they expected me to stand by "my statement"
in the train station that I saw Aaron reach for the gun. I hadn't said
no such thing, but Mr. Sampson said I said it and he said he had
witnesses who heard me say it. "And if you say anything else," he
said, "I can't be responsible for your health. Now you know"—he
put that bloody hand on my shoulder and he smiled his sweet death
smile— "you *know* I wouldn't threaten you, but the boys"—he shook
his head—"the boys are real worked up over this one."

It was long about then that I began to hate Aaron Lott. I'm   42
ashamed to admit it now, but it's true: I hated him. He had lived
his life: he had made his choice. Why should he live my life, too,
and make me choose? It wasn't fair; it wasn't right; it wasn't Christian. What made me so mad was the fact that nothing I said would
help Aaron. He was dead and it wouldn't help one whit for me to
say that he didn't reach for that gun. I tried to explain that to Rachel
when she came to my office, moaning and crying, the night before
the hearing.

"Listen to me, woman," I said. "Listen, Aaron was a good   43
man. He lived a good life. He did a lot of good things, but he's *dead,
dead, dead!* Nothing I say will bring him back. Bull Sampson's got
ten niggers who are going to swear on a stack of Bibles that they
saw Aaron reach for that gun. It won't do me or you or Aaron no
good for me to swear otherwise."

What did I say that for? That woman like to had a fit. She got   44
down on her knees and she begged me to go with Aaron.

"Go wit' him," she cried. "Booker, *Booker!* If you's a man, if
you's a father, if you's a friend, go wit' Aaron."

That woman tore my heart up. I ain't never heard nobody beg
like that.

"Tell the truth, Booker," she said. "That's all I'm asking. Tell
the truth."

"Truth!" I said. "Hah! That's all you niggers talk about: truth.   45
What do you know about truth? Truth is eating good, and sleeping
good. Truth is living, Rachel. Be loyal to the living."

Rachel backed off from me. You would have thought that I   46
had cursed her or something. She didn't say nothing; she just stood
there pressed against the door. She stood there saying nothing for
so long that my nerves snapped.

"Say something," I shouted. "Say something—anything!"   47

She shook her head, slowly at first, and then her head started moving like it wasn't attached to her body. It went back and forth, back and forth, back and forth. I started towards her, but she jerked open the door and ran out into the night, screaming.

48   That did it. I ran across the room to the filing cabinet, opened the bottom drawer, and took out a dusty bottle of Scotch. I started drinking, but the more I drank the soberer I got. I guess I fell asleep 'cause I dreamed I buried Rachel and that everything went along fine until she jumped out of the casket and started screaming. I came awake with a start and knocked over the bottle. I reached for a rag and my hand stopped in mid-air.

49   "Of course," I said out loud and slammed my fist down on the Scotch-soaked papers.

I didn't see nothing.

Why didn't I think of it before?

I didn't see nothing.

50   Jumping up, I walked to and fro in the office. Would it work? I rehearsed it in my mind. All I could see was Aaron's back. I don't know whether he reached for the gun or not. All I know is that *for some reason* the men beat him to death.

51   Rehearsing the thing in my mind, I felt a great weight slip off my shoulders. I did a little jig in the middle of the floor and went upstairs to my bed, whistling. Sarah turned over and looked me up and down.

"What you happy about?"

"Can't a man be happy?" I asked.

52   She sniffed the air, said, "Oh," turned over, and mumbled something in her pillow. It came to me then for the first time that she was 'bout the only person in town who hadn't asked me what I was going to do. I thought about it for a little while, shrugged, and fell into bed with all my clothes on.

53   When I woke up the next morning, I had a terrible headache and my tongue was a piece of sandpaper. For a long while, I couldn't figure out what I was doing laying there with all my clothes on. Then it came to me: this was the big day. I put on my black silk suit, the one I wore for big funerals, and went downstairs to breakfast. I walked into the dining room without looking and bumped into Russell, the last person in the world I wanted to see. He was my only child, but he didn't act like it. He was always finding fault. He didn't like the way I talked to Negroes; he didn't like the way I talked to white folks. He didn't like this; he didn't like that. And

to top it off, the young whippersnapper wanted to be an artist. Undertaking wasn't good enough for him. He wanted to paint pictures.

I sat down and grunted. 54

"Good morning, Papa." He said it like he meant it. He wants something, I thought, looking him over closely, noticing that his right eye was swollen.

"You been fighting again, boy?"

"Yes, Papa."

"You younguns. Education—that's what it is. Education! It's ruining you."

He didn't say nothing. He just sat there, looking down when 55 I looked up and looking up when I looked down. This went on through the grits and the eggs and the second cup of coffee.

"Whatcha looking at?" I asked.

"Nothing, Papa."

"Whatcha thinking?"

"Nothing, Papa."

"You lying, boy. It's written all over your face."

He didn't say nothing.

I dismissed him with a wave of my hand, picked up the paper, 56 and turned to the sports page.

"What are you going to do, Papa?"

The question caught me unawares. I know now that I was 57 expecting it, that I wanted him to ask it; but he put it so bluntly that I was flabbergasted. I pretended I didn't understand.

"Do 'bout what, boy? Speak up!"

"About the trial, Papa."

I didn't say nothing for a long time. There wasn't much, in 58 fact, I could say; so I got mad.

"Questions, questions, questions," I shouted. "That's all I get 59 in this house—questions. You never have a civil word for your pa. I go out of here and work my tail off and you keep yourself shut up in that room of yours looking at them fool books and now soon as your old man gets his back against the wall you join the pack. I expected better than that of you, boy. A son ought to back his pa."

That hurt him. He picked up the coffee pot and poured himself 60 another cup of coffee and his hand trembled. He took a sip and watched me over the rim.

"They say you are going to chicken out, Papa."

"Chicken out? What that mean?"

A red man has courage and fortitude, not regrets and guilt.

"They're betting you'll 'Tom.' "

I leaned back in the chair and took a sip of coffee.

61 "So they're betting, huh?" The idea appealed to me. "Crazy— they'd bet on a funeral."

I saw pain on his face. He sighed and said: "I bet, too, Papa."

The cup fell out of my hand and broke, spilling black water over the tablecloth.

"You did what?"

"I bet you wouldn't 'Tom.' "

62 "You little fool." I fell out laughing and then I stopped suddenly and looked at him closely. "How much you bet?"

"One hundred dollars."

I stood up.

"You're lying," I said. "Where'd you get that kind of money?"

"From Mamma."

63 "Sarah!" I shouted. "Sarah! You get in here. What kind of house you running, sneaking behind my back, giving this boy money to gamble with?"

64 Sarah leaned against the door jamb. She was in her hot iron mood. There was no expression on her face. And her eyes were hard.

65 "I gave it to him, Booker," she said. "They called you an Uncle Tom. He got in a fight about it. He wanted to bet on you, Booker. *He* believes in you."

Suddenly I felt old and used up. I pulled a chair to me and sat down.

"Please," I said, waving my hand. "Please. Go away. Leave me alone. Please."

66 I sat there for maybe ten or fifteen minutes, thinking, praying. The phone rang. It was Mr. Withers, the president of the bank. I had put in for a loan and it had been turned down, but Mr. Withers said there'd been a mistake. "New fellow, you know," he said, clucking his tongue. He said he knew that it was my lifelong dream to build a modern funeral home and to buy a Cadillac hearse. He said he sympathized with that dream, supported it, thought the town needed it, and thought I deserved it. "The loan will go through," he said. "Drop by and see me this morning after the hearing."

67 When I put that phone down, it was wet with sweat. I couldn't turn that new funeral home down and Mr. Withers knew it. My father had raised me on that dream and before he died he made me swear on a Bible I would make it good. And here it was on a platter, just for a word, a word that wouldn't hurt nobody.

I put on my hat and hurried to the courthouse. When they   68
called my name, I walked in with my head held high. The courtroom
was packed. The white folks had all the seats and the colored folks
were standing in the rear. Whoever arranged the seating had set
aside the first two rows for white men. They were sitting almost on
top of each other, looking mean and uncomfortable in their best
white shirts.

I walked up to the bench and swore on the Bible and took a   69
seat. Mr. Rivers gave me a little smile and waited for me to get
myself set.

"State your name," he said.

"Booker Taliaferro Brown." I took a quick look at the first two   70
rows and recognized at least ten of the men who killed Aaron.

"And your age?"

"Fifty-seven."

"You're an undertaker?"

"Yessir."

"You been living in this town all your life?"

"Yessir."

"You like it here, don't you, Booker?"

Was this a threat? I looked Mr. Rivers in the face for the first   71
time. He smiled.

I told the truth. I said, "Yessir."

"Now, calling your attention to the day of May 17th, did any-   72
thing unusual happen on that day?"

The question threw me. I shook my head. Then it dawned on   73
me. He was talking about—

"Yessir," I said. "That's the day Aaron got—" Something in
Mr. Rivers' face warned me and I pulled up—"that's the day of the
trouble at the train station."

Mr. Rivers smiled. He looked like a trainer who'd just put a   74
monkey through a new trick. You could feel the confidence and the
contempt oozing out of him. I looked at his prissy little mustache
and his smiling lips and I got mad. Lifting my head a little bit, I
looked him full in the eyes: I held the eyes for a moment and I tried
to tell the man behind the eyes that I was a man like him and that
he didn't have no right to be using me and laughing about it. But
he didn't get the message. He chuckled softly, turned his back on
me, and faced the audience.

"I believe you were with the preacher that day."   75

The water was getting deep. I scroonched down in my seat, closed the lids of my eyes, and looked dense.

76   "Yessir, Mr. Rivers," I drawled. "Ah was, Ah was."

"Now Booker—" he turned around—"I believe you tried to keep the nigger preacher from getting out of line."

I hesitated. It wasn't a fair question. Finally, I said: "Yessir."

"You begged him not to go to the white side?"

"Yessir."

77   "And when that failed, you went over to *your* side—the *colored* side—and looked through the window?"

"Yessir."

He put his hand in his coat pocket and studied my face.

"You saw *everything*, didn't you?"

"Just about." A muscle on the inside of my thigh started tingling.

78   Mr. Rivers shuffled some papers he had in his hand. He seemed to be thinking real hard. I pushed myself against the back of the chair. Mr. Rivers moved close, quick, and stabbed his finger into my chest.

"Booker, did you see the nigger preacher reach for Mr. Sampson's gun?"

79   He backed away, smiling. I looked away from him and I felt my heart trying to tear out of my skin. I looked out over the courtroom. It was still: wasn't even a fly moving. I looked at the white folks in front and the colored folks in back and I turned the question over in my mind. While I was doing that, waiting, taking my time, I noticed, out of the corner of my eye, that the smile on Mr. Rivers' face was dying away. Suddenly, I had a terrible itch to know what that smile would turn into.

80   I said, "Nosir."

Mr. Rivers stumbled backwards like he had been shot. Old Judge Sloan took off his glasses and pushed his head out over the bench. The whole courtroom seemed to be leaning in to me and I saw Aaron's widow leaning back with her eyes closed and it seemed to me at that distance that her lips were moving in prayer.

81   Mr. Rivers was the first to recover. He put his smile back on and he acted like my answer was in the script.

"You mean," he said, "that you didn't see it. It happened so quickly that you missed it?"

82   I looked at the bait and I ain't gonna lie: I was tempted. He knew as well as I did what I meant, but he was gambling on my

weakness. I had thrown away my funeral home, my hearse, everything I owned, and he was standing there like a magician, pulling them out of a hat, one at a time, dangling them, saying: "Looka here, looka here, don't they look pretty?" I was on top of a house and he was betting that if he gave me a ladder I would come down. He was wrong, but you can't fault him for trying. I looked him in the eye and went the last mile.

"Aaron didn't reach for that gun," I said. "Them people, they just fell on—"   83

"Hold it," he shouted. "I want to remind you that there are laws in this state against perjury. You can go to jail for five years for what you just said. Now I know you've been conferring with those NAACP fellows, but I want to remind you of the statements you made to Sheriff Sampson and me. Judge—" he dismissed me with a wave of his hand—"Judge, this *man*—" he caught himself and it was my turn to smile—"this *boy* is lying. Ten niggers have testified that they saw the preacher reach for the gun. Twenty white people saw it. You've heard their testimony. I want to withdraw this witness and I want to reserve the right to file perjury charges against him."   84

Judge Sloan nodded. He pushed his bottom lip over his top one.   85

"You can step down," he said. "I want to warn you that perjury is a very grave offense. You—"

"Judge, I didn't—"

"Nigger!" He banged his gavel. "Don't you interrupt me. Now git out of here."

Two guards pushed me outside and waved away the reporters. Billy Giles, Mr. Sampson's assistant, came out and told me Mr. Sampson wanted me out of town before sundown. "And he says you'd better get out before the Northern reporters leave. He won't be responsible for your safety after that."   86

I nodded and went on down the stairs and started out the door.

"Booker!"

Rachel and a whole line of Negroes were running down the stairs. I stepped outside and waited for them. Rachel ran up and throwed her arms around me. "It don't take but one, Booker," she said. "It don't take but one." Somebody else said: "They whitewashed it, they whitewashed it, but you spoiled it for 'em."   87

Russell came out then and stood over to the side while the others crowded around to shake my hands. Then the others sensed that he was waiting and they made a little aisle. He walked up to   88

me kind of slow-like and he said, "Thank you, sir." That was the
first time in his whole seventeen years that that boy had said "sir"
to me. I cleared my throat and when I opened my eyes Sarah was
standing beside me. She didn't say nothing; she just put her hand
in mine and stood there. It was long about then, I guess, when I
realized that I wasn't seeing so good. They say I cried, but I don't
believe a word of it. It was such a hot day and the sun was shining
so bright that the sweat rolling down my face blinded me. I wiped
the sweat out of my eyes and some more people came up and said
a lot of foolish things about me showing the white folks and following in Aaron's footsteps. I wasn't doing no such fool thing. Ol'
Man Rivers just put the thing to me in a way it hadn't been put
before—man to man. It was simple, really. Any man would have
done it.

Thinking Critically About This Reading

1. What was Aaron Lott's motive in staging the protest that resulted
   in his murder? Given his background and obvious community
   standing, do you think the motive was sufficiently strong to cause
   him to behave as he did?

2. The narrator mentions that several onlookers, men as well as
   women, witnessed the murder of Aaron Lott at the railway station
   but did nothing to stop it or to testify about it. How do you
   account for such passivity in the face of a brutal murder?

3. What is the civic responsibility of one who lives under an evil
   system that enjoys popular support?

4. What finally convinces the narrator to tell the truth at the hearing?

5. The story ends on an indeterminate note. What do you think
   happened to the narrator and his family after the hearing?

Understanding the Writer's Process

1. The story is written in the first person. Why is this point of view
   particularly suited to this story? What kind of information does
   the first person allow the author to convey efficiently that he
   might not otherwise have been able to do?

2. Early in the story we learn that Aaron Lott is a minister and that
   the narrator is the chairman of the deacons' board of Lott's church.

What is the effect of this information on the reader? How does this information predispose the reader toward the characters?

3. What definition of *manhood* is implicit in this story? In the context of the story, what meaning does *boy* have?
4. What thematic relationship links the beginning of this story with its ending?
5. How is the title of this story related to its theme? Who becomes converted and to what? From what is he or are they converted?

Examining the Writer's Language

1. In paragraph 1, the narrator says that Aaron Lott "felt wood pressing against his back." What does this metaphor mean?
2. Aaron says, in paragraph 3, "I sweated over this thing. I prayed. I got down on my knees and I asked God not to give me this cup. But He said I was the one." What is the meaning of the allusion to the cup?
3. *Verisimilitude* is defined as "the appearance or semblance of truth and actuality"; it means the degree to which a writer creates the appearance of truth. What techniques of language does the writer use to endow his narrator with verisimilitude?
4. How does the narrator foreshadow the martyrdom of Aaron Lott?
5. Throughout the story, the narrator uses the word *nigger* several times as does the Sheriff, the Solicitor, and the Judge. What is the difference in the connotation of that word when used by the narrator and by these other characters?

Writing Assignment Based on "The Convert"

"The Convert" is a story about prejudice. What does *prejudice* mean? Write an essay in which you carefully define this term.

STUDENT ESSAY (IN PROCESS) DEFINITION

Christine Levey

Christine Levey, in her first year of college, recently graduated from high school, where she was an excellent student. In her junior year, she hopes to transfer to Westmont College in California to major in education; Christine wants to become a teacher. At present, she is intensely involved in the Presbyterian Church and in community work.

First Draft   Christine Levey

Eng. 101

(handwritten: Begin with a description of whites beating blacks in Queens in Dec. of 1986.)

What Is Racial Prejudice?

Prejudice of any kind—whether ~~it be~~ directed ~~to~~ *(toward)* food, occupation, nation, or race—implies a preconceived and unreasonable judgment or opinion, usually ~~an~~ unfavorable ~~one~~, *(handwritten: wordy)* marked by suspicion, fear, intolerance, or even hatred. The term prejudice ~~is~~ derived from the Latin praejudicium, formed from prae, meaning "before" and judicium, meaning "judgment." *(handwritten: In other words, judgment is rendered before all the facts are known.)* ~~/People~~ People in general tend to consider their *(handwritten: So?)* personal appearance and behavior as normal as well as desirable. ~~However~~, when they encounter *(handwritten: or act)* other people who do not look the way they do or act differently, distrust and fear *(handwritten: Better parallelism)* are bred, especially if the contrasts are obvious—such as skin color, ~~the~~ shape ~~of the eyes~~, or religion ~~choice~~. The evil aspect of prejudice is that it encourages discrimination, *(handwritten: sharper word)* racism, and segregation. If allowed to spread, it inevitably becomes a ~~massive~~ *(malignant)* tumor on the vital organs of society.

The historical chronicle of prejudice reaches back two thousand years, to the time of ancient Greeks and Romans, who enslaved all

foreigners ~~they~~ considered inferior to them-

selves. When the modern Jewish nation was

formed in 1917, it believed itself to be

superior to other nations because, according

to the ~~Jewish~~ Torah, the Jews were God's chosen

people; thus, they tended to look down on all

gentiles, especially Arabs, as children of a

lesser god. In retaliation for what was consi-

dered Jewish arrogance, gentile nations over

the last several decades have persecuted Jews

for their way of life and religious beliefs. ~~In~~

~~addition,~~ the Chinese regarded Westerners as

"hairy white barbarians" even hundreds of

years after Marco Polo's journey to China.

~~Much later in history,~~ slavery became a

way of life in the southern United States from

the 17th to the middle of the 19th century, as

white citizens enslaved blacks, whom they

often considered little better than beasts of

burden. The slaves were eventually freed dur-

ing the Civil War; however, segregation and

discrimination ~~followed~~. To help bring an end

to this inhumane tradition of prejudice, the

U.S. government eventually passed laws in the

1950's, designed to give blacks the same oppor-

tunities as whites—to have an equal education,

to compete for equal jobs, and to live in equal

neighborhoods. Nonetheless, despite these

measures, the United States today still faces

severe racial problems, exacerbated by con-

tinuous implicit or explicit prejudice.

[Handwritten marginal annotations: "Better transition needed to indicate the passage of time"; "self-evident"; "many centuries later,"; "Transition is too abrupt"; "The Far East, too, has contributed its share of pre-judice to the world."; "For instance,"; "One of the most shameful epochs of prejudice involved our own country."; "better topic sentence"; "give specific examples (buses, restaurants, housing)"; "lingered on"]

Perhaps the worst kind of prejudice is the kind that leads to genocide, the mass murder of an entire race or culture. The most tragic example of attempted genocide is Adolf Hitler's "final solution," a cruel euphemism for his coldblooded plan to eradicate all Jews during World War II. With an obsessive arrogance Hitler proclaimed that Germans were a part of the "superior Nordic race" and that Jews were utterly inferior—so inferiour that they did not deserve to live on this earth. As a result of this proclamation, six million Jews were rounded up like cattle, left to rot in concentration camps, or marched off to gas chambers where they were efficiently murdered.

Conclusion.

↳ Any country claiming to be civilized has no business harboring feelings of racial prejudice, no matter how subtle. A truly human society willingly tolerates racial, national, and religious variety.

Final Draft
Christine Levey
Eng. 101

What Is Racial Prejudice?

Outside the little cafe, with its red neon sign blinking the words "New Park Pizzeria," a police car stands guard while other heavily-armed squad cars patrol the streets of Howard Beach, a New York neighborhood of well-manicured homes still filled with Christmas decorations. This is New Year's Eve, 1986. The atmosphere is full of terror because a few days earlier three black youths were beaten and clubbed outside the pizza parlor by a hysterical white teen–age mob armed with baseball bats and tree limbs. One of the victims, Michael Griffin, was struck by a car as he was fleeing his attackers. The cause of so much chaos and terror? Racial prejudice.

Prejudice of any kind—whether directed toward food, occupation, nation, or race—implies a preconceived and unreasonable judgment or opinion, usually unfavorable, marked by suspicion, fear, intolerance, or even hatred. The term prejudice derives from the Latin praejudicium, formed from prae, meaning "before," and judicium, meaning "judgment." In other words, judgment is rendered before all the facts are known. People in general tend to consider their personal appearance and behavior as normal as well as desirable. However, when they encounter other people who do not look or act the way they do, distrust and fear are bred, especially if the contrasts are obvious—such as skin color, eye shape, or religion. The evil aspect of prejudice is that it encourages discrimination, racism, and segregation. If allowed to spread, it inevitably becomes a malignant tumor on the vital organs of society.

The historical chronicle of prejudice reaches back two thousand years, to the time of ancient Greeks and Romans, who enslaved all

foreigners considered inferior to themselves.
Many centuries later, when the modern Jewish
nation was formed in 1917, it believed itself
to be superior to other nations because, according to the Torah, the Jews were God's chosen people; thus, they tended to look down on
all gentiles, especially Arabs, as children of
a lesser god. In retaliation for what was considered Jewish arrogance, gentile nations over
the last several decades have persecuted Jews
for their way of life and religious beliefs.
The Far East, too, has contributed its share of
prejudice to the world. For instance, the
Chinese regarded Westerners as "hairy white
barbarians" even hundreds of years after Marco
Polo's journey to China.

One of the most shameful epochs of prejudice involves our own country. Slavery became a way of life in the southern United States
from the 17th to the middle of the 19th century,
as white citizens enslaved blacks, whom they
often considered little better than beasts of
burden. Tired pregnant women were pushed to the
back of public buses; thirsty farm hands were
forced to wait in line to drink from their own
"black" water fountains; and hundreds of black
families lived in shamefully run-down shacks
in black shanty towns. The slaves were eventually freed during the Civil War; however,
segregation and discrimination lingered on. To
help bring an end to this inhumane tradition of
prejudice, the U.S. government eventually
passed laws in the 1950's, designed to give

blacks the same opportunities as whites—to have an equal education, to compete for equal jobs, and to live in equal neighborhoods. Nonetheless, despite these measures, the United States today still faces severe racial problems, exacerbated by continuous implicit or explicit prejudice.

Perhaps the worst kind of prejudice is the kind that leads to genocide, the mass murder of an entire race or culture. The most tragic example of attempted genocide is Adolf Hitler's "final solution," a cruel euphemism for his coldblooded plan to eradicate all Jews during World War II. With an obsessive arrogance Hitler proclaimed that Germans were a part of the "superior Nordic race" and that Jews were utterly inferior—so inferior that they did not deserve to live on this earth. As a result of this proclamation, six million Jews were rounded up like cattle, left to rot in concentration camps, or marched off to gas chambers where they were efficiently murdered.

Any country claiming to be civilized has no business harboring feelings of racial prejudice, no matter how subtle. A truly humane society willingly tolerates racial, national, and religious variety.

IN THE HOUSEPLANT CEMETERY

INHERITED WHEN
ROOMMATE MOVED
6/5/81
BOUGHT THE FARM
6/30/81

WON AS DOOR PRIZE
10/6/75
MET ITS MAKER
5/12/76

BOUGHT ON IMPULSE
5/19/88
BIT THE DUST
10/4/88

RECEIVED AS
GIFT
11/14/79
KICKED BUCKET
7/3/80

LEFT BY COLLEGE-BOUND
DAUGHTER
9/8/79
TOOK THE BIG RIDE
1/29/82

R. Chast

Drawing by R. Chast; © 1991 The New Yorker Magazine, Inc.

5

Using Examples

HOW TO WRITE WITH EXAMPLES

Primarily of two types, the example is a kind of specific detail used to support a writer's claims. First, there is the brief example, mentioned in passing, that adds a dollop of fact and substance to a writer's opinion. Consider this paragraph:

> "Women's language" shows up in all levels of English. For example, women are encouraged and allowed to make far more precise discriminations in naming colors than men do. Words like "mauve, beige, ecru, aquamarine, lavender" and so on, are unremarkable in a woman's active vocabulary, but largely absent from that of most men. I know of no evidence suggesting that women actually see a wider range of colors than men do. It is simply that fine discriminations of this sort are relevant to women's vocabularies, but not to men's; to men, who control most of the interesting affairs of the world, such distinctions are trivial—irrelevant.
>
> ROBIN LAKOFF, *"Women's Language"*

The example is brief, to the point, and gives instances of the kinds of color words women routinely use but men don't.

Second, there is the extended example that consumes entire paragraphs or more in pursuit of explanation. Here is such a case:

> Sometimes a writer will contradict what he has already written, and in that case the only thing to do is to investigate what has changed his point of view. For instance, in 1608 Captain John Smith issued a description of his capture by Powhatan, and he made it clear that the Indian chief had treated him with unwavering courtesy and hospitality. In 1624 the story was repeated in Smith's *General History of Virginia*, but the writer's circumstances had changed. Smith needed money, "having a prince's mind imprisoned in a poor man's purse," and he wanted the book to be profitable. Powhatan's daughter, the princess Pocahontas, had recently been in the news, for her visit to England had aroused a great deal of interest among the sort of people that Smith hoped would buy his book. So Smith supplied a new version of the story, in which the once-hospitable Powhatan would have permitted the hero's brains to be dashed out if Pocahontas had not saved his life. It was the second story that achieved fame, and of course it may have been true. But it is impossible to trust it because the desire of the writer is so obviously involved; as Smith said in his pros-

pectus, he needed money and hoped that the book would give "satisfaction."

MARCHETTE CHUTE, *"Getting at the Truth"*

Most of the paragraph is an extended example that amply supports the topic sentence: "Sometimes a writer will contradict what he has already written, and in that case the only thing to do is to investigate what has changed his point of view."

Examples of either kind are used mainly to support generalizations or claims made by a writer about a group, a trend, or a type. But not every assertion or opinion a writer makes needs to be propped up by an example. Modest statements of indisputable fact can stand uncontested or be elaborated on without the formal underpinning of an example. Here the phrase "for instance" is inappropriate because no example follows, only elaboration.

> Without a knowledge of mythology, much of the best literature of our English language cannot be understood. For instance, it cannot be appreciated fully.

Yet "it cannot be appreciated fully" is not really an example, but merely an additional statement of fact. To be an example, the cited material must be a fairly detailed and representative instance that supports the writer's view. Examples should always be smaller assertions than the statement they are intended to support. Nor will writing "for example" before an assertion automatically make it an example.

When to cite or not to cite an example is a judgment call for every writer. A rule of thumb is that you should give examples whenever making some fairly broad claim or asserting a generality about a type, trend, or group. So if you wrote, "Hot dogs are bad for my digestion," that statement will need elaboration but not necessarily in the form of an extended example. You might go on to state, "They often contain heavy starches and artificial flavorings." On the other hand, if you asserted, "Many fast foods are innately unhealthy," that is a generalization about a group—fast foods—and should be supported by examples. Perhaps, "For instance, hot dogs are known to cause digestive problems in the elderly and potato chips are loaded with cholesterol. . . ." Similarly, in the preceding extract the writer's topic sentence made this rather general claim: "Sometimes a writer will contradict what he has already written, and in that case the only thing to do is to investigate what has changed his point of view." This claim is broad enough to require support by example and should be worded so that the reader immediately wonders: Really? How do writers sometimes contradict what they have already written? And so the stage is set for an example.

1. Vary the Introductions to Your Examples

Many writers will automatically write "for example" every time they give an example; although a perfectly useful and handy prefatory remark, overuse makes it predictable and drab. By varying your introductions, you can present your examples with occasional flair and wit. A case in point is John Taylor's essay, "Don't Blame Me." He introduces one example by simply writing, "Take the frat–house drug busts in March at the University of Virginia" (paragraph 6). Later, he introduces another example more formally with, "To give but one example . . ." (paragraph 8). Others essayists in this chapter are equally ingenious. In "Advertisements for Oneself," the author introduces examples variously: "Sometimes the ads are quirkily self–conscious" (paragraph 3); "Humor helps, especially in the form that usually gives off the flat glare of . . ." (paragraph 6), which is followed by quotations from humorous ads. Often no prefatory remark is even necessary, especially when it is contextually clear that the material to follow is an example. Reading "Don't Blame Me" provides many instances of examples that are not formally introduced.

Of course, the point is not to quibble about how an example may be introduced, but merely to suggest alternatives to the cut-and-dried "for example" that most of us immediately think of. So if you can, vary the introductions to your examples; more importantly, however, use examples that are always enlightening and appropriate.

2. Give Appropriate Examples Only

The example itself is not a point, but a series of facts or an anecdote quoted in support of a point. And it should always directly and palpably support the point you are making. In selecting examples, use common sense. Basically, any cited example should be both appropriate to your point and representative of it. So, if you are writing an essay about the hardships to which dorm students are subjected, an example of your mother's unreasonable restrictions on dating will not support that point since your mother regulates *your* behavior only. However, if the plumbing is always clogging up or the furnace always conking out, you can comfortably cite such failures as typical examples of the hardships suffered in your dorm.

3. Find Your Examples Before You Begin Writing

If you know your subject extraordinarily well, this advice is not for you, since examples and facts about it are on the tip of your pen. But most of us are often called on to write about subjects we know only casually and must learn about through research. In such cases, examples ordinarily are found in the preparatory legwork a writer must complete before actually beginning to write. Examples accumulate in the notes and jottings a writer makes during preliminary reading and research. If you neglect such preliminaries and still expect examples to pop into your head while scribbling at your desk, chances are excellent that none will appear. The writer who wails, "I can't think of anything to say," is actually saying, "I don't know enough about this subject." Make it a point to know enough about your subject and you will rarely find yourself in that unhappy predicament. Do your homework on the subject, familiarize yourself with the literature written about it, and you will almost always enjoy an abundant stock of useful quotable examples at your fingertips.

ADVERTISEMENTS FOR ONESELF

Lance Morrow

Lance Morrow (b. 1944), a senior writer for Time, *is a regular contributor to the personal essay feature of the magazine. He is, as well, the author of* Minnesota, a State That Works *(1973).*

Preparing to Read This Selection Critically

Personal ads, commonly found in a wide-ranging list of periodicals, sing the praises of the lonely urban individual who is eager, desperate even, for a companion. Lance Morrow gives us a sampling of such ads, lamenting their popularity and sad usefulness in our time. Note that most of Morrow's examples are drawn from New York publications, some of which you may not know and might wish to look up. As you read, ask yourself if Morrow is describing a northeastern phenomenon or whether this courtship ritual also exists in your particular city or town. Assuming that you do not live in New York, how different do you think similar personals might be worded if written by someone from your hometown? What traits and characteristics would they especially tout?

1   It is an odd and compact art form, and somewhat unnatural. A person feels uncomfortable composing a little song of himself for the classifieds. The personal ad is like haiku of self-celebration, a brief solo played on one's own horn. Someone else should be saying these things. It is for others to pile up the extravagant adjectives ("sensitive, warm, witty, vibrant, successful, handsome, accomplished, incredibly beautiful, cerebral and sultry") while we stand demurely by. But someone has to do it. One competes for attention. One must advertise. One must chum the waters and bait the hook, and go trolling for love and laughter, for caring and sharing, for long walks and quiet talks, for Bach and Brie. Nonsmokers only. Photo a must.

2   There are poetic conventions and clichés and codes in composing a personal ad. One specifies DWF (divorced white female), SBM (single black male), GWM (gay white male) and so on, to describe marital status, race, sex. Readers should understand the euphemisms. "Zaftig" or "Rubenesque," for example, usually means fat. "Unpretentious" is liable to mean boring. "Sensuous" means the party likes sex.

3   Sometimes the ads are quirkily self-conscious. "Ahem," began one suitor in the *New York Review of Books.* "Decent, soft-spoken sort, sanely silly, philosophish, seeks similar." Then he started to hit his stride: "Central Jersey DM WASP professional, 38, 6'2", slow hands, student of movies and Marx, gnosis and news, craves womanish companionship. . . ."

4   The sociology of personals has changed in recent years. One reason that people still feel uncomfortable with the form is that during the '60s and early '70s, personal ads had a slightly sleazy

connotation. They showed up in the back of underground news-papers and sex magazines, the little billboards through which wife swappers and odd sexual specialists communicated. In the past few years, however, personal ads have become a popular and reputable way of shopping for new relationships. The Chicago *Tribune* pub-lishes them. So does the conservative *National Review*, although a note from the publisher advises, "*NR* extends maximum freedom in this column, but *NR's* maximum freedom may be another man's straitjacket. *NR* reserves the right to reject any copy deemed un-suitable." *NR* would likely have turned down a West Coast entreaty: "Kinky Boy Scout seeks Kinky Girl Scout to practice knots. Your rope or mine?" *NR's* personals are notably chaste, but so are those in most other magazines. The emphasis is on "traditional values," on "long-term relationships" and "nest building." The sexual rev-olution has cooled down to a domestic room temperature. The raciest item might call for a woman with "Dolly Parton-like figure." One ad in Los Angeles stated: "Branflake patent holder tired of money and what it can buy seeks intellectual stimulation from big-bosomed brunette. Photo please." The *Village Voice* not long ago rejected the language of a man who wanted a woman with a "big ass." A few days later the man returned with an ad saying he sought a "calli-pygian" woman.

Every week *New York* magazine publishes five or six pages of personals, at $23 a line. The *New York Review of Books* publishes column after column of some of the most entertaining personals. Many of them are suffused with a soft-focus romanticism. Firelight plays over the fantasy. Everyone seems amazingly successful. The columns are populated by Ph.D.s. Sometimes one encounters a mil-lionaire. Occasionally a satirical wit breaks the monotony: "I am DWM, wino, no teeth, smell bad, age 40—look 75. Live in good cardboard box in low-traffic alley. You are under 25, tall, sophisti-cated, beautiful, talented, financially secure, and want more out of life. Come fly with me."

Humor helps, especially in a form that usually gives off a flat glare of one-dimensional optimism. It is hard not to like the "well read, well shaped, well disposed widow, early sixties, not half bad in the dusk with the light behind me." She sought a "companion-able, educated, professional man of wit and taste," and she probably deserved him. Her self-effacement is fairly rare in personals. The ads tend sometimes to be a little nervous and needing, and anxiously hyperbolic. Their rhetoric tends to get overheated and may produce unintended effects. A man's hair stands on end a bit when he encounters "Alarmingly articulate, incorrigibly witty, overeducated but extremely attractive NYC woman." A female reader of *New York* might enjoy a chuckling little shudder at this: "I am here! A caring, knowing, daffy, real, tough, vulnerable and handsome brown-eyed psychoanalyst." One conjures up the patient on the couch and a Freudian in the shape of Daffy Duck shouting: "You're desPICable!"

7   The struggle in composing one's ad is to be distinctive and relentlessly self-confident. What woman could resist the "rugged rascal with masculine determined sensual viewpoint"? An ad should not overreach, however, like the woman who began: "WANTED: One Greek god of refined caliber."

8   Not all the ads are jaunty or dewy-eyed. One begins: "Have herpes?" Some are improbably specialized: "Fishing Jewish woman over 50 seeks single man to share delights of angling." Or: "Literate snorkeler . . . have room in my life for one warm, secure, funny man."

9   Anyone composing a personal ad faces an inherent credibility problem. While we are accustomed to the self-promotions of politicians, say, we sense something bizarre when ordinary people erupt in small rhapsodies of self-celebration that are occasioned by loneliness and longing. One is haunted by almost piteous cries that come with post-office-box number attached: "Is there anyone out there? Anyone out there for me?"

10   Composing an ad with oneself as the product is an interesting psychological exercise, and probably good training in self-assertion. Truth will endure a little decorative writing, perhaps. The personals are a form of courtship that is more efficient, and easier on the liver, than sitting in bars night after night, hoping for a lucky encounter. Yet one feels sometimes a slightly disturbed and forlorn vibration in those columns of chirpy pleading. It is inorganic courtship. There is something severed, a lost connection. One may harbor a buried resentment that there are not parents and aunts and churches and cotillions to arrange the meetings in more seemly style.

11   That, of course, may be mere sentimentalism. Whatever works. Loneliness is the Great Satan. Jane Austen, who knew everything about courtship, would have understood the personals columns perfectly. Her novel *Emma*, in fact, begins, "Emma Woodhouse, handsome, happy, clever, and rich, with a comfortable home and happy disposition." The line might go right into the *New York Review of Books*.

Thinking Critically About This Reading

1. What are some of the rhetorical difficulties with which the writer of a personal ad must cope?
2. For which sex does the personal ad form strike you as being more suitable? Why?
3. What advantages or disadvantages does the personal ad have over more conventional ways of making dates?
4. The author claims the sexual revolution has cooled down to "a domestic room temperature." Do you agree? To what do you attribute this cooling down?
5. The author says "a man's hair stands on end" upon encountering an ad like this one: "Alarmingly articulate, incorrigibly witty, overeducated but extremely attractive NYC woman." Why would a man react with fear to this ad? What does that reaction imply about men?

Understanding the Writer's Process

1. How does the author introduce his many examples? Do his introductions adequately prepare us for the examples that follow?
2. With the exceptions of paragraphs 6 and 11, what do all the paragraph openings of this essay share in common?
3. Whose point of view is reflected in the final two sentences of the opening paragraph?
4. To what literary form does the author compare the personal ad? Do you find this comparison apt or farfetched?
5. Essays are said to be written either to inform, entertain, or persuade. Which of these purposes do you think is behind this particular essay? How does the author carry out his purpose?

Examining the Writer's Language

1. Define the meanings of these words as used in the context of this essay: haiku (paragraph 1), cerebral (1), demurely (1), gnosis (3), suffused (5), self-effacement (6), hyperbolic (6), inherent (9), rhapsodies (9), cotillions (10).
2. In paragraph 1, the author writes: "One must chum the waters and bait the hook, and go trolling for love and laughter, for caring

and sharing, for long walks and quiet talks, for Bach and Brie."
What does this metaphor mean and why is it an apt one for
personal ads?

3. In paragraph 1, the author provides a sample of adjectives commonly used in personal ads—"sensitive, warm, witty, vibrant, successful, handsome, accomplished, incredibly beautiful, cerebral,
sultry." List five adjectives other than these that you would use to
describe yourself in a personal ad.

4. In paragraph 11, the author writes, "Loneliness is the Great Satan." Where does this expression, "the Great Satan" come from?
What is ironic about its use in this context?

Suggestions for Writing

1. Write the ultimate personal ad—an extended ad for yourself—in
essay form, giving examples of your sterling qualities and most
appealing attributes.

2. Peruse the personal ads in any newspaper or magazine mentioned by the author. Select the two ads you think are most and
least appealing. Write an essay analyzing and giving examples
of the phrasing and diction that make each ad good or bad.

THE TRUTH ABOUT LYING

Tom Rickman

*Tom Rickman, Hollywood screenwriter and di-
rector, was born and reared in Sharpe, Kentucky. After
serving for three years in the Marines, he entered Mur-
ray State College as an English major, where he developed an interest in acting and made a movie ad-
aptation of a Flannery O'Connor short story. He
subsequently studied at the American Film Institute.
He has written a number of films, including* Kansas
City Bomber *(1972) and* River Rat *(1984), which he
also directed.*

Preparing to Read This Selection Critically

This is a humorous article, written with a satirical, tongue-in-cheek deftness. But like all good satire, it is based on a kernel of truth we occasionally glimpse peeking through the mockery. Hollywood is the ultimate fantasy land, and people who live there and work in the movie business do have an ethic against telling the truth if it means rocking the boat or possibly making an enemy. As you read, be sensitive to what Rickman is obliquely complaining about even as he satirically lauds the Hollywood cult of lying. Remember that in satire inversion often is used humorously to make a point, and frequently an author will ironically praise the very thing he or she is complaining about.

I am told that many outside the movie industry—the so–called   1
real people—believe that lying is wrong. If true, and I'm unable to confirm it from personal experience, it is this basic misapprehension *more than any other factor* that will stamp the ineradicable brand of "real" on your forehead forever, and condemn you to a lifetime of buying your own lunch and getting flown over by us Movie People jetting back and forth to the coast. If you really want to make it in the industry, the first thing you have to do is divest yourself of the notion that lying is somehow "bad." Forget "bad." For "bad," substitute "good." I'm not going on until you've done this.

OK? Good. Experienced movie people know the truth about   2
lying, that it is not an act of deceit, treachery, malice, cowardice, or self–aggrandizement—although of course any lie worthy of the name is going to contain at least one of these qualities—but that it is the common, humane discourse without which business would be impossible and life unlivable. Lying, in truth, as practiced out here, is the sincere expression of compassion, of kindness and charity. If you don't know this, you belong in another profession, like advertising or law.

Let me begin with the most elementary, everyday illustration   3
of what I mean. Someone you know has opened his movie. You see it. You hate it. "How'd you like it?" he asks. You say, "Great." There. Simple, basic humanity—and it doesn't cost you a penny. Of course, you can elaborate—"I had fun with it; it's a real audience picture," et cetera—but such embellishments can be risky, especially if your

eyes have a tendency to glaze over. "Great" is an unpretentious, all–purpose word that will never let you down. You should memorize this word as soon as possible.

4   That's a very primitive, deep–structure example of the first great category of lies: Lies You Tell Other People. Now let's look at the second great category: Lies Other People Tell You.

5   You have a screenplay at a Major Motion Picture Studio. They read it. They hate it. They hate it *so much* they uncharacteristically cancel their important lunches so they can have more time to ridicule it. It makes their day. They call you. "How'd you like my script?" you ask. "Great," they say. "We had fun with it." They ask for revisions because everybody wants to read it again. This is a near–perfect example of what I'm telling you here. Think if they told you the truth. Think if hell froze over.

6   One more. You direct a movie. It arcs, like an Olympic diver with magnets around his neck, straight into the old steel–lined toilet. Your fellow professionals say they liked it—"Great"—singling out several second–unit shots inserted against your will as having your unmistakable mark. Various agents and studio executives protect your self-esteem by claiming not to have seen the movie *yet*; or, in the ultimate refinement of charity, not mentioning it at all. Thus the community gathers around you and life can go on. If you ask why, then you're ready to hear about the third and most intricate category of lies: Lies You Tell Yourself.

7   You sneak–preview your movie with an invited audience. They laugh in all the wrong places. "Great," you say. "More comedy here than I thought." Ten minutes into the picture, five people walk out. You note that they are demographic misfits and therefore irrelevant: The members of the target audience remain, glued to their seats. When they begin to go, you know exactly why: The free coffee dispensed in the lobby as a goodwill gesture is taking its toll on their kidneys. You know they'll hurry back as quickly as possible, eagerly quizzing their seatmates about what they missed during this untimely call of nature. When they don't come back, you picture them, trapped and desperate, behind restroom doors with jammed locks. You resolve to berate the theater owner about his shoddy facility; then about the decline of exhibitor responsibility in general when you see the last reel come up where the third is supposed to be. When the audience doesn't seem to notice, you know it's because they're completely engrossed, and the out–of–sequence reel does

seem to strengthen the second act. Afterward, you read the questionnaires, the first of which says, "This director couldn't direct lemmings to the beach." But you know that in any random gathering of people, a certain percentage of them are going to be hopelessly psychotic. When the numbers show that eighty percent would recommend the movie to their friends only if bribed or tortured, you remind yourself of the Immortals whose work was also misunderstood by the masses: Griffith, Welles, Pol Pot. Next day, when your agent calls, apologizing for missing the preview ("Had to take my pit bull for shots"), asking you how it went, you say, "Great."

Those of you who are quibbleminded might possibly protest 8
that the above anecdote ends with a clear–cut example of category one, Lies You Tell Other People. In truth, it is a powerfully illustrative instance of the principle that governs all three categories: Lying as Listening to and Agreeing With the Lie That Is Being Told. I'm sure I don't have to point out that without this most indispensable factor, the whole system falls apart. The very essence of lying is, first and foremost, sincerity, however fleeting.

It is vital, therefore, that lying not become second nature to 9
you. It must become first nature. Nothing is more pathetic than an inept liar. Contempt is justly heaped on those who, when lying, lose control of their shifty little eyes or can't stop rubbing their disgusting sweaty palms on their Calvins. Like, you give your script to some bozo to read. "How'd you like it?" "I *loved* it!" he says. "I mean really! What can I tell you—it's wonderful!" You shouldn't even try to stifle the sneer that's going to twist your clenched, white lips. Phony jerk. Give you a break, will you? Serves you right for sucking up to amateurs.

In future columns, I'll return to this topic, exploring the loftiest 10
reaches of lying, such as Mogul Lying, Movie Star Lying, and Lying to the Folks Back Home About How Well You're Doing. Meanwhile, you might fill out the questionnaire below as to your response to this first effort:

I thought Rickman's column was: 11
    a) great
    b) great
    c) great
    d) all of the above
I'll know what you mean. 12

Thinking Critically About This Reading

1. Rickman jocularly suggests that lying as it is practiced in the movie business is "humane." What, in your opinion, is the distinction between a humane and an inhumane lie?

2. What special circumstances in the movie business do you think necessitate the routine telling of lies as Rickman facetiously alleges?

3. If Rickman is right, even if he does exaggerate for humor, what ultimate effect do you think the lying he describes is likely to have on movies and movie–making?

4. What equivalents to the kind of lying Rickman describes can you find in everyday social life?

5. Imagine a society in which everyone is bluntly and brutally truthful. Would such a society be morally superior to our own? Would you like to live in it? Why or why not?

Understanding the Writer's Process

1. How does the persona behind Rickman's article contribute to its humor?

2. How does a reader first know that the aim of the author is primarily humorous?

3. Aside from providing us with examples of the usefulness of lying, what other rhetorical type does the author's tongue–in–cheek treatment of lying practice?

4. The author uses irony throughout the article for humorous effect. Point to at least one example of ironic usage.

5. On what primary tactic does the humor of this piece depend? Give an example.

Examining the Writer's Language

1. Define the meanings of the following words used in this article: ineradicable (paragraph 1), divest (1), self–aggrandizement (2), discourse (2), embellishments (3), demographic (7), berate (7), engrossed (7), quibbleminded (8).

2. Cite the use of at least one humorous metaphor in this article.

3. Who are or were Griffith, Welles, and Pol Pot, the immortals mentioned in paragraph 7 whose work the author says "was also misunderstood by the masses"? What is ironic about this combination of names?

4. The author writes in paragraph 9, "Like, you give your script to some bozo to read." What does "like" mean in this sentence? What happens to the humor if you replace it with the Standard English equivalent?

5. Express in Standard English the following sentence: "Serves you right for sucking up to amateurs."

Suggestions for Writing

1. Write an essay in which you give two *extended* examples of the usefulness of the "white lie" in social situations.

2. Write an essay giving examples of what you mean by "truth."

COURTSHIP THROUGH THE AGES

James Thurber

> *During his long stay at* The New Yorker, *James Thurber (1894–1961) was beloved as writer and cartoonist. His perceptive wit and satirical humor have endeared him to several generations of readers. Thurber's work is still read and admired today in numerous collections, among them* The Thurber Carnival *(1945),* The Thurber Album *(1952), and* Thurber Country *(1957).*

Preparing to Read This Selection Critically

"Courtship Through the Ages," first published in 1939 by *The New Yorker*, is vintage Thurber—an involved discussion of the courtship rituals in the animal kingdom, with Thurber seeing hilarious parallels to the lovesick male of our own species. Although Thurber is writing as

a humorist, the similarities he draws between the courtship rituals of animals and people fit in neatly with the
sexual stereotypes of the 1930s and 1940s. As you read,
ask yourself whether they still apply to courtship in our
day. Are females today as indifferent to sex as Thurber
humorously suggests? Are they as passive and uncaring
about passion and men as they were assumed to be during Thurber's day? Finally, would readers of our own time
find this as funny as Thurber's audience did, or would
they regard it as old-fashioned and corny?

1   Surely nothing in the astonishing scheme of life can have nonplussed Nature so much as the fact that none of the females of any
of the species she created really cared very much for the male, as
such. For the past ten million years Nature has been busily inventing
ways to make the male attractive to the female, but the whole business of courtship, from the marine annelids up to man, still lumbers
heavily along, like a complicated musical comedy. I have been reading the sad and absorbing story in Volume 6 (Cole to Dama) of the
Encyclopedia Britannica. In this volume you can learn about cricket,
cotton, costume designing, crocodiles, crown jewels, and Coleridge,
but none of these subjects is so interesting as the Courtship of Animals, which recounts the sorrowful lengths to which all males must
go to arouse the interest of a lady.

2   We all know, I think, that Nature gave man whiskers and a
mustache with the quaint idea in mind that these would prove attractive to the female. We all know that, far from attracting her,
whiskers and mustaches only made her nervous and gloomy, so that
man had to go in for somersaults, tilting with lances, and performing
feats of parlor magic to win her attention; he also had to bring her
candy, flowers, and the furs of animals. It is common knowledge
that in spite of all these "love displays" the male is constantly being
turned down, insulted, or thrown out of the house. It is rather comforting, then, to discover that the peacock, for all his gorgeous plu-
mage, does not have a particularly easy time in courtship; none of
the males in the world do. The first peahen, it turned out, was only
faintly stirred by her suitor's beautiful train. She would often go
quietly to sleep while he was whisking it around. The *Britannica*
tells us that the peacock actually had to learn a certain little trick
to wake her up and revive her interest: he had to learn to vibrate
his quills so as to make a rustling sound. In ancient times man

himself, observing the ways of the peacock, probably tried vibrating his whiskers to make a rustling sound; if so, it didn't get him anywhere. He had to go in for something else; so, among other things, he went in for gifts. It is not unlikely that he got this idea from certain flies and birds who were making no headway at all with rustling sounds.

One of the flies of the family Empidae, who had tried every- 3 thing, finally hit on something pretty special. He contrived to make a glistening transparent balloon which was even larger than himself. Into this he would put sweetmeats and tidbits and he would carry the whole elaborate envelope through the air to the lady of his choice. This amused her for a time, but she finally got bored with it. She demanded silly little colorful presents, something that you couldn't eat but that would look nice around the house. So the male Empis had to go around gathering flower petals and pieces of bright paper to put into his balloon. On a courtship flight a male Empis cuts quite a figure now, but he can hardly be said to be happy. He never knows how soon the female will demand heavier presents, such as Roman coins and gold collar buttons. It seems probable that one day the courtship of the Empidae will fall down, as man's occasionally does, of its own weight.

The bowerbird is another creature that spends so much time 4 courting the female that he never gets any work done. If all the male bowerbirds became nervous wrecks within the next ten or fifteen years, it would not surprise me. The female bowerbird insists that a playground be built for her with a specially constructed bower at the entrance. This bower is much more elaborate than an ordinary nest and is harder to build; it costs a lot more, too. The female will not come to the playground until the male has filled it up with a great many gifts: silvery leaves, red leaves, rose petals, shells, beads, berries, bones, dice, buttons, cigar bands, Christmas seals, and the Lord knows what else. When the female finally condescends to visit the playground, she is in a coy and silly mood and has to be chased in and out of the bower and up and down the playground before she will quit giggling and stand still long enough even to shake hands. The male bird is, of course, pretty well done in before the chase starts, because he has worn himself out hunting for eyeglass lenses and begonia blossoms. I imagine that many a bowerbird, after chasing a female for two or three hours, says the hell with it and goes home to bed. Next day, of course, he telephones someone else and the same trying ritual is gone through with again. A male bowerbird is as exhausted as a night-club habitué before he is out of his twenties.

5   The male fiddler crab has a somewhat easier time, but it can hardly be said that he is sitting pretty. He has one enormously large and powerful claw, usually brilliantly colored, and you might suppose that all he had to do was reach out and grab some passing cutie. The very earliest fiddler crabs may have tried this, but, if so, they got slapped for their pains. A female fiddler crab will not tolerate any caveman stuff; she never has and she doesn't intend to start now. To attract a female, a fiddler crab has to stand on tiptoe and brandish his claw in the air. If any female in the neighborhood is interested—and you'd be surprised how many are not—she comes over and engages him in light badinage, for which he is not in the mood. As many as a hundred females may pass the time of day with him and go on about their business. By nightfall of an average courting day, a fiddler crab who has been standing on tiptoe for eight or ten hours waving a heavy claw in the air is in pretty sad shape. As in the case of the male of all species, however, he gets out of bed next morning, dashes some water on his face, and tries again.

6   The next time you encounter a male web-spinning spider, stop and reflect that he is too busy worrying about his love life to have any desire to bite you. Male web-spinning spiders have a tougher life than any other males in the animal kingdom. This is because the female web-spinning spiders have very poor eyesight. If a male lands on a female's web, she kills him before he has time to lay down his cane and gloves, mistaking him for a fly or a bumblebee who has tumbled into her trap. Before the species figured out what to do about this, millions of males were murdered by ladies they called on. It is the nature of spiders to perform a little dance in front of the female, but before a male spinner could get near enough for the female to see who he was and what he was up to, she would lash out at him with a flat-iron or a pair of garden shears. One night, nobody knows when, a very bright male spinner lay awake worrying about calling on a lady who had been killing suitors right and left. It came to him that this business of dancing as a love display wasn't getting anybody anywhere except the grave. He decided to go in for web-twitching, or strand-vibrating. The next day he tried it on one of the nearsighted girls. Instead of dropping in on her suddenly, he stayed outside the web and began monkeying with one of its strands. He twitched it up and down and in and out with such a

lilting rhythm that the female was charmed. The serenade worked beautifully; the female let him live. The *Britannica's* spider-watchers, however, report that this system is not always successful. Once in a while, even now, a female will fire three bullets into a suitor or run him through with a kitchen knife. She keeps threatening him from the moment he strikes the first low notes on the outside strings, but usually by the time he has got up to the high notes played around the center of the web, he is going to town and she spares his life.

Even the butterfly, as handsome a fellow as he is, can't always win a mate merely by fluttering around and showing off. Many butterflies have to have scent scales on their wings. Hepialus carries a powder puff in a perfumed pouch. He throws perfume at the ladies when they pass. The male tree cricket, Oecanthus, goes Hepialus one better by carrying a tiny bottle of wine with him and giving drinks to such doxies as he has designs on. One of the male snails throws darts to entertain the girls. So it goes, through the long list of animals, from the bristle worm and his rudimentary dance steps to man and his gift of diamonds and sapphires. The golden-eye drake raises a jet of water with his feet as he flies over a lake; Hepialus has his power puff, Oecanthus his wine bottle, man his etchings. It is a bright and melancholy story, the age-old desire of the male for the female, the age-old desire of the female to be amused and entertained. Of all the creatures on earth, the only males who could be figured as putting any irony into their courtship are the grebes and certain other diving birds. Every now and then a courting grebe slips quietly down to the bottom of a lake and then, with a mighty "Whoosh!" pops out suddenly a few feet from his girl friend, splashing water all over her. She seems to be persuaded that this is a purely loving display, but I like to think that the grebe always has a faint hope of drowning her or scaring her to death.

I will close this investigation into the mournful burdens of the male with *Britannica's* story about a certain Argus pheasant. It appears that the Argus displays himself in front of a female who stands perfectly still without moving a feather. . . . The male Argus the *Britannica* tells about was confined in a cage with a female of another species, a female who kept moving around, emptying ashtrays and fussing with lampshades all the time the male was showing off his talents. Finally, in disgust, he stalked away and began displaying in front of his water trough. He reminds me of a certain male *(Homo sapiens)* of my acquaintance who one night after dinner asked his wife to put down her detective magazine so that he could read a poem of which he was very fond. She sat quietly enough until he was well into the middle of the thing, intoning with great ardor and intensity. Then suddenly there came a sharp, disconcerting *slap!* It turned out that all during the male's display, the female had been intent on a circling mosquito and had finally trapped it between the palms of her hands. The male in this case did not stalk away and display in front of a water trough; he went over to Tim's and had a flock of drinks and recited the poem to the fellas. I am sure they all told bitter stories of their own about how their displays had been interrupted by females. I am also sure that they all ended up singing "Honey, Honey, Bless Your Heart."

Thinking Critically About This Reading

1. This humorous essay is based on the assumption that the male is ardent in romance but the female is basically indifferent. Is this a reasonable assumption, or is the author passing on a male chauvinist stereotype?

2. What effects has women's widespread entry into the workplace had on courtship and the relationship between the sexes?

3. What definition of femininity seems implicit in this essay? Is this definition flattering or demeaning? To whom? Do you find it accurate for our own time?

4. What aspects of the courtship ritual do you think should be left entirely to the man's initiative? To the woman's?

5. If you are a woman, what features and attributes do you think make a man especially attractive? If you are a man, what makes a woman especially attractive?

Understanding the Writer's Process

1. Where do we first learn that this is intended as a comical rather than as a serious essay? What early clue does the author give of his intent?

2. How does Thurber manage to extract humor through his treatment of the many examples of animal courtship?

3. The author specifically mentions that the material on courtship came from an article in the *Encyclopaedia Britannica*. What does this allusion add to his essay?

4. What implicit comparisons do the examples in this essay draw? How are the comparisons used to generate humor?

5. In paragraph 8, the author relates the sad story of the male Argus pheasant and an acquaintance of his from the species *Homo sapiens*. Aside from the predictable frustration both males suffer, what is especially ironic about this discussion?

Examining the Writer's Language

1. Define the meanings of the following words as used in this essay: nonplussed (paragraph 1), contrived (3), habitué (4), badinage (5), rudimentary (7).

2. How does the use of slangy colloquialisms contribute to the humor of this essay? Cite specific examples.

3. Why is *love display* placed within quotation marks only in paragraph 2 and nowhere else?

4. The author frequently uses the biological names of the creatures he is discussing. Why? What does such use contribute to the humor of the piece?

Suggestions for Writing

1. Write an essay about courtship rituals in which you have participated (include specific examples).

2. Write an essay about the rituals some women go through to attract the attention of men.

"DON'T BLAME ME"

John Taylor

John Taylor, a Contributing Editor at New York *magazine, graduated from the University of Chicago in 1977. Born in Japan and reared mainly in Asia, Taylor also has been on the staff of* Newsweek *and* Business Week. *He is the author of* Storming the Magic Kingdom: Wall Street, The Raiders, and The Battle' for

Disney *(1987), and* Circus of Ambition: The Culture
of Wealth and Power in the Eighties *(1989).*

Preparing to Read This Selection Critically

This is an article in which the author tries simultaneously to prove the existence of the very situation he
is lamenting. As Taylor tells it in this piece from *New York*
magazine, Americans, especially those living in urban
areas, have begun to blame others obsessively for their
own bad choices or mistakes. To prove that what he is
alleging is true, Taylor cites numerous examples and re-
gales us with the testimonies of experts who agree with
him. As you read, ask yourself whether Taylor has proven
that the culture of victimization is as widespread as he
alleges. Pay attention to the credentials of the experts he
cites, remembering that, as Taylor admits, "an expert can
be found to testify to the truth of any factual theory, no
matter how frivolous."

1   When Rose Cipollone developed lung cancer after smoking a
pack and a half of cigarettes a day for 40 years, she didn't blame
herself for stupidly ignoring the warning labels on the cigarette
packs, as well as the American Cancer Society's ubiquitous ads decrying the hazards of smoking and the continual barrage of reports
on television and in the papers linking it to death. She didn't accept,
with a shrug, the fact that she had gambled with her health and
lost. No. Don't blame me! she protested, and in her lawsuit against
the Liggett Group and two other tobacco companies, which was
continued by her estate after her death and is now before the Supreme Court, she blamed the cigarette manufacturers for her habit.

2   Don't blame me! I'm a victim of . . .

3   Of what? It's hard to choose. There are so many new categories
of victimization these days. In fact, a truly imaginative person can
find many, many reasons why he shouldn't be blamed for what he's
done. As Marion Barry [then mayor of Washington, D.C.] did.

4   When Barry was caught smoking crack in a Washington, D.C.,
hotel, he didn't blame himself for his bad judgment or weakness of
character. First he blamed the woman he was with, exclaiming to
the police who arrested him, "Bitch set me up!" Then his friends
blamed a "racist" plot by federal agents to try to hound black pol-

iticians out of office. And when none of these excuses succeeded in reconciling people to the videotaped image of the mayor of Washington, D.C., sucking on a crack pipe, Barry blamed his behavior on drugs and alcohol, declaring, "I was a victim."

A case, if a very flimsy case, can be made that Rose Cipollone 5 and Marion Barry should not be held *entirely* responsible for their predicaments. After all, cigarettes are habit-forming, though people quit all the time, and crack is addictive, though Barry, like many of the drug's connoisseurs, appears to have been an occasional user. However lame Cipollone's and Barry's excuses, however cynically they may have resorted to them, addictive chemicals can impede the exercise of free will. And so perhaps the newest, the most perverse, the most outrageous twist in America's evolving culture of victimization is the claim by people who can't come up with an excuse, who can't find a suitable victim category, that they have been treated unfairly just by virtue of the fact that they have been caught doing something wrong.

Take the frat–house drug busts in March at the University of 6 Virginia. James Carter was among the twelve students arrested, but when Fred Carter, James's father, learned of the charge, was he furious at his son for jeopardizing his promising future by breaking the law, for being so dumb, so arrogant, or, at the very least, so careless as to get caught? No. The father's wrath was instead directed primarily at the police. "Why didn't the investigators go to the University of Richmond or Norfolk State?" he asked indignantly. For the police to arrest his son rather than any of the other dealers who happened to be selling drugs in the country at the moment was, he felt, unfair. It was almost a form of discrimination.

THE CULTURE OF VICTIMIZATION

It's a strange phenomenon, this growing compulsion of Amer- 7 icans of all creeds, colors, and incomes, of the young and the old, the infirm and the robust, the guilty as well as the innocent, to ascribe to themselves the status of victims to try to find someone or something else to blame for whatever is wrong or incomplete or just plain unpleasant about their lives. "There's a widely held view that if something bad happens to you, someone else must be responsible," says Roger Conner, the director of the American Alliance for Rights & Responsibilities, a neoliberal social–action lobby in Washington. "This mind–set is a profound deformation of our society, a collective form of paranoia. Bad things do happen to good people."

8   To give but one example, Conner points to the issue of birth
defects. "It used to be that if a child was born with birth defects,
the presumption was that it was in the nature of things," he says.
"Now the obstetrician is all too often held responsible for the production of perfect babies. Victimization takes the place of what used
to be thought of as acts of God."

9   The culture of victimization is largely responsible for the $117
billion spent annually on insurance to protect against litigation, but
the phenomenon extends, of course, far beyond the courts. It is a
major theme in race relations and in the feminist critique of society.
It has spawned a new academic discipline, victimology. It provides
unending fodder for the morbidly voyeuristic audiences of television
talk shows and is responsible for a virtual genre of books that have
titles like *The Cinderella Complex, The Casanova Complex, The Soap
Opera Syndrome, Adult Children of Alcoholics, Beyond Codependency,
Beyond Acceptance,* and *Obsessive Love: When Passion Holds You Prisoner,* and explore the compulsions, maladies, syndromes, and pre-
sumptions that purportedly prevent people from assuming control
of their lives. Without it, a good percentage of the 125,000 psychologists, therapists, and counselors who form the country's gar-
gantuan therapy industry would be out of work.

10   Much of this focus on victimization is commendable. Society
no longer shrugs off battered wives and abused children. Crime
victims are treated with greater consideration. But what began as a
well-meaning attempt to acknowledge the plight of previously ignored victims has developed a momentum of its own. In their rush
to establish ever more categories of victims, lawyers and therapists
are encouraging a grotesquely cynical evasion of the ethic of individual responsibility. The United States is becoming a nation of
belligerent shirkers, of pouting, mewling, finger-pointing crybabies.
"Everyone is a victim these days; no one accepts any responsibility
for anything," says Irving Horowitz, a professor of sociology at Rutgers and the editor of the journal *Society.*

11   But that is because there are, quite simply, enormous advantages to be had today if you can successfully portray yourself as a
victim. Among them are the psychic rewards. "Being a victim delivers to you a certain innocence," Shelby Steele, the black essayist,
has said. Victim status not only confers the moral superiority of
innocence. It enables people to avoid taking responsibility for their
own behavior. "Victimization exempts people from ordinary standards," says Fred Siegel, a professor of humanities at Cooper Union.

Indeed, while much has been made in recent years of the syndrome called "blaming the victim," less attention has been paid to another syndrome, the don't–blame–me–I'm–a–victim syndrome. This trend began in the sixties with the idea that victims of "social injustice" shouldn't be held accountable for the wrongs they do. But it has expanded far beyond that. Criminals now regularly claim that they themselves are the victims of PMS or postpartum depression or that they have suffered from overexposure to television or pornography— serial killer Ted Bundy's excuse. In the famous "Twinkie defense," Dan White, who killed San Francisco mayor George Moscone, argued that he was a victim of temporary insanity brought about by eating junk food.

Enormous financial rewards can accrue once victimization has been established, and this also encourages people to go to extraordinary lengths to present themselves as helpless. Marjorie Thoreson, a former topless dancer, stripper, and alleged prostitute who had been arrested for indecent exposure and lewd conduct, and convicted of tear–gas–gun possession, grand theft auto and passing bad checks, and who became a *Penthouse* Pet under the name Anneka di Lorenzo, was awarded $4 million last year because she claimed she had been the victim of a "Svengali–like" influence that *Penthouse* publisher Bob Guccione exercised on her in persuading her to sleep with a business associate.

But at least Thoreson was arguing that she had actually suffered. The willingness of society to grant victim status to just about anyone troubling to make even the most farfetched claim, and the obvious benefits of these claims, can be seen in a new trend in litigation called "compensating the uninjured." These are people who have suffered nothing but nonetheless claim to be victims because they are afraid they might one day suffer. Four people in California were awarded more than $1 million after claiming that living near a polluted groundwater supply had given them "cancerphobia." And then there is the case of Marc Christian, Rock Hudson's lover, who was awarded $14.5 million because, though he tested negative for the HIV virus, he suffered from fear of AIDS. "Becoming a victim is the greatest thing that's ever happened to a lot of people," says Walter Olson, author of a new book called *The Litigation Explosion*.

RIGHTS INFLATION

The culture of victimization is reinforced by the prevailing intellectual conviction that people are not ever really in control of their

own lives. Marx, Freud, Lacan, Derrida, and Foucault have all promoted this point, arguing that humans are the victims of unconscious
urges or class oppression or patriarchal social systems or the struc-
tures of language. As Ronald Walters, chairman of the department
of political science at Howard University, put it in his summation
of the conventional wisdom, "This business of rugged individualism
really is a sham."

15   According to this view, the idea that men and women should
largely be held responsible for their own lives is not just laughably
naive—it is, in fact, malevolent bourgeois propaganda. Success stories in the Horatio Alger mold, even true ones, amount to nothing
more than opium for the masses that diverts the victims of social
injustice from its true cause—capitalist oppression—by stirring up
fantasies of individual achievement.

16   Oddly enough, given such assumptions, the United States in
the past 25 years has witnessed the most astonishing proliferation
of specific individual freedoms in history. Amitai Etzioni, a sociol-
ogist at George Washington University, refers to it as a "rights inflation," and he attributes it to the "rights industry," that whole
roiling mass of lawyers, lobbyists, and special–interest groups who
swarm over courts and legislatures with their grievances and demands for recognition of an astonishing array of new rights—not
only the rights of women and minorities and illegal immigrants but
the rights of fetuses, the rights of hunters, the rights of non-smokers,
the rights of smokers, the rights of animals, the rights of trees, the
right to own a machine gun, the right of unfashionably dressed men
to be admitted to chic nightclubs, the right of the homeless to shelter,
the right of the insane to wander the streets, the right of drug addicts
to treatment, to name just a few. And then there are the rights *not*
to do certain things—as in the right of geriatrics not to retire, the
right of doctors with AIDS not to inform their patients, the right of
pilots not to be randomly tested for alcohol. The rights list is as
lengthy as the categories of victimization.

17   But that is because "rights" and "victims" are inextricably
linked concepts. If you can establish a right, then prove you are
denied it, you acquire victim status. Most people trouble to assert
their rights, or even to be aware of them, only when they feel those
rights are being violated. Haitians insisted on their "right" to donate
blood only after they were banned from doing so by the federal
government because of the high incidence of AIDS among Haitians.

In fact, rights are proliferating so rapidly that they now often 18 collide. Members of ACT UP, for example, have declared that AIDS victims are being killed not only by the disease itself but by government officials, who are "murdering" those with the affliction by failing to find a cure. This puts them in conflict with certain animal-rights activists who believe—as one of them, Tom Regan, has said—that "we have no basic right not to be harmed by those natural diseases we are heir to."

This only illustrates that rights do not exist in a vacuum. "Each 19 right poses a moral claim on someone else," Amitai Etzioni points out. Indeed, the defining irony of America's culture of victimization is that the spread of new rights, while liberating for certain people, has been a cause of frustration, resentment, and even, yes, victimization for others.

Seven years ago, voters in Washington, D.C., passed an ini- 20 tiative saying every homeless person in the city had an absolute right to shelter. All sorts of criminals promptly flooded in and began dealing drugs and harassing, robbing, and beating the other residents. The shelter managers tried to ban these people for not obeying the rules, but they were prevented from doing so on the grounds that *everyone* had an absolute right to shelter. When that right collided with the rules, it was the rules that had to go. Shelter residents endured this anarchy until last year, when the City Council reformed the law.

This sort of blind defense of absolute rights creates huge num- 21 bers of people who are true victims in the ultimate sense: They are dead. To understand how this has come about, it is worthwhile comparing the National Rifle Association and the American Civil Liberties Union. Though members of the two organizations tend to despise one another, they are, in their determination to protect a limited category of rights they regard as absolute, almost identical.

Both, for example, have done everything in their power to 22 enable the drug trade to flourish. The ACLU has declared drug use a "victimless crime" and argues, in fact, that the war on drugs "is no less than a war on the Constitution." The ACLU's reasoning, of course, is that the government is infringing on the liberties of all Americans when it promotes drug testing, sobriety checkpoints, anti–loitering laws, curfews, and the use of profiles—even nonracial profiles—to apprehend drug smugglers. In cities from Alexandria, Virginia, to Inkster, Michigan, the ACLU has gone to court to stop local police efforts to disrupt open–air crack markets by conducting sweeps, arresting loiterers, or setting up drive–through checkpoints. As a result, those drug markets continue to thrive.

23   The NRA has also come to the aid of drug dealers. It opposes virtually all restrictions on the sale of cheap handguns and semi–automatic rifles, and on the ownership of machine guns, on the grounds that these are absolute rights under the Second Amendment. Consequently, more than 33,000 people were killed in 1989 by guns, and while that figure included 12,000 suicides who would probably have found another way to end their lives (supporting the NRA's contention that guns don't kill people, people kill people), it also included 1,000 who died in accidents and nearly 12,000 who were murdered, among them 56 policemen.

24   The ACLU and the NRA are willing to tolerate the drug trade and its resultant slaughter as the price we have to pay to protect our constitutional freedoms. Both defend their positions by invoking the tired cliché that any attempt to create social order inevitably leads to totalitarianism—to brown shirts, firing squads, and concentration camps. If cars are stopped at checkpoints, the ACLU has declared in its literature, "we will be a long way down the road to a police state." In a similarly hysterical vein, the NRA argues that the Chinese in Tiananmen Square were slaughtered because they didn't have the right to bear arms. "The students of Beijing did not have a Second Amendment right to defend themselves when the soldiers came," the NRA asserted in an ad. "Because tyranny cannot tolerate armed citizens, those brave young Chinese could only hurl words and hold out empty hands against an army."

25   Both organizations console themselves with the fact that, as teenage gang members shoot innocent bystanders as well as each other in inner–city turf wars, and as families collapse under the strains of crack addiction, the civil liberties of all these people are being protected. For the people themselves, however, the consolation is minimal. "I deal in funerals. I deal in corpses. I don't care about civil libertarians," Father George Clements, a priest in Chicago's drug–ridden black slums, recently told a reporter.

THE MEDICALIZATION OF MORALITY

26   The culture of victimization is a uniquely American phenomenon, the inevitable outcome when traditional American optimism is thwarted. "We expect things to turn out well," says Roger Conner. "In Oriental culture, life is regarded as painful, and people learn how to deal with disappointment. Our culture places much more

worth on individual fulfillment." It is also an urban phenomenon. "You leave Chicago, New York, Los Angeles, and go to smaller towns and rural areas, you see responsibility and a sense of community," observes Irving Horowitz. And it parallels the decline of organized religion, which usually emphasized the inevitability of hardship and promised that the reward for enduring it with fortitude would come in the afterlife. "There is no consolation, no sense of continuity and transcendence," Fred Siegel explains.

But the chief reason religion has declined during the past 30 years has been that people came to think that their own individual lives need not be disappointing. The central tenet of the postwar generation, reinforced by Dr. Spock, by television, and by advertising, was that every American was entitled not just to pursue happiness but to *be* happy, to enjoy steadily increasing prosperity, invigorating personal relationships, glowing health, a rich sex life, the respect of peers—in a word, fulfillment. 27

The utopian sixties notion that suffering could be eliminated through social change, as well as the advances in medical technology that drastically improved life–expectancy rates, reinforced this psychology of entitlement. And, of course, a sense of entitlement is a prerequisite for claims of victimization. At the same time, the great therapy movement of the seventies was encouraging a spirit of confession, first in encounter groups, then increasingly on television. It was confession of the Freudian variety, focused on the awful things done to you, rather than of the Catholic variety, in which you confessed your own sins. Confessions of victimization were awarded with applause and television–talk–show appearances. The more graphic and detailed the confession, the greater the applause. By the end of the eighties, *Donahue*, the more earthy *Sally Jessy Raphael* and *The Oprah Winfrey Show* and the shamelessly prurient *Geraldo* were producing daily spectacles of psychic exhibitionism. 28

By then, many Americans had completely succumbed to—or become the victims of—what Christopher Lasch calls "the new paternalism." For the poor, this meant passive dependence on welfare payments and social workers. The middle classes, for their part, were encouraged to think that they were incapable of handling virtually all personal problems on their own, that mourning, job loss, divorce, disorderly children—whatever it was—required some form of therapy or counseling. In one school in Park Slope, a mother who was told her child's difficulties in "socialization" deserved professional treatment learned from other parents that almost half of them had been 29 urged by the school at one point or another to send their children into therapy.

30   The assumption that bad behavior represents a personality disorder or emotional problem is but one aspect of what has been called the medicalization of morality. The fact that the sufferers of chronic fatigue syndrome are disproportionately upper middle class has suggested that at least some of its supposed victims are actually just depressed, or even merely unhappy; they have latched on to the syndrome, according to one argument, because it displaces onto a mysterious virus the responsibility for their vague ennui. In other words, it gives them victim status.

31   So does a claim of addiction, since addiction is now considered a disease. Categories of addiction have proliferated wildly in recent years; gambling, drinking, running up debts, shopping too often, and overeating are all considered addictions. This is largely due to the therapy industry, which creates new markets for itself by establishing that certain types of behavior are the result of disease and that treatment for these problems therefore should be reimbursed by insurance companies.

32   Even sex is an addiction. People now describe themselves as "sex addicts" and "relationship addicts." On a recent show, Sally Jessy Raphael introduced Marion Barry as recovering not only from addictions to drugs and alcohol but also from "his addictions to women and sex." Barry, Raphael went on, was a man who could "sum up the entire addiction decade."

33   The idea that virtually all deviant behavior can be ascribed to some condition of which the deviant is a victim was once the property of a handful of sixties psychiatrists like R. D. Laing and Karl Menninger, who argued in his book *The Crime of Punishment* that what all criminals really needed was therapy. But today, the *Diagnostic & Statistical Manual of Mental Disorders* of American psychiatry lists a whole range of personality disorders, such as the Immature Personality Disorder and the Self–defeating Personality Disorder, that, according to current medical thinking, can force people to do things that they wouldn't otherwise do.

34   When Richard Berendzen, the former president of American University, resigned last year after admitting to having made obscene phone calls from his office, a doctor named Kenneth Grundfast argued in the *Washington Post* that Berendzen deserved public sympathy because he was the victim of an obsessive–compulsive disorder, which often is "caused more by abnormal DNA sequences

within an individual's chromosomes than by the moral lapses commonly described as wickedness, hostility or turpitude." Grundfast went on to say that "the tragedy is more ours than his. We may be the weak and misguided, not Berendzen."

Such an attitude, which radically expands the traditional conception of the insanity defense, is now a common feature of murder defenses. In the aftermath of a series of killings of babies by mothers, Nancy Berchtold, a woman who describes herself as having suffered from postpartum psychosis, and Peter Goldberger, a lawyer (what else?) who has defended women who kill their infants, argued in a letter to the *New York Times* that "the horror of infanticide often leads society to create more victims by responding with anger and punishment. A calmer and more objective view leads to the conclusion that the terrible act, while never justified, should sometimes be excused."

The proposition that a woman's murder of her child should be excused because of a temporary hormonal imbalance is put forward in the name of feminism. But it is, in the view of Kent Bailey, a professor of psychology at Virginia Commonwealth University who has studied pathological criminality, a profoundly anti-feminist view. "It reinforces the idea that women are these creatures who, because of their hormones, are likely to do strange things," he says.

It also erodes traditional morality. "By revising notions of personal responsibility, our disease conceptions undercut moral and legal standards exactly at a time when we suffer most from a general loss of social morality," the psychologist Stanton Peele has written in *Diseasing of America*. "Disease notions . . . legitimize, reinforce, and excuse the behaviors in question—convincing people, contrary to all evidence, that their behavior is not their own."

LITIGATION AS A PANACEA

The culture of victimization can also be directly attributed to specific developments in the law. In the sixties, the long–standing legal tradition of contributory negligence was widely rejected by the courts. Contributory negligence held that if you yourself had contributed to the cause of your injury, you could not claim someone else was responsible. In its stead, the courts began accepting the idea of comparative negligence, in which someone who was partially or even largely responsible for what befell him could still sue. This is best illustrated by the case of the New York man who was mutilated after he deliberately jumped in front of a subway but then received $650,000 because the train hadn't stopped in time to avoid hitting him.

39   Courts also began to endorse the concept of strict liability, which enabled people to claim that manufacturers could be held responsible for design shortcomings in their products even if those weren't the result of negligence. As a result, anyone could go into court to argue that in hindsight a product ought to have been designed differently. Another legal concept that gained currency was inadequate warning, which encouraged anyone who had fallen off a stepladder or cut himself with a power saw to file a claim. Men who injured themselves in refrigerator races—in which large, usually beery guys strap refrigerators to their backs and see who can run the fastest—argued that the warnings against carrying these appliances were insufficient.

40   Fifteen years ago, it might never have occurred to someone who hurt his back in a refrigerator race to sue the manufacturer. And the chances of a lawyer's suggesting such a course of action were much less. Legal ethics, encoded in the rules of the American Bar Association and in court rulings, prevented lawyers from inciting grievances in clients. But when the Supreme Court ruled in 1977 that lawyers could advertise, that traditional restraint was abandoned. The first of the ads that now fill New York subways began to appear, appealing to clients who "may be entitled to compensation."

41   Thereafter, in a series of less publicized but even more significant decisions, the Supreme Court allowed lawyers to solicit particular clients aggressively. In other words, lawyers could go out and persuade someone who had never previously thought of suing that it might be a good idea to do so. Nowadays, according to Walter Olson, lawyers resort more frequently than ever to the time–honored practice of buying police logs of accident and crime victims. They also acquire access to the registries of handicapped children. Then the lawyers begin making cold calls, suggesting lawsuits.

42   Finally, in 1975, Congress changed the Federal Rules of Evidence to accept a much looser definition of expert testimony. Previously, experts needed, in the words of the old rule, to have "gained general acceptance in the particular field" about which they were testifying. The new rule allowed virtually anyone to present himself as an expert. New professions such as "accidentology" and "human–factor engineering" sprang up, giving an aura of authority to the wildest claims. "An expert can be found to testify to the truth

of almost any factual theory, no matter how frivolous," Jack Weinstein, a federal court judge, has said.

Given this general relaxation of standards, it is no surprise that litigation has increased exponentially. According to Jury Verdict Research, a firm that surveys the topic, the number of jury verdicts awarding plaintiffs $1 million or more has risen from 22 in 1974 to 588 in 1989. Since 30 to 40 percent of jury awards go to lawyers in the form of contingency fees, and since it is the public that ultimately pays the bill in the form of higher prices to cover the insurance premiums of manufacturers, all this litigation represents a huge transfer of wealth from average Americans to lawyers. 43

Lawyers, of course, argue the tremendous social benefits of litigation. Why should someone who has been in an accident have to pay his own medical bills, regardless of whether it is his own fault? Isn't it more just, more progressive, for us all to share the cost by having the victim sue a manufacturer and then having the manufacturer raise the price we pay for his products? Litigation, it is also argued, draws attention to wrongdoing and serves as a deterrent to negligence and corporate irresponsibility. In support of this notion, Hofstra law professor Monroe Freedman once actually wrote an essay called "Advertising and Soliciting: The Case for Ambulance Chasing." 44

Similarly, litigation is applauded because it helps advance particular political agendas—another laudable idea easily carried to obnoxious extremes. John Banzhaf, a law professor at George Washington University, offers a course designed to teach students to use, in the words of the course catalogue, "the law as a powerful tool for affecting [sic] social change and advancing the public interest." Banzhaf's students, known around town as Banzhaf's bandits, receive course credit for filing lawsuits. Obsessed with eradicating every imagined vestige of sexual discrimination, some of the students sued three Washington restaurants for requiring men but not women to wear dinner jackets. Others sued two dry-cleaning stores for charging more to clean women's clothes than men's, forcing the tiny establishments to spend thousands of dollars in legal fees. "It's all based on the idea that it can't hurt to introduce more claims of victimization," says Richard Samp, a lawyer with the nonprofit Washington Legal Foundation. 45

But there are practical consequences. Endless lawsuits raise the price of consumer goods and even cause some of them to disappear. Because of liability risks, only one company, Merck Sharp & Dohme, 46 is willing to continue manufacturing the vaccine for measles, mumps, and rubella. Because of the fear of liability, pole vaulting has been outlawed in Iowa high schools, and diving boards have been eliminated at many public pools. Football helmets now cost $150, half of which goes to insurance premiums, and that puts them out of the reach of poor high schools and youth leagues. The wealthy are increasingly reluctant to sponsor Little League teams or join charity boards because they can become targets of lawsuits.

47   The moral assumptions that justify the tide of litigation are also questionable. "Do not bear false witness" is the Seventh Commandment. And American history is full of examples, from the Salem witch trials to the McCarthy hearings, of the harm that can result from false accusations. "The symbolic idea in all of this [litigation] is that it is good to accuse people, even if you're not sure they've done something wrong," says Walter Olson. "But it's bad."

RACIAL VICTIMIZATION

48   In early April, ABC broadcast *Separate but Equal*, an extremely flattering four–hour mini–series about the life of black Supreme Court Justice Thurgood Marshall. For years, blacks have complained that Hollywood hasn't provided enough opportunities for black actors nor created enough characters that can serve as positive role models for black audiences. *Separate but Equal* seemed a step in that direction. But instead of applauding the network for drawing attention to black achievement, Richard Carter, a black former columnist for the *Daily News*, attacked the movie in a *New York Times* op–ed piece as "an insult to African Americans." Carter's reasoning: Thurgood Marshall actually has "very light" skin, while Sidney Poitier, the actor who portrayed him, is "very dark." Carter urged Hollywood to hire "talented black actors—of which there are many— whose color approximates that of the person portrayed."

49   It's not difficult to imagine the uproar that would occur if a black actor was told he had the wrong shade of pigmentation for a certain role. And so, what Carter's piece really demonstrated was the lengths to which some blacks will go to try to prove that white society is hopelessly racist and that it is impossible for blacks to get ahead. That, no matter what happens, blacks are perennial victims.

50   Probably no group has become more tragically enmeshed in the culture of victimization than black Americans. Blacks have been and continue to be victimized by racism. But because of that very fact, and because white society has tried to redress it, victimization

has become a source of power for blacks. "Most groups organized their identity, at least to some extent, around the source of their power," Shelby Steele said during a forum held last fall in Washington by the Progressive Policy Institute. "And for blacks, ironically, that meant organizing our identity around our victimization."

While this was more or less inevitable, as Steele said, it created 51 a conundrum for blacks by giving them a stake in their victimization. While most people would agree that affirmative action programs, which have been made available by white acknowledgment of black victimization, are deserved, they nonetheless foster what Steele calls "a politics of difference." And the problem with the politics of difference, according to Steele, is that it "rewards victimization. It sets up a reward system in which, in order to accept the entitlements that come to you because you are a victim, you continue to escalate your claims of victimization. You get more and more tied into a victim–focused identity, and so, even as you enjoy the benefits of society, your screams of victimization grow louder."

To suggest that blacks have developed any sort of dependency 52 on their victim status is extremely provocative, even inflammatory, given the misery and danger that underclass blacks face every day, and this accounts for the virulent hostility that often greets Steele. Writing in *The Nation,* Yale professor Adolph Reed called him "a Disney World facsimile" who was "ratifying the social prejudice of the wealthy and powerful." But the temptation does exist for blacks to exploit white guilt by invoking racism whenever it is to their advantage, and the temptation is not always successfully resisted. When *Do the Right Thing* failed to win the top prize at Cannes, Spike Lee did not resign himself to the fact the judges liked *sex, lies and videotape* better; instead, he accused them of racism.

This "victim–focused identity"—to use Steele's phrase—has cre- 53 ated a profound ambivalence among many blacks about joining the mainstream. Black students in the slums who work hard in high school are ridiculed for trying to "be white," and adult blacks who join middle–class white society are derisively referred to, by other blacks, as "Afropeans" and "Afrosaxons" and "Incognegros." "Some black leaders have a deep emotional investment in the idea of failure, and no amount of counterevidence is sufficient to overwhelm it," says Will Marshall, president of the Progressive Policy Institute, a Washington think tank with ties to the Democratic Party.

Blacks who do integrate are sometimes accused not just of 54 shedding their race but of actually betraying it. Colin Powell might be considered an outstanding example of the upward mobility available to blacks in society today. But to some blacks, Powell is just a lackey for the white power structure. On a recent *Frontline* show, one black audience member complained that certain blacks felt that having Colin Powell direct the war in the Gulf was equivalent to "the house nigger sending the field niggers to die."

55   Historically, all minorities, from Italians to Jews to Chinese, have wrestled with the fear that in assimilating, they are somehow sacrificing their ethnic identity. But recently, assimilation has come to be seen as a sort of cultural genocide, with minorities claiming victimization because, in order to join mainstream society, they have had to adopt some of its practices. Whites, for example, have been accused of racism for expecting blacks to sit quietly through movies. White audiences, the young black director Mario Van Peebles recently declared, need to "get hip to the extroverted reactions by black audiences to what they are seeing on the screen."

56   But framing the debate in those terms—uptight white repression and outgoing black spontaneity—masks the real issue, which concerns the collapse of commonly held notions of civilized behavior: in this case, the idea of respect for the rights of others. Talking in theaters is harmless enough. But the suggestion that it is inherently racist to insist on common standards of behavior is, like so many other features of the culture of victimization, a recipe for anarchy.

COMPASSION FATIGUE

57   It's been said that Americans are developing an aversion to risk, but that is an incomplete description. Americans are willing to take risks. They are willing to do stupid and dangerous things like holding refrigerator races. What they are not willing to do is accept the consequences of their actions. Nothing more clearly illustrates this spineless hypocrisy than the fact that the Maryland legislature recently rejected a bill requiring motorcycle riders to wear helmets but also rejected a bill requiring motorcycle riders to have medical insurance. That means a motorcycle rider in Maryland can bash in his skull because he isn't wearing a helmet and then go to a hospital and demand free treatment because he can't pay the bills.

58   "If you try to think where we went wrong, it was in delinking rights and responsibilities," says Roger Conner. "People are fixated on their rights but have a shriveled sense of responsibility, so if they

don't have what they want, they assume it must be someone else's fault."

That attitude can exist only so long as someone else is willing 59 to be held responsible. But as the list of victims and rights expands, and as the special–interest groups that promote them grow increasingly numerous, militant, and shrill, the people who constitute what remains of the social mainstream are feeling ever more beleaguered and unsympathetic.

Their well of guilt is running dry, a phenomenon that is known 60 as "compassion fatigue" and is compounded by the fact that federal, state, and local budgets are all being cut. "In the sixties, white liberal guilt could be appealed to as the basis of policy," says William Galston, a professor at the University of Maryland and the former issues director for Walter Mondale. "But people who used to feel guilty and acted on the basis of guilt are now saying, 'To hell with it. I gave at the office.' "

A fledgling movement has arisen to try to dislodge the culture 61 of victimization. Among its members are Galston and his colleague Amitai Etzioni, who recently started a journal called *The Responsive Community,* which argues the need to balance individual rights with community responsibilities. They propose, for example, new divorce laws that would focus on the needs of children rather than the rights of parents. Other ideas include national service, which the Progressive Policy Institute has advocated; tenant management of apartment buildings; and changes in welfare regulations to allow the poor to save money. "The economy *may* work best if everyone is motivated by greed, but society doesn't," says Etzioni, who describes his philosophy as Communitarianism. "Society requires a sense of duty, obligation."

Instilling those values will not be easy. Americans want more 62 social services, but they also want lower taxes. They want jury trials, but they don't want to serve on juries. In a recent study of the attitudes of younger Americans, Democratic pollster Peter Hart interviewed teenagers who "reveal notions of America's unique character that emphasize freedom and license almost to the complete exclusion of service or participation. When asked to name some qualities that make this country special, the young people [in a focus group] sat in silence until one young man offered, 'Cable TV.' Asked how to encourage more young people to vote, one young woman replied, 'Pay them.' "

Thinking Critically About This Reading

1. What is our traditional notion of sin, and how is it affected by the culture of victimization?

2. If it could be shown convincingly that morality is primarily caused not by individual training or belief but by genetics and brain chemistry, how should this knowledge alter our present conception of penology?

3. What conflict, if any, do you see existing between a psychological and a religious view of human actions and choices?

4. What is there about a large urban area that is likely to foster the culture of victimization?

5. A January, 1992, lawsuit filed by death row inmates in San Quentin Prison argues for the right of condemned men to reproduce and petitions the court to allow them to store their sperm for artificial insemination of any willing woman. What is your opinion of this lawsuit?

Understanding the Writer's Process

1. Aside from introducing its theme, what else does the opening paragraph of this essay accomplish with the example of Rose Cipollone?

2. In paragraph 10, the author changes his tune slightly. Why?

3. The author states that a "truly imaginative person can find many, many reasons why he shouldn't be blamed for what he's done." What about this assertion might some editors find objectionable?

4. Aside from his examples, what is the bulk of evidence presented by the author to document what he calls the "culture of victimization"? What is your opinion of the effectiveness of this evidence?

5. Although the author organizes his essay mainly by the presentation of examples, what two other rhetorical strategies does he also use to drive home his point about victimization?

Examining the Writer's Language

1. Define the meanings of the following words used in this essay: ubiquitous (paragraph 1), decrying (1), deformation (7), voyeu-

ristic (9), syndromes (9), inextricably (17), anarchy (20), fortitude (26), transcendence (26), prurient (28), ennui (30), turpitude (34), exponentially (43), eradicating (45), vestige (45), redress (50), conundrum (51).

2. What inferences can be made about the audience of this article by the writer's style, syntax, and vocabulary?

3. In paragraph 11, the author quotes Shelby Steele, whom he identifies as a "black essayist." Why do you think the author chose to mention Steele's race here?

4. The author, in paragraph 11, writes: "Victim status not only confers the moral superiority of innocence. It enables people to avoid taking responsibility for their own behavior." What might make this passage objectionable in formal writing?

5. In paragraph 27 the author argues that the belief that one "was entitled" to be happy is a "central tenet of the postwar generation," reinforced in part by Dr. Spock. Who is Spock, and how did he reinforce this belief?

Suggestions for Writing

1. Write an essay in which you give examples from your own local newspaper of the emerging culture of victimization that Taylor describes.

2. Attack or defend the soundness of Taylor's thesis that a culture of victimization is emerging in the urban centers of the United States.

THE ENORMOUS RADIO

John Cheever

John Cheever (1912–1982), American writer, was born in Quincy, Massachusetts, and educated at Thayer Academy. Known primarily as a writer of exquisitely detailed short stories about the social amoralities of affluent city dwellers, Cheever is also the author of several novels—among them The Wapshot

Chronicle *(1957)*, The Wapshot Scandal *(1964)*, Bullet
Park *(1969)*, *and* Falconer *(1977)*.

Preparing to Read This Selection Critically

"The Enormous Radio" tells the story of an affluent
young couple whose new radio has the ability to pick up
the intimate conversations of their neighbors. The story
builds to a shattering recognition of moral frailty. As you
read, try to find present–day equivalents for these characters, who are prototypes drawn from urban America of
the late 1940s. What broad label would we attach to such
characters today? Do they worry about the same things
we do, or do their concerns seem remote from our own?
What does Irene Westcott find so troubling about her
neighbors, and how would we likely react to similar revelations today?

1   Jim and Irene Westcott were the kind of people who seem to
strike that satisfactory average of income, endeavor, and respectability that is reached by the statistical reports in college alumni bulletins. They were the parents of two young children, they had been
married nine years, they lived on the twelfth floor of an apartment
house near Sutton Place, they went to the theatre on an average of
10.3 times a year, and they hoped someday to live in Westchester.
Irene Westcott was a pleasant, rather plain girl with soft brown hair
and a wide, fine forehead upon which nothing at all had been written, and in the cold weather she wore a coat of fitch skins dyed to
resemble mink. You could not say that Jim Westcott looked younger
than he was, but you could at least say of him that he seemed to
feel younger. He wore his graying hair cut very short, he dressed
in the kind of clothes his class had worn at Andover, and his manner
was earnest, vehement, and intentionally naïve. The Westcotts dif-
fered from their friends, their classmates, and their neighbors only
in an interest they shared in serious music. They went to a great
many concerts—although they seldom mentioned this to anyone—
and they spent a good deal of time listening to music on the radio.

2   Their radio was an old instrument, sensitive, unpredictable,
and beyond repair. Neither of them understood the mechanics of
radio—or of any of the other appliances that surrounded them—and
when the instrument faltered, Jim would strike the side of the cabinet

with his hand. This sometimes helped. One Sunday afternoon, in the middle of a Schubert quartet, the music faded away altogether. Jim struck the cabinet repeatedly, but there was no response; the Schubert was lost to them forever. He promised to buy Irene a new radio, and on Monday when he came home from work he told her that he had got one. He refused to describe it, and said it would be a surprise for her when it came.

The radio was delivered at the kitchen door the following after- 3 noon, and with the assistance of her maid and the handyman Irene uncrated it and brought it into the living room. She was struck at once with the physical ugliness of the large gumwood cabinet. Irene was proud of her living room, she had chosen its furnishings and colors as carefully as she chose her clothes, and now it seemed to her that the new radio stood among her intimate possessions like an aggressive intruder. She was confounded by the number of dials and switches on the instrument panel, and she studied them thoroughly before she put the plug into a wall socket and turned the radio on. The dials flooded with a malevolent green light, and in the distance she heard the music of a piano quintet. The quintet was in the distance for only an instant; it bore down upon her with a speed greater than light and filled the apartment with the noise of music amplified so mightily that it knocked a china ornament from a table to the floor. She rushed to the instrument and reduced the volume. The violent forces that were snared in the ugly gumwood cabinet made her uneasy. Her children came home from school then, and she took them to the Park. It was not until later in the afternoon that she was able to return to the radio.

The maid had given the children their suppers and was su- 4 pervising their baths when Irene turned on the radio, reduced the volume, and sat down to listen to a Mozart quintet that she knew and enjoyed. The music came through clearly. The new instrument had a much purer tone, she thought, than the old one. She decided that tone was most important and that she could conceal the cabinet behind a sofa. But as soon as she had made her peace with the radio, the interference began. A crackling sound like the noise of a burning powder fuse began to accompany the singing of the strings. Beyond the music, there was a rustling that reminded Irene unpleasantly of the sea, and as the quintet progressed, these noises were joined by many others. She tried all the dials and switches but nothing dimmed the interference, and she sat down, disappointed and bewildered, and tried to trace the flight of the melody. The elevator shaft in her building ran beside the living-room wall, and it was the noise of the elevator that gave her a clue to the character of the static. The rattling of the elevator cables and the opening and closing of the elevator doors were reproduced in her loudspeaker, and, realizing that the radio was sensitive to electrical currents of all sorts, she began to discern through the Mozart the ringing of telephone bells, the dialing of phones, and the lamentation of a vacuum cleaner. By listening more carefully, she was able to distinguish doorbells, elevator bells, electric razors, and Waring mixers, whose sounds had been picked up from the apartments that surrounded hers and transmitted through her loudspeaker. The powerful and ugly instrument, with its mistaken sensitivity to discord, was more than she could hope to master, so she turned the thing off and went into the nursery to see her children.

5   When Jim Westcott came home that night, he went to the radio confidently and worked the controls. He had the same sort of experience Irene had had. A man was speaking on the station Jim had chosen, and his voice swung instantly from the distance into a force so powerful that it shook the apartment. Jim turned the volume control and reduced the voice. Then, a minute or two later, the interference began. The ringing of telephones and doorbells set in, joined by the rasp of the elevator doors and the whir of cooking appliances. The character of the noise had changed since Irene had tried the radio earlier; the last of the electric razors was being unplugged, the vacuum cleaners had all been returned to their closets, and the static reflected that change in pace that overtakes the city after the sun goes down. He fiddled with the knobs but couldn't get rid of the noises, so he turned the radio off and told Irene that in the morning he'd call the people who had sold it to him and give them hell.

6   The following afternoon, when Irene returned to the apartment from a luncheon date, the maid told her that a man had come and fixed the radio. Irene went into the living room before she took off her hat or her furs and tried the instrument. From the loudspeaker came a recording of the "Missouri Waltz." It reminded her of the thin, scratchy music from an old-fashioned phonograph that she sometimes heard across the lake where she spent her summers. She waited until the waltz had finished, expecting an explanation of the recording, but there was none. The music was followed by silence, and then the plaintive and scratchy record was repeated. She turned the dial and got a satisfactory burst of Caucasian music—the thump

of bare feet in the dust and the rattle of coin jewelry—but in the background she could hear the ringing of bells and a confusion of voices. Her children came home from school then, and she turned off the radio and went to the nursery.

When Jim came home that night, he was tired, and he took a 7 bath and changed his clothes. Then he joined Irene in the living room. He had just turned on the radio when the maid announced dinner, so he left it on, and he and Irene went to the table.

Jim was too tired to make even a pretense of sociability, and 8 there was nothing about the dinner to hold Irene's interest, so her attention wandered from the food to the deposits of silver polish on the candlesticks and from there to the music in the other room. She listened for a few minutes to a Chopin prelude and then was surprised to hear a man's voice break in. "For Christ's sake, Kathy," he said, "do you always have to play the piano when I get home?" The music stopped abruptly. "It's the only chance I have," a woman said. "I'm at the office all day." "So am I," the man said. He added something obscene about an upright piano, and slammed a door. The passionate and melancholy music began again.

"Did you hear that?" Irene asked. 9

"What?" Jim was eating his dessert.

"The radio. A man said something while the music was still going on—something dirty."

"It's probably a play."

"I don't think it *is* a play," Irene said.

They left the table and took their coffee into the living room. 10 Irene asked Jim to try another station. He turned the knob. "Have you seen my garters?" a man asked. "Button me up," a woman said. "Have you seen my garters?" the man said again. "Just button me up and I'll find your garters," the woman said. Jim shifted to another station. "I wish you wouldn't leave apple cores in the ashtrays," a man said. "I hate the smell."

"This is strange," Jim said.

"Isn't it?" Irene said.

Jim turned the knob again. " 'On the coast of Coromandel 11 where the early pumpkins blow,' " a woman with a pronounced English accent said, " 'in the middle of the woods lived the Yonghy-Bonghy-Bò. Two old chairs, and half a candle, one old jug without a handle . . .' "

"My God!" Irene cried. "That's the Sweeneys' nurse." 12

" 'These were all his worldly goods,' " the British voice continued.

13   "Turn that thing off," Irene said. "Maybe they can hear *us.*"
Jim switched the radio off. "That was Miss Armstrong, the Sweeney's nurse," Irene said. "She must be reading to the little girl. They live in 17-B. I've talked with Miss Armstrong in the Park. I know her voice very well. We must be getting other people's apartments."

14   "That's impossible," Jim said.
"Well, that was the Sweeneys' nurse," Irene said hotly. "I know her voice. I know it very well. I'm wondering if they can hear us."

15   Jim turned the switch. First from a distance and then nearer, nearer, as if borne on the wind, came the pure accents of the Sweeneys' nurse again: " '*Lady Jingly! Lady Jingly!*' " she said, " '*sitting where the pumpkins blow, will you come and be my wife?* said the Yonghy-Bonghy-Bò . . .' "

16   Jim went over to the radio and said "Hello" loudly into the speaker.
" '*I am tired of living singly,*' " the nurse went on, " '*on this coast so wild and shingly, I'm a-weary of my life; if you'll come and be my wife, quite serene would be my life . . .*' "

17   "I guess she can't hear us," Irene said. "Try something else."
Jim turned to another station, and the living room was filled with the uproar of a cocktail party that had overshot its mark. Someone was playing the piano and singing the "Whiffenpoof Song," and the voices that surrounded the piano were vehement and happy. "Eat some more sandwiches," a woman shrieked. There were screams of laughter and a dish of some sort crashed to the floor.

18   "Those must be the Fullers, in 11-E," Irene said. "I knew they were giving a party this afternoon. I saw her in the liquor store. Isn't this too divine? Try something else. See if you can get those people in 18-C."

19   The Westcotts overheard that evening a monologue on salmon fishing in Canada, a bridge game, running comments on home movies of what had apparently been a fortnight at Sea Island, and a bitter family quarrel about an overdraft at the bank. They turned off their radio at midnight and went to bed, weak with laughter. Sometime in the night, their son began to call for a glass of water and Irene got one and took it to his room. It was very early. All the lights in the neighborhood were extinguished, and from the boy's window she could see the empty street. She went into the living room and tried the radio. There was some faint coughing, a moan,

and then a man spoke. "Are you all right, darling?" he asked. "Yes," a woman said wearily. "Yes, I'm all right, I guess," and then she added with great feeling, "But, you know, Charlie, I don't feel like myself any more. Sometimes there are about fifteen or twenty minutes in the week when I feel like myself. I don't like to go to another doctor, because the doctor's bills are so awful already, but I just don't feel like myself, Charlie. I just never feel like myself." They were not young, Irene thought. She guessed from the timbre of their voices that they were middle-aged. The restrained melancholy of the dialogue and the draft from the bedroom window made her shiver, and she went back to bed.

The following morning, Irene cooked breakfast for the family—   20
the maid didn't come up from her room in the basement until ten—braided her daughter's hair, and waited at the door until her children and her husband had been carried away in the elevator. Then she went into the living room and tried the radio. "I don't want to go to school," a child screamed. "I hate school. I won't go to school. I hate school." "You will go to school," an enraged woman said. "We paid eight hundred dollars to get you into that school and you'll go if it kills you." The next number on the dial produced the worn record of the "Missouri Waltz." Irene shifted the control and invaded the privacy of several breakfast tables. She overheard demonstrations of indigestion, carnal love, abysmal vanity, faith, and despair. Irene's life was nearly as simple and sheltered as it appeared to be, and the forthright and sometimes brutal language that came from the loudspeaker that morning astonished and troubled her. She continued to listen until her maid came in. Then she turned off the radio quickly, since this insight, she realized, was a furtive one.

Irene had a luncheon date with a friend that day, and she left   21
her apartment at a little after twelve. There were a number of women in the elevator when it stopped at her floor. She stared at their handsome and impassive faces, their furs, and the cloth flowers in their hats. Which one of them had been to Sea Island? she wondered. Which one had overdrawn her bank account? The elevator stopped at the tenth floor and a woman with a pair of Skye terriers joined them. Her hair was rigged high on her head and she wore a mink cape. She was humming the "Missouri Waltz."

Irene had two Martinis at lunch, and she looked searchingly   22
at her friend and wondered what her secrets were. They had intended to go shopping after lunch, but Irene excused herself and

went home. She told the maid that she was not to be disturbed; then she went into the living room, closed the doors, and switched on the radio. She heard, in the course of the afternoon, the halting conversation of a woman entertaining her aunt, the hysterical conclusion of a luncheon party, and a hostess briefing her maid about some cocktail guests. "Don't give the best Scotch to anyone who hasn't white hair," the hostess said. "See if you can get rid of that liver paste before you pass those hot things, and could you lend me five dollars? I want to tip the elevator man."

23   As the afternoon waned, the conversations increased in intensity. From where Irene sat, she could see the open sky above the East River. There were hundreds of clouds in the sky, as though the south wind had broken the winter into pieces and were blowing it north, and on her radio she could hear the arrival of cocktail guests and the return of children and businessmen from their schools and offices. "I found a good-sized diamond on the bathroom floor this morning," a woman said. "It must have fallen out of that bracelet Mrs. Dunston was wearing last night." "We'll sell it," a man said. "Take it down to the jeweler on Madison Avenue and sell it. Mrs. Dunston won't know the difference, and we could use a couple of hundred bucks . . ." " 'Oranges and lemons, say the bells of St. Clement's,' " the Sweeneys' nurse sang. " 'Halfpence and farthings, say the bells of St. Martin's. When will you pay me? say the bells of old Bailey . . .' " "It's not a hat," a woman cried, and at her back roared a cocktail party. "It's not a hat, it's a love affair. That's what Walter Florell said. He said it's not a hat, it's a love affair," and then, in a lower voice, the same woman added, "Talk to somebody, for Christ's sake, honey, talk to somebody. If she catches you standing here not talking to anybody, she'll take us off her invitation list, and I love these parties."

24   The Westcotts were going out for dinner that night, and when Jim came home, Irene was dressing. She seemed sad and vague, and he brought her a drink. They were dining with friends in the neighborhood, and they walked to where they were going. The sky was broad and filled with light. It was one of those splendid spring evenings that excite memory and desire, and the air that touched their hands and faces felt very soft. A Salvation Army band was on the corner playing "Jesus Is Sweeter." Irene drew on her husband's arm and held him there for a minute, to hear the music. "They're really such nice people, aren't they?" she said. "They have such nice faces. Actually, they're so much nicer than a lot of the people

we know." She took a bill from her purse and walked over and dropped it into the tambourine. There was in her face, when she returned to her husband, a look of radiant melancholy that he was not familiar with. And her conduct at the dinner party that night seemed strange to him, too. She interrupted her hostess rudely and stared at the people across the table from her with an intensity for which she would have punished her children.

It was still mild when they walked home from the party, and   25 Irene looked up at the spring stars. " 'How far that little candle throws its beams,' " she exclaimed. " 'So shines a good deed in a naughty world.' " She waited that night until Jim had fallen asleep, and then went into the living room and turned on the radio.

Jim came home at about six the next night. Emma, the maid,   26 let him in, and he had taken off his hat and was taking off his coat when Irene ran into the hall. Her face was shining with tears and her hair was disordered. "Go up to 16-C, Jim!" she screamed. "Don't take off your coat. Go up to 16-C. Mr. Osborn's beating his wife. They've been quarreling since four o'clock, and now he's hitting her. Go up there and stop him."

From the radio in the living room, Jim heard screams, obscen-   27 ities, and thuds. "You know you don't have to listen to this sort of thing," he said. He strode into the living room and turned the switch. "It's indecent," he said. "It's like looking in windows. You know you don't have to listen to this sort of thing. You can turn it off."

"Oh, it's so horrible, it's so dreadful," Irene was sobbing. "I've   28 been listening all day, and it's so depressing."

"Well, if it's so depressing, why do you listen to it? I bought this damned radio to give you some pleasure," he said. "I paid a great deal of money for it. I thought it might make you happy. I wanted to make you happy."

"Don't, don't, don't, don't quarrel with me," she moaned, and   29 laid her head on his shoulder. "All the others have been quarreling all day. Everybody's been quarreling. They're all worried about money. Mrs. Hutchinson's mother is dying of cancer in Florida and they don't have enough money to send her to the Mayo Clinic. At least, Mr. Hutchinson says they don't have enough money. And some woman in this building is having an affair with the handy-man—with that hideous handyman. It's too disgusting. And Mrs. Melville has heart trouble and Mr. Hendricks is going to lose his job in April and Mrs. Hendricks is horrid about the whole thing and that girl who plays the 'Missouri Waltz' is a whore, a common whore, and the elevator man has tuberculosis and Mr. Osborn has been beating Mrs. Osborn." She wailed, she trembled with grief and checked the stream of tears down her face with the heel of her palm.

30 "Well, why do you have to listen?" Jim asked again. "Why do you have to listen to this stuff if it makes you so miserable?"

31 "Oh, don't, don't, don't," she cried. "Life is too terrible, too sordid and awful. But we've never been like that, have we, darling? Have we? I mean, we've always been good and decent and loving to one another, haven't we? And we have two children, two beautiful children. Our lives aren't sordid, are they, darling? Are they?" She flung her arms around his neck and drew his face down to hers. "We're happy, aren't we, darling? We are happy, aren't we?"

32 "Of course we're happy," he said tiredly. He began to surrender his resentment. "Of course we're happy. I'll have that damned radio fixed or taken away tomorrow." He stroked her soft hair. "My poor girl," he said.

33 "You love me, don't you?" she asked. "And we're not hypercritical or worried about money or dishonest, are we?"

"No, darling," he said.

34 A man came in the morning and fixed the radio. Irene turned it on cautiously and was happy to hear a California-wine commercial and a recording of Beethoven's Ninth Symphony, including Schiller's "Ode to Joy." She kept the radio on all day and nothing untoward came from the speaker.

35 A Spanish suite was being played when Jim came home. "Is everything all right?" he asked. His face was pale, she thought. They had some cocktails and went in to dinner to the "Anvil Chorus" from *Il Trovatore*. This was followed by Debussy's "La Mer."

36 "I paid the bill for the radio today," Jim said. "It cost four hundred dollars. I hope you'll get some enjoyment out of it."

"Oh, I'm sure I will," Irene said.

37 "Four hundred dollars is a good deal more than I can afford," he went on. "I wanted to get something that you'd enjoy. It's the last extravagance we'll be able to indulge in this year. I see that you haven't paid your clothing bills yet. I saw them on your dressing table." He looked directly at her. "Why did you tell me you'd paid them? Why did you lie to me?"

38 "I just didn't want you to worry, Jim," she said. She drank some water. "I'll be able to pay my bills out of this month's allowance. There were the slipcovers last month, and that party."

"You've got to learn to handle the money I give you a little 39
more intelligently, Irene," he said. "You've got to understand that
we won't have as much money this year as we had last. I had a
very sobering talk with Mitchell today. No one is buying anything.
We're spending all our time promoting new issues, and you know
how long that takes. I'm not getting any younger, you know. I'm
thirty-seven. My hair will be gray next year. I haven't done as well
as I'd hoped to do. And I don't suppose things will get any better."
"Yes, dear," she said. 40
"We've got to start cutting down," Jim said. "We've got to think
of the children. To be perfectly frank with you, I worry about money
a great deal. I'm not at all sure of the future. No one is. If anything
should happen to me, there's the insurance, but that wouldn't go
very far today. I've worked awfully hard to give you and the children
a comfortable life," he said bitterly. "I don't like to see all of my
energies, all of my youth, wasted in fur coats and radios and slipcovers and—"
"Please, Jim," she said. "Please. They'll hear us." 41
"*Who'll hear us?* Emma can't hear us."
"The radio."
"Oh, I'm sick!" he shouted. "I'm sick to death of your appre- 42
hensiveness. The radio can't hear us. Nobody can hear us. And what
if they can hear us? Who cares?"
Irene got up from the table and went into the living room. Jim 43
went to the door and shouted at her from there. "Why are you so
Christly all of a sudden? What's turned you overnight into a convent
girl? You stole your mother's jewelry before they probated her will.
You never gave your sister a cent of that money that was intended
for her—not even when she needed it. You made Grace Howland's
life miserable, and where was all your piety and your virtue when
you went to that abortionist? I'll never forget how cool you were.
You packed your bag and went off to have that child murdered as
if you were going to Nassau. If you'd had any reasons, if you'd had
any good reasons—"
Irene stood for a minute before the hideous cabinet, disgraced 44
and sickened, but she held her hand on the switch before she extinguished the music and the voices, hoping that the instrument
might speak to her kindly, that she might hear the Sweeneys' nurse.
Jim continued to shout at her from the door. The voice on the radio
was suave and noncommittal. "An early-morning railroad disaster
in Tokyo," the loudspeaker said, "killed twenty-nine people. A fire

in a Catholic hospital near Buffalo for the care of blind children was extinguished early this morning by nuns. The temperature is forty-seven. The humidity is eighty-nine."

Thinking Critically About This Reading

1. What is Cheever saying about the lives of ordinary people? Do you agree with his view?

2. How would you characterize the Westcotts' marriage?

3. Why does Irene shiver when she overhears the late-night conversation between the middle-aged couple?

4. Why does Irene become so emotional about the Salvation Army band that the Westcotts pass on the street? What does this incident say about her frame of mind?

5. What part does the city seem to play in the moral tone of the Westcotts' life? Do you agree with the English Romantic poets that the city is a corrupting force? Or do you think the moral climate of any life is independent of its surroundings?

Understanding the Writer's Process

1. The story opens by informing us that the Westcotts are statistically average in "income, endeavor, and respectability. . . ." What is the point behind this emphatic reminder that we are dealing with average people?

2. In paragraph 3, how does the author alert us (in his description of it) to the malign possibilities of the new radio?

3. Although the Westcotts, we are told in the first paragraph, have two children, we are never told their names. Why?

4. In paragraph 4, the author writes, "The powerful and ugly instrument, with its mistaken sensitivity to discord, was more than she could hope to master, so she turned the thing off and went into the nursery to see her children." What literary device is the author employing here, and for what reason?

5. We do not learn of Irene Westcott's moral failings until the very end of the story. Why? Were you entirely surprised by the revelations about her?

Examining the Writer's Language

1. Define the meanings of the following words as used in this story: malevolent (paragraph 3), discord (4), timbre (19), carnal (20), abysmal (20), impassive (21), sordid (31).

2. How does the title of this story aptly reflect its theme? In what way is the radio *enormous?*

3. What does the first name of the main female character mean? What is ironic about this name?

4. " 'I am tired of living singly,' " the nurse went on, " 'on this coast so wild and shingly, I'm a-weary of my life; if you'll come and be my wife, quite serene would be my life . . .' " What is especially ironic about this nursery rhyme picked up by the radio?

5. What city is the likely setting for this story? What language hints does the writer give of this setting? What assumption does he make about the reader of this story?

Writing Assignment Based on "The Enormous Radio"

"The Enormous Radio" is a story that peers beneath the surface of respectability and public facade to affirm an often overlooked truth—that things are not always what they seem. Write an essay in which you provide examples from society, nature, or the political structure in support of this truth.

STUDENT ESSAY (IN PROCESS) USING EXAMPLES

Henry Bastone

Henry Bastone is taking his first-year general education requirements leading to a B.A. in journalism. His ambition is to become a newspaper foreign correspondent. During a recent vacation, he had an opportunity to observe pigs on a ranch and became fascinated with their clever antics. When this essay was assigned, he decided to take advantage of his dis-coveries about pigs and include them as one of the examples. We believe his work reflects the value of close observation in preparation for writing.

<u>First draft</u>   Henry Bastone

                                                    Eng. 101

On second thought, "peccaries" is obscure

Illusion in Nature

~~Peccaries are my Kinds of People~~

People are not the only experts in the art of illusion. Among the many other examples in na-ture, three in particular immediately spring to mind. They are the caterpillar, the koala bear, and the pig. ¶ Something about the menacing undulations of a caterpillar's progress across a cabbage leaf can be thoroughly off-putting. Its blobby little suction pads for legs, to-gether with its bilious color, ~~fat,~~ its worm-like shape, and oozy texture, arouse in many people a sense of unease. If by some mischance a cater-pillar should find its way onto the arm of a particularly sensitive person, ~~an agitated outburst~~ a squeal of horror will surely follow, ceasing only when the offensive little creature, looped over the end of a pencil, is removed and slid back onto a leaf. Although ~~Just as~~ one will ~~automatically~~ eagerly reach one's hand to out ~~to~~ touch a flower, ~~so by the same token~~ one will

All three of these categories are not what they seem to be

~~one~~ snatch back that same hand in horror if it inadvertently comes into contact with a caterpillar lurking behind the bloom. But ^Caterpillars are simply ^masters of disguise, ~~though, since they have but two functions to fulfill: to eat, and not be eaten,~~ Consider the swallowtail caterpillar, for instance. Its one desire in life is to eat without ^Its sickly greenish color, being eaten; punctuated with white flecks, makes it almost thus indistinguishable from a disgusting bird-dropping, thereby allowing it to munch away unmolested. Similarly, ^The pussmoth caterpillar looks exactly like the brownish green, velvety plant it lives on. No one could possibly know that the true destiny of ~~this mean little creature~~ these caterpillars with ~~its~~ their voracious appetite, 5--is ~~was~~ to emerge, one bright, sunny day, as a splendid, imperial butterfly— its an amazing ~~insect~~ beings of incomparable beauty. Having magically ^cast off its caterpillar costume ~~during the~~ overnight ~~night~~, the butterfly no longer needs to find food, but now lives ~~only~~ for its ultimate ~~one~~ purpose—to attract a mate and start the whole process over again. Found in spring and early summer, where flowers grow in abundance, butterflies have long been associated with femininity, fecundity, and regeneration, Since ancient times, they have evoked a mood of effulgence as their brilliantly irridescent colors, flirtatious flight. patterns, and tantalizing beauty irrisistably attract the eye and titillate the senses ^of the beholder. Ever since the days of ~~As long ago as~~ the mythical Helen, women have adorned themselves with gold and enamelled butterflies, thus enhancing their

[margin notes:]

I've broken the unity of my thought here.

whose senses?

attract
what?

own beauty and power to attract, *men*. But the ephemeral beauty of the butterfly is as fleeting as the radiance of a young girl in the first bloom of youth. And, just as the graceful Helen was captured, held fast, and borne away to Troy by the dastardly Paris, so butterflies are collected, pinned down, and categorized, ending up with fascinating Latin labels, perhaps now even more beautiful than their own fast-fading colors. So it has been with women—and butterflies—for centuries.

Here I get off the track

The caterpillar's life is a wondrous tale. As Mark Twain's beggar turned out to be a prince, so the ugly caterpillar turns out to be a beautiful butterfly.

Announce a new example

~~One of man's popular misconceptions~~ Another *the* example ~~about~~ nature is the koala bear. For a start, ~~this~~ seemingly gentle, toy-like creature is not a bear, but *a* second cousin to the kangaroo—a marsupial. ~~Like the kangaroo, the koala bear rears its young in its pouch, and is also native to Australia~~. Lucky children everywhere have toy koala bears and love them because they are so cute and cuddly and seem to be endowed with especially amiable, intelligent natures. ~~Not true!~~ Although *real* koala bears are a tremendous tourist attraction in Australia, ~~visitors report that~~ these funny little animals are slow-moving, sluggish, not particularly bright or good humored, and, oftentimes, irritatingly obstinate. The luxuriously soft, grey fur in which the toy koala bears are encased is probably stripped off a poor, docile chinchilla rabbit, if the truth were known. And the notion

This animal fools just about everyone.

irrelevant

What a deception!

that real live koalas are also soft and silky
is patently false. ~~A vacationer, recently back~~
~~from Australia, said that~~ their fur feels like
the upholstery stuffing spilling out of an old
Ford car seat. The long, curved claws, which
enable koalas to cling to the branches of the
eucalyptus trees, on which they live, have also
caused vicious wounds to unwary game wardens.
The men in charge of this now endangered
species know better today. Now they wear cricket pads to protect their legs, and long leather
gloves to protect their arms and hands. As if
this were not enough, koalas are the most compulsive and finnicky eaters. Each adult koala
chews his way through two to three pounds of
special leaves each day. The leaves must be of
a certain age and from a special species of
eucalyptus that grows only in a certain soil
and is found only in a certain region of eastern
Australia. By the way, these leaves also account for the bad tempers of the koala bears because the eucalyptus acts like liquor, causing
the bears to be "hung over" most of the time. At
the turn of the century, literally millions of
koala bears were wiped out by an epidemic
virus, while tens of thousands more were
slaughtered for their fur. Nowadays, although
costly to keep, koalas are on the way back.

In reality [inserted]

transition needed [margin note]

Moreover [inserted]

I found this information interesting, but it is really irrelevant to my thesis. [margin note]

The truth is that koala bears are not at all the sweet pets they appear to be, but instead are rather dangerously perverse. [handwritten]

striking [margin note]

A ~~further~~ example of things not always
being what they seem ~~might include what appears~~

is the [inserted]

~~to be an almost~~ universal^{ly} disdain^{ed} ~~for the~~ pig.
In captivity, the appearance and behavior of
this animal hardly ~~add up~~ *conform* to the general ~~idea~~ *standard*
of what is good, ~~and what is~~ beautiful, or clean.
~~Also,~~ |Unlike the sacred cow of Hinduism, the
swine is nowhere considered holy. On the contrary, certain religious taboos about the consumption of pork, together with the biblical
injunction not to cast pearls before swine, may
well account, in part, for the pig's being one

The active voice here is more direct.

of the most maligned creatures on ~~the planet.~~ *earth.*
Most people consider the pig ~~The pig is usually thought of as being~~ stupid,
fat, and ugly—its appearance made even more
~~disagreeable because of~~ *repulsive by* its pinkish, fleshy
color. It also seems to be greedy, noisy,
short-sighted, and as belligerent as a drunk on
a Saturday night. Even worse, ~~for some,~~ it is
dirty and smells unbelievably awful. Pigs are
also supposed to be untidy and disorderly, like
people whose lives and homes are in a constant
state of disarray. ~~Oddly enough,~~ *Ironically,* the pig is ~~all too~~
often accused of foibles which ~~have~~ *are* pecul-
iarly human ~~qualities.~~ /When left to their own
devices, ~~however,~~ pigs are exceptionally clean
and orderly ~~by nature,~~ so that to liken a person
to a pig is really to insult a remarkable and
worthy creature. In reality, pigs are not in
the least stupid, ranking only second to the
Great Apes, among the mammals, for their mental
abilities. While it is true that they do not see
very well, their exceptional sense of smell
guides them with an almost clairvoyant accu-
racy_x in their quest for food and shelter. Al-

How different is the reality about pigs!

though wild pigs prefer plant food and like to
dig with their muzzles for succulent roots,
they can also hunt and catch small animals with
the deftness and agility of hungry wild cats.
Like humans, pigs are basically gregarious,
preferring to live in groups or pairs, and to
this end they often form large herds. In order
to maint~a~in contact within the herd, pigs vocalize readily, warning each other of danger or
attack. The constant squeaks, grunts, snorts,
and sneezes—all denote *either* distress, satisfaction, ~mating messages~ *affection*, or even perhaps hoggish
humor! Because of this species' extreme adaptability and superior intelligence, pigs can
be found the world over. They often roam vast
distances and are excellent swimmers.

no ¶ The pig's exceptional sense of smell,
coupled with its taste for the exotic, long ago
inspired the frugal farmers of southern France
to employ their farmyard swine in ~the~ tracking
down ~of~ the highly—prized, well—hidden truf-

*Interesting
history but
breaks the
unity of the
paragraph*

fles. ~Wild pigs had discovered and secretely
savored truffles long before people found out
about them and turned the harvesting of truffles into a highly lucrative business~. Buckled
into a harness, with an eager farmer dangling
on the other end of a long leash, the clever
~hunting~ pig will set off at a trot, in search of
the elusive truffle. Leading the farmer across
fields and hedgerows, valleys and swamps—its
muzzle waving in the air like a satellite dish—
the pig will break into a triumphant gallop as
it closes in on its prey, often hidden deep be-

neath the moist, leafy carpet of the forest
floor. The irony is that the very truffles the
pig muzzles up for its master will undoubtedly
end up in the stuffing for a delicious loin of
pork. Who is to say that the pig does not suspect this? Perhaps this is the reason why, in
some areas, pigs are considered too "willful"
to hunt truffles, and dogs have been trained in
their place. At least the dogs can be pretty
sure that they will not end up—trussed, stuffed, roasted, and garnished with truffles—as
the entree for Sunday dinner.

I need a final paragraph that summarizes the essay

¶ The world is full of humans whose lives have been completely misjudged. But other species of nature have been misjudged as well. Perhaps we should heed the advice given to the protagonist in Shakespeare's King Lear: *"See better."*

Final draft   Henry Bastone
                               Eng. 101

Illusions in Nature

People are not the only experts in the
art of illusion. Among the many other examples
in nature, three in particular immediately
spring to mind. They are the caterpillar, the
koala bear, and the pig. All three off these
creatures are not what they seem to be.
Something about the menacing undulations of a caterpillar's progress across a cab-

bage leaf can be thoroughly off-putting. Its blobby little suction pads for legs—together with its bilious color, its worm-like shape, and its oozy texture—arouse in many people a sense of unease. If by some mischance a caterpillar should find its way onto the arm of a particularly sensitive person, a squeal of horror will surely follow, ceasing only when the offensive little creature, looped over the end of a pencil, is removed and slid back onto a leaf. Although one will eagerly reach out one's hand to touch a flower, one will snatch back that same hand in horror if it inadvertently comes into contact with a caterpillar lurking behind the bloom. But caterpillars are simply masters of disguise. Consider the swallowtail caterpillar, for instance. Its one desire in life is to eat without being eaten; thus, its sickly greenish color, punctuated with white flecks, makes it almost indistinguishable from a disgusting bird-dropping, thereby allowing it to munch away unmolested. Similarly, the pussmouth caterpillar looks exactly like the brownish green, velvety plant it lives on. No one could possibly know that the real destiny of these caterpillars—these creatures with their voracious appetites—is to emerge, one bright sunny day, as splendid, imperial butterflies—amazing beings of incomparable beauty. Having magically cast off its caterpillar costume overnight, the butterfly no longer needs to find food, but now lives for its ultimate purpose—to attract a mate and

start the whole process over again. Found in
spring and early summer, where flowers grow in
abundance, butterflies have long been associated with femininity, fecundity, and regeneration. Since ancient times, they have
evoked a mood of effulgence as their brilliantly irridescent colors, flirtatious
flight patterns, and tantalizing beauty irresistibly attract the eye and titillate the
senses of the beholder. Ever since the days of
the mythical Helen, women have adorned themselves with gold and enamelled butterflies,
thus enhancing their own beauty and power to
attract men. The caterpillar's life is a wondrous tale. As Mark Twain's beggar turned out
to be a prince, so the ugly caterpillar turns
out to be a beautiful butterfly.

Another example of an illusion in nature
is the koala bear. This animal fools just about
everyone. For a start, the seemingly gentle,
toy-like little creature is not a bear, but a
marsupial, second cousin to the kangaroo.
Lucky children everywhere have toy koala bears
and love them because they are so cute and
cuddly and seem to be endowed with especially
amiable, intelligent natures. What a deception! Although real koala bears are a tremendous tourist attraction in Australia, these
funny little animals are slow-moving, sluggish, not particularly bright or good humored,
and, oftentimes, irritatingly obstinate. The
luxuriously soft, grey fur in which the toy
koala bears are encased is probably stripped

off a poor, docile chinchilla rabbit, if the truth were known. And the notion that real live koalas are also soft and silky is patently false. In reality their fur feels like the upholstery stuffing spilling out of an old Ford car seat. Moreover, the long, curved claws, which enable koalas to cling to the branches of the eucalyptus trees, on which they live, have also caused vicious wounds to unwary game wardens. The men in charge of this now endangered species wear cricket pads to protect their legs, and long leather gloves to protect their arms and hands. As if this were not enough, koalas are the most compulsive and finnicky eaters. Each adult koala daily chews its way through two to three pounds of special leaves. The leaves must be of a certain age and from a special species of eucalyptus that grows only in a certain soil and is found only in a certain region of eastern Australia. By the way, these leaves also account for the bad tempers of the koala bears because the eucalyptus acts like liquor, causing the bears to be "hung over" most of the time. The truth is that koala bears are not at all the sweet pets they appear to be, but instead are rather dangerously perverse.

A striking example of things not always being what they seem is the universally disdained pig. In captivity, the appearance and behavior of this animal hardly conform to the general standard of what is good, beautiful, or clean. Also, unlike the sacred cow of Hinduism, the swine is nowhere considered holy. On the contrary, certain religious taboos about the consumption of pork, together with the biblical injunction not to cast pearls before swine, may well account, in part, for the pig's being one of the most maligned creatures on earth. Most people consider the pig stupid, fat, and ugly—its appearance made even more repulsive by its pinkish, fleshy color. It also seems to be greedy, noisy, short-sighted, and as belligerent as a drunk on a Saturday night. Even worse, it is dirty and smells unbelievably awful. Pigs are also supposed to be untidy and disorderly, like people whose lives and homes are in a constant state of disarray. Ironically, the pig is all too often accused of foibles which are peculiarly human. How different is the reality about pigs! When left to their own devices, pigs are exceptionally clean and orderly, so that to liken a person to a pig is really to insult a remarkable and worthy creature. In reality, pigs are not in the least stupid, ranking only second to the Great Apes, among the mammals, for their mental abilities. While it is true that pigs do not see very well, their exceptional sense of smell guides them with almost clairvoyant accuracy in their quest for food and shelter. Although wild pigs prefer plant food and like to dig with their muzzles for succulent roots, they can also hunt and catch small animals with the deftness and agility of hungry wild cats. Like humans, pigs are basically gregarious, preferring to live in groups or pairs, and to this end they often

will undoubtedly end up in the stuffing for a
delicious loin of pork. Who is to say that the
pig does not suspect this? Perhaps this is the
reason why, in some areas, pigs are considered
too "willful" to hunt truffles, and dogs have
been trained in their place. At least the dogs
can be pretty sure that they will not end up—
trussed, stuffed, roasted, and garnished with
truffles—as the entree for Sunday dinner.

   The world is full of humans whose lives
have been completely misjudged. But other
species of nature have been misjudged as well.
Perhaps we should heed the advice given to the
protagonist in Shakespeare's <u>King Lear</u>: "See
better."

form large herds. In order to maintain contact
within the herd, pigs vocalize readily, warning each other of danger or attack. Their constant squeaks, grunts, snorts, and sneezes—all
denote either distress, satisfaction, affection, or even perhaps hoggish humor! Because of
this species' extreme adaptability and
superior intelligence, pigs can be found the
world over. They often roam vast distances and
are excellent swimmers. The pig's exceptional
sense of smell, coupled with its taste for the
exotic, long ago inspired the frugal farmers of
southern France to employ their farmyard swine
in tracking down the highly–prized, well–hidden truffles. Buckled into a harness, with an
eager farmer dangling on the other end of a long
leash, the clever hunting pig will set off at a
trot, in search of the elusive truffle. Leading

the farmer across fields and hedgerows, valleys and swamps—its muzzle waving in the air
like a satellite dish—the pig will break into a
triumphant gallop as it closes in on its prey,
often hidden deep beneath the moist, leafy carpet of the forest floor. The irony is that the
very truffles the pig muzzles up for its master

6

Explaining Process

[handwritten marginalia: definition description / may was...]

HOW TO WRITE A PROCESS ESSAY

The process essay is regarded as so elementary a form that many English departments do not even teach it. But as any harassed consumer who has ever struggled to assemble even a child's toy from the written instructions can tell you, process instructions and essays are seldom clear and often maddeningly dense. (Remember that frustrating Christmas Eve, those impossible dollhouse instructions, and the overwhelming urge to *murder* the writer?)

Basically, the process essay is a *how-to* essay with step-by-step advice or instructions on how to do something. Most such essays actually contain the term "how to" in their titles and generally follow a sequential explanation of the steps in the process. Sometimes an essayist follows a process not to instruct a reader in how to do it but rather to say how it typically is done. Such an essay is "Behind the Formaldehyde Curtain," which explains how a mortician goes about preparing a corpse for public viewing. Most of the other essays in this chapter typically focus on sequential instructions for getting something done.

1. Begin with a Clear Statement of What You Are Explaining

Tell the reader exactly what you are going to explain. Spare no detail, for it is essential that the reader know where the essay is leading. "Let us see how dictionaries are made and how the editors arrive at definitions," the writer tells us in "How Dictionaries Are Made." "Almost anyone can substantially reduce his exposure to cold germs and increase his resistance to them," is the opening statement of "How to Fight Cold-Proneness." Then the author tells us how to proceed in the fight against colds.

If you are instructing the reader in how to hoist a sail, how to make a quilt, how to perform the Heimlich maneuver—say so and plainly. Nor does it hurt to say what you are *not* going to explain, as this student did in an essay on how to sail upwind:

> The purpose of this essay is to give instructions on how to sail a boat upwind. My essay assumes a boat with a fixed

keel that is rigged as a sloop. Since sailing a centerboard boat or a two-master rigged either as a ketch or a yawl requires slightly different skills, I will not cover these kinds of boats in this essay.

This is the sort of finite statement of purpose that helps give the reader a precise idea of where an essay is heading.

2. Make Each Step of the Process Clear

While it is always important to link the ideas of an essay with adequate transitions, it is never more so than in the process essay. Generally, the easiest way is to mark the steps of process instructions by numbering them or using headings as Eichenlaub does in "How to Fight Cold–Proneness." This may strike you as "cookbookish" and rather inelegant, but it works.

Also, you can mark the steps of a process explanation with strong transitions, and one of the strongest transitions you can use for this purpose is a new paragraph. You even can begin this new paragraph with an opening sentence that, like a grappling hook, seizes your next topic or step. Here are some examples from "Behind the Formaldehyde Curtain":

> The body is first laid out in the undertaker's morgue—or rather, Mr. Jones is reposing in the preparation room—to be readied to bid the world farewell. (paragraph 7)

> The next step is to have at Mr. Jones with a thing called a trocar. (paragraph 13)

> The embalmer, having allowed an appropriate interval to elapse, returns to the attack, but now he brings into play the skill and equipment of sculptor and cosmetician. (paragraph 15)

Although grim, this process is depicted in unmistakable steps marked by clean transitions.

3. Explain from the Viewpoint of the Innocent

Making unwarranted assumptions about what a reader knows is bad enough in any essay, but generally fatal to the clarity of a process essay. The reader knows nothing about the process; the reader does not understand insider's jargon—these are the only two safe assumptions a process essayist can make. Steps that may seem plain and obvious to you are likely to mystify a beginner. Be careful, then, to explain in detail every single step, to bridge even obvious gaps between the steps, and to take nothing for granted in explaining a process. If bored, your reader can always skim over the obvious. But the baffled reader can only pore over the material while vainly scratching for a glimmer of understanding. Here is a snippet from a process essay that assumes too much:

> The boat heels when sailed into the wind because of complex forces of the wind acting against the sail, making it behave like an airfoil. The sail fills up on the windward side while air rushes past the leeward side creating a vacuum. Directional stability is threatened by the force of the heel, and if the center of effort of the boat is not improperly distributed, the boat will develop strong characteristics of lee helm. . . .

Although this passage might mean volumes to a sailor, to a naive reader it is incomprehensible in its denseness. What is "directional stability"? What does the writer mean by "center of effort," and how can it be "improperly distributed"? What is "lee helm"? Not one of these terms has been explained—up to now—yet the writer blithely assumes the reader will grasp them. This is the kind of mistake writers of instructional manuals typically make, leaving consumers either to mangle the disassembled product, or to trash the manual.

HOW DICTIONARIES ARE MADE

S. I. Hayakawa

Samuel Ichiye Hayakawa (1906–1992) was born in Vancouver, British Columbia, and educated at the University of Wisconsin. From 1969 to 1973, he was president of San Francisco State College, and from 1977 to 1983, a U.S. senator from California. Among his many works on semantics and linguistics are Language in Action *(1939) and* Language in Thought and Action *(1978). The process of dictionary making detailed in this essay by Hayakawa was used originally by Ac-*

cademia della Crusca to prepare the dictionary of the Italian language and later refined by English lexicographer Samuel Johnson for his Dictionary of the English Language *(1755), the first comprehensive work of its kind in English. In the short space of three years, Johnson single-handedly compiled 114,000 quotations that illustrated the definition of 40,000 words. Hundreds of years later, as Hayakawa tells us, Johnson's procedure is still followed by modern dictionary makers.*

Preparing to Read This Selection Critically

Notice at what point in his essay the author invites you to find out how dictionaries are made and how editors arrive at definitions. Your challenge is to follow the steps as the author presents them. You will want to be careful in separating one step from the next because each step may entail several editorial actions. You must note, too, that while explaining how dictionaries define words, the author also defines the term *dictionary* itself.

It is widely believed that every word has a correct meaning, 1 that we learn these meanings principally from teachers and grammarians (except that most of the time we don't bother to, so that we ordinarily speak "sloppy English"), and that dictionaries and grammars are the supreme authority in matters of meaning and usage. Few people ask by what authority the writers of dictionaries and grammars say what they say. I once got into a dispute with an Englishwoman over the pronunciation of a word and offered to look it up in the dictionary. The Englishwoman said firmly "What for? I am English. I was born and brought up in England. The way I speak *is* English." Such self-assurance about one's own language is not uncommon among the English. In the United States, however, anyone who is willing to quarrel with the dictionary is regarded as either eccentric or mad.

Let us see how dictionaries are made and how the editors arrive 2 at definitions. What follows applies, incidentally, only to those dictionary offices where first-hand, original research goes on—not those in which editors simply copy existing dictionaries. The task of writing a dictionary begins with the reading of vast amounts of the literature of the period or subject that the dictionary is to cover. As the editors read, they copy on cards every interesting or rare word, every unusual or peculiar occurrence of a common word, a large number of common words in their ordinary uses, and also the sentences in which each of these words appears, thus:

---

pail

The dairy *pails* bring home increase of milk

Keats, Endymion

1, 44–45

---

3   That is to say, the context of each word is collected, along with the word itself. For a really big job of dictionary writing, such as the *Oxford English Dictionary* (usually bound in about twenty-five volumes), millions of such cards are collected, and the task of editing occupies decades. As the cards are collected, they are alphabetized and sorted. When the sorting is completed, there will be for each word anywhere from two to three to several hundred illustrative quotations, each on its card.

4   To define a word, then, the dictionary editor places before him the stack of cards illustrating that word; each of the cards represents an actual use of the word by a writer of some literary or historical importance. He reads the cards carefully, discards some, rereads the rest, and divides up the stack according to what he thinks are the several senses of the word. Finally, he writes his definitions, following the hard-and-fast rule that each definition *must* be based on what the quotations in front of him reveal about the meaning of the word. The editor cannot be influenced by what *he* thinks a given word *ought* to mean. He must work according to the cards or not at all.

5   The writing of a dictionary, therefore, is not a task of setting up authoritative statements about the "true meanings" of words, but a task of *recording*, to the best of one's ability, what various

words *have meant* to authors in the distant or immediate past. *The writer of a dictionary is a historian, not a lawgiver.* If, for example, we had been writing a dictionary in 1890, or even as late as 1919, we could have said that the word "broadcast" means "to scatter" (seed, for example), but we could not have decreed that from 1921 on, the most common meaning of the word should become "to disseminate audible messages, etc., by radio transmission." To regard the dictionary as an "authority," therefore, is to credit the dictionary writer with gifts of prophecy which neither he nor anyone else possesses. In choosing our words when we speak or write, we can be *guided* by the historical record afforded us by the dictionary, but we cannot be *bound* by it, because new situations, new experiences, new inventions, new feelings, are always compelling us to give new uses to old words. Looking under a "hood," we should ordinarily have found, five hundred years ago, a monk; today, we find a motorcar engine.

Thinking Critically About This Reading

1. What role do word usage and grammar play in our social assessments of people?

2. If dictionaries merely record the way people speak and use words, what do we mean by *bad* grammar? What do we mean by *good* grammar? How may English usage be judged bad or good?

3. Should colleges and universities enforce a single standard of English on everyone, or should they allow dialect users to express themselves freely in their own vernacular?

4. Many writers, such as George Orwell, have written articles decrying the decline of English. What are your own views on this debate? Is English declining or merely changing?

5. Words are said to have denotative or connotative meanings. What is the difference between these two meanings? Which of these meanings are dictionaries better at recording? Why?

Understanding the Writer's Process

1. In paragraph 1, what does the anecdote about the Englishwoman demonstrate? Why do you think the author chose to tell it?

2. What lead-in to his process explanation does the writer use?

3. How does the author make clear his contention that dictionaries cannot predict meaning but can only record it?

4. Although most process explanations use numbers or letters to distinguish between process steps, this one does not. Why?

Examining the Writer's Language

1. Define the meanings of the following words as used in this essay: decreed (paragraph 5), disseminate (5).

2. As an example of how a dictionary maker uses cards, the author reproduces a dictionary card on the word *pail*. What makes a word like *pail* ideal for this example?

3. "As the editors read, they copy on cards every interesting or rare word, every unusual or peculiar occurrence of a common word, a large number of common words in their ordinary uses, and also the sentences in which each of these words appears. . . ." How does the author achieve emphasis in this sentence?

Suggestions for Writing

1. Write an essay outlining any sensible process that can be used to increase one's vocabulary.

2. Write an essay detailing the process you follow in studying for an exam.

AFTERNOON DINNER AT HITLER'S CHANCELLERY

Albert Speer

Albert Speer (1905–1981) was a German architect and National Socialist (Nazi) leader. When Hitler came to power, he chose Speer as his official architect, admiring his grandiose style and highly efficient method of organization. His designs include the stadium at Nuremberg (1934). In 1942, Speer became Minister for Armaments, and the following year he also took on some of Hermann Goering's responsibilities as planner of the German war economy. Using a kind of slave labor for the construction of strategic roads and defenses, Speer caused economic production to reach its peak in 1944, despite Allied bombardment. In the last months of World War II Speer did much to thwart Hitler's willingness to devastate Germany with his "scorched earth" policy. In 1946, Speer was condemned by the Nuremberg war crimes tribunal to Spandau Prison for 20 years. Released in 1966, he died in 1981. Speer is best known for his memoirs, Inside the Third Reich *(translated into English in 1970), from which the excerpt below is reprinted.*

Preparing to Read This Selection Critically

While the selection below does not instruct you in how to accomplish a task, it is nonetheless a process analysis in that it relates how a curious historical tradition took place. You will want to establish in your own mind what steps Hitler took to ensure that dinners at the Chancellery created a certain milieu reflecting a particular taste and atmosphere. Try to conjure up a physical image of the kinds of people invited and then make sure you understand what ideas Hitler wanted to get across to his guests during these informal dinners.

Between forty and fifty persons had access to Hitler's afternoon 1 dinner table in the Chancellery. They needed only to telephone his adjutant and say they would be coming. Usually they were the Gauleiters and Reichsleiters of the party, a few cabinet ministers, the members of the inner circle, but no army officers except for Hitler's Wehrmacht adjutant. More than once this adjutant, Colonel Schmundt, urged Hitler to allow the leading military men to dine with him; but Hitler would not have it. Perhaps he realized that the quality of his regular associates was such that the officers' corps would soon be looking down on them.

I too had free admission to Hitler's residence and often availed 2 myself of it. The policeman at the entrance to the front garden knew my car and opened the gate without making inquiries; I would park my car in the yard and enter the apartment that Troost had rebuilt.

It extended along the right side of the new Chancellery and was connected with it by a hall.

3   The SS member of Hitler's escort squad greeted me familiarly. I would hand him my roll of drawings and then, unaccompanied, like someone who belonged to the household, step into the spacious entrance hall: a room with two groups of comfortable seats, the white walls adorned with tapestries, the dark–red marble floor richly covered with rugs. There would usually be several guests there conversing, while others might be making private telephone calls. In general this room was favored because it was the only one where smoking was permitted.

4   It was not at all customary to use the otherwise mandatory *"Heil Hitler"* in greeting; a *"Guten Tag"* was far more common. The party lapel badge was also little flaunted in this circle, and uniforms were relatively seldom seen. Those who had penetrated as far as this privileged group could allow themselves a certain informality.

5   Through a square reception salon, which thanks to its uncomfortable furniture remained unused, you reached the actual living room, where the guests would be chatting, usually standing. This room, about a thousand square feet in area, was the only one in the entire apartment furnished with a measure of *Gemütlichkeit*.[1] Out of respect for its Bismarckian past it had been preserved during the major reconstruction of 1933–34 and had a beamed ceiling, wood wainscoting, and a fireplace adorned by a Florentine Renaissance coat of arms which Chancellor von Bülow had once brought back from Italy. This was the only fireplace on the lower floor. Around it were grouped a sofa and chairs upholstered in dark leather; behind the sofa stood a largish table with a marble top on which several newspapers usually lay. A tapestry and two paintings by Schinkel hung on the walls. They had been lent by the National Gallery for the Chancellor's apartment.

6   Hitler was royally unreliable about the time of his appearance. The dinner was usually set for about two o'clock, but it was apt to be three or later before Hitler arrived, sometimes from the upper private rooms of the apartment, often from a conference in the Chancellery. His entrance was as informal as that of any private individual. He greeted his guests by shaking hands; everyone gathered in a circle around him. He would express his opinion on one or another problem of the day, with a few favored guests he inquired,

---

[1] German for *comfort*.

usually in a conventional tone, about the well–being of "your spouse." Then he took the news excerpts from his press chief, sat down off to one side, and began to read. Sometimes he would pass an excerpt on to one of the guests because the news seemed especially interesting to him, and would throw out a few casual remarks about it.

The guests would continue to stand around for another fifteen   7
or twenty minutes, until the curtain was drawn away from a glass door that led to the dining room. The house steward, a man with the encouraging bulk of a restaurateur, would inform Hitler quietly, in a tone in keeping with the whole unpublic atmosphere, that dinner was ready. The Fuehrer[2] would lead the way; the others followed him into the dining room without any order of rank.

Of all the rooms in the Chancellor's apartment that Professor   8
Troost had redecorated, this large square dining room (forty by forty feet) was the most harmonious. A wall with three glass doors led out to the garden. Opposite was a large buffet of palisander wood; above it hung a painting by Kaulbach which had a certain charm because it was unfinished; at any rate it was without some of the embarrassing aspects of that eclectic painter. Each of the two other walls was marked by a shallow recess in which, on pedestals of marble, stood nude studies by the Munich sculptor Josef Wackerle. To either side of the recesses were more glass doors which led to the pantry, to a large salon, and into the living room from which we had come. Smoothly plastered walls, painted ivory, and equally light-colored curtains, produced a feeling of openness and brightness. Slight jogs in the walls carried out the clean, austere rhythm; a molding held it all together. The furnishing was restrained and restful: a large round table for about fifteen persons, ringed by simple chairs with dark red leather seats. The chairs were all alike, the host's no more elaborate than the rest. At the corners of the room stood four more small tables, each with from four to six similar chairs. The tableware consisted of light, plain china and simple glasses; both had been selected by Professor Troost before his death. A few flowers in a bowl formed the centerpiece.

Such was the "Merry Chancellor's Restaurant," as Hitler often   9
called it in speaking to his guests. He had his seat on the window side of the room, and before entering would select which of the

---

[2] German for *leader*, a term applied to Hitler.

guests would be seated at his side. All the rest sat down around the table wherever they found a place. If many guests came, the adjutants and persons of lesser importance, among whom I belonged, took seats at the side tables—an advantage, I always thought, since there we could talk with less constraint.

10   The food was emphatically simple. A soup, no appetizer, meat with vegetables and potatoes, a sweet. For beverage we had a choice between mineral water, ordinary Berlin bottled beer, or a cheap wine. Hitler was served his vegetarian food, drank Fachinger mineral water, and those of his guests who wished could imitate him. But few did. It was Hitler himself who insisted on this simplicity. He could count on its being talked about in Germany. Once, when the Helgoland fishermen presented him with a gigantic lobster, this delicacy was served at table, much to the satisfaction of the guests, but Hitler made disapproving remarks about the human error of consuming such ugly monstrosities. Moreover, he wanted to have such luxuries forbidden, he declared.

11   Goering[3] seldom came to these meals. Once, when I left him to go to dinner at the Chancellery, he remarked: "To tell the truth, the food there is too rotten for my taste. And then, these party dullards from Munich! Unbearable."

12   Hess[4] came to table about once every two weeks; he would be followed by his adjutant in a rather weird getup, carrying a tin vessel containing a specially prepared meal which was to be rewarmed in the kitchen. For a long time it was hidden from Hitler that Hess had his own special vegetarian meal served to himself. When someone finally gave the secret away, Hitler turned irritably to Hess in the presence of the assembled company and blustered, "I have a first–class diet cook here. If your doctor has prescribed something special for you, she will be glad to prepare it. But you cannot bring your food with you." Hess, even then inclining to obstinate contrariness, began explaining that the components of his meals had to be of special biodynamic origin. Whereupon Hitler bluntly informed him that in that case he should take his meals at home. Thereafter Hess scarcely ever came to the dinners.

13   When, at the instance of the party, word was sent out that all households in Germany should eat a one-dish meal on Sundays, thereby promoting guns instead of butter, only a tureen of soup was

[3] Hermann Goering, Air Minister of Germany and close friend of Hitler.
[4] Rudolf Hess, Hitler's Deputy Fuehrer.

served at Hitler's table too. The number of Sunday guests thereafter shrank to two or three, which provoked some sarcastic remarks from Hitler about the spirit of sacrifice among his associates. For there would also be a list passed around the table, with every guest pledging his donation to the war effort. Every one-dish meal cost me fifty or a hundred marks.

Thinking Critically About This Reading

1. What gathering, equivalent to these dinners described, do we have in the United States? What purpose do such gatherings achieve? Why were women excluded from these dinners?

2. What general impression did Hitler wish to leave concerning his afternoon dinners? Is the impression of advantage to him or not? Give reasons for your answer.

3. History has treated Hitler as a maniacal man whose greed for power was enormous and whose cruelty toward certain races knew no bounds. For instance, his "final solution" toward Jews, whom he hated, created the nightmare of concentration camps in which entire families were exterminated in gas chambers. Why are none of these aspects of Hitler's character revealed in this description—or are they? Comment on this question.

4. From your knowledge of history, what happened to Hitler's circle of friends invited to the Chancellery? What is your opinion of their fate? What is your philosophy concerning the responsibilities of having power?

5. Hitler referred to his dining room as the "Merry Chancellor's Restaurant." What comments in the selection indicate that not everyone thought of the dinners in such laudatory terms?

Understanding the Writer's Process

1. How does the author organize his process analysis? Divide the process into five or six separate steps.

2. From what point of view is the essay written? What advantage, if any, does it have?

3. Why do you suppose the author spends so much time describing the surroundings of the Chancellery, even including the names of the artists whose works hung on the walls and giving the details of furniture style, wall decoration, and paint color?

4. From the author's description of the dining room, do you agree that it was filled with a measure of comfort? What dominant impression would you ascribe to the place?

5. What effect does the final paragraph have on the entire process analysis?

Examining the Writer's Language

1. Using a dictionary, define the following words as they are used in Speer's essay: adjutant (paragraph 1), Bismarckian (5), wainscoting (5), steward (7), restaurateur (7), jogs (8), constraint (9), blustered (12), contrariness (12).

2. What effect do the German words sprinkled throughout the essay have? Do they prevent you from understanding the essay unless they are translated? Explain your answer.

3. In paragraph 6, what words are important to building a portrait of Hitler? What image do they convey?

4. What do you think the author means by the word "harmonious" as related to the Chancellery dining room? (See paragraph 8.)

5. What is the point of including the details of what Hitler ate and drank?

Suggestions for Writing

1. Write an essay in which you describe the process of dining in unostentatious or even humble surroundings—such as a picnic in the park, a potluck meal in the apartment of a struggling young couple, or a birthday dinner in an ordinary middle–class home. Organize your essay according to the chronological order in which the meal occurs.

2. Using your imagination, describe what you consider an ideal Christmas or Thanksgiving dinner. Organize your description as a process analysis, outlining each step of the event.

HOW TO FIGHT COLD-PRONENESS

John E. Eichenlaub

John E. Eichenlaub (b. 1922) is a physician who
spent years practicing general medicine, taking care of

the many ailments that families are subject to. He did this so successfully that in 1953 he decided to write articles and books that would make his home remedies available to a larger audience than just his private patients. Besides his popular book, A Minnesota Doctor's Home Remedies for Common and Uncommon Ailments *(1960), from which the essay below is reprinted, he also has written a number of articles for popular magazines.*

Preparing to Read This Selection Critically

Because the advice offered in this selection is addressed to anyone prone to the common cold, you will need to place yourself in that category in order to get the most from the selection. As you follow, step by step, what this old-fashioned family doctor has to suggest, compare his advice to television advertisements concerning colds or to your own physician's advice. Ask yourself if heeding the preventions outlined might cause risks to your health. Does the advice run counter to what you know about colds? Would you feel comfortable trying these remedies and recommending them to others? Or does the advice appear to be esoteric and dangerously unscientific?

Almost anyone can substantially reduce his exposure to cold 1 germs and substantially increase his resistance to them. If you are particularly subject to colds, home measures to counteract this tendency usually prove especially worthwhile. These measures are more effective than any cold shot yet devised and involve absolutely no medical expense or risk.

You cannot dodge cold germs simply by avoiding people who 2 sneeze and cough. Colds spread mainly before complaints begin and reach you mainly from members of your own family or close circle of friends. A few germs, even of the worst possible kind, do you no harm. It takes thousands or millions of germs, all from the same germ family, to set up disease. Even one less than the crucial number leads to no trouble at all. You can cut down spread of germs through mouth moisture, improperly sanitized dishes, and close quarters in the firm knowledge that even a few less germs spread may mean a great deal less sickness in your household.

3   **Protect your nose lining against cold germs.** Some home measures for preventing colds are just common sense: enough rest, well–chosen foods, and sufficient warm clothing. Science can add two tremendous aids: extra help for your body's main shield against cold germs, which is your nose lining, and heightened resistance through cold–fighting morale.

4   **How your nose lining protects you against germs.** Your nose lining spreads an invisibly thin sheet of sticky mucus over the entire inside of your nose. When you breathe in germs, most of them stick in the sheet of mucus. Tiny sweeper cells continually brush the mucus back into your throat. A brand new sheet forms every six minutes or so. Meanwhile sweepings pile up at the back of your throat until they make a glob big enough for you to swallow. Your stomach acids kill the germs.

5   In the wintertime, the dry, heated air turns your nose lining's mucus blanket to crusts. It may even dry the nose lining until it cracks, providing completely free access to germs. Moisturization prevents this effect, and thus increases your nose lining's resistance.

6   How can you moisturize your nose lining? Three main methods are worthwhile:

7   1. Add moisture to heated air. Humidifiers or moisturizing pans on the radiators are worthwhile. They at least take the edge off the dryness of indoor air. They cannot do the whole job, since thorough home air moisturization requires evaporation of several gallons of water each day.

8   2. Turn down the heat. When you warm air from 68 degrees to 80 degrees, you increase its drying power more than fourfold. It's best to heat your nose only to 68 degrees and put on extra sweaters or heavier clothes for bodily warmth. At night, you can cool your bedroom five or ten degrees by turning heat down or by ventilation. That gives your nose lining a rest from too-dry, overheated air. Extra blankets keep your body comfortably warm.

9   3. Use home–made moisturizing nose spray. You can banish dry crusts and help your nose's defense by using this moisturing spray:

>   1 tablespoon glycerin, obtained from any drugstore without
>   prescription.
>   1½ tablespoons 70% alcohol (rubbing alcohol strength).
>   1 teaspoon table salt.
>   1 pint tap or distilled water.

If your tap water has a heavy odor of chlorine, let it stand   10
overnight in an open vessel. Mix the ingredients and stir until salt
is thoroughly dissolved. Pour into clean bottle and stopper firmly.

Get a plastic pocket atomizer for about 35¢ at the drugstore,   11
fill it with this solution, and use it several times a day as needed.

Last-minute action to ward off a cold. Can you tell when a   12
cold is just coming on? If you can, you may be able to stop some
colds from getting a real start.

The first thing to try is moisturizing spray (see above). Spray   13
the inside of your nose thoroughly every hour or two. Keep warm
and get a good night's sleep. This program alone will stop some
colds in their tracks.

If you have enough colds to make it worthwhile, one other   14
medicine might help you. It's a combination of codeine and papav-
erine, which are available on prescription only. When used at the
first sign of a cold, it sometimes stops the nose lining responses
which allow germs to get a foothold. When you next see your doctor,
ask if you should have this material on hand and how you should
use it when you feel a cold coming on.

Fight colds by mental measures. Parts of your brain actually   15
govern your circulation and many other bodily functions through
which you fight off germs. Your emotional state greatly influences
these functions. It can thus help or hurt your resistance to all kinds
of infection. This effect is very strong. Just thinking you are liable
to get a cold may tip the balance and make you fall victim to one.

A research expert proved the importance of emotions to the   16
origin of colds without even trying. He wanted to grow cold germs
in the laboratory. In order to tell whether the germs were present
in his culture solution, he decided to spray some into a few people's
noses. The subjects were left in hospital rooms and protected from
new infections until any strong germs they already had acquired
would have shown up. (Some cold germs are probably present in
most people's throats at all times, but not enough to cause a cold
so long as their resistance is normal.) Then he sprayed a few people
with ordinary water telling them the stuff was loaded with germs.
One out of five promptly came down with a cold.

The rest of the experiment proved that strong cold germs were   17
present in the doctor's other mixture. But this very first step proved
a point which is very important to you. It means that even weak
cold germs can be helped along by mental forces until they overcome
your resistance. When you get chilled or feel a draught, the chances

are that you say to yourself: "Now I'm in for it! I'll have a cold tomorrow for sure!" That conviction itself causes concern and emotional response which actually help to give you the cold.

18   **Build your cold–fighting morale.** You can protect yourself against two thirds of all colds by building cold–fighting morale. That's what a team of researchers at Michigan found out when they were experimenting with a new cold vaccine. They thought they had an effective product and designed tests to prove the fact. One group of people got the vaccine. Another group got nothing, and still another got distilled water, being told that they were getting cold shots.

19   When the results were in, the people who took the cold shots reported only one third as many colds as the ones who had nothing at all. But the ones who got the distilled water had even less! The conviction that they would get less colds actually cut tremendously the number of colds these people suffered!

20   What does this mean to you? Certainly not that your colds aren't real: they're real, germ–caused infections. But your resistance may be affected so much by concern about old superstitions that you have many colds which you could otherwise fight off.

21   This need not be. You can use mental forces to *increase* your resistance instead of impair it. You can build your cold–fighting morale to the point where you have many less colds per year.

22   **How to build cold-fighting morale.** Cold–fighting morale is best built on one firm conviction: *nothing that happens to you can give you a cold.* You need never say to yourself: "Drat it! I did thus–and–so, so now I'll probably get a cold!" Absolutely none of the common experiences you might note can give you a cold.

23   Let's look at some of the ideas science has explored in reaching this conclusion:

24   *Draughts, night air, and going without a hat do not cause colds.* The lining of your nose is definitely affected by nerve and emotional balance. Your nose can get stopped up or runny on the basis of pure nerve reflex when you are exposed to wind or cold. It can get stopped up and runny after any uncomfortable nerve–tickling exposure, even through slight draughts. But unless worry or concern add further burdens, your nose lining will usually get back to normal before the ever–present cold germs actually get a start.

25   *Chilling doesn't cause colds.* When I was only a child, I remember my aunt stomping her feet one day as she came in the front door.

"Brrrr—" she said. "I'm chilled clean through. Have a cold 26 tomorrow, like as not."

The next day, sure enough! She had a cold. But today's science 27 says that my aunt probably already had the cold germs in her body, and those germs were already starting disease when she first walked in my door saying "Brrrr—." My aunt almost certainly felt chilly because of a beginning cold; she didn't get the cold because of the chill. But millions of people are positive that whenever they get chilled a cold will certainly follow. If they actually do get chilled, not simply get chilly sensations because of a beginning cold, how many of them actually suffer a cold, not because of the chill, but because of fearful certainty that they are headed for the sickbed?

Have confidence in your body's powers. Of course, it pays 28 to dress yourself warmly to avoid extreme exposure. But it pays to have confidence in your body, too. Take reasonable measures to avoid chilling, then shrug your shoulders and forget it if you find that you've been uncomfortably cool.

Other people's colds aren't easy to catch. Suppose a stranger 29 sneezes at you in a store. What are your chances of getting a cold?

Actually, almost none at all. Children, who take little care to 30 dodge other people's germs, get colds four times out of five when they are right in the household with a cold victim. But as an adult, you will *escape* four times out of five even if you are in close family contact with a cold. Moreover, most people who sneeze or cough at you in public have already passed the early days when their cold can still be spread and could not give you germs no matter how hard they tried. Many people sneeze or cough because of conditions which are impossible to spread, like allergy. Your chance of catching a stranger's cold is almost zero, but your chance of worrying yourself into a cold after he's sneezed in your face is considerable indeed, unless you have become convinced that colds are rarely spread through such contact.

Cold-fighting morale can really protect you. If you are con- 31 vinced that nothing is likely to cause colds, you won't suffer psychologically induced ones. You will probably also increase your resistance against whatever cold-causing germs you meet. So whenever you find yourself thinking that what has just happened might cause a cold, repeat to yourself several times: "Nothing that happens to me can give me a cold. Not draughts, not chilling, not even a victim's sneeze! Nothing that happens to me can give me a cold!" As you go about your daily activities, have confidence in your body's powers of resistance. You will still occasionally meet an over-whelming number of cold germs and suffer an infection. But you can throw off the bulk of cold germs without even a sniffle.

Thinking Critically About This Reading

1. What difference in purpose and approach do you detect in the process analysis of Eichenlaub's essay and that of Albert Speer concerning afternoon dinners with Hitler (see pp. 311–315)?

2. Why do you suppose the author emphasizes the fact that one cannot avoid colds by staying away from anyone who displays cold symptoms? Do you agree with him? Why or why not?

3. What are the strengths of this essay? What are its weaknesses? Explain each. How convincing is the information provided?

4. Have you ever experienced an illness that seemed to be the direct result of your emotional state? If so, describe the situation. Do you believe in the connection between mind and disease or health? Support your answer.

5. Reread paragraph 4 and use it as a model to explain any other natural process with which you are familiar.

Understanding the Writer's Process

1. What techniques does Eichenlaub use to help you follow his organization?

2. Process writing usually involves other kinds of rhetorical developments as well. Which other developments are involved in this essay? Point to individual passages.

3. How is coherence maintained between paragraphs 5 and 6?

4. What sentence best represents the culmination of the author's process of building a cold–fighting morale?

5. What is the thesis of this essay and where is it stated? How effective is this placement?

Examining the Writer's Language

1. The following words are important to an understanding of the essay. Define each word and check your definition against that

of a dictionary: mucus (paragraph 4), humidifiers (7), evaporation (7), culture (16), draught (17), impair (21), induced (31).
2. What audience is addressed in this essay? How can you tell?
3. How does the author create a closeness between him and his audience—as if he were in the reader's home offering personal advice?
4. What is the author's tone throughout the essay? How effective do you find this tone?
5. How does the author avoid using medical terminology in explaining his cure and prevention of colds?

Suggestions for Writing

1. Write a process essay describing your own step–by–step method of fighting a cold or any other illness that has victimized you.
2. Write an essay in which you delineate the steps our government should take to fight epidemics such as AIDS.

BEHIND THE FORMALDEHYDE CURTAIN

Jessica Mitford

Jessica Mitford (b. 1917), born into an aristocratic English family and educated at home, migrated to the United States as a young woman and became a naturalized citizen. She has become known as one of America's foremost muckrakers and has written many books that expose the silliness and corruption in American society. Among her published works are The American Way of Death *(1963) and* Kind and Unusual Punishment: The Prison Business *(1973). She frequently contributes articles to such widely read periodicals as* The Atlantic Monthly *and* Harper's.

Preparing to Read This Selection Critically

"Behind the Formaldehyde Curtain," a title given by some anonymous anthology editor to this widely reprinted excerpt from *The American Way of Death*, offers a close look at the funeral industry. Not for the squeamish, this article recounts in grisly detail the absurd and barbaric, to say nothing of expensive, practice of embalming. To gain a full understanding of this essay, you must be sure to grasp the satirical tone used by its author. This tone, however, does not stop the author from enumerating carefully each step in the process of readying a corpse for viewing. When you have reached the end of the essay, you should be able to state in your own words what purpose the author had in mind for giving such an extravagant and dramatic process analysis.

1   The drama begins to unfold with the arrival of the corpse at the mortuary.

2   Alas, poor Yorick! How surprised he would be to see how his counterpart of today is whisked off to a funeral parlor and is in short order sprayed, sliced, pierced, pickled, trussed, trimmed, creamed, waxed, painted, rouged and neatly dressed—transformed from a common corpse into a Beautiful Memory Picture. This process is known in the trade as embalming and restorative art, and is so universally employed in the United States and Canada that the funeral director does it routinely, without consulting corpse or kin. He regards as eccentric those few who are hardy enough to suggest that it might be dispensed with. Yet no law requires embalming, no religious doctrine commends it, nor is it dictated by considerations of health, sanitation, or even of personal daintiness. In no part of the world but in Northern America is it widely used. The purpose of embalming is to make the corpse presentable for viewing in a suitably costly container; and here too the funeral director routinely, without first consulting the family, prepares the body for public display.

3   Is all this legal? The processes to which a dead body may be subjected are after all to some extent circumscribed by law. In most states, for instance, the signature of next of kin must be obtained before an autopsy may be performed, before the deceased may be cremated, before the body may be turned over to a medical school for research purposes; or such provision must be made in the decedent's will. In the case of embalming, no such permission is required nor is it ever sought. A textbook, *The Principles and Practices of Embalming*, comments on this: "There is some question regarding

the legality of much that is done within the preparation room." The author points out that it would be most unusual for a responsible member of a bereaved family to instruct the mortician, in so many words, to *"embalm"* the body of a deceased relative. The very term "embalming" is so seldom used that the mortician must rely upon custom in the matter. The author concludes that unless the family specifies otherwise, the act of entrusting the body to the care of a funeral establishment carries with it an implied permission to go ahead and embalm.

Embalming is indeed a most extraordinary procedure, and one must wonder at the docility of Americans who each year pay hundreds of millions of dollars for its perpetuation, blissfully ignorant of what it is all about, what is done, how it is done. Not one in ten thousand has any idea of what actually takes place. Books on the subject are extremely hard to come by. They are not to be found in most libraries or bookshops. 4

In an era when huge television audiences watch surgical operations in the comfort of their living rooms, when, thanks to the animated cartoon, the geography of the digestive system has become familiar territory even to the nursery school set, in a land where the satisfaction of curiosity about almost all matters is a national pastime, the secrecy surrounding embalming can, surely, hardly be attributed to the inherent gruesomeness of the subject. Custom in this regard has within this century suffered a complete reversal. In the early days of American embalming, when it was performed in the home of the deceased, it was almost mandatory for some relative to stay by the embalmer's side and witness the procedure. Today, family members who might wish to be in attendance would certainly be dissuaded by the funeral director. All others, except apprentices, are excluded by law from the preparation room. 5

A close look at what does actually take place may explain in large measure the undertaker's intractable reticence concerning a procedure that has become his major *raison d'être*. Is it possible he fears that public information about embalming might lead patrons to wonder if they really want this service? If the funeral men are loath to discuss the subject outside the trade, the reader may, understandably, be equally loath to go on reading at this point. For those who have the stomach for it, let us part the formaldehyde curtain. . . . 6

The body is first laid out in the undertaker's morgue—or rather, Mr. Jones is reposing in the preparation room—to be readied to bid the world farewell. 7

8   The preparation room in any of the better funeral establishments has the tiled and sterile look of a surgery, and indeed the embalmer-restorative artist who does his chores there is beginning to adopt the term "dermasurgeon" (appropriately corrupted by some mortician-writers as "demi-surgeon") to describe his calling. His equipment, consisting of scalpels, scissors, augers, forceps, clamps, needles, pumps, tubes, bowls and basins, is crudely imitative of the surgeon's, as is his technique, acquired in a nine- or twelve-month post-high-school course in an embalming school. He is supplied by an advanced chemical industry with a bewildering array of fluids, sprays, pastes, oils, powders, creams, to fix or soften tissue, shrink or distend it as needed, dry it here, restore the moisture there. There are cosmetics, waxes and paints to fill and cover features, even plaster of Paris to replace entire limbs. There are ingenious aids to prop and stabilize the cadaver: a Vari-Pose Head Rest, the Edwards Arm and Hand Positioner, the Repose Block (to support the shoulders during the embalming), and the Throop Foot Positioner, which resembles an old-fashioned stocks.

9   Mr. John H. Eckels, president of the Eckels College of Mortuary Science, thus describes the first part of the embalming procedure: "In the hands of a skilled practitioner, this work may be done in a comparatively short time and without mutilating the body other than by slight incision—so slight that it scarcely would cause serious inconvenience if made upon a living person. It is necessary to remove the blood, and doing this not only helps in the disinfecting, but removes the principal cause of disfigurements due to discoloration."

10   Another textbook discusses the all-important time element: "The earlier this is done, the better, for every hour that elapses between death and embalming will add to the problems and complications encountered. . . ." Just how soon should one get going on the embalming? The author tells us, "On the basis of such scanty information made available to this profession through its rudimentary and haphazard system of technical research, we must conclude that the best results are to be obtained if the subject is embalmed before life is completely extinct—that is, before cellular death has occurred. In the average case, this would mean within an hour after somatic death." For those who feel that there is something a little rudimentary, not to say haphazard, about this advice, a comforting thought is offered by another writer. Speaking of fears entertained in early days of premature burial, he points out, "One of the effects

of embalming by chemical injection, however, has been to dispel fears of live burial." How true; once the blood is removed, chances of live burial are indeed remote.

To return to Mr. Jones, the blood is drained out through the 11 veins and replaced by embalming fluid pumped in through the arteries. As noted in *The Principles and Practices of Embalming,* "every operator has a favorite injection and drainage point—a fact which becomes a handicap only if he fails or refuses to forsake his favorites when conditions demand it." Typical favorites are the carotid artery, femoral artery, jugular vein, subclavian vein. There are various choices of embalming fluid. If Flextone is used, it will produce a "mild, flexible rigidity. The skin retains a velvety softness, the tissues are rubbery and pliable. Ideal for women and children." It may be blended with B. and G. Products Company's Lyf-Lyk tint, which is guaranteed to reproduce "nature's own skin texture . . . the velvety appearance of living tissue." Suntone comes in three separate tints: Suntan; Special Cosmetic tint, a pink shade "especially indicated for young female subjects"; and Regular Cosmetic Tint, moderately pink.

About three to six gallons of a dyed and perfumed solution of 12 formaldehyde, glycerin, borax, phenol, alcohol and water is soon circulating through Mr. Jones, whose mouth has been sewn together with a "needle directed upward between the upper lip and gum and brought out through the left nostril," with the corners raised slightly "for a more pleasant expression." If he should be bucktoothed, his teeth are cleaned with Bon Ami and coated with colorless nail polish. His eyes, meanwhile, are closed with flesh-tinted eye caps and eye cement.

The next step is to have at Mr. Jones with a thing called a trocar. 13 This is a long, hollow needle attached to a tube. It is jabbed into the abdomen, poked around the entrails and chest cavity, the contents of which are pumped out and replaced with "cavity fluid." This done, and the hole in the abdomen sewn up, Mr. Jones's face is heavily creamed (to protect the skin from burns which may be caused by leakage of the chemicals), and he is covered with a sheet and left unmolested for a while. But not for long—there is more, much more, in store for him. He has been embalmed, but not yet restored, and the best time to start the restorative work is eight to ten hours after embalming, when the tissues have become firm and dry.

The object of all this attention to the corpse, it must be re- 14 membered, is to make it presentable for viewing in an attitude of healthy repose. "Our customs require the presentation of our dead in the semblance of normality . . . unmarred by the ravages of illness, disease or mutilation," says Mr. J. Sheridan Mayer in his *Restorative Art*. This is rather a large order since few people die in the full bloom of health, unravaged by illness and unmarked by some disfigurement. The funeral industry is equal to the challenge: "In some cases the gruesome appearance of a mutilated or disease-ridden subject may be quite discouraging. The task of restoration may seem impossible and shake the confidence of the embalmer. This is the time for intestinal fortitude and determination. Once the formative work is begun and affected tissues are cleaned or removed, all doubts of success vanish. It is surprising and gratifying to discover the results which may be obtained."

15   The embalmer, having allowed an appropriate interval to elapse, returns to the attack, but now he brings into play the skill and equipment of sculptor and cosmetician. Is a hand missing? Casting one in plaster of Paris is a simple matter. "For replacement purposes, only a cast of the back of the hand is necessary; this is within the ability of the average operator and is quite adequate." If a lip or two, a nose or an ear should be missing, the embalmer has at hand a variety of restorative waxes with which to model replacements. Pores and skin texture are simulated by stippling with a little brush, and over this cosmetics are laid on. Head off? Decapitation cases are rather routinely handled. Ragged edges are trimmed, and head joined to torso with a series of splints, wires and sutures. It is a good idea to have a little something at the neck—a scarf or a high collar—when time for viewing comes. Swollen mouth? Cut out tissue as needed from inside the lips. If too much is removed, the surface contour can easily be restored by padding with cotton. Swollen necks and cheeks are reduced by removing tissue through vertical incisions made down each side of the neck. "When the deceased is casketed, the pillow will hide the suture incisions . . . as an extra precaution against leakage, the suture may be painted with liquid sealer."

16   The opposite condition is more likely to present itself—that of emaciation. His hypodermic syringe now loaded with massage cream, the embalmer seeks out and fills the hollowed and sunken areas by injection. In this procedure the backs of the hands and fingers and the under-chin area should not be neglected.

17   Positioning the lips is a problem that recurrently challenges the ingenuity of the embalmer. Closed too tightly, they tend to give a stern, even disapproving expression. Ideally, embalmers feel, the

lips should give the impression of being ever so slightly parted, the upper lip protruding slightly for a more youthful appearance. This takes some engineering, however, as the lips tend to drift apart. Lip drift can sometimes be remedied by pushing one or two straight pins through the inner margin of the lower lip and then inserting them between the two front upper teeth. If Mr. Jones happens to have no teeth, the pins can just as easily be anchored in his Armstrong Face Former and Denture Replacer. Another method to maintain lip closure is to dislocate the lower jaw, which is then held in its new position by a wire run through holes which have been drilled through the upper and lower jaws at the midline. As the French are fond of saying, *il faut souffrir pour être belle.*[1]

If Mr. Jones has died of jaundice, the embalming fluid will very   18 likely turn him green. Does this deter the embalmer? Not if he has intestinal fortitude. Masking pastes and cosmetics are heavily laid on, burial garments and casket interiors are color-correlated with particular care, and Jones is displayed beneath rose-colored lights. Friends will say "How *well* he looks." Death by carbon monoxide, on the other hand, can be rather a good thing from the embalmer's viewpoint: "One advantage is the fact that this type of discoloration is an exaggerated form of a natural pink coloration." This is nice because the healthy glow is already present and needs but little attention.

The patching and filling completed, Mr. Jones is now shaved,   19 washed and dressed. Cream-based cosmetic, available in pink, flesh, suntan, brunette and blond, is applied to his hands and face, his hair is shampooed and combed (and, in the case of Mrs. Jones, set), his hands manicured. For the horny-handed son of toil special care must be taken; cream should be applied to remove ingrained grime, and the nails cleaned. "If he were not in the habit of having them manicured in life, trimming and shaping is advised for better appearance—never questioned by kin."

Jones is now ready for casketing (this is the present participle   20 of the verb "to casket"). In this operation his right shoulder should be depressed slightly "to turn the body a bit to the right and soften the appearance of lying flat on the back." Positioning the hands is a matter of importance, and special rubber positioning blocks may be used. The hands should be cupped slightly for a more lifelike, relaxed appearance. Proper placement of the body requires a delicate

---

[1] You have to suffer to be beautiful.

sense of balance. It should lie as high as possible in the casket, yet not so high that the lid, when lowered, will hit the nose. On the other hand, we are cautioned, placing the body too low "creates the impression that the body is in a box."

21   Jones is next wheeled into the appointed slumber room where a few last touches may be added—his favorite pipe placed in his hand or, if he was a great reader, a book propped into position. (In the case of little Master Jones a Teddy bear may be clutched.) Here he will hold open house for a few days, visiting hours 10 A.M. to 9 P.M.

22   All now being in readiness, the funeral director calls a staff conference to make sure that each assistant knows his precise duties. Mr. Wilber Kriege writes: "This makes your staff feel that they are a part of the team, with a definite assignment that must be properly carried out if the whole plan is to succeed. You never heard of a football coach who failed to talk to his entire team before they go on the field. They have drilled on the plays they are to execute for hours and days, and yet the successful coach knows the importance of making even the bench-warming third-string substitute feel that he is important if the game is to be won." The winning of *this* game is predicated upon glass-smooth handling of the logistics. The funeral director has notified the pallbearers whose names were furnished by the family, has arranged for the presence of clergyman, organist, and soloist, has provided transportation for everybody, has organized and listed the flowers sent by friends. In *Psychology of Funeral Service* Mr. Edward A. Martin points out: "He may not always do as much as the family thinks he is doing, but it is his helpful guidance that they appreciate in knowing they are proceeding as they should. . . . The important thing is how well his services can be used to make the family believe they are giving unlimited expression to their own sentiment."

23   The religious service may be held in a church or in the chapel of the funeral home; the funeral director vastly prefers the latter arrangement, for not only is it more convenient for him but it affords him the opportunity to show off his beautiful facilities to the gathered mourners. After the clergyman has had his say, the mourners queue up to file past the casket for a last look at the deceased. The family is *never* asked whether they want an open-casket ceremony; in the absence of their instruction to the contrary, this is taken for granted. Consequently well over 90 percent of all American funerals feature the open casket—a custom unknown in other parts of the

world. Foreigners are astonished by it. An English woman living in San Francisco described her reaction in a letter to the writer:

> I myself have attended only one funeral—that of an elderly fellow worker of mine. After the service I could not understand why everyone was walking towards the coffin (sorry, I mean casket), but thought I had better follow the crowd. It shook me rigid to get there and find the casket open and poor old Oscar lying there in his brown tweed suit, wearing a suntan makeup and just the wrong shade of lipstick. If I had not been extremely fond of the old boy, I have a horrible feeling that I might have giggled. Then and there I decided that I could never face another American funeral—even dead.

The casket (which has been resting throughout the service on   24 a Classic Beauty Ultra Metal Casket Bier) is now transferred by a hydraulically operated device called Porto-Lift to a balloon-tired, Glide Easy casket carriage which will wheel it to yet another conveyance, the Cadillac Funeral Coach. This may be lavender, cream, light green—anything but black. Interiors, of course, are color-correlated, "for the man who cannot stop short of perfection."

At graveside, the casket is lowered into the earth. This office,   25 once the prerogative of friends of the deceased, is now performed by a patented mechanical lowering device. A "Lifetime Green" artificial grass mat is at the ready to conceal the sere earth, and overhead, to conceal the sky, is a portable Steril Chapel Tent ("resists the intense heat and humidity of summer and the terrific storms of winter . . . available in Silver Grey, Rose or Evergreen"). Now is the time for the ritual scattering of earth over the coffin, as the solemn words "earth to earth, ashes to ashes, dust to dust" are pronounced by the officiating cleric. This can today be accomplished "with a mere flick of the wrist with the Gordon Leak-Proof Earth Dispenser. No grasping of a handful of dirt, no soiled fingers. Simple, dignified, beautiful, reverent! The modern way!" The Gordon Earth Dispenser (at $5) is of nickel-plated brass construction. It is not only "attractive to the eye and long wearing"; it is also "one of the 'tools' for building better public relations" if presented as "an appropriate non-commercial gift" to the clergyman. It is shaped something like a salt-shaker.

Untouched by human hand, the coffin and the earth are now   26 united.

It is in the function of directing the participants through this   27 maze of gadgetry that the funeral director has assigned to himself his relatively new role of "grief therapist." He has relieved the family of every detail, he has revamped the corpse to look like a living doll, he has arranged for it to nap for a few days in a slumber room, he has put on a well-oiled performance in which the concept of *death* has played no part whatsoever—unless it was inconsiderately mentioned by the clergyman who conducted the religious service. He has done everything in his power to make the funeral a real pleasure for everybody concerned. He and his team have given their all to score an upset victory over death.

Thinking Critically About This Reading

1. If embalming is legally suspect while being expensive and pointless as well, why has it become such a universal custom in our society?

2. What motive does the author imply is behind the entire embalming and funeral procedure she describes? What motive do you think accounts for its widespread popularity?

3. The author claims that funeral directors are reticent to discuss embalming because they fear public knowledge of the procedure will make people wonder if they really want this service. Now that you know about the procedure, how do you feel about it?

4. What alternatives to the standard practice of funerals in America do you consider more dignified and decent?

5. Many states are lax in regulating the funeral industry. What laws do you think should be enacted to regulate this industry?

Understanding the Writer's Process

1. Jessica Mitford is widely regarded as one of America's foremost muckrakers. What is a muckraker? In what way is this article squarely in the muckraking tradition?

2. Who was Yorick? Why does the author invoke his name in paragraph 2? What is this invocation called?

3. Throughout her article, the author refers to the corpse as *Mr. Jones*. What does this add to her discussion?

4. In paragraph 8, what techniques does the author employ to show vividly the undertaker's grisly and ugly trade?

5. Why does so much of this article consist of quotations? What do the quotations add to the author's revelations about the embalming business?

Examining the Writer's Language

1. Define the following words as used in this article: circumscribed (paragraph 3), inherent (5), intractable (6), disfigurements (9), rudimentary (10), haphazard (10), unravaged (14), queue (23).
2. What is ironic about the title of this piece? On what allusion is it based?
3. Why is *Beautiful Memory Picture* initially capitalized in paragraph 2? What do the capital letters imply?
4. Throughout this piece, the author frequently resorts to verbal irony. Cite some examples of verbal irony in this article.
5. In paragraph 20, the author tells us that *casketing* is the present participle of the verb *to casket*. What point is she making with this grammatical aside?

Suggestions for Writing

1. Write an essay proposing steps you think should be taken to prevent funeral directors from extorting silly and expensive burial practices from bereaved relatives.
2. Taking any familiar ritual or custom of American life that you think ridiculous (for example: marriage ceremonies, dating, family get-togethers, and so forth), write a satirical process explanation of how it is carried out.

SIX FEET OF THE COUNTRY

Nadine Gordimer

> *Nadine Gordimer (b. 1923) is a Nobel Prize-winning novelist and short-story writer. She grew up in the gold-mining country of South Africa, graduating from the University of the Witwatersrand in*

Johannesburg, where she now lives with her husband.
She has written several novels, including The Voice
of the Serpent *(1953),* The Late Bourgeois World
(1966), The Guest of Honor *(1970), and* The Conser-
vationist *(1975). But it is her short stories, exploring*
the theme of clashing relationships among the races of
her native land, that have won her a wide following
overseas. She offers no moral hope for whites who live
under the apartheid system, and she conveys in great
artistic detail certain complex psychological moments
in the life of South Africans. The selection below is
taken from her volume Six Feet of the Country *(1953).*

Preparing to Read This Selection Critically

Pay close attention to the setting of the story and
to the point of view of the narrator. It is important to
notice that he is a white, married man from the city. The
story quickly focuses on the relationship between blacks
and whites. Try to understand the underlying assumptions and biases in both races. All groups described represent certain views and values as they confront each
other. Try to determine what these views and values are.
Notice also what characteristics the writer attributes to
Lerice, who is a woman.

1   My wife and I are not real farmers—not even Lerice, really. We
bought our place, ten miles out of Johannesburg on one of the main
roads, to change something in ourselves, I suppose; you seem to
rattle about so much within a marriage like ours. You long to hear
nothing but a deep satisfying silence when you sound a marriage.
The farm hasn't managed that for us, of course, but it has done
other things, unexpected, illogical. Lerice, who I thought would retire there in Chekhovian sadness for a month or two, and then leave
the place to the servants while she tried yet again to get a part she
wanted and become the actress she would like to be, has sunk into
the business of running the farm with all the serious intensity with
which she once imbued the shadows in a playwright's mind. I should
have given it up long ago if it had not been for her. Her hands, once
small and plain and well kept—she was not the sort of actress who
wears red paint and diamond rings—are hard as a dog's pads.

I, of course, am there only in the evenings and on weekends. 2
I am a partner in a luxury-travel agency, which is flourishing—needs
to be, as I tell Lerice, in order to carry the farm. Still, though I know
we can't afford it, and though the sweetish smell of the fowls Lerice
breeds sickens me, so that I avoid going past their runs, the farm
is beautiful in a way I had almost forgotten—especially on a Sunday
morning when I get up and go out into the paddock and see not
the palm trees and fishpond and imitation-stone birdbath of the
suburbs but white ducks on the dam, the alfalfa field brilliant as
window dresser's grass, and the little, stocky, mean-eyed bull, lustful
but bored, having his face tenderly licked by one of his ladies. Lerice
comes out with her hair uncombed, in her hand a stick dripping
with cattle dip. She will stand and look dreamily for a moment, the
way she would pretend to look sometimes in those plays. "They'll
mate tomorrow," she will say. "This is their second day. Look how
she loves him, my little Napoleon." So that when people come out
to see us on Sunday afternoon, I am likely to hear myself saying as
I pour out the drinks, "When I drive back home from the city every
day, past those rows of suburban houses, I wonder how the devil
we ever did stand it. . . . Would you care to look around?" And there
I am, taking some pretty girl and her young husband stumbling
down to our riverbank, the girl catching her stockings on the mealie-
stooks and stepping over cow turds humming with jewel-green files
while she says, ". . . the *tensions* of the damned city. And you're
near enough to get into town to a show, too! I think it's wonderful.
Why, you've got it both ways!" And for a moment I accept the
triumph as if I *had* managed it—the impossibility that I've been trying
for all my life—just as if the truth was that you could get it "both
ways," instead of finding yourself with not even one way or the
other but a third, one you had not provided for at all.

But even in our saner moments, when I find Lerice's earthy 3
enthusiasms just as irritating as I once found her histrionical ones,
and she finds what she calls my "jealousy" of her capacity for enthusiasm as big a proof of my inadequacy for her as a mate as ever
it was, we do believe that we have at least honestly escaped those
tensions peculiar to the city about which our visitors speak. When
Johannesburg people speak of "tension," they don't mean hurrying
people in crowded streets, the struggle for money, or the general
competitive character of city life. They mean the guns under the white
men's pillows and the burglar bars on the white men's windows.

They mean those strange moments on city pavements when a black man won't stand aside for a white man.

4   Out in the country, even ten miles out, life is better than that. In the country, there is a lingering remnant of the pretransitional stage; our relationship with the blacks is almost feudal. Wrong, I suppose, obsolete, but more comfortable all around. We have no burglar bars, no gun. Lerice's farm boys have their wives and their piccanins living with them on the land. They brew their sour beer without the fear of police raids. In fact, we've always rather prided ourselves that the poor devils have nothing much to fear, being with us; Lerice even keeps an eye on their children, with all the competence of a woman who has never had a child of her own, and she certainly doctors them all—children and adults—like babies whenever they happen to be sick.

5   It was because of this that we were not particularly startled one night last winter when the boy Albert came knocking at our window long after we had gone to bed. I wasn't in our bed but sleeping in the little dressing-room-*cum*-linen-room next door, because Lerice had annoyed me and I didn't want to find myself softening toward her simply because of the sweet smell of the talcum powder on her flesh after her bath.

6   She came and woke me up. "Albert says one of the boys is very sick," she said. "I think you'd better go down and see. He wouldn't get us up at this hour for nothing."

7   "What time is it?"

8   "What does it matter?" Lerice is maddeningly logical.

9   I got up awkwardly as she watched me—how is it I always feel a fool when I have deserted her bed? After all, I know from the way she never looks at me when she talks to me at breakfast the next day that she is hurt and humiliated at my not wanting her—and I went out, clumsy with sleep.

10   "Which of the boys is it?" I asked Albert as we followed the dance of my torch.

11   "He's too sick. Very sick, *Baas*," he said.

12   "But who? Franz?" I remembered Franz had had a bad cough for the past week.

13   Albert did not answer; he had given me the path, and was walking along beside me in the tall dead grass. When the light of the torch caught his face, I saw that he looked acutely embarrassed. "What's this all about?" I said.

He lowered his head under the glance of the light. "It's not 14
me, *Baas*. I don't know. Petrus he send me."

Irritated, I hurried him along to the huts. And there, on Petrus's 15
iron bedstead, with its brick stilts, was a young man, dead. On his
forehead there was still a light, cold sweat; his body was warm. The
boys stood around as they do in the kitchen when it is discovered
that someone has broken a dish—uncooperative, silent. Somebody's
wife hung about in the shadows, her hands wrung together under
her apron.

I had not seen a dead man since the war. This was very dif- 16
ferent. I felt like the others—extraneous, useless. "What was the
matter?" I asked.

The woman patted at her chest and shook her head to indicate 17
the painful impossibility of breathing.

He must have died of pneumonia. 18

I turned to Petrus. "Who was this boy? What was he doing 19
here?" The light of a candle on the floor showed that Petrus was
weeping. He followed me out the door.

When we were outside, in the dark, I waited for him to speak. 20
But he didn't. "Now, come on, Petrus, you must tell me who this
boy was. Was he a friend of yours?"

"He's my brother, *Baas*. He came from Rhodesia to look for 21
work."

The story startled Lerice and me a little. The young boy had 22
walked down from Rhodesia to look for work in Johannesburg, had
caught a chill from sleeping out along the way, and had lain ill in
his brother Petrus's hut since his arrival three days before. Our boys
had been frightened to ask us for help for him because we had never
been intended ever to know of his presence. Rhodesian natives are
barred from entering the Union unless they have a permit; the young
man was an illegal immigrant. No doubt our boys had managed the
whole thing successfully several times before; a number of relatives
must have walked the seven or eight hundred miles from poverty
to the paradise of zoot suits, police raids, and black slum townships
that is their *Egoli*, City of Gold—the Bantu name for Johannesburg.
It was merely a matter of getting such a man to lie low on our farm
until a job could be found with someone who would be glad to take
the risk of prosecution for employing an illegal immigrant in exchange for the services of someone as yet untainted by the city.

Well, this was one who would never get up again. 23

24   "You would think they would have felt they could tell *us*,"
said Lerice next morning. "Once the man was ill. You would have
thought at least—" When she is getting intense over something, she
has a way of standing in the middle of a room as people do when
they are shortly to leave on a journey, looking searchingly about
her at the most familiar objects as if she had never seen them before.
I had noticed that in Petrus's presence in the kitchen, earlier, she
had had the air of being almost offended with him, almost hurt.

25   In any case, I really haven't the time or inclination anymore
to go into everything in our life that I know Lerice, from those
alarmed and pressing eyes of hers, would like us to go into. She is
the kind of woman who doesn't mind if she looks plain, or odd; I
don't suppose she would even care if she knew how strange she
looks when her whole face is out of proportion with urgent uncer-
tainty. I said, "Now I'm the one who'll have to do all the dirty work,
I suppose."

26   She was still staring at me, trying me out with those eyes—
wasting her time, if she only knew. "I'll have to notify the health
authorities," I said calmly. "They can't just cart him off and bury
him. After all, we don't really know what he died of."

27   She simply stood there, as if she had given up—simply ceased
to see me at all.

28   I don't know when I've been so irritated. "It might have been
something contagious," I said. "God knows." There was no answer.

29   I am not enamored of holding conversations with myself. I
went out to shout to one of the boys to open the garage and get
the car ready for my morning drive to town.

30   As I had expected, it turned out to be quite a business. I had
to notify the police as well as the health authorities, and answer a
lot of tedious questions: How was it I was ignorant of the boy's
presence? If I did not supervise my native quarters, how did I know
that that sort of thing didn't go on all the time? Et cetera, et cetera.
And when I flared up and told them that so long as my natives did
their work, I didn't think it my right or concern to poke my nose
into their private lives, I got from the coarse, dull-witted police
sergeant one of those looks that come not from any thinking process
going on in the brain but from that faculty common to all who are
possessed by the master-race theory—a look of insanely inane certainty. He grinned at me with a mixture of scorn and delight at my
stupidity.

Then I had to explain to Petrus why the health authorities had 31
to take away the body for a postmortem—and, in fact, what a postmortem was. When I telephoned the health department some days
later to find out the result, I was told that the cause of death was,
as we had thought, pneumonia, and that the body had been suitably
disposed of. I went out to where Petrus was mixing a mash for the
fowls and told him that it was all right, there would be no trouble;
his brother had died from that pain in his chest. Petrus put down
the paraffin can and said, "When can we go to fetch him, *Baas?*"

"To fetch him?"   32

"Will the *Baas* please ask them when we must come?"   33

I went back inside and called Lerice, all over the house. She   34
came down the stairs from the spare bedrooms, and I said, "*Now*
what am I going to do? When I told Petrus, he just asked calmly
when they could go and fetch the body. They think they're going
to bury him themselves."

"Well, go back and tell him," said Lerice. "You must tell him.   35
Why didn't you tell him then?"

When I found Petrus again, he looked up politely. "Look, Pe-   36
trus," I said. "You can't go to fetch your brother. They've done it
already—they've *buried* him, you understand?"

"Where?" he said slowly, dully, as if he thought that perhaps   37
he was getting this wrong.

"You see, he was a stranger. They knew he wasn't from here,   38
and they didn't know he had some of his people here so they thought
they must bury him." It was difficult to make a pauper's grave sound
like a privilege.

"Please, *Baas*, the *Baas* must ask them." But he did not mean   39
that he wanted to know the burial place. He simply ignored the
incomprehensible machinery I told him had set to work on his dead
brother; he wanted the brother back.

"But, Petrus," I said, "how can I? Your brother is buried al-   40
ready. I can't ask them now."

"Oh, *Baas!*" he said. He stood with his bran-smeared hands   41
uncurled at his sides, one corner of his mouth twitching.

"Good God, Petrus, they won't listen to me! They can't, any-   42
way. I'm sorry, but I can't do it. You understand?"

He just kept on looking at me, out of his knowledge that white   43
men have everything, can do anything; if they don't, it is because
they won't.

44   And then, at dinner, Lerice started. "You could at least phone," she said.

45   "Christ, what d'you think I am? Am I supposed to bring the dead back to life?"

46   But I could not exaggerate my way out of this ridiculous responsibility that had been thrust on me. "Phone them up," she went on. "And at least you'll be able to tell him you've done it and they've explained that it's impossible."

47   She disappeared somewhere into the kitchen quarters after coffee. A little later she came back to tell me, "The old father's coming down from Rhodesia to be at the funeral. He's got a permit and he's already on his way."

48   Unfortunately, it was not impossible to get the body back. The authorities said that it was somewhat irregular, but that since the hygiene conditions had been fulfilled, they could not refuse permission for exhumation. I found out that, with the undertaker's charges, it would cost twenty pounds. Ah, I thought, that settles it. On five pounds a month, Petrus won't have twenty pounds—and just as well, since it couldn't do the dead any good. Certainly I should not offer it to him myself. Twenty pounds—or anything else within reason, for that matter—I would have spent without grudging it on doctors or medicines that might have helped the boy when he was alive. Once he was dead, I had no intention of encouraging Petrus to throw away, on a gesture, more than he spent to clothe his whole family in a year.

49   When I told him, in the kitchen that night, he said, "Twenty pounds?"

50   I said, "Yes, that's right, twenty pounds."

51   For a moment, I had the feeling, from the look on his face, that he was calculating. But when he spoke again I thought I must have imagined it.

52   "We must pay twenty pounds!" he said in the faraway voice in which a person speaks of something so unattainable that it does not bear thinking about.

53   "All right, Petrus," I said, and went back to the living room.

54   The next morning before I went to town, Petrus asked to see me. "Please, *Baas*," he said, awkwardly handing me a bundle of notes. They're so seldom on the giving rather than the receiving side, poor devils, that they don't really know how to hand money to a white man. There it was, the twenty pounds, in ones and halves, some creased and folded until they were soft as dirty rags, others

smooth and fairly new—Franz's money, I suppose, and Albert's, and Dora the cook's, and Jacob the gardener's, and God knows who else's besides, from all the farms and small holdings round about. I took it in irritation more than in astonishment, really—irritation at the waste, the uselessness of this sacrifice by people so poor. Just like the poor everywhere, I thought, who stint themselves the decencies of life in order to ensure themselves the decencies of death. So incomprehensible to people like Lerice and me, who regard life as something to be spent extravagantly and, if we think about death at all, regard it as the final bankruptcy.

The servants don't work on Saturday afternoon anyway, so it 55 was a good day for the funeral. Petrus and his father had borrowed our donkey cart to fetch the coffin from the city, where, Petrus told Lerice on their return, everything was "nice"—the coffin waiting for them, already sealed up to save them from what must have been a rather unpleasant sight after two weeks' interment. (It had taken all that time for the authorities and the undertaker to make the final arrangements for moving the body.) All morning, the coffin lay in Petrus's hut, awaiting the trip to the little old burial ground, just outside the eastern boundary of our farm, that was a relic of the days when this was a real farming district rather than a fashionable rural estate. It was pure chance that I happened to be down there near the fence when the procession came past; once again Lerice had forgotten her promise to me and had made the house uninhabitable on a Saturday afternoon. I had come home and been infuriated to find her in a pair of filthy old slacks and with her hair uncombed since the night before, having all the varnish scraped off the living-room floor, if you please. So I had taken my number-8 iron and gone off to practice my approach shots. In my annoyance, I had forgotten about the funeral, and was reminded only when I saw the procession coming up the path along the outside of the fence toward me; from where I was standing, you can see the graves quite clearly, and that day the sun glinted on bits of broken pottery, a lopsided homemade cross, and jam jars brown with rainwater and dead flowers.

I felt a little awkward, and did not know whether to go on 56 hitting my golf ball or stop at least until the whole gathering was decently past. The donkey cart creaks and screeches with every revolution of the wheels, and it came along in a slow, halting fashion somehow peculiarly suited to the two donkeys who drew it, their little potbellies rubbed and rough, their heads sunk between the shafts, and their ears flattened back with an air submissive and downcast; peculiarly suited, too, to the group of men and women who came along slowly behind. The patient ass. Watching, I thought, You can see now why the creature became a Biblical symbol. Then the procession drew level with me and stopped, so I had to put down my club. The coffin was taken down off the cart—it was a shiny, yellow-varnished wood, like cheap furniture—and the donkeys twitched their ears against the flies. Petrus, Franz, Albert, and the old father from Rhodesia hoisted it on their shoulders and the procession moved on, on foot. It was really a very awkward moment. I stood there rather foolishly at the fence, quite still, and slowly they filed past, not looking up, the four men bent beneath the shiny wooden box, and the straggling troop of mourners. All of them were servants or neighbors' servants whom I knew as casual, easygoing gossipers about our lands or kitchen. I heard the old man's breathing.

57   I had just bent to pick up my club again when there was a sort of jar in the flowing solemnity of their processional mood; I felt it at once, like a wave of heat along the air, or one of those sudden currents of cold catching at your legs in a placid stream. The old man's voice was muttering something; the people had stopped, confused, and they bumped into one another, some pressing to go on, others hissing them to be still. I could see that they were embarrassed, but they could not ignore the voice; it was much the way that the mumblings of a prophet, though not clear at first, arrest the mind. The corner of the coffin the old man carried was sagging at an angle; he seemed to be trying to get out from under the weight of it. Now Petrus expostulated with him.

58   The little boy who had been left to watch the donkeys dropped the reins and ran to see. I don't know why—unless it was for the same reason people crowd around someone who has fainted in a cinema—but I parted the wires of the fence and went through, after him.

59   Petrus lifted his eyes to me—to anybody—with distress and horror. The old man from Rhodesia had let go of the coffin entirely, and the three others, unable to support it on their own, had laid it on the ground, in the pathway. Already there was a film of dust lightly wavering up its shiny sides. I did not understand what the old man was saying; I hesitated to interfere. But now the whole seething group turned on my silence. The old man himself came over to me, with his hands outspread and shaking, and spoke di-

rectly to me, saying something that I could tell from the tone, without understanding the words, was shocking and extraordinary.

"What is it, Petrus? What's wrong?" I appealed. 60

Petrus threw up his hands, bowed his head in a series of hys- 61 terical shakes, then thrust his face up at me suddenly. "He says, 'My son was not so heavy.' "

Silence. I could hear the old man breathing; he kept his mouth 62 a little open, as old people do.

"My son was young and thin," he said at last, in English. 63

Again silence. Then babble broke out. The old man thundered 64 against everybody; his teeth were yellowed and few, and he had one of those fine, grizzled, sweeping mustaches that one doesn't often see nowadays, which must have been grown in emulation of early Empire builders. It seemed to frame all his utterances with a special validity, perhaps merely because it was the symbol of the traditional wisdom of age—an idea so fearfully rooted that it carries still something awesome beyond reason. He shocked them; they thought he was mad, but they had to listen to him.

With his own hands he began to prize the lid off the coffin 65 and three of the men came forward to help him. Then he sat down on the ground; very old, very weak, and unable to speak, he merely lifted a trembling hand toward what was there. He abdicated, he handed it over to them; he was no good anymore.

They crowded round to look (and so did I), and now they 66 forgot the nature of this surprise and the occasion of grief to which it belonged, and for a few minutes were carried up in the delightful astonishment of the surprise itself. They gasped and flared noisily with excitement. I even noticed the little boy who had held the donkeys jumping up and down, almost weeping with rage because the backs of the grown-ups crowded him out of his view.

In the coffin was someone no one had ever seen before: a 67 heavily built, rather light-skinned native with a neatly stitched scar on his forehead—perhaps from a blow in a brawl that had also dealt him some other, slower-working injury, which had killed him.

I wrangled with the authorities for a week over that body. I 68 had the feeling that they were shocked, in a laconic fashion, by their own mistake, but that in the confusion of their anonymous dead they were helpless to put it right. They said to me, "We are trying to find out," and "We are still making inquiries." It was as if at any moment they might conduct me into their mortuary and say, "There!

Lift up the sheets; look for him—your poultry boy's brother. There are so many black faces—surely one will do?"

69   And every evening when I got home, Petrus was waiting in the kitchen. "Well, they're trying. They're still looking. The *Baas* is seeing to it for you, Petrus," I would tell him. "God, half the time I should be in the office I'm driving around the back end of the town chasing after this affair," I added aside, to Lerice, one night.

70   She and Petrus both kept their eyes turned on me as I spoke, and, oddly, for those moments they looked exactly alike, though it sounds impossible: my wife, with her high, white forehead and her attenuated Englishwoman's body, and the poultry boy, with his horny bare feet below khaki trousers tied at the knee with string and the peculiar rankness of his nervous sweat coming from his skin.

71   "What makes you so indignant, so determined about this now?" said Lerice suddenly.

72   I stared at her. "It's a matter of principle. Why should they get away with a swindle? It's time these officials had a jolt from someone who'll bother to take the trouble."

73   She said, "Oh." And as Petrus slowly opened the kitchen door to leave, sensing that the talk had gone beyond him, she turned away, too.

74   I continued to pass on assurances to Petrus every evening, but although what I said was the same and the voice in which I said it was the same, every evening it sounded weaker. At last, it became clear that we would never get Petrus's brother back, because nobody really knew where he was. Somewhere in a graveyard as uniform as a housing scheme, somewhere under a number that didn't belong to him, or in the medical school, perhaps, laboriously reduced to layers of muscle and strings of nerve? Goodness knows. He had no identity in this world anyway.

75   It was only then, and in a voice of shame, that Petrus asked me to try and get the money back.

76   "From the way he asks, you'd think he was robbing his dead brother," I said to Lerice later. But as I've said, Lerice had got so intense about this business that she couldn't even appreciate a little ironic smile.

77   I tried to get the money; Lerice tried. We both telephoned and wrote and argued, but nothing came of it. It appeared that the main expense had been the undertaker, and after all he had done his job.

So the whole thing was a complete waste, even more of a waste for the poor devils than I had thought it would be.

The old man from Rhodesia was about Lerice's father's size, 78 so she gave him one of her father's old suits, and he went back home rather better off, for the winter, than he had come.

Thinking Critically About This Reading

1. The narrator opens his story by telling us that his wife and he bought a farm ten miles out of Johannesburg in order to change something in themselves. What do you suppose they wanted to change? Did they succeed?

2. What does the author mean when he states (paragraph 4) that "our relationship with the blacks is almost feudal." Why is such a relationship more "comfortable" than the relationship in the city? What is your view of this relationship?

3. Why was it so important that Petrus have his brother's body properly buried?

4. Reread Jessica Mitford's "Behind the Formaldehyde Curtain" (pp. 323–332). What, if any, assumptions does that essay have in common with this piece by Gordimer?

5. State your position for or against traditional funeral services. What is the good or bad of them? Should people spend hard-earned money on funerals—why or why not?

Understanding the Writer's Process

1. Why do you suppose the author titled her story "Six Feet of the Country"? Suggest another, less ambiguous title you think might appeal to readers.

2. What paragraph signals the beginning of the conflict and the rising action of the story? What purpose do the preliminary paragraphs serve?

3. In hiding behind the persona of the husband, what has the narrator achieved that she could not by being the wife?

4. How does the narrator describe Lerice's looks? What does this description contribute to the meaning of the story?

5. What is the importance of paragraph 74? How does this paragraph fit into the theme of the story?

Examining the Writer's Language

1. Find a more common synonym for the following words found in the story: imbued (paragraph 1), extraneous (16), interment (55), emulation (64), validity (64), attenuated (70).
2. What is the meaning of the expression "Chekhovian sadness" in paragraph 1?
3. What impression of country life is conveyed through the words in paragraph 2?
4. In paragraph 8, the narrator describes Lerice as "maddeningly logical." Is this description supported by her role in the story? Explain your answer.
5. What words convey the emotional climax of the story? In which paragraph do they occur? What is the effect on the reader?

Writing Assignment Based on "Six Feet of the Country"

As a sensitive reader, you cannot escape noticing that in this story, using the burial of a young Rhodesian, the author shows great sympathy to the cause of poor blacks. Write an essay in which you describe the burial of some wealthy, but not admirable, person. Try to draw the reader's sympathy away from this person by emphasizing those aspects of the funeral that are pompous and hypocritical.

STUDENT ESSAY (IN PROCESS)
EXPLAINING PROCESS

Roberta Jean Gwinn

> *Roberta Jean Gwinn is a mature student, having entered college thirty-five years after graduating from high school. She has reared six children and has worked at various occupations, including bookkeeper, jazz musician, and quilting instructor. She is working toward a B.A. in cultural anthropology and plans on attending the university for an advanced degree in folklore and mythology—subjects about which she has written sev-*

*eral essays. The one reproduced below is on another
of her favorite subjects, quilting.*

First draft   Roberta Gwinn
                               Eng. 101

How to Make a Quilt
~~Quilting~~

*Too abrupt—
transition
would help*

Few people take quilting lessons, these
days, because they need to make warm covers.
after all,
ᴧDepartment stores, discount outlets, and even
supermarkets have inexpensive warm covers for
sale. Quilts are made as an expression of love,

cluttered

caring concern, and~~, not incidentally, the~~ ar-
impulse   *who would have*
tistic ~~ability of the maker~~. Many women ᴧtakeᴧup
          a
quilting as ᴧcreative outletₓsay~~ing~~ "I'm just
making bed covers." It is as though they need
an excuse to be artistic. Dabbling in oils or
watercolors would be a frivolous waste of
money, in their eyes, but money invested in

be direct

fabric and lessons will result in a durable
                    take up quilting
family heirloom. Men who ~~enter this field~~, such
as internationally recognized quilt maker and

*show
contrast*

quilting expert, Michael James, unabashedly
proclaim their creations to be Wall Art and
                        most women quilters, however,
file copyright papers on their designs.ᴧ~~Women~~
view this copyrighting of design as heresy.
They have been sharing patterns, including
ones of their own design, quite freely for hundreds of years. There are tens of thousands of

patterns in public domain, but now a few men are
saying that there are certain patterns~~x~~ reserved for individual use. Why has this happened? ^*Because* Quilting has finally been recognized as
a creative art and, fortunately, one which al-
learn with
~~agreement~~ most anyone can ~~indulge in to their hearts~~ de-
if the proper steps are followed.
~~number)~~ light. *Step One: Gathering the materials*
~~all steps.~~ *First,* ~~To get started~~, you have to have some-
Use a thing to quilt. Until the 1770's, just prior to
heading for the American Revolution, all quilts were ~~what~~
each step. ~~are called~~ "whole-cloth" quilts. They weren't
pieced patchwork or applique. They consisted
of one whole piece for the top, another for the
back of the quilt, and some sort of filler or
stuffing to go in between. Then, the whole business was sewn together through all the layers
to keep the stuffing from shifting around, the
the quilt
edged were hemmed together, and ~~it~~ was ready to
go on a bed. The big change ~~in quilting~~ to patterned and appliqued tops, came about during
the Stamp Act period, when George III insisted
we send our raw wool and flax to London to be
woven; then, if we needed whole cloth, we could
buy it back. Needless to say, patched garments
fashionable
and bedding became ~~the in thing~~. What seemed a
great deprivation, at the time, actually led to
a great leap forward, artistically, in
quilting.

    Since whole-cloth quilts are so easy to
do, they make a great first project. I would
recommend a modest-size wall hanging, say 18"
x 18" or 24" x 36". *Here are the materials*
you must assemble:

~~You will need~~

From the ~~F~~abric ~~S~~tore~~X~~

Permanently—pressed, pre—shrunk, un—bleached muslin 5/8 yard for the smaller size, 1½ yds. for the larger size.

One small oll of <u>bonded</u> polyester batting.

One box of rust—proof pins.

One package of <u>#7 betweens</u> needles.

A spool of muslin quilting or embroidery thread.

A scrap of three squares to the inch ~~X~~ check material.

From the ~~H~~ardware or ~~L~~umber ~~Y~~ard::

Four straight ~~one by twos (pine)~~ *1" x 2" pine boards,* two of them ~~should be~~ six inches longer than the shorter side of ~~your~~ project~~;~~ the other two ~~should be~~ six inches longer than the long side ∧ *of your project.*

Four ~~two-inch~~ C clamps.

Three or four cards of thumb tacks.

From the ~~S~~tationery ~~S~~tore

A piece of poster board as big as your project

A medium—line black marker, a graphite (regular #2) pencil, and ∧*assorted* color pencils. (~~as sorted~~)

Step Two: Creating the design *your design*
~~Work first on your design.~~ You can sketch ~~it~~ directly on the poster board. ~~Or~~ if you have absolutely no talent at sketching, you can cheat as

I do. I hunt up a slide ~ color or black and
white ~ *of some compositional pattern I like* ~~that I really like – good composition –~~
and drop it in the slide projector. Then I tape
the poster board to the wall, shine the slide
on it, and pencil onto the poster board what I

Had better suggest more examples

want from the slide. *For instance,* You can ~~also trace over,~~ *use* a
picture of ~~some~~ flowers, *of a bird, of some geometric shape, or* ~~or~~ what~~s~~ever strikes *of*
your fancy, and then transfer the design to the
poster board. You don't want ~~it~~ *the design* to be too busy
and it does not have to extend to the edges;
don't be concerned with filling up all the
space. When you are satisfied with your design,

trace
go over the lines you are going to use with the
black marker.

   If you are doing the 18 x 18 size, *quilt* cut
your fabric on the fold and you will have a
front and back. If you are doing the larger
size, open your fabric and fold the long side,
so the finished edges (selvedges) are together, and cut across the middle. *Since* The pieces
are supposed to be bigger than the finished
product, ~~but not that big.~~ Trim the 18 inches to
21½-inches square and the 24 x 36 to 27 x 39.
Find the middle of your design and the middle
of your fabric. *Next* Lay the fabric on the poster
board, matching the centers and squar*ing* up the
sides. Now tape the fabric down. *Then* Transfer the
design lightly onto the fabric with the
graphite pencil *(Don't worry;* you will be able to see it
through the muslin)

Step Three: Fastening your project to the frame

Mark the middle of each board, then find
the middle of each side of the piece you didn't
mark the design on (the back piece). Match the
center of a short side to one of the shorter
pine boards at its center mark and thumb tack
out from the center every three inches or so,
all the way to the ends of the fabric., Do the
same with the opposite end (other short side).
Lay all four boards on the floor or on a big
table to form a rectangle. The fabric on the
sides should cover about one inch of the inner
edge of the long boards. Match middles and
thumb tack the centers; then stretch the material tight and C clamp the boards together at the
corners. You may have to unclamp a corner or two
and reclamp to get the back tight and squared
up at the corners. Unroll your batting on the
back and trim off what you don't need. Lay the
top piece, with the design right side up on top
of the batting, matching middles of sides to
the middles of the sides of the back. Pin the
top to the back, pointing the pins in toward the
middles on the long sides, but parallel to the
boards on the short sides. If your back is in
the frames the right tightness, you will have
to pull abit to get the top to fit all the way
around. Now you are ready to quilt.

Re Write for better clarity

Step Four: The actual quilting

Since You want both hands free for ~~this/so~~ quilting, you
won't be able to hold onto the frame ~~too~~. I have

regular quilt stands I inherited a short while
ago. They look like saw horses that are hinged
at the top with piano hinges so I can make them
lower or higher by spreading the legs apart or
bringing them closer together. If you don't
have anything like that, ~~or four chairs of even
height you can set your frame on,~~ you could do
as I did for years. Set one end of your frame on
a table and the other end on your ironing board ^--
or something similar.

~~This~~ *Quilting* is the best part. ~~Up 'til now you
have been cutting things apart or just getting
ready, now you are finally getting it together.~~) *not neces- sary*
Thread up a #7 between needle and take the piece
of ^*scrap* check cloth. ~~No need to make a knot~~. Weave
the needle in and out of the check, hitting each
~~and every~~ corner in a straight line, aiming for
~~8~~ *eight* stitches to the inch. When you think you have
the gauge down pat and you can hit the corners
with regularity, leave the thread in the material and just cut it off. You want to keep this
practice piece on ~~the~~ top of the quilt to check
back to frequently. The trick to making an impressive piece is to be consistent and neat.

not really necessary to the process | Museum quality is judged to be a minimum of ele-
ven stitches to the inch. This gauge is not that
much bigger and, unless some picky person gets
out a ruler and counts your stitch in each inch,
who's to know but you and me? Thread up again
and make a very tiny knot in the end of the
thread. *# Now, do the same thing to the actual quilt.*
 ←―― Fan out your fingers and lay your hand
down on the quilt top sideways, with your thumb

at the edge pointing at your chest. Lay your
scissors or the needle pack down at the outer
edge of your little finger. That is ~~all the~~
as far
~~farther~~ away from you that you will ever want
to quilt, or you will give yourself a kink in
your back. About an inch away from where you
want to start working on your design, slide
your needle point into the top and come up on a
line of the design. Now quilt along all of the
lines you marked in your design. Don't go all
the way through to the back. You will do all the
work from the top. Now give a the thread a little jerk so the knot disappears inside, so you
won't have any knots showing on the front or the
back. It is imperative that you wear a thimble.
Now just weave in and out as you did with the
check material. ~~Yes, it is thicker. If you are~~
Insert ~~right handed, your left hand should be under~~
to make ~~the quilt to help tip the needle back up. A~~
the process ~~piece of tape on the index finger of you left~~
seem ~~hand will cut down on your getting pricked by~~
like more ~~the needle.~~ Continue quilting until you run out
fun. of thread; then make the tiniest knot possible
under the last stitch, put the needle back on
the work, but only under the top, and come out
away from the design. Pull gently on the tail
end of the thread and snip it with the scissors,
taking great care not to cut the fabric. Rub the
spot with your finger nail and the end will disappear inside. When you have quilted a hands
span in all around the edges, carefully loosen
the clamps on one end of the frame, remove the
pins along the long sides a hands span and a

half, ~~worth~~ and fold the board under once or
twice, whatever is needed to get you to a place
not yet quilted. Tighten the clamps and go on
quilting. Some people like to alternate the
quilting of each end, but I like to stay at one
end and quilt up to the middle and then turn the
frame around and quilt the other half. ~~That's~~
You choose your own system.
~~up to you.~~ ∧

    When all of your design is quilted, take
out the pins on the sides that haven't already
been pulled as you went along, unclamp and unroll the boards, and unpin the ends. The only
thing left to do is to turn the outside edges of

* *In time your needle will continue to move as though
self-propelled--in and out of the fabric, eight stitches to
the inch, flowing effortlessly, stitching along your
design. Your mind can already be planning the next
quilt -- warm colors this time for a winter quilt. "I'll
choose browns, gold, orange, and maybe a touch of red,"
you may muse. You fantasize about doing a Georgetown circle or a "good ole" bear's paw.*

the fabric to each other ∧ with the raw edges on
the inside, of course ∧ and neatly hem them

               closed. *Now, sit back and admire your handiwork.*
End on   (*Your design should stand out like a sculpture*
a happy   *on a frieze. If you have followed the directions*
note --   *carefully, you will have produced a genuine piece*
             of old-fashioned American art-- a nostalgic
             reminiscence of bygone days.

Final draft   Alberta Gwinn

                                              Eng. 101

                 How to Make a Quilt

     Few people these days take quilting les-
sons in order to make warm covers. After all,
department stores, discount outlets, and even
supermarkets have inexpensive warm covers for
sale. Quilts are made as an expression of love,
caring concern, and artistic impulse. Many
women who have taken up quilting as a creative
outlet say, "I'm just making bed covers." It is
as though they needed an excuse to be artistic.
Dabbling in oils or watercolors would be a
frivolous waste of money, in their eyes, but
money invested in fabric and lessons will result in a durable family heirloom. Men who take
up quilting, such as internationally recognized quilt maker Michael James, unabashedly
proclaim their creations to be wall art and
file copyright papers on their designs. Most
women quilters, however, view this copyrighting of design as heresy. They have been sharing
patterns, including ones of their own design,
quite freely for hundreds of years. There are
tens of thousands of patterns in public domain,
but now a few men are saying that there are certain patterns reserved for individual use. Why
has this happened? Because quilting has finally been recognized as a creative art and,
fortunately, one which almost anyone can learn
with delight if the proper steps are followed.

<u>Step one</u>: <u>Gathering the materials</u>

First, you have to have something to quilt. Until the 1770's, just prior to the American Revolution, all quilts were "whole-cloth" quilts, not pieced patchwork or applique. Rather, they consisted of one whole piece for the top, another for the back of the quilt, and some sort of filler or stuffing to go in between. Then the whole business was sewn together through all the layers to keep the stuffing from shifting around, the edges were hemmed together, and the quilt was ready to go on a bed. The big change, to patterned and appliqued tops, came about during the Stamp Act period, when George III insisted that we send our raw wool and flax to London for weaving; then, if we needed whole cloth, we could buy it back. Needless to say, patched garments and bedding became fashionable. What seemed a great deprivation at the time actually led to a great leap forward, artistically, in quilting.

Since whole-cloth quilts are so easy to do, they make a great first project. I recommend a modest-size wall hanging, say 18" x 18" or 24" x 36." Here are the materials you must assemble:

<u>From the fabric store</u>

Permanently-pressed, pre-shrunk, un-bleached muslin, 5/8 yard for the smaller size, 1½ yds. for the larger size.

One small roll of <u>bonded</u> polyester batting.

One box of rust-proof pins.

One package of <u>#7 betweens</u> needles.

A spool of muslin quilting or embroidery thread.

A scrap of three-squares-to-the-inch check material.

From the hardware store

Or lumber yard

Four straight 1" x 2" pine boards, two of them six inches longer than the short side of your project, the other six inches longer than the long side of your project.

Four two-inch C clamps.

Three or four cards of thumb tacks.

From the Stationary Store

A piece of poster board as big as your project.

A medium-line black marker, a graphite (regular #2) pencil, and assorted color pencils.

Step two: Creating the design

You can sketch your design directly on the poster board. If you have absolutely no talent at sketching, you can cheat as I do. I hunt up a slide—color or black and white—of some compositional pattern I like and I drop it in the slide projector. Then I tape the poster board to the wall, shine the slide on it, and pencil onto the poster board what I want from the slide. For instance, you can use a picture of flowers, of a bird, of some geometric shape, or of whatever strikes your fancy, and then transfer the design to the poster board. You don't want the design to be too busy and it does not have to extend to the edges; don't be concerned with filling up all the space. When you are satisfied with your design, trace the lines you are going to use with the black marker.

If you are doing the 18 x 18 size quilt, cut your fabric on the fold and you will have a front and back. If you are doing the larger size, open your fabric and fold the long side, so the finished edges (selvedges) are together, and then cut across the middle. Since the pieces are supposed to be bigger than the finished product, trim the 18 inches to 21½-inch squares and the 24 x 26 to 27 x 39. Find the middle of your design and the middle of your fabric. Next, lay the fabric on the poster board, matching the centers, and squaring up the sides. Now tape the fabric down. Then, transfer the design lightly onto the fabric with the graphite pencil. (Don't worry; you will be able to see it through the muslin).

Step three: Fastening your project into the frame
Now you are ready to put your project into the frames. You have a choice here of either thumbtacking the back of your project to the

frames or wrapping the frames with muslin and then pinning the back of your project to the wrapping around the frames. If you decide to do the latter, now is the time to wrap your boards. After wrapping them, or leaving them bare, lay them on the floor in the shape of a rectangle. The two sides which are opposite each other should either be on top, or they should both be on the bottom. (See diagram at end of essay.) Let the ends of the boards extend about three inches past where they overlap, and clamp them together where they overlap. This is the simplest frame you can make and the most practical. Center the sides of the back of your project and pin or thumbtack out from the centers of each side. You may have to adjust the clamping point when you get to the corners. It is important that the back be stretched tight in the frames and that this frame be fully adjustable. When you have the back in to your satisfaction, cut a piece of batting the same size and just lay it on the back; no need to pin it down. Now, place the top piece on the batting, with the design you have drawn on it right side up. Match the middles of the sides of the top to the middles of the sides of the back and pin the top to the back. Pin from the middle of the sides out to the corners, stretching the fabric tight so that the top and back match exactly. For easy removal later, you should put your pins into the top piece of fabric, parallel to the side

boards which are on top of the other two boards.
Now you are ready to quilt.

Step four: The actual quilting
Since you want both hands free for quilting,
you won't be able to hold onto the frame. I have
regular quilt stands I inherited a short while
ago. They look like saw horses hinged at the top
with piano hinges so I can make them lower or
higher by spreading the legs apart or bringing
them closer together. If you don't have anything like that, you could do as I did for
years: Set one end of your frame on a table and
the other end on your ironing board—or something similar.

    Quilting is the best part. Thread up a
#7 between needle and take the piece of scrap
check cloth. Weave the needle in and out of the
check, hitting each corner in a straight line,
aiming for eight stitches to the inch. When you
think you have the gauge down pat and you can
hit the corners with regularity, leave the
thread in the material and just cut it off. You
want to keep this practice piece on top of the
quilt to check back to frequently. The trick to
making an impressive piece is to be consistent
and neat.

    Now do the same thing to the actual
quilt. Fan out your fingers and lay your hand
down on the quilt top, sideways with your thumb
at the edge pointing at your chest. Lay your

scissors or the needle pack down at the outer edge of your little finger. That is as far away from you that you ever want to quilt, or you will give yourself a kink in your back. About an inch away from where you want to start working on your design, slide your needle point into the top and come up on a line of the design. Now quilt along all of the lines you marked in your design. Don't go all the way through to the back. You will do all the work from the top. Now give the thread a little jerk so that the knot disappears inside, and you won't have any knots showing on the front or the back. It is imperative that you wear a thimble. Now just weave in and out as you did with the check material.

In time your needle will continue to move as though self-propelled—in and out of the fabric, eight stitches to the inch, flowing effortlessly, constantly working in squares. Your mind can already be planning the next quilt—warm colors this time for a winter quilt. "I'll choose browns, gold, orange, and maybe a touch of red," you may muse. You fantasize about doing a Georgetown circle or a "good ole" bear's paw.

Continue quilting until you run out of thread; then make the tiniest knot possible under the last stitch, put the needle back on the work—but only under the top—and come out away from the design. Pull gently on the tail

end of the thread and snip it with the scissors,
taking great care not to cut the fabric. Rub the
spot with your finger nail and the end will disappear inside. When you have quilted a hand's
span in all around the edges, carefully loosen
the clamps on one end of the frame, remove the
pins along the long sides a hand's span and a
half, and fold the board under once or twice,
whatever is needed to get you to a place not yet
quilted. Tighten the clamps and go on quilting.
Some people like to alternate the quilting of
each end, but I like to stay at one end and quilt
up to the middle and then turn the frame around
and quilt the other half. You choose your own
system.

Step five: Enjoying the finished product
When all of your design is quilted, take out the
pins on the sides that haven't already been
pulled as you went along, unclamp and unroll
the boards, and unpin the ends. The only thing
left to do is to turn the outside edges of the
fabric to each other—with the raw edges on the
inside, of course—and neatly hem them closed.
Now, sit back and admire your handiwork. Your
design should stand out like a sculpture on a
frieze. If you have followed the directions
carefully, you will have produced a genuine

piece of old–fashioned American art—a nostal–
gic reminiscence of bygone days.

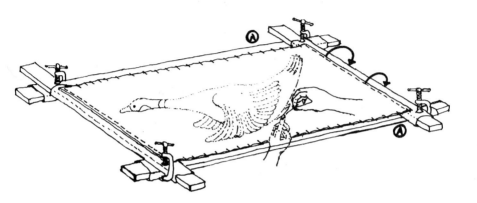

"Genial, outgoing Gil Wheat, I guess you know everybody: quiet, mild-mannered John Lilienthal; mordant, sardonic Geoff Relf; compact, dynamic Jim Stockton; serious, high-minded Art Herzog; brilliant, mercurial John Motheral; and me, of course—long-winded, boring Stan Norton."

7

Classification

HOW TO WRITE A CLASSIFICATION

Classification, also known as division, is familiar and useful to virtually everyone and is employed to various effects by different disciplines. Basically, classification means to subdivide a subject into its types, kinds, divisions, or groups. In the life sciences, classification is used to sort animals and plants into genera and species. In anthropology, it is used to group the artifacts of early peoples by developmental techniques. In criticism, it is used to divide English literature into such periods as the Neoclassical, the Romantic, or the Victorian, each of which has distinctly identifying characteristics.

Indeed, an essential hallmark of a logical classification is the use of some distinguishing feature to separate one set of items from another. A type or group can have no meaning if its members do not share some exclusive trait or characteristic not present in others. Thus, in English literature the restraint and formalism in the work of Alexander Pope identify him as belonging to the neoclassical poets, who stressed form and structure over sentiment. A poet like William Wordsworth, whose work reflects a loose and unstructured form but revels in sentiment, would be excluded automatically from that group.

In freshman composition classes, the classification assignment is mainly intended as an exercise in informal thinking. More often than not, it will ask you to exercise some disciplined thought about an event or circumstance from everyday life with which you are likely to be familiar. The essay "College Pressures" by William Zinsser, reproduced in this chapter, is the typical sort of classification assignment you might be asked to do for English. Although all students are painfully aware of college pressures, it is only through careful thinking that Zinsser is able to sort these pressures by cause and so arrive at his pressure types: economic, parental, peer, and self-induced. The essay that flows from this thinking is typically enlightening. Classification enables us to see things clearer—to identify the pattern behind seemingly random events or occurrences and therefore to better control their impact on our lives.

1. Choose a Single Principle for the Classification

By the principle of a classification, we mean the distinguishing feature used to determine membership in its types, kinds, or groups. For example, to classify your nonrelatives you might use their degree of closeness to you as a classifying principle, arriving at the categories of acquaintances, friends, and intimates. A psychologist might classify people by their body type, be it endomorph, mesomorph, or ectomorph. A geographer might classify the climatic regions of the earth by average annual rainfall. In each case, the classification yields types whose members are all selected by the same single principle.

The principle used to make a classification cannot be trivial, however, or the resulting categories will be meaningless. For example, pharmacology classifies drugs into chemical groups based on their effectiveness in treating certain diseases. That is a significant principle, since it is plainly important for a physician to know which disease can be treated by which drug. On the other hand, a classification of drugs based only on weight correspondingly would be useless and worthless. Similarly, if you wrote an essay classifying your acquaintances by their height, the result most likely would be pointless since height is a random quality that can reveal nothing significant about your choice and range of friendships.

To classify properly, then, your types or groups must result from sorting by means of a significant single principle, and the principle applied must yield pure and important groups or types. An essay classifying rocks according to whether or not they can be skipped across water is of no use to a geologist. On the other hand, an essay classifying rocks by their likely origin or chemical composition could be very useful. One student wrote an essay classifying the life forms found in a tide pool by their color—a trivial principle that resulted in trivial types. Another student classified these same life forms by their method of propulsion in the water—yielding creatures that floated (plankton and various protozoa), swam (fish and other aquatic animals), crawled (types of crustaceans), or were permanently attached to a rock or reef (members of the Cirripedia subclass of shellfish). The result was both a useful classification and an inventive essay.

2. Keep Your Categories Intact and Separate

The categories of a classification must not overlap or contain items already contained within another entry. For example, an essay classifying your nonrelatives by their degree of closeness to you would be flawed if it listed coworkers as a separate category along with acquaintances, friends, and intimates (a coworker could also be an acquaintance, friend, or even an intimate). Here is an excerpt from a classification whose categories overlap:

> Unhappy union workers have four avenues for making their opposition or wishes known to management: protest voiced by the union, organized response to the company, job slowdown, and outright strike. The first of these, protest voiced by the union spokesperson, is likely.

By "organized response to the company," the student meant a course of action already subsumed under job slowdown or outright strike.

3. Make the Classification Complete

A classification is incomplete if it leaves out an important category or type. If you wrote an essay about types of treatment available for corns and calluses of the feet and stated there were two—better-fitting shoes and ointments for softening the affected areas—you would be omitting an important third alternative: surgical removal of corns and calluses. With some classifications, however, especially those based on personal observation or opinion, incompleteness is not and cannot be an issue. For example, Max Eastman wrote an essay in which he argued that there were two types of human nature—the poetic and the practical. But is this true? And can a contrary position ever be proved? How many types of human nature are there, and how may that alleged number be demonstrated with verifiable certainty? The answer is that no one knows, and that it cannot be. Nor, for that matter, should one even try to drag science or certainty into that kind of speculation. Internal consistency and a forceful presentation is all one can expect from a classifying essay about such a speculative topic.

4. Give Equal Space to Equal Entries

For the sake of symmetry, a classifying essay must give approximately equal treatment to every category. If you are classifying addictive drugs into four types—narcotics, depressants, stimulants, and hallucinogens—you are obliged to write evenly and equally about all four. To spend four pages on narcotics and dismiss the remaining three in a paragraph is to write a badly unbalanced essay that will leave a reader puzzling over its focus.

Remember that classification is chiefly an exercise in thinking. If you have not thought carefully about your categories, if you have been careless in selecting a classifying principle to apply to your subject, your essay is likely to reflect these weaknesses. Time devoted to prethinking and prewriting the classification essay is generally time well spent.

THINKING AS A HOBBY

William Golding

William Golding (b. 1911) is an Oxford–educated British novelist best known for Lord of the Flies *(1954), a fictional story about the primitive savagery displayed by a group of boys stranded on an island. In 1983, Golding received the Nobel Prize for Literature. Among the works that have won him praise from many critics are* The Pyramid *(1964),* The Scorpion God *(1971), and* Paper Work *(1984). Golding once declared that his hobbies were "thinking, classical Greek, sailing, and archeology." In the essay that follows, he proposes that thinking can be classified into three types and then proceeds to tell some anecdotes to prove his point.*

Preparing to Read This Selection Critically

Classification is often a way of thinking and looking at the world so as to gain control of the amazing diversity in every aspect of life. In this essay, for example, William Golding proposes that there are three grades of thinking. Has he really divided the entire "pie"? Are there really only three grades of thinking? The answer is actually beside the purpose of the essay, which is to influence the reader to acknowledge that certain ways of thinking are pernicious whereas others are beneficial to society. Golding has taken the huge diversity in people's ways of thinking and condensed it into three major types, but you must make sure that you understand the implications and snares of each type.

1   While I was still a boy, I came to the conclusion that there were three grades of thinking; and since I was later to claim thinking as my hobby, I came to an even stranger conclusion—namely, that I myself could not think at all.

2   I must have been an unsatisfactory child for grownups to deal with. I remember how incomprehensible they appeared to me at first, but not, of course, how I appeared to them. It was the headmaster of my grammar school who first brought the subject of thinking before me—though neither in the way, nor with the result he intended. He had some statuettes in his study. They stood on a high cupboard behind his desk. One was a lady wearing nothing but a bath towel. She seemed frozen in an eternal panic lest the bath towel slip down any farther, and since she had no arms, she was in an unfortunate position to pull the towel up again. Next to her, crouched the statuette of a leopard, ready to spring down at the top drawer of a filing cabinet labeled A—AH. My innocence interpreted this as the victim's last, despairing cry. Beyond the leopard was a naked, muscular gentleman, who sat, looking down, with his chin on his fist and his elbow on his knee. He seemed utterly miserable.

3   Some time later, I learned about these statuettes. The headmaster had placed them where they would face delinquent children, because they symbolized to him the whole of life. The naked lady was the Venus of Milo. She was Love. She was not worried about the towel. She was just busy being beautiful. The leopard was Nature, and he was being natural. The naked, muscular gentleman was not miserable. He was Rodin's Thinker, an image of pure thought. It is easy to buy small plaster models of what you think life is like.

4   I had better explain that I was a frequent visitor to the headmaster's study, because of the latest thing I had done or left undone. As we now say, I was not integrated. I was, if anything, disintegrated; and I was puzzled. Grownups never made sense. Whenever I found myself in a penal position before the headmaster's desk, with the statuettes glimmering whitely above him, I would sink my head, clasp my hands behind my back and writhe one shoe over the other.

5   The headmaster would look opaquely at me through flashing spectacles. "What are we going to do with you?"

6   Well, what *were* they going to do with me? I would writhe my shoe some more and stare down at the worn rug.

7   "Look up, boy! Can't you look up?"

Then I would look up at the cupboard, where the naked lady 8
was frozen in her panic and the muscular gentleman contemplated
the hindquarters of the leopard in endless gloom. I had nothing to
say to the headmaster. His spectacles caught the light so that you
could see nothing human behind them. There was no possibility of
communication.

"Don't you ever think at all?" 9

No, I didn't think, wasn't thinking, couldn't think—I was sim- 10
ply waiting in anguish for the interview to stop.

"Then you'd better learn—hadn't you?" 11

On one occasion the headmaster leaped to his feet, reached 12
up and plonked Rodin's masterpiece on the desk before me.

"That's what a man looks like when he's really thinking." 13

I surveyed the gentleman without interest or comprehension. 14

"Go back to your class." 15

Clearly there was something missing in me. Nature had en- 16
dowed the rest of the human race with a sixth sense and left me
out. This must be so, I mused, on my way back to the class, since
whether I had broken a window, or failed to remember Boyle's Law,
or been late for school, my teachers produced me one, adult answer:
"Why can't you think?"

As I saw the case, I had broken the window because I had 17
tried to hit Jack Arney with a cricket ball and missed him; I could
not remember Boyle's Law because I had never bothered to learn
it; and I was late for school because I preferred looking over the
bridge into the river. In fact, I was wicked. Were my teachers, perhaps, so good that they could not understand the depths of my
depravity? Were they clear, untormented people who could direct
their every action by this mysterious business of thinking? The
whole thing was incomprehensible. In my earlier years, I found even
the statuette of the Thinker confusing. I did not believe any of my
teachers were naked, ever. Like someone born deaf, but bitterly
determined to find out about sound, I watched my teachers to find
out about thought.

There was Mr. Houghton. He was always telling me to think. 18
With a modest satisfaction, he would tell me that he had thought
a bit himself. Then why did he spend so much time drinking? Or
was there more sense in drinking than there appeared to be? But if
not, and if drinking were in fact ruinous to health—and Mr. Houghton was ruined, there was no doubt about that—why was he always
talking about the clean life and the virtues of fresh air? He would

spread his arms wide with the action of a man who habitually spent his time striding along mountain ridges.

19   "Open air does me good, boys—I know it!"

20   Sometimes, exalted by his own oratory, he would leap from his desk and hustle us outside into a hideous wind.

21   "Now, boys! Deep breaths! Feel it right down inside you—huge draughts of God's good air!"

22   He would stand before us, rejoicing in his perfect health, an open-air man. He would put his hands on his waist and take a tremendous breath. You could hear the wind, trapped in the cavern of his chest and struggling with all the unnatural impediments. His body would reel with shock and his ruined face go white at the unaccustomed visitation. He would stagger back to his desk and collapse there, useless for the rest of the morning.

23   Mr. Houghton was given to high-minded monologues about the good life, sexless and full of duty. Yet in the middle of one of these monologues, if a girl passed the window, tapping along on her neat little feet, he would interrupt his discourse, his neck would turn of itself and he would watch her out of sight. In this instance, he seemed to me ruled not by thought but by an invisible and irresistible spring in his nape.

24   His neck was an object of great interest to me. Normally it bulged a bit over his collar. But Mr. Houghton had fought in the First World War alongside both Americans and French, and had come—by who knows what illogic?—to a settled detestation of both countries. If either country happened to be prominent in current affairs, no argument could make Mr. Houghton think well of it. He would bang the desk, his neck would bulge still further and go red. "You can say what you like," he would cry, "but I've thought about this—and I know what I think!"

25   Mr. Houghton thought with his neck.

26   There was Miss Parsons. She assured us that her dearest wish was our welfare, but I knew even then, with the mysterious clair-voyance of childhood, that what she wanted most was the husband she never got. There was Mr. Hands—and so on.

27   I have dealt at length with my teachers because this was my introduction to the nature of what is commonly called thought. Through them I discovered that thought is often full of unconscious prejudice, ignorance and hypocrisy. It will lecture on disinterested purity while its neck is being remorselessly twisted toward a skirt. Technically, it is about as proficient as most businessmen's golf, as

honest as most politicians' intentions, or—to come near my own preoccupation—as coherent as most books that get written. It is what I came to call grade-three thinking, though more properly, it is feeling, rather than thought.

True, often there is a kind of innocence in prejudices, but in those days I viewed grade-three thinking with an intolerant contempt and an incautious mockery. I delighted to confront a pious lady who hated the Germans with the proposition that we should love our enemies. She taught me a great truth in dealing with grade-three thinkers; because of her, I no longer dismiss lightly a mental process which for nine-tenths of the population is the nearest they will ever get to thought. They have immense solidarity. We had better respect them, for we are outnumbered and surrounded. A crowd of grade-three thinkers, all shouting the same thing, all warming their hands at the fire of their own prejudices, will not thank you for pointing out the contradictions in their beliefs. Man is a gregarious animal, and enjoys agreement as cows will graze all the same way on the side of a hill.

Grade-two thinking is the detection of contradictions. I reached grade two when I trapped the poor, pious lady. Grade-two thinkers do not stampede easily, though often they fall into the other fault and lag behind. Grade-two thinking is a withdrawal, with eyes and ears open. It became my hobby and brought satisfaction and loneliness in either hand. For grade-two thinking destroys without having the power to create. It set me watching the crowds cheering His Majesty the King and asking myself what all the fuss was about, without giving me anything positive to put in the place of that heady patriotism. But there were compensations. To hear people justify their habit of hunting foxes and tearing them to pieces by claiming that the foxes like it. To hear our Prime Minister talk about the great benefit we conferred on India by jailing people like Pandit Nehru and Gandhi. To hear American politicians talk about peace in one sentence and refuse to join the League of Nations in the next. Yes, there were moments of delight.

But I was growing toward adolescence and had to admit that Mr. Houghton was not the only one with an irresistible spring in his neck. I, too, felt the compulsive hand of nature and began to find that pointing out contradiction could be costly as well as fun. There was Ruth, for example, a serious and attractive girl. I was an atheist at the time. Grade-two thinking is a menace to religion and knocks down sects like skittles. I put myself in a position to be converted by her with an hypocrisy worthy of grade three. She was a Methodist—or at least, her parents were, and Ruth had to follow suit. But, alas, instead of relying on the Holy Spirit to convert me, Ruth was foolish enough to open her pretty mouth in argument. She claimed that the Bible (King James Version) was literally inspired. I countered by saying that the Catholics believed in the literal inspiration of Saint Jerome's *Vulgate*, and the two books were different. Argument flagged.

31   At last she remarked that there were an awful lot of Methodists, and they couldn't be wrong, could they—not all those millions? That was too easy, said I restively (for the nearer you were to Ruth, the nicer she was to be near to) since there were more Roman Catholics than Methodists anyway; and they couldn't be wrong, could they— not all those hundreds of millions? An awful flicker of doubt appeared in her eyes. I slid my arm around her waist and murmured breathlessly that if we were counting heads, the Buddhists were the boys for my money. But Ruth had *really* wanted to do me good, because I was so nice. She fled. The combination of my arm and those countless Buddhists was too much for her.

32   That night her father visited my father and left, red-cheeked and indignant. I was given the third degree to find out what had happened. It was lucky we were both of us only fourteen. I lost Ruth and gained an undeserved reputation as a potential libertine.

33   So grade-two thinking could be dangerous. It was in this knowledge, at the age of fifteen, that I remember making a comment from the heights of grade two, on the limitations of grade three. One evening I found myself alone in the school hall, preparing it for a party. The door of the headmaster's study was open. I went in. The headmaster had ceased to thump Rodin's Thinker down on the desk as an example to the young. Perhaps he had not found any more candidates, but the statuettes were still there, glimmering and gathering dust on top of the cupboard. I stood on a chair and rearranged them. I stood Venus in her bath towel on the filing cabinet, so that now the top drawer caught its breath in a gasp of sexy excitement. "A-ah!" The portentous Thinker I placed on the edge of the cupboard so that he looked down at the bath towel and waited for it to slip.

34   Grade-two thinking, though it filled life with fun and excitement, did not make for content. To find out the deficiencies of our elders bolsters the young ego but does not make for personal security. I found that grade two was not only the power to point out

contradictions. It took the swimmer some distance from the shore and left him there, out of his depth. I decided that Pontius Pilate was a typical grade-two thinker. "What is truth?" he said, a very common grade-two thought, but one that is used always as the end of an argument instead of the beginning. There is a still higher grade of thought which says, "What is truth?" and sets out to find it.

But these grade-one thinkers were few and far between. They 35 did not visit my grammar school in the flesh though they were there in books. I aspired to them, partly because I was ambitious and partly because I now saw my hobby as an unsatisfactory thing if it went no further. If you set out to climb a mountain, however high you climb, you have failed if you cannot reach the top.

I *did* meet an undeniably grade-one thinker in my first year at 36 Oxford. I was looking over a small bridge in Magdalen Deer Park, and a tiny mustached and hatted figure came and stood by my side. He was a German who had just fled from the Nazis to Oxford as a temporary refuge. His name was Einstein.

But Professor Einstein knew no English at that time and I knew 37 only two words of German. I beamed at him, trying wordlessly to convey by my bearing all the affection and respect that the English felt for him. It is possible—and I have to make the admission—that I felt here were two grade-one thinkers standing side by side; yet I doubt if my face conveyed more than a formless awe. I would have given my Greek and Latin and French and a good slice of my English for enough German to communicate. But we were divided; he was as inscrutable as my headmaster. For perhaps five minutes we stood together on the bridge, undeniable grade-one thinker and breathless aspirant. With true greatness, Professor Einstein realized that any contact was better than none. He pointed to a trout wavering in midstream.

He spoke: "Fisch." 38

My brain reeled. Here I was, mingling with the great, and yet 39 helpless as the veriest grade-three thinker. Desperately I sought for some sign by which I might convey that I, too, revered pure reason. I nodded vehemently. In a brilliant flash I used up half of my German vocabulary. "*Fisch. Ja. Ja.*"

For perhaps another five minutes we stood side by side. Then 40 Professor Einstein, his whole figure still conveying good will and amiability, drifted away out of sight.

I, too, would be a grade-one thinker. I was irreverent at the 41 best of times. Political and religious systems, social customs, loyalties and traditions, they all came tumbling down like so many rotten apples off a tree. This was a fine hobby and a sensible substitute for cricket, since you could play it all the year round. I came up in the end with what must always remain the justification for grade-one thinking, its sign, seal and charter. I devised a coherent system for living. It was a moral system, which was wholly logical. Of course, as I readily admitted, conversion of the world to my way of thinking might be difficult, since my system did away with a number of trifles, such as big business, centralized government, armies, marriage. . . .

42   It was Ruth all over again. I had some very good friends who stood by me, and still do. But my acquaintances vanished, taking the girls with them. Young women seemed oddly contented with the world as it was. They valued the meaningless ceremony with a ring. Young men, while willing to concede the chaining sordidness of marriage, were hesitant about abandoning the organizations which they hoped would give them a career. A young man on the first rung of the Royal Navy, while perfectly agreeable to doing away with big business and marriage, got as red-necked as Mr. Houghton when I proposed a world without any battleships in it.

43   Had the game gone too far? Was it a game any longer? In those prewar days, I stood to lose a great deal, for the sake of a hobby.

44   Now you are expecting me to describe how I saw the folly of my ways and came back to the warm nest, where prejudices are so often called loyalties, where pointless actions are hallowed into custom by repetition, where we are content to say we think when all we do is feel.

45   But you would be wrong. I dropped my hobby and turned professional.

46   If I were to go back to the headmaster's study and find the dusty statuettes still there, I would arrange them differently. I would dust Venus and put her aside, for I have come to love her and know her for the fair thing she is. But I would put the Thinker, sunk in his desperate thought, where there were shadows before him—and at his back, I would put the leopard, crouched and ready to spring.

Thinking Critically About This Reading

1. William Golding classifies thinking into three types. Using your own words, how would you describe each type? Is there a value judgment implied in the classification? If so, what is it?

2. Using Golding's system of classifying thought, what grade of thinking would you attribute to a crowd of students on your college campus chanting slogans against world hunger and against exploitation of the poor in Third World countries?

3. Why does Golding use anecdotes about elementary school teachers as the focal point of his classification? How are these teachers related to the purpose of the essay?

4. Describe someone whom you consider a grade-one thinker. Why is it so difficult to find grade-one thinkers?

5. Golding implies that true grade-one thinking threatens the convention of marriage (paragraph 41). Do you agree? Disagree? Why? Why not?

Understanding the Writer's Process

1. Three symbolic statuettes play a significant role throughout Golding's essay. In which paragraph are the statuettes first introduced? How are they subsequently interpreted?

2. How does Golding render a scene vivid when he writes about his various youthful encounters? How effective is the technique? Why?

3. What symbol is used to represent Mr. Houghton's primitive instincts? Miss Parsons's? What do both symbols have in common?

4. What tone pervades Golding's essay? How does the tone contribute to the effectiveness of the message?

5. What specific examples does Golding use to illustrate grade-two thinking?

Examining the Writer's Language

1. Define the meanings of the following words as used in this essay: integrated (paragraph 4), opaquely (5), detestation (24), clairvoyance (26), solidarity (28), Pandit (29), restively (31), libertine (32), inscrutable (37).

2. What is meant by the figure of speech: "Mr. Houghton thought with his neck"?

3. In your own words, explain what the author means when he states that "grade-two thinking is a menace to religion and knocks down sects like skittles." What other simile does he use later in the essay to describe grade-one thinking?

4. What distinction does the author draw between thinking as a *hobby* and thinking as a *profession?* What do these terms mean in the context in which they are used?

Suggestions for Writing

1. Write an essay in which you establish your own classifications or typical ways of thinking. Be sure to supply vivid examples for each classification.
2. Describe a person whom you consider a true grade-three thinker. Give examples of his or her thinking.

or

Describe a person whom you consider a true grade-one thinker. Give examples of his or her thinking.

LOVE IS A FALLACY

Max Shulman

Max Shulman (b. 1919) is a free-lance writer who has been involved in writing and producing for cinema as well as for television. A year after receiving his bachelor's degree, he wrote the successful play, Barefoot Boy with Cheek *(1943), which was later turned into a popular musical. Shulman's other plays are* Feather Merchants *(1944),* Zebra Derby *(1946),* Sleep 'Til Noon *(1949), and* Rally Round the Flag, Boys! *(1957). But he is perhaps best known for his unforgettable TV series,* Affairs of Dobey Gillis, Half a Hero.

Preparing to Read This Selection Critically

First of all, you will be delighted by Shulman's well-known humor. But if you read carefully, you will become aware that at the same time that he is narrating a college love triangle, he also is classifying the most common logical fallacies according to their official types. Shulman also is demonstrating something about logic. What is it?

You should be able to answer this question after reading the essay.

Cool was I and logical. Keen, calculating, perspicacious, acute 1 and astute—I was all of these. My brain was as powerful as a dynamo, as precise as a chemist's scales, as penetrating as a scalpel. And—think of it!—I was only eighteen.

It is not often that one so young has such a giant intellect. 2 Take, for example, Petey Burch, my roommate at the University of Minnesota. Same age, same background, but dumb as an ox. A nice enough fellow, you understand, but nothing upstairs. Emotional type. Unstable. Impressionable. Worst of all, a faddist. Fads, I submit, are the very negation of reason. To be swept up in every new craze that comes along, to surrender yourself to idiocy just because everybody else is doing it—this, to me, is the acme of mindlessness. Not, however, to Petey.

One afternoon I found Petey lying on his bed with an expres- 3 sion of such distress on his face that I immediately diagnosed appendicitis. "Don't move," I said. "Don't take a laxative. I'll get a doctor."

"Raccoon," he mumbled thickly. 4

"Raccoon?" I said, pausing in my flight. 5

"I want a raccoon coat," he wailed. 6

I perceived that his trouble was not physical, but mental. "Why 7 do you want a raccoon coat?"

"I should have known it," he cried, pounding his temples. "I 8 should have known they'd come back when the Charleston came back. Like a fool I spent all my money for textbooks, and now I can't get a raccoon coat."

"Can you mean," I said incredulously, "that people are actually 9 wearing raccoon coats again?"

"All the Big Men on Campus are wearing them. Where've you 10 been?"

"In the library," I said, naming a place not frequented by Big 11 Men on Campus.

He leaped from the bed and paced the room. "I've got to have 12 a raccoon coat," he said passionately, "I've got to!"

"Petey, why? Look at it rationally. Raccoon coats are unsan- 13 itary. They shed. They smell bad. They weigh too much. They're unsightly. They—"

14   "You don't understand," he interrupted impatiently. "It's the thing to do. Don't you want to be in the swim?"

15   "No," I said truthfully.

16   "Well, I do," he declared. "I'd give anything for a raccoon coat. Anything!"

17   My brain, that precision instrument, slipped into high gear. "Anything?" I asked, looking at him narrowly.

18   "Anything," he affirmed in ringing tones.

19   I stroked my chin thoughtfully. It so happened that I knew where to get my hands on a raccoon coat. My father had had one in his undergraduate days; it lay now in a trunk in the attic back home. It also happened that Petey had something I wanted. He didn't *have* it exactly, but at least he had first rights on it. I refer to his girl, Polly Espy.

20   I had long coveted Polly Espy. Let me emphasize that my desire for this young woman was not emotional in nature. She was, to be sure, a girl who excited the emotions, but I was not one to let my heart rule my head. I wanted Polly for a shrewdly calculated, entirely cerebral reason.

21   I was a freshman in law school. In a few years I would be out in practice. I was well aware of the importance of the right kind of wife in furthering a lawyer's career. The successful lawyers I had observed were, almost without exception, married to beautiful, gracious, intelligent women. With one omission, Polly fitted these specifications perfectly.

22   Beautiful she was. She was not yet of pin-up proportions, but I felt sure that time would supply the lack. She already had the makings.

23   Gracious she was. By gracious I mean full of graces. She had an erectness of carriage, an ease of bearing, a poise that clearly indicated the best of breeding. At table her manners were exquisite. I had seen her at the Kozy Kampus Korner eating the specialty of the house—a sandwich that contained scraps of pot roast, gravy, chopped nuts, and a dipper of sauerkraut—without even getting her fingers moist.

24   Intelligent she was not. In fact, she veered in the opposite direction. But I believed that under my guidance she would smarten up. At any rate, it was worth a try. It is, after all, easier to make a beautiful dumb girl smart than to make an ugly smart girl beautiful.

25   "Petey," I said, "are you in love with Polly Espy?"

"I think she's a keen kid," he replied, "but I don't know if 26
you'd call it love. Why?"

"Do you," I asked, "have any kind of formal arrangement with 27
her? I mean are you going steady or anything like that?"

"No. We see each other quite a bit, but we both have other 28
dates. Why?"

"Is there," I asked, "any other man for whom she has a par- 29
ticular fondness?"

"Not that I know of. Why?" 30

I nodded with satisfaction. "In other words, if you were out 31
of the picture, the field would be open. Is that right?"

"I guess so. What are you getting at?" 32

"Nothing, nothing," I said innocently, and took my suitcase 33
out of the closet.

"Where are you going?" asked Petey. 34

"Home for the weekend." I threw a few things into the bag. 35

"Listen," he said, clutching my arm eagerly, "while you're 36
home, you couldn't get some money from your old man, could you,
and lend it to me so I can buy a raccoon coat?"

"I may do better than that," I said with a mysterious wink and 37
closed my bag and left.

"Look," I said to Petey when I got back Monday morning. I 38
threw open the suitcase and revealed the huge, hairy, gamy object
that my father had worn in his Stutz Bearcat in 1925.

"Holy Toledo!" said Petey reverently. He plunged his hands 39
into the raccoon coat and then his face. "Holy Toledo!" he repeated
fifteen or twenty times.

"Would you like it?" I asked. 40

"Oh yes!" he cried, clutching the greasy pelt to him. Then a 41
canny look came into his eyes. "What do you want for it?"

"Your girl," I said, mincing no words. 42

"Polly?" he said in a horrified whisper. "You want Polly?" 43

"That's right." 44

He flung the coat from him. "Never," he said stoutly. 45

I shrugged. "Okay. If you don't want to be in the swim, I guess 46
it's your business."

I sat down in a chair and pretended to read a book, but out 47
of the corner of my eye I kept watching Petey. He was a torn man.
First he looked at the coat with the expression of a waif at a bakery
window. Then he turned away and set his jaw resolutely. Then he
looked back at the coat, with even more longing in his face. Then

he turned away, but with not so much resolution this time. Back and forth his head swiveled, desire waxing, resolution waning. Finally he didn't turn away at all; he just stood and stared with mad lust at the coat.

48   "It isn't as though I was in love with Polly," he said thickly. "Or going steady or anything like that."

49   "That's right," I murmured.

50   "What's Polly to me, or me to Polly?"

51   "Not a thing," said I.

52   "It's just been a casual kick—just a few laughs, that's all."

53   "Try on the coat," said I.

54   He complied. The coat bunched high over his ears and dropped all the way down to his shoe tops. He looked like a mound of dead raccoons. "Fits fine," he said happily.

55   I rose from my chair. "Is it a deal?" I asked, extending my hand.

56   He swallowed. "It's a deal," he said and shook my hand.

57   I had my first date with Polly the following evening. This was in the nature of a survey; I wanted to find out just how much work I had to do to get her mind up to the standard I required. I took her first to dinner. "Gee, that was a delish dinner," she said as we left the restaurant. Then I took her to a movie. "Gee, that was a marvy movie," she said as we left the theater. And then I took her home. "Gee, I had a sensaysh time," she said as she bade me good night.

58   I went back to my room with a heavy heart. I had gravely underestimated the size of my task. This girl's lack of information was terrifying. First she had to be taught to *think*. This loomed as a project of no small dimensions, and at first I was tempted to give her back to Petey. But then I got to thinking about her abundant physical charms and about the way she entered a room and the way she handled a knife and fork, and I decided to make an effort.

59   I went about it, as in all things, systematically. I gave her a course in logic. It happened that I, as a law student, was taking a course in logic myself, so I had all the facts at my finger tips. "Polly," I said to her when I picked her up on our next date, "tonight we are going over to the Knoll and talk."

60   "Oo, terrif," she replied. One thing I will say for this girl: you would go far to find another so agreeable.

61   We went to the Knoll, the campus trysting place, and we sat down under an old oak, and she looked at me expectantly. "What are we going to talk about?" she asked.

"Logic." 62

She thought this over for a minute and decided she liked it. 63
"Magnif," she said.

"Logic," I said, clearing my throat, "is the science of thinking. 64
Before we can think correctly, we must first learn to recognize the
common fallacies of logic. These we will take up tonight."

"Wow-dow!" she cried, clapping her hands delightedly. 65

I winced, but went bravely on. "First let us examine the fallacy 66
called Dicto Simpliciter."

"By all means," she urged, batting her lashes eagerly. 67

"Dicto Simpliciter means an argument based on an unqualified 68
generalization. For example: Exercise is good. Therefore everybody
should exercise."

"I agree," said Polly earnestly. "I mean exercise is wonderful. 69
I mean it builds the body and everything."

"Polly," I said gently, "the argument is a fallacy. *Exercise is* 70
good is an unqualified generalization. For instance, if you have heart
disease, exercise is bad, not good. Many people are ordered by their
doctors *not* to exercise. You must *qualify* the generalization. You must
say exercise is *usually* good, or exercise is good *for most* people.
Otherwise you have committed a Dicto Simpliciter. Do you see?"

"No," she confessed. "But this is marvy. Do more! Do more!" 71

"It will be better if you stop tugging at my sleeve," I told her, 72
and when she desisted, I continued. "Next we take up a fallacy
called Hasty Generalization. Listen carefully: You can't speak
French. I can't speak French. Petey Burch can't speak French. I must
therefore conclude that nobody at the University of Minnesota can
speak French."

"Really?" said Polly, amazed. "*Nobody?*" 73

I hid my exasperation. "Polly, it's a fallacy. The generalization 74
is reached too hastily. There are too few instances to support such
a conclusion."

"Know any more fallacies?" she asked breathlessly. "This is 75
more fun than dancing even."

I fought off a wave of despair. I was getting nowhere with this 76
girl, absolutely nowhere. Still, I am nothing if not persistent. I continued. "Next comes Post Hoc. Listen to this: Let's not take Bill on
our picnic. Every time we take him out with us, it rains."

"I know somebody just like that," she exclaimed. "A girl back 77
home—Eula Becker, her name is. It never fails. Every single time we
take her on a picnic—"

78   "Polly," I said sharply, "it's a fallacy. Eula Becker doesn't *cause* the rain. She has no connection with the rain. You are guilty of Post Hoc if you blame Eula Becker."

79   "I'll never do it again," she promised contritely. "Are you mad at me?"

80   I sighed deeply. "No, Polly, I'm not mad."

81   "Then tell me some more fallacies."

82   "All right. Let's try Contradictory Premises."

83   "Yes, let's," she chirped, blinking her eyes happily.

84   I frowned, but plunged ahead. "Here's an example of Contradictory Premises: If God can do anything, can He make a stone so heavy that He won't be able to lift it?"

85   "Of course," she replied promptly.

86   "But if He can do anything, He can lift the stone," I pointed out.

87   "Yeah," she said thoughtfully. "Well, then I guess He can't make the stone."

88   "But He can do anything," I reminded her.

89   She scratched her pretty, empty head. "I'm all confused," she admitted.

90   "Of course you are. Because when the premises of an argument contradict each other, there can be no argument. If there is an irresistible force, there can be no immovable object. If there is an immovable object, there can be no irresistible force. Get it?"

91   "Tell me some more of this keen stuff," she said eagerly.

92   I consulted my watch. "I think we'd better call it a night. I'll take you home now, and you go over all the things you've learned. We'll have another session tomorrow night."

93   I deposited her at the girl's dormitory, where she assured me that she had had a perfect terrif evening, and I went glumly home to my room. Petey lay snoring in his bed, the raccoon coat huddled like a great hairy beast at his feet. For a moment I considered waking him and telling him that he could have his girl back. It seemed clear that my project was doomed to failure. The girl simply had a logic-proof head.

94   But then I reconsidered. I had wasted one evening; I might as well waste another. Who knew? Maybe somewhere in the extinct crater of her mind, a few embers still smoldered. Maybe somehow I could fan them into flame. Admittedly it was not a prospect fraught with hope, but I decided to give it one more try.

Seated under the oak the next evening I said, "Our first fallacy   95
tonight is called Ad Misericordiam."

She quivered with delight.   96

"Listen closely," I said. "A man applies for a job. When the   97
boss asks him what his qualifications are, he replies that he has a
wife and six children at home, the wife is a helpless cripple, the
children have nothing to eat, no clothes to wear, no shoes on their
feet, there are no beds in the house, no coal in the cellar, and winter
is coming."

A tear rolled down each of Polly's pink cheeks. "Oh, this is   98
awful, awful," she sobbed.

"Yes, it's awful," I agreed, "but it's no argument. The man   99
never answered the boss's question about his qualifications. Instead
he appealed to the boss's sympathy. He committed the fallacy of
Ad Misericordiam. Do you understand?"

"Have you got a handkerchief?" she blubbered.   100

I handed her a handkerchief and tried to keep from screaming   101
while she wiped her eyes. "Next," I said in a carefully controlled
tone, "we will discuss False Analogy. Here is an example: Students
should be allowed to look at their textbooks during examinations.
After all, surgeons have X-rays to guide them during an operation,
lawyers have briefs to guide them during a trial, carpenters have
blueprints to guide them when they are building a house. Why,
then, shouldn't students be allowed to look at their textbooks during
an examination?"

"There now," she said enthusiastically, "is the most marvy   102
idea I've heard in years."

"Polly," I said testily, "the argument is all wrong. Doctors,   103
lawyers, and carpenters aren't taking a test to see how much they
have learned, but students are. The situations are altogether different, and you can't make an analogy between them."

"I still think it's a good idea," said Polly.   104

"Nuts," I muttered. Doggedly I pressed on. "Next we'll try   105
Hypothesis Contrary to Fact."

"Sounds yummy," was Polly's reaction.   106

"Listen: If Madame Curie had not happened to leave a pho-   107
tographic plate in a drawer with a chunk of pitchblende, the world
today would not know about radium."

"True, true," said Polly, nodding her head. "Did you see the   108
movie? Oh, it just knocked me out. That Walter Pidgeon is so
dreamy. I mean he fractures me."

109   "If you can forget Mr. Pidgeon for a moment," I said coldly, "I would like to point out that the statement is a fallacy. Maybe Madame Curie would have discovered radium at some later date. Maybe somebody else would have discovered it. Maybe any number of things would have happened. You can't start with a hypothesis that is not true and then draw any supportable conclusions from it."

110   "They ought to put Walter Pidgeon in more pictures," said Polly. "I hardly ever see him any more."

111   One more chance, I decided. But just one more. There is a limit to what flesh and blood can bear. "The next fallacy is called Poisoning the Well."

112   "How cute!" she gurgled.

113   "Two men are having a debate. The first one gets up and says, 'My opponent is a notorious liar. You can't believe a word that he is going to say.' . . . Now, Polly, think. Think hard. What's wrong?"

114   I watched her closely as she knit her creamy brow in concentration. Suddenly a glimmer of intelligence—the first I had seen—came into her eyes. "It's not fair," she said with indignation. "It's not a bit fair. What chance has the second man got if the first man calls him a liar before he even begins talking?"

115   "Right!" I cried exultantly. "One hundred percent right. It's not fair. The first man has *poisoned the well* before anybody could drink from it. He has hamstrung his opponent before he could even start. . . . Polly, I'm proud of you."

116   "Pshaw," she murmured, blushing with pleasure.

117   "You see, my dear, these things aren't so hard. All you have to do is concentrate. Think—examine—evaluate. Come now, let's review everything we have learned."

118   "Fire away," she said with an airy wave of her hand.

119   Heartened by the knowledge that Polly was not altogether a cretin, I began a long, patient review of all I had told her. Over and over and over again I cited instances, pointed out flaws, kept hammering away without letup. It was like digging a tunnel. At first everything was work, sweat, and darkness. I had no idea when I would reach the light, or even *if* I would. But I persisted. I pounded and clawed and scraped, and finally I was rewarded. I saw a chink of light. And then the chink got bigger and the sun came pouring in and all was bright.

120   Five grueling nights this took, but it was worth it. I had made a logician out of Polly; I had taught her to think. My job was done. She was worthy of me at last. She was a fit wife for me, a proper

hostess for my many mansions, a suitable mother for my well-heeled children.

It must not be thought that I was without love for this girl. 121 Quite the contrary. Just as Pygmalion loved the perfect woman he had fashioned, so I loved mine. I determined to acquaint her with my feelings at our very next meeting. The time had come to change our relationship from academic to romantic.

"Polly," I said when next we sat beneath our oak, "tonight we 122 will not discuss fallacies."

"Aw, gee," she said, disappointed. 123

"My dear," I said, favoring her with a smile, "we have now 124 spent five evenings together. We have gotten along splendidly. It is clear that we are well matched."

"Hasty Generalization," said Polly brightly. 125

"I beg your pardon," said I. 126

"Hasty Generalization," she repeated. "How can you say that 127 we are well matched on the basis of only five dates?"

I chuckled with amusement. The dear child had learned her 128 lessons well. "My dear," I said patting her hand in a tolerant manner, "five dates is plenty. After all, you don't have to eat a whole cake to know that it's good."

"False Analogy," said Polly promptly. "I'm not a cake. I'm a 129 girl."

I chuckled with somewhat less amusement. The dear child had 130 learned her lessons perhaps too well. I decided to change tactics. Obviously the best approach was a simple, strong, direct declaration of love. I paused for a moment while my massive brain chose the proper words. Then I began:

"Polly, I love you. You are the whole world to me, and the 131 moon and the stars and the constellations of outer space. Please, my darling, say that you will go steady with me, for if you will not, life will be meaningless. I will languish. I will refuse my meals. I will wander the face of the earth, a shambling, hollow-eyed hulk."

There, I thought, folding my arms, that ought to do it. 132

"Ad Misericordiam," said Polly. 133

I ground my teeth. I was not Pygmalion; I was Frankenstein, 134 and my monster had me by the throat. Frantically I fought back the tide of panic surging through me. At all costs I had to keep cool.

"Well, Polly," I said, forcing a smile, "you certainly have 135 learned your fallacies."

"You're darn right," she said with a vigorous nod. 136

137   "And who taught them to you, Polly?"

138   "You did."

139   "That's right. So you do owe me something, don't you, my dear? If I hadn't come along you never would have learned about fallacies."

140   "Hypothesis Contrary to Fact," she said instantly.

141   I dashed perspiration from my brow. "Polly," I croaked, "you mustn't take all these things so literally. I mean this is just classroom stuff. You know that the things you learn in school don't have anything to do with life."

142   "Dicto Simpliciter," she said, wagging her finger at me playfully.

143   That did it. I leaped to my feet, bellowing like a bull. "Will you or will you not go steady with me?"

144   "I will not," she replied.

145   "Why not?" I demanded.

146   "Because this afternoon I promised Petey Burch that I would go steady with him."

147   I reeled back, overcome with the infamy of it. After he promised, after he made a deal, after he shook my hand! "The rat!" I shrieked, kicking up great chunks of turf. "You can't go with him, Polly. He's a liar. He's a cheat. He's a rat."

148   "Poisoning the well," said Polly, "and stop shouting. I think shouting must be a fallacy too."

149   With an immense effort of will, I modulated my voice. "All right," I said. "You're a logician. Let's look at this thing logically. How could you choose Petey Burch over me? Look at me—a brilliant student, a tremendous intellectual, a man with an assured future. Look at Petey—a knothead, a jitterbug, a guy who'll never know where his next meal is coming from. Can you give me one logical reason why you should go steady with Petey Burch?"

150   "I certainly can," declared Polly. "He's got a raccoon coat."

Thinking Critically About This Reading

1. With the characters in the essay seeming either naive or supercilious, what keeps the essay from being trivial?

2. During which decade does the relationship between the narrator and Polly Espy take place? What facts identify the times? What might replace these facts today?

3. On which of the logical fallacies discussed is prejudice based? Explain your answer by using an appropriate example.
4. What is the most efficient way to refute an argument based on logical fallacies?
5. Politically ambitious persons are often accused of using logical fallacies, especially when attacking an opponent. What example from a recent campaign can you cite?

Understanding the Writer's Process

1. What technique does the author use repeatedly to create humor? Give two or three specific examples.
2. How does the author assure that the reader will understand the logical fallacies?
3. What, if anything, does the dialogue add to the success of the essay? How does it affect the portrait of Polly?
4. What difference is there between the comments made by the narrator and those made by Polly? What purpose does the difference serve?

Examining the Writer's Language

1. In the context of the essay, define each of the following words: perspicacious (paragraph 1), cerebral (20), trysting (61), pitch-blende (107), shambling (131), infamy (147), modulated (149).
2. Which of the logical fallacies consists of a poetic metaphor? What advantage, if any, does it have over the others?
3. In the second sentence of the essay, how does the author achieve harmony and balance? Comment on the style.
4. In paragraph 93, Petey is described as lying in bed snoring, "the raccoon coat huddled like a great hairy beast at his feet." What kind of image is this?
5. What are some other effective images or figures of speech found throughout Shulman's essay? Single out two or three and explicate them.

Suggestions for Writing

1. Choosing one of the following logical fallacies, define the fallacy, state how it misconstrues truth, and give two or three examples

of its use in ordinary conversation: *dicto simpliciter,* poisoning the well, *post hoc.*

2. Write a satirical political speech in which you purposely use glaring logical fallacies.

COLLEGE PRESSURES

William Zinsser

William K. Zinsser (b. 1922) is a writer, editor, and teacher. He began his career with the New York Herald Tribune *and was also a columnist for* Look, Life, *and the* New York Times. *During the 1970s, Zinsser taught writing at Yale University, where he was master of Branford College. He is presently executive editor of Book-of-the-Month Club. Among Zinsser's books are* Pop Goes America *(1966),* The Lunacy Boom *(1970), and* On Writing Well *(1980), which became a best-seller because of its lucid and practical advice on how to avoid writing in a laborious, jargonized style. Zinsser has published numerous essays on various aspects of American life, among which is the essay that follows. In it he identifies four types of pressures exerted on college students.*

Preparing to Read This Selection Critically

This selection, as so many others in this book, can be misread because on a superficial, literal level the author seems to be promoting failure or dropping out among college students. Actually, he has something quite different in mind: He wants students to enjoy the various opportunities offered in college and he wants them to be free of pressures that make them frantic and miserable. It is these pressures, along with their consequences, that you must discern in this essay. Once you grasp them, you then can ponder whether or not the author is right.

Dear Carlos: I desperately need a dean's excuse for my chem midterm which will begin in about 1 hour. All I can say is that I totally blew it this week. I've fallen incredibly, inconceivably behind.

Carlos: Help! I'm anxious to hear from you. I'll be in my room and won't leave it until I hear from you. Tomorrow is the last day for . . .

Carlos: I left town because I started bugging out again. I stayed up all night to finish a take home make-up exam & am typing it to hand in on the 10th. It was due on the 5th. P.S. I'm going to the dentist. Pain is pretty bad.

Carlos: Probably by Friday I'll be able to get back to my studies. Right now I'm going to take a long walk. This whole thing has taken a lot out of me.

Carlos: I'm really up the proverbial creek. The problem is I really *bombed* the history final. Since I need that course for my major . . .

Carlos: Here follows a tale of woe. I went home this weekend, had to help my Mom, & caught a fever so didn't have much time to study. My professor . . .

Carlos: Aargh! Trouble. Nothing original but everything's piling up at once. To be brief, my job interview . . .

Hey Carlos, good news! I've got mononucleosis.

Who are these wretched supplicants, scribbling notes so laden   1
with anxiety, seeking such miracles of postponement and balm? They are men and women who belong to Branford College, one of the twelve residential colleges at Yale University, and the messages are just a few of the hundreds that they left for their dean, Carlos Hortas—often slipped under his door at 4 A.M.—last year.

But students like the ones who wrote those notes can also be   2
found on campuses from coast to coast—especially in New England and at many other private colleges across the country that have high academic standards and highly motivated students. Nobody could doubt that the notes are real. In their urgency and their gallows humor they are authentic voices of a generation that is panicky to succeed.

3   My own connection with the message writers is that I am
master of Branford College. I live in its Gothic quadrangle and know
the students well. (We have 485 of them.) I am privy to their hopes
and fears—and also to their stereo music and their piercing cries in
the dead of night ("Does anybody *ca-a-are?*"). If they went to Carlos
to ask how to get through tomorrow, they come to me to ask how
to get through the rest of their lives.

4   Mainly I try to remind them that the road ahead is a long one
and that it will have more unexpected turns than they think. There
will be plenty of time to change jobs, change careers, change whole
attitudes and approaches. They don't want to hear such liberating
news. They want a map—right now—that they can follow unswerv-
ingly to career security, financial security, Social Security and, presumably, a prepaid grave.

5   What I wish for all students is some release from the clammy
grip of the future. I wish them a chance to savor each segment of
their education as an experience in itself and not as a grim preparation for the next step. I wish them the right to experiment, to trip
and fall, to learn that defeat is as instructive as victory and is not
the end of the world.

6   My wish, of course, is naive. One of the few rights that America
does not proclaim is the right to fail. Achievement is the national
god, venerated in our media—the million-dollar athlete, the wealthy
executive—and glorified in our praise of possessions. In the presence
of such a potent state religion, the young are growing up old.

7   I see four kinds of pressure working on college students today;
economic pressure, parental pressure, peer pressure, and self-induced pressure. It is easy to look around for villains—to blame the
colleges for charging too much money, the professors for assigning
too much work, the parents for pushing their children too far, the
students for driving themselves too hard. But there are no villains;
only victims.

8   "In the late 1960s," one dean told me, "the typical question
that I got from students was 'Why is there so much suffering in the
world?' or 'How can I make a contribution?' Today it's 'Do you think
it would look better for getting into law school if I did a double
major in history and political science, or just majored in one of
them?' " Many other deans confirmed this pattern. One said:
"They're trying to find an edge—the intangible something that will
look better on paper if two students are about equal."

Note the emphasis on looking better. The transcript has be- 9
come a sacred document, the passport to security. How one appears
on paper is more important than how one appears in person. *A* is
for Admirable and *B* is for Borderline, even though, in Yale's official
system of grading, *A* means "excellent" and *B* means "very good."
Today, looking very good is no longer good enough, especially for
students who hope to go on to law school or medical school. They
know that entrance into the better schools will be an entrance into
the better law firms and better medical practices where they will
make a lot of money. They also know that the odds are harsh. Yale
Law School, for instance, matriculates 170 students from an appli-
cant pool of 3,700; Harvard enrolls 550 from a pool of 7,000.

It's all very well for those of us who write letters of recom- 10
mendation for our students to stress the qualities of humanity that
will make them good lawyers or doctors. And it's nice to think that
admission officers are really reading our letters and looking for the
extra dimension of commitment or concern. Still, it would be hard
for a student not to visualize these officers shuffling so many tran-
scripts studded with *A*s that they regard a *B* as positively shameful.

The pressure is almost as heavy on students who just want to 11
graduate and get a job. Long gone are the days of the "gentleman's
C," when students journeyed through college with a certain relaxation, sampling a wide variety of courses—music, art, philosophy,
classics, anthropology, poetry, religion—that would send them out
as liberally educated men and women. If I were an employer I would
rather employ graduates who have this range and curiosity than
those who narrowly pursued safe subjects and high grades. I know
countless students whose inquiring minds exhilarate me. I like to
hear the play of their ideas. I don't know if they are getting *A*s or
*C*s, and I don't care. I also like them as people. The country needs
them, and they will find satisfying jobs. I tell them to relax. They
can't.

Nor can I blame them. They live in a brutal economy. Tuition, 12
room, and board at most private colleges now comes to at least
$7,000, not counting books and fees. This might seem to suggest
that the colleges are getting rich. But they are equally battered by
inflation. Tuition covers only 60 percent of what it costs to educate
a student, and ordinarily the remainder comes from what colleges
receive in endowments, grants, and gifts. Now the remainder keeps
being swallowed by the cruel costs—higher every year—of just opening the doors. Heating oil is up. Insurance is up. Postage is up.

Health-premium costs are up. Everything is up. Deficits are up. We are witnessing in America the creation of a brotherhood of paupers—colleges, parents, and students, joined by the common bond of debt.

13   Today it is not unusual for a student, even if he works part time at college and full time during the summer, to accrue $5,000 in loans after four years—loans that he must start to repay within one year after graduation. Exhorted at commencement to go forth into the world, he is already behind as he goes forth. How could he not feel under pressure throughout college to prepare for this day of reckoning? I have used "he," incidentally, only for brevity. Women at Yale are under no less pressure to justify their expensive education to themselves, their parents, and society. In fact, they are probably under more pressure. For although they leave college superbly equipped to bring fresh leadership to traditionally male jobs, society hasn't yet caught up with this fact.

14   Along with economic pressure goes parental pressure. Inevitably, the two are deeply intertwined.

15   I see many students taking pre-medical courses with joyless tenacity. They go off to their labs as if they were going to the dentist. It saddens me because I know them in other corners of their life as cheerful people.

16   "Do you want to go to medical school?" I ask them.

17   "I guess so," they say, without conviction, or "Not really."

18   "Then why are you going?"

19   "Well, my parents want me to be a doctor. They're paying all this money and . . ."

20   Poor students, poor parents. They are caught in one of the oldest webs of love and duty and guilt. The parents mean well, they are trying to steer their sons and daughters toward a secure future. But the sons and daughters want to major in history or classics or philosophy—subjects with no "practical" value. Where's the payoff on the humanities? It's not easy to persuade such loving parents that the humanities do indeed pay off. The intellectual faculties developed by studying subjects like history and classics—an ability to synthesize and relate, to weigh cause and effect, to see events in perspective—are just the faculties that make creative leaders in business or almost any general field. Still, many fathers would rather put their money on courses that point toward a specific profession—courses that are pre-law, pre-medical, pre-business, or, as I sometimes heard it put, "pre-rich."

But the pressure on students is severe. They are truly torn.   21
One part of them feels obligated to fulfill their parents' expectations;
after all, their parents are older and presumably wiser. Another part
tells them that the expectations that are right for their parents are
not right for them.

I know a student who wants to be an artist. She is very ob-   22
viously an artist and will be a good one—she has already had several
modest local exhibits. Meanwhile she is growing as a well-rounded
person and taking humanistic subjects that will enrich the inner
resources out of which her art will grow. But her father is strongly
opposed. He thinks that an artist is a "dumb" thing to be. The
student vacillates and tries to please everybody. She keeps up with
her art somewhat furtively and takes some of the "dumb" courses
her father wants her to take—at least they are dumb courses for her.
She is a free spirit on a campus of tense students—no small achievement in itself—and she deserves to follow her muse.

Peer pressure and self-induced pressure are also intertwined,   23
and they begin almost at the beginning of freshman year.

"I had a freshman student I'll call Linda," one dean told me,   24
"who came in and said she was under terrible pressure because her
roommate, Barbara, was much brighter and studied all the time. I
couldn't tell her that Barbara had come in two hours earlier to say
the same thing about Linda."

The story is almost funny—except that it's not. It's symptomatic   25
of all the pressures put together. When every student thinks every
other student is working harder and doing better, the only solution
is to study harder still. I see students going off to the library every
night after dinner and coming back when it closes at midnight. I
wish they could sometimes forget about their peers and go to a
movie. I hear the clacking of typewriters in the hours before dawn.
I see the tension in their eyes when exams are approaching and
papers are due: *"Will I get everything done?"*

Probably they won't. They will get sick. They will get   26
"blocked." They will sleep. They will oversleep. They will bug out.
Hey, Carlos, help!

Part of the problem is that they do more than they are expected   27
to do. A professor will assign five-page papers. Several students will
start writing ten-page papers to impress him. Then more students
will write ten-page papers, and a few will raise the ante to fifteen.
Pity the poor student who is still just doing the assignment.

28   "Once you have twenty or thirty percent of the student population deliberately overexerting," one dean points out, "it's bad for
everybody. When a teacher gets more and more effort from his class,
the student who is doing normal work can be perceived as not doing
well. The tactic works, psychologically."

29   Why can't the professor just cut back and not accept longer
papers? He can, and he probably will. But by then the term will be
half over and the damage done. Grade fever is highly contagious
and not easily reversed. Besides, the professor's main concern is
with his course. He knows his students only in relation to the course
and doesn't know that they are also overexerting in their other
courses. Nor is it really his business. He didn't sign up for dealing
with the student as a whole person and with all the emotional baggage the student brought along from home. That's what deans, masters, chaplains, and psychiatrists are for.

30   To some extent this is nothing new: a certain number of professors have always been self-contained islands of scholarship and
shyness, more comfortable with books than with people. But the
new pauperism has widened the gap still further, for professors who
actually like to spend time with students don't have as much time
to spend. They also are overexerting. If they are young, they are
busy trying to publish in order not to perish, hanging by their fingernails onto a shrinking profession. If they are old and tenured,
they are buried under the duties of administering departments—as
departmental chairmen or members of committees—that have been
thinned out by the budgetary axe.

31   Ultimately it will be the students' own business to break the
circles in which they are trapped. They are too young to be prisoners
of their parents' dreams and their classmates' fears. They must be
jolted into believing in themselves as unique men and women who
have the power to shape their own future.

32   "Violence is being done to the undergraduate experience," says
Carlos Hortas. "College should be open-ended: at the end it should
open many, many roads. Instead, students are choosing their goal
in advance, and their choices narrow as they go along. It's almost
as if they think that the country has been codified in the type of
jobs that exist—that they've got to fit into certain slots. Therefore,
fit into the best-paying slot.

33   "They ought to take chances. Not taking chances will lead to
a life of colorless mediocrity. They'll be comfortable. But something
in the spirit will be missing."

I have painted too drab a portrait of today's students, making   34
them seem a solemn lot. That is only half of their story; if they were
so dreary I wouldn't so thoroughly enjoy their company. The other
half is that they are easy to like. They are quick to laugh and to
offer friendship. They are not introverts. They are usually kind and
are more considerate of one another than any student generation I
have known.

Nor are they so obsessed with their studies that they avoid   35
sports and extracurricular activities. On the contrary, they juggle
their crowded hours to play on a variety of teams, perform with
musical and dramatic groups, and write for campus publications.
But this in turn is one more cause of anxiety. There are too many
choices. Academically, they have 1,300 courses to select from; outside class they have to decide how much spare time they can spare
and how to spend it.

This means that they engage in fewer extracurricular pursuits   36
than their predecessors did. If they want to row on the crew and
play in the symphony they will eliminate one; in the '60s they would
have done both. They also tend to choose activities that are self-
limiting. Drama, for instance, is flourishing in all twelve of Yale's
residential colleges as it never has before. Students hurl themselves
into these productions—as actors, directors, carpenters, and technicians—with a dedication to create the best possible play, knowing
that the day will come when the run will end and they can get back
to their studies.

They also can't afford to be the willing slave of organizations   37
like the *Yale Daily News.* Last spring at the one-hundredth anniversary banquet of that paper—whose past chairmen include such once
and future kings as Potter Stewart, Kingman Brewster, and William
F. Buckley, Jr.[1]—much was made of the fact that the editorial staff
used to be small and totally committed and that "newsies" routinely
worked fifty hours a week. In effect they belonged to a club; Newsies
is how they defined themselves at Yale. Today's student will write
one or two articles a week, when he can, and he defines himself as
a student. I've never heard the word Newsie except at the banquet.

If I have described the modern undergraduate primarily as a   38
driven creature who is largely ignoring the blithe spirit inside who

[1] Stewart (b. 1915) is a retired justice of the U.S. Supreme Court; Brewster (b. 1919)
is a former president of Yale; and Buckley (b. 1925) is an influential editor and
columnist.

keeps trying to come out and play, it's because that's where the crunch is, not only at Yale but throughout American education. It's why I think we should all be worried about the values that are nurturing a generation so fearful of risk and so goal-obsessed at such an early age.

39   I tell students that there is no one "right" way to get ahead—that each of them is a different person, starting from a different point and bound for a different destination. I tell them that change is a tonic and that all the slots are not codified nor the frontiers closed. One of my ways of telling them is to invite men and women who have achieved success outside the academic world to come and talk informally with my students during the year. They are heads of companies or ad agencies, editors of magazines, politicians, public officials, television magnates, labor leaders, business executives, Broadway producers, artists, writers, economists, photographers, scientists, historians—a mixed bag of achievers.

40   I ask them to say a few words about how they got started. The students assume that they started in their present profession and knew all along that it was what they wanted to do. Luckily for me, most of them got into their field by a circuitous route, to their surprise, after many detours. The students are startled. They can hardly conceive of a career that was not pre-planned. They can hardly imagine allowing the hand of God or chance to nudge them down some unforeseen trail.

Thinking Critically About This Reading

1. What is the main purpose of Zinsser's classification? Do you agree with his assessment? Why? Why not?

2. Which of the pressures described do you consider the most oppressive? Give reasons for your choice.

3. In your view, what factors have caused the transcript to become the influential document it now is?

4. Not all critics of education agree with Zinsser that students are too competitive and work too hard at being successful in college. Contrarily, many critics have complained of a rising tide of mediocre students who cannot read, write, or calculate adequately. Which view is correct? Give reasons for your answer.

5. What do you consider the required ingredients of a curriculum designed to help students develop freely by listening to their

inner voices so they can choose a lifework that truly appeals to them?

Understanding the Writer's Process

1. Zinsser's essay does not begin with a formal introduction in which he announces his purpose; instead, it starts with a list of notes written by college students. What advantage, if any, does this opening have? Why do you suppose the author chose this method of starting his essay?
2. Where does the author state his argument in thesis form? How does the wording help both the writer and the reader?
3. Why does the author devote three full paragraphs to discussing the college transcript (paragraphs 9, 10, and 11)? How does the discussion keep from breaking the unity of the essay?
4. In paragraph 20, Zinsser asks the question, "Where's the payoff on the humanities?" Is this merely a rhetorical question? What purpose does the question serve?
5. In paragraph 5, how does the author achieve coherence and harmony? Comment on how the author achieves coherence in some other paragraph.

Examining the Writer's Language

1. In the context of Zinsser's essay, define the following words: supplicants (paragraph 1), intangible (8), matriculates (9), exhilarate (11), endowments (12), vacillates (22), furtively (22), circuitous (40).
2. In paragraph 5, the author uses the expression "release from the clammy grip of the future." What kind of figure of speech is this? How do you interpret its meaning?
3. In paragraph 12, the author uses the term "brotherhood of paupers." Where else in the essay are references made to poverty?
4. What does the author mean when he accuses some college professors of being "self-contained islands of scholarship" (paragraph 30)?
5. William Zinsser spent many years at Yale teaching students how to write with clarity and conciseness. Does his own writing reflect these qualities? How would you describe his style?

Suggestions for Writing

1. Choosing one of the following areas, write an essay in which you classify the pressures related to that area: job, church, family, social life, or love life.

2. Write an essay in which you suggest steps to lessen the pressures described in William Zinsser's essay.

WHAT, ME? SHOWING OFF?

Judith Viorst

> *Judith Viorst is a poet, journalist, and writer of children's books. Born in New Jersey and educated at Rutgers University, she has contributed a regular column to* Redbook *magazine and to various other periodicals. In 1970 she won an Emmy Award for her poetic monologues in the CBS special entitled "Annie, The Women in the Life of a Man." Viorst's other writings include a book of poetry entitled* It's Hard to Be Hip Over Thirty, and Other Tragedies of Married Life *(1968) and* Yes, Married, a Saga of Love and Complaint *(1972), which contains some of her best prose pieces. Because of her wry and amusing poems, Judith Viorst has been described as a "rhymeless latter-day Dorothy Parker."*

Preparing to Read This Selection Critically

While the essay that follows is a humorous treatment of how people unwittingly like to show off in various circumstances, it also contains some important psychological insights into human nature. You might ask yourself if it is true, as the author insists, that all human beings have a need to show off. If so, what causes the need and can it be eradicated? Is there such a characteristic as being too humble or too self–effacing? Be prepared to discuss specific examples of the kind of showing off you find particularly repulsive and how you handle people who reveal this behavior.

We're at the Biedermans' annual blast, and over at the far end   1
of the living room an intense young woman with blazing eyes and a throbbing voice is decrying poverty, war, injustice and human suffering. Indeed, she expresses such anguish at the anguish of mankind that attention quickly shifts from the moral issues she is expounding to how very, very, very deeply she cares about them.

She's showing off.   2

Down at the other end of the room an insistently scholarly   3
fellow has just used *angst, hubris,* Kierkegaard and *epistemology* in the same sentence. Meanwhile our resident expert in wine meditatively sips, then pushes away, a glass of unacceptable Beaujolais.

They're showing off.   4

And then there's us, complaining about how tired we are today   5
because we went to work, rushed back to see our son's school play, shopped at the market and hurried home in order to cook gourmet, and then needlepointed another dining-room chair.

And what we also are doing is showing off.   6

Indeed everyone, I would like to propose, has some sort of   7
need to show off. No one's completely immune. Not you. And not I. And although we've been taught that it's bad to boast, that it's trashy to toot our own horn, that nice people don't strut their stuff, seek attention or name-drop, there are times when showing off may be forgivable and maybe even acceptable.

But first let's take a look at showing off that *is* obnoxious, that's   8
not acceptable, that's *never* nice. Like showoffs motivated by a fierce, I'm-gonna-blow-you-away competitiveness. And like narcissistic showoffs who are willing to do anything to be—and stay—the center of attention.

Competitive showoffs want to be the best of every bunch.   9
Competitive showoffs must outshine all others. Whatever is being discussed, they have more—expertise or money or even aggravation—and better—periodontists or children or marriages or recipes for pesto—and deeper—love of animals or concern for human suffering or orgasms. Competitive showoffs are people who reside in a permanent state of sibling rivalry, insisting on playing Hertz to everyone else's Avis.

(You're finishing a story, for instance, about the sweet little   10
card that your five-year-old recently made for your birthday when

the CSO interrupts to relate how *her* daughter not only made her a sweet little card, but also brought her breakfast in bed and saved her allowance for months and months in order to buy her—obviously much more beloved—mother a beautiful scarf for her birthday. *Grrr*.)

11   Narcissistic showoffs, however, don't bother to compete because they don't even notice there's anyone there to compete with. They talk nonstop, they brag, they dance, they sometimes quote Homer in Greek, and they'll even go stand on their head if attention should flag. Narcissistic showoffs want to be the star while everyone else is the audience. And yes, they are often adorable and charming and amusing—but only until around the age of six.

12   (I've actually seen an NSO get up and leave the room when the conversation shifted from his accomplishments. "What's the matter?" I asked when I found him standing on the terrace, brooding darkly. "Oh, I don't know," he replied, "but all of a sudden the talk started getting so superficial." *Aagh!*)

13   Another group of showoffs—much more sympathetic types—are showoffs who are basically insecure. And while there is no easy way to distinguish the insecure from the narcissists and competitors, you may figure out which are which by whether you have the urge to reassure or to strangle them.

14   Insecure showoffs show off because, as one close friend explained, "How will they know that I'm good unless I tell them about it?" And whatever the message—I'm smart, I'm a fine human being, I'm this incredibly passionate lover—showoffs have many different techniques for telling about it.

15   Take smart, for example.

16   A person can show off explicitly by using flashy words, like the hubris-Kierkegaard fellow I mentioned before.

17   Or a person can show off implicitly, by saying not a word and just wearing a low-cut dress with her Phi Beta Kappa key gleaming softly in the cleavage.

18   A person can show off satirically, by mocking showing off: "My name is Bill Sawyer," one young man announces to every new acquaintance, "and I'm bright bright bright bright bright."

19   Or a person can show off complainingly: "I'm sorry my daughter takes after me. Men are just so frightened of smart women."

20   Another way showoffs show off about smart is to drop a Very Smart Name—if this brain is my friend, goes the message, I must be a brain too. And indeed, a popular showing-off ploy—whether

you're showing off smartness or anything else—is to name-drop a glittery name in the hope of acquiring some gilt by association.

The theory seems to be that Presidents, movie stars, Walter 21 Cronkite and Princess Di could be friends, if they chose, with anyone in the world, and that if these luminaries have selected plain old Stanley Stone to be friends with, Stanley Stone must be one hell of a guy. (Needless to say, old Stanley Stone might also be a very dreary fellow, but if Walt and Di don't mind him, why should I?)

Though no one that I know hangs out with Presidents and 22 movie stars, they do (I too!) sometimes drop famous names.

As in: "I go to John Travolta's dermatologist." 23

Or: "I own the exact same sweater that Jackie Onassis wore 24 in a newspaper photograph last week."

Or: "My uncle once repaired a roof for Sandra Day O'Connor." 25

Or: "My cousin's neighbor's sister-in-law has a child who is 26 Robert Redford's son's best friend."

We're claiming we've got gilt—though by a very indirect as- 27 sociation. And I think that when we do, we're showing off.

Sometimes showoffs ask for cheers to which they're not en- 28 titled. Sometimes showoffs earn the praise they seek. And sometimes folks achieve great things and nonetheless do not show off about it.

Now *that's* impressive. 29

Indeed, when we discover that the quiet mother of four with 30 whom we've been talking intimately all evening has recently been elected to the state senate—*and she never even mentioned it!*—we are filled with admiration, with astonishment, with awe.

What self-restraint! 31

For we know damn well—*I* certainly know—that if we'd been 32 that lucky lady, we'd have worked our triumph into the conversation. As a matter of fact, I'll lay my cards right on the table and confess that the first time some poems of mine were published, I not only worked my triumph into every conversation for months and months, but I also called almost every human being I'd ever known to proclaim the glad tidings both local and long distance. Furthermore—let me really confess—if a stranger happened to stop me on the street and all he wanted to know was the time or directions, I tried to detain him long enough to enlighten him with the news that the person to whom he was speaking was a Real Live Genuine Honest-to-God Published Poet.

33   Fortunately for everyone, I eventually—it took me awhile—calmed down.

34   Now, I don't intend to defend myself—I was showing off, I was bragging and I wasn't the slightest bit shy or self-restrained, but a golden, glowing, glorious thing had happened in my life and I had an overwhelming need to exult. Exulting, however (as I intend to argue farther on), may be a permissible form of showing off.

35   Exulting is what my child does when he comes home with an A on his history paper ("Julius Caesar was 50," it began, "and his good looks was pretty much demolished") and wants to read me the entire masterpiece while I murmur appreciative comments at frequent intervals.

36   Exulting is what my husband does when he cooks me one of his cheese-and-scallion omelets and practically does a tap dance as he carries it from the kitchen stove to the table, setting it before me with the purely objective assessment that this may be the greatest omelet ever created.

37   Exulting is what my mother did when she took her first grandson to visit all her friends, and announced as she walked into the room, "Is he gorgeous? Is that a gorgeous baby? Is that the most gorgeous baby you ever saw?"

38   And exulting is what that mother of four would have done if she'd smiled and said, "Don't call me 'Marge' any more. Call me 'Senator.' "

39   Exulting is shamelessly shouting our talents or triumphs to the world. It's saying: I'm taking a bow and I'd like to hear clapping. And I think if we don't overdo it (stopping strangers to say you've been published is overdoing it), and I think if we know when to quit ("Enough about me. Let's talk about you. So what do you think about me?" does not count as quitting), and I think if we don't get addicted (i.e., crave a praise-fix for every poem or A or omelet), and I think if we're able to walk off the stage (and clap and cheer while others take their bows), then I think we're allowed, from time to time, to exult.

40   Though showing off can range from very gross to very subtle, and though the point of showing off is sometimes nasty, sometimes needy, sometimes nice, showoffs always run the risk of being thought immodest, of being harshly viewed as . . . well . . . showoffs. And so for folks who want applause without relinquishing their sense of modesty, the trick is keeping quiet and allowing someone else to show off *for* you.

And I've seen a lot of marriages where wives show off for 41
husbands and where husbands, in return, show off for wives. Where
Joan, for instance, mentions Dick's promotion and his running time
in the marathon. And where Dick, for instance, mentions all the
paintings Joanie sold at her last art show. And where both of them
lean back with self-effacing shrugs and smiles and never once show
off about themselves.

Friends also may show off for friends, and parents for their 42
children, though letting parents toot our horns is risky. Consider,
for example, this sad tale of Elliott, who was a fearless and feisty
public-interest lawyer:

"My son," his proud mother explained to his friends, "has 43
always been independent." (Her son blushed modestly.)

"My son," his proud mother continued, "was the kind of per- 44
son who always knew his own mind." (Her son blushed modestly.)

"My son," his proud mother went on, "was never afraid. He 45
never kowtowed to those in authority." (Her son blushed modestly.)

"My son," his proud mother concluded, "was so independent 46
and stubborn and unafraid of authority that we couldn't get him toilet-
trained—he wet his pants till he was well past four." (Her son . . .)

But showing off is always a risk, whether we do it ourselves 47
or whether somebody else is doing it for us. And perhaps we ought
to consider the words Lord Chesterfield wrote to his sons: "Modesty
is the only sure bait when you angle for praise."

And yes, of course he's right, we know he's right, he must be 48
right. But sometimes it's so hard to be restrained. For no matter what
we do, we always have a lapse or two. So let's try to forgive each
other for showing off.

Thinking Critically About This Reading

1. Can you suggest a personality trait, displayed in public, that is
   worse than showing off? If yes, what is it? If no, why do you
   consider showing off the worst?

2. What techniques can you propose for dealing with competitive
   showoffs at a social gathering? Provide an example of one such
   successful technique.

3. Do you agree that excessive humility can be as annoying as excessive showing off? Give reasons for your answer.

4. What factors or influences in a person's life contribute most toward minimizing a person's need to show off? Give reasons for your answer.

5. The author confesses to having showed off when her dream of having her poems published became a reality. Can you remember an incident when you or a friend showed off? What were the circumstances or causes?

Understanding the Writer's Process

1. At what level of education and literary sophistication is this essay targeted? Give reasons for your answer.

2. The author begins her essay with an anecdote. Do you find it an appropriate opening? Why? Why not? Substitute a different opening and compare its effectiveness with that of the original.

3. How does the author give unity to the three unrelated examples in paragraphs 1, 3, and 5?

4. How does the author differentiate between the words *showing off* and *exulting*?

Examining the Writer's Language

1. In the context of the essay, briefly define each of the following terms: *angst* (paragraph 3), *hubris* (3), Kierkegaard (3), *epistemology* (3), narcissistic (8), periodontists (9), luminaries (21).

2. What three terms does the author use to describe the various types of showoffs? Which of the terms has an etymology that traces its origin back to Greek mythology?

3. What allusions indicate that the essay could not have been written before 1980?

4. Where in paragraph 20 is there a pun? Explain it.

Suggestions for Writing

1. Write an essay in which you draw a contrast between *exulting* and *showing off*. Use appropriate examples to clarify the difference.

2. Write an essay in which you classify one of the following subjects into its major types: humility, humor, snobbery, personality.

THE OPEN WINDOW

Saki (H. H. Munro)

Hector Hugh Munro (1870–1916) was an English author born in Burma. He started his writing career by writing political satires for the Westminster Gazette. *In 1901 he became a foreign correspondent, attached to the Tory* Morningpost, *a job he held for seven years. Using the pseudonym of Saki, Munro was best known and loved for his witty and often bitingly satirical short stories involving youngsters who outsmart the adult set. Among his collections are* Reginald *(1904),* The Chronicles of Clovis *(1911), and* Beasts and Super–Beasts *(1914). He also wrote two novels,* The Unbearable Bassington *(1912) and* When William Came *(1914). Saki was killed fighting in World War I.*

Preparing to Read This Selection Critically

The story is believable only because the author sets the stage for the surprise humorous catastrophe that follows. Study the details that make it possible for the reader to believe what otherwise might seem preposterous. The most important character to watch is the fifteen–year–old girl, who sets the conflict in motion. Pay close attention to her tone and words. When you finish reading the story, formulate in your mind the dominant impression she conveys.

"My Aunt will be down presently, Mr. Nuttel," said a very 1
self-possessed young lady of fifteen; "in the meantime you must try and put up with me."

Framton Nuttel endeavored to say the correct something which 2
should duly flatter the niece of the moment without unduly discounting the aunt that was to come. Privately he doubted more than ever whether these formal visits on a succession of total strangers would do much towards helping the nerve cure which he was supposed to be undergoing.

"I know how it will be," his sister had said when he was 3
preparing to migrate to this rural retreat; "you will bury yourself

down there and not speak to a living soul, and your nerves will be worse than ever from moping. I shall just give you letters of introduction to all the people I know there. Some of them, as far as I can remember, were quite nice." Framton wondered whether Mrs. Sappleton, the lady to whom he was presenting one of the letters of introduction, came into the nice division.

4   "Do you know many of the people round here?" asked the niece, when she judged that they had had sufficient silent communion.

5   "Hardly a soul," said Framton. "My sister was staying here, at the rectory, you know, some four years ago, and she gave me letters of introduction to some of the people here."

6   He made the last statement in a tone of distinct regret.

7   "Then you know practically nothing about my aunt?" pursued the self-possessed young lady.

8   "Only her name and address," admitted the caller. He was wondering whether Mrs. Sappleton was in the married or widowed state. An undefinable something about the room seemed to suggest masculine habitation.

9   "Her great tragedy happened just three years ago," said the child; "that would be since your sister's time."

10   "Her tragedy?" asked Framton; somehow in this restful country spot tragedies seemed out of place.

11   "You may wonder why we keep that window wide open on an October afternoon," said the niece, indicating a large French window that opened onto a lawn.

12   "It is quite warm for the time of the year," said Framton; "but has that window got anything to do with the tragedy?"

13   "Out through that window, three years ago to a day, her husband and her two young brothers went off for their day's shooting. They never came back. In crossing the moor to their favorite snipe-shooting ground they were all three engulfed in a treacherous piece of bog. It had been that dreadful wet summer, you know, and places that were safe in other years gave way suddenly without warning. Their bodies were never recovered. That was the dreadful part of it." Here the child's voice lost its self-possessed note and became falteringly human. "Poor aunt always thinks that they will come back some day, they and the little brown spaniel that was lost with them, and walk in at that window just as they used to do. That is why the window is kept open every evening till it is quite dusk. Poor dear aunt, she has often told me how they went out, her husband with his white waterproof coat over his arm, and Ronnie, her

youngest brother, singing, 'Bertie, why do you bound?' as he always did to tease her, because she said it got on her nerves. Do you know, sometimes on still, quiet evenings like this, I almost get a creepy feeling that they will all walk in through that window—"

She broke off with a little shudder. It was a relief to Framton 14 when the aunt bustled into the room with a whirl of apologies for being late in making her appearance.

"I hope Vera has been amusing you?" she said. 15

"She has been very interesting," said Framton. 16

"I hope you don't mind the open window," said Mrs. Sapple- 17 ton briskly; "my husband and brothers will be home directly from shooting, and they always come in this way. They've been out for snipe in the marshes today, so they'll make a fine mess over my poor carpets. So like you menfolk, isn't it?" She rattled on cheerfully about the shooting and the scarcity of birds, and the prospects for duck in the winter. To Framton it was all purely horrible. He made a desperate effort to turn the talk onto a less ghastly topic; he was conscious that his hostess was giving him only a fragment of her attention, and her eyes were constantly straying past him to the open window and the lawn beyond. It was certainly an unfortunate coincidence that he should have paid his visit on this tragic anniversary.

"The doctors agree in ordering me complete rest, an absence 18 of mental excitement, and avoidance of any violent physical exercise," announced Framton, who labored under the tolerably widespread delusion that total strangers and chance acquaintances are hungry for the least detail of one's ailments and infirmities. "On the matter of diet they are not so much in agreement," he continued.

"No?" said Mrs. Sappleton, in a voice which only replaced a 19 yawn at the last moment. Then she suddenly brightened into alert attention—but not to what Framton was saying.

"Here they are at last!" she cried. "Just in time for tea, and 20 don't they look as if they were muddy up to the eyes!"

Framton shivered slightly and turned towards the niece with 21 a look intended to convey sympathetic comprehension. The child was staring out through the open window with dazed horror in her eyes. In a chill shock of nameless fear Framton swung round in his seat and looked in the same direction.

In the deepening twilight three figures were walking across 22 the lawn towards the window; they all carried guns under their arms, and one of them was additionally burdened with a white coat hung over his shoulders. A tired brown spaniel kept close at their heels. Noiselessly they neared the house, and then a hoarse young voice chanted out of the dusk: "I said, Bertie, why do you bound?"

23   Framton grabbed wildly at his stick and hat; the hall door, the gravel drive, and the front gate were dimly noted stages in his headlong retreat. A cyclist coming along the road had to run into the hedge to avoid imminent collision.

24   "Here we are, my dear," said the bearer of the white mackintosh, coming in through the window; "fairly muddy, but most of it's dry. Who was that who bolted out as we came up?"

25   "A most extraordinary man, a Mr. Nuttel," said Mrs. Sappleton; "could only talk about his illnesses, and dashed off without a word of good-by or apology when you arrived. One would think he had seen a ghost."

26   "I expect it was the spaniel," said the niece calmly; "he told me he had a horror of dogs. He was once hunted into a cemetery somewhere on the banks of the Ganges by a pack of pariah dogs, and had to spend the night in a newly dug grave with the creatures snarling and grinning and foaming just above him. Enough to make anyone lose their nerve."

27   Romance at short notice was her speciality.

Thinking Critically About This Reading

1. On what aspects of humor is this story based? In other words, why is it possible for you to laugh at the outcome?

2. Imagine that Mr. Nuttel were your father. Would the story still seem humorous to you? Why? Why not?

3. Who besides the author/narrator knows what the girl is up to? What technique is the author using in choosing which characters know and which do not?

4. What facts make it possible for the girl to pull off her delusion?

5. What difference, if any, does it make that the protagonist of the story is an adolescent? Explain your answer.

Understanding the Writer's Process

1. Where does the climax of the story take place? What was your personal reaction?

2. What keeps the story from horrifying the reader or from being pathetic? Support your answer with examples from the text.
3. The action of the story takes place in an upper–class setting. What advantage does this setting have over, say, a slum or a factory?
4. How effective is the concluding sentence of the story? Explain your judgment.
5. What is the meaning and purpose of paragraph 26?

Examining the Writer's Language

1. Choose at least three adjectives the narrator uses to create a dominant impression of the girl. What, in your own words, is this dominant impression? Formulate it in a single sentence.
2. What does the dialogue contribute to the story?
3. Of all the characters who speak in the story, whose comments dominate? Why?
4. What kind of language does the narrator of the story use? Is it colloquial? Formal? Journalistic? Slang?
5. Do the events in the story justify the title "The Open Window"? Explain your answer.

Writing Assignment Based on "The Open Window"

"The Open Window" is a humorous classification of upper–class English society. Several types are described. Write an essay in which you imagine a weekend with people from your social milieu. Classify these people into three or four types, describing specific people as typical of each type. For instance, you might describe Mrs. Jones as being the eternal gossip who assassinates character by innuendo. Or, you might describe Mr. Smith, who is grossly obese, as being so interested in food that he waits for every meal as if it were his last. Try to be humorous, like Saki.

STUDENT ESSAY (IN PROCESS) CLASSIFICATION

Christine Lavoie

Christine Lavoie is attending college in order to pursue a career in computer technology. Between high school and college, she worked briefly as a pharmacist's assistant, an insurance claims examiner, and a book-keeper. Her hobbies include cooking, music, reading, and gardening. She also enjoys observing children and their psychological traits.

First Draft   Christine Lavoie

                                           English 101

                    Four Types of Children

    While taking a stroll one morning, I de-
cided to stop and watch some neighborhood children playing on the playground. Quite soon I
found myself engrossed in a scenario fit for
the movies. Though the script had never been
rehearsed, the actors knew their parts by heart
and spoke their lines perfectly. I became so
enthralled that I have returned to this theatre
many times. ~~During each visit, four main character types stood out above the rest.~~ *After only a few visits, I began to single out four main types: the bully, the clown, the con artist, and the scapegoat. I rather suspect that these types will play their acquired roles throughout life.* John is a husky boy, about four feet
tall, with dark hair and brown eyes. When he
~~walks~~ *swaggers* onto the scene, ~~it seems as if~~ he ~~wants to~~ *seems capable of*
~~knock~~ *knocking* down anyone or anything that might get in
his way. As he enters the play area the other
children scatter as if John were some sort of
god. When finally he reaches the swings, three
children leap from their seats. *Without apology,* John hops onto
one seat and begins to ~~sway~~ *swing* back and forth. As
he ~~observes~~ *watches* the other children playing with
jittery nervousness, *caused by* ~~just from being aware of~~

Rewrite thesis to predict the essay.

awesome

his presence, a self-satisfied grin ~~suddenly~~ *gradually*

Make description more vivid → spreads across his face. He looks like a tyrant hovering over his kingdom. "David, get me a Coke," he yells. David, *like a well-programmed robot,* without question, jumps up and trots off toward the snack bar. He, like all the other children, lives in constant fear of the consequences of disobeying John.

Name specific consequences → *Doing so could mean a bloody nose, a scratched chin, or a bruised eye.* ~~John thinks nothing of using brute force to get his way.~~ John is the bully type.

↑↑ Chris, on the other hand, ~~obtains~~ *gets* his satisfaction from amusing the other children. With short sandy ~~blond~~ hair, round green eyes, and an elastic face, Chris can turn the entire playground into uproarious laughter

transition needed → whenever he chooses to perform his funny antics. ~~For instance~~ *For instance,* When another child, (Betty,) is harshly scolded by her mother for throwing sand, Chris waits until the mother's back is turned and then he stands up and ~~begins to mimic her.~~ *the parental scolding including tone of voice and gestures,* Instantly, all of the children start to snicker and giggle. Much to my amazement even a few parents join in ~~on the laughter,~~ somehow condoning *this sly comedic* ~~his~~ behavior. Chris does not get laughs only at the expense of others; quite willingly he often turns himself into a laughing stock—just for attention.

Give some examples. State the type. → *If, for instance, the audience suits him, he will cross his eyes, screw his face into a grimace, or hobble like a cripple. Chris is the clown type.*

Sandra is a pretty girl, with auburn hair cascading down her back to her waist. ~~She is a very complex young lady.~~ Her popularity

Omit irrelevant sentence → among the (other children) ~~helps her to~~ earns ~~the~~ *her admiration* ~~trust~~ and ~~support~~ *envy* of the (others ~~although she is~~)

Use an image to bring her to life.

~~also envied.~~ All the children want to play with her and be her best friend. *She is the Cleopatra of the playground.* Once she has spun her web, the real games begin. During each play session, Sandra will choose only one or two friends to play with—and only if they acquiesce

Approach Jimmy coyly and whisper, "I won't play with you unless you give me your candy bar." Enchanted and ensnared, Jimmy answers, "O.K., here it is."

Use direct dialogue to be more vivid.

immediately to her demands. She may ~~tell Jimmy that she will not play with him if he does not give her his candy bar.~~ He gives her the candy and is rewarded with ~~her company.~~ *her flirtatious smile and a brief moment of her illusive attention.* This little *of "entrap and conquel"* game continues without any of the children wising up to Sandra's *scheming* ~~tactics.~~ ~~Not only are the~~ *are not the only ones* Children ~~are~~ lured into this trap; ~~but so are~~ adults *are too* One hears them comment, "Isn't that just the most adorable little girl you've ever seen?" This ~~girl~~ *Child* can be the most well-behaved and charming ~~nymph~~ *Siren* imaginable—in order to obtain what she wants. Sandra is the con artist type.

better Clarity

rep

Betty is not a pretty girl. In fact, she is rather scrawny and awkward. My sympathies go out to her because she is always getting blamed for ~~things she had no part in.~~ *disasters she did not create. The* ~~Some~~ kids decide to fill balloons with water, hide in the bushes, and throw ~~them~~ *the balloons* at *unsuspecting* passersby. Betty, of course, is appointed to do the dirty work of filling the balloons with water. During her quest, Betty is caught in the act by the park supervisor, who sternly orders *her* to "stop horsing around with all that water." She is discip-

be specific ref

lined severely but does not ~~acknowledge~~ *tattle on* the other ~~children's involvement~~ *Children*. She accepts the blame—as she always does. By shouldering blame, she hopes to receive praise from her peers. A few ~~thank you~~'s *apologies* may come her way, but *for the most part the children take her self sacrifice for granted. She* ~~things will not have changed very much.~~ Betty *is always to blame.* *for being skinny, for* is constantly pick~~ed~~ on by the others ~~for things~~ *being a bungler, for being stupid* *be specific what don't they like?* ~~they don't like about her.~~ She is often the butt of Chris's jokes. He calls her "Jerky Turkey" or "Dizzy Lizzy." John loves to frighten her *— throw a live lizard at her or muddy her clean dress —* *give examples* with the threat of what he might do if she does not follow his bidding. And she is drawn into *except she is Sandra's official slave.* Sandra's web time and ~~time~~ again. The sadde~~st~~ part of all is that this type of personality can become a self-fulfilling prophecy. ~~Sandra~~ *Betty* may go through life feeling unworthy. ~~Sandra~~ *Betty* is the scapegoat type.

//   These four personality types—the bully, the clown, the con artist, and *the* scapegoat—may seem quite different *one from the other;* ~~but~~ they have one characteristics in common: They all have deep feelings of insecurity or worthlessness; therefore, they crave any kind of attention, ~~nega~~ *bad* *Stronger* ~~tive~~ or *good* ~~positive. The most amazing thing to me~~ *Conclusion* ~~is the number of ways they go about getting this~~ *needed* ~~attention.~~

I wonder what each child will be twenty years from now.

<u>Final Draft</u>   Christine Lavoie

English 101

Four Types of Children

While taking a stroll one morning, I decided to stop and watch some neighborhood children playing on the playground. Quite soon I
found myself engrossed in a scenario fit for
the movies. Though the script had never been
rehearsed, the actors knew their parts by heart
and spoke their lines perfectly. I became so
enthralled that I have returned to this theatre
many times. After only a few visits, I began to
single out four main types: the bully, the
clown, the con artist, and the scapegoat. I
rather suspect that these types will play their
acquired roles throughout life.

John is a husky boy, about four feet
tall, with dark hair and brown eyes. When he
swaggers onto the scene, he seems capable of
knocking down anyone or anything that might get
in his way. As he enters the play area, the
other children scatter as if John were some
sort of god. When finally he reaches the
swings, three children leap from their seats.
Without apology, John hops onto one seat and
begins to swing back and forth. As he watches
the other children playing with jittery nervousness, caused by his awesome presence, a
self-satisfied grin gradually spreads across
his face. He looks like a tyrant hovering over
his kingdom. "David, get me a Coke," he yells.

David, like a well-programmed robot, jumps up
and trots off toward the snack bar. He, like all
the other children, lives in constant fear of
the consequences of disobeying John. Doing so
could mean a bloody nose, a scratched chin, or
a bruised eye. John is the bully type.

Chris, on the other hand, gets his
satisfaction from amusing the other children.
With short sandy hair, round green eyes, and an
elastic face, Chris can turn the entire playground into uproarious laughter whenever he
chooses to perform his funny antics. For instance, when Betty, another child, is harshly
scolded by her mother for throwing sand, Chris
waits until the mother's back is turned and
then he stands up and mimicks the parental
scolding, including tone of voice and gestures. Instantly, all of the children start to
snicker and giggle. Much to my amazement even a
few parents join in, somehow condoning this
sly, comedic behavior. Chris does not get
laughs only at the expense of others; quite
willingly he often turns himself into a laughing stock—just for attention. If, for instance, the audience suits him, he will cross
his eyes, screw his face into a grimace, or hobble like a cripple. Chris is the clown type.

Sandra is a pretty girl, with auburn
hair cascading down her back. Her popularity
earns her the admiration and envy of the other
children. All the children want to play with
her and be her best friend. She is the Cleopatra
of the playground. Once she has begun to spin

her web, the real games begin. During each play session, Sandra will choose only one or two friends to play with—and only if they acquiesce immediately to her demands. She may approach Jimmy coyly and whisper, "I won't play with you unless you give me your candy bar." Enchanted and ensnared, Jimmy answers, "O.K., here it is." He gives her the candy and is rewarded with her flirtatious smile and a brief moment of her illusive attention. This little game of en-trap and conquer continues without any of the children wising up to Sandra's scheming tac-tics. Children are not the only ones lured into this trap; adults are too. One hears them com-ment, "Isn't that just the most adorable little girl you've ever seen?" This child can be the most well-behaved and charming siren imagina-ble—in order to get what she wants. Sandra is the con artist type.

Betty is not a pretty girl. In fact, she is rather scrawny and awkward. My sympathies go out to her because she is always getting blamed for disasters she did not create. The kids de-cide to fill balloons with water, hide in the bushes, and throw the balloons at unsuspecting passersby. Betty, of course, is appointed to do the dirty work of filling the balloons with water. During her quest, Betty is caught in the act by the park supervisor, who sternly orders her to "stop horsing around with all that water." She is disciplined severely but does not tattle on the other children. She accepts the blame—as she always does. By shouldering blame, she hopes to receive praise from her peers. A few apologies may come her way, but for the most part the children take her self-sacrifice for granted. She is always to blame. Betty is constantly picked on by the others—for being skinny, for being a bungler, for being stupid. She is often the butt of Chris's jokes. He calls her "Jerky Turkey" or "Dizzy Lizzy." John loves to frighten her with the threat of what he might do—throw a live lizard at her or muddy her clean dress—if she does not follow his bidding. And she is drawn into Sandra's web time and again. In fact, she is Sandra's official slave. The saddest part of all is that this type of personality can become a self-fulfilling prophecy. Betty may go through life feeling unworthy. Betty is the scapegoat type.

These four personality types—the bully, the clown, the con artist, and the scapegoat—may seem quite different one from the other, but they have one characteristics in common: They all have deep feelings of insecurity or worthlessness; therefore, they crave any kind of attention, bad or good. I wonder what each child will be twenty years from now.

Drawing by Jonik; © 1991 The New Yorker Magazine, Inc.

8

Comparing/Contrasting

HOW TO WRITE A COMPARISON/ CONTRAST

Consciously or unconsciously, we spend many of our waking hours engaged in the common thought process known as comparison/contrast. When we compare, we look for similarities between two subjects; when we contrast, we focus on finding their dissimilarities. But as a practical matter, most comparisons involve a dual search for both likenesses and unlikenesses and seldom are concentrated exclusively on uncovering one or the other. We compare shoes in a store, actors in a play, apartments and houses we have lived in, instructors we have had, books we have read, and parties we have attended. Comparing is fundamental to virtually every judgment, decision, or opinion we form throughout the course of daily life.

The written comparison differs from the mental comparison of daily life in degree rather than in kind. It is likely to be more systematically made, with more forethought, and with greater care and precision. Yet it is essentially the same thought process, involving the scrutiny of two items, ideas, events, people, objects, or concepts for their similarities and differences.

1. Choose the Basis of Your Comparison/Contrast

While *comparison*, strictly considered, means showing likenesses between two items, and *contrast* means showing differences, the term *comparison* is commonly used as a catchword for either approach. The basis of a comparison is simply the gauge you use to match up your two subjects. You might compare two friends on the bases of personality, personal appearance, and religious belief. You might compare an apple with an orange for composition of healthful fiber, for cost per pound, or for vitamin C content. To be fair and logical, a comparison/contrast must be made on bases by which the compared items can be judged impartially and equally. You cannot compare one writer's essays with another writer's poetry, but you can compare their literary outputs on the basis of similarity of theme.

Choosing the bases of your comparison/contrast essay requires a great deal of initial prethinking. You should first discern what the bases of your comparison are to be and then list them. If you have the temperament for detailed planning, draw two columns side by side and label each with the name of the item being compared. In the left margin, write down the bases of your comparison/contrast. Then simply fill in the blanks, moving from one column to the other. A chart comparing sailboats with power boats might look like this:

Bases	Sailboats	Powerboats
Cost:		
Ease of operation:		
Recreational use:		

The chart is a rough comparison/contrast list for sailboats and powerboats structured on the bases of cost, ease of operation, and recreational use. To plan your comparison/contrast, you merely fill in the blanks under the respective headings (sailboats and powerboats), listing how they compare to or differ from your three chosen bases.

Many writers automatically begin a comparison/contrast by immediately declaring its basis. Consider an example:

> I am quite positive that of the two, humor is the more comfortable and livable quality. Humorous persons, if their gift is genuine and not a mere shine upon the surface, are always agreeable companions and they sit through the evening best. They have pleasant mouths turned up at the corners. To these corners the great Master of marionettes has fixed strings, and he holds them in his nimblest fingers to twitch them at the slightest jest. But the mouth of the merely witty man is hard and sour until the moment of its discharge. Nor is the flash from a witty man always comforting, whereas a humorous man radiates a general pleasure and is like another candle in the room.
>
> CHARLES BROOKS, *"On the Difference Between Wit and Humor"*

The comparison/contrast in this paragraph between wit and humor is made on the basis of what the writer calls their "more comfortable and livable quality."

2. Use Words and Phrases That Clearly Draw a Comparison/Contrast

Strict comparisons are drawn by using such words and phrases as *like, similar to, in comparison, likewise.* Contrasts are etched by using such words and phrases as *in contrast, yet, however, but, on the other hand, on the contrary, although,* and *otherwise.* Any comparison/contrast may be given a graceful and elegant turn if you are deft in the use of appropriate words and phrases. The following is an example:

> Lenin, with whom I had a long conversation in Moscow in 1920, was, superficially, very *unlike* Gladstone, *and yet,* allowing for the difference in time and place and creed, the two men *had much in common. To begin with the differences:* Lenin was cruel, which Gladstone was not; Lenin had no respect for tradition, *whereas* Gladstone had a great deal; Lenin considered all means legitimate for securing the victory of his party, *whereas* for Gladstone politics was a game with certain rules that must be observed [italics added].
>
> BERTRAND RUSSELL, *"Lenin and Gladstone"*

The italicized expressions mark the twists and turns in the author's unfolding thoughts.

3. Draw the Comparison/Contrast Either Between or Within Paragraphs

The foregoing excerpt is an example of a comparison/contrast drawn wholly within a single paragraph. This kind of organization is used mainly in brief comparisons or in comparisons that touch lightly on several minor points of similarity or difference between subjects. A comparison also may be organized in separate paragraphs that alternately match up compared subjects on a particular basis. Here is an example:

> Ross was an oak of prudence and industry. He rarely drank and never smoked. He excelled at everything he did. He had married his hometown sweetheart, was proudly faithful to her and produced four fine children. After a sampling of success on both coasts he had gone home to the Indiana of his parents and childhood friends.
>
> Tom Heggen had a taste for low life. He had been divorced, had no children and shared bachelor quarters in New York with an ex-actor and screenwriter, Dorothy Parker's estranged husband, Alan Campbell. Tom was a drinker and a pill addict. He turned up regularly at the fashionable restaurant "21," usually bringing along a new girl, a dancer or an actress.
>
> JOHN LEGGETT, *"Ross and Tom"*

The lifestyles of these two writers form the basis of comparison and each comparison forms a separate paragraph.

The decision on whether to draw a comparison within a single paragraph or between separate paragraphs depends largely on personal style and on the complexity of the basis used to compare the two subjects. You may use either method, both, or alternate them and so add a touch of variety to your essay.

4. Deal Fairly and Equally with Both Sides

Although perhaps too obvious to be highlighted as a separate point, it is an odd fact that many otherwise good comparisons are ruined by the writer's slighting one side while lopsidedly favoring the other. Fairness requires that you expend equal amounts of ink on both sides of a comparison. If you are comparing Samuel Johnson's dictionary of the English language with Noah Webster's later effort in North America, you should not write two pages on Johnson's work and only one on Webster's. Nor will you be tempted to make this mistake if you plan your essay with the chart recommended earlier.

JUST SAY "NO," JUST HEAR "NO"

Carol Sanger

> *Carol Sanger is a law professor at Santa Clara University and a visiting scholar at the Institute for Research on Women and Gender at Stanford University. Much of her writing has centered on women's role in society and the problems created by being a female. For instance, in 1985 she published* Day Care Center Licensing and Child Care, *a work intended for providers of children's day care.*

Preparing to Read This Selection Critically

The subject of sexual harassment and rape recently has taken up much space in all segments of the media—

newspapers, magazines, and television. Whereas in the past a woman who had been sexually harassed or even raped by an employer or someone else in authority would be too ashamed or afraid to admit the crime, today women are coming forward in a much more courageous and forthright manner to face the perpetrators of these acts. As you read Sanger's views, ask yourself whether you agree with her basic distinction between rape and sex and whether her distinction will lead to a more fair judgment of alleged sex crimes when they are presented in court. Think also about whether the new trend might end up being unfair to males. Search your memory for personal experiences or experiences of friends that might shed light on the argument.

1   We are a culture that has learned to think in slogans, and bumper stickers may be a truer gauge of what matters to Americans than newspaper editorials. I am sure about one thing that matters a lot. No surprise here—it is sex.

2   Pick any occupation and there is a bumper sticker bragging about how plumbers or lawyers or cement pourers or accountants "do it": with their briefs on, with their slide rules out, under water, in the air. Lots of people seem to be doing it, or at least thinking about it, and plastering the news on their fenders. We ride around habituated to these casual, public and slightly sniggering announcements about sex.

3   There is also another familiar bumper sticker—the "Just Say No" message of drug education fame. We teach children that what they say counts, that if they "just say no," they will be in control, their decisions not to participate will be respected, and they will be safe from the harms of drugs.

4   Saying "no" may work for kids declining drugs. But it often works less well for women who say "no" to sex, women who do not want to "do it." Saying "yes" or "no" matters tremendously here. It is the difference between sexual intercourse and rape.

5   Some people seem confused about the difference between sexual intercourse and rape. The first is a voluntary, often intimate association. The second is a criminal act. The difference between them is not the time of day or the location or what either person was wearing—or what their grades in high school were. The essential difference is consent.

Consent—agreeing to something—is usually not a hard concept   6
to understand. It may at first appear more complex in the context
of rape. One reason is simply its unexpected presence. There is no
other crime defined in terms of consent. Only in rape is the victim
asked, "Did you agree to it?" Compare "Did you agree to be punched
in the face?" "Did you agree to be mugged?"

A second problem has been the language of consent, in most   7
other circumstances no problem at all. Parties to an agreement signal
consent by saying "yes." But, so the story goes, everyone knows
that women say "no" when they really mean "yes" because "no"
is the acceptable social response. With one word—"no"—supposedly
standing in for both "yes" and "no," men have understood their
job to be to persuade the woman into "yes," and if that fails, to
take her "no" for the "yes" that they thought was there anyway,
no matter what she said.

Here the law is a grim conspirator. In most jurisdictions, rape   8
is defined not just as sexual intercourse without the woman's consent
but as sexual intercourse without consent *and* as a result of force or
the threat of force. So, saying "no" may not be enough. You have
to say no, then wait and fear being overpowered, and then resist
(complexities that don't fit on a bumper sticker).

By refusing to accept a verbal "no" as the end of the matter,   9
the law requires women to be afraid. Fear is, of course, nothing new
to women. We incorporate it into how we negotiate quite ordinary
events—where we park, how late we stay, whether we smile at a
stranger. Women can inventory the events of any day and list the
ways they have been careful, the routinized responses to fear. Rape
laws formalize fear. By burdening simple consent with the requirement of resistance, they keep women afraid.

Rape laws undermine consent in another way, too. There are   10
few instances where consenting to something once means you have
agreed to it forever. Remember, rape is still defined in many states
as sexual intercourse with a woman who is not one's wife, without
her consent and as a result of force or threat of force. So, for married
women, having agreed to marry means they have agreed to sex for
the duration. In effect, marriage is a waiver of the protection of rape
laws. Saying "no" to a husband may not matter at all.

The idea that there is a free zone, like marriage, in which rape   11
can occur without consent leads to yet another problem with the way
consent to sexual intercourse is popularly understood—specificity. The
law says that rape is sexual intercourse without the woman's consent.

That ought to mean that the woman has to consent to the intercourse itself—not just to a ride home, a movie or a walk around the block. Without this explicit consent, every time, intercourse is rape, as much a crime as punching someone in the face without her consent. Yet juries and prosecutors routinely infer consent to sex from the fact that a woman agrees to go on a date, or from the fact that she has chosen to be in a certain place at a certain time.

12   There are other, less legal reasons why decisions by women to decline sex are not taken seriously. Go back to the bumper stickers. In many ways we seem to take the view that sex is no big deal, a funny subject for puns on car bumpers. What's the problem? Who wouldn't want it?

13   I think the answer is "lots of people," but I'm only sure about lots of women.

14   Imagine a society—or a legal system—where saying "yes" to intercourse is regarded as skeptically as saying "no" is now. In this imaginary society, spoken words are accompanied by cartoon–like bubbles over one's head that tell what the speaker really wants. We might learn that women consent for many reasons. Sometimes "yes" would mean "Yes, I want to." But other times, I'd bet that "yes" would mean "What's the point in saying 'no'? It's going to happen anyway." Or, "If I say 'no,' he'll get angry, and then what?"

15   In our world, "yes" always signifies "yes" with regard to sex. That's OK. But if "yes" means "yes," then "no"—just "no"—has got to mean "no." Otherwise, both are confusing. Let's try *that* on a few bumper stickers.

Thinking Critically About This Reading

1. In her essay, the author takes great pains to draw a distinction between the words *yes* and *no*. Why is there no room for *maybe* in her analysis?

2. According to the author, the difference between sexual intercourse and rape has nothing to do with time of day, apparel worn, or school grades earned. What is she alluding to by using those particular examples?

3. On pages 546–552 of this book, Anita Hill, a lawyer who worked for Judge Clarence Thomas, then Assistant Secretary of Education for the United States Government and now a U.S. Supreme Court justice, accuses her former boss of having harassed her sexually.

Reread her speech and judge her response in terms of the "no" mentioned by Sanger. What is your opinion of the Hill–Thomas relationship? Do you believe the woman was sexually harassed or not? Be specific in your answer.

4. In paragraph 9, the author mentions areas of everyday life in which women negotiate out of fear. What example, from your own experience or that of someone you know, can you cite either to support or refute the author's view?

5. Do you believe rape laws should apply to husbands as well as to other males who force sex on women? Give reasons for your answer.

Understanding the Writer's Process

1. Where in the essay does the author announce her analysis of the difference between sexual intercourse and rape? What purpose does the announcement serve?

2. What other rhetorical mode (besides comparison/contrast) does the author use in order to clarify the difference between sexual intercourse and rape? Is it necessary? Explain your answer.

3. Where has the author placed the thesis of her essay? Is the placement effective? Why or why not?

4. Why does the author refer to bumper stickers in the final sentence of her essay?

5. What difference do you perceive between bumper stickers and editorials?

Examining the Writer's Language

1. From the list that follows, choose four words that are not normally part of your writing vocabulary and place each word in a sentence: slogans (1), gauge (1), habituated (2), conspirator (8), inventory (9), routinized (9), waiver (10), specificity (11).

2. What figure of speech is used in paragraph 8 when the law is termed "a grim conspirator"? What is its purpose?

3. In paragraph 9, what is the purpose of the sudden shift to the "we" point of view?

4. What is the purpose of the parenthetical clause in paragraph 8?

5. How would you describe the general level of language used in this essay? Is it formal, informal, or colloquial? What kind of audience does it address?

Suggestions for Writing

1. In 500 words or less, delineate the difference between "infatuation" and "love." Use examples to clarify your points.
2. Write an essay in which you differentiate between a woman's clear consent to having sex and her half–hearted consent as a result of fear or reticence.

THE PRISONER'S DILEMMA

Stephen Chapman

Stephen Chapman (b. 1907) was for many years Associate Editor of The New Republic, *for which he wrote numerous influential articles on political as well as social issues. In the following essay, Chapman takes the unusual position that although most U.S. citizens have come to view the punishments prescribed for Islamic countries guided by the Koran as barbaric and unnecessarily cruel, in actuality the practices of Western democracies, including our country, are equally, and perhaps even more, barbaric. The essay originally appeared in the March 8, 1980, issue of* The New Republic.

Preparing to Read This Selection Critically

The idea of punishment as a means of reform has been studied by scholars of every kind—religious, philosophical, social, political, and sociological. Some people support the ancient idea of an eye for an eye and a tooth for a tooth; others believe that love and kindness is the way to cure evil; still others support psychotherapy as the only hope for criminal behavior, construing it as a mental disease. The essay that follows, with its surprising arguments, is well worth pondering. No one can point proudly to our American prison system and say that it is successful—not with all of the recidivism leading to repeat rapes, arson, robbery, and murder. So what about other ways of dealing with crime, such as the one adopted in Islamic countries, where the general system is to let the punishment fit the crime, exactly and without deviation? Can that tradition really be worse than the sadistic tradition in the United States of keeping a criminal in solitary confinement for years, or the ineffective tradition of turning prisons into country clubs as soon as the inmates complain that they need better meals, better television sets, and better sports activities? This essay begs you to find a solution to the problem of how best to treat people who break the law. Think about it and formulate a plan you can support.

If the punitive laws of Islam were applied for only one year, all the devastating injustices would be uprooted. Misdeeds must be punished by the law of retaliation: cut off the hands of the thief; kill the murderers; flog the adulterous woman or man. Your concerns, your "humanitarian" scruples are more childish than reasonable. Under the terms of Koranic law, any judge fulfilling the seven requirements (that he have reached puberty, be a believer, know the Koranic laws perfectly, be just, and not be affected by amnesia, or be a bastard, or be of the female sex) is qualified to be a judge in any type of case. He can thus judge and dispose of twenty trials in a single day, whereas the Occidental justice might take years to argue them out.

FROM *Sayings of the Ayatollah Khomeini*

One of the amusements of life in the modern West is the opportunity to observe the barbaric rituals of countries that are attached to the customs of the dark ages. Take Pakistan, for example, our newest ally and client state in Asia. Last October President Zia, in harmony with the Islamic fervor that is sweeping his part of the world, revived the traditional Moslem practice of flogging lawbreakers in public. In Pakistan, this qualified as mass entertainment, and no fewer than 10,000 law-abiding Pakistanis turned out to see justice done to 26 convicts. To Western sensibilities the spectacle seemed barbaric—both in the sense of cruel and in the sense of pre-civilized. In keeping with Islamic custom each of the unfortunates—who had been caught in prostitution raids the previous night and summarily convicted and sentenced—was stripped down to a pair of white shorts, which were painted with a red stripe across the buttocks (the target). Then he was shackled against an easel, with pads thoughtfully placed over the kidneys to prevent injury. The floggers were muscular, fierce-looking sorts—convicted murderers, as it happens—who paraded around the flogging platform in colorful loincloths. When the time for the ceremony began, one of the floggers took a running start and brought a five-foot stave down across the first victim's buttocks, eliciting screams from the convict and murmurs from the audience. Each of the 26 received from five to 15 lashes. One had to be carried from the stage unconscious.

2   Flogging is one of the punishments stipulated by Koranic law, which has made it a popular penological device in several Moslem countries, including Pakistan, Saudi Arabia, and, most recently, the ayatollah's Iran. Flogging, or *ta'zir*, is the general punishment prescribed for offenses that don't carry an explicit Koranic penalty. Some crimes carry automatic *hadd* punishments—stoning or scourging (a severe whipping) for illicit sex, scourging for drinking alcoholic beverages, amputation of the hands for theft. Other crimes—as varied as murder and abandoning Islam—carry the death penalty (usually carried out in public). Colorful practices like these have given the Islamic world an image in the West, as described by historian G. H. Jansen, "of blood dripping from the stumps of amputated hands and from the striped backs of malefactors, and piles of stones barely concealing the battered bodies of adulterous couples." Jansen, whose book *Militant Islam* is generally effusive in its praise of Islamic practices, grows squeamish when considering devices like flogging, amputation, and stoning. But they are given enthusiastic endorsement by the Koran itself.

3   Such traditions, we all must agree, are no sign of an advanced civilization. In the West, we have replaced these various punishments (including the death penalty in most cases) with a single device. Our custom is to confine criminals in prison for varying lengths of time. In Illinois, a reasonably typical state, grand theft carries a punishment of three to five years; armed robbery can get you from six to 30. The lowest form of felony theft is punishable by one to three years in prison. Most states impose longer sentences on habitual offenders. In Kentucky, for example, habitual offenders can be sentenced to life in prison. Other states are less brazen, preferring the more genteel sounding "indeterminate sentence," which

allows parole boards to keep inmates locked up for as long as life. It was under an indeterminate sentence of one to 14 years that George Jackson served 12 years in California prisons for committing a $70 armed robbery. Under a Texas law imposing an automatic life sentence for a third felony conviction, a man was sent to jail for life last year because of three thefts adding up to less than $300 in property value. Texas also is famous for occasionally imposing extravagantly long sentences, often running into hundreds or thousands of years. This gives Texas a leg up on Maryland, which used to sentence some criminals to life plus a day—a distinctive if superfluous flourish.

The punishment *intended* by Western societies in sending their 4 criminals to prison is the loss of freedom. But, as everyone knows, the actual punishment in most American prisons is of a wholly different order. The February 2 [1980] riot at New Mexico's state prison in Santa Fe, one of several bloody prison riots in the nine years since the Attica bloodbath, once again dramatized the conditions of life in an American prison. Four hundred prisoners seized control of the prison before dawn. By sunset the next day 33 inmates had died at the hands of other convicts and another 40 people (including five guards) had been seriously hurt. Macabre stories came out of prisoners being hanged, murdered with blowtorches, decapitated, tortured, and mutilated in a variety of gruesome ways by drug-crazed rioters.

The Santa Fe penitentiary was typical of most maximum-se- 5 curity facilities, with prisoners subject to overcrowding, filthy conditions, and routine violence. It also housed first-time, non-violent offenders, like check forgers and drug dealers, with murderers serving life sentences. In a recent lawsuit, the American Civil Liberties Union called the prison "totally unfit for human habitation." But the ACLU says New Mexico's penitentiary is far from the nation's worst.

That American prisons are a disgrace is taken for granted by 6 experts of every ideological stripe. Conservative James Q. Wilson has criticized our "[c]rowded, antiquated prisons that require men and women to live in fear of one another and to suffer not only deprivation of liberty but a brutalizing regimen." Leftist Jessica Mitford has called our prisons "the ultimate expression of injustice and inhumanity." In 1973 a national commission concluded that "the American correctional system today appears to offer minimum protection to the public and maximum harm to the offender." Federal courts have ruled that confinement in prisons in 16 different states violates the constitutional ban on "cruel and unusual punishment."

7   What are the advantages of being a convicted criminal in an advanced culture? First there is the overcrowding in prisons. One Tennessee prison, for example, has a capacity of 806, according to accepted space standards, but it houses 2300 inmates. One Louisiana facility has confined four and five prisoners in a single six-foot-by-six foot cell. Then there is the disease caused by overcrowding, unsanitary conditions, and poor or inadequate medical care. A federal appeals court noted that the Tennessee prison had suffered frequent outbreaks of infectious diseases like hepatitis and tuberculosis. But the most distinctive element of American prison life is its constant violence. In his book *Criminal Violence, Criminal Justice*, Charles Silberman noted that in one Louisiana prison, there were 211 stabbings in only three years, 11 of them fatal. There were 15 slayings in a prison in Massachusetts between 1972 and 1975. According to a federal court, in Alabama's penitentiaries (as in many others), "robbery, rape, extortion, theft and assault are everyday occurrences."

8   At least in regard to cruelty, it's not at all clear that the system of punishment that has evolved in the West is less barbaric than the grotesque practices of Islam. Skeptical? Ask yourself: would you rather be subjected to a few minutes of intense pain and considerable public humiliation, or be locked away for two or three years in a prison cell crowded with ill-tempered sociopaths? Would you rather lose a hand or spend 10 years or more in a typical state prison? I have taken my own survey on this matter. I have found no one who does not find the Islamic system hideous. And I have found no one who, given the choices mentioned above, would not prefer its penalties to our own.

9   The great divergence between Western and Islamic fashions in punishment is relatively recent. Until roughly the end of the 18th century, criminals in Western countries rarely were sent to prison. Instead they were subject to an ingenious assortment of penalties. Many perpetrators of a variety of crimes simply were executed, usually by some imaginative and extremely unpleasant method involving prolonged torture, such as breaking on the wheel, burning at the stake, or drawing and quartering. Michel Foucault's book *Discipline and Punish: The Birth of the Prison* notes one form of capital punishment in which the condemned man's "belly was opened up, his entrails quickly ripped out, so that he had time to see them, with

his own eyes, being thrown on the fire; in which he was finally decapitated and his body quartered." Some criminals were forced to serve on slave galleys. But in most cases various corporal measures such as pillorying, flogging, and branding sufficed.

In time, however, public sentiment recoiled against these mea-   10
sures. They were replaced by imprisonment, which was thought to have two advantages. First, it was considered to be more humane. Second, and more important, prison was supposed to hold out the possibility of rehabilitation—purging the criminal of his criminality—something that less civilized punishments did not even aspire to. An 1854 report by inspectors of the Pennsylvania prison system illustrates the hopes nurtured by humanitarian reformers.

> Depraved tendencies, characteristic of the convict, have been restrained by the absence of vicious association, and in the mild teaching of Christianity, the unhappy criminal finds a solace for an involuntary exile from the comforts of social life. If hungry, he is fed; if naked, he is clothed; if destitute of the first rudiments of education, he is taught to read and write; and if he has never been blessed with a means of livelihood, he is schooled in a mechanical art, which in after life may be to him the source of profit and respectability. Employment is not his toil nor labor, weariness. He embraces them with alacrity, as contributing to his moral and mental elevation.

Imprisonment is now the universal method of punishing crim-   11
inals in the United States. It is thought to perform five functions, each of which has been given a label by criminologists. First, there is simple *retribution:* punishing the lawbreaker to serve society's sense of justice and to satisfy the victims' desire for revenge. Second, there is *specific deterrence:* discouraging the offender from misbehaving in the future. Third, *general deterrence:* using the offender as an example to discourage others from turning to crime. Fourth, *prevention:* at least during the time he is kept off the streets, the criminal cannot victimize other members of society. Finally, and most important, there is *rehabilitation:* reforming the criminal so that when he returns to society he will be inclined to obey the laws and able to make an honest living.

How satisfactorily do American prisons perform by these cri-   12
teria? Well, of course, they do punish. But on the other scores they don't do so well. Their effect in discouraging future criminality by the prisoner or others is the subject of much debate, but the soaring rates of the last 20 years suggest that prisons are not a dramatically

effective deterrent to criminal behavior. Prisons do isolate convicted criminals, but only to divert crime from ordinary citizens to prison guards and fellow inmates. Almost no one contends any more that prisons rehabilitate their inmates. If anything, they probably impede rehabilitation by forcing inmates into prolonged and almost exclusive association with other criminals. And prisons cost a lot of money. Housing a typical prisoner in a typical prison costs far more than a stint at a top university. This cost would be justified if prisons did the job they were intended for. But it is clear to all that prisons fail on the very grounds—humanity and hope of rehabilitation—that caused them to replace earlier, cheaper forms of punishment.

13   The universal acknowledgment that prisons do not rehabilitate criminals has produced two responses. The first is to retain the hope of rehabilitation but do away with imprisonment as much as possible and replace it with various forms of "alternative treatment," such as psychotherapy, supervised probation, and vocational training. Psychiatrist Karl Menninger, one of the principal critics of American penology, has suggested even more unconventional approaches, such as "a new job opportunity or a vacation trip, a course of reducing exercises, a cosmetic surgical operation or a herniotomy, some night school courses, a wedding in the family (even one for the patient!), an inspiring sermon." This starry-eyed approach naturally has produced a backlash from critics on the right, who think that it's time to abandon the goal of rehabilitation. They argue that prisons perform an important service just by keeping criminals off the streets, and thus should be used with that purpose alone in mind.

14   So the debate continues to rage in all the same old ruts. No one, of course, would think of copying the medieval practices of Islamic nations and experimenting with punishments such as flogging and amputation. But let us consider them anyway. How do they compare with our American prison system in achieving the ostensible objectives of punishment? First, do they punish? Obviously they do, and in a uniquely painful and memorable way. Of course any sensible person, given the choice, would prefer suffering these punishments to years of incarceration in a typical American prison. But presumably no Western penologist would criticize Islamic punishments on the grounds that they are not barbaric enough. Do they deter crime? Yes, and probably more effectively than sending convicts off to prison. Now we read about a prison sentence in the newspaper, then think no more about the criminal's payment for

his crimes until, perhaps, years later we read a small item reporting his release. By contrast, one can easily imagine the vivid impression it would leave to be wandering through a local shopping center and to stumble onto the scene of some poor wretch being lustily flogged. And the occasional sight of an habitual offender walking around with a bloody stump at the end of his arm no doubt also would serve as a forceful reminder that crime does not pay.

Do flogging and amputation discourage recidivism? No one 15 knows whether the scars on his back would dissuade a criminal from risking another crime, but it is hard to imagine that corporal measures could stimulate a higher rate of recidivism than already exists. Islamic forms of punishment do not serve the favorite new right goal of simply isolating criminals from the rest of society, but they may achieve the same purpose of making further crimes impossible. In the movie *Bonnie and Clyde*, Warren Beatty successfully robs a bank with his arm in a sling, but this must be dismissed as artistic license. It must be extraordinarily difficult, at the very least, to perform much violent crime with only one hand.

Do these medieval forms of punishment rehabilitate the crim- 16 inal? Plainly not. But long prison terms do not rehabilitate either. And it is just as plain that typical Islamic punishments are no crueler to the convict than incarceration in the typical American state prison.

Of course there are other reasons besides its bizarre forms of 17 punishment that the Islamic system of justice seems uncivilized to the Western mind. One is the absence of due process. Another is the long list of offenses—such as drinking, adultery, blasphemy, "profiteering," and so on—that can bring on conviction and punishment. A third is all the ritualistic mumbo-jumbo in pronouncements of Islamic law (like that talk about puberty and amnesia in the ayatollah's quotation at the beginning of this article). Even in these matters, however, a little cultural modesty is called for. The vast majority of American criminals are convicted and sentenced as a result of plea bargaining, in which due process plays almost no role. It has been only half a century since a wave of religious fundamentalism stirred this country to outlaw the consumption of alcoholic beverages. Most states also still have laws imposing austere constraints on sexual conduct. Only two weeks ago the *Washington Post* reported that the FBI had spent two and a half years and untold amounts of money to break up a nationwide pornography ring. Flogging the clients of prostitutes, as the Pakistanis did, does seem silly. But only a few months ago Mayor Koch of New York was proposing that clients caught in his own city have their names broadcast by radio stations. We are not so far advanced on such matters as we often like to think. Finally, my lawyer friends assure me that the rules of jurisdiction for American courts contain plenty of petty requirements and bizarre distinctions that would sound silly enough to foreign ears.

18   Perhaps it sounds barbaric to talk of flogging and amputation, and perhaps it is. But our system of punishment also is barbaric, and probably more so. Only cultural smugness about their system and willful ignorance about our own make it easy to regard the one as cruel and the other as civilized. We inflict our cruelties away from public view, while nations like Pakistan stage them in front of 10,000 onlookers. Their outrages are visible; ours are not. Most Americans can live their lives for years without having their peace of mind disturbed by the knowledge of what goes on in our prisons. To choose imprisonment over flogging and amputation is not to choose human kindness over cruelty, but merely to prefer that our cruelties be kept out of sight, and out of mind.

19   Public flogging and amputation may be more barbaric forms of punishment than imprisonment, even if they are not more cruel. Society may pay a higher price for them, even if the particular criminal does not. Revulsion against officially sanctioned violence and infliction of pain derives from something deeply ingrained in the Western conscience, and clearly it is something admirable. Grotesque displays of the sort that occur in Islamic countries probably breed a greater tolerance for physical cruelty, for example, which prisons do not do precisely because they conceal their cruelties. In fact it is our admirable intolerance for calculated violence that makes it necessary for us to conceal what we have not been able to do away with. In a way this is a good thing, since it holds out the hope that we may eventually find a way to do away with it. But in another way it is a bad thing, since it permits us to congratulate ourselves on our civilized humanitarianism while violating its norms in this one area of our national life.

Thinking Critically About This Reading

1. What underlying assumptions cause the contrasts in attitude between Islamic countries and the United States toward punishing crimes?

2. What aspects of prison life in our country does the author consider just as barbaric as the floggings and amputations of wrongdoers by Islamic governments? Do you agree with this view? Why? Why not?

3. In paragraph 8, the author asks: ". . . would you rather be subjected to a few minutes of intense pain and considerable public humiliation, or be locked away for two or three years in a prison cell crowded with ill-tempered sociopaths? Would you rather lose a hand or spend 10 years or more in a typical state prison?" What is your answer to both these questions? Give reasons for your answers.

4. Chapman's essay was published in 1980. What evidence is there, if any, to indicate that prison reform has improved deterrence, prevention, and rehabilitation since the author wrote his essay? Give supportive evidence for your answer.

5. As you consider the present international scene, do you believe the United States can take pride in any significant humanitarian advances? If you believe we can, what specific advances? If you don't believe we can, what positive suggestions for improvement can you offer?

Understanding the Writer's Process

1. Where in the essay does the author state his thesis? Comment on the strategy of this placement.

2. In addition to citing examples, how does the author strengthen his argument that U.S. punishment is often more barbaric than that of Islamic countries?

3. How does the author try to capture the reader's attention at the beginning of the essay? In your view, does he succeed? Why? Why not?

4. How is coherence maintained between paragraphs 2 and 3?

5. Paragraph 7 begins with a question. What kind of question is this? How does the author answer it?

Examining the Writer's Language

1. Choose five of the following terms and use each in a sentence of your own: sensibilities (paragraph 1), summarily (1), loincloths

(1), stave (1), stipulated (2), scourging (2), malefactors (2), decapitated (4), sociopaths (8), ingenious (9), perpetrators (9), recidivism (15), dissuade (15). If you do not recognize a word, check it in a college dictionary.

2. In paragraph 17, the author uses the term "plea bargaining." How does *plea bargaining* differ from *immunity?* What do the terms share in common?

3. In paragraph 2, how does the author use the word "colorful"? Is the word appropriately used?

4. What are the connotations of *macabre*, as used in paragraph 4?

5. In several paragraphs throughout the essay, Chapman vividly describes gruesome methods of killing or torturing. What is his purpose in doing so? Would the essay lose its effectiveness if he used more euphemistic language?

Suggestions for Writing

1. Write an essay in which you contrast an effective prison with an ineffective one. (They can both be imaginary.) Be sure to establish the bases of your contrast and to deal fairly with both sides.

2. Imagine yourself a prisoner of war in a concentration camp located in a totalitarian country. Write an essay in which you describe what happens to you and how you handle yourself. (Good background reading for this essay is Jacobo Timerman's *Prisoner Without a Name, Cell Without a Number* [1981].)

OF SPEED READERS AND LIP-MOVERS

William H. Gass

William H. Gass (b. 1924) is an American author and college professor. Born in Fargo, North Dakota, he received his B.A. from Kenyon College and his Ph.D. from Cornell University. In 1954 he moved to Purdue University to teach philosophy, but also started to write fiction, which became his primary interest. In 1969 he won a Guggenheim fellowship and accepted a position as professor of philosophy at Washington University in St. Louis, where he remains today. His fiction has been compared to Sherwood Anderson's in its treatment of "grotesque" characters and to James Joyce's in its treatment of language. Among his novels are Omensetter's Luck *(1966) and* Willie Master's Lonesome Wife *(1968). In 1968 he also brought out a much–praised volume of short stories,* In the Heart of the Heart of the Country. *More recently, he has written a volume of literary criticism,* Fiction and Figures of Life *(1970), and has been a regular contributor to such magazines as* The Nation, South Atlantic Quarterly, *and* The New York Times Book Review.

Preparing to Read This Selection Critically

Most of us have envied people who can read a 400–page novel in one afternoon as if they were skimming the front page of a newspaper. In the essay below, originally published in *The New York Times Book Review* (1984), a well–known professor and novelist examines the advantages of being a slow reader. As you absorb what Gass tells you, think of those writings that have influenced your life most profoundly and consider whether those writings could be fully appreciated if they had been read at a high speed. For instance, is it worthwhile to read a book like the Bible by skimming along at a top rate or does it require you to stop and analyze the meaning and philosophy underlying the words? Likewise, can Shakespeare be fully appreciated when he is read so quickly that the beautiful language never has time to sink in? Gass's own essay can serve as a test: Can it be read speedily in order to get the gist, or must it be pondered to enjoy the nuances?

I was never much of an athlete, but I was once the member 1 of a team. Indeed, I was its star, and we were champions. During high school I belonged to a squad of speed readers in Ohio, although I was never awarded a letter for it. Still, we took on the top 10 in our territory and read as rapidly as possible every time we were challenged to a match, hoping to finish in front of that towheaded punk from Canton, the tomato–cheeked girl from Marietta, or that silent pair of sisters, all spectacles and squints, who looked tough as German script and who hailed from Shaker Heights or some other rough neighborhood full of swift, mean raveners of text.

2   We called ourselves the Speeders. Of course. Everybody did. There were the Sharon Speeders, the Steubenville Speeders and the Niles Nouns. They never won. How could they? I lost a match myself once to a kid with green teeth. And that's the way, I'm afraid, we appeared to others—as creeps with squints, bad posture, unclean complexions, unscrubbed teeth, tousled hair. We never had dates, we only memorized them; and when any real sports team went on the road to represent the high school, we carried the socks, the Tootsie Rolls, the towels for them. My nemesis with the green teeth had a head of thin red hair like rust on a saw; he revolved a suggestive little finger in his large fungiform ears. My God, I thought . . . and the shame of that defeat still rushes to my face whenever I remember it. Nevertheless, even today I possess a substantial, gold-colored medallion on which one sunbeaming eye seems hung above a book like a spider. Both book and eye are open—wide. I take that open, streaming eye to be an omen.

3   Our reading life has its salad days, its autumnal times. At first, of course, we do it badly, scarcely keeping our balance, toddling along behind our finger, so intent on remembering what each word is supposed to mean that the sentence is no longer a path, and we arrive at its end without having gone anywhere. Thus it is with all the things we learn, for at first they passively oppose us; they lie outside us like mist or the laws of nature; we have to issue orders to our eyes, our limbs, our understanding: Lift this, shift that, thumb the space bar, let up on the clutch—easy! There go the gears!—and don't forget to modify the verb, or remember what an escudo's worth. After a while, we find we like standing up, riding a bike, singing "Don Giovanni," making puff pastry, puppy love or model planes. Then we are indeed like the adolescent in our eager green enthusiasms: They are plentiful as leaves. Every page is a pasture, and we are let out to graze like hungry herds.

4   Do you remember what magic the word *thigh* could work on you, showing up in the middle of a passage suddenly, like a whiff of cologne in a theater? I admit it: The widening of the upper thigh remains a miracle, and, honestly, many of us once read the word *thigh* as if we were exploring Africa, seeking the source of the Nile. No volume was too hefty then, no style too verbal. The weight of

a big book was more comforting than Christmas candy, though you had to be lucky, strike the right text at the right time, because the special excitement Thomas Wolfe provides, for instance, can be felt only in the teens. And when, again, will any of us possess the energy, the patience, the inner sympathy for volcanic bombast to read— enjoy—Carlyle?

Repeating was automatic. Who needed Gertrude Stein? I must 5 have rushed through a pleasant little baseball book called "The Crimson Pennant" at least a dozen times, consuming a cake I had already cut into crumbs, yet that big base hit was never better than on that final occasion when its hero and I ran round those bases, and he shyly doffed his hat to the crowd.

No one threatened to whack our rumps if we didn't read an- 6 other Nancy Drew by Tuesday; no sour–faced virgin browbeat us with "The Blithedale Romance" or held out "The Cloister and the Hearth" like a cold plate of good–for–you food. We were on our own. I read Swinburne and the "Adventures of the Shadow." I read Havelock Ellis and Tom Swift and "The Idylls of the King." I read whatever came to hand, and what came to hand were a lot of naughty French novels, detective stories, medical adventures, books about bees, biographies of Napoleon, and "Thus Spake Zarathustra" like a bolt of lightning.

I read them all, whatever they were, with an ease that defies 7 the goat's digestion, and with an ease that is now so easily forgotten, just as we forget the wild wobble in our bikes' wheels, or the hu- miliating falls we took when we began our life on spokes. That wind I felt, when I finally stayed upright around the block, continuously reaffirmed the basic joy of cycling. It told me not merely that I was moving, but that I was moving *under my own power;* just as later, when I'd passed my driver's test, I would feel another sort of ex- hilaration—an intense, addictive, dangerous one—that of command, of my ability to control the energy produced by another thing or person, to direct the life contained in another creature.

Yes, in those early word–drunk years, I would down a book 8 or two a day as though they were gins. I read for adventure, ex- citement, to sample the exotic and the strange, for climax and res- olution, to participate in otherwise forbidden passions. I forgot what it was to be under my own power, under my own steam. I was, like so many adolescents, as eager to leap from my ordinary life as the salmon is to get upstream. I sought a replacement for the world.

With a surreptitious lamp lit, I stayed awake to dream. I grew reckless. I read for speed.

9 When you read for speed you do not read recursively, looping along the line like a sewing machine, stitching something together—say, the panel of a bodice to a sleeve—linking a pair of terms, the contents of a clause, closing a seam by following the internal directions of the sentence so that the word *you* is first fastened to the word *read*, and then the phrase *for speed* is attached to both in order that the entire expression can be finally fronted by a grandly capitalized *When* . . . while all of that, in turn, is gathered up to await the completion of the later segment that begins *you do not read recursively.* You can hear how long it seems to take—this patient process—and how confusing it can become. Nor do you linger over language, repeating some especially pleasant little passage, in the enjoyment, perhaps, of a modest rhyme (for example, the small clause, *when you read for speed*), or a particularly apt turn of phrase (an image, for instance, such as the one that dealt with Green Teeth's thin red hair—like rust on a saw). None of that, when you read for speed.

10 Nor, naturally, do you move your lips as you read the word *read* or the words *moving your lips*, so that the poor fellow next to you in the reading room has to watch intently to see what your lips are saying: Are you asking him out? For the loan of his Plutarch's "Lives"? And of course the poor fellow is flummoxed to find that you are moving your lips to say *moving your lips.* What can that mean? The lip–mover—O, such a person is low on our skill–scale. We are taught to have scorn for him, for her.

11 On the other hand, the speeding reader drops diagonally down across the page, on a slant like a skier, cuts across the text the way a butcher prefers to slice sausage, so that a small round can be made to yield a misleading larger oval piece. The speeding reader is after the kernel, the heart, the gist. Paragraphs become a country the eye flies over looking for landmarks, reference points, airports, restrooms, passages of sex. The speeding reader guts a book the way the skillful clean fish. The gills are gone, the tail, the scales, the fins; then the filet slides away swiftly as though fed to a seal. And only the slow reader, whose finger falters in front of long words, who moves the lips, who dances the text, will notice the odd crowd of images—flier, skier, butcher, seal—that have gathered to comment on the aims and activities of the speeding reader, perhaps like gossips at a wedding.

To the speeding reader, this jostle of images, this crazy collision   12
of ideas—of landing strip, kernel, heart, guts, sex—will not be felt,
because it is only the inner core of meaning he's after; it is the gist
she wants. And the gist is: Readers who read rapidly read only for
the most generalized, stereotyped sense. For them, meaning floats
over the page like fluffy clouds. Cliché is forever in fashion. They
read, as we say, synonymously, seeking sameness; and, indeed, it
is all the same to them if they are said in one moment to be greedy
as seals, and in another moment likened to descalers of fish. They—
you, I, we—"get" the idea.

A speed–reading match had two halves. (I say "had" because   13
I believe these matches long ago lit their last light.) The first consisted
of the rapid reading itself, through which, of course, I whizzzzed,
all the while making the sound of closing covers in order to dis-
concert Green Teeth or the silent Shaker Heights sisters, who were
to think I had completed my reading already. I didn't wear glasses
then, but I carried a glasses case to every match, and always dropped
it at a pertinent moment.

Next we were required to answer questions about what we   14
claimed we'd covered, and here quickness was again essential. The
questions, however, soon disclosed their biases. They had a structure, their own gist; and it became possible, after some experience,
to guess what would be asked about a text almost before it had been
begun. Is it "Goldilocks" we're skimming? Then what is the favorite
breakfast food of the three bears? How does Goldilocks escape from
the house? Why weren't the three bears at home when Goldilocks
came calling? The multiple answers we could choose from also had
their own tired tilt and, like the questions, gave themselves away.
The favorite breakfast foods, for instance, were: (a) Quaker Oats
(which this year is paying for the prizes, and in this sly fashion gets
its name in); (b) Just Rite (written like a brand name); (c) porridge
(usually misspelled); (d) sugar–coated curds and whey. No one ever
wondered whether Goldilocks was suffering from sibling rivalry;
why she had become a teenie–trasher; or why mother bear's bowl
of porridge was cold when baby bear's smaller bowl was still warm
and Just Rite.

There were many other mysteries, but not for these quiz mas-   15
ters who didn't even want to know the sexual significance of Cinderella's slipper, or why it had to be made of glass. I won my cham-
pionship medal by ignoring the text entirely (it was a section from
Volume Two of Oswald Spengler's "Decline of the West," the part

that begins, "Regard the flowers at eventide as, one after the other, they close in the setting sun. . . ." But then, of course, you remember that celebrated passage). I skipped the questions as well, and simply encircled the gloomiest alternatives offered. Won in record time. No one's got through Spengler with such dispatch since.

16   What did these matches, with their quizzes for comprehension, their love of literal learning, tell me? They told me that time was money (a speed reader's clearest idea); they told me what the world wanted me to read when I read, eat when I ate, see when I saw. Like the glutton, I was to get everything in and out in a hurry. Turnover was topmost. What the world wanted me to get was the gist, but the gist was nothing but an idea of trade—an idea so drearily uniform and emaciated it might have modeled dresses.

17   There is another way of reading I'd like to recommend. It's slow, old–fashioned, not easy either, rarely practiced. It must be learned. It is a way of life. What!—I hear your hearts exclaim—is the old wart going to go on some more about reading? Reading? When we can see the rings around his eyes for every year he's worn them out . . . reading? When we are commencing from college, leaving books, book bags, bicycles behind like pretty scenes along the highway? Yes. Just so. That's true. Most of you *are* through. Farewell, chemistry. Farewell, "Canterbury Tales." Imagine reading *that* again. Or "The Faerie Queene" even the first time. Farewell, Sir Philip Sydney, and your golden lines:

> Farewell O Sunn, Arcadias clearest light;
> Farewell O pearl, the poore mans plenteous treasure:
> Farewell O golden staffe, the weake mans might:
> Farewell O joy, the joyfulls onely pleasure.
> Wisdom farewell, the skillesse mans direction:
> Farewell with thee, farewell all our affection.

18   Now "Paradise" is "Lost." Who cares if molecular genetics has revolutionized biology? Farewell, philosophy. Farewell, free love. From now on there will be an interest, a carrying, a handling charge. Farewell, "A Farewell to Arms." "Goodbye, Columbus."

19   You may have noticed that I am now speaking in sentence fragments. The speed reader hates subordination, qualification, re-finement, deployment, ritual, decoration, order, mother, inference, country, logic, family, flag, God. Here is a little test: In that last list, what word will the speed reader pick out to stand for the rest of

it—to be its gist? *God*, you guess? No. Wrong. Nor *flag*, though that's
appealing. *Mother* will be the word we want.

    All right. I heard your hearts heave like a slow sea. I'm adapt-   20
able. Let's talk about drinking. I belonged to a drinking club once.
Defeated the Fraternal Order of Eagles on their own turf. The Chug-
a-lugs, we were called. Inevitably. You don't plan, I'm sure, to give
up drinking. Or reading—not altogether—I imagine. Not the letters
to *Penthouse*. The inky pages of *The Washington Post*. *TV Guide*. Legal
briefs. Medical romances. Business lore.

    Well, there is another way of drinking I'd like to recommend.   21
We've already dealt with the first way. Gulp. Get the gist. And the
gist is the level of alcohol in your blood, the pixilated breath you
blow into the test balloon. It makes appropriate the expression: Have
a belt. We can toss down a text, a time of life, a love affair, that walk
in the park that gets us from here to there. We can chug–a–lug them.
You have, perhaps, had to travel sometime with a person whose
passion was that simple: It was *getting there*. You have no doubt
encountered people who impatiently wait for the payoff, they urge
you to come to the point; at dinner, the early courses merely delay
dessert; they look only at the bottom line (that obscene phrase); they
are persons consumed by consequences; they want to climax without
crescendo.

    But we can read and walk and write and look in quite a different   22
way. It is possible. I was saved from sameness by Immanuel Kant.
You can't speed–read "The Critique of Pure Reason." You can't
speed–read Wallace Stevens. There is no gist, no simple translation,
no key concept that will unlock these works; actually, there is no
lock, no door, no wall, no room, no house, no world.

    Reading is a complicated, profound, silent, still, very personal,   23
very private, very solitary yet civilizing activity. Nothing is more
social than speech—we are bound together by our common sounds
more securely than even by our laws. Nevertheless, no one is more
aware of the isolated self than the reader, for a reader communes
with the word heard immaterially in that hollow of the head made
only for hearing, a room nowhere in the body in any ordinary sense.
On the bus, everyone of us may be deep in something different.
Sitting next to a priest, I can still enjoy my pornography, though I
may keep a thumb discreetly on top of the title.

    I've grown larger, if not wiser. My vices now are visionary.   24
That baseball book, "The Crimson Pennant," has become "The
Crimson Cancan." What do I care if Father McIvie is reading about

investments? Yet while all of us, in our verbal recreations, are full
of respect for the privacy of our neighbors, the placards advertising
perfume or footwear invade the public space like a visual smell;
Muzak fills every unstoppered ear the way the static of the street
does. The movies, the radio, television, theater, music: All run on
at their own rate, and the listener or the viewer must attend, keep
up, or lose out—but not the reader. The reader is free. The reader
is in charge and pedals the cycle. It is easy for a reader to announce
that his present run of Proust has been postponed until the holidays.

25   Reading, that is, is not a public imposition. Of course, when
we read, many of us squirm and fidget. One of the closest friends
of my youth would sensuously wind and unwind on his forefinger
the long blond strands of his hair. How he read—that is how I
remember him. Yes, our postures are often provocative, perverse.
Yet these outward movements of the body really testify to the importance of the inner movements of the mind; and even those rapid
flickers of the eye, as we shift from word to word, phrase to phrase
and clause to clause, hoping to keep our head afloat on a flood of
Faulkner or Proust or Joyce or James, are registers of reason. For
reading is reasoning, figuring things out through thoughts, making
arrangements out of arrangements until we've understood a text so
fully it is nothing but feeling and pure response, until its conceptual
turns are like the reversals of mood in a marriage—petty, sad, ecstatic, commonplace, foreseeable, amazing.

26   In order to have this experience, however, one must learn to
perform the text, say, sing, shout the words to oneself, give them,
with *our* minds, *their* body. Otherwise the eye skates over every
syllable like the speeder. There can be no doubt that often what we
read should be skimmed, as what we are frequently asked to drink
should be spilled. But the speeding reader is alone in another, less
satisfactory way, one quite different from that of the reader who
says the words to herself, because as we read we divide into a
theater: There is the performer who shapes those silent sounds,
moving the muscles of the larynx almost invisibly, and there is the
listener who hears them said and who responds to their passion or
their wisdom.

27   Such a reader sees every text as unique, greets every work as
a familiar stranger. Such a reader is willing to allow another's words
to become hers, his.

28   In the next moment, let us read a wine, since I promised I
would talk about drinking. We have prepared for the occasion, of

course. The bottle has been allowed to breathe. Books need to breathe, too. They should be opened properly, hefted, thumbed. The paper, print, layout, should be appreciated. But now we decant the text into our wide-open and welcoming eyes. We warm the wine in the bowl of the glass with our hand. We let its bouquet collect above it just as the red of red roses seems to stain the air. We wade— shoeless, to be sure—through the color it has liquefied. We roll a bit of it about in our mouths. We sip. We savor. We say some sentences of Sir Thomas Browne: "We tearme sleepe a death, and yet it is waking that kils us, and destroyed those spirits which are the house of life. Tis indeed a part of life that best expresseth death, for every man truely lives so long as hee acts his nature, or someway makes good the faculties of himself. . . ."

Are these words not from a fine field, in a splendid year? There   29
is, of course, a sameness in all these words: *life/death, man/nature.* We get the drift. But the differences! The differences make all the difference, the way nose and eyes and cheekbones form a face, the way a muscle makes emotion pass across it. It is the differences we read. Differences are not only identifiable, distinct; they are epidemic: The wine is light, perhaps, spicy, slow to release its grip upon itself, the upper thigh is widening wonderfully, the night air has hands, words fly out of our mouths like birds. "But who knows the fate of his bones," Browne says, "or how often he is to be buried."

Yet as I say his soul out loud, he lives again; he has risen up   30
in me, and I can be, for him, that temporary savior that every real reader is, putting his words in my mouth; not nervously, notice, as though they were pieces of gum, but in that way that is necessary if the heart is to hear them. And though they are his words and his soul, then, that return through me, I am in charge. He has asked nothing of me; his words move because I move them. It is like cycling, reading is. Can you feel the air, the pure passage of the spirit past the exposed skin?

So this reading will be like living, then—the living each of you   31
will be off in a moment to be busy with, not always speedily, I hope, or in the continuous anxiety of consequence, the sullenness of inattention, the annoying static of distraction. But it will be only a semblance of living—this living—nevertheless, the way unspoken reading is a semblance, unless, from time to time, you perform the outer world within. Because only in that manner can it deliver itself to us. As Rainer Maria Rilke once commanded: "Dance the taste of

the fruit you have been tasting. Dance the orange." I should like to multiply that charge, even past all possibility. Speak the street to yourself sometimes, hear the horns in the forest, read the breeze aloud and make that inner wind yours, because, whether Nature, Man or God has given us the text, we independently possess the ability to read, to read really well, and to move our own mind freely in tune to the moving world.

Thinking Critically About This Reading

1. In paragraph 25, Gass defines reading as "reasoning, figuring things out through thoughts, making arrangements out of arrangements until we've understood a text so fully it is nothing but feeling and pure response. . . ." *The American Heritage Dictionary* defines reading as "to comprehend or take in the meaning of something written or printed." Do these two definitions contradict each other? Why or why not? Which definition helps you to understand the act of reading better? If you have a third definition of your own, compare it with the two just cited.

2. The author indicates that he was an avid reader in his youth. Assuming that his experience was typical of most youthful readers, what was the great attraction to books? Is the experience beneficial or harmful? Explain your answers based on your own experience or that of your friends.

3. What does the author mean when he says that "the reader is free"? (See paragraph 24.) Why is this freedom important?

4. The author admits that he is by nature a speed reader, having won many speed–reading contests. Yet, he recommends another kind of reading to us. Why is this second kind necessary?

5. Why do lip–movers tend to be considered with scorn? How does the author change that view?

Understanding the Writer's Process

1. Where does the author actually begin his comparison/contrast of speed reading versus slow reading? How is the comparison/contrast handled—by block or alternating? What do the preliminary paragraphs contribute to the essay?

2. Gass uses analogies to clarify his vision of reading. What are some of the analogies? How effective are they?

3. The author's final paragraph is filled with paradoxical images. What meaning does it convey? Summarize the meaning in your own words.

4. What is the purpose of the autobiographical incidents related in the opening section of the essay? Do they add to or detract from the main purpose of the essay, which is to compare speed reading with slow reading? Explain your opinions.

5. How does the author maintain coherence between his description of speed reading and slow reading?

Examining the Writer's Language

1. Find one appropriate synonym for the following words used in the essay: nemesis (paragraph 2), bombast (4), doffed (5), flummoxed (10), inference (19), provocative (25).

2. What kind of language does the author use? Is it prosaic, poetic, or scientific? Give examples of what you mean.

3. In paragraph 5, what is the meaning of the question, "Who needed Gertrude Stein?"

4. Why do you suppose the word "thigh" was so intriguing to the author? (See paragraph 4.)

5. What is the meaning of "salad days" and "autumnal times" as used in paragraph 3?

6. Why does the author use the metaphor "word-drunk years" in paragraph 8? Explain the meaning of the image.

Suggestions for Writing

1. Using literary works with which you are familiar, write an essay contrasting material that can be read speedily with material that must be absorbed slowly. Be sure to clarify why each category requires a certain pace.

2. Choosing two essays from this book, contrast them in terms of the speed with which each must be read in order to reap maximum benefits.

DIOGENES AND ALEXANDER

Gilbert Highet

> *Gilbert Highet (1906–1978), American classicist,*
> *was born and educated in Scotland. He taught Greek*
> *and Latin at Columbia University from 1938 until his*
> *death in 1978. His wife is famed novelist Helen*
> *McInnes. Among Highet's best-known works are* The
> Classical Tradition *(1949)*, The Art of Teaching
> *(1950), and* The Anatomy of Satire *(1962). The fol-*
> *lowing essay, reprinted from* Horizon *magazine, draws*
> *a sharp contrast between two famous personalities—*
> *one young and one old—who influenced Greek history.*

Preparing to Read This Selection Critically

The following portraits of two famous Greeks is not
so much a contrast of personalities as of values. Beyond
the obvious differences in the two men's looks, ages, and
social bearings, there are values to consider. Think of
Diogenes's values and then think of Alexander's. Which
do you consider more conducive to a happy life and a
healthy society? Choose the best characteristics of each
man and form an imaginary composite. Would such a
person be an ideal member of today's society, one young
people should model themselves after? What men, if any,
today reveal the virtues you admire? Be prepared to state
what these virtues are and why they are important.

1   Lying on the bare earth, shoeless, bearded, half-naked, he
looked like a beggar or a lunatic. He was one, but not the other. He
had opened his eyes with the sun at dawn, scratched, done his
business like a dog at the roadside, washed at the public fountain,
begged a piece of breakfast bread and a few olives, eaten them
squatting on the ground, and washed them down with a few hand-
fuls of water scooped from the spring. (Long ago he had owned a
rough wooden cup, but he threw it away when he saw a boy drinking out of his hollowed hands.) Having no work to go to and no
family to provide for, he was free. As the market place filled up with
shoppers and merchants and gossipers and sharpers and slaves and

foreigners, he had strolled through it for an hour or two. Everybody knew him, or knew of him. They would throw sharp questions at him and get sharper answers. Sometimes they threw jeers, and got jibes; sometimes bits of food, and got scant thanks; sometimes a mischievous pebble, and got a shower of stones and abuse. They were not quite sure whether he was mad or not. He knew they were mad, each in a different way; they amused him. Now he was back at his home.

It was not a house, not even a squatter's hut. He thought 2
everybody lived far too elaborately, expensively, anxiously. What good is a house? No one needs privacy; natural acts are not shameful; we all do the same things, and need not hide them. No one needs beds and chairs and such furniture: the animals live healthy lives and sleep on the ground. All we require, since nature did not dress us properly, is one garment to keep us warm, and some shelter from rain and wind. So he had one blanket—to dress him in the daytime and cover him at night—and he slept in a cask. His name was Diogenes. He was the founder of the creed called Cynicism (the word means "doggishness"); he spent much of his life in the rich, lazy, corrupt Greek city of Corinth, mocking and satirizing its people, and occasionally converting one of them.

His home was not a barrel made of wood: too expensive. It 3
was a storage jar made of earthenware, something like a modern fuel tank—no doubt discarded because a break had made it useless. He was not the first to inhabit such a thing: the refugees driven into Athens by the Spartan invasion had been forced to sleep in casks. But he was the first who ever did so by choice, out of principle.

Diogenes was not a degenerate or a maniac. He was a philos- 4
opher who wrote plays and poems and essays expounding his doctrine; he talked to those who cared to listen; he had pupils who admired him. But he taught chiefly by example. All should live naturally, he said, for what is natural is normal and cannot possibly be evil or shameful. Live without conventions, which are artificial and false; escape complexities and superfluities and extravagances: only so can you live a free life. The rich man believes he possesses his big house with its many rooms and its elaborate furniture, his pictures and his expensive clothes, his horses and his servants and his bank accounts. He does not. He depends on them, he worries about them, he spends most of his life's energy looking after them; the thought of losing them makes him sick with anxiety. They possess him. He is their slave. In order to procure a quantity of false,

perishable goods he has sold the only true, lasting good, his own independence.

5   There have been many men who grew tired of human society with its complications, and went away to live simply—on a small farm, in a quiet village, in a hermit's cave, or in the darkness of anonymity. Not so Diogenes. He was not a recluse, or a stylite, or a beatnik. He was a missionary. His life's aim was clear to him: it was "to restamp the currency." (He and his father had once been convicted for counterfeiting, long before he turned to philosophy, and this phrase was Diogenes's bold, unembarrassed joke on the subject.) To restamp the currency: to take the clean metal of human life, to erase the old false conventional markings, and to imprint it with its true values.

6   The other great philosophers of the fourth century before Christ taught mainly their own private pupils. In the shady groves and cool sanctuaries of the Academy, Plato discoursed to a chosen few on the unreality of this contingent existence. Aristotle, among the books and instruments and specimens and archives and re-search-workers of his Lyceum, pursued investigations and gave lectures that were rightly named *esoteric* "for those within the walls." But for Diogenes, laboratory and specimens and lecture halls and pupils were all to be found in a crowd of ordinary people. Therefore he chose to live in Athens or in the rich city of Corinth, where travelers from all over the Mediterranean world constantly came and went. And, by design, he publicly behaved in such ways as to show people what real life was. He would constantly take up their spiritual coin, ring it on a stone, and laugh at its false superscription.

7   He thought most people were only half-alive, most men only half-men. At bright noonday he walked through the market place carrying a lighted lamp and inspecting the face of everyone he met. They asked him why. Diogenes answered, "I am trying to find a *man.*"

8   To a gentleman whose servant was putting on his shoes for him, Diogenes said, "You won't be really happy until he wipes your nose for you: that will come after you lose the use of your hands."

9   Once there was a war scare so serious that it stirred even the lazy, profit-happy Corinthians. They began to drill, clean their weapons, and rebuild their neglected fortifications. Diogenes took his old cask and began to roll it up and down, back and forward. "When you are all so busy," he said, "I felt I ought to do *something!*"

And so he lived—like a dog, some said, because he cared nothing   10
for privacy and other human conventions, and because he showed
his teeth and barked at those whom he disliked. Now he was lying
in the sunlight, as contented as a dog on the warm ground, happier
(he himself used to boast) than the Shah of Persia. Although he knew
he was going to have an important visitor, he would not move.

The little square began to fill with people. Page boys elegantly   11
dressed, spearmen speaking a rough foreign dialect, discreet secretaries, hard-browed officers, suave diplomats, they all gradually
formed a circle centered on Diogenes. He looked them over, as a
sober man looks at a crowd of tottering drunks, and shook his head.
He knew who they were. They were the attendants of the conqueror
of Greece, the servants of Alexander, the Macedonian king, who
was visiting his newly subdued realm.

Only twenty, Alexander was far older and wiser than his years.   12
Like all Macedonians he loved drinking, but he could usually handle
it; and toward women he was nobly restrained and chivalrous. Like
all Macedonians he loved fighting; he was a magnificent commander, but he was not merely a military automaton. He could
think. At thirteen he had become a pupil of the greatest mind in
Greece, Aristotle. No exact record of his schooling survives. It is
clear, though, that Aristotle took the passionate, half-barbarous boy
and gave him the best of Greek culture. He taught Alexander poetry:
the young prince slept with the *Iliad* under his pillow and longed
to emulate Achilles, who brought the mighty power of Asia to ruin.
He taught him philosophy, in particular the shapes and uses of
political power: a few years later Alexander was to create a supranational empire that was not merely a power system but a vehicle
for the exchange of Greek and Middle Eastern cultures.

Aristotle taught him the principles of scientific research: during   13
his invasion of the Persian domains Alexander took with him a large
corps of scientists, and shipped hundreds of zoological specimens
back to Greece for study. Indeed, it was from Aristotle that Alexander learned to seek out everything strange which might be instructive. Jugglers and stunt artists and virtuosos of the absurd he
dismissed with a shrug; but on reaching India he was to spend hours
discussing the problems of life and death with naked Hindu mystics,
and later to see one demonstrate Yoga self-command by burning
himself impassively to death.

Now, Alexander was in Corinth to take command of the   14
League of Greek States which, after conquering them, his father

Philip had created as a disguise for the New Macedonian Order. He was welcomed and honored and flattered. He was the man of the hour, of the century: he was unanimously appointed commander-in-chief of a new expedition against old, rich, corrupt Asia. Nearly everyone crowded to Corinth in order to congratulate him, to seek employment with him, even simply to see him: soldiers and statesmen, artists and merchants, poets and philosophers. He received their compliments graciously. Only Diogenes, although he lived in Corinth, did not visit the new monarch. With that generosity which Aristotle had taught him was a quality of the truly magnanimous man, Alexander determined to call upon Diogenes. Surely Diogenes, the God-born, would acknowledge the conqueror's power by some gift of hoarded wisdom.

15   With his handsome face, his fiery glance, his strong supple body, his purple and gold cloak, and his air of destiny, he moved through the parting crowd, toward the Dog's kennel. When a king approaches, all rise in respect. Diogenes did not rise, he merely sat up on one elbow. When a monarch enters a precinct, all greet him with a bow or an acclamation. Diogenes said nothing.

16   There was a silence. Some years later Alexander speared his best friend to the wall, for objecting to the exaggerated honors paid to His Majesty; but now he was still young and civil. He spoke first, with a kindly greeting. Looking at the poor broken cask, the single ragged garment, and the rough figure lying on the ground, he said: "Is there anything I can do for you, Diogenes?"

17   "Yes," said the Dog. "Stand to one side. You're blocking the sunlight."

18   There was silence, not the ominous silence preceding a burst of fury, but a hush of amazement. Slowly, Alexander turned away. A titter broke out from the elegant Greeks, who were already beginning to make jokes about the Cur that looked at the King. The Macedonian officers, after deciding that Diogenes was not worth the trouble of kicking, were starting to guffaw and nudge one another. Alexander was still silent. To those nearest him he said quietly, "If I were not Alexander, I should be Diogenes." They took it as a paradox, designed to close the awkward little scene with a polite curtain line. But Alexander meant it. He understood Cynicism as the others could not. Later he took one of Diogenes's pupils with him to India as a philosophical interpreter (it was he who spoke to the naked *saddhus*). He was what Diogenes called himself, a *cosmopolitēs*, "citizen of the world." Like Diogenes, he admired the

heroic figure of Hercules, the mighty conqueror who labors to help mankind while all others toil and sweat only for themselves. He knew that of all men then alive in the world only Alexander the conqueror and Diogenes the beggar were truly free.

Thinking Critically About This Reading

1. Although Diogenes and Alexander were in many ways different from one another, what aspects did they share in common?
2. Alexander is reputed to have made the remark, "If I were not Alexander, I should be Diogenes." What did he mean?
3. If you had the choice of being either Diogenes or Alexander today, which one would you choose to be? Give specific reasons for your choice. Describe the kind of life you would be living in our society.
4. Do you agree with Diogenes's view that the more a man owns, the more enslaved be becomes (paragraph 4)? Give reasons for your answer. What major advantages do the rich have over the poor? What major disadvantages?
5. Diogenes flouted conventions whereas Alexander abided by them. What is your view of conventions? How important are they to our society?

Understanding the Writer's Process

1. How does the author organize his contrast? What other system could he have used?
2. What are the bases on which Highet draws his contrast?
3. What is the meaning of the allusion in paragraph 10?
4. Paragraph 15 flows smoothly. What techniques enhance its coherence? What other paragraph uses the same techniques?
5. How effective is the author's conclusion? Write a different conclusion and compare it with the original.

Examining the Writer's Language

1. Using a college dictionary, define the following terms: expounding (paragraph 4), superfluities (4), stylite (5), discoursed (6),

contingent (6), archives (6), superscription (6), supranational (12), virtuosos (13).

2. What four uncommon words does the author define within the context of the essay?

3. What is meant by the phrase "to restamp the currency" in paragraph 5?

4. What descriptive details contribute toward the portrait of Alexander as an impressive emperor?

5. What does the term "man of the hour" (paragraph 14) connote?

Suggestions for Writing

1. Write an essay in which you contrast one of the following pairs: two famous statesmen, two feminist leaders, two great artists, two living political leaders.

2. Write an essay in which you contrast any two people whom you admire.

THE COLONEL'S LADY

W. Somerset Maugham

W. Somerset Maugham (1874–1965) was a famous British writer of plays, short stories, and novels. The son of a British diplomat, Maugham was born in Paris and spoke French before he spoke English. His fiction reveals the psychological depths and exotic settings of his wide–ranging trips all over the world. Recognized as a dramatist before turning to short stories and novels, Maugham's successful plays include The Circle *(1921),* Our Betters *(1923), and* The Constant Wife *(1927). He had written eight novels before his masterpiece,* Of Human Bondage *(1915), appeared. His other well–known novels are* The Moon and Sixpence *(1919),* Cakes and Ale *(1930), and* The Razor's Edge *(1944). The story that follows is taken from a collection of short stories entitled* Creatures of Circumstance *(1946).*

Preparing to Read This Selection Critically

It will not escape your attention that in the story that follows a marked contrast is drawn between the colonel and his wife. What may escape your notice is the fact that as the husband describes his wife, he really reveals much about himself. In reading, try to establish some bases for the developing contrast. For example, on the basis of attitude toward romance, how do the two differ? What about the basis of compassion or sympathy? Find other bases, and mentally list his characteristics and then hers. Also, try to figure out what part of the story is fantasy and what part is actuality. Moreover, judge the characters in terms of which one you would prefer to have as your friend.

All this happened two or three years before the outbreak of the war. 1

The Peregrines were having breakfast. Though they were alone 2 and the table was long they sat at opposite ends of it. From the walls George Peregrine's ancestors, painted by the fashionable painters of the day, looked down upon them. The butler brought in the morning post. There were several letters for the colonel, business letters, *The Times* and a small parcel for his wife Evie. He looked at his letters and then, opening *The Times*, began to read it. They finished breakfast and rose from the table. He noticed that his wife hadn't opened the parcel.

"What's that?" he asked. 3

"Only some books." 4

"Shall I open it for you?" 5

"If you like." 6

He hated to cut string and so with some difficulty untied the 7 knots.

"But they're all the same," he said when he had unwrapped 8 the parcel. "What on earth d'you want six copies of the same book for?" He opened one of them. "Poetry." Then he looked at the title page. *When Pyramids Decay*, he read, by E. K. Hamilton. Eva Katherine Hamilton: that was his wife's maiden name. He looked at her with smiling surprise. "Have you written a book, Evie? You are a slyboots."

9   "I didn't think it would interest you very much. Would you like a copy?"

10   "Well, you know poetry isn't much in my line, but—yes, I'd like a copy; I'll read it. I'll take it along to my study. I've got a lot to do this morning."

11   He gathered up *The Times*, his letters and the book, and went out. His study was a large and comfortable room, with a big desk, leather arm-chairs and what he called "trophies of the chase" on the walls. On the bookshelves were works of reference, books on farming, gardening, fishing and shooting, and books on the last war, in which he had won an M.C. and a D.S.O. For before his marriage he had been in the Welsh Guards. At the end of the war he retired and settled down to the life of a country gentleman in the spacious house, some twenty miles from Sheffield, which one of his forebears had built in the reign of George III. George Peregrine had an estate of some fifteen hundred acres which he managed with ability; he was a Justice of the Peace and performed his duties conscientiously. During the season he rode to hounds two days a week. He was a good shot, a golfer and though now a little over fifty could still play a hard game of tennis. He could describe himself with propriety as an all-around sportsman.

12   He had been putting on weight lately, but was still a fine figure of a man; tall, with grey curly hair, only just beginning to grow thin on the crown, frank blue eyes, good features and a high colour. He was a public-spirited man, chairman of any number of local organisations and, as became his class and station, a loyal member of the Conservative Party. He looked upon it as his duty to see to the welfare of the people on his estate and it was a satisfaction to him to know that Evie could be trusted to tend the sick and succour the poor. He had built a cottage hospital on the outskirts of the village and paid the wages of a nurse out of his own pocket. All he asked of the recipients of his bounty was that at elections, county or general, they should vote for his candidate. He was a friendly man, affable to his inferiors, considerate with his tenants and popular with the neighbouring gentry. He would have been pleased and at the same time slightly embarrassed if someone had told him he was a jolly good fellow. That was what he wanted to be. He desired no higher praise.

It was hard luck that he had no children. He would have been 13 an excellent father, kindly but strict, and would have brought up his sons as gentlemen's sons should be brought up, sent them to Eton, you know, taught them to fish, shoot and ride. As it was, his heir was a nephew, son of his brother killed in a motor accident, not a bad boy, but not a chip off the old block, no, sir, far from it; and would you believe it, his fool of a mother was sending him to a co-educational school. Evie had been a sad disappointment to him. Of course she was a lady, and she had a bit of money of her own; she managed the house uncommonly well and she was a good hostess. The village people adored her. She had been a pretty little thing when he married her, with a creamy skin, light brown hair and a trim figure, healthy too and not a bad tennis player; he couldn't understand why she'd had no children; of course she was faded now, she must be getting on for five and forty; her skin was drab, her hair had lost its sheen and she was as thin as a rail. She was always neat and suitably dressed, but she didn't seem to bother how she looked, she wore no make-up and didn't even use lipstick; sometimes at night when she dolled herself up for a party you could tell that once she'd been quite attractive, but ordinarily she was—well, the sort of woman you simply didn't notice. A nice woman, of course, a good wife, and it wasn't her fault if she was barren, but it was tough on a fellow who wanted an heir of his own loins; she hadn't any vitality, that's what was the matter with her. He supposed he'd been in love with her when he asked her to marry him, at least sufficiently in love for a man who wanted to marry and settle down, but with time he discovered that they had nothing much in common. She didn't care about hunting, and fishing bored her. Naturally they'd drifted apart. He had to do her the justice to admit that she'd never bothered him. There'd been no scenes. They had no quarrels. She seemed to take it for granted that he should go his own way. When he went up to London now and then she never wanted to come with him. He had a girl there, well, she wasn't exactly a girl, she was thirty-five if she was a day, but she was blonde and luscious and he only had to wire ahead of time and they'd dine, do a show and spend the night together. Well, a man, a healthy normal man had to have some fun in his life. The thought crossed his mind that if Evie hadn't been such a good woman she'd have been a better wife; but it was not the sort of thought that he welcomed and he put it away from him.

14   George Peregrine finished his *Times* and being a considerate fellow rang the bell and told the butler to take it to Evie. Then he looked at his watch. It was half-past ten and at eleven he had an appointment with one of his tenants. He had half an hour to spare.

15   "I'd better have a look at Evie's book," he said to himself.

16   He took it up with a smile. Evie had a lot of highbrow books in her sitting-room, not the sort of books that interested him, but if they amused her he had no objection to her reading them. He noticed that the volume he now held in his hand contained no more than ninety pages. That was all to the good. He shared Edgar Allan Poe's opinion that poems should be short. But as he turned the pages he noticed that several of Evie's had long lines of irregular length and didn't rhyme. He didn't like that. At his first school, when he was a little boy, he remembered learning a poem that began: *The boy stood on the burning deck,* and later, at Eton, one that started: *Ruin seize thee, ruthless king;* and then there was Henry V; they'd had to take that, one half. He stared at Evie's pages with consternation.

17   "That's not what I call poetry," he said.

18   Fortunately it wasn't all like that. Interspersed with the pieces that looked so odd, lines of three or four words and then a line of ten or fifteen, there were little poems, quite short, that rhymed, thank God, with the lines all the same length. Several of the pages were just headed with the word *Sonnet,* and out of curiosity he counted the lines; there were fourteen of them. He read them. They seemed all right, but he didn't quite know what they were all about. He repeated to himself: *Ruin seize thee, ruthless king.*

19   "Poor Evie," he sighed.

20   At that moment the farmer he was expecting was ushered into the study, and putting the book down he made him welcome. They embarked on their business.

21   "I read your book, Evie," he said as they sat down to lunch. "Jolly good. Did it cost you a packet to have it printed?"

22   "No, I was lucky. I sent it to a publisher and he took it."

23   "Not much money in poetry, my dear," he said in his good-natured, hearty way.

24   "No, I don't suppose there is. What did Bannock want to see you about this morning?"

25   Bannock was the tenant who had interrupted his reading of Evie's poems.

26   "He's asked me to advance the money for a pedigree bull he wants to buy. He's a good man and I've half a mind to do it."

George Peregrine saw that Evie didn't want to talk about her   27
book and he was not sorry to change the subject. He was glad she
had used her maiden name on the title page; he didn't suppose
anyone would ever hear about the book, but he was proud of his
own unusual name and he wouldn't have liked it if some damned
penny-a-liner had made fun of Evie's effort in one of the papers.

During the few weeks that followed he thought it tactful not to   28
ask Evie any questions about her venture into verse and she never
referred to it. It might have been a discreditable incident that they
had silently agreed not to mention. But then a strange thing happened.
He had to go to London on business and he took Daphne out to
dinner. That was the name of the girl with whom he was in the habit
of passing a few agreeable hours whenever he went to town.

"Oh, George," she said, "is that your wife who's written a   29
book they're all talking about?"

"What on earth d'you mean?"   30

"Well, there's a fellow I know who's a critic. He took me out   31
to dinner the other night and he had a book with him. 'Got anything
for me to read?' I said. 'What's that?' 'Oh, I don't think that's your
cup of tea,' he said, 'It's poetry. I've just been reviewing it.' 'No
poetry for me,' I said. 'It's about the hottest stuff I ever read,' he
said. 'Selling like hot cakes. And it's damned good.' "

"Who's the book by?" asked George.   32

"A woman called Hamilton. My friend told me that wasn't her   33
real name. He said her real name was Peregrine. 'Funny,' I said, 'I
know a fellow called Peregrine.' 'Colonel in the army,' he said. 'Lives
near Sheffield.' "

"I'd just as soon you didn't talk about me to your friends,"   34
said George with a frown of vexation.

"Keep your shirt on, dearie. Who d'you take me for? I just   35
said: 'It's not the same one.' " Daphne giggled. "My friend said:
'They say he's a regular Colonel Blimp.' "

George had a keen sense of humour.   36

"You could tell them better than that," he laughed. "If my wife   37
had written a book I'd be the first to know about it, wouldn't I?"

"I suppose you would."   38

Anyhow the matter didn't interest her and when the colonel   39
began to talk of other things she forgot about it. He put it out of
his mind too. There was nothing to it, he decided, and that silly
fool of a critic had just been pulling Daphne's leg. He was amused
at the thought of her tackling that book because she had been told

it was hot stuff and then finding it just a lot of bosh cut up into unequal lines.

40   He was a member of several clubs and next day he thought he'd lunch at one in St. James's Street. He was catching a train back to Sheffield early in the afternoon. He was sitting in a comfortable armchair having a glass of sherry before going into the dining-room when an old friend came up to him.

41   "Well, old boy, how's life?" he said. "How d'you like being the husband of a celebrity?"

42   George Peregrine looked at his friend. He thought he saw an amused twinkle in his eyes.

43   "I don't know what you're talking about," he answered.

44   "Come off it, George. Everyone knows E. K. Hamilton is your wife. Not often a book of verse has a success like that. Look here, Henry Dashwood is lunching with me. He'd like to meet you."

45   "Who the devil is Henry Dashwood and why should he want to meet me?"

46   "Oh, my dear fellow, what do you do with yourself all the time in the country? Henry's about the best critic we've got. He wrote a wonderful review of Evie's book. D'you mean to say she didn't show it you?"

47   Before George could answer his friend had called a man over. A tall, thin man, with a high forehead, a beard, a long nose and a stoop, just the sort of man whom George was prepared to dislike at first sight. Introductions were effected. Henry Dashwood sat down.

48   "Is Mrs. Peregrine in London by any chance? I should very much like to meet her," he said.

49   "No, my wife doesn't like London. She prefers the country," said George stiffly.

50   "She wrote me a very nice letter about my review. I was pleased. You know, we critics get more kicks than halfpence. I was simply bowled over by her book. It's so fresh and original, very modern without being obscure. She seems to be as much at her ease in free verse as in the classical metres." Then because he was a critic he thought he should criticise. "Sometimes her ear is a trifle at fault, but you can say the same of Emily Dickinson. There are several of those short lyrics of hers that might have been written by Landor."

51   All this was gibberish to George Peregrine. The man was nothing but a disgusting highbrow. But the colonel had good manners

and he answered with proper civility: Henry Dashwood went on as though he hadn't spoken.

"But what makes the book so outstanding is the passion that throbs in every line. So many of these young poets are so anaemic, cold, bloodless, dully intellectual, but here you have real naked, earthy passion; of course deep, sincere emotion like that is tragic—ah, my dear Colonel, how right Heine was when he said that the poet makes little songs out of his great sorrows. You know, now and then, as I read and reread those heart-rending pages I thought of Sappho." 52

This was too much for George Peregrine and he got up. 53

"Well, it's jolly nice of you to say such nice things about my wife's little book. I'm sure she'll be delighted. But I must bolt, I've got to catch a train and I want to get a bite of lunch." 54

"Damned fool," he said irritably to himself as he walked upstairs to the dining-room. 55

He got home in time for dinner and after Evie had gone to bed he went into his study and looked for her book. He thought he'd just glance through it again to see for himself what they were making such a fuss about, but he couldn't find it. Evie must have taken it away.

"Silly," he muttered. 56

He'd told her he thought it jolly good. What more could a fellow be expected to say? Well, it didn't matter. He lit his pipe and read the *Field* till he felt sleepy. But a week or so later it happened that he had to go into Sheffield for the day. He lunched there at his club. He had nearly finished when the Duke of Haverel came in. This was the great local magnate and of course the colonel knew him, but only to say how d'you do to; and he was surprised when the Duke stopped at his table. 57

"We're so sorry your wife couldn't come to us for the week-end," he said, with a sort of shy cordiality. "We're expecting rather a nice lot of people." 58

George was taken aback. He guessed that the Haverels had asked him and Evie over for the week-end and Evie, without saying a word to him about it, had refused. He had the presence of mind to say he was sorry too. 59

"Better luck next time," said the Duke pleasantly and moved on. 60

Colonel Peregrine was very angry and when he got home he said to his wife: 61

62   "Look here, what's this about our being asked over to Haverel? Why on earth did you say we couldn't go? We've never been asked before and it's the best shooting in the country."

63   "I didn't think of that. I thought it would only bore you."

64   "Damn it all, you might at least have asked me if I wanted to go."

65   "I'm sorry."

66   He looked at her closely. There was something in her expression that he didn't quite understand. He frowned.

67   "I suppose *I* was asked?" he barked.

68   Evie flushed a little.

69   "Well, in point of fact you weren't."

70   "I call it damned rude of them to ask you without asking me."

71   "I suppose they thought it wasn't your sort of party. The Duchess is rather fond of writers and people like that, you know. She's having Henry Dashwood, the critic, and for some reason he wants to meet me."

72   "It was damned nice of you to refuse, Evie."

73   "It's the least I could do," she smiled. She hesitated a moment. "George, my publishers want to give a little dinner party for me one day towards the end of the month and of course they want you to come too."

74   "Oh, I don't think that's quite my mark. I'll come up to London with you if you like. I'll find someone to dine with."

75   Daphne.

76   "I expect it'll be very dull, but they're making rather a point of it. And the day after, the American publisher who's taken my book is giving a cocktail party at Claridge's. I'd like you to come to that if you wouldn't mind."

77   "Sounds like a crashing bore, but if you really want me to come I'll come."

78   "It would be sweet of you."

79   George Peregrine was dazed by the cocktail party. There were a lot of people. Some of them didn't look so bad, a few of the women were decently turned out, but the men seemed to him pretty awful. He was introduced to everyone as Colonel Peregrine, E. K. Hamilton's husband, you know. The men didn't seem to have anything to say to him, but the women gushed.

80   "You *must* be proud of your wife. Isn't it *wonderful*? You know, I read it right through at a sitting. I simply couldn't put it down,

and when I'd finished I started again at the beginning and read it
right through a second time. I was simply *thrilled*."

The English publisher said to him: 81
"We've not had a success like this with a book of verse for   82
twenty years. I've never seen such reviews."

The American publisher said to him: 83
"It's swell. It'll be a smash hit in America. You wait and see."   84

The American publisher had sent Evie a great spray of orchids.   85
Damned ridiculous, thought George. As they came in, people were
taken up to Evie, and it was evident that they said flattering things
to her, which she took with a pleasant smile and a word or two of
thanks. She was a trifle flushed with the excitement, but seemed
quite at her ease. Though he thought the whole thing a lot of stuff
and nonsense George noted with approval that his wife was carrying
it off in just the right way.

"Well, there's one thing," he said to himself, "you can see she's   86
a lady and that's a damned sight more than you can say of anyone
else here."

He drank a good many cocktails. But there was one thing that   87
bothered him. He had a notion that some of the people he was
introduced to looked at him in rather a funny sort of way, he couldn't
quite make out what it meant, and once when he strolled by two
women who were sitting together on a sofa he had the impression
that they were talking about him and after he passed he was almost
certain they tittered. He was very glad when the party came to an
end.

In the taxi on their way back to their hotel Evie said to him: 88
"You were wonderful, dear. You made quite a hit. The girls   89
simply raved about you: they thought you so handsome."

"Girls," he said bitterly. "Old hags."   90
"Were you bored, dear?"   91
"Stiff."   92

She pressed his hand in a gesture of sympathy.   93
"I hope you won't mind if we wait and go down by the after-   94
noon train. I've got some things to do in the morning."

"No, that's all right. Shopping?"   95
"I do want to buy one or two things, but I've got to go and   96
be photographed. I hate the idea, but they think I ought to be. For
America, you know."

He said nothing. But he thought. He thought it would be a   97
shock to the American public when they saw the portrait of the

homely, desiccated little woman who was his wife. He'd always been under the impression that they liked glamour in America.

98   He went on thinking, and next morning when Evie had gone out he went to his club and up to the library. There he looked up recent numbers of *The Times Literary Supplement, The New Statesman* and *The Spectator.* Presently he found reviews of Evie's book. He didn't read them very carefully, but enough to see that they were extremely favourable. Then he went to the bookseller's in Piccadilly where he occasionally bought books. He'd made up his mind that he had to read this damned thing of Evie's properly, but he didn't want to ask her what she'd done with the copy she'd given him. He'd buy one for himself. Before going in he looked in the window and the first thing he saw was a display of *When Pyramids Decay.* Damned silly title! He went in. A young man came forward and asked if he could help him.

99   "No, I'm just having a look around." It embarrassed him to ask for Evie's book and he thought he'd find it for himself and then take it to the salesman. But he couldn't see it anywhere and at last, finding the young man near him, he said in a carefully casual tone: "By the way, have you got a book called *When Pyramids Decay?*"

100   "The new edition came in this morning. I'll get a copy."

101   In a moment the young man returned with it. He was a short, rather stout young man, with a shock of untidy carroty hair and spectacles. George Peregrine, tall, upstanding, very military, towered over him.

102   "Is this a new edition then?" he asked.

103   "Yes, sir. The fifth. It might be a novel the way it's selling."

104   George Peregrine hesitated a moment.

105   "Why d'you suppose it's such a success? I've always been told no one reads poetry."

106   "Well, it's good, you know. I've read it meself." The young man, though obviously cultured, had a slight Cockney accent, and George quite instinctively adopted a patronising attitude. "It's the story they like. Sexy, you know, but tragic."

107   George frowned a little. He was coming to the conclusion that the young man was rather impertinent. No one had told him anything about there being a story in the damned book and he had not gathered that from reading the reviews. The young man went on:

108   "Of course it's only a flash in the pan, if you know what I mean. The way I look at it, she was sort of inspired like by a personal

experience, like Housman was with *The Shropshire Lad.* She'll never write anything else."

"How much is the book?" said George coldly to stop his chat- 109 ter. "You needn't wrap it up, I'll just slip it into my pocket."

The November morning was raw and he was wearing a great- 110 coat.

At the station he bought the evening papers and magazines 111 and he and Evie settled themselves comfortably in opposite corners of a first-class carriage and read. At five o'clock they went along to the restaurant car to have tea and chatted a little. They arrived. They drove home in the car which was waiting for them. They bathed, dressed for dinner, and after dinner Evie, saying she was tired out, went to bed. She kissed him, as was her habit, on the forehead. Then he went into the hall, took Evie's book out of his greatcoat pocket and going into the study began to read it. He didn't read verse very easily and though he read with attention, every word of it, the impression he received was far from clear. Then he began at the beginning again and read it a second time. He read with increasing malaise, but he was not a stupid man and when he had finished he had a distinct understanding of what it was all about. Part of the book was in free verse, part in conventional metres, but the story it related was coherent and plain to the meanest intelligence. It was the story of a passionate love affair between an older woman, married, and a young man. George Peregrine made out the steps of it as easily as if he had been doing a sum in simple addition.

Written in the first person, it began with the tremulous surprise 112 of the woman, past her youth, when it dawned upon her that the young man was in love with her. She hesitated to believe it. She thought she must be deceiving herself. And she was terrified when on a sudden she discovered that she was passionately in love with him. She told herself it was absurd; with the disparity of age between them nothing but unhappiness could come to her if she yielded to her emotion. She tried to prevent him from speaking but the day came when he told her that he loved her and forced her to tell him that she loved him too. He begged her to run away with him. She couldn't leave her husband, her home; and what life could they look forward to, she an ageing woman, he so young? How could she expect his love to last? She begged him to have mercy on her. But his love was impetuous. He wanted her, he wanted her with all his heart, and at last trembling, afraid, desirous, she yielded to him. Then there was a period of ecstatic happiness. The world, the dull, humdrum world of every day, blazed with glory. Love songs flowed from her pen. The woman worshipped the young, virile body of her lover. George flushed darkly when she praised his broad chest and slim flanks, the beauty of his legs and the flatness of his belly.

113   Hot stuff, Daphne's friend had said. It was that all right. Disgusting.

114   There were sad little pieces in which she lamented the emptiness of her life when as must happen he left her, but they ended with a cry that all she had to suffer would be worth it for the bliss that for a while had been hers. She wrote of the long, tremulous nights they passed together and the languor that lulled them to sleep in one another's arms. She wrote of the rapture of brief stolen moments when, braving all danger, their passion overwhelmed them and they surrendered to its call.

115   She thought it would be an affair of a few weeks, but miraculously it lasted. One of the poems referred to three years having gone by without lessening the love that filled their hearts. It looked as though he continued to press her to go away with him, far away, to a hill town in Italy, a Greek island, a walled city in Tunisia, so that they could be together always, for in another of the poems she besought him to let things be as they were. Their happiness was precarious. Perhaps it was owing to the difficulties they had to encounter and the rarity of their meetings that their love had retained for so long its first enchanting ardour. Then on a sudden the young man died. How, when or where George could not discover. There followed a long, heart-broken cry of bitter grief, grief she could not indulge in, grief that had to be hidden. She had to be cheerful, give dinner-parties and go out to dinner, behave as she had always behaved, though the light had gone out of her life and she was bowed down with anguish. The last poem of all was a set of four short stanzas in which the writer, sadly resigned to her loss, thanked the dark powers that rule man's destiny that she had been privileged at least for a while to enjoy the greatest happiness that we poor human beings can ever hope to know.

116   It was three o'clock in the morning when George Peregrine finally put the book down. It had seemed to him that he heard Evie's voice in every line, over and over again he came upon turns of phrase he had heard her use, there were details that were as familiar to him as to her; there was no doubt about it; it was her own story she had told, and it was as plain as anything could be that she had had a lover and her lover had died. It was not anger so much that

he felt, nor horror or dismay, though he was dismayed and he was horrified, but amazement. It was as inconceivable that Evie should have had a love affair, and a wildly passionate one at that, as that the trout in a glass case over the chimney piece in his study, the finest he had ever caught, should suddenly wag its tail. He understood now the meaning of the amused look he had seen in the eyes of that man he had spoken to at the club, he understood why Daphne when she was talking about the book had seemed to be enjoying a private joke, and why those two women at the cocktail party had tittered when he strolled past them.

He broke out into a sweat. Then on a sudden he was seized 117 with fury and he jumped up to go and awake Evie and ask her sternly for an explanation. But he stopped at the door. After all, what proof had he? A book. He remembered that he'd told Evie he thought it jolly good. True, he hadn't read it, but he'd pretended he had. He would look a perfect fool if he had to admit that.

"I must watch my step," he muttered. 118

He made up his mind to wait for two or three days and think 119 it all over. Then he'd decide what to do. He went to bed, but he couldn't sleep for a long time.

"Evie," he kept on saying to himself. "Evie, of all people." 120

They met at breakfast next morning as usual. Evie was as she 121 always was, quiet, demure and self-possessed, a middle-aged woman who made no effort to look younger than she was, a woman who had nothing of what he still called It. He looked at her as he hadn't looked at her for years. She had her usual placid serenity. Her pale blue eyes were untroubled. There was no sign of guilt on her candid brow. She made the same little casual remarks she always made.

"It's nice to get back to the country again after those two hectic 122 days in London. What are you going to do this morning?"

It was incomprehensible. 123

Three days later he went to see his solicitor. Henry Blane was 124 an old friend of George's as well as his lawyer. He had a place not far from Peregrine's and for years they had shot over one another's preserves. For two days a week he was a country gentleman and for the other five a busy lawyer in Sheffield. He was a tall, robust fellow, with a boisterous manner and a jovial laugh, which suggested that he liked to be looked upon essentially as a sportsman and a good fellow and only incidentally as a lawyer. But he was shrewd and worldly-wise.

125   "Well, George, what's brought you here today?" he boomed as the colonel was showed into his office. "Have a good time in London? I'm taking my missus up for a few days next week. How's Evie?"

126   "It's about Evie I've come to see you," said Peregrine, giving him a suspicious look. "Have you read her book?"

127   His sensitivity had been sharpened during those last days of troubled thought and he was conscious of a faint change in the lawyer's expression. It was as though he were suddenly on his guard.

128   "Yes, I've read it. Great success, isn't it? Fancy Evie breaking out into poetry. Wonders will never cease."

129   George Peregrine was inclined to lose his temper.

130   "It's made me look a perfect damned fool."

131   "Oh, what nonsense, George! There's no harm in Evie's writing a book. You ought to be jolly proud of her."

132   "Don't talk such rot. It's her own story. You know it and everyone else knows it. I suppose I'm the only one who doesn't know who her lover was."

133   "There is such a thing as imagination, old boy. There's no reason to suppose the whole thing isn't made up."

134   "Look here, Henry, we've known one another all our lives. We've had all sorts of good times together. Be honest with me. Can you look me in the face and tell me you believe it's a made-up story?"

135   Harry Blane moved uneasily in his chair. He was disturbed by the distress in old George's voice.

136   "You've got no right to ask me a question like that. Ask Evie."

137   "I daren't," George answered after an anguished pause. "I'm afraid she'd tell me the truth."

138   There was an uncomfortable silence.

139   "Who was the chap?"

140   Harry Blane looked at him straight in the eye.

141   "I don't know, and if I did I wouldn't tell you."

142   "You swine. Don't you see what a position I'm in? Do you think it's very pleasant to be made absolutely ridiculous?"

143   The lawyer lit a cigarette and for some moments silently puffed it.

144   "I don't see what I can do for you," he said at last.

145   "You've got private detectives you employ, I suppose. I want you to put them on the job and let them find everything out."

"It's not very pretty to put detectives on one's wife, old boy; 146
and besides, taking for granted for a moment that Evie had an affair,
it was a good many years ago and I don't suppose it would be
possible to find out a thing. They seem to have covered their tracks
pretty carefully."

"I don't care. You put the detectives on. I want to know the 147
truth."

"I won't, George. If you're determined to do that you'd better 148
consult someone else. And look here, even if you got evidence that
Evie had been unfaithful to you what would you do with it? You'd
look rather silly divorcing your wife because she'd committed adultery ten years ago."

"At all events I could have it out with her." 149

"You can do that now, but you know just as well as I do that 150
if you do she'll leave you. D'you want her to do that?"

George gave him an unhappy look. 151

"I don't know. I always thought she'd been a damned good 152
wife to me. She runs the house perfectly, we never have any servant
trouble; she's done wonders with the garden and she's splendid
with all the village people. But damn it, I have my self-respect to
think of. How can I go on living with her when I know that she
was grossly unfaithful to me?"

"Have you always been faithful to her?" 153

"More or less, you know. After all, we've been married for 154
nearly twenty-four years and Evie was never much for bed."

The solicitor slightly raised his eyebrows, but George was too 155
intent on what he was saying to notice.

"I don't deny that I've had a bit of fun now and then. A man 156
wants it. Women are different."

"We only have men's word for that," said Harry Blane, with 157
a faint smile.

"Evie's absolutely the last woman I'd have suspected of kicking 158
over the traces. I mean, she's a very fastidious, reticent woman.
What on earth made her write the damned book?"

"I suppose it was a very poignant experience and perhaps it 159
was a relief to her to get it off her chest like that."

"Well, if she had to write it why the devil didn't she write it 160
under an assumed name?"

"She used her maiden name. I suppose she thought that was 161
enough, and it would have been if the book hadn't had this amazing
boom."

162   George Peregrine and the lawyer were sitting opposite one another with a desk between them. George, his elbow on the desk, his cheek on his hand, frowned at his thought.

163   "It's so rotten not to know what sort of a chap he was. One can't even tell if he was by way of being a gentleman. I mean, for all I know he may have been a farm-hand or a clerk in a lawyer's office."

164   Harry Blane did not permit himself to smile and when he answered there was in his eyes a kindly, tolerant look.

165   "Knowing Evie so well I think the probabilities are that he was all right. Anyhow I'm sure he wasn't a clerk in my office."

166   "It's been a shock to me," the colonel sighed. "I thought she was fond of me. She couldn't have written that book unless she hated me."

167   "Oh, I don't believe that. I don't think she's capable of hatred."

168   "You're not going to pretend that she loves me."

169   "No."

170   "Well, what does she feel for me?"

171   Harry Blane leaned back in his swivel chair and looked at George reflectively.

172   "Indifference, I should say."

173   The colonel gave a little shudder and reddened.

174   "After all, you're not in love with her, are you?"

175   George Peregrine did not answer directly.

176   "It's been a great blow to me not to have any children, but I've never let her see that I think she's let me down. I've always been kind to her. Within reasonable limits I've tried to do my duty by her."

177   The lawyer passed a large hand over his mouth to conceal the smile that trembled on his lips.

178   "It's been such an awful shock to me," Peregrine went on. "Damn it all, even ten years ago Evie was no chicken and God knows, she wasn't much to look at. It's so ugly." He sighed deeply. "What would *you* do in my place?"

179   "Nothing."

180   George Peregrine drew himself bolt upright in his chair and he looked at Harry with the stern set face that he must have worn when he inspected his regiment.

181   "I can't overlook a thing like this. I've been made a laughing-stock. I can never hold up my head again."

"Nonsense," said the lawyer sharply, and then in a pleasant,   182
kindly manner, "Listen, old boy: the man's dead; it all happened a
long while back. Forget it. Talk to people about Evie's book, rave
about it, tell 'em how proud you are of her. Behave as though you
had so much confidence in her, you *knew* she could never have been
unfaithful to you. The world moves so quickly and people's memories are so short. They'll forget."

"I shan't forget."   183

"You're both middle-aged people. She probably does a great   184
deal more for you than you think and you'd be awfully lonely without her. I don't think it matters if you don't forget. It'll be all to the
good if you can get it into that thick head of yours that there's a lot
more in Evie than you ever had the gumption to see."

"Damn it all, you talk as if *I* was to blame."   185

"No, I don't think you were to blame, but I'm not so sure that   186
Evie was either. I don't suppose she wanted to fall in love with this
boy. D'you remember those verses right at the end? The impression
they gave me was that though she was shattered by his death, in
a strange sort of way she welcomed it. All through she'd been aware
of the fragility of the tie that bound them. He died in the full flush
of his first love and had never known that love so seldom endures;
he'd only known its bliss and beauty. In her own bitter grief she
found solace in the thought that he'd been spared all sorrow."

"All that's a bit above my head, old boy. I see more or less   187
what you mean."

George Peregrine stared unhappily at the inkstand on the desk.   188
He was silent and the lawyer looked at him with curious, yet sympathetic, eyes.

"Do you realise what courage she must have had never by a   189
sign to show how dreadfully unhappy she was?" he said gently.

Colonel Peregrine sighed.   190

"I'm broken. I suppose you're right; it's no good crying over   191
spilt milk and it would only make things worse if I made a fuss."

"Well?"   192

George Peregrine gave him a pitiful little smile.   193

"I'll take your advice. I'll do nothing. Let them think me a   194
damned fool and to hell with them. The truth is, I don't know what
I'd do without Evie. But I'll tell you what, there's one thing I shall
never understand till my dying day: What in the name of heaven
did the fellow ever see in her?"

Thinking Critically About This Reading

1. What insight into life does this story about the Peregrines offer? Do you believe this insight is psychologically realistic? Give reasons for your answer.

2. Colonel Peregrine and his wife, Evie, have entirely opposite natures. What are the traits of one as opposed to the traits of the other? List them in two columns.

3. Do you believe that Evie actually had the passionate love affair described in her book? Give reasons for your answer.

4. What is Colonel Peregrine's view of a wife's role? How do you feel about this view? Be specific in answering this question.

5. What does the final sentence of the story reveal about the Colonel?

Understanding the Writer's Process

1. In several pieces on literary criticism, Maugham stated that it was a kind of literary snobbery to scorn plot when telling a story. How does "The Colonel's Lady" reveal a concern or lack of concern for plot? Refer to specific elements.

2. From whose point of view is the story told? How effective is this angle?

3. What role does Henry Dashwood play in the story? Are his views necessary to the plot?

4. How are the characters in the story developed? Mention as many ways as you can detect.

5. What passage do you consider the point of highest tension in the story? Give reasons for your answer.

Examining the Writer's Language

1. Study the following expressions that refer to Evie: "slyboots" (paragraph 8), "pretty little thing" (13), "poor Evie" (19), "my wife's little book" (54), "the homely, desiccated little woman who was his wife" (97). What do these expressions share in common?

2. What references in the story indicate that Colonel Peregrine is a member of the privileged class of British society?

3. What is the meaning of the fish analogy in paragraph 116?

4. What is the antecedent to *this* in the opening sentence of paragraph 51?

5. What is the significance of the word "nothing" in paragraph 179?

Writing Assignment Based on "The Colonel's Lady"

"The Colonel's Lady" is a fascinating fictional study in contrast between two people whose personalities are at extreme opposites. History is filled with real-life contrasts between people who hold the same jobs, have the same talents, or come from the same social and economic backgrounds. Select two well-known people—either from history or the present—and write an essay drawing a sharp contrast between them. You might consider two artists, two sports figures, two national leaders, or even two criminals. Choose clear bases of contrast and deal evenly with both sides.

STUDENT ESSAY (IN PROCESS)
COMPARISON/CONTRAST

Steven Corpuz

Steven Corpuz has recently finished high school and is pursuing an A.A. degree in management part-time: Later he plans to earn an M.B.A. in business markets. His outside interests include physical fitness and marksmanship.

First Draft   Steven Corpuz

                                                  English 101

Supply title — *Mohammud Ali vs. Mike Tyson*

Mohammud Ali and Mike Tyson will never

Rewrite for *Furthermore,*

quater / clarity meet in a boxing ring. ~~Yet, although~~ their

backgrounds, boxing styles, and personalities

Markedly *yet* *these two famous men*

are different, ~~they~~ exemplify the standard by

today

which all other boxers are measured.

stress Ali's

Mohammud Ali was born Cassius Clay on

He spent

"Normal" "January 18, 1942, in Louisville, Kentucky. His

Background

early years ~~were not unlike those of any~~ like any other black
boy growing up in the 40's and 50's, in a family of normal, happy people. At the age
of ten he began his boxing career. Within four
years he went on to capture many boxing awards,
including two Kentucky Golden Gloves and two
National Amateur titles in the light-heavy
weight division. Then in the 1960 Olympic Games he
represented the United States and won a gold
medal. After winning the gold medal, he turned
professional, and on February 25, 1964, an un-
derrated Muhammud Ali, then still Cassius
Clay, defeated a savage punching Sonny Liston
to win the World Heavy weight title. By this time the whole world was watching him breathlessly Ali went at ring side or on television
on to accumulate a record of fifty-six wins and
four losses, and is the only man to win the
World Heavy weight title on three separate
occasions. Unlike Ali ~~On the other hand~~, Mike Tyson's spent his childhood under circumstances that were ~~was~~ anything but normal. ~~He was~~ Born the
youngest of three children to Lorna Tyson and a
father he never met. His family lived in a rough
part of Brooklyn, New York. Hungry for attention and love, He turned to crime
to win the friendship of older boys. At first
the crimes were petty, but soon they turned
into felonies, such as burglaries and muggings.
At the age of thirteen, Mike was sent to the
Tryon reform school for boys in upstate New
York. There he was introduced to the legendary boxing trainer Cus D'Amato, who was quickly impressed by Tyson's natural size and ability.
D'Amato trained Tyson through a lack luster
amateur career, in which Tyson finished second
to the eventual Olympic heavyweight champion

Henry Tilman. In October of 1984 Mike Tyson turned professional, an event that changed boxing forever. He went on to accumulate a record that had never been accomplished before: he won his first twenty fights by knockout. Tyson finally received a title shot after twenty seven fights without a single loss. He eventually destroyed Trevor Brebick in less than six minutes to become the youngest heavy weight champion at the age of twenty.

The boxing styles these two fighters used were distinctly different. On one hand, there was an elegant, smooth "champion", Mohammud Ali, a boxer in the true sense of the word. On the other hand, there was Mike Tyson, a brawler with powerful defensive skills. whereas Mohammad Ali had many weapons in his arsenal—his long reach, his fancy foot work, his endurance, and his magical anticipation and timing, Mike Tyson had only two weapons his tenacity and his explosive punching power. If Ali was a leaping panther, then Tyson was a charging bull. While the background of a fighter is recorded for posterity and his style wins fights, a fighter is also remembered for his personality in and out of the ring. Mohammad Ali is remembered for his flamboyant, arrogant, proud personality, for being a fighter who boasted that he was the worlds "prettiest" man and that he "floated" like a butterfly" and "stung" like a bee." On the other hand Mike Tyson will be remembered for his quiet manner, and his icy stare, the silenced his opponents with his iron fist. Let us remember that these brilliant two fighters came from different backgrounds and that they revealed two unique styles and personalities. Al-

though boxing careers are short, these two
fighters will always be remembered as
champions. *They are both stars in the annals
of boxing*

Tie them together as a conclusion.

*He dazzled his opponent with words as
well as with punches.*

Final Draft   Steven Corpuz

English 101

Mohammud Ali vs. Mike Tyson

Mohammud Ali and Mike Tyson will never
meet in a boxing ring. Furthermore, their backgrounds, boxing styles, and personalities are
markedly different. Yet these two famous men
exemplified the standard by which today all
other boxers are measured.

Mohammud Ali was born Cassius Clay on
January 18, 1942, in Louisville, Kentucky. He
spent his early years like any other black boy
growing up in the 40's and 50's in a family of
normal, happy people. At the age of ten he began
his boxing career. Within four years he went on
to capture many boxing awards, including two
Kentucky Golden Gloves and two National
Amateur titles in the light-heavy weight division. Then, in the 1960 Olympic Games, he represented the United States and won a gold
medal. After winning the gold medal, he turned
professional, and on February 25, 1964, an un-
derrated Mohammud Ali, then still Cassius
Clay, defeated a savage punching Sonny Liston

to win the World Heavy Weight title. By this
time the whole world was watching him
breathlessly—at ring side or on television.
Ali went on to accumulate a record of fifty six
wins and four losses, and is the only man to win
the World Heavy weight title on three separate
occasions.

Unlike Ali, Mike Tyson spent his childhood under circumstances that were anything
but normal. Born the youngest of three children
to Lorna Tyson and a father he never met, his
family lived in a rough part of Brooklyn, New
York. Hungry for attention and love, he turned
to crime to win the friendship of older boys.
At first the crimes were petty, but soon they
turned into felonies, such as burglaries and
muggings. At the age of thirteen, Mike was sent
to the Tryon reform school for boys in Upstate
New York. There he was introduced to the legendary boxing trainer, Cus D'Amato, who was
quickly impressed by Tyson's size and natural
ability. D'Amato trained Tyson through a
lackluster amateur career, in which Tyson
finished second to the eventual Olympic
heavyweight champion, Henry Tilman. In October
of 1984, Mike Tyson turned professional, an
event that changed his boxing career. He went
on to accumulate a record that had never been
accomplished before: He won his first twenty
fights by knockout. Tyson finally received a
title shot after twenty-seven fights without a
single loss. He eventually destroyed Trevor
Brebick in less than six minutes, to become the
youngest heavy weight champion at the age of

twenty.

The boxing styles of these two fighters were distinctly different. On one hand, there was Mohammud Ali, an elegant, smooth "champion," in the true sense of the word. On the other hand, there was Mike Tyson, a brawler with powerful defensive skills. Whereas Mohammud Ali had many weapons in his arsenal--his long reach, his fancy foot work, his endurance, and his magical anticipation and timing, Mike Tyson had only two weapons -- his tenacity and his explosive punching power. If Ali was a leaping panther, then Tyson was a charging bull.

While the background of a fighter is recorded for posterity, and his style wins the fights, a fighter is also remembered for his personality in and out of the ring. Mohammud Ali is remembered for his flamboyantly arrogant personality, for being a fighter who boasted that he was the world's "prettiest man" and that he floated "like a butterfly" and stung "like a bee." He dazzled his opponent with words as well as with punches. Mike Tyson, on the other hand, will be remembered for his quiet manner and his icy stare. He silenced his opponents with his iron fist.

Let us remember that these two brilliant fighters came from different backgrounds and that they revealed two unique styles and personalities. Although boxing careers are short, these two fighters will always be remembered as champions. They are both stars in the annals of boxing.

Drawing by Stevenson; © 1991 The New Yorker Magazine, Inc.

9

Analyzing Cause

HOW TO WRITE A CAUSAL ANALYSIS

The causal analysis essay either explains cause or predicts effect. Explaining cause means analyzing the reasons underlying an event that already has occurred. Predicting effect means gauging the consequences of an event that has yet to occur. The following schematic clarifies the difference between cause and effect:

Cause (past) ← Situation → Effect (future)

A causal analysis to explain the sinking of the *Titanic* therefore would inquire into why the ocean liner struck the iceberg, why the water–tight compartments failed to keep her afloat, and why she did not carry enough lifeboats to save all the passengers. On the other hand, if you wrote an essay based on the question "What are the likely consequences of a modern ocean liner striking an iceberg in the North Atlantic?" you would be analyzing effect.

The essay that analyzes cause or predicts effect (*causal analysis* is a blanket term that refers to both) is an exercise in thinking and is thus prone to numerous logical flaws. Cause is no easy subject, neither is effect. Both are abstract concepts that require of the writer a careful and methodical turn of mind.

1. Be Specific in Your Analysis but Not Dogmatic

A common mistake in analyzing cause is the confusion of dogmatic beliefs with genuine answers. Some people think that excessive television viewing is the cause of violent behavior, that declining church membership is the prime reason behind the epidemic of failed marriages, that sparing the rod inevitably spoils the child. We do not know if any of these assertions is true; definitive scientific answers are still pending. So if you wrote a paper flatly supporting any one of these assertions without providing substantial evidence for your position, you would have based the thesis mainly on dogmatic belief.

In fact, complex problems are seldom resolved by dogma. Because most events have not one cause but several converging causes, it is a simplistic misunderstanding of reality to think otherwise. The following paragraph, for example, rashly asserts an insupportable cause for the declining birthrate:

Abortion has led to consequences that were unforeseen in *Roe v. Wade*, the Supreme Court decision that legalized abortions. Abortion led to a decline in birthrate from 72.5 million during the postwar period to 56.6 million between 1965 and 1980. Because of abortion, between 1975 and 1985 there was a 13% drop in the number of schoolchildren between the ages of 6 and 18. One demographic analyst predicts that because of the decline in birthrate, during the 1990s the housing industry will be "tearing its hair out." He also predicts enormous problems with the funding of Social Security.

But blaming the decline in U.S. birthrate solely on abortion ignores other significant causes: the advent of the pill and of other effective contraceptive means; the increase in career opportunities for women, which has led many to postpone childbearing; and the shift away from the traditional family.

As a model for asserting cause, we recommend the cautious and delicate reasoning in Oliver Sacks's essay, "The Man Who Mistook His Wife for a Hat," the second selection presented in this chapter. In struggling to grasp the causes behind the evolution of a brain-damaged patient's art form from representational to abstract, Sacks reports that the patient's wife bluntly told him: "Ach, you doctors, you're such philistines! Can you not see *artistic development*—how he renounced the realism of his earlier years, and advanced into abstract, non-representational art?" Consider how Sacks ponders the causes behind the strange evolution of the patient's art:

And yet, I wondered, was she not partly right? For there is often a struggle, and sometimes, even more interestingly, a collusion between the powers of pathology and creation. Perhaps, in his cubist period, there might have been both artistic and pathological development, colluding to engender an original form; for, as he lost the concrete, so he might have gained in the abstract, developing a greater sensitivity to all the structural elements of line, boundary, contour—an almost Picasso-like power to see, and equally depict, those abstract organizations embedded in, and normally lost in, the concrete.... Though in the final pictures, I feared, there was only chaos and agnosia.

OLIVER SACKS, *"The Man Who Mistook His Wife*
for a Hat"

Here we get no dogmatic assertions, but a careful weighing of probable causes.

Being cautious does not mean being wishy-washy, straddling the fence, or loading your prose with a wagon train of qualifiers (humble hedgers) such as *In my opinion's, I think's,* and *It is only my personal view's.* Mainly, it means sticking to the tale told by the evidence and drawing no hasty conclusions based solely on personal and insupportable belief.

2. Use Words and Phrases That Indicate a Cause or Effect Relationship

If you are analyzing cause, you should come right out and say so by using various phrases and expressions that make plain your purpose and thinking. Such words and phrases as *because, reason why, the effect of,* and so on, can make clear to the reader what you are about. Consider this passage, for example, in which the writer uses the italicized phrases and their words to clarify the intent of the essay:

> Anyone who claims that it is impossible to get rid of the random violence of today's mean streets may be telling the truth, but is also missing the point. Street crime may be normal in the U.S., but it is not inevitable at such advanced levels, and the fact is that *there are specific reasons* for the nation's incapacity to keep its street crime down. Almost all *these reasons can be traced* to the American criminal justice system. It is not that there are no mechanisms in place to deal with American crime, merely that the existing ones are impractical, inefficient, anachronistic, uncooperative, and often lead to as much civic destruction as they are meant to curtail.
> *Why does the system fail?* For one thing, the. . . .
>
> ROGER ROSENBLATT, *"Why The Justice System Fails"*

It also does no harm to specify in the working title that your essay is an attempt at causal analysis. In the preceding example it is evident from the title that reasons will be given for the breakdown of the criminal justice system. Effective titles can contribute markedly to a reader's understanding of a writer's purpose, and thus make an essay easier to follow.

3. Focus on the Immediate Rather Than the Remote Cause

The poet may well be right that we cannot pluck a flower without disturbing a star. Many Eastern religions adhere to just such unseen relationships between and among all things—a view that tends considerably to muddle our Western view of proximate and actual causation. However, if such invisible bonds exist, their effect appears so inconsequential that one may safely spend a lifetime uprooting row after row of flowers without causing the faintest heavenly quiver.

Common sense therefore suggests that any causal analysis be focused on the nearest reasonable and available cause that explains an event or effect, giving only occasional honorable mention to more distant possibilities. For example, you may argue that one reason for a midair collision between a commercial jet and a private plane is the FAA's firing of hundreds of striking experienced controllers and replacing them with newly trained recruits. Even so, the more immediate cause may be the pilot error that brought the private aircraft blundering into the restricted airspace properly occupied by the commercial jet. But for that blunder, the collision would not have occurred. Perhaps a more experienced controller would have spotted the converging aircraft and prevented the disaster. *Perhaps,* however, is only speculation. What is definitely known and established is that many other aircraft, under the guidance of the new controllers, have passed one another safely in the skies. That these two collided must be, therefore, the result of something more immediate (a more proximate cause) than the air traffic controllers' inexperience. To determine that *thing* and explain it is to focus your analysis properly, and your essay, on the immediate rather than the remote cause.

WHAT YOU WILL BE

Milton Mayer

> *Milton Mayer (1908–1986) was an American educator, journalist, editor, and author. He was best known for his probing works on the individual in relation to politics, religion, and self-realization. For his work as a journalist he received a George Polk Memorial Award and a Benjamin Franklin Citation. Mayer also taught at the University of Massachusetts,*

*at Amherst, and at Windham College. Among his books
are* They Thought They Were Free: The Germans,
1933–1945 *(1955),* What Can A Man Do? *(1964),* If
Men Were Angels *(1972), and* The Nature of the
Beast *(1975).*

Preparing to Read This Selection Critically

The following commencement address is easy to
misread and thus be depressing. Essential to a correct
interpretation of the content is the author's ironic tone.
He is saying one thing but actually hoping for the opposite. Keep that in mind and try to formulate what this
opposite is. Despite Mayer's hostile persona and his intellectual positions that go against the average person's
preconceptions, your challenge is to understand the pitfalls he points out and to map a course for avoiding them;
only then can you escape the despair such an address
could elicit.

1   As you are now, so I once was; as I am now, so you will be.
You will be tempted to smile when I tell you that I am middle–aged
and corrupt. You should resist the temptation. Twenty–five years
from now you will be ineluctably middle–aged and, unless you hear
and heed what I say today, just as ineluctably corrupt. You will not
believe me, and you should not, because what I say at my age should
be unbelievable at yours. But you should hear me out because I
know more than you do in one respect: you know only what it is
to be young, while I know what it is to be both young and old. In
any case, I will not lie to you in order to make you feel good. You
will be old much longer than you are young, and I would rather
that you believed me the longer time than the shorter.

2   I tell you today that instantly is not a moment too soon if you
are going to escape the fate I predict for you and embody myself.
For what was said long ago is still true, that corruption runs faster
than death and the faster runner overtakes the slower. It may indeed
be too late already, unless you mend your ways this least of all likely
moments. I once heard Robert Hutchins tell a graduating class that
they were closer to the truth that day than they would ever be again.
I did not believe him. But I have seen most of the members of that
class since, and I regret to inform you that Hutchins was right. Mind

you, he did not say that they were close to the truth; he only said that they would never be so close again. They had been taught what right and wrong were and had not yet had a chance to do what e. e. cummings calls "up grow and down forget." If my own history and the history of the race is instructive, this commencement is for nearly every last one of you the commencement of disintegration. A cynic once said that he would not give a hang for a man who wasn't a socialist before he was twenty or who was one after that. I do not know if socialism is a good ideal, but I know that it is an ideal and I know that the cynic was confident that you would lose your ideals. You may even have trifled, in your springtime, with such radical aberrations as pacifism. But you will soon stop trifling; and when, at thirty, you have already begun to molder, your friends will tell you that you have mellowed.

All societies are deplorable, and history indicates that they   3 always will be. You have lived twenty years in a deplorable society. You have lived sheltered lives, but you have had no one to shelter you from your parents and teachers. Your parents have done what they could to adjust you to the deplorable society to which they, as their advanced age testifies, have successfully adjusted themselves. When they said you were improving, they meant that you were getting to be like them. When they said they hoped you would keep out of trouble, they meant that you should not do anything that they wouldn't do. But some of the things that they wouldn't do should have been done. The condition of the society to which they have accommodated their lives is the proof of their criminal negligence. Your teachers have been no better, and no better an influence on you, than your parents. They may have had higher ideals; it takes higher ideals to teach children than to have them. But your teachers' survival (like your parents') testifies to their adjustability. They have done as they were told, and in a deplorable society there are some things that men are told to do that no man should do. A high-school teacher in California told me that not one of his colleagues wanted to take the anti-Communist oath required of teachers in that state, and neither did he; but every one of them took it in order to hold his job and escape the national black list. As they are now, so you will be.

Like your teachers and your parents before you, you will be   4 told to do bad things in order to hold your job. In college you may have quit the campus daily or defied the old fraternity on principle. It will be harder to quit the metropolitan daily or defy the old country on principle; it will be easier to forget the principle. And if, in addition to holding your job, you want to be promoted, you will think of bad things to do on your own. And you will have good reasons for doing them. You will have wives (at least one apiece) and children to maintain. You will have a home and mortgage to enlarge. And life insurance, purchased against the certainty of death, dread of which in turn adds preciousness to staying alive at any price. And neighbors who are having their children's teeth straightened. Your dentists' bills alone will corrupt you. You will have doctors' bills to pay, and they will increase as you grow older, becoming extremely heavy when you are moribund and powerless to earn money. You will have lusts, as you have now, to gratify, but the lusts you have now are relatively inexpensive and they will give way to more expensive if less gratifying lusts. You will have worthy philanthropies to support and the respect of people whose respect depends on your supporting those philanthropies. You will have an automobile (if you are so wretched as to be a one–car family), and you might as well turn it in every year because the new model will be so revolutionary that it will depreciate the old one to the point where there's no point in keeping it.

5   Some of the things you will be expected to do (or will expect yourself to do) for the sake of your wife and children, your community, your health, or your burial are bad things. You will have to have good reasons for doing them; and, thanks to your education, you will have them. The trouble with education is that it teaches you rhetoric while you are young. When, for rhetorical purposes, you embrace the doctrine of the lesser evil, you ignore its fatal flaw of present certainty and future contingency; being young, you think you will live forever, so that you may do bad things today in order to do good things tomorrow. But today is certain, tomorrow contingent; and this night an old man's soul may be required of him. When you are old, and too tired to embrace doctrines for rhetorical purposes, you will find that the doctrine of the lesser evil has embraced you and destroyed you. You protest my melancholy prediction, but the Great Actuarial Table is against you. Twenty–five years from now nine out of ten of you (or all ten) will tolerate an existence which, if you could foresee it now, you would call intolerable. If such an existence has any virtue at all, it has only one: it will give you a wistful old age. You will look back to your springtime, fifty years gone, and say, "Those were the days." And you will be right.

The only thing that will save you from wistfulness is the one   6
talent whose lack now redeems you—the talent for self-deception.
You won't even know that you are corrupt. You will be no worse
than your neighbors, and you will be sure to have some that you
won't be as bad as. You will have friends who praise in you the
characteristics you have in common with them. They will persuade
you that there is nothing wrong with either hoarding or squandering
as much money as you can get legally. And if, some sudden night,
you go berserk and bawl out that life is a sell, they will put you to
bed with the assurance that you will be all right in the morning.
And you will be. Worse than being corrupt, you will be contented
in your corruption.

Twenty-five years from now you will celebrate your twentieth   7
wedding anniversary. Because you love your wife—still more if you
don't—you will want to celebrate it in style. You will reserve a window table for two at the choicest restaurant in town, and the champagne bucket will be at the table when you arrive. You will not be
the cynosure of all eyes, but you will think you are. The head waiter
(or maitre d', as he is known here) will address you by name. As
your eye travels down the menu it will be distracted by something
outside the window, which will prove to be a hungry man. What
will you do? Do you know what you will do then, twenty-five years
from now? You will call the maitre d' and tell him to have the drapes
pulled, and he will tell the waiter, and he will tell the bus boy, who
will do it.

Your table, even before you have ordered, will be laden with   8
rolls and crackers (of several sorts) and butter pats on butter plates.
Hungry, and a little nervous, as you should be, you will break up
a roll and butter it and eat it as you wait for your wife to make up
her confounded mind. The waiter will ask you if you want the
champagne poured, and you will say yes; and he will open it with
a pop which, beneath the dinner din, will be unheard by the rest
of the diners (but you won't know that). Thirsty, and a little nervous
still, you will sip your glass, forgetting to toast your wife, and resume
your study of the menu. And then, for the first time, you will see,
in fine italic print at the bottom, the words "The Management reserves the right to refuse service to anyone." And then you will
know (for you will be an educated man) that you are sitting in a
Jim Crow restaurant—that being the meaning of the words "The
Management, etc."

9   Now the country in which you were raised calls itself a Christian country, and the parents who raised you up called themselves Christian people, and the church whose vestry has just elected you calls itself a Christian church, and you call yourself a Christian. Jim Crowism is un–Christian. It is also un–American, and you call yourself an American. What will you do? What will you do then, twenty–five years from now?

10   The champagne is open and sipped. The roll is buttered, half–eaten. Will you get up from the table and tell your wife to get up and tell her why, and tell the waiter and the maitre d', and maybe the management, that you are leaving the restaurant and why, and pay for the champagne and the rolls and the butter pats and, if necessary, for the dinner, but refuse to eat there? Or will you pretend, as the management (by printing the notice in fine italic type) intended you to pretend, that you did not see the notice? You will stay at the table and order your dinner and eat it.

11   You will have been measured for corruption and found to fit. You may be the man who raised the flag on Iwo Jima—a hero abroad but not at home, where it's harder to be a hero. At Iwo Jima you had either to raise the flag or drop it. It was publicly shameful to drop it. But the night of your anniversary dinner it would have been publicly shameful to *raise* the flag by leaving the restaurant. And public shame was what you could not bear, either at Iwo Jima or in the restaurant.

12   There are a lot of involuntary, non–voluntary or reflexive heroes. I am one myself. I do not doubt that I would have raised the flag at Iwo Jima rather than let it drop in public. But I was the man who took his wife to dinner at the Jim Crow restaurant. Believe me, there is no contradiction between the corruption which will consume you, day by day, in the face of unpopularity or public shame and the heroism of the moment accompanied by public praise. And when you have been measured often enough and long enough for corruption, you will like what you see in the mirror. I don't mean that you won't continue to have good impulses. You will. But you will have persuasive reasons for suppressing them. From time to time, as the vestige of your springtime idealism stirs you, you will want to do the right thing. But you will have to put off doing it until you have buried your father, and then your mother, your brother, your children, and your grandchildren. You may live to be very old, but you will not outlive the last descendant for whose sake you will suppress your good impulses.

What life did to me, because there was no one to tell me what   13
I am telling you now, it will do to you if you do not at once adopt
Principiis obsta as your motto and spurn every other. "Resist the
beginnings." At twenty I was what you are; I had had all the middle–
class care that a middle–class society and a middle–class home could
provide. My parents wanted me to have what they took to be advantages, and I had them. But my advantages were of no use to me
at all when life came down on me, as it will upon you, like a ton
of bricks. I had studied morality, just as you have, but it was the
easy morality designed to sustain my character in an easy world. I
would not steal another man's watch unless my children were starving, and my children would never be starving. Nor will yours if,
with what your parents call your advantages, you do as you are told
and get to the top. The reason your children will not be starving is
that you will have been corrupted. Your corruption will save you
from having to decide whether to steal another man's watch. I was
prepared, like you, to be a hero the instant heroism was required
of me. I saw myself at Iwo Jima, at Gettysburg, at Concord. But I
did not see myself at home, so weakened by the corrosive years
ahead that I would not be able to stand up on my hind legs and
say no when I had to do it alone. Never knowing—as you do not
know—that my needs would be limitless, I never imagined that my
surrender would be complete.

My education prepared me to say no to my enemies. It did not   14
prepare me to say no to my friends, still less to myself, to my own
limitless need for a little more status, a little more security, and a
little more of the immediate pleasure that status and security provide. Corruption is accompanied by immediate pleasure. When you
feel good, you are probably, if not necessarily, doing bad. But happiness is activity in accordance with virtue, and the practice of virtue
is painful. The pursuit of happiness requires a man to undertake
suffering. Your intelligence, or your psychiatrist's, will tell you
whether you are suffering for the right reason. But it will not move
you to undertake the suffering.

God is said to come to us in little things. The Devil is no fool: 15
he comes that way too. The Devil has only one objective, and if he
can persuade you to justify your derelictions by saying "I'm only
human," he has achieved it. He will have got you to deny the Christ
within you, and that is all he wants. If you are only human you are
his. The Devil will keep you quiet when you ought to talk by reminding you that nobody asked you to say anything. He will keep

you in your chair when you ought to get up and out by reminding you that you love your wife and it's your twentieth anniversary. He will give you the oath to take and say, "As long as you're loyal, why not say so?" He will tell you that the beggar outside the restaurant would only spend the money on whiskey. The Devil has come to me in little things for twenty-five years—and now I say and do the things in which, when he first began coming, he had to instruct me.

16   I tell you that you are in mortal jeopardy today, and anyone who tells you differently is selling you to the Devil. It is written on Plato's ring that it is easier to form good habits than to break bad ones. Your habits are not yet fully formed. You are, in some measure still, only potentially corrupt. Life will actualize and habitualize every bit of your corruptibility. If you do not begin to cultivate the habit of heroism today—and habits are formed by acts—you never will. You may delude yourselves, as I did, by setting about to change the world. But for all that you do or do not do, you will leave the world, as I do, no better than you found it and yourselves considerably worse. For the world will change you faster, more easily, and more durably than you will change it. If you undertake only to keep the world from changing you—not to lick 'em but to avoid j'ining 'em—you will have your hands full.

17   Other, more agreeable commencement orators have warned you of life's pitfalls. I tell you that you are marked for them. I believe you will not escape them because I see nothing in your environment that has prepared you even to recognize them. Your elders tell you to compare yourselves with the Russians and see how much worse the Russians are; this is not the way to prepare you to recognize pitfalls. Your elders tell you to be technologists because the Russians are technologists and your country is technologically backward; this is no way to prepare you to recognize pitfalls. You are marked for the pit. The Great Actuarial Table is against you.

18   What you need (and the Russians with you) is neither pharisaism nor technology. What you need is what the psalmist knew he needed—a heart, not a head, of wisdom. What you need is what Bismarck said was the only thing the Germans needed—civilian courage. I do not know where you will get it. If I did, I would get it myself. You were divinely endowed to know right and to do right, and you have before you, in the tradition of your country and of human history, the vision to help you if you will turn to it. But no one will compel you to turn to it, and no one can. The dictates of

your society, of any society, will not serve you. They are dictates that corrupted your parents and your teachers. If Socrates did not know where virtue came from—and he didn't—neither do I. He pursued it earlier and harder than anyone else and concluded that it was the gift of God. In despair of your parents and your society, of your teachers and your studies, of your neighbors and your friends, and above all of your fallen nature and the Old Adam in you, I bespeak for you the gift of God.

Thinking Critically About This Reading

1. Mayer makes growing old seem gloomy and futile—or does he? What is your personal response to this sermonlike commencement address? What would your reaction be if you were in the audience?

2. How would you counter Mayer's argument that all young people are ineluctably headed for corruption? What evidence would you cite to prove the opposite view?

3. What, in your view, are the strongest temptations that might lead young people to the corruption described by Mayer? How can these temptations be resisted?

4. Reread William Golding's "Thinking as a Hobby." Which kind of thinking would Mayer encourage? Which would he consider corrupting? Give reasons for your answers.

5. What is your reaction to Mayer's insistence that the talent for self–deception causes people to be content in their inevitable corruption? Assuming that Mayer is right, what can be done by our social institutions—education, religion, and family—to counteract self–deception?

Understanding the Writer's Process

1. What evidence does the author use to convince his readers of the danger they face in the future? How convincing is the evidence? What kind of evidence, if any, does he leave out?

2. In his analysis of cause, what causes does the author cite for the effect (corruption) he predicts?

3. What is the author's thesis and where is it stated? Is the placement significant? Why or why not?

4. What evidence does the author produce for his judgment that "all societies are deplorable"? Do you agree or disagree? Support your answer.
5. What is the purpose of the long anecdote related in paragraphs 7–11? What is your reaction to it?

Examining the Writer's Language

1. The following words are not a common part of most people's vocabulary. Try to use each one in a sentence without sounding awkward: ineluctably (1), cynic (2), moribund (4), cynosure (7), vestige (12), corrosive (13).
2. How does the author achieve a sense of intimacy between him and his audience?
3. In paragraph 4, how does the author achieve a sense of rhetorical harmony and balance?
4. What is the purpose of the long question posed in the third sentence of paragraph 10?
5. In paragraph 12, what is the difference between an "involuntary" and a "non–voluntary" hero? How does this difference fit the author's thesis?
6. What is the meaning of the word *bespeak* as used in the final paragraph of the address?

Suggestions for Writing

1. Write an essay in which you project our society twenty years from now, analyzing the effects of one of the following situations: (1) our relationship with Russia and the Commonwealth, (2) ecological damage, (3) urban overcrowding.
2. Using Mayer's essay as a model, compose a 500–word high school graduation address, preparing your listeners for the kinds of social problems you believe they will face in college.

THE MAN WHO MISTOOK HIS WIFE FOR A HAT

Oliver Sacks

Oliver Sacks (b. 1933) is professor of clinical neurology at the Albert Einstein College of Medicine and consults on neurological disorders for numerous New York hospitals. Born in London and educated in England, as well as in the United States, Dr. Sacks has specialized in migraine headaches and other more complex neurological disorders. His deep interest in the individual experience of his patients has led to his writing such books as Migraine, a Common Disorder *(1970);* Awakening *(1973);* A Leg to Stand On *(1984); and* The Man Who Mistook His Wife for a Hat *(1986), from which the following essay is taken. In this essay, Dr. Sacks analyzes the cause of an unusual neurological affliction that actually resulted in a musician's inability to view space normally.*

Preparing to Read This Selection Critically

The strange neurological illness described in the following essay points out how under certain circumstances the powers of illness cooperate with the powers of artistic creation. In other words, a mad poet may create a beautiful sonnet or a mad painter place something extraordinarily symbolic on canvas. The interest of Dr. Sacks's research lies not so much in the neurological cause of pathology he discovers as in its fascinating effects. Here is a great musician who successfully teaches music, yet cannot recognize his own shoe, a glove, or the faces of his loved ones. You need to sort out in your own mind what is tragic and what is amazing about the professor's illness; doing so will help you establish a philosophical vision of life and its ultimate value.

Dr P. was a musician of distinction, well-known for many years   1
as a singer, and then, at the local School of Music, as a teacher. It was here, in relation to his students, that certain strange problems were first observed. Sometimes a student would present himself, and Dr P. would not recognise him; or, specifically, would not recognise his face. The moment the student spoke, he would be recognised by his voice. Such incidents multiplied, causing embarrassment, perplexity, fear—and, sometimes, comedy. For not only did Dr P. increasingly fail to see faces, but he saw faces when there were no faces to see: genially, Magoo-like when in the street, he

might pat the heads of water-hydrants and parking-meters, taking these to be the heads of children; he would amiably address carved knobs on the furniture, and be astounded when they did not reply. At first these odd mistakes were laughed off as jokes, not least by Dr P. himself. Had he not always had a quirky sense of humour, and been given to Zen-like paradoxes and jests? His musical powers were as dazzling as ever; he did not feel ill—he had never felt better; and the mistakes were so ludicrous—and so ingenious—that they could hardly be serious or betoken anything serious. The notion of there being "something the matter" did not emerge until some three years later, when diabetes developed. Well aware that diabetes could affect his eyes, Dr P. consulted an ophthalmologist, who took a careful history, and examined his eyes closely. "There's nothing the matter with your eyes," the doctor concluded. "But there is trouble with the visual parts of your brain. You don't need my help, you must see a neurologist." And so, as a result of this referral, Dr P. came to me.

2   It was obvious within a few seconds of meeting him that there was no trace of dementia in the ordinary sense. He was a man of great cultivation and charm, who talked well and fluently, with imagination and humour. I couldn't think why he had been referred to our clinic.

3   And yet there *was* something a bit odd. He faced me as he spoke, was oriented towards me, and yet there was something the matter—it was difficult to formulate. He faced me with his *ears*, I came to think, but not with his eyes. These, instead of looking, gazing, at me, "taking me in," in the normal way, made sudden strange fixations—on my nose, on my right ear, down to my chin, up to my right eye—as if noting (even studying) these individual features, but not seeing my whole face, its changing expressions, "me", as a whole. I am not sure that I fully realised this at the time— there was just a teasing strangeness, some failure in the normal interplay of gaze and expression. He saw me, he *scanned* me, and yet . . .

4   "What seems to be the matter?" I asked him at length.

5   "Nothing that I know of," he replied with a smile, "but people seem to think there's something wrong with my eyes."

6   "But *you* don't recognise any visual problems?"

7   "No, not directly, but I occasionally make mistakes."

8   I left the room briefly, to talk to his wife. When I came back Dr P. was sitting placidly by the window, attentive, listening rather

than looking out. "Traffic," he said, "street sounds, distant trains—
they make a sort of symphony, do they not? You know Honegger's
Pacific 234?"

What a lovely man, I thought to myself. How can there be 9
anything seriously the matter? Would he permit me to examine him?

"Yes, of course, Dr Sacks." 10

I stilled my disquiet, his perhaps too, in the soothing routine 11
of a neurological exam—muscle strength, co-ordination, reflexes,
tone . . . It was while examining his reflexes—a trifle abnormal on
the left side—that the first bizarre experience occurred. I had taken
off his left shoe and scratched the sole of his foot with a key—a
frivolous-seeming but essential test of a reflex—and then, excusing
myself to screw my ophthalmoscope together, left him to put on
the shoe himself. To my surprise, a minute later, he had not done
this.

"Can I help?" I asked. 12

"Help what? Help whom?" 13

'Help you put on your shoe." 14

"Ach," he said, "I had forgotten the shoe", adding, *sotto voce,* 15
"The shoe? The shoe?" He seemed baffled.

"Your shoe," I repeated. "Perhaps you'd put it on." 16

He continued to look downwards, though not at the shoe, with 17
an intense but misplaced concentration. Finally his gaze settled on
his foot: "That is my shoe, yes?"

Did I mis-hear? Did he mis-see? 18

"My eyes," he explained, and put a hand to his foot. "*This* is 19
my shoe, no?"

"No, it is not. That is your foot. *There* is your shoe." 20

"Ah! I thought that was my foot." 21

Was he joking? Was he mad? Was he blind? If this was one of 22
his "strange mistakes," it was the strangest mistake I had ever come
across.

I helped him on with his shoe (his foot), to avoid further com- 23
plication. Dr P. himself seemed untroubled, indifferent, maybe
amused. I resumed my examination. His visual acuity was good: he
had no difficulty seeing a pin on the floor, though sometimes he
missed it if it was placed to his left.

He saw all right, but what did he see? I opened out a copy of 24
the *National Geographic Magazine,* and asked him to describe some
pictures in it.

25   His responses here were very curious. His eyes would dart from one thing to another, picking up tiny features, individual features, as they had done with my face. A striking brightness, a colour, a shape would arrest his attention and elicit comment—but in no case did he get the scene-as-a-whole. He failed to see the whole, seeing only details, which he spotted like blips on a radar screen. He never entered into relation with the picture as a whole—never faced, so to speak, *its* physiognomy. He had no sense whatever of a landscape or scene.

26   I showed him the cover, an unbroken expanse of Sahara dunes.

27   "What do you see here?" I asked.

28   "I see a river," he said. "And a little guest-house with its terrace on the water. People are dining out on the terrace. I see coloured parasols here and there." He was looking, if it was "looking," right off the cover, into mid-air and confabulating non-existent features, as if the absence of features in the actual picture had driven him to imagine the river and the terrace and the coloured parasols.

29   I must have looked aghast, but he seemed to think he had done rather well. There was a hint of a smile on his face. He also appeared to have decided that the examination was over, and started to look round for his hat. He reached out his hand, and took hold of his wife's head, tried to lift it off, to put it on. He had apparently mistaken his wife for a hat! His wife looked as if she was used to such things.

30   I could make no sense of what had occurred, in terms of conventional neurology (or neuropsychology). In some ways he seemed perfectly preserved, and in others absolutely, incomprehensibly devastated. How could he, on the one hand, mistake his wife for a hat and, on the other, function, as apparently he still did, as a teacher at the Music School?

31   I had to think, to see him again—and to see him in his own familiar habitat, at home.

32   A few days later I called on Dr P. and his wife at home, with the score of the *Dichterliebe* in my briefcase (I knew he liked Schumann), and a variety of odd objects for the testing of perception. Mrs P. showed me into a lofty apartment, which recalled fin-de-siècle Berlin. A magnificent old Bösendorfer stood in state in the centre of the room, and all round it were music-stands, instruments, scores . . . There were books, there were paintings, but the music was central. Dr P. came in and, distracted, advanced with outstretched hand to the grandfather clock, but, hearing my voice, cor-

rected himself, and shook hands with me. We exchanged greetings, and chatted a little of current concerts and performances. Diffidently, I asked him if he would sing.

"The *Dichterliebe!*" he exclaimed. "But I can no longer read   33
music. You will play them, yes?"

I said I would try. On that wonderful old piano even my play-   34
ing sounded right, and Dr P. was an aged, but infinitely mellow Fischer-Dieskau, combining a perfect ear and voice with the most incisive musical intelligence. It was clear that the Music School was not keeping him on out of charity.

Dr P.'s temporal lobes were obviously intact: he had a won-   35
derful musical cortex. What, I wondered, was going on in his parietal and occipital lobes, especially in those areas where visual processing occurred? I carry the Platonic solids in my neurological kit, and decided to start with these.

"What is this?" I asked, drawing out the first one.   36

"A cube, of course."   37

"Now this?" I asked, brandishing another.   38

He asked if he might examine it, which he did swiftly and   39
systematically: "A dodecahedron, of course. And don't bother with the others—I'll get the eikosihedron too."

Abstract shapes clearly presented no problems. What about   40
faces? I took out a pack of cards. All of these he identified instantly, including the jacks, queens, kings, and the joker. But these, after all, are stylised designs, and it was impossible to tell whether he saw faces or merely patterns. I decided I would show him a volume of cartoons which I had in my briefcase. Here, again, for the most part, he did well. Churchill's cigar, Schnozzle's nose: as soon as he had picked out a key feature he could identify the face. But cartoons, again, are formal and schematic. It remained to be seen how he would do with real faces, realistically represented.

I turned on the television, keeping the sound off, and found   41
an early Bette Davis film. A love scene was in progress. Dr P. failed to identify the actress—but this could have been because she had never entered his world. What was more striking was that he failed to identify the expressions on her face or her partner's, though in the course of a single torrid scene these passed from sultry yearning through passion, surprise, disgust and fury to a melting reconcili-ation. Dr P. could make nothing of any of this. He was very unclear as to what was going on, or who was who or even what sex they were. His comments on the scene were positively Martian.

42   It was just possible that some of his difficulties were associated with the unreality of a celluloid, Hollywood world; and it occurred to me that he might be more successful in identifying faces from his own life. On the walls of the apartment there were photographs of his family, his colleagues, his pupils, himself. I gathered a pile of these together and, with some misgivings, presented them to him. What had been funny, or farcical, in relation to the movie, was tragic in relation to real life. By and large, he recognised nobody: neither his family, nor his colleagues, nor his pupils, nor himself. He recognised a portrait of Einstein, because he picked up the characteristic hair and moustache; and the same thing happened with one or two other people. "Ach, Paul!" he said, when shown a portrait of his brother. "That square jaw, those big teeth, I would know Paul anywhere!" But was it Paul he recognised, or one or two of his features, on the basis of which he could make a reasonable guess as to the subject's identity? In the absence of obvious "markers," he was utterly lost. But it was not merely the cognition, the *gnosis*, at fault; there was something radically wrong with the whole way he proceeded. For he approached these faces—even of those near and dear—as if they were abstract puzzles or tests. He did not relate to them, he did not behold. No face was familiar to him, seen as a "thou," being just identified as a set of features, an "it". Thus there was formal, but no trace of personal, gnosis. And with this went his indifference, or blindness, to expression. A face, to us, is a person looking out—we see, as it were, the person through his *persona*, his face. But for Dr P. there was no *persona* in this sense—no outward *persona*, and no person within.

43   I had stopped at a florist on my way to his apartment and bought myself an extravagant red rose for my buttonhole. Now I removed this and handed it to him. He took it like a botanist or morphologist given a specimen, not like a person given a flower.

44   "About six inches in length," he commented. "A convoluted red form with a linear green attachment."

45   "Yes," I said encouragingly, "and what do you think it *is*, Dr P.?"

46   "Not easy to say." He seemed perplexed. "It lacks the simple symmetry of the Platonic solids, although it may have a higher symmetry of its own . . . I think this could be an inflorescence or flower."

47   "Could be?" I queried.

48   "Could be," he confirmed.

"Smell it," I suggested, and he again looked somewhat puz- 49
zled, as if I had asked him to smell a higher symmetry. But he
complied courteously, and took it to his nose. Now, suddenly, he
came to life.

"Beautiful!" he exclaimed, "An early rose. What a heavenly 50
smell!" He started to hum "Die Rose, die Lillie ..." Reality, it
seemed, might be conveyed by smell, not by sight.

I tried one final test. It was still a cold day, in early spring, 51
and I had thrown my coat and gloves on the sofa.

"What is this?" I asked, holding up a glove. 52

"May I examine it?" he asked, and, taking it from me, he 53
proceeded to examine it as he had examined the geometrical shapes.

"A continuous surface," he announced at last, "infolded on 54
itself. It appears to have"—he hesitated—"five outpouchings, if this
is the word."

"Yes," I said cautiously. "You have given me a description. 55
Now tell me what it is."

"A container of some sort?" 56

"Yes," I said, "and what would it contain?" 57

"It would contain its contents!" said Dr P., with a laugh. "There 58
are many possibilities. It could be a change-purse, for example, for
coins of five sizes. It could ..."

I interrupted the barmy flow. "Does it not look familiar? Do 59
you think it might contain, might fit, a part of your body?"

No light of recognition dawned on his face.[1] 60

No child would have the power to see and speak of "a con- 61
tinuous surface ... infolded on itself," but any child, any infant,
would immediately know a glove as a glove, see it as familiar, as
going with a hand. Dr P. didn't. He saw nothing as familiar. Visually,
he was lost in a world of lifeless abstractions. Indeed he did not
have a real visual world, as he did not have a real visual self. He
could speak about things, but did not see them face-to-face. Hughl-
ings Jackson, discussing patients with aphasia and left-hemisphere
lesions, says they have lost "abstract" and "propositional" thought—
and compares them with dogs (or, rather, he compares dogs to patients with aphasia). Dr P., on the other hand, functioned precisely
as a machine functions. It wasn't merely that he displayed the same

---

[1] Later, by accident, he got it on, and exclaimed, "My God, it's a glove!" This was
reminiscent of Kurt Goldstein's patient "Lanuti", who could only recognise objects
by trying to use them in action.

indifference to the visual word as a computer but—even more strikingly—he construed the world as a computer construes it, by means of key features and schematic relationships. The scheme might be identified—in an "identiti-kit" way—without the reality being grasped at all.

62   The testing I had done so far told me nothing about Dr P.'s inner world. Was it possible that his visual memory and imagination were still intact? I asked him to imagine entering one of our local squares from the north side, to walk through it, in imagination or in memory, and tell me the buildings he might pass as he walked. He listed the buildings on his right side, but none of those on his left. I then asked him to imagine entering the square from the south. Again he mentioned only those buildings that were on the right side, although these were the very buildings he had omitted before. Those he had "seen" internally before were not mentioned now presumably, they were no longer "seen." It was evident that his difficulties with leftness, his visual field deficits, were as much internal as external, bisecting his visual memory and imagination.

63   What, at a higher level, of his internal visualisation? Thinking of the almost hallucinatory intensity with which Tolstoy visualises and animates his characters, I questioned Dr P. about *Anna Karenina*.[2] He could remember incidents without difficulty, had an undiminished grasp of the plot, but completely omitted visual characteristics, visual narrative or scenes. He remembered the words of the characters, but not their faces; and though, when asked, he could quote, with his remarkable and almost verbatim memory, the original visual descriptions, these were, it became apparent, quite empty for him, and lacked sensorial, imaginal, or emotional reality. Thus there was an internal agnosia as well.[3]

But this was only the case, it became clear, with certain sorts of visualisation. The visualisation of faces and scenes, of visual nar-

---

[2] Novel by Leo Tolstoy.

[3] I have often wondered about Helen Keller's visual descriptions, whether these, for all their eloquence, are somehow empty as well? Or whether, by the transference of images from the tactile to the visual, or, yet more extraordinarily, from the verbal and the metaphorical to the sensorial and the visual, she *did* achieve a power of visual imagery, even though her visual cortex had never been stimulated, directly, by the eyes? But in Dr P.'s case it is precisely the cortex that was damaged, the organic prerequisite of all pictorial imagery. Interestingly and typically he no longer dreamed pictorially—the "message" of the dream being conveyed in non-visual terms.

rative and drama—this was profoundly impaired, almost absent. But the visualisation of *schemata* was preserved, perhaps enhanced. Thus when I engaged him in a game of mental chess, he had no difficulty visualising the chessboard or the moves—indeed, no difficulty in beating me soundly.

Luria said of Zazetsky that he had entirely lost his capacity to 64 play games but that his "vivid imagination" was unimpaired. Zazetsky and Dr P. lived in worlds which were mirror images of each other. But the saddest difference between them was that Zazetsky, as Luria said, "fought to regain his lost faculties with the indomitable tenacity of the damned," whereas Dr P. was not fighting, did not know what was lost, did not indeed know that anything was lost. But who was more tragic, or who was more damned—the man who knew it, or the man who did not?

When the examination was over, Mrs P. called us to the table, 65 where there was coffee and a delicious spread of little cakes. Hungrily, hummingly, Dr P. started on the cakes. Swiftly, fluently, unthinkingly, melodiously, he pulled the plates towards him, and took this and that, in a great gurgling stream, an edible song of food, until, suddenly, there came an interruption: a loud, peremptory rat-tat-tat at the door. Startled, taken aback, arrested, by the interruption, Dr P. stopped eating, and sat frozen, motionless, at the table, with an indifferent, blind, bewilderment on his face. He saw, but no longer saw, the table; no longer perceived it as a table laden with cakes. His wife poured him some coffee: the smell titillated his nose, and brought him back to reality. The melody of eating resumed.

How does he do anything, I wondered to myself? What hap- 66 pens when he's dressing, goes to the lavatory, has a bath? I followed his wife into the kitchen and asked her how, for instance, he managed to dress himself. "It's just like the eating," she explained. "I put his usual clothes out, in all the usual places, and he dresses without difficulty, singing to himself. He does everything singing to himself. But if he is interrupted and loses the thread, he comes to a complete stop, doesn't know his clothes—or his own body. He sings all the time—eating songs, dressing songs, bathing songs, everything. He can't do anything unless he makes it a song."

While we were talking my attention was caught by the pictures 67 on the walls.

"Yes," Mrs P. said, "he was a gifted painter as well as a singer. 68 The School exhibited his pictures every year."

69   I strolled past them curiously—they were in chronological order. All his earlier work was naturalistic and realistic, with vivid mood and atmosphere, but finely detailed and concrete. Then, years later, they became less vivid, less concrete, less realistic and naturalistic; but far more abstract, even geometrical and cubist. Finally, in the last paintings, the canvasses became nonsense, or nonsense to me—mere chaotic lines and blotches of paint. I commented on this to Mrs P.

70   "Ach, you doctors, you're such philistines!" she exclaimed. "Can you not see *artistic development*—how he renounced the realism of his earlier years, and advanced into abstract, non-representational art?"

71   "No, that's not it," I said to myself (but forbore to say it to poor Mrs P.). He had indeed moved from realism to non-representation to the abstract, but this was not the artist, but the pathology, advancing—advancing towards a profound visual agnosia, in which all powers of representation and imagery, all sense of the concrete, all sense of reality, were being destroyed. This wall of paintings was a tragic pathological exhibit, which belonged to neurology, not art.

72   And yet, I wondered, was she not partly right? For there is often a struggle, and sometimes, even more interestingly, a collusion between the powers of pathology and creation. Perhaps, in his cubist period, there might have been both artistic and pathological development, colluding to engender an original form; for as he lost the concrete, so he might have gained in the abstract, developing a greater sensitivity to all the structural elements of line, boundary, contour—an almost Picasso-like power to see, and equally depict, those abstract organizations embedded in, and normally lost in, the concrete . . . Though in the final pictures, I feared, there was only chaos and agnosia.

73   We returned to the great music-room, with the Bösendorfer in the centre, and Dr P. humming the last torte.

74   "Well, Dr Sacks," he said to me. "You find me an interesting case, I perceive. Can you tell me what you find wrong, make recommendations?"

75   "I can't tell you what I find wrong," I replied, "but I'll say what I find right. You are a wonderful musician, and music is your life. What I would prescribe, in a case such as yours, is a life which consists entirely of music. Music has been the centre, now make it the whole, of your life."

This was four years ago—I never saw him again, but I often 76
wondered how he apprehended the world, given his strange loss of
image, visuality, and the perfect preservation of a great musicality.
I think that music, for him, had taken the place of image. He had
no body-image, he had body-music: this is why he could move and
act as fluently as he did, but came to a total confused stop if the
"inner music" stopped. And equally with the outside, the world . . .

In *The World as Representation and Will* Schopenhauer speaks 77
of music as "pure will". How fascinated he would have been by Dr
P., a man who had wholly lost the world as representation, but
wholly preserved it as music or will.

And this, mercifully, held to the end—for despite the gradual 78
advance of his disease (a massive tumour or degenerative process
in the visual parts of his brain) Dr P. lived and taught music to the
last days of his life.

Thinking Critically About This Reading

1. In this causal analysis, which is the cause and which the effect?
   Why is it so difficult to determine cause and effect in cases such
   as this? What other difficulty can you perceive?

2. Why did Dr. P. refuse to take his own health condition seriously?
   How do you respond to your own health problems? When you
   have unusual symptoms, do you stick your head in the sand or
   do you see a physician immediately?

3. What are the bizarre aspects of Dr. P.'s malady? What keeps them
   from being farcical? What attitude do most of your acquaintances
   display toward persons with bizarre health problems?

4. How is the scientific method revealed in this narration?

5. Do you agree with the author (paragraph 72) that "there is often
   a struggle, and sometimes, even more interestingly, a collusion
   between the powers of pathology and creation."? What artists
   reveal a life in which illness and art seem to collude? Cite examples from your knowledge of art history.

Understanding the Writer's Process

1. What is the relationship between the title and content of this
   essay? What is your opinion of the choice of title?

2. What is the author's reason for using multiple dashes in paragraph 3? Why the ellipsis at the end of the paragraph?

3. Paragraph 3 asks a significant question. Where in the essay is the question answered?

4. Which does the narrator apparently consider more significant—the cause or the effect of Dr. P.'s condition? Provide reasons for your answer.

5. What is the purpose of the rather lengthy paragraph 42?

Examining the Writer's Language

1. Using a college dictionary, define the following terms: ludicrous (paragraph 1), ingenious (1), physiognomy (25), confabulating (28), habitat (31), celluloid (42), persona (42), convoluted (43), linear (43), schemata (64), peremptory (65), collusion (72).

2. From the following list of scientific terms (extracted from the essay), choose those that you do not recognize, study their meanings in an appropriate dictionary, and use them in a sentence of your own: ophthalmologist, dementia, physiognomy, neuropsychology, temporal lobe, parietal lobe, occipital lobe, morphologist, aphasia, agnosia, schemata.

3. What are *Zen-like paradoxes* (paragraph 1)? Cite an example.

4. What is the meaning of *Magoo-like* (paragraph 1)?

5. What is the meaning of the figure of speech: "Dr. P. was an aged, but infinitely mellow Fischer-Dieskau"?

Suggestions for Writing

1. Write an essay in which you describe the painful effects of a physical or emotional illness you personally experienced. As best you can, trace the illness to a cause.

2. Write an essay analyzing the life of a famous artist who suffered from a serious physical or mental condition. Focus on how the artist overcame the condition.

THE CRUEL LOGIC OF LIBERATION

Joseph Sobran

Joseph Sobran (b. 1946) is a free-lance writer, syndicated with United Press International. A long-time senior editor of National Review, *Sobran is also a contributing editor to the* Human Life Review *and has written for numerous magazines, among them* Harper's *and* The American Spectator. *He follows in the conservative tradition of William F. Buckley, Jr., James J. Kilpatrick, and Michael Novak as he wrestles with such social issues of contemporary life as pornography, abortion, and public prayer; or as he analyzes the problems of history, literature, and public personalities.*

Preparing to Read This Selection Critically

Sobran's position doubtlessly will cause some readers to bristle with irritation and others to smile with understanding. Your own reaction will depend on how you confront the issue of women's rights versus those of men. Continuous research among sociologists, psychologists, and biologists still has not yielded a definitive answer to the question of whether the differences between men and women are mostly biological or cultural. In response to Sobran's views, we suggest you consider the practicalities of the present rather than the conflicting views of research on the brain, DNA, or biological behavior. In other words, think about whether it is fair to deny the father a voice in abortion and whether it is good for society to achieve complete genetic equality. You need to ponder these matters and come to some conclusion.

Maybe it would be an exaggeration to say that men have only 1
themselves to blame for feminism. But I think there's something
in it.

One of the big (and ugly) feminist issues is abortion. I recently 2
got into a debate with a feminist who contended that men should
have no say in the matter, that it was strictly a women's concern.

Very well, I rejoined: in that case women shouldn't be able to file paternity suits.

3   Why not? she demanded. Because, I said, if motherhood is going to be optional, then no woman who chooses it should be able to impose the consequence of her choice on an unwilling man. If a pregnant woman has nine months in which to decide whether to bear a child, during which time she need neither consult nor inform the father (even if he's her husband) and during which time he can't have any say in the matter, it seems grossly unfair to require him to support the child she alone decided to bring into this world.

4   Put otherwise, we have disjoined sex from procreation. Officially, a human fetus is no longer a human being: no objective social penalty attaches to killing it. It's now a matter of law that a sexual act can't commit a woman to motherhood: she can repudiate the consequences of her act. (It's "her body.") So it seems like an illogical residue of an older code to say that the same act that commits her to nothing can simultaneously commit her partner to fatherhood. The paternity suit is a vestige of the code that presumed that the whole point of sex, not to mention the foreseeable result, was reproduction. If women shouldn't be burdened with unwanted children, neither should men. Especially not at the whim of the woman.

5   My interlocutor was distressed by this line of argument, but she had no reply. So I tried it out on a radio broadcast. The only answer I got was that my logic was cruel. But the logic wasn't particularly mine and, besides, a syllogism is under no obligation to be humanitarian: abortion is nasty, so we shouldn't be surprised if the consistent application of its rationale turns out to be equally nasty.

6   Which was exactly the point I set out to make. I agree that people shouldn't be forced to have unwanted children. But once they've begotten a child, they have a child. If either party has a "right" to renounce it, the other should have the same right. Or there is no such right, for anyone.

7   I feel compassion for the woman who is distressed by her pregnancy. But I also feel compassion for the man who can't prevent his child from being aborted, and above all for the child, who has least choice in the matter. As far as that goes, I feel compassion for the poor girl, herself seduced and abandoned, who abandons her infant. But I don't therefore approve of the act that merely passes the injustice along to an innocent party.

8   A good deal of contemporary feminism (by no means all of it) can be traced to the sense of modern life's injustice to woman.

Abortion is inherent in the sexual revolution: we were promised a cheap intimacy, an intimacy without commitment, by erotic utopians like Hugh Hefner.

But like most revolutions and utopias, the sexual one went awry. 9 The burden of it fell most heavily on women: when accidents happen, they happen to women. That is not a good reason for making the children pay. It's an excellent reason for doing something else: namely, challenging the dogmatic premises of sexual "liberation."

Correct me if I'm wrong, but my strong impression is that the 10 new morality hasn't increased the sum total of human bliss. The rates of divorce, abortion and venereal disease are up, up, up, and the pornography trade that has bought Hefner his jet planes and mansions seems to me to testify not to more romance but to more intense loneliness, of a somewhat morbid and sordid kind.

It's time to insist that the promises of the sexual utopians have 11 been as false as those of the social utopians, and as disastrous. If we haven't noticed this, maybe it's because the disasters have occurred on a smaller scale.

Thinking Critically About This Reading

1. What is the writer's proposition? Where is it stated? What necessary changes does it imply? Do you agree with his proposition? Why? Why not? If you (whether you are male or female) should beget a child, what position would you take on this issue?

2. In paragraph 6, the author takes the position that once a child is begotten, father and mother have equal rights to renounce it. Do you support this view? Give reasons or illustrations to clarify your answer.

3. According to the author, what is the legal status of a fetus? What rights does it have? Has the author correctly interpreted the Supreme Court ruling on legalized abortion?

4. The author considers it grossly unfair to permit a woman to decide whether she wants her conceived child to be born or aborted—yet to force a man through a paternity suit to play the role of a father. Do you believe the author really wants to give men the right to abort children they have conceived, or does he have another purpose in mind? Explain your answers.

5. Inasmuch as statistics clearly indicate the *new morality* has not noticeably increased the sum total of human bliss, are you willing

to return to the days of unreliable contraceptives and forced marriages because of pregnancy? Focusing on the subject of sexual relations, what suggestions have you for the future happiness of families and couples?

Understanding the Writer's Process

1. How does the title of the essay fit the argument of the author? What other creative title do you suggest?

2. Sobran begins the essay by stating that men have only themselves to blame for feminism, but drops that issue in favor of an argument against a woman's exclusive right to decide whether to have an abortion. Did the author become unwittingly sidetracked? If not, how is his argument related to the opening sentence?

3. The author compares the promises of the sexual liberation movement with those of the social utopians. What commonality does the author see? Do you agree with his view? Why? Why not?

Examining the Writer's Language

1. Choose one of the following terms and define it in a brief paragraph: feminism, motherhood, utopia, intimacy.

2. How would you characterize the author's style? Is it formal or informal? Simple or ornate? Roundabout or straightforward? Cite specific passages to support your description.

3. What is the purpose of the parentheses in paragraph 4?

Suggestions for Writing

1. Write an essay either supporting or attacking the following proposition: If women can choose not to have the child they have conceived, then men should have that same choice. Follow the rules of logic in presenting your argument.

2. Write an essay for or against the modern idea of liberated sex. Present ample evidence in defense of your position.

WHY WE FALL IN LOVE

M. Scott Peck

*M. Scott Peck (b. 1936) is medical director of the
New Milford Hospital Mental Health Clinic and a psychiatrist in private practice in New Milford, Connecticut. He earned a B.A. from Harvard and an M.D. from
Case Western Reserve. Two books,* The Road Less
Traveled *(1978) and* The People of the Lie *(1980)—
both drawing heavily on case histories from Dr. Peck's
psychoanalytic practice—have made him sought after
nationally as a lecturer and group discussion leader.
In the first book, Dr. Peck clarifies the difference between true love and mere dependency, and helps the
reader confront personal problems through spiritual
growth. In the second book, he probes man's response
to the darker side of existence, insisting that we call
this darker side by its true name, evil, in order to heal
it. The following essay is excerpted from* The Road
Less Traveled, *and suggests both the cause and effect
of falling in love.*

Preparing to Read This Selection Critically

Before you can analyze this essay critically, you
must follow the author's description of what happens
when one falls in love. Be sure that you understand the
concept of "ego boundaries" and the illusions created by
falling in love. Although the excerpt does not include
Peck's definition of love (as opposed to falling in love),
you readily can supply this definition by converting
Scott's negative definition—that is, saying what falling in
love is not—into a positive one. Ask yourself if you willingly would give up falling in love if the sacrifice would
guarantee true love. Try to play devil's advocate by making a case for the act of falling in love as an integral part
of true love.

Of all the misconceptions about love the most powerful and   1
pervasive is the belief that "falling in love" is love or at least one

of the manifestations of love. It is a potent misconception, because falling in love is subjectively experienced in a very powerful fashion as an experience of love. When a person falls in love what he or she certainly feels is "I love him" or "I love her." But two problems are immediately apparent. The first is that the experience of falling in love is specifically a sex-linked erotic experience. We do not fall in love with our children even though we may love them very deeply. We do not fall in love with our friends of the same sex—unless we are homosexually oriented—even though we may care for them greatly. We fall in love only when we are consciously or unconsciously sexually motivated. The second problem is that the experience of falling in love is invariably temporary. No matter whom we fall in love with, we sooner or later fall out of love if the relationship continues long enough. This is not to say that we invariably cease loving the person with whom we fell in love. But it is to say that the feeling of ecstatic lovingness that characterizes the experience of falling in love always passes. The honeymoon always ends. The bloom of romance always fades.

2   To understand the nature of the phenomenon of falling in love and the inevitability of its ending, it is necessary to examine the nature of what psychiatrists call ego boundaries. From what we can ascertain by indirect evidence, it appears that the newborn infant during the first few months of its life does not distinguish between itself and the rest of the universe. When it moves its arms and legs, the world is moving. When it is hungry, the world is hungry. When it sees its mother move, it is as if it is moving. When its mother sings, the baby does not know that it is itself not making the sound. It cannot distinguish itself from the crib, the room and its parents. The animate and the inanimate are the same. There is no distinction yet between I and thou. It and the world are one. There are no boundaries, no separations. There is no identity.

3   But with experience the child begins to experience itself—namely, as an entity separate from the rest of the world. When it is hungry, mother doesn't always appear to feed it. When it is playful, mother doesn't always want to play. The child then has the experience of its wishes not being its mother's command. Its will is experienced as something separate from its mother's behavior. A sense of the "me" begins to develop. This interaction between the infant and the mother is believed to be the ground out of which the child's sense of identity begins to grow. It has been observed that when the interaction between the infant and its mother is grossly

disturbed—for example, when there is no mother, no satisfactory mother substitute or when because of her own mental illness the mother is totally uncaring or uninterested—then the infant grows into a child or adult whose sense of identity is grossly defective in the most basic ways.

As the infant recognizes its will to be its own and not that of 4 the universe, it begins to make other distinctions between itself and the world. When it wills movement, its arm waves before its eyes, but neither the crib nor the ceiling move. Thus the child learns that its arm and its will are connected, and therefore that its arm is *its* and not something or someone else's. In this manner, during the first year of life, we learn the fundamentals of who we are and who we are not, what we are and what we are not. By the end of our first year we know that this is my arm, my foot, my head, my tongue, my eyes and even my viewpoint, my voice, my thoughts, my stomachache, and my feelings. We know our size and our physical limits. These limits are our boundaries. The knowledge of these limits inside our minds is what is meant by ego boundaries.

The development of ego boundaries is a process that continues 5 through childhood into adolescence and even into adulthood, but the boundaries established later are more psychic than physical. For instance, the age between two and three is typically a time when the child comes to terms with the limits of its power. While before this time the child has learned that its wish is not necessarily its mother's command, it still clings to the possibility that its wish might be its mother's command and the feeling that its wish should be her command. It is because of this hope and feeling that the two-year-old usually attempts to act like a tyrant and autocrat, trying to give orders to its parents, siblings and family pets as if they were menials in its own private army, and responds with regal fury when they won't be dictated to. Thus parents speak of this age as "the terrible twos." By the age of three the child has usually become more tractable and mellow as a result of an acceptance of the reality of its own relative powerlessness. Still, the possibility of omnipotence is such a sweet, sweet dream that it cannot be completely given up even after several years of very painful confrontation with one's own impotence. Although the child of three has come to accept the reality of the boundaries of its power, it will continue to escape occasionally for some years to come into a world of fantasy in which the possibility of omnipotence (particularly its own) still exists. This is the world of Superman and Captain Marvel. Yet gradually even the superheroes are given up, and by the time of mid-adolescence, young people know that they are individuals, confined to the boundaries of their flesh and the limits of their power, each one a relatively frail and impotent organism, existing only by cooperation within a group of fellow organisms called society. Within this group they are not particularly distinguished, yet they are isolated from others by their individual identities, boundaries and limits.

6   It is lonely behind these boundaries. Some people—particularly those whom psychiatrists call schizoid—because of unpleasant, traumatizing experiences in childhood, perceive the world outside of themselves as unredeemably dangerous, hostile, confusing and unnurturing. Such people feel their boundaries to be protecting and comforting and find a sense of safety in their loneliness. But most of us feel our loneliness to be painful and yearn to escape from behind the walls of our individual identities to a condition in which we can be more unified with the world outside of ourselves. The experience of falling in love allows us this escape—temporarily. The essence of the phenomenon of falling in love is a sudden collapse of a section of an individual's ego boundaries, permitting one to merge his or her identity with that of another person. The sudden release of oneself from oneself, the explosive pouring out of oneself into the beloved, and the dramatic surcease of loneliness accompanying this collapse of ego boundaries is experienced by most of us as ecstatic. We and our beloved are one! Loneliness is no more!

7   In some respects (but certainly not in all) the act of falling in love is an act of regression. The experience of merging with the loved one has in it echoes from the time when we were merged with our mothers in infancy. Along with the merging we also reexperience the sense of omnipotence which we had to give up in our journey out of childhood. All things seem possible! United with our beloved we feel we can conquer all obstacles. We believe that the strength of our love will cause the forces of opposition to bow down in submission and melt away into the darkness. All problems will be overcome. The future will be all light. The unreality of these feelings when we have fallen in love is essentially the same as the unreality of the two-year-old who feels itself to be king of the family and the world with power unlimited.

8   Just as reality intrudes upon the two-year-old's fantasy of omnipotence so does reality intrude upon the fantastic unity of the couple who have fallen in love. Sooner or later, in response to the problems of daily living, individual will reassert itself. He wants

to have sex; she doesn't. She wants to go to the movies; he doesn't. He wants to put money in the bank; she wants a dishwasher. She wants to talk about her job; he wants to talk about his. She doesn't like his friends; he doesn't like hers. So both of them, in the privacy of their hearts, begin to come to the sickening realization that they are not one with the beloved, that the beloved has and will continue to have his or her own desires, tastes, prejudices and timing different from the other's. One by one, gradually or suddenly, the ego boundaries snap back into place; gradually or suddenly, they fall out of love. Once again they are two separate individuals. At this point they begin either to dissolve the ties of their relationship or to initiate the work of real loving.

By my use of the word "real" I am implying that the perception 9 that we are loving when we fall in love is a false perception—that our subjective sense of lovingness is an illusion. Full elaboration of real love will be deferred until later in this section. However, by stating that it is when a couple falls out of love they may begin to really love I am also implying that real love does not have its roots in a feeling of love. To the contrary, real love often occurs in a context in which the feeling of love is lacking, when we act lovingly despite the fact that we don't feel loving. Assuming the reality of the definition of love with which we started, the experience of "falling in love" is not real love for the several reasons that follow.

Falling in love is not an act of will. It is not a conscious choice. 10 No matter how open to or eager for it we may be, the experience may still elude us. Contrarily, the experience may capture us at times when we are definitely not seeking it, when it is inconvenient and undesirable. We are as likely to fall in love with someone with whom we are obviously ill matched as with someone more suitable. Indeed, we may not even like or admire the object of our passion, yet, try as we might, we may not be able to fall in love with a person whom we deeply respect and with whom a deep relationship would be in all ways desirable. This is not to say that the experience of falling in love is immune to discipline. Psychiatrists, for instance, frequently fall in love with their patients, just as their patients fall in love with them, yet out of duty to the patient and their role they are usually able to abort the collapse of their ego boundaries and give up the patient as a romantic object. The struggle and suffering of the discipline involved may be enormous. But discipline and will can only control the experience; they cannot create it. We can choose how to respond to the experience of falling in love, but we cannot choose the experience itself.

11   Falling in love is not an extension of one's limits or boundaries; it is a partial and temporary collapse of them. The extension of one's limits requires effort; falling in love is effortless. Lazy and undisciplined individuals are as likely to fall in love as energetic and dedicated ones. Once the precious moment of falling in love has passed and the boundaries have snapped back into place, the individual may be disillusioned, but is usually none the larger for the experience. When limits are extended or stretched, however, they tend to stay stretched. Real love is a permanently self-enlarging experience. Falling in love is not.

12   Falling in love has little to do with purposively nurturing one's spiritual development. If we have any purpose in mind when we fall in love it is to terminate our own loneliness and perhaps insure this result through marriage. Certainly we are not thinking of spiritual development. Indeed, after we have fallen in love and before we have fallen out of love again we feel that we have arrived, that the heights have been attained, that there is both no need and no possibility of going higher. We do not feel ourselves to be in any need of development; we are totally content to be where we are. Our spirit is at peace. Nor do we perceive our beloved as being in need of spiritual development. To the contrary, we perceive him or her as perfect, as having been perfected. If we see any faults in our beloved, we perceive them as insignificant—little quirks or darling eccentricities that only add color and charm.

13   If falling in love is not love, then what is it other than a temporary and partial collapse of ego boundaries? I do not know. But the sexual specificity of the phenomenon leads me to suspect that it is a genetically determined instinctual component of mating behavior. In other words, the temporary collapse of ego boundaries that constitutes falling in love is a stereotypic response of human beings to a configuration of internal sexual drives and external sexual stimuli, which serves to increase the probability of sexual pairing and bonding so as to enhance the survival of the species. Or to put it in another, rather crass way, falling in love is a trick that our genes pull on our otherwise perceptive mind to hoodwink or trap us into marriage. Frequently the trick goes awry one way or another, as when the sexual drives and stimuli are homosexual or when other forces—parental interference, mental illness, conflicting responsibilities or mature self-discipline—supervene to prevent the bonding.

On the other hand, without this trick, this illusory and inevitably temporary (it would not be practical were it not temporary) regression to infantile merging and omnipotence, many of us who are happily or unhappily married today would have retreated in wholehearted terror from the realism of the marriage vows.

Thinking Critically About This Reading

1. Throughout the essay, Dr. Peck suggests that *falling in love* is not at all the same as *being in love*. In your opinion, what is the major difference? Give examples that support your answer.

2. Although Dr. Peck himself is not completely sure why people have been falling in love throughout recorded history, he suspects why. What is his suspicion? Do you agree or disagree with his view? Give reasons that support your answers.

3. Do you agree with the author's argument that falling in love promises far more than it delivers? Support your answer with examples from personal experience or observation.

4. Dr. Scott states that the typical two-year-old acts like a tyrant because the child believes she or he is omnipotent. What other theories could be proposed to explain such behavior?

5. What results flow from the collapse of ego boundaries when a person falls in love? Describe several results you personally have experienced or observed. What are the advantages and disadvantages of the collapse? Will Dr. Peck's essay help you avoid the pitfalls of falling in love? Why? Why not?

Understanding the Writer's Process

1. On which does the author place more emphasis—the cause or the effect of falling in love? Why?

2. The author provides a definition of love in paragraphs 10, 11, and 12. How does he go about his definition? How effective is this method?

3. How does the author support the proposition that sooner or later reality intrudes upon the love fantasy?

4. How does Dr. Peck attempt to prove that falling in love is an act of immaturity?

5. What is the purpose of the exclamations at the end of paragraph 6? What is the purpose of the parentheses at the beginning of paragraph 7?

Examining the Writer's Language

1. Write a brief definitional paragraph on each of the following terms: ego boundaries (paragraphs 2 and 5), the world of Superman and Captain Marvel (paragraph 5), "the terrible twos" (paragraph 5).
2. Although Dr. Peck never formally defines *schizoid personality* (paragraph 6), he provides clues through the use of context. What did you learn about schizoid personality from the context in which the term is used?
3. How does the language of paragraph 7 suit the subject that is being discussed?
4. How is the transition made from paragraph 9 to paragraph 10?
5. In paragraph 11, what key words indicate the difference between *real love* and *falling in love*?

Suggestions for Writing

1. Write an essay in which you answer the question: How does being in love differ from falling in love?
2. Write an essay in which you suggest the major causes of falling in love.

LIKE A WINDING SHEET

Ann Petry

Ann Petry (b. 1912) is an American news reporter and fiction writer. Born and reared in Connecticut, she was educated at the University of Connecticut and at Columbia University. At the age of twenty-six, after having spent some time working as a pharmacist, she decided that writing was her vocation and went to work

as a reporter for the Amsterdam News *and later for*
The People's Voice. *In 1943 she covered the Harlem
riot, on which she based her first short novel,* In Darkness. *It was followed by a full-length novel,* The Street
*(1946), also based on her experiences while living in
Harlem. This novel established Petry as a fiction writer
of note. She is much admired for the way her stories
treat race relationships in the United States—focusing
not only on the political context but also on the complex
psychological and social implications. She has a brilliant capacity for making her readers feel the oppression and victimization of the characters she portrays.*

Preparing to Read This Selection Critically

When reading this story, you will be tempted to
judge Johnson harshly because his act of violence seems
unprovoked and brutally savage. Delay such a judgment
until you have placed yourself in his position, feeling
every event of the day he has spent at home and at work.

He had planned to get up before Mae did and surprise her by   1
fixing breakfast. Instead he went back to sleep and she got out of
bed so quietly he didn't know she wasn't there beside him until he
woke up and heard the queer soft gurgle of water running out of
the sink in the bathroom.

He knew he ought to get up but instead he put his arms across   2
his forehead to shut the afternoon sunlight out of his eyes, pulled
his legs up close to his body, testing them to see if the ache was
still in them.

Mae had finished in the bathroom. He could tell because she   3
never closed the door when she was in there and now the sweet
smell of talcum powder was drifting down the hall and into the
bedroom. Then he heard her coming down the hall.

"Hi, babe," she said affectionately.   4

"Hum," he grunted, and moved his arms away from his head,   5
opened one eye.

"It's a nice morning."   6

"Yeah." He rolled over and the sheet twisted around him,   7
outlining his thighs, his chest. "You mean afternoon, don't ya?"

8   Mae looked at the twisted sheet and giggled. "Looks like a winding sheet," she said. "A shroud—" Laughter tangled with her words and she had to pause for a moment before she could continue. "You look like a huckleberry—in a winding sheet—"

9   "That's no way to talk. Early in the day like this," he protested.

10   He looked at his arms silhouetted against the white of the sheets. They were inky black by contrast and he had to smile in spite of himself and he lay there smiling and savoring the sweet sound of Mae's giggling.

11   "Early?" She pointed a finger at the alarm clock on the table near the bed and giggled again. "It's almost four o'clock. And if you don't spring up out of there, you're going to be late again."

12   "What do you mean 'again'?"

13   "Twice last week. Three times the week before. And once the week before and—"

14   "I can't get used to sleeping in the daytime," he said fretfully. He pushed his legs out from under the covers experimentally. Some of the ache had gone out of them but they weren't really rested yet. "It's too light for good sleeping. And all that standing beats the hell out of my legs."

15   "After two years you oughta be used to it," Mae said.

16   He watched her as she fixed her hair, powdered her face, slipped into a pair of blue denim overalls. She moved quickly and yet she didn't seem to hurry.

17   "You look like you'd had plenty of sleep," he said lazily. He had to get up but he kept putting the moment off, not wanting to move, yet he didn't dare let his legs go completely limp because if he did he'd go back to sleep. It was getting later and later but the thought of putting his weight on his legs kept him lying there.

18   When he finally got up he had to hurry, and he gulped his breakfast so fast that he wondered if his stomach could possibly use food thrown at it at such a rate of speed. He was still wondering about it as he and Mae were putting their coats on in the hall.

19   Mae paused to look at the calendar. "It's the thirteenth," she said. Then a faint excitement in her voice, "Why, it's Friday the thirteenth." She had one arm in her coat sleeve and she held it there while she stared at the calendar. "I oughta stay home," she said. "I shouldn't go outa the house."

20   "Aw, don't be a fool," he said. "Today's payday. And payday is a good luck day everywhere, any way you look at it." And as she stood hesitating he said, "Aw, come on."

And he was late for work again because they spent fifteen 21
minutes arguing before he could convince her she ought to go to
work just the same. He had to talk persuasively, urging her gently,
and it took time. But he couldn't bring himself to talk to her roughly
or threaten to strike her like a lot of men might have done. He
wasn't made that way.

So when he reached the plant he was late and he had to wait 22
to punch the time clock because the day–shift workers were streaming
out in long lines, in groups and bunches that impeded his progress.

Even now just starting his workday his legs ached. He had to 23
force himself to struggle past the outgoing workers, punch the time
clock, and get the little cart he pushed around all night, because he
kept toying with the idea of going home and getting back in bed.

He pushed the cart out on the concrete floor, thinking that if 24
this was his plant he'd make a lot of changes in it. There were too
many standing–up jobs for one thing. He'd figure out some way
most of 'em could be done sitting down and he'd put a lot more
benches around. And this job he had—this job that forced him to
walk ten hours a night, pushing this little cart, well, he'd turn it
into a sitting–down job. One of those little trucks they used around
railroad stations would be good for a job like this. Guys sat on a
seat and the thing moved easily, taking up little room and turning
in hardly any space at all, like on a dime.

He pushed the cart near the foreman. He never could remem- 25
ber to refer to her as the forelady even in his mind. It was funny
to have a white woman for a boss in a plant like this one.

She was sore about something. He could tell by the way her 26
face was red and her eyes were half–shut until they were slits.
Probably been out late and didn't get enough sleep. He avoided
looking at her and hurried a little, head down, as he passed her
though he couldn't resist stealing a glance at her out of the corner
of his eye. He saw the edge of the light–colored slacks she wore
and the tip end of a big tan shoe.

"Hey, Johnson!" the woman said. 27

The machines had started full blast. The whirr and the grinding 28
made the building shake, made it impossible to hear conversations.
The men and women at the machines talked to each other but looking at them from just a little distance away, they appeared to be
simply moving their lips because you couldn't hear what they were
saying. Yet the woman's voice cut across the machine sounds—harsh,
angry.

29   He turned his head slowly. "Good evenin', Mrs. Scott," he said, and waited.

30   "You're late again."

31   "That's right. My legs were bothering me."

32   The woman's face grew redder, angrier looking. "Half this shift comes in late," she said. "And you're the worst one of all. You're always late. Whatsa matter with ya?"

33   "It's my legs," he said. "Somehow they don't ever get rested. I don't seem to get used to sleeping days. And I just can't get started."

34   "Excuses. You guys always got excuses," her anger grew and spread. "Every guy comes in here late always has an excuse. His wife's sick or his grandmother died or somebody in the family had to go to the hospital," she paused, drew a deep breath. "And the niggers is the worse. I don't care what's wrong with your legs. You get in here on time. I'm sick of you niggers—"

35   "You got the right to get mad," he interrupted softly. "You got the right to cuss me four ways to Sunday but I ain't letting nobody call me a nigger."

36   He stepped closer to her. His fists were doubled. His lips were drawn back in a thin narrow line. A vein in his forehead stood out swollen, thick.

37   And the woman backed away from him, not hurriedly but slowly—two, three steps back.

38   "Aw, forget it," she said. "I didn't mean nothing by it. It slipped out. It was accident." The red of her face deepened until the small blood vessels in her cheeks were purple. "Go on and get to work," she urged. And she took three more slow backward steps.

39   He stood motionless for a moment and then turned away from the sight of the red lipstick on her mouth that made him remember that the foreman was a woman. And he couldn't bring himself to hit a woman. He felt a curious tingling in his fingers and he looked down at his hands. They were clenched tight, hard, ready to smash some of those small purple veins in her face.

40   He pushed the cart ahead of him, walking slowly. When he turned his head, she was staring in his direction, mopping her forehead with a dark blue handkerchief. Their eyes met and then they both looked away.

41   He didn't glance in her direction again but moved past the long work benches, carefully collecting the finished parts, going slowly and steadily up and down, and back and forth the length of

the building, and as he walked he forced himself to swallow his anger, get rid of it.

And he succeeded so that he was able to think about what had happened without getting upset about it. An hour went by but the tension stayed in his hands. They were clenched and knotted on the handles of the cart as though ready to aim a blow.

And he thought he should have hit her anyway, smacked her hard in the face, felt the soft flesh of her face give under the hardness of his hands. He tried to make his hands relax by offering them a description of what it would have been like to strike her because he had the queer feeling that his hands were not exactly a part of him anymore—they had developed a separate life of their own over which he had no control. So he dwelt on the pleasure his hands would have felt—both of them cracking at her, first one and then the other. If he had done that his hands would have felt good now—relaxed, rested.

And he decided that even if he'd lost his job for it, he should have let her have it and it would have been a long time, maybe the rest of her life, before she called anybody else a nigger.

The only trouble was he couldn't hit a woman. A woman couldn't hit back the same way a man did. But it would have been a deeply satisfying thing to have cracked her narrow lips wide open with just one blow, beautifully timed and with all his weight in back of it. That way he would have gotten rid of all the energy and tension his anger had created in him. He kept remembering how his heart had started pumping blood so fast he had felt it tingle even in the tips of his fingers.

With the approach of night, fatigue nibbled at him. The corners of his mouth drooped, the frown between his eyes deepened, his shoulders sagged; but his hands stayed tight and tense. As the hours dragged by he noticed that the women workers had started to snap and snarl at each other. He couldn't hear what they said because of the sound of machines but he could see the quick lip movements that sent words tumbling from the sides of their mouths. They gestured irritably with their hands and scowled as their mouths moved.

Their violent jerky motions told him that it was getting close on to quitting time but somehow he felt that the night still stretched ahead of him, composed of endless hours of steady walking on his aching legs. When the whistle finally blew he went on pushing the cart, unable to believe that it had sounded. The whirring of the machines died away to a murmur and he knew then that he'd really heard the whistle. He stood still for a moment, filled with a relief that made him sigh.

48   Then he moved briskly, putting the cart in the storeroom, hurrying to take his place in the line forming before the paymaster. That was another thing he'd change, he thought. He'd have the pay envelopes handed to the people right at their benches so there wouldn't be ten or fifteen minutes lost waiting for the pay. He always got home about fifteen minutes late on payday. They did it better in the plant where Mae worked, brought the money right to them at their benches.

49   He stuck his pay envelope in his pants' pocket and followed the line of workers heading for the subway in a slow–moving stream. He glanced up at the sky. It was a nice night, the sky looked packed full to running over with stars. And he thought if he and Mae would go right to bed when they got home from work they'd catch a few hours of darkness for sleeping. But they never did. They fooled around—cooking and eating and listening to the radio and he always stayed in a big chair in the living room and went almost but not quite to sleep and when they finally got to bed it was five or six in the morning and daylight was already seeping around the edges of the sky.

50   He walked slowly, putting off the moment when he would have to plunge into the crowd hurrying toward the subway. It was a long ride to Harlem and tonight the thought of it appalled him. He paused outside an all–night restaurant to kill time, so that some of the first rush of workers would be gone when he reached the subway.

51   The lights in the restaurant were brilliant, enticing. There was life and motion inside. And as he looked through the window he thought that everything within range of his eyes gleamed—the long imitation marble counter, the tall stools, the white porcelain–topped tables and especially the big metal coffee urn right near the window. Steam issued from its top and a gas flame flickered under it—a lively, dancing, blue flame.

52   A lot of the workers from his shift—men and women—were lining up near the coffee urn. He watched them walk to the porcelain–topped tables carrying steaming cups of coffee and he saw that just the smell of the coffee lessened the fatigue lines in their faces. After the first sip their faces softened, they smiled, they began to talk and laugh.

On a sudden impulse he shoved the door open and joined the   53
line in front of the coffee urn. The line moved slowly. And as he
stood there the smell of the coffee, the sound of the laughter and
of the voices, helped dull the sharp ache in his legs.

He didn't pay any attention to the white girl who was serving   54
the coffee at the urn. He kept looking at the cups in the hands of
the men who had been ahead of him. Each time a man stepped out
of the line with one of the thick white cups the fragrant steam got
in his nostrils. He saw that they walked carefully so as not to spill
a single drop. There was a froth of bubbles at the top of each cup
and he thought about how he would let the bubbles break against
his lips before he actually took a big deep swallow.

Then it was his turn. "A cup of coffee," he said, just as he had   55
heard the others say.

The white girl looked past him, put her hands up to her head
and gently lifted her hair away from the back of her neck, tossing
her head back a little. "No more coffee for a while," she said.

He wasn't certain he'd heard her correctly and he said "What?"   56
blankly.

"No more coffee for a while," she repeated.   57

There was silence behind him and then uneasy movement. He   58
thought someone would say something, ask why or protest, but
there was only silence and then a faint shuffling sound as though
the men standing behind him had simultaneously shifted their
weight from one foot to the other.

He looked at the girl without saying anything. He felt his hands   59
begin to tingle and the tingling went all the way down to his finger
tips so that he glanced down at them. They were clenched tight,
hard, into fists. Then he looked at the girl again. What he wanted
to do was hit her so hard that the scarlet lipstick on her mouth
would smear and spread over her nose, her chin, out toward her
cheeks, so hard that she would never toss her head again and refuse
a man a cup of coffee because he was black.

He estimated the distance across the counter and reached for-   60
ward, balancing his weight on the balls of his feet, ready to let the
blow go. And then his hands fell back down to his sides because
he forced himself to lower them, to unclench them and make them
dangle loose. The effort took his breath away because his hands
fought against him. But he couldn't hit her. He couldn't even now
bring himself to hit a woman, not even this one, who had refused
him a cup of coffee with a toss of her head. He kept seeing the

gesture with which she had lifted the length of her blond hair from the back of her neck as expressive of her contempt for him.

61   When he went out the door he didn't look back. If he had he would have seen the flickering blue flame under the shiny coffee urn being extinguished. The line of men who had stood behind him lingered a moment to watch the people drinking coffee at the tables and then they left just as he had without having had the coffee they wanted so badly. The girl behind the counter poured water in the urn and swabbed it out and as she waited for the water to run out, she lifted her hair gently from the back of her neck and tossed her head before she began making a fresh lot of coffee.

62   But he had walked away without a backward look, his head down, his hands in his pockets, raging at himself and whatever it was inside of him that had forced him to stand quiet and still when he wanted to strike out.

63   The subway was crowded and he had to stand. He tried grasping an overhead strap and his hands were too tense to grip it. So he moved near the train door and stood there swaying back and forth with the rocking of the train. The roar of the train beat inside his head, making it ache and throb, and the pain in his legs clawed up into his groin so that he seemed to be bursting with pain and he told himself that it was due to all that anger–born energy that had piled up in him and not been used and so it had spread through him like a poison—from his feet and legs all the way up to his head.

64   Mae was in the house before he was. He knew she was home before he put the key in the door of the apartment. The radio was going. She had it tuned up loud and she was singing along with it.

65   "Hello, babe," she called out, as soon as he opened the door.

66   He tried to say "hello" and it came out half grunt and half sigh.

67   "You sure sound cheerful," she said.

68   She was in the bedroom and he went and leaned against the doorjamb. The denim overalls she wore to work were carefully draped over the back of a chair by the bed. She was standing in front of the dresser, tying the sash of a yellow housecoat around her waist and chewing gum vigorously as she admired her reflection in the mirror over the dresser.

69   "Whatsa matter?" she said. "You get bawled out by the boss or somep'n?"

70   "Just tired," he said slowly. "For God's sake, do you have to crack that gum like that?"

"You don't have to lissen to me," she said complacently. She 71
patted a curl in place near the side of her head and then lifted her
hair away from the back of her neck, ducking her head forward and
then back.

He winced away from the gesture. "What you got to be always 72
fooling with your hair for?" he protested.

"Say, what's the matter with you anyway?" She turned away 73
from the mirror to face him, put her hands on her hips. "You ain't
been in the house two minutes and you're picking on me."

He didn't answer her because her eyes were angry and he 74
didn't want to quarrel with her. They'd been married too long and
got along too well and so he walked all the way into the room and
sat down in the chair by the bed and stretched his legs out in front
of him, putting his weight on the heels of his shoes, leaning way
back in the chair, not saying anything.

"Lissen," she said sharply. "I've got to wear those overalls 75
again tomorrow. You're going to get them all wrinkled up leaning
against them like that."

He didn't move. He was too tired and his legs were throbbing 76
now that he had sat down. Besides the overalls were already wrinkled and dirty, he thought. They couldn't help but be for she'd worn
them all week. He leaned farther back in the chair.

"Come on, get up," she ordered. 77

"Oh, what the hell," he said wearily, and got up from the 78
chair. "I'd just as soon live in a subway. There'd be just as much
place to sit down."

He saw that her sense of humor was struggling with her anger. 79
But her sense of humor won because she giggled.

"Aw, come on and eat," she said. There was a coaxing note 80
in her voice. "You're nothing but an old hungry nigger trying to act
tough and—" she paused to giggle and then continued, "You—"

He had always found her giggling pleasant and deliberately 81
said things that might amuse her and then waited, listening for the
delicate sound to emerge from her throat. This time he didn't even
hear the giggle. He didn't let her finish what she was saying. She
was standing close to him and that funny tingling started in his
finger tips, went fast up his arms and sent his fist shooting straight
for her face.

There was the smacking sound of soft flesh being struck by a 82
hard object and it wasn't until she screamed that he realized he had
hit her in the mouth—so hard that the dark red lipstick had blurred

and spread over her full lips, reaching up toward the tip of her nose, down toward her chin, out toward her cheeks.

83   The knowledge that he had struck her seeped through him slowly and he was appalled but he couldn't drag his hands away from her face. He kept striking her and he thought with horror that something inside him was holding him, binding him to this act, wrapping and twisting about him so that he had to continue it. He had lost all control over his hands. And he groped for a phrase, a word, something to describe what this thing was like that was happening to him and he thought it was like being enmeshed in a winding sheet—that was it—like a winding sheet. And even as the thought formed in his mind, his hands reached for her face again and yet again.

Thinking Critically About This Reading

1. What is the real cause of Johnson's eruption of violence? Does he secretly hate his wife? Or are there other reasons that led to the terrible final scene between him and her?

2. After analyzing fully the entire confrontation between Johnson and his wife, how justified do you feel he was in his actions? What is your judgment of what he did? What alternative action could he have taken?

3. What other contexts beside the context of personal interaction does the author use as a backdrop to her story? Is her narration realistic or does she seem to create an imaginary, fantastic world?

4. What steps can any neighborhood take to lessen the stress and tension that lead to explosive race reactions? Is it important to use preventive measures or should those in power have the right to force the powerless to serve them?

5. The foreman at the plant where Johnson works is a woman. What, if anything, does her gender add to the development of the story? Would it change the story significantly if she had been a man? Why or why not?

Understanding the Writer's Process

1. How does this fictional account differ from a more prosaic causal analysis, such as, say, the one by Scott Peck titled "Why We Fall in Love" (see pp. 512–518)?

2. How does the author convey the emotions building up inside Johnson?

3. How is the title of the story related to its theme or meaning?

4. Good stories always consist of some kind of conflict which is resolved in a climax. What is the conflict in this story and when is it resolved?

Examining the Writer's Language

1. Choose the correct use of the following italicized words, taken from the story:

    a. The dark horse was *silhouetted* against the lighted sky.

    b. All of the children *silhouetted* the food rapidly.

    c. He laughed so hard that he *silhouetted* himself.

    a. All the toys were *impeded* to the cellar.

    b. Anyone who gets *impeded* will arrive first.

    c. My grades *impeded* my progress in college.

    a. In a shrill voice, he yelled *complacently*.

    b. She sat by the fireplace, reading *complacently*.

    c. Because it was snowing, they shivered *complacently*.

    a. The buyer was *appalled* by the high price of food.

    b. Every student was warmly *appalled* by the movie.

    c. I was delighted and *appalled* to find the money.

    a. To be *enmeshed* means to be free and clear.

    b. To be *enmeshed* means to be warned.

    c. To be *enmeshed* means to be entangled.

2. What does the language of paragraphs 34 and 38 reveal about the forewoman who is Johnson's boss?

3. What is the importance of the word "hands" in paragraphs 42 and 43?

4. What words does the author use to reveal the fatigue Johnson feels?

5. What is the dominant impression created by the language of paragraph 51?

Writing Assignment Based on "Like a Winding Sheet"

Reread "Like a Winding Sheet," focusing your attention on all of the characters in the story. Then write a literary paper analyzing the causes leading to the enormous anger displayed by Johnson. Your thesis should include both the cause and effect involved in your analysis. Be sure to back your views with specific passages from the story.

STUDENT ESSAY (IN PROCESS) ANALYZING CAUSE

Sharon R. Aldridge

Sharon R. Aldridge has entered college to pursue a career in psychology. She brings to her studies an inquiring spirit and an enthusiasm for learning. Reflecting her determination to develop better skills, Sharon has taken great pains to improve her writing through careful editing.

First Draft   Sharon Aldridge

English 101

The Marriage of Anne

Set against a backdrop of tradition and convention are the unusual, out-of-the ordinary human behaviors we may often wonder at, and speculate upon. Included in these is a cat-

I need a sharper paragraph

*See below

egory that involves unconventional marital partnerships. A May-December romance, as one such example, may involve other lesser known factors for existing than the expected monetary gain.

conciseness lacking

Anne had a bright future before her. At twenty-four, she was ~~an attractive, red haired, young lady who had~~ *a lovely redhead, with* a number of young men for suitors and the choice of several ~~interesting~~ *promising* careers ~~she was vacillating between.~~ *Furthermore,* It was a time when women were ~~trying~~ *being allowed* to define their roles in society. ~~Woman was being declared~~ *they were proclaimed* "Liberated".

Transition needed

~~Suddenly~~ *But* Suddenly Anne became engaged to a grey-haired, paunchy, elderly man forty years her senior. Her decision to settle down and get married was startling to her friends, while her choice of partners was *utterly* shocking. Although everyone liked and admired her fiance, ~~John, who was~~ a retired screen writer and respected *author* ~~writer~~ of fiction, ~~they~~ *friends and family* questioned Anne's ~~possible~~ motives for making so firm a commitment to such ~~a~~ *an eccentric* relationship. ~~The relationship for~~

edit for smoothness

Anne, ~~had,~~ however, ~~three powerful dynamics~~ *had* three powerful dynamics that seduced her unwittingly into the union. ~~Anne's~~ *deep* insecurity, ~~her~~ *a strong* conflict ~~of~~ *between* dependency, *and* independency, and ~~her~~ *a* fear of intimacy ~~were stabilized by his maturity and guiding force.~~

*Because society is mired in tradition and convention, any human behavior that flouts the norm will usually cause either passionate outrage or endless notoriety. Marriages, for instance, cannot break certain unspoken but sacred rules without baffling or even hurting those close to the alliance. The marriage *of Anne illustrates this point. Anne married a man forty years her senior; yet, she did not do so for money. What, then, were the causes leading to this May-December romance?*

misplaced clause

fine-tuning

Anne felt with John a renewed sense of self-confidence, along with a clearer focus on who she was and where she wanted to go. Her sense of ~~her~~ self had been shaken ~~from the~~ *by recurrent* shift~~ing of~~ *s in* values and attitudes she had undergone in her late teens and early twenties as she explored relationships and tried on new roles.

misplaced phrase

A few failures along the way with men had left her bruised and wary. An over-rigid moral up- *choked* bringing still ~~pulled at~~ her, even as ~~Anne hun~~ *she gasped* ~~gorily sought~~ for *fresh* philosophical ~~expansion~~ *freezes*. At this ~~ripe~~ *critical* moment in her life, ~~John stepped in~~ *John's influence* ~~and~~ seemed to open ~~so many new~~ *into exciting new territory* doors ~~for her~~, teaching her from the vastness of his experience about art, literature, and philosophy.

more colorful diction needed

Be specific here. What did he teach her?

John introduced Anne to the poetry of T.S. Eliot, Robert Frost, and Emily Dickinson. Together they pored of the novels of William Faulkner and F. Scott Fitzgerald. He took her to exotic plays, to fascinating lectures, and to soul-quenching symphonies. In short, through John, Anne explored new worlds of intellectual and cultural riches.

His attention flattered her, his encouragement strengthened her, and his *gentleness* ~~caring~~ put salve to her wounds. At time went on, ~~paradoxically~~, she felt a return to innocence and wonder as new worlds opened to her. Also, *John's* ~~his~~ intelligent perceptions helped trigger in her depths she had never dreamed ~~of~~. *existed. To her amazement, she realized that she had a brain capable of understanding*

In John, Anne found ~~an excellent solu-tion~~ *a resolution* to her conflicting needs for independence *Plato, Emerson, Sartre, and many others*

and dependenc~~y~~e. At ~~his age~~ sixty-five, John was content to
sit back and ~~take things easy~~ live serenely, doing a bit of
writing from time to time and bus~~i~~ying himself
with a few hobbies and reading. *He was not compelled to burn the candle at both ends like younger men were.* Thus, Anne was free
to pursue her career, socialize, and in gen-
eral, to do ~~things~~ as she pleased. ~~But always,~~ However,
She could enroll in a college mythology class; she could learn to use a computer, or she could go to a movie by herself.
always John
there was ~~someone~~ to come home to, talk about
her day with, and unburden her problems to. ~~He~~ John
was a shoulder to lean on, and, ah yes, he was the ~~a~~ father she sometimes needed, and that rare ~~husband and friend~~ confidant
who would listen to her ideas. Early in the relationship, Anne could see that John offered
her a protection few other men ~~who knew~~ could
offer, and without risk to that fierce and
stubborn need in her to be her own person. John,
with a certain cunning wisdom, spotted her conflict of needing to need as well as her not
needing to need and he gave her space so that she never
felt like a caged bird.

Intimacy ~~was~~ a big problem for Anne, and
most particularly, intimacy with the opposite
sex. In John she found a way to fulfill ~~a~~ need
~~for~~ related~~ness~~ while still maintaining a certain distance. The age difference between them
became an asset. The young men she had known and
dated had been so demanding, both physically
and emotionally. On the other hand, John was
patient and careful, giving Anne the choice to
draw near as she chose or to put distance between them. This gave her a ~~greater~~ sense of

[margin annotations:] Transition needed · unnecessary

control in their relationship, something that had been missing ~~before in her life.~~ *in her romances with other men.* ~~It~~ *We* also gave her the opportunity to be more forward and aggressive in intimate moments if she *so* desired and to be challenged by a male who could be cool at times. Most of all, ~~His~~ *John's* respect for her privacy *Anne* gave ~~her~~ courage to be more open and vulnerable, to take risks in sharing herself with him, and to learn to trust her instincts in an intimate relationship. ~~This was another major issue that helped sway her to marry him.~~

Stronger conclusion needed

Tongues wagged and the neighbors took bets on how soon this odd love affair would sour. But it never did. John died and took with him Anne's undivided love and infinite gratitude. He was her Henry Higgins; she was his Eliza Doolittle

---

<u>Final Draft</u>   Sharon Aldridge

                                         English 101

The Marriage of Anne

Because society is mired in tradition and convention, any human behavior that flouts the norm will usually cause either passionate outrage or endless notoriety. Marriages, for instance, cannot break certain unspoken but sacred rules without baffling or even hurting those close to the alliance. The marriage of Anne illustrates that point. Anne married a man forty years her senior; yet, she did not do so for money. What, then, were the causes leading to this May–December romance?

Anne had a bright future before her. At twenty-four, she was a lovely redhead, with a number of young suitors and the choice of several promising careers. Furthermore, it was a time when women were being allowed to define their roles in society; they were proclaimed "liberated." But suddenly Anne became engaged to a grey-haired, paunchy, elderly man forty years her senior. Her decision to settle down and get married was startling to her friends while her choice of partners was utterly shocking. Although everyone liked and admired her fiance, a retired screen writer and respected author of fiction, friends and family questioned Anne's motives for making so firm a commitment to such an eccentric relationship. For Anne, however, the relationship had three powerful dynamics that seduced her unwittingly into the union: deep insecurity, a strong conflict between dependency and independency, and a fear of intimacy.

With John, Anne felt a renewed sense of self-confidence, along with a clearer focus on who she was and where she wanted to go. Her sense of self had been shaken by recurrent shifts in values and attitudes she had undergone in her late teens and early twenties as she explored relationships and tried new roles. Along the way, a few failures with men had left her bruised and wary. An over-rigid moral upbringing still choked her, even as she gasped for fresh philosophical breezes. At this critical moment in her life, John's influence

seemed to open doors into exciting new territory, teaching her from the vastness of his experience   about   art,   literature,   and
philosophy. John introduced Anne to the poetry
of T.S. Eliot, Robert Frost, and Emily Dickinson. Together they pored of the novels of William Faulkner and F. Scott Fitzgerald. He took
her to exotic plays, to fascinating lectures,
and to soul-quenching symphonies. In short,
through John, Anne explored new worlds of intellectual and cultural riches. His attention
flattered her, his encouragement strengthened
her, and his gentleness put salve to her
wounds. At time went on, she felt a return to
innocence and wonder as new worlds opened to
her. Also, John's intelligent perceptions
helped trigger in her depths she had never
dreamed existed. To her amazement, she
realized that she had a brain capable of understanding Plato, Emerson, Sartre, and many
others.

In John, Anne found a resolution to her
conflicting needs for independence and dependence. At sixty-five, John was content to sit
back and live serenely, doing a bit of writing
from time to time and busying himself with a few
hobbies and reading. He was not compelled to
burn the candle at both ends like younger men
were. Thus, Anne was free to pursue her career,
to socialize, and in general, to do as she
pleased. She could enroll in a college mythology class, she could learn to use a computer,
or she could go to a movie by herself. However,

there was always John to come home to, talk about her day with, and unburden her problems to. John was a shoulder to lean on, and, ah yes, he was the father she sometimes needed, and that rare confidant who would listen to her ideas. Early in the relationship, Anne could see that John offered her a protection few other men could offer, and without risk to that fierce and stubborn need in her to be her own person. John, with a certain cunning wisdom, spotted her conflict of needing to need as well as her not needing to need, and he gave her space so that she never felt like a caged bird.

Intimacy had always been a big problem for Anne, and most particularly, intimacy with the opposite sex. In John she found a way to fulfill her need to relate to a man while still maintaining a certain distance between her and him. The age difference between them became an asset. The young men she had known and dated had been so demanding, both physically and emotionally. They were tiring in their primitive urge to turn conversation into sex. On the other hand, John was patient and careful, giving Anne the choice to draw near as she chose, or to put distance between them. This gave her a sense of control in their relationship, something that had been missing in her romances with other men. He also gave her the opportunity to be more forward and aggressive in intimate moments if she so desired and to be challenged by a male who could be cool at times. Most of all, John's respect for her privacy gave Anne courage to be more open and vulnerable, to take risks in sharing herself with him, and to learn to trust her instincts in an intimate relationship.

Tongues wagged, and the neighbors took bets on how soon this odd love affair would sour. But it never did. John died and took with him Anne's undivided love and infinite gratitude. He was her Henry Higgins; she was his Eliza Doolittle.

"And this is the final question:
What, in your opinion, is to become of us all?"

10

Argumentation

HOW TO WRITE AN ARGUMENT

The written argument is an ancient composite form that harks back to the dawn of literacy. Its ultimate goal is to persuade the listener or reader to embrace a viewpoint. How to achieve this goal most effectively varies with audience and subject. Nevertheless, chances are that during the course of an argument you also will have to describe a point, draw a contrast, explain a process, or define a term—making your presentation a composite of techniques commonly practiced in other rhetorical modes.

Oral or written, an argument is essentially composed of appeals—either pleas made on behalf of your case or evidence cited in its support. However, common sense tells us that the strength and effectiveness of an appeal vary considerably with an audience's stake in an issue. For example, when arguing in favor of a zoning change to permit commercial building in a neighborhood that suffers high unemployment, the most effective appeal focuses on how the new zoning would create jobs. On the other hand, when arguing in favor of commercial zoning in a wealthy and historic district, the appeal should focus on allaying the fears of residents that the new building will be unsightly and inharmonious with its surroundings. Effective arguments always tailor their appeals to suit the circumstances of the issue and the disposition of the likely audience.

1. Begin with an Arguable Proposition

Some issues can be argued logically and some cannot. Among the unarguable are subjects grounded in personal value or faith, subjects unprovable by rational means, and subjects already decisively settled in the public consciousness. For example, you will never succeed in proving conclusively to everyone's satisfaction that abortion is a sin: that is strictly a personal belief. It is also extremely unlikely you will ever succeed in flatly demonstrating that spirits can communicate through mediums: Such a claim thus far has been impossible to settle by rational debate. Nor is it likely you could ever succeed in making a convincing case of the view that the planet Earth is flat. The Flat Earth Society notwithstanding, that issue is already so firmly established in the public consciousness that it is no longer rationally arguable.

In essence, then, you must make sure the proposition you intend to argue is in fact arguable. Sometimes only a slight shift in emphasis turns an unarguable issue into one that is arguable. Consider the following propositions:

Unarguable	Female prostitutes should be subject to registration and regular medical examinations because men have the right to know that the sex they're paying for is safe.
Arguable	Female prostitutes should be subject to registration and regular medical examinations as a preventative measure to check the spread of AIDS.
Unarguable	Hockey is surely the most loathsome "sport" ever invented.
Arguable	Because hockey has lately been marred by increasing outbreaks of violence among players during matches, the penalty of expulsion from the league should be levied against those players who are chronic brawlers.

First, men have none of the rights alleged in the first proposition. Second, that hockey is the "most loathsome" sport is an assertion of personal distaste, and as such cannot be made the basis of a logical argument.

Finally, avoid writing an essay on the obvious issue. Most students doubtless will write essays for or against such time-honored wrangles as abortion, nuclear disarmament, or capital punishment. Although compelling topics, they have been rehashed so often in student papers that long-suffering composition teachers dread reading about them. If you select an issue that your teacher either has never or only rarely seen before, chances are your essay will get a sympathetic reading—if only because it provides relief from the humdrum and the expected. One student of ours wrote an excellent essay arguing for prohibitive licensing fees to discourage recombitant DNA experiments; another wrote an intriguing essay arguing that the complete plays of Shakespeare should be mandatory reading for all high school students. Both essays were a welcome change from the usual cannon fodder of the argumentative essay.

2. Support Your Points

To assert a point is neither to support it automatically nor to prove it. If you declare that Shakespeare should be mandatory reading for all high school students because all speakers of English occasionally quote Shakespeare, you have done nothing more than make an empty and vain assertion. To advance the argument, you must provide proof. You might do so by writing a paragraph like this one:

> If you cannot understand my argument, and declare, "It's Greek to me," you are quoting Shakespeare; if you claim to be more sinned against than sinning, you are quoting Shakespeare; if you recall your salad days, you are quoting Shakespeare; if you act more in sorrow than in anger, if your wish is father to the thought, if your property has vanished into thin air, you are quoting Shakespeare; if you have ever refused to budge an inch or suffered from green-eyed jealousy, if you have played fast and loose, if you have been tongue-tied, a tower of strength, hood-winked or in a pickle, if you have knitted your brows, made a virtue of necessity, insisted on fair play, slept not one wink, stood on ceremony, danced attendance (on your lord and master), laughed yourself into stitches, had short shrift, cold comfort or too much of a good thing, if you have seen better days or lived in a fool's paradise—why, be that as it may, the more fool you, for it is a foregone conclusion that you are (as good luck would have it) quoting Shakespeare.
>
> BERNARD LEVIN, *Enthusiasms*

The writer's examples irresistibly prove his point: that without knowing it, most speakers of English regularly quote Shakespeare.

Examples aside, a writer may also support a point with facts, statistics, expert testimony, and logical reasoning. A fact is a statement that is true and verifiable (as opposed to an opinion, which is not). Facts are useful ammunition in some arguments, mere fluff in others. Although no recital of facts can convincingly settle an argument that hinges on disagreement over belief or value, in some arguments facts are compelling. Here, for example, is a sample of facts cited by a blue-ribbon committee commissioned by the President to study the condition of education in the United States:

> International comparisons of student achievement, completed a decade ago, reveal that on 19 academic tests American students were never first or second and, in comparison with other industrialized nations, were last seven times.

> Some 23 million American adults are functionally illiterate by the simple tests of everyday reading, writing, and comprehension.

The College Board's Scholastic Aptitude Tests (SAT) demonstrate a virtually unbroken decline from 1963 to 1980. Average verbal scores fell over 50 points and average mathematics
scores dropped nearly 40 points.

DAVID P. GARDNER, *A Nation At Risk*

And remember, cited facts must always be accompanied by sources
that a curious or interested reader may check.

Expert testimony, consisting of the opinions of acknowledged
authorities who agree with your position, can also be useful evidence
in an argument. To support his argument that an unjust law is unworthy of support, Martin Luther King, Jr., in "Letter from Birmingham Jail," quoted the opinion of St. Augustine that "an unjust
law is no law at all." To back his contention that UFO visits have
occurred, astronomer Robert Jastrow, in an essay entitled "The Case
for UFO's," cited the views of veteran UFO researcher Dr. Allen
Hyneck that several UFO sightings are of unmistakable authenticity.
The expert you cite should be a recognized authority with sterling
credentials, which you should summarize briefly unless the expert
is of such renown as to require no introduction (as examples, Aristotle, Queen Victoria, Jesus Christ).

Logical reasoning also may be used in support of an argument
and is, in fact, the major prop behind the case made in "The Cruel
Logic of Liberation." Exposing what Sobran considers to be a logical
inconsistency in the feminist position forms the heart of the writer's
argument:

> One of the big (and ugly) feminist issues is abortion. I
> recently got into a debate with a feminist who contended that
> men should have no say in the matter, that it was strictly a
> woman's concern. Very well, I rejoined: in that case women
> shouldn't be allowed to file paternity suits.
>
> Why not? she demanded. Because, I said, if motherhood
> is going to be optional, then no woman who chooses it should
> be able to impose the consequence of her choice on an unwilling
> man. If a pregnant woman has nine months in which to decide
> whether to bear a child, during which time she need neither
> consult nor inform the father (even if he's her husband) and
> during which time he can't have any say in the matter, it seems
> grossly unfair to require him to support the child she alone
> decided to bring into this world.
>
> JOSEPH SOBRAN, "The Cruel Logic of Liberation"

Some arguments may be settled by this kind of logical fencing—the thrust and parry of propositions and rebuttals—but the vast majority of issues can be decided only by more substantial evidence and by more realistic appeals.

3. Anticipate the Opposition

Anticipating the opposition is a favored ploy of debaters—stealing an opponent's thunder by replying to it before even the first roar is sounded. One common way to anticipate the opposition is to reflect its stand in a rhetorical question, which you then rebut with an answer. The following is an example from the essay "Why I Am an Agnostic":

> To say that God made the universe gives no explanation of the beginnings of things. If we are told that God made the universe, the question immediately arises: Who made God? Did he always exist, or was there some power back of that? Did he create matter out of nothing, or is his existence coextensive with matter? The problem is still there. What is the origin of it all? If, on the other hand, one says that the universe was not made by God, that it always existed, he has the same difficulty to confront. To say that the universe was here last year, or millions of years ago, does not explain its origin. This is still a mystery. As to the question of the origin of things, man can only wonder and doubt and guess.
>
> CLARENCE DARROW, "Why I Am an Agnostic"

Anticipating the opposition demonstrates you are familiar with your opponent's reasoning but still reject its claims. Your presentation is likely to seem more sophisticated and carefully thought out when you reflect and rebut your opponent's arguments than when you simply march forward with your own case.

ANITA HILL'S STATEMENT TO THE SENATE JUDICIARY COMMITTEE

Anita Hill

Anita Hill (b. 1956) has been a law professor at Oral Roberts University in Tulsa, Oklahoma, and is

*now a professor of law at the University of Oklahoma.
She received her legal training at Yale University, prac-
ticing law in the firm of Ward, Hardraker & Ross until
her appointment as an assistant to Judge Clarence
Thomas during his tenure as Assistant Secretary of
Education for Civil Rights in the U.S. Department of
Education. Anita Hill was brought to public attention
when on October 11 of 1991 she stood before the U.S.
Senate Judiciary Committee to accuse Clarence
Thomas, then seeking an appointment as a justice of
the U.S. Supreme Court, of sexual harassment. For several days the American people were glued to their television sets as they watched this woman describe in
vivid detail the judge's improper sexual behavior
toward her. In the end, Thomas was not censured and
was appointed to the Supreme Court, a position he still
holds.*

Preparing to Read This Selection Critically

While you will be in a better position to judge the
debate between Hill and Thomas after you have pondered and analyzed both sides, you should read the following text as objectively as possible, asking yourself if
this woman is believable or not. Pay attention to her
credentials, her opinions, and her attitudes. Heed what
she states and perhaps also what she leaves unstated. Try
to play devil's advocate by placing yourself in the position
of the man she is accusing. Above all, try to be fair in
your judgment.

Mr. Chairman, Sen. Thurmond, members of the committee, my   1
name is Anita F. Hill, and I am a professor of law at the University
of Oklahoma. I was born on a farm in Okmulgee County, Okla., in
1956. I am the youngest of 13 children. I had my early education in
Okmulgee County. My father, Albert Hill, is a farmer in that area.
My mother's name is Erma Hill. She is also a farmer and a housewife.

My childhood was one of a lot of hard work and not much   2
money, but it was one of solid family affection, as represented by
my parents. I was reared in a religious atmosphere in the Baptist
faith, and I have been a member of the Antioch Baptist Church in

Tulsa, Okla., since 1983. It is a very warm part of my life at the present time.

3   For my undergraduate work, I went to Oklahoma State University and graduated from there in 1977. I am attaching to this statement a copy of my resume for further details of my education.

4   I graduated from the university with academic honors and proceeded to the Yale Law School, where I received my JD degree in 1980. Upon graduation from law school, I became a practicing lawyer with the Washington, D.C., firm of Ward, Hardraker & Ross.

5   In 1981, I was introduced to now Judge Thomas by a mutual friend. Judge Thomas told me that he was anticipating a political appointment, and he asked if I would be interested in working with him. He was, in fact, appointed as assistant secretary of education for civil rights. After he had taken that post, he asked if I would become his assistant, and I accepted that position.

6   In my early period there, I had two major projects. The first was an article I wrote for Judge Thomas's signature on the education of minority students. The second was the organization of a seminar on high–risk students which was abandoned because Judge Thomas transferred to the EEOC where he became the chairman of that office.

7   During this period at the Department of Education, my working relationship with Judge Thomas was positive. I had a good deal of responsibility and independence. I thought he respected my work and that he trusted my judgment. After approximately three months of working there, he asked me to go out socially with him.

8   What happened next and telling the world about it are the two most difficult things, experiences of my life. It is only after a great deal of agonizing consideration and sleepless number—a great number of sleepless nights that I am able to talk of these unpleasant matters to anyone but my close friends.

9   I declined the invitation to go out socially with him and explained to him that I thought it would jeopardize what at the time I considered to be a very good working relationship. I had a normal social life with other men outside of the office. I believed then, as now, that having a social relationship with a person who was supervising my work would be ill–advised. I was very uncomfortable with the idea and told him so.

10   I thought that by saying no and explaining my reasons my employer would abandon his social suggestions. However, to my regret, in the following few weeks, he continued to ask me out on

several occasions. He pressed me to justify my reasons for saying no to him. These incidents took place in his office or mine. They were in the form of private conversations which would not have been overheard by anyone else.

My working relationship became even more strained when 11 Judge Thomas began to use work situations to discuss sex. On these occasions, he would call me into his office for reports on education issues and projects, or he might suggest that, because of the time pressures of his schedule, we go to lunch to a government cafeteria.

After a brief discussion of work, he would turn the conver- 12 sation to a discussion of sexual matters.

His conversations were very vivid. He spoke about acts that 13 he had seen in pornographic films involving such matters as women having sex with animals and films showing group sex or rape scenes.

He talked about pornographic materials depicting individuals 14 with large penises or large breasts involved in various sex acts. On several occasions, Thomas told me graphically of his own sexual prowess.

Because I was extremely uncomfortable talking about sex with 15 him at all and particularly in such a graphic way, I told him that I did not want to talk about these subjects. I would also try to change the subject to education matters or to non-sexual personal matters such as his background or his beliefs. My efforts to change the subject were rarely successful.

Throughout the period of these conversations, he also from 16 time to time asked me for social engagements. My reaction to these conversations was to avoid them by eliminating opportunities for us to engage in extended conversations. This was difficult because at the time I was his only assistant at the Office of Education—or Office for Civil Rights.

During the latter part of my time at the Department of Edu- 17 cation, the social pressures and any conversation of his offensive behavior ended. I began both to believe and hope that our working relationship could be a proper, cordial, and professional one.

When Judge Thomas was made chair of the EEOC, I needed 18 to face the question of whether to go with him. I was asked to do so, and I did. The work itself was interesting, and at that time it appeared that the sexual overtures which had so troubled me had ended. I also faced the realistic fact that I had no alternative job. While I might have gone back to private practice, perhaps in my old firm or at another, I was dedicated to civil rights work, and my first choice was to be in that field. Moreover, the Department of Education itself was a dubious venture. President Reagan was seeking to abolish the entire department.

19   For my first months at the EEOC, where I continued to be an assistant to Judge Thomas, there were no sexual conversations or overtures. However, during the fall and winter of 1982, these began again. The comments were random and ranged from pressing me about why I didn't go out with him to remarks about my personal appearance. I remember his saying that some day I would have to tell him the real reason that I wouldn't go out with him.

20   He began to show displeasure in his tone and voice and his demeanor and his continued pressure for an explanation. He commented on what I was wearing in terms of whether it made me more or less sexually attractive. The incidents occurred in his inner office at the EEOC.

21   One of the oddest episodes I remember was an occasion in which Thomas was drinking a Coke in his office. He got up from the table at which we were working, went over to his desk to get the Coke, looked at the can and asked, "Who has put pubic hair on my Coke?" On other occasions, he referred to the size of his own penis as being larger than normal, and he also spoke on some occasions of the pleasures he had given to women with oral sex.

22   At this point, late 1982, I began to feel severe stress on the job. I began to be concerned that Clarence Thomas might take out his anger with me by degrading me or not giving me important assignments. I also thought that he might find an excuse for dismissing me.

23   In January of 1983, I began looking for another job. I was handicapped because I feared that, if he found out, he might make it difficult for me to find other employment and I might be dismissed from the job I had. Another factor that made my search more difficult was that there was a period—this was during a period of a hiring freeze in the government. In February of 1983, I was hospitalized for five days on an emergency basis for acute stomach pain which I attributed to stress on the job.

24   Once out of the hospital, I became more committed to find other employment and sought further to minimize my contact with Thomas. This became easier when Allison Duncan became office director, because most of my work was then funneled through her and I had contact with Clarence Thomas mostly in staff meetings.

In the spring of 1983, an opportunity to teach at Oral Roberts 25
University opened up. I participated in a seminar—taught an afternoon session and seminar at Oral Roberts University. The dean of
the university saw me teaching and inquired as to whether I would
be interested in furthering—pursuing a career in teaching, beginning
at Oral Roberts University. I agreed to take the job in large part
because of my desire to escape the pressures I felt at the EEOC due
to Judge Thomas.

When I informed him that I was leaving in July, I recall that 26
his response was that now I would no longer have an excuse for not
going out with him. I told him that I still preferred not to do so.

At some time after that meeting, he asked if he could take me 27
to dinner at the end of the term. When I declined, he assured me
that the dinner was a professional courtesy only and not a social
invitation.

I reluctantly agreed to accept that invitation, but only if it was 28
at the very end of a working day.

On, as I recall, the last day of my employment at the EEOC 29
in the summer of 1983, I did have dinner with Clarence Thomas.
We went directly from work to a restaurant near the office. We talked
about the work I had done, both at Education and at the EEOC. He
told me that he was pleased with all of it except for an article and
speech that I had done for him while we were at the Office for Civil
Rights. Finally, he made a comment that I will vividly remember.

He said that if I ever told anyone of his behavior that it would 30
ruin his career. This was not an apology, nor was it an explanation.
That was his last remark about the possibility of our going out or
reference to his behavior.

In July of 1983, I left the Washington, D.C., area and have had 31
minimal contact with Judge Clarence Thomas since. I am of course
aware from the press that some questions have been raised about
conversations I had with Judge Clarence Thomas after I left the
EEOC. From 1983 until today, I have seen Judge Thomas only twice.

On one occasion, I needed to get a reference from him, and 32
on another he made a public appearance in Tulsa.

On one occasion he called me at home and we had an incon- 33
sequential conversation. On one occasion he called me without
reaching me, and I returned the call without reaching him, and
nothing came of it. I have on at least three occasions, been asked
to act as a conduit to him for others.

34   I knew his secretary, Diane Holt. We had worked together at both EEOC and Education. There were occasions on which I spoke to her, and on some of these occasions undoubtedly I passed on some casual comment to then Chairman Thomas. There were a series of calls in the first three months of 1985, occasioned by a group in Tulsa, which wished to have a civil rights conference. They wanted Judge Thomas to be the speaker and enlisted my assistance for this purpose.

35   I did call in January and February to no effect, and finally suggested to the person directly involved, Susan Cahal, that she put the matter into her own hands and call directly. She did so in March of 1985. In connection with that March invitation, Ms. Cahal wanted conference materials for the seminar and some research was needed. I was asked to try to get the information and did attempt to do so.

36   There was another call about another possible conference in July of 1985. In August of 1987, I was in Washington, D.C., and I did call Diane Holt. In the course of this conversation, she asked me how long I was going to be in town and I told her. It is recorded in the message as Aug. 15. It was, in fact, Aug. 20. She told me about Judge Thomas's marriage and I did say congratulate him.

37   It is only after a great deal of agonizing consideration that I am able to talk of these unpleasant matters to anyone except my closest friends. As I've said before, these last few days have been very trying and very hard for me and it hasn't just been the last few days this week. It has actually been over a month now that I have been under the strain of this issue.

38   Telling the world is the most difficult experience of my life, but it is very close to having to live through the experience that occasioned this meeting. I may have used poor judgment early on in my relationship with this issue. I was aware, however, that telling at any point in my career could adversely affect my future career. And I did not want early on to burn all the bridges to the EEOC.

39   As I said, I may have used poor judgment. Perhaps I should have taken angry or even militant steps, both when I was in the agency, or after I left it. But I must confess to the world that the course that I took seemed the better as well as the easier approach.

40   I declined any comment to newspapers, but later when Senate staff asked me about these matters I felt I had a duty to report. I have no personal vendetta against Clarence Thomas. I seek only to provide the committee with information which it may regard as relevant.

It would have been more comfortable to remain silent. I took   41
no initiative to inform anyone. But when I was asked by a representative of this committee to report my experience, I felt that I had
to tell the truth. I could not keep silent.

Thinking Critically About This Reading

1. What bearing does all of Hill's autobiographical information have
   on her argument? Would her accusation be just as forceful without
   it?
2. What facts, if any, make Hill's accusations believable? What facts,
   if any, make her accusations difficult to believe?
3. How effective do you consider Hill's attempts to avoid Thomas's
   alleged sexual advances? Could she have been more aggressive,
   more deliberate, more direct?
4. How believable are the reasons for Hill's move to the EEOC
   (Equal Employment Opportunity Commission) with Thomas after he had sexually harassed her?
5. Hill ends her accusation by stating that she has no personal vendetta against Clarence Thomas, but that she merely seeks to provide the committee with relevant information. Do you consider
   the information she presented as relevant to a Supreme Court
   justice's appointment? Give reasons for your answer.

Understanding the Writer's Process

1. How does Hill organize her address? Into what major topics is
   it divided? Do you find the organization effective or can you
   suggest a better method of developing the case against Thomas?
2. Why does Hill dwell on the enormous emotional difficulty of
   revealing her experience? For instance, why does she admit that
   she agonized and spent sleepless nights over the issue? How does
   such suffering affect her argument?
3. Why do you suppose Hill is so graphic in her depiction of Thomas's behavior, detailing such incidents as his boasting of the size
   of his sexual organ and alluding to oral and bestial sex?
4. In paragraph 23 Hill refers to her hospitalization as the result of
   severe stress on the job. How might such a revelation work
   against Hill?

5. How strong is Hill's conclusion? Is it typical of the methods used by attorneys in court? Or is it different and if so, why?

Examining the Writer's Language

1. Use each of the the following words in a sentence whose context will help clarify the word's meaning: jeopardize (paragraph 9), graphically (14), prowess (14), overtures (18), venture (18), demeanor (20), inconsequential (33), militant (39).
2. What is the most outstanding characteristic of the writer's language? Provide examples of the characteristic.
3. How is the word "handicapped" used in paragraph 23?
4. What reaction do you think Hill hoped to get from her audience when she alluded to the "pubic hair" incident (see paragraph 21)?
5. In paragraph 17, what do you think Hill meant by the term "professional"?

Suggestions for Writing

1. Write an essay in which you support either Anita Hill's or Clarence Thomas's side in the issue at stake. You may research news articles written at the time of the Senate Judiciary Committee's inquiry in order to bolster your argument.
2. Write an argument in which you support either stringent laws to protect women from sexual harassment or the idea that women need more training to deal forcefully with sexual harassment.

CLARENCE THOMAS'S STATEMENT TO THE SENATE JUDICIARY COMMITTEE

Clarence Thomas

> *Clarence Thomas (b. 1948) is a United States Supreme Court Justice, having been appointed to the bench by President George Bush in 1991, following weeks of highly publicized hearings in front of a Senate*

Judiciary Committee charged with deciding whether or not to confirm Thomas. The most spectacular part of the hearings took place when one of Thomas's former assistants at the Department of Education, Anita Hill, accused him of having sexually harassed her ten years earlier by pressuring her for dates and by holding pornographic conversations with her concerning such matters as oral sex, bestial sex, and Thomas's own sexual prowess. The thousands of Americans who became fascinated with the hearings were deeply divided in their attitudes toward Thomas—some accusing him of being a pervert, others accusing Hill of being an erotomaniac similar to the woman in the popular movie Fatal Attraction. *After graduating from law school, Thomas held the following positions: Assistant Secretary of Civil Rights for the U.S. Department of Education, Chairman of the U.S. Equal Employment Opportunity Commission, and judge on the U.S. Court of Appeals for the District of Columbia Circuit.*

Preparing to Read This Selection Critically

The full record of what actually happened between Anita Hill and Clarence Thomas probably will never be revealed. What the public record does tell is enough to challenge anyone who likes a lively debate. On one extreme side are critics like Robert Bly, who suggested that President Bush now has the honor of having "a self–piteously lying porno freak on the Supreme Court." On the other side are defenders like Peggy Noonan, who wrote an editorial in the *New York Times* suggesting that the average normal woman supported Thomas. Your reading of both addresses should engage your thoughts on several issues, the most obvious being sexual harassment, women's rights, and the responsibilities of public office. The following questions are relevant to the Hill–Thomas case: What is sexual harassment? Is there cause for women to be afraid of male power in the workplace? Does a person seeking high public office have a responsibility to be morally respectable?

1   Mr. Chairman, Sen. Thurmond, members of the committee. As excruciatingly difficult as the last two weeks have been, I welcome the opportunity to clear my name today. No one other than my wife and Sen. Danforth, to whom I read this statement at 6:30 a.m., has seen or heard this statement. No handlers, no advisers.

2   The first I learned of the allegations by Prof. Anita Hill was on Sept. 25, 1991, when the FBI came to my home to investigate her allegations. When informed by the FBI agent of the nature of the allegations and the person making them, I was shocked, surprised, hurt and enormously saddened. I have not been the same since that day.

3   For almost a decade, my responsibilities included enforcing the rights of victims of sexual harassment. As a boss, as a friend and as a human being, I was proud that I had never had such an allegation leveled against me, even as I sought to promote women and minorities into non–traditional jobs.

4   In addition, several of my friends who are women have confided in me about the horror of harassment on the job or elsewhere. I thought I really understood the anguish, the fears, the doubts, the seriousness of the matter. But, since Sept. 25th, I have suffered immensely as these very serious charges were leveled against me. I have been racking my brains and eating my insides out trying to think of what I could have said or done to Anita Hill to lead her to allege that I was interested in her in more than a professional way and that I talked with her about pornographic or X–rated films.

5   Contrary to some press reports, I categorically denied all of the allegations and denied that I ever attempted to date Anita Hill when first interviewed by the FBI. I strongly reaffirm that denial.

6   Let me describe my relationship with Anita Hill. In 1981, after I went to the Department of Education as an assistant secretary in the Office of Civil Rights, one of my closest friends from both college and law school, Gil Hardy, brought Anita Hill to my attention. As I remember, he indicated that she was dissatisfied with her law firm and wanted to work in government.

7   Based primarily, if not solely, on Gil's recommendation, I hired Anita Hill.

8   During my tenure at the Department of Education, Anita Hill was an attorney adviser who worked directly with me. She worked on special projects, as well as day–to–day matters. As I recall, she was one of two professionals working directly with me at the time.

As a result, we worked closely on numerous matters. I recall 9
being pleased with her work product and the professional but cordial
relationship which we enjoyed at work. I also recall engaging in
discussions about politics and current events.

Upon my nomination to become chairman of the Equal Em- 10
ployment Opportunity Commission, Anita Hill, to the best of my
recollection, assisted me in the nomination and confirmation process. After my confirmation, she and Diane Holt, then my secretary,
joined me at EEOC. I do not recall that there was any question or
doubt that she would become a special assistant to me at EEOC,
although, as a career employee, she retained the option of remaining
at the Department of Education.

At EEOC, our relationship was more distant and our contacts 11
less frequent as a result of the increased size of my personal staff
and the dramatic increase and diversity of my day–to–day responsibilities. Upon reflection, I recall that she seemed to have had some
difficulty adjusting to this change in her role. In any case, our relationship remained both cordial and professional.

At no time did I become aware, either directly or indirectly, 12
that she felt I had said or done anything to change the cordial nature
of our relationship. I detected nothing from her or from my staff,
or from Gil Hardy, our mutual friend, with whom I maintained
regular contact. I am certain that, had any statement or conduct on
my part been brought to my attention, I would remember it clearly
because of the nature and seriousness of such conduct, as well as
my adamant opposition to sex discrimination and sexual harassment.
But there were no such statements.

In the spring of 1983, Mr. Charles Kothe contacted me to speak 13
at the law school at Oral Roberts University in Tulsa, Okla.

Anita Hill, who is from Oklahoma, accompanied me on that 14
trip. It was not unusual that individuals on my staff would travel
with me occasionally. Anita Hill accompanied me on that trip primarily because this was an opportunity to combine business and a
visit to her home.

As I recall, during our visit at Oral Roberts University, Mr. 15
Kothe mentioned to me the possibility of approaching Anita Hill to
join the faculty at Oral Roberts University Law School. I encouraged
him to do so and noted to him, as I recall, that Anita Hill would do
well in teaching. I recommended her highly and she eventually was
offered a teaching position.

16   Although I did not see Anita Hill often after she left EEOC, I did see her on one or two subsequent visits to Tulsa, Okla.

17   And, on one visit, I believe, she drove me to the airport. I also occasionally received telephone calls from her. She would speak directly with me or with my secretary, Diane Holt. Since Anita Hill and Diane Holt had been with me at the Department of Education, they were fairly close personally and I believe they occasionally socialized together. I would also hear about her through Linda Jackson, then Linda Lambert, whom both Anita Hill and I met at the Department of Education, and I would hear of her from my friend, Gil.

18   Throughout the time that Anita Hill worked with me, I treated her as I treated my other special assistants. I tried to treat them all cordially, professionally and respectfully, and I tried to support them in their endeavors and be interested in and supportive of their success. I had no reason or basis to believe my relationship with Anita Hill was anything but this way until the FBI visited me a little more than two weeks ago.

19   I find it particularly troubling that she never raised any hint that she was uncomfortable with me. She did not raise or mention it when considering moving with me to EEOC from the Department of Education, and she'd never raised it with me when she left EEOC and was moving on in her life. And, to my fullest knowledge, she did not speak to any other women working with or around me who would feel comfortable enough to raise it with me, especially Diane Holt, to whom she seemed closest on my personal staff. Nor did she raise it with mutual friends such as Linda Jackson and Gil Hardy.

20   This is a person I have helped at every turn in the road since we met. She seemed to appreciate the continued cordial relationship we had since Day 1. She sought my advice and counsel, as did virtually all of the members of my personal staff.

21   During my tenure in the executive branch as a manager, as a policy–maker and as a person, I have adamantly condemned sex harassment. There is no member of this committee or this Senate who feels stronger about sex harassment than I do. As a manager, I made every effort to take swift and decisive action when sex harassment raised or reared its ugly head. The fact that I feel so very strongly about sex harassment and spoke loudly at EEOC has made these allegations doubly hard on me. I cannot imagine anything that I said or did to Anita Hill that could have been mistaken for sexual harassment.

But, with that said, if there is anything that I have said that   22
has been misconstrued by Anita Hill or anyone else to be sexual
harassment, then I can say that I am so very sorry and I wish I had
known. If I did know, I would have stopped immediately and I
would not, as I've done over the past two weeks, have to tear away
at myself, trying to think of what I could possibly have done. But
I have not said or done the things that Anita Hill has alleged. God
has gotten me through the days since Sept. 25th, and he is my judge.

Mr. Chairman, something has happened to me in the dark days   23
that have followed since the FBI agents informed me about these
allegations. And the days have grown darker as this very serious,
very explosive and very sensitive allegation—or these sensitive allegations were selectively leaked in a distorted way to the media
over the past weekend. As if the confidential allegations themselves
were not enough, this apparently calculated public disclosure has
caused me, my family and my friends enormous pain and great
harm. I have never in all my life felt such hurt, such pain, such
agony. My family and I have been done a grave and irreparable
injustice.

During the past two weeks, I lost the belief that, if I did my   24
best, all would work out. I called upon the strength that helped me
get here from Pin Point, and it was all sapped out of me. It was
sapped out of me because Anita Hill was a person I considered a
friend whom I admired and thought I had treated fairly and with
the utmost respect. Perhaps I could have been—better weathered
this if it was from someone else. But here was someone I truly felt
I had done my best with. Though I am by no means a perfect person,
I have not done what she has alleged, and I still don't know what
I could possibly have done to cause her to make these allegations.

When I stood next to the President in Kennebunkport being   25
nominated to the Supreme Court of the United States, that was a
high honor; but, as I sit here before you 103 days later, that honor
has been crushed. From the very beginning, charges were leveled
against me from the shadows, charges of drug abuse, anti-Semitism,
wife beating, drug use by family members, that I was a quota appointment, confirmation conversion, and much, much more. And
now, this.

I have complied with the rules. I responded to a document   26
request that produced over 30,000 pages of documents, and I have
testified for five full days under oath. I have endured this ordeal for
103 days. Reporters sneaking into my garage to examine books I

read. Reporters and interest groups swarming over divorce papers looking for dirt. Unnamed people starting preposterous and damaging rumors. Calls all over the country specifically requesting dirt.

27   This is not American; this is Kafkaesque. It has got to stop. It must stop for the benefit of future nominees and our country. Enough is enough.

28   I'm not going to allow myself to be further humiliated in order to be confirmed. I am here specifically to respond to allegations of sex harassment in the workplace. I am not here to be further humiliated by this committee or anyone else, or to put my private life on display for prurient interests or other reasons. I will not allow this committee or anyone else to probe into my private life. This is not what America is all about.

29   To ask me to do that would be to ask me to go beyond fundamental fairness.

30   Yesterday, I called my mother. She was confined to her bed, unable to work and unable to stop crying. Enough is enough.

31   Mr. Chairman, in my 43 years on this Earth I have been able with the help of others and with the help of God to defy poverty, avoid prison, overcome segregation, bigotry, racism and obtain one of the finest educations available in this country, but I have not been able to overcome this process. This is worse than any obstacle or anything that I have ever faced.

32   Throughout my life, I have been energized by the expectation and the hope that in this country I would be treated fairly in all endeavors. When there was segregation, I hoped there would be fairness one day or some day. When there was bigotry and prejudice, I hoped that there would be tolerance and understanding some day.

33   Mr. Chairman, I am proud of my life, proud of what I have done and what I have accomplished, proud of my family—and this process, this process is trying to destroy it all. No job is worth what I have been through, no job. No horror in my life has been so debilitating. Confirm me if you want. Don't confirm me if you are so led, but let this process end. Let me and my family regain our lives.

34   I never asked to be nominated. It was an honor. Little did I know the price, but it is too high.

35   I enjoy and appreciate my current position and I am comfortable with the prospect of returning to my work as a judge on the U.S. Court of Appeals for the D.C. Circuit and to my friends there. Each of these positions is public service, and I have given at the

office. I want my life and my family's life back, and I want them returned expeditiously. I have experienced the exhilaration of new heights from the moment I was called to Kennebunkport by the President to have lunch and he nominated me. That was the high point. At that time, I was told eye–to–eye that, "Clarence, you made it this far on merit. The rest is going to be politics." And it surely has been.

There have been other highs. The outpouring of support from   36
my friends of long standing; a bonding like I have never experienced with my old boss, Sen. Danforth; the wonderful support of those who have worked with me. There have been prayers said for my family and me by people I know and people I will never meet, prayers that were heard and that sustained not only me, but also my wife and my entire family.

Instead of understanding and appreciating the great honor be-   37
stowed upon me, I find myself here today defending my name, my integrity, because somehow select portions of confidential documents dealing with this matter were leaked to the public.

Mr. Chairman, I am a victim of this process. My name has   38
been harmed. My integrity has been harmed. My character has been harmed. My family has been harmed. My friends have been harmed.

There is nothing this committee, this body or this country can   39
do to give me my good name back. Nothing.

I will not provide the rope for my own lynching or for further   40
humiliation. I am not going to engage in discussions nor will I submit to roving questions of what goes on in the most intimate parts of my private life or the sanctity of my bedroom. These are the most intimate parts of my privacy, and they will remain just that, private.

Thinking Critically About This Reading

1. Judge Clarence Thomas does not provide his audience with the detailed autobiographical background that Anita Hill did. Is this an oversight, or was Thomas's objective different from Hill's? Explain your answer.

2. What irony does Thomas point out early in his address? Is the irony relevant, or should Thomas have saved his comments for more important defense information?

3. Thomas repeatedly praises Anita Hill and states that he respected and admired her enough to help her career in every way he could.

Would it have been more effective if he had denounced and repudiated her or accused her of seeking fame by attaching herself to his public image? How would you have handled the situation?

4. Why is it difficult, after hearing both sides of the issue, to decide beyond any reasonable doubt which one of the two persons is lying?

5. What is your own definition of sexual harassment and how do you think it can be prevented?

Understanding the Writer's Process

1. If you were to summarize Thomas's address into one sentence, what would you say?

2. How does Thomas organize his address? What are its major components?

3. What is the purpose of paragraph 31? How effective is it?

4. Why do you suppose the speaker refers to some of the good things that have happened to him during the difficulties associated with the hearings? (See paragraphs 35 and 36.)

5. Why does Thomas mention that he has complied with the rules (see paragraph 26)?

6. Which address do you consider more forceful, Hill's or Thomas's? Give reasons for your judgment.

Examining the Writer's Language

1. Using a dictionary, write a definition of the following words found in Thomas's address: categorically (paragraph 5), confirmation (10), adamant (12), distorted (23), energized (32), expeditiously (35), exhilaration (35).

2. In paragraph 23, the author uses three words that essentially have the same lexical meaning. What is the idea being defined? What is the point of such repetition?

3. In paragraph 33, what rhetorical purpose does the word *proud* serve?

4. What is "the prurient interest" referred to in paragraph 28?

5. What is the rhetorical as well as emotional effect of the last three sentences in paragraph 33?

Suggestions for Writing

1. In an essay of approximately 500 words, argue either for or against the notion that the personal morality of a person striving for public office must be taken into account by those whose votes assure that person's position.

2. After carefully reviewing both Anita Hill's and Clarence Thomas's speeches write an argument in which you support one side over the other. Be sure to allude to specific passages in the texts.

WHY I AM AN AGNOSTIC

Clarence Darrow

Clarence Darrow (1857–1938), celebrated American trial lawyer, practiced first throughout Ohio and later in Chicago. Bitterly opposed to the death penalty, Darrow defended hundreds of clients against charges of murder—and not one was ever sentenced to death. Long an agnostic, Darrow constantly fought fundamentalist tenets. He gained national prominence when, pitted against William Jennings Bryan, he unsuccessfully defended John T. Scopes's right to teach evolution in a Tennessee classroom. Darrow wrote a novel entitled Farmington *(1904) and a treatise entitled* Crime: Its Cause and Treatment. *The essay that follows reveals both Darrow's concise, sarcastic style and his contempt for Biblical fundamentalism.*

Preparing to Read This Selection Critically

The argument for or against God, immortality, and the Bible is usually futile because the scientific or objective evidence required to prove the proposition one way or another does not exist. In the end, it is a matter of personal faith. However, Darrow's argument certainly can be judged on the basis of its effectiveness. For instance, you can judge the effectiveness of his tone, his examples, and even the validity (if not truth) of his arguments. Also, you need to ascertain some of the basic assumptions on which he constructs his case, such as his agnostic position and his hostility toward unquestioning faith in the Christian religion.

1   An agnostic is a doubter. The word is generally applied to those who doubt the verity of accepted religious creeds of faiths. Everyone is an agnostic as to the beliefs or creeds they do not accept. Catholics are agnostic to the Protestant creeds, and the Protestants are agnostic to the Catholic creed. Anyone who thinks is an agnostic about something, otherwise he must believe that he is possessed of all knowledge. And the proper place for such a person is in the madhouse or the home for the feeble-minded. In a popular way, in the western world, an agnostic is one who doubts or disbelieves the main tenets of the Christian faith.

2   I would say that belief in at least three tenets is necessary to the faith of a Christian: a belief in God, a belief in immortality, and a belief in a supernatural book. Various Christian sects require much more, but it is difficult to imagine that one could be a Christian, under any intelligent meaning of the word, with less. Yet there are some people who claim to be Christians who do not accept the literal interpretation of all the Bible, and who give more credence to some portions of the book than to others.

3   I am an agnostic as to the question of God. I think that it is impossible for the human mind to believe in an object or thing unless it can form a mental picture of such object or thing. Since man ceased to worship openly an anthropomorphic God and talked vaguely and not intelligently about some force in the universe, higher than man, that is responsible for the existence of man and the universe, he cannot be said to believe in God. One cannot believe in a force excepting as a force that pervades matter and is not an individual entity. To believe in a thing, an image of the thing must be stamped on the mind. If one is asked if he believes in such an animal as a camel, there immediately arises in his mind an image of the camel. This image has come from experience or knowledge of the animal gathered in some way or other. No such image comes, or can come, with the idea of a God who is described as a force.

4   Man has always speculated upon the origin of the universe, including himself. I feel, with Herbert Spencer, that whether the universe had an origin—and if it had—what the origin is will never be known by man. The Christian says that the universe could not

make itself; that there must have been some higher power to call it into being. Christians have been obsessed for many years by Paley's argument that if a person passing through a desert should find a watch and examine its spring, its hands, its case and its crystal, he would at once be satisfied that some intelligent being capable of design had made the watch. No doubt this is true. No civilized man would question that someone made the watch. The reason he would not doubt it is because he is familiar with watches and other appliances made by man. The savage was once unfamiliar with a watch and would have had no idea upon the subject. There are plenty of crystals and rocks of natural formation that are as intricate as a watch, but even to intelligent man they carry no implication that some intelligent power must have made them. They carry no such implication because no one has any knowledge or experience of someone having made these natural objects which everywhere abound.

To say that God made the universe gives us no explanation of   5 the beginnings of things. If we are told that God made the universe, the question immediately arises: Who made God? Did he always exist, or was there some power back of that? Did he create matter out of nothing, or is his existence coextensive with matter? The problem is still there. What is the origin of it all? If, on the other hand, one says that the universe was not made by God, that it always existed, he has the same difficulty to confront. To say that the universe was here last year, or millions of years ago, does not explain its origin. This is still a mystery. As to the question of the origin of things, man can only wonder and doubt and guess.

As to the existence of the soul, all people may either believe   6 or disbelieve. Everyone knows the origin of the human being. They know that it came from a single cell in the body of the mother, and that the cell was one out of ten thousand in the mother's body. Before gestation the cell must have been fertilized by a spermatozoön from the body of the father. This was one out of perhaps a billion spermatozoa that was the capacity of the father. When the cell is fertilized a chemical process begins. The cell divides and multiplies and increases into millions of cells, and finally a child is born. Cells die and are born during the life of the individual until they finally drop apart, and this is death.

If there is a soul, what is it, and where did it come from, and   7 where does it go? Can anyone who is guided by his reason possibly imagine a soul independent of a body, or the place of its residence, or the character of it, or anything concerning it? If man is justified in any belief or disbelief on any subject, he is warranted in the disbelief in a soul. Not one scrap of evidence exists to prove any such impossible thing.

8   Many Christians base the belief of a soul and God upon the Bible. Strictly speaking, there is no such book. To make the Bible, sixty-six books are bound into one volume. These books are written by many people at different times, and no one knows the time or the identity of any author. Some of the books were written by several authors at various times. These books contain all sorts of contradictory concepts of life and morals and the origin of things. Between the first and the last nearly a thousand years intervened, a longer time than has passed since the discovery of America by Columbus.

9   When I was a boy the theologians used to assert that the proof of the divine inspiration of the Bible rested on miracles and prophecies. But a miracle means a violation of a natural law, and there can be no proof imagined that could be sufficient to show the violation of a natural law; even though proof seemed to show violation, it would only show that we were not acquainted with all natural laws. One believes in the truthfulness of a man because of his long experience with the man, and because the man has always told a consistent story. But no man has told so consistent a story as nature.

10   If one should say that the sun did not rise, to use the ordinary expression, on the day before, his hearer would not believe it, even though he had slept all day and knew that his informant was a man of the strictest veracity. He would not believe it because the story is inconsistent with the conduct of the sun in all the ages past.

11   Primitive and even civilized people have grown so accustomed to believing in miracles that they often attribute the simplest manifestations of nature to agencies of which they know nothing. They do this when the belief is utterly inconsistent with knowledge and logic. They believe in old miracles and new ones. Preachers pray for rain, knowing full well that no such prayer was ever answered. When a politician is sick, they pray for God to cure him, and the politician almost invariably dies. The modern clergyman who prays for rain and for the health of the politician is no more intelligent in this matter than the primitive man who saw a separate miracle in the rising and setting of the sun, in the birth of an individual, in the growth of a plant, in the stroke of lightning, in the flood, in every manifestation of nature and life.

As to prophecies, intelligent writers gave them up long ago.   12
In all prophecies facts are made to suit the prophecy, or the prophecy
was made after the facts, or the events have no relation to the
prophecy. Weird and strange and unreasonable interpretations are
used to explain simple statements, that a prophecy may be claimed.

Can any rational person believe that the Bible is anything but   13
a human document? We now know pretty well where the various
books came from, and about when they were written. We know that
they were written by human beings who had no knowledge of science, little knowledge of life, and were influenced by the barbarous
morality of primitive times, and were grossly ignorant of most things
that men know today. For instance, Genesis says that God made
the earth, and he made the sun to light the day and the moon to
light the night, and in one clause disposes of the stars by saying
that "he made the stars also." This was plainly written by someone
who had no conception of the stars. Man, by the aid of his telescope,
has looked out into the heavens and found stars whose diameter is
as great as the distance between the earth and the sun. We know
that the universe is filled with stars and suns and planets and systems. Every new telescope looking further into the heavens only
discovers more and more worlds and suns and systems in the endless
reaches of space. The men who wrote Genesis believed, of course,
that this tiny speck of mud that we call the earth was the center of
the universe, the only world in space, and made for man, who was
the only being worth considering. These men believed that the stars
were only a little way above the earth, and were set in the firmament
for man to look at, and for nothing else. Everyone today knows that
this conception is not true.

The origin of the human race is not as blind a subject as it   14
once was. Let alone God creating Adam out of hand, from the dust
of the earth, does anyone believe that Eve was made from Adam's
rib—that the snake walked and spoke in the Garden of Eden—that
he tempted Eve to persuade Adam to eat an apple, and that it is on
that account that the whole human race was doomed to hell—that
for four thousand years there was no chance for any human to be
saved, though none of them had anything whatever to do with the
temptation; and that finally men were saved only through God's
son dying for them, and that unless human beings believed this
silly, impossible and wicked story they were doomed to hell? Can
anyone with intelligence really believe that a child born today

should be doomed because the snake tempted Eve and Eve tempted Adam? To believe that is not God-worship; it is devil-worship.

15   Can anyone call this scheme of creation and damnation moral? It defies every principle of morality, as man conceives morality. Can anyone believe today that the whole world was destroyed by flood, save only Noah and his family and a male and female of each species of animal that entered the Ark? There are almost a million species of insects alone. How did Noah match these up and make sure of getting male and female to reproduce life in the world after the flood had spent its force? And why should all the lower animals have been destroyed? Were they included in the sinning of man? This is a story which could not beguile a fairly bright child of five years of age today.

16   Do intelligent people believe that the various languages spoken by man on earth came from the confusion of tongues at the Tower of Babel, some four thousand years ago? Human languages were dispersed all over the face of the earth long before that time. Evidences of civilizations are in existence now that were old long before the date that romancers fix for the building of the Tower, and even before the date claimed for the flood.

17   Do Christians believe that Joshua made the sun stand still, so that the day could be lengthened, that a battle might be finished? What kind of person wrote that story, and what did he know about astronomy? It is perfectly plain that the author thought that the earth was the center of the universe and stood still in the heavens, and that the sun either went around it or was pulled across its path each day, and that the stopping of the sun would lengthen the day. We know now that had the sun stopped when Joshua commanded it, and had it stood still until now, it would not have lengthened the day. We know that the day is determined by the rotation of the earth upon its axis, and not by the movement of the sun. Everyone knows that this story simply is not true, and not many even pretend to believe the childish fable.

18   What of the tale of Balaam's ass speaking to him, probably in Hebrew? Is it true, or is it a fable? Many asses have spoken, and doubtless some in Hebrew, but they have not been that breed of asses. Is salvation to depend on a belief in a monstrosity like this?

19   Above all the rest, would any human being today believe that a child was born without a father? Yet this story was not all unreasonable in the ancient world; at least three or four miraculous births are recorded in the Bible, including John the Baptist and Samson.

Immaculate conceptions were common in the Roman world at the time and at the place where Christianity really had its nativity. Women were taken to the temples to be inoculated of God so that their sons might be heroes, which meant, generally, wholesale butchers. Julius Caesar was a miraculous conception—indeed, they were common all over the world. How many miraculous-birth stories is a Christian now expected to believe?

In the days of the formation of the Christian religion, disease   20 meant the possession of human beings by devils. Christ cured a sick man by casting out the devils, who ran into the swine, and the swine ran into the sea. Is there any question but what that was simply the attitude and belief of a primitive people? Does anyone believe that sickness means the possession of the body by devils, and that the devils must be cast out of the human being that he may be cured? Does anyone believe that a dead person can come to life? The miracles recorded in the Bible are not the only instances of dead men coming to life. All over the world one finds testimony of such miracles: miracles which no person is expected to believe, unless it is his kind of a miracle. Still at Lourdes today, and all over the present world, from New York to Los Angeles and up and down the lands, people believe in miraculous occurrences, and even in the return of the dead. Superstition is everywhere prevalent in the world. It has been so from the beginning, and most likely will be so unto the end.

The reasons for agnosticism are abundant and compelling. Fan-   21 tastic and foolish and impossible consequences are freely claimed for the belief in religion. All the civilization of any period is put down as a result of religion. All the cruelty and error and ignorance of the period has no relation to religion. The truth is that the origin of what we call civilization is not due to religion but to skepticism. So long as men accepted miracles without question, so long as they believed in original sin and the road to salvation, so long as they believed in a hell where man would be kept for eternity on account of Eve, there was no reason whatever for civilization: life was short, and eternity was long, and the business of life was preparation for eternity.

When every event was a miracle, when there was no order or   22 system or law, there was no occasion for studying any subject, or being interested in anything excepting a religion which took care of the soul. As man doubted the primitive conceptions about religion, and no longer accepted the literal, miraculous teachings of ancient books, he set himself to understand nature. We no longer cure disease by casting out devils. Since that time, men have studied the human body, have built hospitals and treated illness in a scientific way. Science is responsible for the building of railroads and bridges, of steamships, of telegraph lines, of cities, towns, large buildings and small, plumbing and sanitation, of the food supply, and the countless thousands of useful things that we now deem necessary to life. Without skepticism and doubt, none of these things could have been given to the world.

23   The fear of God is not the beginning of wisdom. The fear of God is the death of wisdom. Skepticism and doubt lead to study and investigation, and investigation is the beginning of wisdom.

24   The modern world is the child of doubt and inquiry, as the ancient world was the child of fear and faith.

Thinking Critically About This Reading

1. What are the strengths of the writer's argument? What are its weaknesses? Cite specific passages to support your answer.

2. Darrow defines an agnostic as a doubter. What is your opinion concerning the value of doubt? Where is it appropriate and where is it not?

3. What is your reaction to paragraph 5? Can you provide the answers to the questions posed? How? Why not?

4. In paragraph 11, the author states that primitive, and even some civilized, people have become so accustomed to believing in miracles that they will call something a miracle when it is totally inconsistent with knowledge and logic. What is your definition of a miracle? Give an example of what you would consider a miracle.

5. To what extent do you agree with the author that "The modern world is the child of doubt and inquiry, as the ancient world was the child of fear and faith"? Provide examples from personal experience showing how faith is more important than knowledge or vice versa.

Understanding the Writer's Process

1. How does Darrow organize his argument? List the major divisions and their topics.

2. How does the author treat anyone who does not agree with him? How do you feel about this attitude on the part of the author?

3. What is the purpose of paragraph 18?

4. What is the purpose of the references to Spencer and Paley in paragraph 4?

5. What topic does the question at the beginning of paragraph 19 permit the author to introduce? How relevant is the topic?

Examining the Writer's Language

1. Use each of the following words in a sentence that indicates clearly your knowledge of what the word means: verity (paragraph 1), tenets (1), credence (2), anthropomorphic (3), veracity (10), skepticism (21).

2. The author does not think it possible to believe in an object or a thing unless the human mind can form an image of that object or thing. What figure of speech does Darrow use to make his idea concrete?

3. What does the term "coextensive" mean in paragraph 5?

4. What does the phrase "inoculated of God" mean in paragraph 19?

5. When the author says "The fear of God is the death of wisdom" in paragraph 23, how is he manipulating language?

Suggestions for Writing

1. Write an essay in which you explain either why you do or why you do not appreciate Darrow's argument.

2. Write an essay in which you extol the Bible by explaining its historical role in the fight against "evil."

LETTER FROM BIRMINGHAM JAIL

Martin Luther King, Jr.

Martin Luther King, Jr. (1929–1968) was a Baptist minister and president of the Southern Christian

*Leadership Conference, an organization actively in-
volved in the defense of equal rights for blacks. King
was born in Atlanta, Georgia, where he spent a good
share of his life. He was educated at Moorehouse College, Crozer Theological Seminary, and Boston University, from which he earned a Ph.D. In 1964, King's
unflagging struggle for peaceful resistance to White
oppression won him the Nobel Peace Prize. Since his
1968 assassination in Memphis, Tennessee, King's
name has often been linked with that of Mahatma Gandhi as a world figure symbolizing compassion for the
lot of all oppressed minorities. In 1986, President Ronald Reagan declared Martin Luther King Day a national
holiday. Two documents by King have become rhetorical classics: the famous speech, "I Have a Dream,"
and the moving and persuasive letter, reprinted here,
addressed to King's ministerial colleagues and written
while King was incarcerated for participation in civil
rights protests in Birmingham, Alabama.*

Preparing to Read This Selection Critically

The fact that the following selection is a letter addressed to King's colleagues places it in a special category
of argumentation. As you read, focus on those techniques
often used in correspondence and see how they affect the
tone and content of the work. Try to understand how
King's own experience as a black person advances his
argument. King believes in the interrelatedness of all
communities. How does this belief affect his argument
and do you agree with his basic assumptions? Try to
answer these questions as you progress through the letter.
Moreover, think of alternative actions to the one King
chose as a way of settling the racial issue examined in
the letter.

My Dear Fellow Clergymen:

1   While confined here in the Birmingham city jail, I came across
your recent statement calling my present activities "unwise and untimely." Seldom do I pause to answer criticism of my work and
ideas. If I sought to answer all the criticisms that cross my desk, my

secretaries would have little time for anything other than such correspondence in the course of the day, and I would have no time for constructive work. But since I feel that you are men of genuine good will and that your criticisms are sincerely set forth, I want to try to answer your statement in what I hope will be patient and reasonable terms.

I think I should indicate why I am here in Birmingham, since 2
you have been influenced by the view which argues against "outsiders coming in." I have the honor of serving as president of the Southern Christian Leadership Conference, an organization operating in every southern state, with headquarters in Atlanta, Georgia. We have some eighty-five affiliated organizations across the South, and one of them is the Alabama Christian Movement for Human Rights. Frequently we share staff, educational, and financial resources with our affiliates. Several months ago the affiliate here in Birmingham asked us to be on call to engage in a nonviolent direct-action program if such were deemed necessary. We readily consented, and when the hour came, we lived up to our promise. So I, along with several members of my staff, am here because I was invited here. I am here because I have organizational ties here.

But more basically, I am in Birmingham because injustice is 3
here. Just as the prophets of the eighth century B.C. left their villages and carried their "thus saith the Lord" far beyond the boundaries of their home towns, and just as the Apostle Paul left his village of Tarsus and carried the gospel of Jesus Christ to the far corners of the Greco-Roman world, so am I compelled to carry the gospel of freedom beyond my own home town. Like Paul, I must constantly respond to the Macedonian call for aid.

Moreover, I am cognizant of the interrelatedness of all com- 4
munities and states. I cannot sit idly by in Atlanta and not be concerned about what happens in Birmingham. Injustice anywhere is a threat to justice everywhere. We are caught in an inescapable network of mutuality, tied in a single garment of destiny. Whatever affects one directly, affects all indirectly. Never again can we afford to live with the narrow, provincial "outside agitator" idea. Anyone who lives inside the United States can never be considered an outsider anywhere within its bounds.

You deplore the demonstrations taking place in Birmingham. 5
But your statement, I am sorry to say, fails to express a similar concern for the conditions that brought about the demonstrations. I am sure that none of you would want to rest content with the

superficial kind of social analysis that deals merely with effects and does not grapple with underlying causes. It is unfortunate that demonstrations are taking place in Birmingham, but it is even more unfortunate that the city's white power structure left the Negro community with no alternative.

6   In any nonviolent campaign there are four basic steps: collection of the facts to determine whether injustices exist; negotiation; self-purification; and direct action. We have gone through all these steps in Birmingham. There can be no gainsaying the fact that racial injustice engulfs this community. Birmingham is probably the most thoroughly segregated city in the United States. Its ugly record of brutality is widely known. Negroes have experienced grossly unjust treatment in the courts. There have been more unsolved bombings of Negro homes and churches in Birmingham than in any other city in the nation. These are the hard, brutal facts of the case. On the basis of these conditions, Negro leaders sought to negotiate with the city fathers. But the latter consistently refused to engage in good-faith negotiation.

7   Then, last September, came the opportunity to talk with leaders of Birmingham's economic community. In the course of the negotiations, certain promises were made by the merchants—for example, to remove the stores' humiliating racial signs. On the basis of these promises, the Reverend Fred Shuttlesworth and the leaders of the Alabama Christian Movement for Human Rights agreed to a moratorium on all demonstrations. As the weeks and months went by, we realized that we were the victims of a broken promise. A few signs, briefly removed, returned; the others remained.

8   As in so many past experiences, our hopes had been blasted, and the shadow of deep disappointment settled upon us. We had no alternative except to prepare for direct action, whereby we would present our very bodies as a means of laying our case before the conscience of the local and the national community. Mindful of the difficulties involved, we decided to undertake a process of self-purification. We began a series of workshops on nonviolence, and we repeatedly asked ourselves: "Are you able to accept blows without retaliating?" "Are you able to endure the ordeal of jail?" We decided to schedule our direct-action program for the Easter season, realizing that except for Christmas, this is the main shopping period of the year. Knowing that a strong economic-withdrawal program would be the by product of direct action, we felt that this would be the

best time to bring pressure to bear on the merchants for the needed change.

Then it occurred to us that Birmingham's mayoral election was 9
coming up in March, and we speedily decided to postpone action until after election day. When we discovered that the Commissioner of Public Safety, Eugene "Bull" Connor, had piled up enough votes to be in the run-off, we decided again to postpone action until the day after the run-off so that the demonstrations could not be used to cloud the issues. Like many others, we waited to see Mr. Connor defeated, and to this end we endured postponement after postponement. Having aided in this community need, we felt that our direct-action program could be delayed no longer.

You may well ask, "Why direct action? Why sit-ins, marches, 10
and so forth? Isn't negotiation a better path?" You are quite right in calling for negotiation. Indeed, this is the very purpose of direct action. Nonviolent direct action seeks to create such a crisis and foster such a tension that a community which has constantly refused to negotiate is forced to confront the issue. It seeks so to dramatize the issue that it can no longer be ignored. My citing the creation of tension as part of the work of the nonviolent-resister may sound rather shocking. But I must confess that I am not afraid of the word "tension." I have earnestly opposed violent tension, but there is a type of constructive, nonviolent tension which is necessary for growth. Just as Socrates felt that it was necessary to create a tension in the mind so that individuals could rise from the bondage of myths and half-truths to the unfettered realm of creative analysis and objective appraisal, so must we see the need for nonviolent gadflies to create the kind of tension in society that will help men rise from the dark depths of prejudice and racism to the majestic heights of understanding and brotherhood.

The purpose of our direct-action program is to create a situation 11
so crisis-packed that it will inevitably open the door to negotiation. I therefore concur with you in your call for negotiation. Too long has our beloved Southland been bogged down in a tragic effort to live in monologue rather than dialogue.

One of the basic points in your statement is that the action 12
that I and my associates have taken in Birmingham is untimely. Some have asked: "Why didn't you give the new city administration time to act?" The only answer that I can give to this query is that the new Birmingham administration must be prodded about as much as the outgoing one, before it will act. We are sadly mistaken if we

feel that the election of Albert Boutwell as mayor will bring the millennium to Birmingham. While Mr. Boutwell is a much more gentle person than Mr. Connor, they are both segregationists, dedicated to maintenance of the status quo. I have hoped that Mr. Boutwell will be reasonable enough to see the futility of massive resistance to desegregation. But he will not see this without pressure from devotees of civil rights. My friends, I must say to you that we have not made a single gain in civil rights without determined legal and nonviolent pressure. Lamentably, it is an historical fact that privileged groups seldom give up their privileges voluntarily. Individuals may see the moral light and voluntarily give up their unjust posture; but, as Reinhold Niebuhr has reminded us, groups tend to be more immoral than individuals.

13   We know through painful experience that freedom is never voluntarily given by the oppressor; it must be demanded by the oppressed. Frankly, I have yet to engage in a direct-action campaign that was "well timed" in the view of those who have not suffered unduly from the disease of segregation. For years now I have heard the word "Wait!" It rings in the ear of every Negro with piercing familiarity. This "Wait" has almost always meant "Never." We must come to see, with one of our distinguished jurists, that "justice too long delayed is justice denied."

14   We have waited for more than 340 years for our constitutional and God-given rights. The nations of Asia and Africa are moving with jetlike speed toward gaining political independence, but we still creep at horse-and-buggy pace toward gaining a cup of coffee at a lunch counter. Perhaps it is easy for those who have never felt the stinging darts of segregation to say, "Wait." But when you have seen vicious mobs lynch your mothers and fathers at will and drown your sisters and brothers at whim; when you have seen hate-filled policemen curse, kick, and even kill your black brothers and sisters; when you see the vast majority of your twenty million Negro brothers smothering in an airtight cage of poverty in the midst of an affluent society; when you suddenly find your tongue twisted and your speech stammering as you seek to explain to your six-year-old daughter why she can't go to the public amusement park that has just been advertised on television, and see tears welling up in her eyes when she is told that Funtown is closed to colored children, and see ominous clouds of inferiority beginning to form in her little mental sky, and see her beginning to distort her personality by developing an unconscious bitterness toward white people; when

you have to concoct an answer for a five-year-old son who is asking "Daddy, why do white people treat colored people so mean?"; when you take a cross-country drive and find it necessary to sleep night after night in the uncomfortable corners of your automobile because no motel will accept you; when you are humiliated day in and day out by nagging signs reading "white" and "colored"; when your first name becomes "nigger," your middle name becomes "boy" (however old you are) and your last name becomes "John," and your wife and mother are never given the respected title "Mrs."; when you are harried by day and haunted by night by the fact that you are a Negro, living constantly at tiptoe stance, never quite knowing what to expect next, and are plagued with inner fears and outer resentments; when you are forever fighting a degenerating sense of "nobodiness"—then you will understand why we find it difficult to wait. There comes a time when the cup of endurance runs over, and men are no longer willing to be plunged into the abyss of despair. I hope, sirs, you can understand our legitimate and unavoidable impatience.

You express a great deal of anxiety over our willingness to break   15
laws. This is certainly a legitimate concern. Since we so diligently urge people to obey the Supreme Court's decision of 1954 outlawing segregation in the public schools, at first glance it may seem rather paradoxical for us consciously to break laws. One may well ask: "How can you advocate breaking some laws and obeying others?" The answer lies in the fact that there are two types of laws: just and unjust. I would be the first to advocate obeying just laws. One has not only a legal but a moral responsibility to obey just laws. Conversely, one has a moral responsibility to disobey unjust laws. I would agree with St. Augustine that "an unjust law is no law at all."

Now, what is the difference between the two? How does one   16
determine whether a law is just or unjust? A just law is a man-made code that squares with the moral law or the law of God. An unjust law is a code that is out of harmony with the moral law. To put it in the terms of St. Thomas Aquinas: An unjust law is a human law that is not rooted in eternal law and natural law. Any law that uplifts human personality is just. Any law that degrades human personality is unjust. All segregation statutes are unjust because segregation distorts the soul and damages the personality. It gives the segregator a false sense of superiority and the segregated a false sense of inferiority. Segregation, to use the terminology of the Jewish philosopher Martin Buber, substitutes "I-it" relationship for an "I-thou"

relationship and ends up relegating persons to the status of things. Hence segregation is not only politically, economically, and sociologically unsound, it is morally wrong and sinful. Paul Tillich has said that sin is separation. Is not segregation an existential expression of man's tragic separation, his awful estrangement, his terrible sinfulness? Thus it is that I can urge men to obey the 1954 decision of the Supreme Court, for it is morally right; and I can urge them to disobey segregation ordinances, for they are morally wrong.

17   Let us consider a more concrete example of just and unjust laws. An unjust law is a code that a numerical or power majority group compels a minority group to obey but does not make binding on itself. This is *difference* made legal. By the same token, a just law is a code that a majority compels a minority to follow and that it is willing to follow itself. This is *sameness* made legal.

18   Let me give another explanation. A law is unjust if it is inflicted on a minority that, as a result of being denied the right to vote, had no part in enacting or devising the law. Who can say that the legislature of Alabama which set up that state's segregation laws was democratically elected? Throughout Alabama all sorts of devious methods are used to prevent Negroes from becoming registered voters, and there are some counties in which, even though Negroes constitute a majority of the population, not a single Negro is registered. Can any law enacted under such circumstances be considered democratically structured?

19   Sometimes a law is just on its face and unjust in its application. For instance, I have been arrested on a charge of parading without a permit. Now, there is nothing wrong in having an ordinance which requires a permit for a parade. But such an ordinance becomes unjust when it is used to maintain segregation and to deny citizens the First-Amendment privilege of peaceful assembly and protest.

20   I hope you are able to see the distinction I am trying to point out. In no sense do I advocate evading or defying the law, as would the rabid segregationist. That would lead to anarchy. One who breaks an unjust law must do so openly, lovingly, and with a willingness to accept the penalty. I submit that an individual who breaks a law that conscience tells him is unjust, and who willingly accepts the penalty of imprisonment in order to arouse the conscience of the community over its injustice, is in reality expressing the highest respect for law.

21   Of course, there is nothing new about this kind of civil disobedience. It was evidenced sublimely in the refusal of Shadrach,

Meshach, and Abednego to obey the laws of Nebuchadnezzar, on the ground that a higher moral law was at stake. It was practiced superbly by the early Christians, who were willing to face hungry lions and the excruciating pain of chopping blocks rather than submit to certain unjust laws of the Roman Empire. To a degree, academic freedom is a reality today because Socrates practiced civil disobedience. In our own nation, the Boston Tea Party represented a massive act of civil disobedience.

We should never forget that everything Adolf Hitler did in 22 Germany was "legal" and everything the Hungarian freedom fighters did in Hungary was "illegal." It was "illegal" to aid and comfort a Jew in Hitler's Germany. Even so, I am sure that, had I lived in Germany at the time, I would have aided and comforted my Jewish brothers. If today I lived in a Communist country where certain principles dear to the Christian faith are suppressed, I would openly advocate disobeying that country's anti-religious laws.

I must make two honest confessions to you, my Christian and 23 Jewish brothers. First, I must confess that over the past few years I have been gravely disappointed with the white moderate. I have almost reached the regrettable conclusion that the Negro's great stumbling block in his stride toward freedom is not the White Citizen's Counciler or the Ku Klux Klanner, but the white moderate, who is more devoted to "order" than to justice; who prefers a negative peace which is the absence of tension to a positive peace which is the presence of justice; who constantly says, "I agree with you in the goal you seek, but I cannot agree with your methods of direct action"; who paternalistically believes he can set the timetable for another man's freedom; who lives by a mythical concept of time and who constantly advises the Negro to wait for a "more convenient season." Shallow understanding from people of good will is more frustrating than absolute misunderstanding from people of ill will. Lukewarm acceptance is much more bewildering than outright rejection.

I had hoped that the white moderate would understand that 24 law and order exist for the purpose of establishing justice and that when they fail in this purpose they become the dangerously structured dams that block the flow of social progress. I had hoped that the white moderate would understand that the present tension in the South is a necessary phase of the transition from an obnoxious negative peace, in which the Negro passively accepted his unjust plight, to a substantive and positive peace, in which all men will respect the dignity and worth of human personality. Actually, we who engage in nonviolent direction action are not the creators of tension. We merely bring to the surface the hidden tension that is already alive. We bring it out in the open, where it can be seen and dealt with. Like a boil that can never be cured so long as it is covered up but must be opened with all its ugliness to the natural medicines of air and light, injustice must be exposed, with all the tension its exposure creates, to the light of human conscience and the air of national opinion, before it can be cured.

25   In your statement you assert that our actions, even though peaceful, must be condemned because they precipitate violence. But is this a logical assertion? Isn't this like condemning a robbed man because his possession of money precipitated the evil act of robbery? Isn't this like condemning Socrates because his unswerving commitment to truth and his philosophical inquiries precipitated the act by the misguided populace in which they made him drink hemlock? Isn't this like condemning Jesus because his unique God-consciousness and never-ceasing devotion to God's will precipitated the evil act of crucifixion? We must come to see that, as the federal courts have consistently affirmed, it is wrong to urge an individual to cease his efforts to gain his basic constitutional rights because the quest may precipitate violence. Society must protect the robbed and punish the robber.

26   I had also hoped that the white moderate would reject the myth concerning time in relation to the struggle for freedom. I have just received a letter from a white brother in Texas. He writes: "All Christians know that the colored people will receive equal rights eventually, but it is possible that you are in too great a religious hurry. It has taken Christianity almost two thousand years to accomplish what it has. The teachings of Christ take time to come to earth." Such an attitude stems from a tragic misconception of time, from the strangely irrational notion that there is something in the very flow of time that will inevitably cure all ills. Actually, time itself is neutral; it can be used either destructively or constructively. More and more I feel that the people of ill will have used time much more effectively than have the people of good will. We will have to repent in this generation not merely for the hateful words and actions of the bad people, but for the appalling silence of the good people. Human progress never rolls in on wheels of inevitability; it comes through the tireless efforts of men willing to be co-workers with God, and without this hard work, time itself becomes an ally

of the forces of social stagnation. We must use time creatively, in the knowledge that the time is always ripe to do right. Now is the time to make real the promise of democracy and transform our pending national elegy into a creative psalm of brotherhood. Now is the time to lift our national policy from the quicksand of racial injustice to the solid rock of human dignity.

You speak of our activity in Birmingham as extreme. At first I was rather disappointed that fellow clergymen would see my non-violent efforts as those of an extremist. I began thinking about the fact that I stand in the middle of two opposing forces in the Negro community. One is a force of complacency, made up in part of Negroes who, as a result of long years of oppression, are so drained of self-respect and a sense of "somebodiness" that they have adjusted to segregation; and in part of a few middle-class Negroes who, because of a degree of academic and economic security and because in some ways they profit by segregation, have become insensitive to the problems of the masses. The other force is one of bitterness and hatred, and it comes perilously close to advocating violence. It is expressed in the various black nationalist groups that are springing up across the nation, the largest and best-known being Elijah Muhammad's Muslim movement. Nourished by the Negro's frustration over the continued existence of racial discrimination, this movement is made up of people who have lost faith in America, who have absolutely repudiated Christianity, and who have concluded that the white man is an incorrigible "devil."

I have tried to stand between these two forces, saying that we need emulate neither the "do-nothingism" of the complacent nor the hatred and despair of the black nationalist. For there is the more excellent way of love and nonviolent protest. I am grateful to God that, through the influence of the Negro church, the way of nonviolence became an integral part of our struggle.

If this philosophy had not emerged, by now many streets of the South would, I am convinced, be flowing with blood. And I am further convinced that if our white brothers dismiss as "rabble-rousers" and "outside agitators" those of us who employ nonviolent direct action, and if they refuse to support our nonviolent efforts, millions of Negroes will, out of frustration and despair, seek solace and security in Black-nationalist ideologies—a development that would inevitably lead to a frightening racial nightmare.

Oppressed people cannot remain oppressed forever. The yearning for freedom eventually manifests itself, and that is what

27

28

29

30

has happened to the American Negro. Something within has reminded him of his birthright of freedom, and something without has reminded him that it can be gained. Consciously or unconsciously, he has been caught up by the *Zeitgeist*, and with his black brothers of Africa and his brown and yellow brothers of Asia, South America, and the Caribbean, the United States Negro is moving with a sense of great urgency toward the promised land of racial justice. If one recognizes this vital urge that has engulfed the Negro community, one should readily understand why public demonstrations are taking place. The Negro has many pent-up resentments and latent frustrations, and he must release them. So let him march; let him make prayer pilgrimages to the city hall; let him go on freedom rides—and try to understand why he must do so. If his repressed emotions are not released in nonviolent ways, they will seek expression through violence; this is not a threat but a fact of history. So I have not said to my people, "Get rid of your discontent." Rather, I have tried to say that this normal and healthy discontent can be channeled into the creative outlet of nonviolent direct action. And now this approach is being termed extremist.

31   But though I was initially disappointed at being categorized as an extremist, as I continued to think about the matter I gradually gained a measure of satisfaction from the label. Was not Jesus an extremist for love: "Love your enemies, bless them that curse you, do good to them that hate you, and pray for them which despitefully use you, and persecute you." Was not Amos an extremist for justice: "Let justice roll down like waters and righteousness like an ever-flowing stream." Was not Paul an extremist for the Christian gospel: "I bear in my body the marks of the Lord Jesus." Was not Martin Luther an extremist: "Here I stand; I cannot do otherwise, so help me God." And John Bunyan: "I will stay in jail to the end of my days before I make a butchery of my conscience." And Abraham Lincoln: "This nation cannot survive half slave and half free." And Thomas Jefferson: "We hold these truths to be self-evident, that all men are created equal. . . ." So the question is not whether we will be extremists, but what kind of extremists we will be. Will we be extremists for hate or for love? Will we be extremists for the preservation of injustice or for the extension of justice? In that dramatic scene on Calvary's hill three men were crucified. We must never forget that all three were crucified for the same crime—the crime of extremism. Two were extremists for immorality, and thus fell below their environment. The other, Jesus Christ, was an extremist for love,

truth, and goodness, and thereby rose above his environment. Perhaps the South, the nation, and the world are in dire need of creative extremists.

I had hoped that the white moderate would see this need. 32 Perhaps I was too optimistic; perhaps I expected too much. I suppose I should have realized that few members of the oppressor race can understand the deep groans and passionate yearnings of the oppressed race, and still fewer have the vision to see that injustice must be rooted out by strong, persistent, and determined action. I am thankful, however, that some of our white brothers in the South have grasped the meaning of this social revolution and committed themselves to it. They are still all too few in quantity, but they are big in quality. Some—such as Ralph McGill, Lillian Smith, Harry Golden, James McBride Dabbs, Anne Braden, and Sarah Patton Boyle—have written about our struggle in eloquent and prophetic terms. Others have marched with us down nameless streets of the South. They have languished in filthy, roach-infested jails, suffering the abuse and brutality of policemen who view them as "dirty nigger-lovers." Unlike so many of their moderate brothers and sisters, they have recognized the urgency of the moment and sensed the need for powerful "action" antidotes to combat the disease of segregation.

Let me take note of my other major disappointment. I have 33 been so greatly disappointed with the white church and its leadership. Of course, there are some notable exceptions. I am not unmindful of the fact that each of you has taken some significant stands on this issue. I commend you, Reverend Stallings, for your Christian stand on this past Sunday, in welcoming Negroes to your worship service on a nonsegregated basis. I commend the Catholic leaders of this state for integrating Spring Hill College several years ago.

But despite these notable exceptions, I must honestly reiterate 34 that I have been disappointed with the church. I do not say this as one of those negative critics who can always find something wrong with the church. I say this as a minister of the gospel, who loves the church; who was nurtured in its bosom; who has been sustained by its spiritual blessings and who will remain true to it as long as the cord of life shall lengthen.

When I was suddenly catapulted into the leadership of the bus 35 protest in Montgomery, Alabama, a few years ago, I felt we would be supported by the white church. I felt that the white ministers, priests, and rabbis of the South would be among our strongest allies.

Instead, some have been outright opponents, refusing to understand the freedom movement and misrepresenting its leaders; all too many others have been more cautious than courageous and have remained silent behind the anesthetizing security of stained glass windows.

36   In spite of my shattered dreams, I came to Birmingham with the hope that the white religious leadership of this community would see the justice of our cause and, with deep moral concern, would serve as the channel through which our just grievances could reach the power structure. I had hoped that each of you would understand. But again I have been disappointed.

37   I have heard numerous southern religious leaders admonish their worshipers to comply with a desegregation decision because it is the law, but I have longed to hear white ministers declare: "Follow this decree because integration is morally right and because the Negro is your brother." In the midst of blatant injustices inflicted upon the Negro, I have watched white churchmen stand on the sideline and mouth pious irrelevancies and sanctimonious trivialities. In the midst of a mighty struggle to rid our nation of racial and economic injustice I have heard many ministers say: "Those are social issues, with which the gospel has no real concern." And I have watched many churches commit themselves to a completely otherworldly religion which makes a strange, un-Biblical distinction between body and soul, between the sacred and the secular.

38   I have traveled the length and breadth of Alabama, Mississippi, and all the other southern states. On sweltering summer days and crisp autumn mornings I have looked at the South's beautiful churches with their lofty spires pointing heavenward. I have beheld the impressive outlines of her massive religious-education buildings. Over and over I have found myself asking: "What kind of people worship here? Who is their God? Where were their voices when the lips of Governor Barnett dripped with words of interposition and nullification? Where were they when Governor Wallace gave a clarion call for defiance and hatred? Where were their voices of support when bruised and weary Negro men and women decided to rise from the dark dungeons of complacency to the bright hills of creative protest?"

39   Yes, these questions are still in my mind. In deep disappointment I have wept over the laxity of the church. But be assured that my tears have been tears of love. There can be no deep disappointment where there is not deep love. Yes, I love the church. How could I do otherwise? I am in the rather unique position of being the son,

the grandson, and the great-grandson of preachers. Yes, I see the church as the body of Christ. But, oh! How we have blemished and scarred that body through social neglect and through fear of being nonconformists.

There was a time when the church was very powerful—in the   40
time when the early Christians rejoiced at being deemed worthy to suffer for what they believed. In those days the church was not merely a thermometer that recorded the ideas and principles of popular opinion; it was a thermostat that transformed the mores of society. Whenever the early Christians entered a town, the people in power became disturbed and immediately sought to convict the Christians for being "disturbers of the peace" and "outside agitators." But the Christians pressed on, in the conviction that they were "a colony of heaven," called to obey God rather than man. Small in number, they were big in commitment. They were too God-intoxicated to be "astronomically intimidated." By their effort and example they brought an end to such ancient evils as infanticide and gladiatorial contests.

Things are different now. So often the contemporary church   41
is a weak, ineffectual voice with an uncertain sound. So often it is an archdefender of the status quo. Far from being disturbed by the presence of the church, the power structure of the average community is consoled by the church's silent—and often even vocal—sanction of things as they are.

But the judgment of God is upon the church as never before.   42
If today's church does not recapture the sacrificial spirit of the early church, it will lose its authenticity, forfeit the loyalty of millions, and be dismissed as an irrelevant social club with no meaning for the twentieth century. Every day I meet young people whose disappointment with the church has turned into outright disgust.

Perhaps I have once again been too optimistic. Is organized   43
religion too inextricably bound to the status quo to save our nation and the world? Perhaps I must turn my faith to the inner spiritual church, the church within the church, as the true *ekklesia*[1] and the hope of the world. But again I am thankful to God that some noble souls from the ranks of organized religion have broken loose from the paralyzing chains of conformity and joined us as active partners in the struggle for freedom. They have left their secure congregations and walked the streets of Albany, Georgia, with us. They have gone

[1] The Greek New Testament word for the early Christian church.

down the highways of the South on tortuous rides for freedom. Yes, they have gone to jail with us. Some have been dismissed from their churches, have lost the support of their bishops and fellow ministers. But they have acted in the faith that right defeated is stronger than evil triumphant. Their witness has been the spiritual salt that has preserved the true meaning of the gospel in these troubled times. They have carved a tunnel of hope through the dark mountain of disappointment.

44   I hope the church as a whole will meet the challenge of this decisive hour. But even if the church does not come to the aid of justice, I have no despair about the future. I have no fear about the outcome of our struggle in Birmingham, even if our motives are at present misunderstood. We will reach the goal of freedom in Birmingham and all over the nation, because the goal of America is freedom. Abused and scorned though we may be, our destiny is tied up with America's destiny. Before the pilgrims landed at Plymouth, we were here. Before the pen of Jefferson etched the majestic words of the Declaration of Independence across the pages of history, we were here. For more than two centuries our forebears labored in this country without wages; they made cotton king; they built the homes of their masters while suffering gross injustice and shameful humiliation—and yet out of a bottomless vitality they continued to thrive and develop. If the inexpressible cruelties of slavery could not stop us, the opposition we now face will surely fail. We will win our freedom because the sacred heritage of our nation and the eternal will of God are embodied in our echoing demands.

45   Before closing I feel impelled to mention one other point in your statement that has troubled me profoundly. You warmly commended the Birmingham police force for keeping "order" and "preventing violence." I doubt that you would have so warmly commended the police force if you had seen its dogs sinking their teeth into unarmed, nonviolent Negroes. I doubt that you would so quickly commend the policemen if you were to observe their ugly and inhumane treatment of Negroes here in the city jail; if you were to watch them push and curse old Negro women and young Negro girls; if you were to see them slap and kick old Negro men and young boys; if you were to observe them, as they did on two occasions, refuse to give us food because we wanted to sing our grace together. I cannot join you in your praise of the Birmingham police department.

It is true that the police have exercised a degree of discipline   46
in handling the demonstrators. In this sense they have conducted
themselves rather "nonviolently" in public. But for what purpose?
To preserve the evil system of segregation. Over the past few years
I have consistently preached that nonviolence demands that the
means we use must be as pure as the ends we seek. I have tried to
make clear that it is wrong to use immoral means to attain moral
ends. But now I must affirm that it is just as wrong, or perhaps even
more so, to use moral means to preserve immoral ends. Perhaps Mr.
Connor and his policemen have been rather nonviolent in public,
as was Chief Pritchett in Albany, Georgia, but they have used the
moral means of nonviolence to maintain the immoral end of racial
injustice. As T. S. Eliot has said, "The last temptation is the greatest
treason: To do the right deed for the wrong reason."

I wish you had commended the Negro sit-inners and dem-   47
onstrators of Birmingham for their sublime courage, their willingness
to suffer, and their amazing discipline in the midst of great prov-
ocation. One day the South will recognize its real heroes. They will
be the James Merediths, with the noble sense of purpose that enables
them to face jeering and hostile mobs, and with the agonizing loneliness that characterizes the life of the pioneer. They will be old,
oppressed, battered Negro women, symbolized in a seventy-two-
year-old woman in Montgomery, Alabama, who rose up with a
sense of dignity and with her people decided not to ride segregated
buses, and who responded with ungrammatical profundity to one
who inquired about her weariness: "My feets is tired, but my soul
is at rest." They will be the young high school and college students,
the young ministers of the gospel and a host of their elders, cou-
rageously and nonviolently sitting in at lunch counters and willingly
going to jail for conscience' sake. One day the South will know that
when these disinherited children of God sat down at lunch counters,
they were in reality standing up for what is best in the American
dream and for the most sacred values in our Judaeo-Christian heritage, thereby bringing our nation back to those great wells of democracy which were dug deep by the founding fathers in their for-
mulation of the Constitution and the Declaration of Independence.

Never before have I written so long a letter. I'm afraid it is   48
much too long to take your precious time. I can assure you that it
would have been much shorter if I had been writing from a comfortable desk, but what else can one do when he is alone in a narrow

jail cell, other than write long letters, think long thoughts, and pray long prayers?

49   If I have said anything in this letter that overstates the truth and indicates an unreasonable impatience, I beg you to forgive me. If I have said anything that understates the truth and indicates my having a patience that allows me to settle for anything less than brotherhood, I beg God to forgive me.

50   I hope this letter finds you strong in the faith. I also hope that circumstances will soon make it possible for me to meet each of you, not as an integrationist or a civil-rights leader but as a fellow clergyman and a Christian brother. Let us all hope that the dark clouds of racial prejudice will soon pass away and the deep fog of misunderstanding will be lifted from our fear-drenched communities, and in some not too distant tomorrow the radiant stars of love and brotherhood will shine over our great nation with all their scintillating beauty.

Yours for the cause of Peace and Brotherhood,

MARTIN LUTHER KING, JR.

Thinking Critically About This Reading

1. What reasons does King give his colleagues for his being in Alabama? Why does he feel compelled to offer them reasons? What is your view of his reasons?

2. In paragraph 6, King indicates that four steps must be completed before taking direct action against racial abuse. What is your critical evaluation of these steps? Which step do you consider the most important? What does King mean by *self-purification?* What other steps, if any, do you suggest?

3. According to King, what is the purpose of demonstrations, sit-ins, and marches? Do you agree with these means? Why? Why not?

4. Do you agree with King's view, expressed in paragraph 12, that privileged groups seldom give up their privileges voluntarily? Provide historical examples to support your answer.

5. Do you agree with King that if a law of the land is unjust, you should break it? What alternative do you suggest? What contemporary laws, if any, do you consider unjust? What do you suggest doing about them?

Understanding the Writer's Process

1. What is the relationship of the title to the content of the letter?
2. What kinds of analogies does the author continuously draw throughout his letter? How effective or fair are they?
3. King devotes considerable space to an issue that has caused him painful disappointment. What issue is this? Which paragraphs deal with the issue?
4. What is the purpose and effect of paragraph 14?
5. Is King's ending appropriate to his purpose? How effective is it? Evaluate the ending from a literary point of view.

Examining the Writer's Language

1. Explain the following expressions used by King: "tied in a single garment of destiny" (paragraph 4), "nonviolent gadflies" (10), "stinging darts" (14), "mythical concept of time" (23), "frightening racial nightmare" (29), "anesthetizing security of stained glass windows" (35).
2. What is the effect of addressing his readers as "My Dear Fellow Clergymen"?
3. To whom is King referring when he uses the phrase "these disinherited children of God" in paragraph 47? In what way are they disinherited?
4. What language in the letter reveals that King is addressing clergymen with more than a passing acquaintance with theology? What is the purpose of this language?
5. What about King's language and style reveals the fact that he was an experienced preacher? Cite specific passages.

Suggestions for Writing

1. Write an essay in which you argue against some racial prejudice of which you are aware in your personal environment. Use strong evidence (vivid examples, facts, quotations from authorities, and personal experience) to strengthen your argument.
2. Pretending that King's letter is addressed to you, answer it in approximately 500 words.

HILLS LIKE WHITE ELEPHANTS

Ernest Hemingway

Ernest Hemingway (1899–1961) was one of American's most celebrated twentieth–century novelists and short–story writers. The son of a country doctor, he worked as a reporter for the Kansas City Star, *where he began to develop his matchless reportorial style. During World War I, he served as an ambulance driver in France and in Italy. Later—while working in Paris as a correspondent for the* Toronto Star—*he became friends with Gertrude Stein and her circle of expatriate Americans, a group he describes in his novel* The Sun Also Rises *(1926). His next important novel was* A Farewell to Arms *(1929), which explores a tragic wartime love affair between an ambulance driver and a British nurse. During the Spanish Civil War, Hemingway worked as a correspondent on the Loyalist side and recorded his experiences in* For Whom the Bell Tolls *(1940). In 1954, Hemingway was awarded the Nobel Prize in Literature. Hemingway is also known for his many excellent short stories, which often focus on people who live dangerously and who face tragic experiences with profound stoicism. Among such stories is the following work concerning two lovers who come to a crossroads in their relationship.*

Preparing to Read This Selection Critically

As it dawns on you what problem the two characters in this story are facing, you will see that the narrative can form a nice jumping–off point to a social argument still debated in social, psychological, religious, and political circles today. You must pay close attention to every word spoken by both the man and the woman in the story so as not to misread what is happening. Once you understand the problem and discern the attitudes subtly revealed by both parties, the story should provide you with considerable emotional fuel for a strong position either for or against the action contemplated.

The hills across the valley of the Ebro were long and white. 1
On this side there was no shade and no trees and the station was
between two lines of rails in the sun. Close against the side of the
station there was the warm shadow of the building and a curtain,
made of strings of bamboo beads, hung across the open door into
the bar, to keep out flies. The American and the girl with him sat
at a table in the shade, outside the building. It was very hot and
the express from Barcelona would come in forty minutes. It stopped
at this junction for two minutes and went on to Madrid.

"What should we drink?" the girl asked. She had taken off 2
her hat and put it on the table.

"It's pretty hot," the man said. 3

"Let's drink beer." 4

"Dos cervezas," the man said into the curtain. 5

"Big ones?" a woman asked from the doorway. 6

"Yes. Two big ones." 7

The woman brought two glasses of beer and two felt pads. 8
She put the felt pads and the beer glasses on the table and looked
at the man and the girl. The girl was looking off at the line of hills.
They were white in the sun and the country was brown and dry.

"They look like white elephants," she said. 9

"I've never seen one," the man drank his beer. 10

"No, you wouldn't have." 11

"I might have," the man said. "Just because you say I wouldn't 12
have doesn't prove anything."

The girl looked at the bead curtain. "They've painted some- 13
thing on it," she said. "What does it say?"

"Anis del Toro. It's a drink." 14

"Could we try it?" 15

The man called "Listen" through the curtain. The woman came 16
out from the bar.

"Four reales." 17

"We want two Anis del Toro." 18

"With water?" 19

"Do you want it with water?" 20

"I don't know," the girl said. "Is it good with water?" 21

"It's all right." 22

"You want them with water?" asked the woman. 23

"Yes, with water." 24

"It tastes like licorice," the girl said and put the glass down. 25

"That's the way with everything." 26

27   "Yes," said the girl. "Everything tastes of licorice. Especially all the things you've waited so long for, like absinthe."

28   "Oh, cut it out."

29   "You started it," the girl said. "I was being amused. I was having a fine time."

30   "Well, let's try and have a fine time."

31   "All right. I was trying. I said the mountains looked like white elephants. Wasn't that bright?"

32   "That was bright."

33   "I wanted to try this new drink. That's all we do, isn't it—look at things and try new drinks?"

34   "I guess so."

35   The girl looked across at the hills.

36   "They're lovely hills," she said. "They don't really look like white elephants. I just meant the coloring of their skin through the trees."

37   "Should we have another drink?"

38   "All right."

39   The warm wind blew the bead curtain against the table.

40   "The beer's nice and cool," the man said.

41   "It's lovely," the girl said.

42   "It's really an awfully simple operation, Jig," the man said. "It's not really an operation at all."

43   The girl looked at the ground the table legs rested on.

44   "I know you wouldn't mind it, Jig. It's really not anything. It's just to let the air in."

45   The girl did not say anything.

46   "I'll go with you and I'll stay with you all the time. They just let the air in and then it's all perfectly natural."

47   "Then what will we do afterward?"

48   "We'll be fine afterward. Just like we were before."

49   "What makes you think so?"

50   "That's the only thing that bothers us. It's the only thing that's made us unhappy."

51   The girl looked at the bead curtain, put her hand out and took hold of two of the strings of beads.

52   "And you think then we'll be all right and be happy."

53   "I know we will. You don't have to be afraid. I've known lots of people that have done it."

54   "So have I," said the girl. "And afterward they were all so happy."

"Well," the man said, "if you don't want to you don't have to.   55
I wouldn't have you do it if you didn't want to. But I know it's
perfectly simple."

"And you really want to?"   56

"I think it's the best thing to do. But I don't want you to do   57
it if you don't really want to."

"And if I do it you'll be happy and things will be like they   58
were and you'll love me?"

"I love you now. You know I love you."   59

"I know. But if I do it, then it will be nice again if I say things   60
are like white elephants, and you'll like it?"

"I'll love it. I love it now but I just can't think about it. You   61
know how I get when I worry."

"If I do it you won't ever worry?"   62

"I won't worry about that because it's perfectly simple."   63

"Then I'll do it. Because I don't care about me."   64

"What do you mean?"   65

"I don't care about me."   66

"Well, I care about you."   67

"Oh, yes. But I don't care about me. And I'll do it and then   68
everything will be fine."

"I don't want you to do it if you feel that way."   69

The girl stood up and walked to the end of the station. Across,   70
on the other side, were fields of grain and trees along the banks of
the Ebro. Far away, beyond the river, were mountains. The shadow
of a cloud moved across the field of grain and she saw the river
through the trees.

"And we could have all this," she said. "And we could have   71
everything and every day we make it more impossible."

"What did you say?"   72

"I said we could have everything."   73

"We can have everything."   74

"No, we can't."   75

"We can have the whole world."   76

"No, we can't."   77

"We can go everywhere."   78

"No, we can't. It isn't ours any more."   79

"It's ours."   80

"No, it isn't. And once they take it away, you never get it   81
back."

"But they haven't taken it away."   82

83 "We'll wait and see."

84 "Come on back in the shade," he said. "You mustn't feel that way."

85 "I don't feel any way," the girl said. "I just know things."

86 "I don't want you to do anything that you don't want to do—"

87 "Nor that isn't good for me," she said. "I know. Could we have another beer?"

88 "All right. But you've got to realize—"

89 "I realize," the girl said. "Can't we maybe stop talking?"

90 They sat down at the table and the girl looked across at the hills on the dry side of the valley and the man looked at her and at the table.

91 "You've got to realize," he said, "that I don't want you to do it if you don't want to. I'm perfectly willing to go through with it if it means anything to you."

92 "Doesn't it mean anything to you? We could get along."

93 "Of course it does. But I don't want anybody but you. I don't want any one else. And I know it's perfectly simple."

94 "Yes, you know it's perfectly simple."

95 "It's all right for you to say that, but I do know it."

96 "Would you do something for me now?"

97 "I'd do anything for you."

98 "Would you please please please please please please please stop talking?"

99 He did not say anything but looked at the bags against the wall of the station. There were labels on them from all the hotels where they had spent nights.

100 "But I don't want you to," he said, "I don't care anything about it."

101 "I'll scream," the girl said.

102 The woman came out through the curtains with two glasses of beer and put them down on the damp felt pads. "The train comes in five minutes," she said.

103 "What did she say?" asked the girl.

104 "That the train is coming in five minutes."

105 The girl smiled brightly at the woman, to thank her.

106 "I'd better take the bags over to the other side of the station," the man said. She smiled at him.

107 "All right. Then come back and we'll finish the beer."

108 He picked up the two heavy bags and carried them around the station to the other tracks. He looked up the tracks but could

not see the train. Coming back, he walked through the barroom, where people waiting for the train were drinking. He drank an Anis at the bar and looked at the people. They were all waiting reasonably for the train. He went out through the bead curtain. She was sitting at the table and smiled at him.

"Do you feel better?" he asked. 109

"I feel fine," she said. "There's nothing wrong with me. I feel 110 fine."

Thinking Critically About This Reading

1. Although stories usually have no formal argument, they have a theme: They argue a point about life. What, then, is the point of this story? What does it tell you about life?

2. Where in the story is the first hint of a problem? What is the problem? What people have you known personally who have faced a similar problem? What was their response?

3. What does the man mean when he says, "It's perfectly simple"? Do you believe he is convinced that *it* really is simple? Give reasons for your answer.

4. What difference in attitude exists between the woman and the man? Does this difference seem realistic? Would the situation be different today? Explain your answers.

5. The story ends with this comment by the woman: "There's nothing wrong with me. I feel fine." Has she convinced you? Why? Why not? What do you think will happen? Describe life for this couple one year hence.

Understanding the Writer's Process

1. Viewed superficially, this story seems to be excessively simple and to go nowhere. How does the author add depth to the story?

2. What relevance does the title have to the meaning of the story?

3. What is the purpose of the dialogue in paragraphs 71–85? How crucial is the dialogue? Explain your answer fully.

4. Paragraph 8 ends with the man's sentence not completed. What was he going to say when the woman interrupted? Why did she interrupt?

5. Why does the author leave the ending of the story so unresolved?

Examining the Writer's Language

1. How would you describe the style in which this story is written? Compare it with the style of some other author you have read.
2. What is the ratio of dialogue to narrative commentary? What effect does this ratio have?
3. A substantial proportion of dialogue deals with the seemingly trivial issue of choosing a drink. How do you explain so much ado about nothing?
4. How is *licorice* used in the conversation about the drink Anis del Toro (paragraphs 16–28)?

Writing Assignment Based on "Hills Like White Elephants"

"Hills Like White Elephants" deals subtly with a highly charged social issue about which various factions disagree, often vehemently. Write an essay in which you argue for or against some other moral, social, or political issue currently debated in our society.

STUDENT ESSAY (IN PROCESS) ARGUMENTATION

Jeannie Pugmire

> *Jeannie Pugmire is in her first year of college and as yet has not declared a major, preferring first to complete her general education requirements. One of her favorite pastimes is reading and discussing current issues, especially those affecting societal ethics. Jeannie became emotionally as well as intellectually involved in the "Baby M" case when it gained considerable media coverage. In the essay that follows, she clearly states her position.*

First Draft   Jeannie Pugmire

                                        English 101

awkward title   ~~Better Contracts for Surrogate Mothers~~
                   ~~Surrogate Mother Contracts need to Be Revised~~

                                        The issue is Surrogate Motherhood

what issue?   A highly emotional and controversial
I'd better say   issue has lately captivated the attention of
                   the media as well as the public. Because ~~the~~
                   it
                   ~~issue~~ is charged with ethical and moral impli-   *People are*
                   cations never before faced by modern courts,   *firmly*
                                                                          divided
                   some people applaud surrogate motherhood as a   *in their*
                                                              just   *opinions*
                   modern miracle whereas others see it as ~~yet~~   *on the*
                                                depravity   *subject.*
                   another sign of contemporary ~~degeneration~~.
                   Now, a surrogate mother is a woman who agrees
                   to have a baby for another woman. The surrogate
                   is usually artificially inseminated by the
                   other woman's husband. A contract is drawn up,
                   usually stating that, for a certain sum of
                   money, the surrogate agrees to give up her baby
                   upon birth.

                   No ¶ This arrangement sounds very cut and
                                    it is not. Many ramifications obscure
                   dried, but ~~one could not be further from the~~
                   the landscape, and
                   ~~truth if he or she believes this~~. Strong oppos-
                   ition to the whole idea is rapidly spreading.
                   Questions are constantly popping up: Is it
                   right or natural for the biological mother to
                                            Doesn't   whole   boil down to
                   "give away" her child? ~~Isn't~~ the process il-
                   legal adoption of a child? Isn't surrogate
                   mothering simply a form of adultery?
                                        at the center of this murky
                       The real problem, ~~in this entire~~ situa-
                   tion is the contract itself. It is the cause of
                            difficulties
                   many ~~problems~~ for both parties involved after
                   the baby is born. Most contracts state that the

natural mother must give up the baby, upon
birth, to the couple she agreed to have it for.
The contracts do not allow the woman who gave
birth any period of time to reconsider her decision to give her own child away. If surrogate
motherhood is to become an accepted way for a
childless couple to become parents, then the
contracts must be revised to ~~reflect~~ *resemble* adoption
laws, since surrogate mothering is similar to
adopting. Adoption agreements give the natural
mother time to reconsider her decision to give
up her baby and to change her mind. This time *is essential and*
for reflection and psychological probing must
be allowed.

A classic current case—the case of "Baby
M"—involves Rick and Marybeth Whitehead ~~and~~ *versus*
William and Elizabeth Stern. Having agreed to
"rent her womb" to the Sterns, Marybeth
Whitehead was artifically inseminated by William Stern. A contract was drawn up, stating
that for the price of $10,000 Whitehead would
surrender the baby, upon birth, to the Sterns.
The contract said absolutely nothing about allowing Whitehead time to think about what she
was doing. But, after giving birth to a baby
girl on March 17, 1986, Whitehead refused to
give up the baby, claiming that unforeseen in-
stinctive urges caused her to become so attached to her baby that she would "lose her
mind" if she gave her up. On the other side, the
Sterns were taking care of the baby and had become bonded to her as well. The result was a
catastrophic legal battle, which to date has

not been resolved fully, although the New Jersey court awarded preliminary custody to the Sterns, based on the contract provisions.

I sympathize with Marybeth Whitehead. She carried that baby in her womb for nine months and, as is nature's way, she had grown to love the stirrings inside her, as all mothers learn to love a child forming within them. The contract she had signed became an obligation she simply could not fulfill. It was too businesslike and too cold. It allowed no opportunity for ~~Whitehead~~ her to sort out her feelings after the baby was born—and that is wrong. Whitehead is the natural mother of this infant and here she is forced to live up to an agreement ~~which was~~ made before the decisive factors in the case were available. The opposition might argue that William Stern has rights, too, since he is the biological father, but psychologists and obstetricians alike agree that a father's bonding to the fetus forming inside a womb is not as obsessive as that of the mother. As Dr. William Faraday, the obstetrician in Los Angeles, observed, "The protective instinct of a mother after birth is one of the fiercest powers in nature."

Many thoughtful persons are seeing the evil side of present surrogate mother contracts. For instance, William Pierce, who is president of the National Committee for Adoption, has taken a strong stand against the present way of drawing up surrogate mother contracts. He states, "It commercializes a very

[handwritten margin notes:]
I need more explanation

not being clairvoyant, she did not anticipate the affection that would well up once she saw and held her baby.

add something — emotional — perhaps lines from a poem

private thing. It should not take place at all." Most lawyers and psychologists who have studied the problem agree that surrogate mother contracts, in their present forms, are confusing and blatantly unfair. First and foremost, the natural mother is expected (to) coldbloodedly part with her baby. *Furthermore,* Sometimes the couple waiting for their baby never receive him or her. William Handel, an attorney who works in Beverly Hills, California, and who has arranged thirty surrogate births, says that "the adopting couple may be ordered to pay lifetime medical expenses or child support for a child they don't get." This is unfair to both the surrogate mother and to the couple for whom she is having the child. On one hand, the surrogate mother has no time to reconsider her choice of giving away her baby; on the other hand, the adoptive parents may not get the child for which they paid big money.

I do not disapprove of surrogate motherhood, but I strongly disapprove of the present amateurish way of writing contracts filled with loopholes and never covering the most important issues—the rights of the natural mother and the rights of the adoptive parents. Surrogate mother contracts should closely imitate adoption papers—including terms that carefully protect both parties. At the present time, such matters as payment to the surrogate mother *are* is illegal, so that the whole contract is tainted with "underground" black market *manifestations* overtones. Therefore, the contracts *are* have often

Moved image

been called invalid. What is needed is for a committee of competent and wise lawyers to sit down and come up with a valid contract that would understand the basic assumption that we are not dealing with a car or a piece of furniture, but a child whose life and happiness is at stake. With proper revising, surrogate mother contracts could be written that would assure fairness to both the surrogate mother and to the adoptive parents. Of crucial importance in this contract is a clause that will allow the surrogate mother some time to reassess her decision to give up the baby to which she gave birth. Only with decent contracts can both natural mothers and children-loving couples enjoy the beautiful gift of a newborn life.

Final Draft   Jeannie Pugmire

English 101

Better Contracts for Surrogate Mothers

A highly emotional and controversial issue has lately captivated the attention of the media as well as the public. The issue is surrogate motherhood. Because it is charged with ethical and moral implications never before faced by modern courts, people are firmly divided on their opinions on the subject. Some

applaud surrogate motherhood as a modern miracle whereas others see it as just another sign
of contemporary depravity. Now, a surrogate
mother is a woman who agrees to have a baby for
another woman. The surrogate is usually artificially inseminated by the other woman's husband. A contract is drawn up, usually stating
that, for a certain sum of money, the surrogate
agrees to give up her baby upon birth. This
agreement sounds very cut and dried, but it is
not. Many ramifications obscure the landscape,
and strong opposition to the whole idea is
rapidly spreading. Questions are constantly
popping up: Is it right or natural for the
biological mother to "give away" her child?
Doesn't the whole process boil down to illegal
adoption of a child? Isn't surrogate mothering
simply a form of adultery?

The real problem at the center of this
murky situation is the contract itself. It is
the cause of many difficulties for both parties
involved after the baby is born. Most contracts
state that the natural mother must give up the
baby, upon birth, to the couple she agreed to
have it for. The contracts do not allow the
woman who gave birth any period of time to reconsider her decision to give her own child
away. If surrogate motherhood is to become an
accepted way for a childless couple to become
parents, then the contracts must be revised to
resemble adoption laws, since surrogate
mothering is similar to adopting. Adoption
agreements give the natural mother time to re-

consider her decision to give up her baby and to change her mind. This time for reflection and psychological probing is essential and must be allowed.

A classic current case—the case of "Baby M"—involves Rick and Marybeth Whitehead versus William and Elizabeth Stern. Having agreed to "rent her womb" to the Sterns, Marybeth Whitehead was artificially inseminated by William Stern. A contract was drawn up, stating that for the price of $10,000 Whitehead would surrender the baby, upon birth, to the Sterns. The contract said absolutely nothing about allowing Whitehead time to think about what she was doing. But, after giving birth to a baby girl on March 17, 1986, Whitehead refused to give up the baby, claiming that unforeseen instinctive urges caused her to become so attached to her baby that she would "lose her mind" if she gave her up. On the other side, the Sterns were taking care of the baby and had become bonded to her as well. The result was a catastrophic legal battle, which to date has not been resolved fully, although the New Jersey court awarded preliminary custody to the Sterns, based on the contract provisions.

I sympathize with Marybeth Whitehead. She carried that baby in her womb for nine months and, as is nature's way, she had grown to love the stirrings inside her, as all mothers learn to love a child forming within them. The contract she had signed became an obligation she simply could not fulfill. It was

too businesslike and too cold. It allowed no
opportunity for her to sort out her feelings
after the baby was born—and that is wrong.
Whitehead is the natural mother of this infant
and here she is forced to live up to an agreement made before the decisive factors in the
case were available. Not being clairvoyant,
she did not anticipate the affection that would
well up once she saw and held her baby. The opposition might argue that William Stern has
rights, too, since he is the biological father,
but psychologists and obstetricians alike
agree that a father's bonding to the fetus
forming inside a womb is not as obsessive as
that of the mother. As Dr. William Faraday, an
obstetrician in Los Angeles, observed, "The
protective instinct of a mother is one of the
fiercest powers in nature." Or, in the words of
a mother's poetic lines,

> There is none,
> In all this cold and hollow
> world, no fount
> Of deep, strong, deathless
> love, save that within
> A mother's heart.
> —Mrs. Hemans

Many thoughtful persons are seeing the
evil side of present surrogate mother contracts. For instance, William Pierce, who is
President of the National Committee for Adoption, has taken a strong stand against the pres-

ent way of drawing up surrogate mother contracts. He states, "It commercializes a very private thing. It should not take place at all." Most lawyers and psychologists who have studied the problem agree that surrogate mother contracts, in their present forms, are confusing and blatantly unfair. First and foremost, the natural mother is expected cold-bloodedly to part with her baby. Furthermore, sometimes the couple waiting for their baby never receive him or her. William Handel, an attorney who works in Beverly Hills, California, and who has arranged thirty surrogate births, says, that "the adopting couple may be ordered to pay lifetime medical expenses or child support for a child they don't get." This is unfair to both the surrogate mother and to the couple for whom she is having the child. On one hand, the surrogate mother has no time to reconsider her choice of giving away her baby; on the other hand, the adoptive parents may not get the baby for which they paid big money.

I do not disapprove of surrogate motherhood, but I strongly disapprove of the present amateurish way of writing contracts filled with loopholes and never covering the most important issues—the rights of the natural mother and the rights of the adoptive parents. Surrogate mother contracts should closely imitate adoption papers—including terms that carefully protect both parties. At the present time, such matters as payment to the surrogate mother are illegal, so that the whole contract

is tainted with black market manisfestations.
Therefore, the contracts are often called invalid. What is needed is for a committee of competent and wise lawyers to sit down and come up
with a valid contract grounded in the basic assumption that we are not dealing with a car or
a piece of furniture, but with a child whose
life and happiness are at stake. With proper
revising, surrogate mother contracts could assure fairness to both the surrogate mother and
to the adoptive parents. Of crucial importance
in this contract is a clause that will allow the
surrogate mother some time to reassess her decision to give up the baby to which she gave
birth. Only with decent contracts can both natural mothers and children-loving couples enjoy
the beautiful gift of a newborn life.

Copyrights and Acknowledgments

Index